Pivot of the Uni

Pivot of the Universe

Pivot of the Universe

Nasir al-Din Shah Qajar and the
Iranian Monarchy

ABBAS AMANAT

I.B. TAURIS

LONDON · NEW YORK

Reprinted in 2008 by I.B.Tauris & Co Ltd
6 Salem Road
London W2 4BU
175 Fifth Avenue
New York, NY 10010
www.ibtauris.com

New paperback edition published in 2008 by I.B.Tauris & Co Ltd
Published in hardback in 1997 by I.B.Tauris & Co Ltd

Part of chapter 4 of this book was published in an earlier version as "The Downfall of Mirza Taqi Khan Amir Kabir and the Problem of Ministerial Authority in Qajar Iran," *International Journal of Middle East Studies* 23 (1991): 577–99.

A full CIP record for this book is available from the British Library.

A full CIP record for this book is available from the Library of Congress.

Library of Congress catalog card number: available

ISBN 978 1 84511 828 0

Printed and bound in India by Thomson Press India Ltd

To Mousa and Besharat Amanat

By the tavern's trail camp astute wanderers,
Who seize and award the royal crown.
If they offer you the paupers' throne,
Your domain encircles the fish and the moon.

Hafiz

The publisher gratefully acknowledges the assistance of the Frederick W. Hilles Publications Fund of Yale University.

Contents

Illustrations

Preface

This book is about the institution of monarchy in modern Iran. It focuses on the life and times of Nasir al-Din Shah Qajar (1831–1896) during the first phase of his reign between 1848 and 1871. In this study I have tried to answer a fundamental question. How did monarchy, the centerpiece of an ancient political order, withstand and adjust to the challenges of modern times, both international and domestic? Nasir al-Din Shah's life and career, his upbringing and personality, and his political conduct provide remarkable materials for such a study. His life reflects dilemmas and vulnerabilities shared by most rulers of the Islamic world in the nineteenth century, though few shared his resilience in facing the hazards and upheavals that characterized the early part of his long reign. By examining how he was transformed from an insecure crown prince and, later, an erratic boy-king in the 1840s and 1850s into a ruler with substantial control over his government and foreign policy in the 1860s and beyond, this study attempts to explore a pattern in the consolidation of traditional monarchies that often perpetuated, rather than being hampered by, the forces of modernity.

European impact during the reign of Nasir al-Din Shah was not only limited to military expansion and diplomatic competition between Iran's two powerful neighbors, Russia and Britain. Europe also offered an alternative model to the traditional concept and practice of government to which rulers such as Nasir al-Din Shah were accustomed. Preserving the balance between tradition and modernity, resisting the West yet conforming to it, thus became a vital concern for Nasir al-Din Shah, adding a new dimension to his task of maintaining the delicate sociopolitical equilibrium. Increasing popular dissent, ministerial autonomy under Amir Kabir and Mirza Aqa Khan Nuri, the endemic factionalism of the Qajar polity, and the shah's personal vulnerabilities were other strains upon the fragile "cycle of equity," the upkeep of which was the shah's ancient duty.

Yet against these odds Nasir al-Din Shah survived on his throne for nearly fifty years (1848–1896). Indeed it is possible to suggest that Nasir al-Din's reign was the beginning of monarchical absolutism in modern sense. The shah combined shrewd diplomacy, often playing off rival Euaropean powers against each other, with selective reforms and equally shrewd weakening of traditional checks and balances to increase his own political power at the expense of ministerial autonomy. With the exception of some important lapses during the Constitutional Revolution, the same process continued to hamper state modernization into the late twentieth century. The fall of the premier Musaddiq in 1953, almost 100 years after the fall of Amir Kabir, and the subsequent consolidation of Muhammad Riza Shah Pahlavi was yet another episode in the struggle between the monarch and minister for the control of the government.

More than a decade after the dramatic collapse of the Pahlavi dynasty (and beyond the political setting in which ancient monarchy was glorified and the Qajar period despised), we can put into historical perspective an institution that for more than twenty-five centuries constituted the most fundamental component of Persian political identity. It is sanguine to believe that the demise of monarchy entailed the immediate loss of its most pervasive elements from Iran's political culture, even though it was reamoved by an anti-monarchical revolution. That the Persian monarchy was one of the oldest and most influential in history only sanctions the enadurance of this legacy, which is evident even in the way power is perceived and practiced in the post-monarchical period. Ingrained deeply into Persian historical consciousness, the mythological dimensions of kingship also have received a new lease on life. *Shahnama*, one of the greatest epics of all times, is, after all, the "book of the kings."

Even on a personal level, the reign of Nasir al-Din Shah still has tangible effects. When I was a young boy growing up in Tehran I once asked my grandfather about his age. With a familiar pose that must have given him time to return to old memories, he could only give his approximate age. "I was a boy of six or seven playing ball in my hometown, Kashan, when the news of Nasir al-Din Shah's assassination arrived." Even at that young age I found it fascinating that the death of a ruler should serve as the starting point in my grandfather's personal history. Some four decades later I can see why that was a turning point for the people of his generation. The break with the ancient past of which Nasir al-Din was a symbol was as swift as the bullet fired from his assassin's pistol. My grandfather was a living link between me and that moment, only a life span away from the reign of Iran's last traditional monarch. In these post-monarchical days, after a century of change and the tumult of two revolutions, that age seems to us even more remote. But remoteness has diminished neither its relaevance nor its fascination for all those who seek answers to Iran's, and in a broader sense the Middle East's, transition to modernity in the crucial decades of the latter half of the past century.

Recognizing the position of monarchy in Perso-Islamic political experience is not to abide by the essentially misconceived notion of "Persian despotism." From Herodotus and Aristotle to Montesquieu and Hegel, the stereotype of an omnipotent "oriental despot" with the powers of life and death over his prostrating subjects captured Western imaginations for reasons having more to do with philosophical and political ideals in the West than with historical realities in the East. As early as the Greco-Persian wars of the fifth century B.C., the West looked upon Persian monarchy as its political "other," contrived in order to augment its own political consciousness. Even up to the present time, the complexity of the Persian kingship model and the functional position of the ruler is often overlooked in the works of nonspecialists in favor of the more fascinating but less historically applicable notion of divine kingship and the position of the shah (or sultan) as the "shadow of God on earth."

Throughout the course of Islamic history, this functional model of kingship served almost unanimously to reconcile the temporal power with the premises of Islam. The fact that the Qajar state was one of the last, if not the last, to be faithful to this model of government makes it all the more interesting. In contrast to renowned rulers of ancient and Islamic eras who presented the archetypes of traditional monarchy in largely self-contained settings, Nasir al-Din Shah and his counterparts in the Ottoman Empire, Egypt, and elsewhere were facing essentially different circumstances. Nasir al-Din lived in the age of Europe's imperial advances, its growing technological edge, and its penetrating profusion of new ideas and institutions. He ruled over a society weakened by economic stagnation and civil strife, discontented with political and clerical repression but still profoundly bound by patriarchal norms and values. Nasir al-Din's views and conduct thus exemplified the dilemma of rulers with the unenviable task of implementing change from above.

Nasir al-Din's long reign in the age of high imperialism and internal instability raises another question: Why was he not overthrown by more potent pretenders to the Qajar throne or by potentially powerful movements of popular dissent? Why was his throne not overrun by the advancing armies of his northern neighbor nor annexed by his neighbor in the south? Except for the almost inevitable peripheral losses in Herat and Marv, why did the frontiers of the Guarded Domains of Iran remain intact? Given the government's overall inefficiency and obvious symptoms of misgovernment, the answers to such questions are even more intriguing.

Was it merely, as has often been argued, the balance of power between the competing imperial neighbors and their shared desire to preserve a buffer state that prolonged the life of another "sick man," this one on the threshold of India? Or did Nasir al-Din's domestic and foreign policies effectively arrest European advances?

Selective reforms and a weakening of the old checks and balances allowed the shah to put a distinctive, personal mark on the sociopolitical system. Nasir al-Din's royal touch was more profound than that which meets the eye at first glance. During his reign the monarch's symbolic centrality to his own world—as reflected in the royal epithet "the pivot of the universe" (*qibla-yi 'alam*)—took on an even more assertive character. His fears and suspicions, which were rooted in his troubled upbringing, were sharpened by the political insecurities of his reign. His emotional losses were compensated for by vengeful rejection of his fatherly ministers. Such motives had an irreversible impact on his reign and the decades that followed. The execution of his first premier, Mirza Taqi Khan Amir Kabir, serves as only one example. His narcissistic dispositions and profligacy as motives for military ventures or granting economic concessions were further examples. On the positive side, the same personal characteristics, when grafted onto his originally nomadic survival talents, led him to resist foreign advances. This nascent patriotism helped preserve his kingdom's territorial integrity. His cultural and artistic interests and religious leanings also helped sustain a cultural heritage still agile and confident of its own norms and worldview. Amplified in the historical space far beyond his human stature, Nasir al-Din was still the center of his own universe.

One hundred years after his death, the image of Nasir al-Din Shah still lingers, not only in popular history books and other literature of "decline" but also in oral anecdotes and comical stories. The air of fantasy and farce that surrounds his image is a curious switch from the image of the tyrant nurtured by his contemporary sources. It is equally distant from the "Martyr King" (*Shah-i Shahid*) persona created in the decades following his assassination. Thanks to what may be called a moralistic historiography, aspects of gullibility and greed were attached to his battered image beyond all realistic proportions. The sympathetic *Shah Baba* (literally, "Papa King") rendered in Sadiq Hidayat's masterpiece *Tup-i Murvari*, by contrast, betrays a nostalgia for patrimonial kingship. Yet Hidayat's portrayal of Nasir al-Din Shah, when set against the parody of the modernity of the Pahlavi era, religious obscurantism, and colonial legacy, more accurately highlights the plights and pleasures of that age. The current revival of interest in the Qajar era and particularly the enthusiasm for Nasir al-Din

Shah beyond sheer entertainment value reflects Hidayat's preoccupation with the dilemma of modernity. In this study I try to depict that past in a light of objectivity often missing from accounts of the Nasiri era and after.

Demonstrating the interaction between the political and the personal in the career of Nasir al-Din Shah and making sense of it as a case study of monarchy in transition thus poses a challenge far more taxing than writing a conventional political biography or an intimate account of his life. For a comprehensive study of Nasir al-Din Shah, the vast amount of primary material on the political history of his reign is as relevant as the most intimate memoirs, diaries, and travelogues. Direct involvement in the government made the shah's personal touch detectable in the most essential issues as well as in the most mundane. The peculiar fashion by which the official and unofficial dimensions of his rule intermingled poses an additional challenge to the historian not only in terms of coverage and organization but also in trying to chart the boundaries of the shah's authority and intervention. This ground, in spite of its richness, has remained largely unexplored. Studies of diplomacy, reform, bureaucracy, religion, and economy in the Nasir al-Din period carried out by Lambton, Kazemzadeh, Keddie, Bakhash, Algar and others, in spite of their significance by virtue of their very focus, were only marginally interested in the ruler's function and the interaction between its formal and private aspects. By relying on primary sources, most of them unknown or scarcely utilized, and taking a fresh look at better-known primary accounts, I hope to contribute to the biographical studies in the Middle East as well to modern Iranian historiography.

To this author, the charm of history lies in its totality, in its multifaceted intricacy, and in the mysterious reality that emerges only when seemingly innocuous facts are brought together. Thus, at times I found it necessary to cross the divisional barriers that often place a work of history in one or another category in order to demonstrate the complexity of Nasir al-Din Shah's character and his age.

For research and writing of this book I am indebted to many individuals and institutions. My deepest gratitude goes to the late Albert Hourani, who from the outset of this project was a source of inspiration to me, read an earlier draft of this book, and made insightful comments. His vivid memory remained a source of moral support and encouragement to me. My gratitude is also due to Fereshteh Bibi Amanat for all her support and assistance over the years. I am especially indebted to Farhad and Firoozeh Diba, whose hospitality during my months of residing in their house while re-searching in London cannot be reciprocated in a few words. Farhad gen-erously allowed me to make use of his excellent collection of books, news-papers, and photographs. To Haynie Wheeler I am especially grateful for her patient and thorough reading of this manuscript and for making valuable comments. Amin Neshati has been of great assistance to me throughout. I am thankful to both of them.

Hossamedin Khoromi of Tehran kindly offered me books and other material from his collection of Qajar manuscripts, documents, and litho-graphs. My thanks are also due to Sirus Amirmokri, Ahmad and Azar Ashraf, Juan Cole, Mnucher Farmanfarmaian, Houchang Chehabi, Af-saneh Najmabadi, Basil Robinson, Franz Rosenthal, and Jonathan Spence. I remember the late Seyyedeh Nasr-Kowssar for her help in acquiring primary material from Iran and the late Sue Stienburg for her assistance at the Sterling Memorial Library at Yale.

A Morse Fellowship at Yale University in 1985–1986 allowed me to begin my work on this book. In 1989 I also received a Griswold grant from The Whitney Humanities Center, Yale University, for research on this book.

Abbas Amanat
New Haven, Connecticut

Preface to the Paperback Edition

The story of this book – the life and times of Nasir al-Din Shah Qajar – above all is the story of power and its illusive nature; how it is gained, how it is held in the face of many odds, and how it is lost to inertia and popular discontent. Nasir al-Din Shah is perhaps a ruler remembered most by posterity, often too harshly, as the embodiment of lost opportunities. His portrayal is often contrasted in the Iranian grand narrative with that of his first premier, Amir Kabir, perhaps the most iconic figure of Persian modern history, whose rise and tragic downfall is depicted in the following pages. This book is also about other men and women who loyally served the shah, abided by his whims and wishes, threatened and manipulated him and fell victim to his fears and suspicions.

A decade after the first publication of *Pivot of the Universe*, I am pleased to note that the specialists and the general public read it not only for an alternative look at the Qajar political landscape but for its relevance to the nature of power even in our time. Here we read about the upbringing, family and dynastic ties and political career of a nineteenth-century ruler who was largely bound by the norms and practices of the ancient institution of Persian kingship and yet at the same time faced numerous modern challenges at home from his own subjects and from European imperial powers. The old dilemma of preserving a domestic balance of power loomed larger for him than his ancestors in the face of court intrigues, vagaries of governance, dire finances and fundamental obstacles to change.

Without subscribing to an essentialist view of history and without assuming that the same political pattern unchangeably persisted over centuries, the parallels with the later rulers of Iran are instructive and at times striking. Economy aside, challenges to Nasir al-Din Shah may resemble similar ones in the twentieth century posed to the Pahlavi ruler Muhammad Reza Shah (as depicted for instance in the recently-published secret diaries of Asadollah Alam, the influential courts minister) or even the conduct of today's actors in Iran's Islamic Republic. Drawing such a parallel is revealing because of Iran's geopolitically pivotal location, then and now. Today's Iran, more than a century after the death of Nasir al-Din Shah, still struggles to hold its ground in a highly volatile regional surrounding (which in the twentieth century is somewhat inadequately defined as the Middle East).

Iran still has to maintain a complex power balance between its northern and southern frontiers while remaining wary of the perils that linger to its east and to its west. The frontiers of Russian empire, true, have now nearly shrunken to its pre-imperial age. After nearly three hundred years, Iran no longer shares common borders with its powerful and often intrusive neighbour to the north. Yet Russia certainly remains an important counterforce to Western powers then and now. One of the redeeming qualities of Nasir al-Din Shah was to master the art of counterbalancing rival superpowers of his time and maintain his own margin of survival in the hostile world of high imperialism. His nearly half-century of rule was a quest to learn this hard-to-prefect art of preserving the equilibrium.

The imperial Britain of Nasir al-Din Shah's time, with all its meddling in Iran's domestic affairs and its condescending attitude to the Persian state, too, has long disappeared (except for a brief mis-adventure during the recent invasion of Iraq) though it left behind in West Asia, South Asia, and the Persian Gulf lasting legacies of conflict and contention. The Ottoman Empire too – another source of anxiety to the Qajar state – has long disappeared and been replaced with several nation-states that still carry the troubling burden of that imperial demise. Iraq is one such example. Nasir al-Din Shah, who liked to call himself the "king of the Shi`ites," realized how the destiny of Iraq and its Shi`ite and Kurdish populations were crucial to the stability of Iran's western frontiers; a fact that badly eludes the American administration today. For nearly two millennia, perhaps as early as the Roman-Parthian wars of the first century, rulers of the Iranian world resisted, and often contested, threats coming from the Mesopotamian low-lands. The peace treaties of Amasiya in 1555, Zobah in 1639, and Erzerum in 1847, as well as the Algerian declaration of 1977 between Muhammad Reza Shah Pahlavi and Saddam Husain, and the ceasefire agreement of 1988 that ended the horrendous Iraq-Iran war were but a few signposts in this troubled history.

Equally important and misunderstood in the West (and by the current US administration in particular) is how the Iranian state historically was vulnerable to dangers in its eastern and northeastern boarders and especially the Afghan frontier. This was demonstrated by the Galzhai Afghan invasion of 1722 that destroyed the Safavid state and plunged Iran into many decades of turmoil and civil war. Subsequently, the same threat led to harsh measures by Nadir Shah Afshar to pacify the Qandahar province and beyond. In the nineteenth century the permanent loss to Iran of its historic Herat province was followed by the emergence of a united Afghanistan. The former was one of the bleakest moments in Nasir al-Din Shah's reign while the latter proved to be a source of relief for the security of eastern Iran. More than a century later, a series of events triggered by the 1980 Soviet invasion of Afghanistan, and subsequently the resistance movement against Soviet occupation, rekindled Iran's old anxieties about its eastern neighbour. The Afghan refugee crisis that obligated Iran to admit more than one and a half million refugees, and finally the ominous rise of Saudi-backed Taliban with expressed hostility to the Shi`ites and the Iranians, were the later ominous developments.

Nasir al-Din Shah of course is not remembered, somewhat unfairly, for his diplomatic skills. His reign is often labeled as an era of submissiveness toward foreign powers in the same way that his domestic policies are identified with stagnation and decadence. The hostile treatment in the historiography of the Pahlavi era, inspired by the Western positivist narrative, have had a fair share in such portrayal. And no doubt the obvious shortcomings and blind spots of Nasir al-Din's rule were too many to be denied or ignored. The murder of his first premier, Mirza Taqi Khan Amir Kabir, has gained a mythical dimension overshadowing almost all other aspects of Nasir al-Din's reign. This display of hero-worshiping – embellished by the nationalist narrative of earlier decades – came at the expense of any balanced assessment of Nasir al-Din's long rule or a realistic view of Amir Kabir's success and failures.

The reader of *Pivot of the Universe* in its Persian translation (it first appeared in Tehran in 2004 as *Qibla-i `Alam*) was offered an alternative interpretation to this excessive glorification. This translation generated a fair amount of interest among the book-reading public to the extent that it was ranked by the Iranian press as "one of the most-widely debated books" of 2005. Even though some Iranian conspiracy theorists diagnosed a plot to blemish the image of an Iranian national icon, the urge for a more realistic reading of the past seems to have prevailed; evidence of some healthy intellectual vibrancy among the Iranian readership who have bought three editions of this book in two years.

Oddly enough, the customary negative portrayal of Nasir al-Din Shah goes hand in hand with some curious commemoration of his popular image. At a time when the Islamic Republic tries hard to obliterate images of the Iranian monarchy (but apparently not hard enough), the poorly-manufactured iconic images of Nasir al-Din Shah abound on fake Qajaresque porcelain and china tea sets, tea pots, water-pipes, decorative plates, vases, and trays; a far cry from the old Gardner china label manufactured in Russia in the nineteenth century and the Bohemian glass popularized after Nasir al-Din Shah's first trip to Europe in 1873. He should at least be congratulated for imprinting himself indelibly on the Iranian popular memory, more successfully perhaps than any other historical or even mythical figure. That there is a kind of mindless quality to these faddish reproductions may tell us something about a collective desire, almost subliminal, to celebrate a bygone epoch, of which now only a shadowy mystique lingers.

Not to bolster such generic images – in textbooks or on teacups – this book aims toward a more accurate and dispassionate depiction of that epoch without, I hope, removing its story-like luster. As is the case with any serious biography – and there are not too many of them about personalities in the Persianate world – this book is meant to be critical without being over-burdened with "analysis". As the reader will see it does not include preamble with the recantation of a fashionable theory and it does not dutifully invoke big names. For those who are interested in historiographical themes, however, there is an ample amount underneath the narrative – for instance in the blend of political with personal histories; a deliberate attempt to break down the formalistic divide in biographical narratives. To this end, there is a new approach toward understanding of the man and his time and, of course, the political institutions and the society that shaped him and in turn he helped to shape for the posterity.

AA
North Haven,
Connecticut

Note on Transliteration and Style

The transliteration system adopted for Persian and Arabic is that of the *International Journal of Middle East Studies* but without diacritical marks. The silent *h* in Persian and Arabic is represented by *a* and the silent *waw* in Persian with *w*. The letter *'ayn* is represented by ' and *hamza*, regardless of its bearer, by '. The Persian *izafa* in proper names and titles is not represented except when necessary. With few exceptions the Arabic definite article *al-* is not assimilated to the noun. Persian works with Arabic titles are transliterated in Arabic. Whenever possible Russian proper names were used in their anglicized form.

Well-known place names are written in their common form (as in the *Oxford Atlas*), and less familiar place names are transliterated. *Iran* instead of *Persia* is used throughout, but *Persian* is preferred over *Iranian* for individuals (regardless of their ethnic origins) as well as for culture, society, and government. All Persian and European civil and military titles are omitted except where necessary. Following the usage of the time, both "autograph" and "autographed note" are used for royal decrees, letters, and other documents signed by the shah (*dast-khatt*). "Prime minister" and "premier" are preferred to "grand vizier" as translations for *sadr-i a'zam*.

Dates in Islamic lunar calendar indicated with Q. (for *Qamari*). Dates with no lunar signifier are in the Persian solar calendar. In all instances equivalents were given in Christian (Gregorian) calendar.

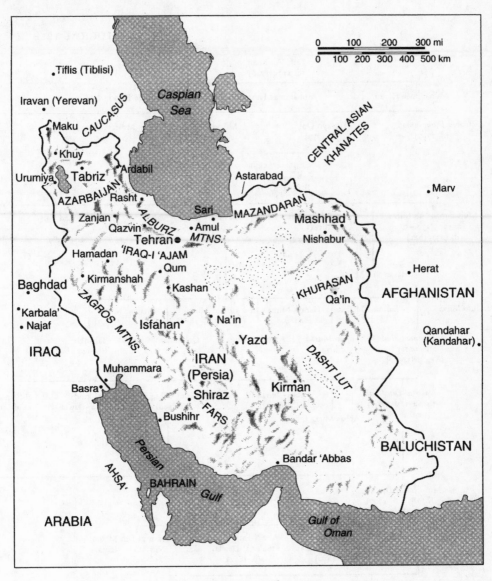

Iran in the nineteenth century

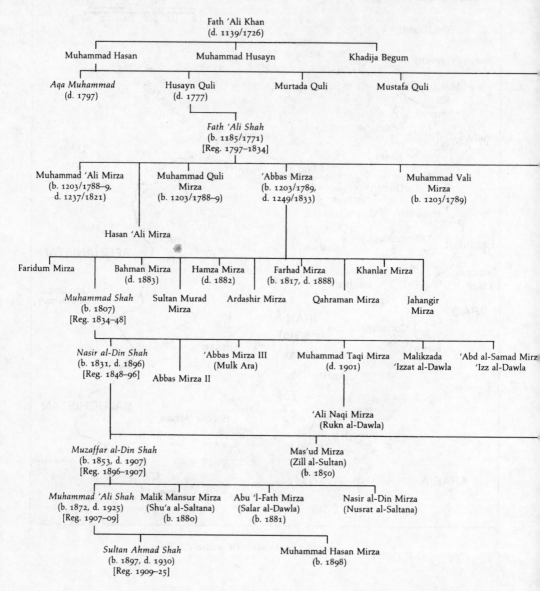

Fath 'Ali Khan
(d. 1139/1726)

Muhammad Hasan   Muhammad Husayn   Khadija Begum

Aqa Muhammad
(d. 1797)

Husayn Quli
(d. 1777)

Murtada Quli

Mustafa Quli

Fath 'Ali Shah
(b. 1185/1771)
[Reg. 1797–1834]

Muhammad 'Ali Mirza
(b. 1203/1788–9,
d. 1237/1821)

Muhammad Quli
Mirza
(b. 1203/1788–9)

'Abbas Mirza
(b. 1203/1789,
d. 1249/1833)

Muhammad Vali
Mirza
(b. 1203/1789)

Hasan 'Ali Mirza

Faridum Mirza

Bahman Mirza
(d. 1883)

Hamza Mirza
(d. 1882)

Farhad Mirza
(b. 1817, d. 1888)

Khanlar Mirza

Muhammad Shah
(b. 1807)
[Reg. 1834–48]

Sultan Murad
Mirza

Ardashir Mirza

Qahraman Mirza

Jahangir
Mirza

Nasir al-Din Shah
(b. 1831, d. 1896)
[Reg. 1848–96]

Abbas Mirza II

'Abbas Mirza III
(Mulk Ara)

Muhammad Taqi Mirza
(d. 1901)

Malikzada
'Izzat al-Dawla

'Abd al-Samad Mirza
'Izz al-Dawla

'Ali Naqi Mirza
(Rukn al-Dawla)

Muzaffar al-Din Shah
(b. 1853, d. 1907)
[Reg. 1896–1907]

Mas'ud Mirza
(Zill al-Sultan)
(b. 1850)

Muhammad 'Ali Shah
(b. 1872, d. 1925)
[Reg. 1907–09]

Malik Mansur Mirza
(Shu'a al-Saltana)
(b. 1880)

Abu 'l-Fath Mirza
(Salar al-Dawla)
(b. 1881)

Nasir al-Din Mirza
(Nusrat al-Saltana)

Sultan Ahmad Shah
(b. 1897, d. 1930)
[Reg. 1909–25]

Muhammad Hasan Mirza
(b. 1898)

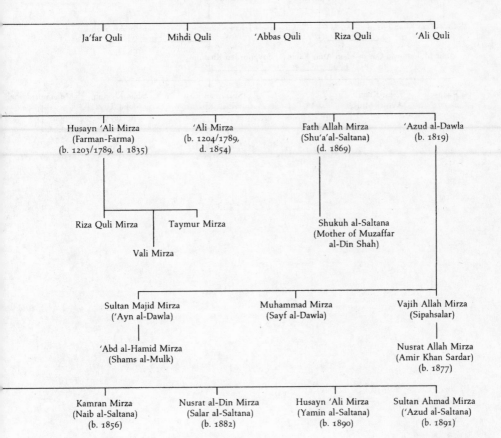

Ja'far Quli   Mihdi Quli   'Abbas Quli   Riza Quli   'Ali Quli

Husayn 'Ali Mirza
(Farman-Farma)
(b. 1203/1789, d. 1835)

'Ali Mirza
(b. 1204/1789,
d. 1854)

Fath Allah Mirza
(Shu'a'al-Saltana)
(d. 1869)

'Azud al-Dawla
(b. 1819)

Riza Quli Mirza   Taymur Mirza

Vali Mirza

Shukuh al-Saltana
(Mother of Muzaffar
al-Din Shah)

Sultan Majid Mirza
('Ayn al-Dawla)

Muhammad Mirza
(Sayf al-Dawla)

Vajih Allah Mirza
(Sipahsalar)

'Abd al-Hamid Mirza
(Shams al-Mulk)

Nusrat Allah Mirza
(Amir Khan Sardar)
(b. 1877)

Kamran Mirza
(Naib al-Saltana)
(b. 1856)

Nusrat al-Din Mirza
(Salar al-Saltana)
(b. 1882)

Husayn 'Ali Mirza
(Yamin al-Saltana)
(b. 1890)

Sultan Ahmad Mirza
('Azud al-Saltana)
(b. 1891)

THE MATERNAL BRANCH OF NASIR AL-DIN SHAH'S GENEALOGICAL TREE

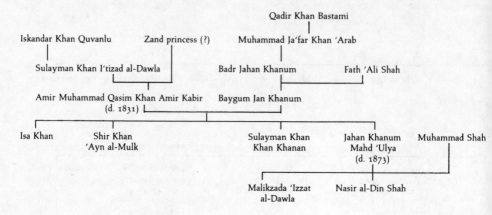

Introduction: The Royal Domain

The long reign of Nasir al-Din Shah (1848–1896), the fourth monarch of the Qajar dynasty (1785–1925), in many respects epitomized the transitional nature of Qajar rule. The world that emerged under the Qajars bridged the Safavid (1501–1722) and post-Safavid periods with the Iran of the twentieth century. During the early Qajar era Iran (Persia, as it was then known to the West) emerged from the political turmoil and economic decline of the late eighteenth century with a relatively stable central government, increased social homogeneity, an expanding economy, and gleams of cultural and religious revival. From the first quarter of the nineteenth century Iran also experienced diverse challenges from outside its borders. Russia and Britain came into extensive contact with Iran in its northern and southern frontiers, not only through war, diplomacy, and trade but later by introducing new social and political ideas and institutions. Unlike India to its southeast and the Caucasus and Central Asia to its north, Iran was never conquered or colonized by its European neighbors, but like the Ottoman Empire to its west, it never remained immune from the European powers' all-embracing, and often intrusive, presence. It did not abandon its own political system, culture, and way of life, yet it did not shun altogether Europe's material, and later cultural, dominance. Gradual awareness of, yet ambivalence toward, the West's pervasive ways was at the heart of the Qajar experience.

It is not by mere coincidence that Europe's "long century"—as the period between the 1789 French Revolution and the 1914 outbreak of World War I is known—finds a certain resonance in the Qajar period. The Persian long century began in earnest in 1785 with the accession to the throne of Aqa Muhammad Khan (1785–1797), the founder of the Qajar dynasty, and came to an effective end with the Constitutional Revolution (1906–1911). The establishment of the Qajar dynasty under Aqa Muhammad Khan unified the country and created an enduring equilibrium after nearly half a century of chronic upheaval. The Constitutional Revolution, by contrast, was an attempt to develop democratic institutions based on the rule of law, conscious nationalism, and secular reforms. The period in

1

between witnessed a long, often painful process of transformation and adjustment to the internal and external realities that defined modern Iran as a state and a nation.

During the first six decades of Qajar rule, three overlapping themes shaped the Persian state and society. In rough chronological order, the first of these was the loosening of tribal loyalties and their gradual replacement with traditional patterns of monarchy and bureaucracy; the second was the encounter with European powers and subsequent adjustment to their strategic and economic contingencies; and the third was the state's interaction with indigenous social and religious forces that sometimes challenged its legitimacy. None of these themes proved detrimental to the survival of the Qajar state, but they combined to produce a serious crisis in the decade leading up to Nasir al-Din's accession.[1]

FROM THE TENT TO THE THRONE

In the 126 years between the fall of the Safavid state in 1722 and the accession of Nasir al-Din Shah, the Qajars evolved from a shepherd-warrior tribe with strongholds in northern Iran into a Persian dynasty with all the trappings of a Perso-Islamic monarchy. Before Aqa Muhammad Khan could place the Kayanid crown on his head in 1785, three generations of the Qajars had lost their lives in the struggle for the throne. As a prominent contingent within the Qizilbash confederacy (the military elite of the Safavid era), the Qajar chiefs considered themselves legitimate candidates for royal power. During the three interregnums in the eighteenth century, they fought bloody contests with other claimants to the Persian crown, first with Nadir Shah (1736–1747) and his Afsharid successors and then with Karim Khan Zand (1750–1779) and his successors. It was not just out of flattery that court chroniclers of later decades reconstructed the early history of the Qajar dynasty. By elevating three generations of Qajar chiefs to the rank of full-fledged kings, they tried to depict the Qajars as legitimate successors to the Safavids, whose right to the throne was usurped by rival dynasties.[2]

Aqa Muhammad Khan (see Pl. 1), who was castrated in his youth by an Afsharid pretender to the throne (a common practice for disqualifying accession), spent years in the Zand court in Shiraz as a hostage for his clan's shaky loyalty. But immediately after Karim Khan's death in 1779, Aqa Muhammad took refuge with his tribe in Astarabad and began a resurgence that eventually made him the master of Iran. In a series of campaigns that took nearly two decades of his life and continued up to the time of his own assassination in 1797, he managed first to subdue the north and then to supplant Zand rule in the south and overcome all but the most persistent of his domestic rivals. When in 1786 he chose Tehran as his capital, he had unified under his rule nearly all of the interior of Iran, though most of the peripheral regions of Azarbaijan and the Caucasus, Khurasan, and the Persian Gulf littoral remained outside his reach. Aqa Muhammad Khan's long and sometimes destructive campaigns were in part motivated by desire for conquest and booty and a sense of vengeance against his rivals. Yet he was also an empire builder with a consistent and clear vision. Notwithstanding his infamous greed and cruelty, which brought about the destruction of many of his enemies and some of his supporters, he should be credited for ultimately bringing back security and peace to a country much abused by civil war, famine, and depopulation.[3]

The Qajar bid for power was the third successive attempt to create a political order in place of and on the model of the Safavid empire. Being the last in a struggle for domination that since the second decade of the eighteenth century had exhausted the Afghans, Afshars, Zands, and numerous other tribal forces on the Iranian periphery no doubt was an advantage to the Qajars. Aqa Muhammad Khan won the last phase of the contest because he had been able to build up a potent war machine at the back of his own quarreling Qajar tribal forces and their allies. There were other reasons, too. The Qajars' rapid adoption of a versatile model of government helped them achieve a state-tribe optimum that had been inconceivable even under a peaceful ruler such as Karim Khan Zand. Moreover, with the emergence of the two European powers on the Iranian horizon at the outset of Qajar rule, the regional climate favored greater stability.

Aqa Muhammad Khan learned from the failures of his predecessors some important lessons in government. He appreciated the collective nature of a tribal enterprise that allowed him to pave the long and bloody way between the Qajar tent camp in Astarabad and Gulistan Palace in Tehran. Yet in his own lifetime he had witnessed the internecine feuding that destroyed previous ruling houses. He thus tried his best to eliminate within and without the Qajar house all actual and potential threats to his designated successor. His nephew and heir apparent, Baba Khan, later known as Fath 'Ali Shah (1797–1834), was the prime beneficiary of Aqa Muhammad Khan's actions. It took another half-century before the Qajars could fully eradicate all rivalries within their own house, but the seed of royal supremacy was already sown.

The reign of Fath 'Ali Shah marked a clear shift from the tribal warring tradition to a model of kingship. Under his rule the Qajar state was able to expand its control to the peripheries of Azarbaijan, Khurasan, and southern Fars. It also managed to establish an extensive court and administration with all the trappings of a Persian royal system. Fath 'Ali Shah's personality and his taste for luxury and royal extravagance, in contrast to the warlike austerity of his uncle, proved remarkably suitable for reconstruction of such a royal system (see Pl. 2).[4]

The early Qajars viewed "the men of the sword" as prime tools of their domination over the land they conquered. The army created by Aqa Muhammad Khan from a conglomerate of northern tribal forces and maintained by Fath 'Ali Shah proved a resilient instrument in the face of early internal dissension and external challenges. Aqa Muhammad Khan's ambition was to restore the old boundaries of the Safavid empire in the Iranian periphery to include principalities of Afghanistan and Central Asia, the Ottoman Iraq, all of the Kurdish region and frontiers of Anatolia, the Caucasian provinces, and the Iranian coasts and islands of the Persian Gulf. This plan was only partially modified under Fath 'Ali Shah. The same spirit of warfare as the basis of imperial domination remained a part of the Qajar ethos under Muhammad Shah (1834–1848; see Pl. 3) and during Nasir al-Din's early reign.

The early Qajars were also keenly aware of the value of "the men of the pen," who were responsible for the government administration (*divan*). Aqa Muhammad Khan's callous treatment of many real and potential rivals seldom was aimed at state officials. He soon began to appreciate the role of officialdom in creating the state apparatus and overseeing its fiscal and military functions. Fath 'Ali Shah was even more consistent in recruiting into his administration secretaries and city officials from Mazandaran and Iraq 'Ajam and from remnants of the Zand bureaucratic families of Fars. These officials often held strong bonds with the 'ulama, the merchants of the bazaar, and with other notables and served as channels of communication with these groups. In Fath 'Ali Shah's service there was also a contingent of Georgians and other Caucasians of slave origin as well as those who had immigrated from the Caucasus to Azarbaijan after the Persian defeat in war with Russia. Some served as eunuchs and servants of the inner court, and others were in the army. Under Muhammad Shah a number of these Georgians, along with Kurdish and other peripheral elements, were recruited into important government posts.

By the middle of the nineteenth century there was an entrenched class of officials acutely aware of its own interests and privileges. Based largely on regional and clan allegiances, they were divided into four informal factions. With a few exceptions, most members of this class were conservative in their worldview and jealously preserved the secrets of their specialized skills. In spite of the enormous power ministers and state accountants wielded throughout the Qajar era, these factions never fully integrated into a unified administrative entity distinct from the court. Their power remained, both in theory and in practice, momentary and contingent on the shah's arbitrary wishes and thus vulnerable to the machinations of the court and the nobility. They were, as they often wished to assert, a class of servants (*tabaqa-yi naukar*) in the shah's retinue.[5]

From Nadir's mistakes the early Qajars also learned the need to court the increasingly influential Shi'ite establishment, the 'ulama, the "men of [religious] learning." Even more than Aqa Muhammad Khan, his successor, Fath 'Ali Shah, ensured their loyalty through patronage, by dispensing gifts and land tenures and sanctioning their judicial authority. As has often been noted, the Qajars clearly felt they needed the 'ulama's consent and cooperation in order to buttress their own precarious legitimacy as successors to the Safavids. Whatever the drawbacks of complying with the 'ulama's wishes and whatever the 'ulama's ambivalence in collaborating with the Qajar shahs, both sides benefited from this symbiosis. The shahs successfully presented themselves as patrons of the faith and defenders of the Shi'ite kingdom, whereas the 'ulama consolidated their social base under the aegis of the state. Greater integration of Shi'ism in the Qajar era as the religion of the state and of a vast majority of people reinforced the state-'ulama bonds.[6]

The shah and his court, the princes and the nobility, the army chiefs and the officials, and to an extent the 'ulama constituted the ruling elite of the Qajar state. Yet in practice the effectiveness of the government was hampered by inherent limitations. Throughout the Qajar period the state suffered from inefficiencies and malfunctions caused by financial restraints, factionalism, organizational confusion, and intrinsic corruption. The state's financial weakness was essentially caused by Iran's stagnant agrarian economy and obstacles to the growth of trade and industrialization, which in turn handicapped the government's ability to raise taxes and improve its archaic methods of expenditure. Moreover, the court and the nobility treated state revenues from the land and other sources as legitimate spoils of the conquest that primarily were to be spent for their upkeep. Little revenue therefore was allocated toward meaningful expansion of the state. The officials shared these spoils with the royalty and the Qajar nobility to maintain their economic privileges and ensure monopoly over the bureaucratic machinery.

Impediments to strong government were deepened by obstacles at the provincial level. Local power bases, whether chiefs of tribal confederacies or prince governors of the Qajar house, reserved a certain degree of autonomy in the provinces. The shah maintained a fragile control over these domains, though it is wrong to believe that such control was merely nominal. Depending on the strength of the ruler and his administration he could maneuver, negotiate, or coerce, whichever was expedient, thus holding indirect sway over the provinces. Yet they could not, and indeed did not wish to, reverse the delicate balance between the center and the periphery. Such devolution of power was seen as cost-efficient and pragmatic. Through practices such as assigning provincial governments to the highest bidder, allotting land and hereditary pensions to the nobility, army officers, and court and government officials, and awarding gifts to the 'ulama, the shah exercised his royal power in preserving this precarious balance. Punitive measures such as the dismissal, banishment, and execution of guilty officials and chiefs (or whoever posed or was presumed to pose a threat to the royal hegemony) were among other royal options. So was the increasingly abused practice of bestowing grandiose titles to the nobility and to all servants of the state.[7] In exchange the Qajar elite and the officialdom demonstrated devotion to the shah not only through military and civil service but by paying symbolic and material homage. Such displays of loyalty ranged from substantial gifts (*pishkish*) presented to the shah on special occasions to perpetual assurances of humility, devotion, and flattery.

That such a system of reciprocal favoritism was prone to serious abuses was acknowledged even by its practitioners. The shah and his ministers resigned themselves to the fact that no reform measure could remedy the defects of this time-honored system. Increasingly from the second quarter of nineteenth century, and more so after the breakdown of the princely system of Fath 'Ali Shah's time, governorships of provinces were auctioned off to the highest bidders among princes of the blood, Qajar chiefs, and bureaucrats. From a purely utilitarian standpoint, the Qajar shahs viewed this annual farming out of provincial offices as an efficient way to raise revenue without directly involving the central government in the costly and laborious practice of collecting taxes. Revolving governorships had for the shah the additional advantage of weakening the semiautonomous power bases of princes and members of the nobility. Yet this system routinely exposed the public, particularly the villagers, to the indiscretion and avarice of provincial and district governors and their tax collectors. Governors tended to look upon their posts as transitory means of generating income not only to recoup the initial sums they pledged to the central government but also to amass a surplus income (*madakhil*) for themselves and their agents. In such a hierarchy of oppression there was little incentive for fairness and compassion. As the central government's ability to raise income dwindled, officials' incentive to maximize their surplus earnings swelled, thus turning the *madakhil* into an institutionalized form of corruption at every level of government.

THE SHAH AND HIS SUBJECTS

Even as late as the Qajar period the monarchy was profoundly influenced by the ancient tradition of Persian kingship. Yet it is unrealistic to assume that the Qajar monarchy remained unaffected by forces that altered the makeup and function of the state in modern times. By the middle of the nineteenth century four dimensions of royal authority underscored Iran's historical experiences. The first was the pre-Islamic tradition of kingship as transmitted through political culture and practice of government and through manuals of government, general histories, and epic legends such as Firdawsi's *Shahnama*. The second was the Islamic, and more specifically the Shi'ite, dimension of government, which essentially aimed at reconciling Persian kingship with the complex notion of political authority in Islam. The third was the nomadic concept of power and leadership, which at least since the Turkish and Mongol invasions of the eleventh to fourteenth centuries had been a persistent feature of the Islamic state. The final influence was the modern Western model of government and examples of European kingship as they became known to Persian (and other Middle Eastern) rulers from the early decades of the nineteenth century.

The Persian monarchical model, a legacy of the Sassanian period (244–640) and before, persisted for centuries in the Islamic world with few interruptions. After the decline of the Abbasid caliphate in the ninth century, for all intents and purposes the institution of the sultanate was a revival of the Persian model. But even before that the Buyid rulers of central and southern Iran (932–1062), who were of Shi'ite persuasion, had adopted the Persian imperial title of "king of kings" (*shahanshah*), whereas their Sunni rivals, the Samanids of Khurasan and Central Asia (819–1005), proud of their Sassanian lineage, had upheld the old courtly practices and patronized the revival of Persian language and culture. In the heyday of the Ghaznavid (998–1050) and the Saljuqid (1038–1194) empires, when loyalty to the caliphate was strong and when the Turkish ancestry of the sultans was pronounced, and later during the Ilkhanid period (1256–1335), Persian ministers were successful in persuading the rulers to embrace a traditional kingly posture and to observe the norms of monarchical rule. The celebrated Persian minister Khwaja Abu-'Ali Hasan Nizam al-Mulk

(d. 1092), who considered the symbiosis between monarchy and "good religion" as a basis for social stability, was indeed advocating a theory set forth by Zoroastrian writers of the sixth century.

This aspect of kingship, the need for compatibility between state and religion, was further stressed in the Safavid period, with the Shi'ite shahs claiming a dual authority. They were viewed both as temporal rulers presiding over the state and, at least up to the early seventeenth century, as deputies of the Shi'ite Imam and thus as custodians of the Shi'ite community. Safavid rulers enhanced such a merging of temporal and religious spheres by granting patronage to Twelver Shi'ite 'ulama and incorporating them into the state apparatus. However, the Safavid shahs did not abandon their royal premises and practices. The subjects of the Safavid empire regarded the monarchy, if not the person of the shah, as an exalted institution crucial for preserving Shi'ism within its oft-threatened boundaries. That there were attempts to resuscitate the Safavid monarchy—including several by pretenders claiming Safavid descent—attests to the endurance of this temporal-religious model for at least half a century after that dynasty's demise. The early Qajars did not claim to be of Safavid descent, nor did they pretend to rule on behalf of a nominal Safavid shah—as did Nadir in his early days and Karim Khan, the *vakil* (deputy), throughout his rule—but they nevertheless tired to sustain an air of legitimacy as protectors of the Shi'ite domain and upholders of the Shi'ite religious order.

Equally important for the Qajar dynasty's survival, however, was its ability to maintain a notion of social justice in its dealings with its subjects. Around the patrimonial figure of the shah were shaped the institutions of government, and through him the bonds with his subjects were forged. The early Qajar rulers honored, at least in principle, the paradigm that divided the state (*dawlat*) from the subjects (*ra'iyat*) and defined the place and functions of each of the two components. The shah viewed his bond with the subjects—the peasants, the urbanites, and the nomads—as one of a social contract; in exchange for the state's providing security and order, the subjects were expected to remain obedient and economically productive. In such a model the shah was at the top of the social pyramid and the ultimate exemplar within a hierarchy that replicated his patriarchal authority at all lower urban, tribal, and familial levels. Every man of stature and authority—the 'ulama, landlords, chiefs of tribes, city wardens, chiefs of the merchants, masters of the guilds, and leaders of the sufi orders—was expected to mind his flock and be responsible for its conduct.

Notwithstanding the patrimonial nature of royal authority, the Perso-Islamic model of state summed up the duties of the ruler in two complementary functions: defense of the kingdom from external threats and administration of justice within the kingdom. In reality, defense of the land required nothing more than mustering the military forces necessary to quell any invasion or organized rebellion (often of a nomadic nature), whereas dispensing justice was synonymous with preserving the societal order against forces of religious sedition and popular chaos. Discharging these duties required a basic division between the ruler and the ruled, which in turn necessitated intermediary agencies to enforce the royal authority. The rationale for the tripartite interplay between the ruler, the government agents, and the subjects was therefore explained in the form of a causal cycle, the so-called "cycle of equity," the maintenance of which was the ruler's responsibility. The kingdom's survival and that of the king as its head, it was argued, required maintaining an army and a bureaucracy in order to defend the land, enforcing the ruler's command, and collecting taxes. But the revenue could only be generated by the subjects if they lived in peace and security. It was thus incumbent upon the king to ensure that the subjects were treated justly and were immune from his agents' natural tendencies toward oppression. If he failed to do so, the kings were warned in no unsure terms by the authors of government manuals, he would foster popular sedition and rebellion, which would soon remove him from the throne and destroy his dynasty.

This rudimentary formula engendered a certain tension within the institution of kingship. It required the ruler to supervise the government apparatus and yet keep a distance from it in order to protect the subjects against the excesses of his own agents. This was often resolved by the ruler's being partially excluded from the routine of governing. Practical power was delegated to ministers and high-ranking officials, but the ruler reserved for himself the discretionary rights of dismissing and promoting, punishing and rewarding. These rights were bestowed upon him because he was considered the locus of divine glory and possessor of royal charisma (*farr-i shahi*). He was the "shadow of God [*zillullah*] on earth," but if he was not capable of maintaining the delicate balance between the government and the subjects he was destined to lose his divine mandate and with it his glory and his throne.[8]

In principle the Qajar shahs, like their predecessors, were aware of these royal duties and recognized the conditionality of their divine mandate. Yet contingencies of their office inevitably occasioned a certain political isolation against which it was hard to prevail. This was intensified by elaborate court protocol, by bureaucratic practices that limited public access to the shahs, and by their desire for material gains, their fears and insecurities, and their own private lifestyles. Even though they made occasional attempts to break through the strictures of their office by reducing the power of their officials or eliminating administrative and courtly barriers by personally hearing the grievances of their subjects, they could hardly escape the mores of the monarchy itself. The spectacle of kingly glory on which the ruler's authority rested required from him lofty gestures of generosity and tempered severity but seriously limited his ultimate task of preserving the balance between the ruling elite and the ruled.

The self-image of the Qajar shah as the nucleus of the ruling elite and as the supreme regulator with divine rights is evident in the use of titles and honorifics and the way these evolved over time. Although the chronicles of the Qajar period showered Aqa Muhammad Khan with many grand appellations, during his own time as ruler he adopted no more grand a title than *khan* and later *shah*. By contrast, his successor, Fath 'Ali Shah, adopted not only the ancient Persian title of *shahanshah* ("king of kings") but also the Torco-Mongol title of *khaqan* ("the khan of the khans"), symbolizing claims over both the throne and the tribes. This lineage was underscored among Fath 'Ali Shah's successors: Muhammad Shah was referred to as "Khaqan son of Khaqan," Nasir al-Din Shah as "Khaqan son of Khaqan son of Khaqan." These royal titles were embellished with an array of other honorifics reflecting the rulers' desire to present a sense of historical continuity and hence legitimacy. Drawing on the glories of the Persian mythical and dynastic past, the Qajar shah was acclaimed by court chroniclers and in official records as a "world conqueror" (*gity sitan*) of "Alexandrian magnitude" (*sikandar sha'n*), a possessor of Jamshid's glory (*Jam jah*), of Faridun's charisma (*Faridun farr*), and of Khusraw's splendor (*Kisra shawkat*). During times of war and punishment he was a Turk with the ferocity of Genghis (*Changiz sawlat*) and the vehemence of Tamerlane (*Timur satwat*). In peacetime he was acknowledged as a "joyous king" (*shahryar-i kamkar*) and a fortuitous sultan (*sultan-i sahab-qaran*) whose religious and civil duties were also couched in his titles. Above all he was the "shadow of God" (*zillullah*) upon earth, a "refuge of Islam" (*Islam panah*) and a "shield of the Islamic shari'a" (*shari'at panah*), but he was also a "guardian of the Persian kingdom" (*hafiz-i mulk-i 'ajam*) and more frequently the king (*padshah*) of the "Guarded Domains" (*mamalik-i mahrusa*) of Iran.

Ample use of grand titles was a practice not limited to the ruler. All the princes of the royal family, members of the nobility, courtiers, government officials, and army officers—and later, under Nasir al-Din, the shah's chief wives, all the servants of the inner court, and even those casually connected to the sprawling Qajar court—held titles often unsuitable to their stature and function. For the early Qajar rulers, conferring titles was a way of enhancing the image of royal magnificence. For the recipients it was a means of acquiring legitimacy in place of rendering service and loyalty. In the highly ceremonious court of Fath 'Ali Shah there was some rationale for granting titles, but by the late Nasir al-Din period and that of his successor, Muzaffar al-Din Shah (1896–1906), there was little meaning in such titles beyond the size of the gift presented to the shah or the ruler's personal favor toward the recipient.[9]

The society over which the early Qajars ruled bore the scars of Iran's ravages of earlier decades. By the middle of the nineteenth century the population of the country was barely more than 6 million, of which more than 80 percent resided in the countryside as nomads and villagers. About two-thirds of the population inhabited the northern and central provinces, with heavier concentrations in Azarbaijan, Kirmanshah, northern Khurasan, and Isfahan. The sparsely populated cities and towns throughout the country served as marketplaces for agricultural products of the hinterlands, for regional trade, and for traditional industries with limited access to other domestic or foreign centers. As the century progressed, a semblance of a national economy began to emerge through a commercial network that allowed larger movements of population and goods between provinces. In the northwest lay Tabriz, Iran's largest and the most prosperous city, with a population of more than 100,000 in the 1850s. It was the country's major gateway to the outside world, through which trade was conducted with Russia, the Ottoman Empire, and Europe. In the central-southern part of the country Isfahan, the great capital of the Safavid empire, with a population no larger than 60,000, still preserved its religious and to some extent its cultural and commercial predominance, even though it had suffered greatly in the turbulent interregnums of the post-Safavid period. By the early decades of the Qajar era, Shiraz, the provincial center of the ancient Fars province and the capital of the Zand dynasty, also maintained something of its flourishing past because of the revival of the Persian Gulf trade. Other centers, such as Yazd in central-southern Iran, Kirman in the southeast, Mashhad in the northeast, and Qazvin in the central north, also enjoyed economic revivals primarily because of trade with neighboring lands. Commercial seaports such as Muhammarah, Bushihr, and Bandar 'Abbas along the Persian Gulf possessed some vitality due to maritime trade with British India and Masqat (Muscat). Barfurush and Rasht in the north also benefited from the Caspian trade with Russia and the Caucasus.[10]

Tehran, the new capital inaugurated by Aqa Muhammad Khan in 1786, even after half a century of Qajar rule barely accommodated a population of more than 80,000. Originally a resort hamlet in the southern foothills of the central Alburz Range north of the old city of Rayy (Rages of ancient times), Tehran first emerged in the middle of the seventeenth century as a Safavid garrison town because of its strategic position as a gateway to the north. Karim Khan Zand had built a small residence there to keep a closer watch over powerful northern tribes such as the Qajars. Aqa Muhammad Khan's choice of his capital was based on a similar concern for control of both the northern and southern regions. He was aware of the loyalties of the inhabitants of previous capitals, Isfahan and Shiraz, to the Safavid and Zand dynasties, respectively, and was wary of the power of the notables in these cities. He probably viewed Tehran's lack of a substantial urban structure as a blessing, because it minimized the chances of resistance to his rule by the notables and by the general public. These cities were also vulnerable to the onslaughts of the Bakhtiyaris of Isfahan and the tribes of central and southern Fars. Moreover, the Qajar ruler was anxious to maintain his firm hold over his own power base in Astarabad and to remain within close reach of Azarbaijan and the Caucasus.

That Tehran was designated in the Fath 'Ali Shah era both the "abode of monarchy" (*dar al-saltana*) and the "abode of the caliphate" (*dar al-khilafah*) reflects the Qajars' view of their capital as the seat of a dual authority—the temporal sovereignty of the shah and the religious custo-dianship (caliphate) that the Qajar ruler hoped to uphold on the Safavid model. The Qajars tried to follow the Safavid example not only by naming their capital grandly but also by physically brandishing its image. Under Fath 'Ali Shah Gulistan Palace was enlarged and beautified, the citadel (*arg*) was extended to include new barracks, and other palaces were built in the vicinity of the capital.[11] The old city quarters were expanded and new quarters developed to house the growing population. Tehran bazaar was renovated and enlarged, and as a sign of Qajar patronage a royal mosque and a central square were constructed adjacent to the citadel. Yet despite these improvements Tehran's development was hindered by the lack of substantial commercial and other economic enterprises. As Iran's political capital it was overshadowed by Tabriz and Isfahan, a fact that explains the Qajars' recognition of Tabriz, the seat of the crown prince since the beginning of the nineteenth century, as another *dar al-saltana*, a designation that also symbolized a sharing of royal power between the ruler and his crown prince.

Persian cities were divided into city wards, each with its own headman (*kadkhuda*), who served under a magistrate or mayor (*kalantar*), who himself answered to the provincial governor. The villagers and tribespeople were organized under similar leaders who were responsible to provincial authorities. Though the Qajar period suffered from a degree of administrative chaos, informal power structure, and confused definition of offices, the basic precepts of a patrimonial hierarchy remained intact. In the cities the guild organizations (*asnaf*) also served as a parallel urban structure, representing professional interests recognized by the state for taxation and other purposes.[12]

The shah's informal hold over the city notables, the bazaar, and the 'ulama, as well as his indirect control over the nomads and the peasants in the countryside, naturally restricted the sphere of his effective power. Instead the symbolic essence of his office as a supreme regulator was reinforced. Increasingly the Qajar shah upheld his royal supremacy over the "Guarded Domains" of Iran not so much by military force and administrative surveillance as by royal grandiosity, symbolic punishments and rewards, and sheer political maneuvering. This curious mix of formal facade and informal practice was visible at every level of the government in its treatment of its subjects.

WITHIN FRAGILE FRONTIERS

An element of continuity in Iran's political order is best observed in the endurance of its geopolitical boundaries. The Qajar territorial equilibrium, which with the exception of some losses on the periphery continued throughout the nineteenth century, was founded on tangible historical precedence. The frontiers of the "Guarded Domains of Iran" (*Mamalik-i Mahrusa-yi Iran*), as the country had been defined since Safavid times, were almost the same as those in the fifth-century definition of *Iranshahr* in the Sassanian manual, *Nama-yi Tansar*, and those outlined by four-teenth-century geographer Hamdullah Mustawfi, the author of *Nazhat al-Qulub*.[13]

In Qajar times Iran's boarders with the Ottoman Empire stretched across the western Caucasus and eastern Anatolia along the Zagrus Range to the northwestern tip of the Persian Gulf. In spite of serious challenges from both sides, which led to several episodes of occupation of Iran's western provinces by the Ottomans, these common frontiers proved to be essentially unalterable. Nadir's largely unsuccessful campaigns against the

Ottomans in Iraq in the 1730s and Karim Khan's abortive attempt to conquer Basra in 1775–1779 exhibited Iran's handicap in securing permanent territorial gains beyond the Zagrus Range. The early Qajar shahs and their contemporary Ottoman sultans entertained expansionist ambitions along these turbulent frontiers, yet despite disputes over Kurdish and Arab tribes of Kurdistan and Khuzistan and over the Persian pilgrims to the Shi'ite holy cities of Iraq there was no significant shift in boundary lines, which were set as early as the Treaty of Amasiya in 1555.

In spite of instability along the Perso-Ottoman borders, during the nineteenth century there was growth in commercial and human exchanges between the two countries. Most significant, there was an increase in the volume of the Persian pilgrimage traffic to the shrine cities of Najaf and Karbala in Ottoman Iraq. Veneration for the Shi'ite imams, whose shrines were adorned by the rulers of Iran, made the Persian public more aware of its Shi'ite identity. Pilgrims to these holy cities also paid homage to the 'ulama, who since the late eighteenth century had been residing there in greater numbers. They presided over teaching circles, which attracted large numbers of students from Iran. Through these students, who returned to Iran to occupy religious positions in their local communities, senior jurists (mujtahids) in Iraq were able to exercise wider authority over the religious affairs of Iran. Their followers throughout the Shi'ite world also grew larger once the means of communication with them improved. At times the decisions of these religious dignitaries clashed with the policies of the Persian state, but by and large they relied on the Qajar rulers to be their protectors and benefactors.

Throughout the Qajar era the Ottoman Empire also served as a window to Europe and an important conduit for the adoption of Western-style administrative and other measures. Nearly all reform-minded statesmen of the Qajar period were exposed at some stage in their careers to modernization efforts in the neighboring empire. These men looked upon the reforms of Mahmud II and the Tanzimat era as models for state-sponsored reforms in their own country. The Qajar shahs, however, viewed these attempts in their neighboring empire with ambivalence. They often saw such measures as hazardous departures from the old ways, changes that could jeopardize the security of their realm and the survival of their throne. The loss of Ottoman provinces to nationalist movements in the Balkans and growing European intervention in the internal affairs of the Ottoman Empire dampened whatever enthusiasm they entertained for change. The two worlds of the Persians and Ottomans thus remained essentially divided along a religiolinguistic chasm that could only be crossed by an intellectual minority.[14]

Iran's eastern frontiers were more volatile and culturally barren. From the Central Asian khanates of Khiva, Marv, and Bukhara in the northeast to Herat and Kandahar in the east to Baluchistan and Makran in the southeast, the Persian frontiers witnessed persistent nomadic incursions. Turkoman, Afghan, and occasionally Baluch encroachments into the interiors of Khurasan and neighboring provinces ravaged the countryside and interrupted the flow of eastern trade with India and Central Asia. The Sunni Turkoman raiders' common practice of abducting villagers and townsmen of Khurasan to sell in the slave markets of Khiva and Bukhara in Central Asia was a major menace to the Qajar government and damaged its reputation. Retaliatory campaigns to quell the Turkoman threat and to reassert sovereignty over eastern principalities, most notably Herat and Marv, were of limited effect and a constant drain on the state's limited resources. Down to the closing decades of the nineteenth century, when Russia completed the annexation of the khanates of Central Asia and a partially integrated Afghanistan emerged under British custody, the threat to the Persian eastern frontiers remained unabated. The Turkoman and Afghan raids weakened Iran's old ties with Transoxania and in effect contributed to Khurasan's cultural and commercial decline. The fervent upholding of Sunni Islam in Central Asia did not ease off after the demise of the Uzbek kingdom of the sixteenth and seventeenth centuries. Shi'ite Iran thus continued to be enveloped on its eastern front by an unsympathetic, if not hostile, Sunni creed in much the same way as it was surrounded on its western front by the Sunni Ottomans. As a legacy of the Safavid era, Iran's ethnoreligious solitude only reaffirmed its national integration. The notion of Guarded Domains thus represented a sense of territorial and political homogeneity in a country in which the Persian language, culture, kingship, and culture and the Shi'ite religious creed became inseparable parts of the evolving national identity.

The fact that Iran's neighbors on its northern and southern frontiers were two rival powers, Russia and Britain, also reflected its geopolitical containment. Highly influential in the political, economic, and sociocultural making of modern Iran, these powers came into wider contact with Iran when it was about to recover from the political malaise and isolation of earlier decades. Since the eighteenth century Russia's ambitions in the Caucasus and on the Caspian coast had been a matter of occasional concern for the Safavids and their successor states; but in the first quarter of the nineteenth century the Qajar state was compelled to give the greatest priority to the threat coming from the northern neighbor. Loss of territory and prestige during two rounds of Russo-Persian wars (1805–1813 and 1826–1828), combined with the ensuing bankruptcy, culminated in the Turkmanchay Treaty of 1828. This treaty permanently severed the Caucasian provinces from Iran and settled the Russo-Persian northwestern boundary along the Aras River. It also imposed on Iran enduring capitulatory and other types of restrictions alien to the Persian notion of sovereignty. The psychological impact of defeat was only magnified by Russia's conquests on the northeastern periphery in the following decades and its postures of advancing toward the northern provinces of Iran proper.

In Iran's nineteenth-century political history there have been few events as pivotal as war with Russia. The Qajar government and society were quick to recognize the Russian threat but came to terms with it with difficulty. The Griboidov incident in 1829, in the aftermath of the war, when a Russian diplomatic mission was massacred by the Tehran mob, was one symptom of public disenchantment with the humiliating submission to a Christian power. In the following decades with varying intensity Russia held the implicit threat of military occupation as a Damoclean sword over the Qajar state in order to accomplish diplomatic and other objectives. Russian advances in the khanates of Central Asia from the early 1860s to late 1880s were seen in Tehran as a mixed blessing. The Qajars were alarmed at the possibility of losing Khurasan and the Caspian provinces to Russia while at the same time being relieved of the Turkoman menace on their frontiers.[15]

With British India stretching by the 1820s as far as Iran's southeastern flank and soon afterward dominating the Persian Gulf, Qajar Iran was bound to view such colonial ascendancy with mixed sentiments. The Persian government viewed Britain as a potential threat to Iran's southern provinces yet considered it a natural ally, a counterbalance against the belligerent northern neighbor. In turn Britain treated Iran with a mixture of accord and distrust. It recognized Iran's value as an ally in pacifying India's northwestern frontiers at the turn of the nineteenth century and soon after as a buffer state against the potential Russian threat to India. Yet over time British authorities became increasingly suspicious of Iran and the possibility that it might succumb to Russian pressure. In the first quarter of the nineteenth century a level of cooperation in defense and commerce existed between the two neighbors, even though Britain reneged on some of its defense commitments during the Russo-Persian wars. British diplomatic relations with Iran, first officially launched by Sir John Malcolm and his mission in 1800, were primarily aimed at safeguarding the interests of the British East India Company. The British emissaries were admired in the Persian court for their resourcefulness and prudence and were viewed with an esteem only matched by the Persians' grudging fear of Russian diplomats and generals.[16]

What made the relations between Iran and both its neighbors problematic in the decades following defeat in wars with Russia was a change in Europe's image of Iran from a mighty and enduring empire to a weak and vulnerable buffer state. The Anglo-Russian contest for supremacy over Central Asia and excessive British concern for the defense of India turned Iran in the eyes of its European neighbors into a pawn in the Great Game. The Persian state came to be seen condescendingly as one that ought to be contained within its frontiers, coaxed by diplomacy at the center, and, if need be, driven into submission (but not militarily conquered) by punitive action. For the British, the Qajar handicap for withstanding the Russian military thrust was concomitant with Iran's obedience to Russian wishes, a prospect Britain tried to resist at all costs. The Russians entertained the same concern in reverse. Throughout the Qajar era, then, Iran became the center stage for a power rivalry between Russia and Britain that often involved concerns for prestige, petty frictions between the representatives of the European powers, and the wishes and interests of the faction-ridden Qajar ruling elite.

Given the bipolar nature of Iran's diplomacy, it was natural for the Persian government to utilize the Anglo-Russian rivalry to safeguard its own interests and maximize its otherwise meager diplomatic gains. Yet such a course of policy was interpreted by both European powers as evidence of intrigue and malicious intent. Thus, to counter the supposed or real influence of the rival party, both powers regarded meddling in Iran's internal affairs a legitimate extension of their diplomacy. More often by direct pressure on the Persian government but also through protégés and proxies, British and Russian envoys began influencing domestic issues ranging from dynastic succession and court protocol to litigation, citizenship, and customs tariffs. Such foreign meddlings were facilitated by structural weaknesses in the Qajar government, by intrinsic corruption and disloyalty among officials, and by rising discontent among the Persian public. From the second quarter of the nineteenth century on, Qajar rulers and many of their high officials were encouraged to rely on foreign backing in order to compensate for their diminishing support among the populace.

Beyond the sphere of diplomacy, elements of Western-style reform began to influence a small but powerful upper crust of the state elite beginning in the early decades of Qajar rule. Defeat in the war with Russia made the Qajars more aware of their military deficiencies and encouraged them to adopt modern weaponry and elements of European warfare in organization of the troops. Most significant, the creation of the New Army (Nizam-i Jadid) under the crown prince 'Abbas Mirza in Azarbaijan after 1813, and elsewhere under other prince-governors, reinforced the Qajar war ethos and transformed the state's perceptions of its power in dealings with its own subjects and with its neighbors. Throughout the nineteenth century the desire for military reform brought into the Iranian environment a host of generals, drill officers, and military advisers from Britain, France, Russia, Austria, Italy, and elsewhere. Together with European diplomats, merchants, and missionaries, they were the most important channels through which the Persians acquired an early knowledge of the West.

For the Qajar Shah and the princely elite from 'Abbas Mirza onward, images of European power took the form not only of military hardware and troop formation but of dress and appearance as well. They adopted European dress for themselves and their New Army to underscore their readiness to defend the land and the faith. The stark contrast between Fath 'Ali Shah's traditional appearance, which included an ornamented Persian long robe, high heels, and a long beard, and the appearance of his successor, Muhammad Shah, who sported semi-Europeanized dress and a short beard, clearly speaks to this change of the royal image. After an initial squabble even the 'ulama reluctantly consented to the Qajar adoption of European dress. The early Qajar statesmen argued that the shah's duties obligated him, and the men of the sword in general, to adopt necessary means against the eminent threat of foreign aggression and that the change of dress was a necessary symbol for the overhaul of the country's defense. The symbolism of the royal shift to European outfits in a culture deeply observant of its dress code went beyond sheer military need. Gradual adoption of European dress heralded a Qajar desire to set forth a new example of monarchy that was more disciplined and forceful, an image deemed necessary to mend the injured legitimacy of the monarchy and mindful of Iran's need to bridge its growing material gap with the outside world.

NOBILITY AND THE PROBLEM OF SUCCESSION

The early Qajars were successful in securing a certain degree of stability by sharing power with princes of the blood and other influential members of the dominant clan. Yet the greatest quandary for them was the question of succession and the rule of primogeniture, the exclusive right of the firstborn to the throne. For more than half a century, between Aqa Muhammad Khan's reign and Nasir al-Din's accession in 1848, diverse forces accelerated or hindered the process of succession. Chief among them were intertribal divisions, tensions within the royal family, the wishes of the foreign powers, and the vested interests of the bureaucracy.

Conscious of the ever-present threat of tribal discord, as early as 1789 Aqa Muhammad Khan stipulated that the crown should pass to the first son born of the bond between the two powerful clans of the Qajar house: the Quvanlu and the Davalu. Aqa Muhammad Khan's aspirations for the continuity of his empire were thus projected in the progenitive capacities of his successor. With similar considerations in mind, Fath 'Ali Shah married his son and celebrated heir, 'Abbas Mirza, to a daughter of Davalu. He also instructed other princes of the royal family to take brides from other Qajar branches.

Healing the age-old tribal rifts between the two chief branches of the Qajar tribe was no doubt the immediate aim for these unions. The ruling family was initially from the Quvanlu (or Quyunlu), the sheep clan that was the principal lineage of the six clans of the Ashaqah-bash ("the downstream settlers") subtribe of the Qajar tribe. By contrast, the Davalu, the camel clan, was the chief clan of the Yukhari-bash ("the upstream settlers").[17] The hostility between the two clans intensified in the late eighteenth century. When the Qajars came to power, the memories of defections and betrayals that had cost the lives of three successive Quvanlu leaders and had caused much fratricide and bloodshed among the Qajars of Astarabad still rankled, especially in the minds of the mothers, sisters, and daughters of the slain warriors. Aqa Muhammad Khan's merciless struggle against his Qajar rivals, both Davalu and Quvanlu, further exacerbated these ill feelings.[18]

Fath 'Ali Shah could not have fulfilled the expectations of his predecessor more fittingly. During the forty-seven years of his adult life, thirty-five of which he spent on the throne, he single-handedly generated a royal family of unprecedented size. He brought close to 1,000 wives of diverse origin, class, age, and function to his royal harem.[19] He married not only the daughters of the Qajars and other tribal chiefs, including ex-wives of his paternal uncles, but also the daughters of high-ranking officials, merchants, and urban notables, women captured in wars with the remnants of the vanquished dynasties (the Afsharids and the Zands), Persian and Georgian slave girls, and a host of concubines, entertainers, and women servants who crowded the expanding inner quarters (*andarun*) of the shah. They bore him offspring at a rate that truly made Fath 'Ali Shah one of the most fertile men in history. Between January and November 1789 alone, shortly after his official designation to apparency, his wives gave birth to no less than seven sons, three of whom (including 'Abbas Mirza) were born within ten days. By the time of his death in 1834, he left behind some sixty sons and more than forty daughters.[20]

The record of Fath 'Ali Shah's children is no less impressive. His first ten sons, the most powerful princes of the royal house, had between them a total of 333 children: 175 sons and 158 daughters.[21] The assessment of the court historian Sipihr, who placed the number of Fath 'Ali's surviving offspring in 1834 at 786, does not seem to be an exaggeration. "It is not implausible," he added, "that by now they have multiplied to ten thousand."[22] Thanks to Fath 'Ali and his sons, in the relatively short period of half a century and over a span of five generations between Aqa Muhammad Khan and Nasir al-Din Shah a new royal nobility was created that could reduce to uneasy submission all rival forces, both within and outside of the Qajar tribe.

The aptitude of Fath 'Ali Shah and the royal princes to assemble households of such proportion certainly went beyond the boundaries of family love or lustful pleasure, the latter becoming the subject of frequent criticism and ridicule by later observers. In many instances, sheer political expediency was the only motivation to marry women of diverse tribal origins. These were wives whom the king and the royal princes often disliked for their odious arrogance but nonetheless tolerated for their worth as pawns, or hostages, in a complicated political game.[23] Union as such was an effective method by which to consolidate the Qajar throne. Discussing the high-ranking wives of his father, Ahmad Mirza 'Azud al-Dawla, the forty-ninth son of Fath 'Ali Shah, noted: "It was merely for the peaceful unification of the tribes and clans, and for the expression of kingly mercy, that these wives became the subjects of royal favor and respect."[24] For all the blame and criticism Fath 'Ali Shah often receives for his life of extravagance and pleasure seeking, he should be credited for transforming, largely by peaceful means, the Qajar tribe from a diffuse oligarchy with shaky loyalties into a closely knit patrimony.

The earliest attempts to enforce a rule of succession proved to be ineffective in relaxing the tension between the shah's numerous sons.[25] Not until Nasir al-Din Shah's reign did the Qajars fully replace the custom of free and often bloody contest for succession with the norm of primogeniture. Although 'Abbas Mirza's nomination was seldom disputed openly by Fath 'Ali Shah himself, the crown prince was periodically challenged by his powerful brothers, who felt they were equally justified in their claim to apparency. The system of provincial tutelage under Fath 'Ali in practice divided Iran among the senior princes of the Qajar house, allowing them to have their miniature court and administration and a large measure of independence in the conduct of their affairs. By the 1820s there were at least four other potential candidates for succession among the sons of the shah, three of whom were eligible because of their maternal Qajar lineage, their proximity in age to the crown prince, and above all their political leverage over the shah. Fath 'Ali himself, who increasingly felt the pressure brought on him by his sons, fostered a level of competition among them—a competition that was not without its later costs to the crown and the country.

Fraternal strife among the Qajar princes in turn introduced new factors into the process of succession, of which the most important was the prospect of foreign intercession. 'Abbas Mirza's position as the crown prince, the viceregent (*na'ib al-saltana*), and the governor general of the province of Azarbaijan was no doubt the strongest among senior princes, even though it was complicated by the burdensome task of defending the northwestern frontiers against Russia. The sobering experience of defeat in the first round of the Russo-Persian wars (1805–1813) and the loss of territories in the Caucasus had already jeopardized his predominance. In subsequent years, the anxious prince tried to consolidate his position by making himself equally indispensable to Fath 'Ali Shah in Tehran, to the tsar in St. Petersburg, and to the British government in London. He began to appreciate the benefits of maintaining friendly relations with Iran's northern neighbor, although such relations did not wholly extinguish his chronic desire to recapture lost territories.[26]

The Treaty of Gulistan (1813), which ended the first round of Russo-Persian wars, guaranteed the tsar's support for the crown prince of Iran, but it also barred the Russian sovereign from interfering in the choice of the heir apparent should a dispute develop among the princes.[27] At about the same time the treaties of 1812 and 1814 with England stipulated similar assurances. Although these provisions seemed intended to strengthen 'Abbas Mirza's hand, they also left the door open for future challenges by his brothers. Such uncertainties in the event of a dispute indicated that in the early decades of Fath 'Ali's reign the question of apparency was still not fully resolved; a free-for-all contest between the qualified princes was still to determine the future of the throne.

Ironically, the humiliating defeat in the second round of the war with Russia altered this situation in favor of primogeniture. The peace treaty of Turkmanchay in 1828 turned out to be an unforeseen opportunity for 'Abbas Mirza to secure his own, and his descendants', succession. At the end of the war the remaining parts of the Caucasus and most of Azarbaijan (including the provincial capital Tabriz) were under Russian occupation. The near elimination of the Persian army and the Russian demand for a burdensome war retribution were further causes of distress to the shah and the crown prince. Such terrible losses even obliged Fath 'Ali to succumb temporarily to the claims of one of his sons, the bellicose Hasan 'Ali Mirza Shaja' al-Saltana, then the governor general of Khurasan, in his bid to replace 'Abbas Mirza. If nothing else, this challenge persuaded 'Abbas Mirza and his minister and chief negotiator, the celebrated Mirza Abul-Qasim Qa'im Maqam, to hasten the peace negotiations with the Russians. In return for accepting nearly all the terms proposed by Russia, the prince and his minister obtained unequivocal recognition of 'Abbas Mirza as the legitimate heir apparent to the throne. Article 7 of the Treaty of Turk-manchay (1828) thus declared:

> His Majesty the Shah of Persia, having judged it fitting to appoint as his successor and heir presumptive his august son Prince Abbas Mirza, His Majesty the Emperor of all the Russia, with a view to giving to His Majesty the Shah public evidence of his friendly dispositions and his desire to contribute to the consolidation of this order of succession, undertake to recognize . . . Prince Abbas Mirza, the successor and heir presumptive of the crown of Persia and to consider him the legitimate sovereign to this kingdom from his accession to the throne.[28]

This article suited both sides. It suited the Russians because it put within their reach a weaker and more vulnerable crown prince receptive to their persuasions. Moreover, clear recognition of 'Abbas Mirza as the new heir apparent was a precautionary measure by Russia, and soon after by Britain, to preempt a dynastic war after the death of the ruling monarch. 'Abbas Mirza himself, understandably apprehensive of his father's uncertainties and of the intrigues of the Tehran court, looked also for alternative support. The second defeat had reduced his popularity, both in Azarbaijan and in the capital, and acknowledgment of his legitimacy by the victorious Russians was necessary if he was to survive the challenge of his jealous brothers.

An even more important outcome of the above article was the future continuity of succession among 'Abbas Mirza's descendants. Although Article 7 of Turkmanchay did not stipulate any such guarantees, its interpretation in favor of 'Abbas Mirza's house, which came about in 1833 with his premature death, was of lasting significance. Fath 'Ali Shah designated Muhammad Mirza, 'Abbas's son, as heir apparent, but the near equal seniority of at least three of the shah's own sons made compliance with the rule of primogeniture a risky enterprise. To justify the unconventional choice of the grandson as heir, Qajar historians (including Jahangir Mirza, another son of 'Abbas Mirza who himself later was a casualty of the struggle for succession) resorted to seeking precedent in Iran's history from Timurid and Safavid times.[29] The shah's decision was tenuously viewed by the neighboring powers as a legitimate interpretation of the spirit of the Turkmanchay treaty.[30]

Predictably, such interpretation was not accepted without serious dissent within the royal family. Upon the death of Fath 'Ali Shah in 1834, a war of succession broke out that involved at least three pretenders to the throne from among the sons of the late shah. These formidable pretenders were overcome through a combination of domestic and foreign assistance that Muhammad Shah and his aids and officials managed to muster. When he set out from Tabriz in 1834 to capture the capital, Muhammad Shah had in his company the European-trained New Army of Azarbaijan, the British and Russian officers and diplomats supportive of his claim, and statesmen of his father's court. These were formidable forces that put Muhammad Mirza's contestants at a clear disadvantage.

The defeat of the pretenders in Tehran, Isfahan, and Shiraz was followed by a rapid shift of loyalties among the associated nobles and officials to Muhammad Shah's camp. The prevalence of 'Abbas Mirza's house thus marked the effective political end for most, if not all, other princes of the Fath 'Ali Shah line (and their descendants), whose meager means from land tenure and pensions could barely meet their needs. However, the house of 'Abbas Mirza, the final winner of the struggle for succession, was never entirely free from internal tension. Brothers of Muhammad Shah proved to be formidable challenges not only to the young shah but even more so to Nasir al-Din Mirza, his heir to the throne.

1 The Child of Turkmanchay

In September 1819 the Qajar ruler of Iran, Fath 'Ali Shah, summoned to the capital his grandson Muhammad Mirza, the twelve-year-old son of crown prince 'Abbas Mirza, to marry him with Malik Jahan, a fourteen-year-old bride of the Quvanlu branch of the ruling dynasty. Muhammad Mirza and Malik Jahan were Nasir al-Din's parents. The marital bond, part of an ambitious scheme of genealogical engineering undertaken by the monarch, was calculated to heal the internecine conflicts that divided the early Qajars. At least three sources considered it important to record the alleged instructions for establishing marriage bonds between the royal house and the rival factions of the Qajar tribe. Proclaimed by Aqa Muhammad Khan, the castrated founder of the dynasty, the instructions were passed on to his superprocreant nephew and successor, Fath 'Ali Shah.

> Marry the daughter of Mirza Muhammad Khan Baglarbagi Davalu to your son and crown prince 'Abbas Mirza—who himself is from his distaff side a Davalu—so that his son, who shall bear my name, Muhammad, will descend from both houses of the Qajar like his father. My uncle Sulayman Khan [Quvanlu] has faithfully toiled at the service of our state. Give one of your daughters to one of his sons, and the child of this union will bear a daughter who shall be betrothed to Muhammad Mirza. The son who, God willing, will be born of this union will be your great-grandson from both sides. Then all [will be] Quvanlu, all [will be] Quvanlu.[1]

This prognostic testimony, at least in its embellished version, sounds more like an apocryphal report produced by court chroniclers anxious to sanctify the right of the dominant Quvanlu, and in particular 'Abbas Mirza's progeny, to the throne. More important, it meant to attach a predestined impeccability to the noble origins of Nasir al-Din Shah, the fourth ruler of the Qajar dynasty and the final product of this complex marital scheme (see genealogical tree).

UNHAPPY UNION

Nasir al-Din Mirza, the first surviving child of Muhammad Mirza and Malik Jahan, was born on 17 July 1831/6 Safar 1247 Q. in the village of

25

Kuhnamir, some fifteen miles south of Tabriz.[2] The pregnant Malik Jahan
must have been driven to the summer resort to escape the heat, or possibly
an outbreak of cholera, in the provincial capital. Giving birth to a child in
a remote village was not unusual for the Qajar royal family, still accustomed to spending weeks, even months, out in the country. Muhammad
Mirza, meanwhile, in the company of his father, 'Abbas Mirza, the crown
prince, was out campaigning against the tribal warlords of northeastern
Khurasan.[3] Indeed, the very name Nasir al-Din ("the Helper [or Supporter]
of the Faith") may have been given to the child, instead of an ancestral
name, in anticipation of his father's victory over the unruly Sunni Turkoman tribes of the northern frontiers. The royal army released more than
20,000 Shi'ite captives who were to have been sold in the slave markets of
Central Asia, and this benevolent action must have given the campaigning
Muhammad Mirza cause for pride. Nasir al-Din's great-grandfather, Fath
'Ali Shah, concurrently reviewing his troops in a camp in central Iran,
celebrated the new birth, as the chronicler Hidayat puts it, "on the emerald-
like meadow," with "the melted ruby" wine.[4] The shah must have been
pleased with the news of yet another addition to the royal flock, but perhaps
neither he nor 'Abbas Mirza or Muhammad Mirza ever expected such a
sudden turn of events as those that in less than four years made the infant
prince, from among numerous contestants, first in line to the Qajar throne.

In spite of "the auspicious birth" of the prince, and in spite of all the
good wishes of Fath 'Ali Shah and the crown prince, 'Abbas Mirza, the
marriage of convenience between Muhammad Mirza and Malik Jahan
proved an unhappy one even by the standards of royal unions. The widening gap between the prince and his wife seemed predictable from the start
given the sheer weight of political benefits the royal family expected from
this bond. The tension between the prince's Davalu mother and his
Quvanlu bride did not help to smooth the couple's married life. Moreover,
a personality conflict between the prince and his bride was exacerbated over
the years by the bitter experience of losing several infant children.[5] By the
time their two surviving children, Nasir al-Din and his sister, Malikzada
(later 'Izzat al-Dawla), were born, some twelve years after the couple's
ceremonial matrimony in 1819, they had both developed personalities of
their own with dispositions distinctly at odds with one another. Nasir
al-Din Mirza was the unfavored child of this problematic union. The
adverse effects of the couple's discord remained visible not only in his
troubled childhood but throughout his adult life. The contrasting personalities of his parents—the introverted and impressionable Muhammad
Mirza versus the energetic and domineering Malik Jahan—were exacer-

bated by other factors, primarily the factional tension between the Quvanlu and Davalu families and the ominous shadow of the premier, Hajji Mirza Aqasi, over Muhammad Shah as moral mentor and fatherly authority.

Muhammad Mirza, the eldest of 'Abbas Mirza's twenty-five sons, was born in 1808 in Tabriz. As far as can be determined about his childhood and youth, he was a taciturn and rather remote boy with no obvious ambition for leadership. His upbringing in Tabriz typified the traditional courtly education that some princes of his time received from the articulate government officials and scribes in the crown prince's service. Even more distant than their father's generation from the habits and manners of the nomadic Qajars, Muhammad Mirza and his brothers were well exposed to the subtleties of Persian civil life. At a strikingly short remove from the uncouth tent dwellers of Astarabad, as brief as a mere decade, the princes of the royal family were busy studying classical texts of Persian literature, the intricacies of Arabic syntax, the rudiments of the Shi'ite religion, and the art of calligraphy. The latter subject was particularly favored by Muhammad Mirza, who, like his father, his grandfather, and a few of his uncles and brothers, was a calligrapher of some skill.[6] Later in life, in tune with his ascetic lifestyle, he developed a somewhat anti-European attitude, though, being the son of 'Abbas Mirza and living in the Tabriz of the 1820s and 1830s, he was well exposed to European ways.

The English traveler and observer James Baillie Fraser, who met Muhammad Mirza in 1834, just before his appointment as heir apparent, describes him as "the worthiest of all the numerous descendants of Fath 'Ali Shah, particularly in the point of morals and private character." Although in talent, Fraser stated condescendingly, Muhammad Mirza could not claim an abundance, "in military affairs he bids fair for competence at least. Take him for all in all, as a *Prince* and a *Qajar*, he is a rarity in Persia." Fraser described him as "gracious and smiling" and found his manner void of all those blustering assumptions of greatness that were so offensive in many of the royal family.[7]

The credit for Muhammad Mirza's accomplishments, as well as for his presiding over a period of cultural revival, reforms, and contact with Europe, no doubt goes to his enlightened and responsive father, 'Abbas Mirza. The credit for transmitting the Persian court culture to the Qajars and educating the princes of 'Abbas Mirza's house, however, belongs to that class of officialdom, "the men of the pen," of whom Mirza 'Isa (Mirza Buzurg) Farahani, Qa'im Maqam I (d. 1821), and his celebrated son Mirza Abul-Qasim, Qa'im Maqam II (d. 1835), were two examples.[8] Encouraged by 'Abbas Mirza's emphasis on educating his sons and flourishing under the supervision of the Qa'im Maqams (both father and son), a number of Muhammad Mirza's brothers went beyond a rudimentary education. At least two of them became writers of some repute.[9] Some of that literary and scholarly interest survived up to the time of Nasir al-Din's governorship of Azarbaijan in 1848 and affected his intellectual formation.

The refinement of literary taste and adherence to courtly manners, however, was difficult to divorce from the time-honored war ethos that marked the life of the early Qajars. Muhammad Mirza was still the product of a mixed milieu in which learning and leisure were merged with ferociousness on the battlefield. The expansionist vision of Aqa Muhammad Khan, the founder of the dynasty, and that of his father, Husayn Quli Khan Jahansuz (literally, "the world burner"), the adventurous warlord of Astarabad, was modeled out of the world-conquering aspirations of Ghengiz and Timur (Tamerlane). Even by the late nineteenth century this vision had not altogether vanished from the collective Qajar mentality. Though mellowed by military inferiority and defeat, the Qajar aggression still found expression in dreams of restoring the lost territories of the Safavid and Afsharid empires as well as in domestic military expeditions and in modes of punishment and torture.

To this odd mixture of civility and belligerence Muhammad Mirza added a third element, one perhaps less typical of the Qajars but of crucial importance in the formation of his character. A mystical attachment to Hajji Mirza Aqasi, an eccentric dervish (and later his prime minister), proved to be as decisive in the prince's private life as in the shaping of his political career and the early life of his future son, Nasir al-Din Mirza. In the large households maintained by the shah and his sons, attachments to spiritual figures often compensated for the lack of intimate family relations. More than intellectual curiosity, emotional needs were the driving force behind Muhammad Mirza's search for spiritual guidance.[10]

The appearance of Hajji 'Abbas Iravani on the Tabriz horizon around 1810 has been attributed to Mirza Buzurg's curiosity for the esoteric.[11] A Caucasian emigré of tribal lineage, Mulla 'Abbas had put behind him a life of adventure and pupilage before slipping into a mulla's attire and being chosen as a tutor to one of Qa'im Maqam's sons. His mixed bag of popularized sufi aphorisms and semiformal religious teachings were attractive enough to earn him, in 1821, the title of *aqasi* (chief officer of the household) and, three years later, the chief tutorship of the crown prince's sons. By this time he had secured sufficient political clout to act as one of 'Abbas Mirza's councilors.[12]

Muhammad Mirza's acquaintance with Aqasi began at an early age when he and his brothers attended the mentor's tutorials. Taking into account Muhammad Mirza's seniority and the fading health of his father, it was not hard for Aqasi to forecast the eventual accession of his pupil to the Qajar throne. In the eyes of the impressionable prince, this simple noncommittal prediction, perhaps with a little persuasion from Aqasi, was seen as evidence of the teacher's miraculous powers. Over the years Muhammad's devotion to his teacher and his moral dependence on him was reinforced by similar prognostications.[13] By the age of twenty Muhammad Mirza was completely devoted to the largely improvised sufi teachings of his master. "At this time," wrote Jahangir Mirza,

> the Hajji [i.e., Aqasi] had entirely conquered the temperaments of the late shah [the term by which the author refers to his deceased brother Muhammad Shah]. By means of mysticism, piety and asceticism he convinced the late shah that he is one of the saints. Since the late shah by nature was ready to acquire apparent and spiritual accomplishments, he recognized the claims of the Hajji and planted the seed of his affection in his noble heart. He too modeled his majestic quest upon piety and abstinence. Most lunches and dinners he sufficed partaking a piece of bread and some vinegar. He avoided European dresses and delicacies and for the rest of his life abstained from taking Russian sugar and refused to wear European fabrics without first purifying them. Gradually, these devotional observations became so obvious that the Crown Prince [i.e., 'Abbas Mirza] could attribute this change of behavior to Hajji's influence. The Crown Prince did not favor especially those matters, such as refraining from punishments and other necessities of sovereignty, which were contrary to temporal kingship. He occasionally rebuked the late shah and even obliged him to eat meat and fatty dishes.[14]

Asceticism, a vegetarian diet (which may have been observed for health reasons), and observation of the Shi'ite code of ritual purity were not the only instructions the ailing Muhammad Mirza received from his mentor. "In secret," adds Jahangir Mirza, "Hajji used to complain to the late shah of his own condition and the undue hostility of Mirza Abul-Qasim [Qa'im Maqam II]. . . . He was frequently making such complaints hoping that one day they would bear fruit."[15]

Qa'im Maqam's rigorous ascendancy over the crown prince's household must have given Muhammad Mirza cause for concern. To the minister's authoritarian conduct Aqasi offered a soothing alternative. Soft-hearted and reassuring, the old tutor was a refuge for the prince, a source of solace and renewed confidence. Muhammad Mirza's fondness for Aqasi manifested itself as though he was trying to replace the harsh and demanding authority of his own father (and that of Qa'im Maqam) with Aqasi's affectionate and fatherly care, a pattern which later repeated itself in the life of his son.

Muhammad Mirza's devotion, one may suspect, was not without connection to the prince's problematic marriage. References to Malik Jahan's unfaithfulness, albeit retrospective, suggest an initial sexual incompatibility if not impotence. Physical mortification was assuaged by a special intimacy with Aqasi and thus served for Muhammad Mirza as a refuge from another source of tension and antagonism. This may partly explain the deep suspicion Malik Jahan reserved for Aqasi. Bitterness and rivalry between the two was unavoidable, as Malik Jahan failed to make a dent in the tutor's moral monopoly over her husband.

Malik Jahan (see Pl. 4), the child of a union between the Quvanlu chief Amir Qasim Khan and Fath 'Ali Shah's second daughter, was much more than just a component in the reproductive machinery of the Qajar royal harem. Highly conscious of her Quvanlu lineage, she consistently resisted efforts by her husband's Davalu relatives to dismiss her as the insignificant property of her spouse. Her paternal grandfather, Sulayman Khan I'tizad al-Dawla, the chief of the Ashaqa-bash division of the Qajar tribe, had played a key role in the establishment of the Qajars. As the governor general of Azarbaijan and, later, chief tutor (atabak) to 'Abbas Mirza, he wielded great influence over the Qajar monarch.[16] Her paternal grandmother belonged to the vanquished house of Zand and probably was awarded as war booty to Sulayman Khan in exchange for his loyal services. Malik Jahan's father, Amir Qasim Khan, who held the supreme position of amir(-i) kabir (grand army chief), served all his life in the Qajar army, though his death in 1831 may have caused a demotion in the Quvanlu status. On the maternal side, Malik Jahan's background featured a union between captor and captive as well. Her grandmother, Fath 'Ali Shah's first wife, was the daughter of a tribal chief humbled by the Qajars and kept as a hostage in the harem to guarantee the good conduct of her tribe. Besides giving birth to Malik Jahan's mother, she had borne for Fath 'Ali two of the shah's most powerful sons: Husayn 'Ali Mirza Farmanfarma and Hasan 'Ali Shaja' al-Saltana.[17]

Often noted for her intelligence and shrewdness, Malik Jahan, like some other women of her status, benefited from some education in the harem. Her writing style, her handwriting, and her interest in poetry (she employed a female poet laureate in her private court) testify to her taste and sophistication. Her ambitions, however, went far beyond the seclusion of her husband's inner quarters. From the time of Muhammad Shah's accession to the throne, her presence among the women of the court was second only to that of her mother-in-law, who was of Davalu lineage. More often an advocate of her son than of her husband, Malik Jahan demonstrated her drive for power through her efforts to secure Nasir al-Din's succession. Her supervision of the interim government in the months following the death of Muhammad Shah in 1848 also testifies to her political talents. Although her part in effecting the fall and execution of Mirza Taqi Khan Amir Kabir has tarnished her image beyond repair, her presence behind Nasir al-Din's throne should not be underestimated. By all accounts she was probably the most influential woman of the Qajar era, gaining an almost independent political stature.[18]

With such a powerful lineage and strong personality, it was not difficult for Malik Jahan to see herself as an equal to Muhammad Mirza and, after 1833, as a legitimate partner in his rising fortune. Being the mother of Muhammad Mirza's first son no doubt enhanced her independent stance as the future queen mother (*mahd-i 'ulya*: "the sublime cradle") once the heir apparency of Muhammad Mirza was confirmed. Nevertheless, her husband continued to avoid her and gradually grew to dislike her independence and her pride as much as her lack of physical beauty. The tensions in this marital relationship were bound to intensify in the environment of the royal harem, where the prominence of a Davalu queen mother—Muhammad Shah's mother—and the competition of other royal wives and children could very well reduce Malik Jahan and her son to the level of insignificance. Nasir al-Din was not untouched by these tensions.

LONESOME CHILDHOOD

In the spring of 1834, Jahangir Mirza, the learned prince and historian of the early Qajar period, anxious to register loyalty to his elder brother Muhammad Mirza, paid a tributary visit to Muhammad's three-year-old son, whom he addressed with his later titles: "the king of the universe, the essence of security, sultan son of sultan and *khaqan* son of *khaqan*, Nasir al-Din *padshah*, may God immortalize his reign." But the symbolic show of submission to the infant prince was to no avail. Five months later, soon after Fath 'Ali Shah's death, the ill-fated Jahangir, Bahman Mirza, and three other sons of 'Abbas Mirza were arrested and imprisoned in the Ardabil citadel in order to preempt plots for the overthrow of the new king, Muhammad Shah. Some months later, Jahangir and his brother Khusraw were blinded by order of Qa'im Maqam I. The new premier justified this gruesome act as a way of consolidating his master's throne in the face of formidable challenges from within the royal family. Ironically, the earliest surviving eyewitness account of Nasir al-Din thus proved to be one of Jahangir's last visual memories. Deprived of the "light of the sight," Jahangir became an early victim in the second round of struggle for succession that ultimately brought Nasir al-Din to the throne. The blinded prince wisely chose to record the history of the struggle rather than take further part in it.[19]

The precious little that is known of Nasir al-Din's early childhood in Tabriz was recorded because of his nomination to apparency in 1835. A year before, upon the accession of Muhammad Shah, the predictable dispute over succession placed Nasir al-Din for the first time at the center of a prolonged controversy. Two of the shah's full brothers, Qahraman and Bahman, who enjoyed the backing of the queen mother and the entire Davalu clan, argued with some vehemence that "in the eye of the foreign powers, a three-year-old child who is still bound to the cradle is not fit to be nominated the crown prince."[20] Such was the attitude of their maternal uncle and scion of the Davalu, Asaf al-Dawla, who, fearing "the departure of the royal blood from the house of Davalu and the ultimate domination of the Quvanlu," was determined to prevent Nasir al-Din's nomination.[21] But Muhammad Shah, still exposed to danger from his rebellious uncles (brothers of 'Abbas Mirza), was reluctant to abide by the Davalu pressure. The appointment to apparency of anyone but the shah's son would have violated the same rule of primogeniture that first legitimized his own accession. In principle the representatives of the foreign powers were supportive of the shah's rationale, for it complied with the European orders of succession. Yet the foreign representatives, particularly Russia's, were also inclined to utilize the existing tension within 'Abbas Mirza's house for their own ends by advocating the appointment of an adult viceroy or regent (na'ib al-saltana) in the person of the shah's brother Qahraman Mirza.

The position of Qa'im Maqam, the shah's first prime minister, was at best uncertain. Less than a year after his appointment he was already under attack from his rivals, most notably Asaf al-Dawla and Hajji Mirza Aqasi. Isolated within the court and unpopular with the bureaucracy as well as with the foreign envoys, he was clearly losing influence with the shah, who was always apprehensive of his authoritarian conduct. Qa'im Maqam's policy of centralization and resistance to foreign and domestic pressure had already made him enemies within the Russian and British legations and among the Davalu dignitaries. Under the circumstances, facilitating the appointment of the young and powerless Nasir al-Din was not his first priority. Instead, he seems to have been promoting the cause of the shah's once-powerful uncles, particularly 'Ali Mirza Zill al-Sultan, who, after his unsuccessful bid for the throne and peaceful surrender, was permitted to reside in Tehran. It is not sheer coincidence that the final nomination of Nasir al-Din came immediately after Qa'im Maqam's downfall. One may suspect that in attempting to restore his control over the shah, the bold premier toyed with the idea of appointing Zill al-Sultan as regent, a move that literally hammered the last nail in the minister's coffin. Cruel and capricious as it was, the secret strangling of the capable and cultivated Qa'im Maqam in the crypt of Nigaristan Palace in the spring of 1835 was the culmination of years of aggravation and ill feeling between minister and monarch perpetuated by the mischiefs of the rival Aqasi.[22]

The appointment of Hajji Mirza Aqasi to the office of premier was the shah's next step and a move that entailed more than just political benefits. By replacing the authoritarian and highly independent minister with the accommodating and at times innovative tutor, the shah registered a crucial shift of power from the traditional bureaucratic classes to the inner circles of the court. It was the reverse, at least temporarily, of the policy pursued by Qa'im Maqam "to monopolize for the premier and the council of the ministers all the appointments, dismissals, disjoining and rejoining of matters, the execution of the government affairs, the allocation of salaries and assignment of offices."[23]

The appointment of Nasir al-Din was a move in the same direction, strengthening the hand of the shah vis-à-vis the Qajar royal family. The decree of nomination was read to an assembly of army chiefs and provincial officials in Tabriz, where the prince was then residing.[24] The ceremonial insignias of the heir apparency, most revived during Fath 'Ali Shah's reign for 'Abbas Mirza—the Kayanid ornamental robe named after the myth-ological dynasty of the *Shahnama*, the dagger, the amulet, and the dec-oration of the Lion and Sun, now the official state emblem—were also bestowed upon the young prince.[25]

The nomination, approved by the "trustees of the sublime state" and the foreign missions, temporarily frustrated "the hopes of those who envisaged themselves as regent and king maker." No doubt this was a reference to the objection raised by Faridun Mirza, another half-brother of the shah and Aqasi's ex-pupil. Apparently he was set up by his tutor to challenge, unsuccessfully, the Russian-backed Qahraman Mirza. In the end, Nasir al-Din's nomination was ratified by representatives of the foreign powers only when Qahraman Mirza was granted the acting governorship of Az-arbaijan, a position that acknowledged his de facto regency over the minor crown prince.[26] Mirza Muhammad Khan Zangina, the commander in chief of the New Army of Azarbaijan (*amir(-i) nizam*), was also reinstated in his post as the steward (*pishkar*) to Qahraman, a typical move by the shah to place a check on Qahraman's autonomy.[27] The young Nasir al-Din had to wait a long time before his heir apparency assumed any real meaning.

In the same year, however, shortly after the official nomination, when Captain Stuart, the secretary of the British mission, paid a visit to the young prince in Tabriz, there was little doubt as to Nasir al-Din's nominal status as the heir apparent. "I never saw so beautiful a child," wrote the Englishman with a taint of exaggeration. "The expression of his countenance is mournful, and the poor thing was evidently shy."[28] A year later, in 1836, when Stuart returned to Azarbaijan, he found the same "beautiful but mournful cast of countenance," but this time the prince was "terribly bored."[29] The mournful countenance may have very well been conditioned by Nasir al-Din's fragile physique.[30] His frail appearance was grave enough to elicit a comment by Tsar Nicholas I (r. 1825–1856) when he met the prince in Iravan (Erevan) in October 1838 (see Fig. 1). Qajar chroniclers noted the tsar's concern for Nasir al-Din's "feeble health and weak frame."[31] No particular malady or disability has been reported, but it is hard to dissociate this state of health from the emotional setbacks Nasir al-Din experienced in his early childhood.

Nasir al-Din's short visit to Iravan during the tsar's tour of the newly conquered Caucasian provinces was his first official engagement. On this mission he was accompanied by a small group of state officials and personal aides, including Muhammad Khan Zangina, the Amir Nizam; 'Isa Khan Quvanlu, the crown prince's maternal uncle; his tutor, Mulla Mahmud Nizam al-'Ulama Tabrizi, the Mulla-bashi; and Mirza Taqi Khan Farahani, the army secretary (*vazir(-i) nizam*) of Azarbaijan and later Nasir al-Din's first prime minister. The mission's objective was to convey the shah's good wishes to Nicholas. At a time when the shah's preparations for reestablishing sovereignty over Herat, long an objective of the Qajar rulers, had aroused strong British opposition, the Persian government felt it expedient to respond favorably to the Russian emperor's friendly gesture. By dispatching the crown prince to greet the tsar—ironically, in the same provinces taken from Iran less than a decade before—the shah was also hoping to secure the approval of his northern neighbor for his choice of the heir apparent.[32]

Upon arrival in Uch Kilisa, outside Iravan, the Persian mission decided to stay in its own tents rather than in the quarters assigned by the Russians. The prince's polite refusal to reside in the town citadel was cherished by

Figure 1. Nasir al-Din Mirza and Tsar Nicholas I of Russia in Iravan (Erevan) in 1838. Lacquer work by Muhammad Isma'il, the royal painter (*naqqash-bashi*). Top: Walls of Iravan and its environs eight years after the city's capture by the Russians. Middle: Young Nasir al-Din Mirza on tsar's lap. The Persian statesmen on the left are probably Muhammad Khan Amir Nizam Zangana and Mirza Taqi Khan Farahani (later Amir Kabir). Bottom: The Persian camp set up outside the city walls. B. W. Robinson, "A Lacquer Mirror of 1854," *Iran: Journal of the British Institute of Persian Studies* V (1967), pl. I, opp. p. 2.

the court historians as an early sign of his alertness and wit. With his usual ornate style, Sipihr quotes Nasir al-Din as saying: "We prefer the lush verdure of the meadow and the affluence of the stream to the dense enclosure of the citadel."[33] The young prince must have decided on his preference for the outdoors, an irrepressible habit of his, very early in life, but his decision may also have been influenced by some of his companions' patriotic sentiments.

The audience with Nicholas was amicable enough. The young child was led to an adjacent hall, where he was privately received. The emperor sat the shy prince on his lap and "persuaded him to smile and talk." As a sign of affection, he gave him his own diamond ring with his portrait engraved underneath. He also assured him that in the future his "great uncle," the emperor, would fulfill all his wishes. Conversing with the members of the mission, the tsar's attitude was informal and yet rather patronizing, almost as though he were receiving officials of a neighboring vassalage. To the prince's tutor he "entrusted the education of the crown prince," and tapping the shoulder of an "old friend" he even exchanged a few friendly words in Russian with Mirza Taqi Khan, whom he knew from an earlier visit in the company of Khusraw Mirza in 1830.[34]

The reception of the Persian mission, however, did not seem to have impressed Mirza Taqi Khan, who a year later, in his private discussion with the British consul in Tabriz, complained of "how little regard and distinction" the crown prince had received "as compared to the attention shown to Khusraw Mirza."[35] After the mission returned to Tabriz, however, the tsar sent the crown prince a royal eagle decoration and a diamond hat pin (jiqqa). Despite Mirza Taqi Khan's impression, the Russians' reception of the mission and the royal gifts they bestowed on the crown prince were interpreted in Tehran as signs of the tsar's approval of Nasir al-Din's apparency—an issue of grave importance to the shah. The gifts were also taken as symbols of Russian support for the Herat enterprise.[36]

Despite the tsar's caution, the issue of the crown prince's upbringing did not receive high priority in the eyes of the shah and his ministers. In his early years, Nasir al-Din received only a haphazard education, one less thorough than his father's. Largely isolated from the outside up to the age of six or seven, he was confined to his mother's residential quarters, where a host of eunuchs, maids, and playmates compensated for the noticeable lack of parental care. An Abyssinian eunuch, Bashir Khan, a purchased slave of Malik Jahan's, was in charge of overseeing the prince's affairs. Bashir, like other black eunuchs in the Qajar harem, was treated with a peculiar mixture of awe and intimacy. Bashir was a capable manager whose severe side was complemented by a sentimental, sometimes childish temperament. Later on, when he became the shah's chief eunuch, Bashir took pride in his personal attendance to Nasir al-Din over the years, even boasting of having changed his diapers.[37] By contrast, a combination of gratitude, pity, and old grudges best characterized Nasir al-Din's ambivalent attitude toward his eunuch. Judging by his unfortunate end—Bashir was executed under orders from Nasir al-Din in 1859 in an outburst of kingly rage—it is hard not to detect the prevalence of negative feelings.[38]

The rest of the crown prince's childhood attendants were treated with greater compassion. A Tabrizi maid of Malik Jahan who nursed the prince in his infancy was later honored to be the mother of the shah's first concubine (*mut'a*). Her daughter, 'Iffat al-Saltana ("the Chastity of the Sovereign"), bore the shah his most powerful son, Mas'ud Mirza Zill al-Sultan.[39] The son of another childhood maid from Hamadan later became one of the shah's favorite pages of the inner court (*khalwat*) and was to write a didactic treatise, full of boring truisms, on the education of royal princes.[40] Another bedroom maid was close enough to the shah to be included in the royal entourage during his first European tour in 1873; unfortunately, in order not to embarrass his hosts by breaching European etiquette, the shah was obliged in Moscow to part with his bedside companion.[41] Ibrahim Khan, another member of the entourage, was the shah's closest childhood playmate and confidant. He was the son of a Georgian captive belonging to Malik Jahan's household and, as Amin al-Sultan (I), later rose in rank to become the powerful butler and court minister of the mid-Nasiri period. His son, 'Ali Asghar Khan Amin al-Sultan (II), the premier of the late Nasiri period, received a royal attention reserved for the shah's most favored sons.[42]

Intimacy with maids and servants and their children, who often were his playmates, may explain Nasir al-Din's unreserved reliance in later life on the servant class. It was this class that first introduced him to the outside world and taught him values of friendship and loyalty. In a society accustomed to treating children as miniature adults, princes even more than other children were in need of moral support to take them through the difficult passage of early adulthood. The sheer political demands on Nasir al-Din to behave majestically, particularly when his apparency was perpetually under question, required that he adopt a mask of solemnness and gravity that could only be put aside in the private company of his attendants. "Even from early childhood," recalls Sipihr, "the crown prince's royal grandeur was such that in his presence even the princes and the notables of Iran were not permitted to sit."[43] This self-imposed facade of grandeur, so characteristic of Nasir al-Din Shah's public life, was a defense mechanism painfully developed in his childhood and rehearsed in the privacy of his inner court to conceal his shyness and vulnerability.

In the summer of 1839, when the eight-year-old Nasir al-Din was summoned to the capital, it had been nearly five years since he had last seen his father.[44] Although no specific reason is recorded, one may surmise that the crown prince's recall had more to do with the grave political situation in which his father found himself after the Herat campaign than with any feelings of fatherly affection. The humiliating setback in Herat and evacuation of Persian troops under British pressure had caused Muhammad Shah utter disillusionment. The retaliatory British expedition in the Persian Gulf and the ensuing occupation of Kharg Island and the port of Bushihr drove the shah's already precarious foreign policy to the brink of total disaster. The disheartening news of Ibrahim Pasha's defeat in the Syrian campaign, Egypt's surrender to the sovereignty of the British-backed Ottoman sultan, and the emergence of a new Anglo-Russian accord over the Eastern Question further demoralized the shah, who now came to realize that he had little choice but to mend fences with Britain. The shah's conciliatory conduct toward the British, however, provided an ideal time for the rival Russians to press for new concessions of their own. Typical of the diplomatic crises augmented by competing powers, one power's act of aggression resulted in growing pressure by the other. The Russian government, contrary to its earlier approval of Nasir al-Din's apparency (at least, as the Persian government saw it), now resorted to a policy of lionizing a rival claimant—in this case, the shah's ambitious and capable brother Qahraman Mirza. This policy shift, which was motivated by the Russian desire to manipulate Qahraman in exchange for a vague promise to support his apparency, became a Damoclean sword over the head of the desperate monarch. The removal of Nasir al-Din from Azarbaijan thus became a necessity in order to fulfill the Russians' design for Qahraman and to consolidate his supremacy over the province.[45]

The dangers of such a move could not have gone unnoticed by acute observers in Azarbaijan. As early as January 1838, in the heat of the Herat campaign and immediately before the break in relations with Britain, Mirza Taqi Khan Farahani, then the province's Secretary of the Army, warned the British consul in Tabriz, Edward Bonham, in a private conversation of the grave repercussions of removing Nasir al-Din and appointing Qahraman independently to the governorship of Azarbaijan. Conveying in part the views of his superior, Muhammad Khan Zangina, Mirza Taqi Khan wished to transmit to the British foreign secretary, Lord Palmerston, that any

British compromise on this issue would result in a Russian advantage and ultimately another war of succession.

In reply to Bonham's inquiry about what might happen after the shah's death (not too remote a possibility because of the shah's deteriorating health), Mirza Taqi Khan stated bluntly: "What can occur but difficulties? If that animal of a shah had placed the Valiahd [*vali'ahd:* "the guardian of the age"; i.e., the crown prince] here with the Amir [i.e., Amir Nizam Zangina] alone, he could have placed him on the throne. All Azarbaijan, at least, would have joined him. But now he has sent Caraman [Qahraman] Mirza here. He has all the power and Amir has none. He wants the throne for himself and has a party ready to assist him in Tabriz and in other parts of Azarbaijan."[46] The strong language Mirza Taqi Khan used in reference to the shah no doubt reflected his disappointment with the Persian government's surrender to Russian demands. He warned that Russian assistance to Qahraman would have grave results for the crown prince. "It all depends on half an hour," stressed Mirza Taqi Khan, "if the Amir receives the first news, he will seize Caraman Mirza and proclaim the Valiahd. If he has not time [sic] for that, he will endeavor to escape himself. . . . There are many others who will not acknowledge a Kajar [i.e., Qajar] king again, unless it be the Valiahd."[47]

In lieu of Russian support for Qahraman, Mirza Taqi Khan held the view that without British "consent no one can reign here" and "no Shah could control" the country. The gravity of the situation in Azarbaijan and concern over the fate of Nasir al-Din prompted Mirza Taqi Khan to share this confidential information with the British representative and, moreover, to call for British intervention. This earliest record of Mirza Taqi Khan's contact with a European mission reflects not only his political preference and his recognition of the crucial part the neighboring powers were playing in Iran's internal affairs but also his long-term wish (as part of the Azarbaijan army administration) to use Nasir al-Din as a vehicle for ascending the political ladder, an ambition that took another decade to be fulfilled.

Not all the officials of high rank shared Mirza Taqi Khan's aspirations for the young prince, and Aqasi seems to have been least excited by the prince's prospects. Nasir al-Din's residence in the capital for the next nine years, up to the time of his reappointment to the governorship of Azarbaijan in 1848, proved to be a period of virtual eclipse. He and his mother had to resist constant efforts aimed at undermining the prince's position. A combination of personal and political factors not only deprived Nasir al-Din of his seat in Azarbaijan, a province traditionally assigned to the heir apparent, but also cast serious doubt over his future succession.

The political situation in the capital was of little assistance to the crown prince. The Aqasi regime, chaotic and unpredictable, was only in nominal control of large sectors of the government administration. The conflict between the prime minister's policy of centralization and his political rivals' efforts in the provinces to preserve their autonomy brought the Qajar state to a virtual standstill. The Davalu contingent in Khurasan under Asaf al-Dawla and his sons was holding out against Aqasi's sorties. The Davalu allies, along with Qahraman and, later, his brother Bahman, were in practical control of Azarbaijan, and perhaps more than ever this coalition in the north was relishing the hope of an eventual takeover. The central and southwestern provinces, by contrast, were in the hands of Manuchihr Khan Mu'tamad al-Dawla, a Georgian eunuch of great political talent whose earlier draconian measures to pacify the south were rewarded with long-term tenure over Isfahan and a vast region in its vicinity that was equally impenetrable to Aqasi.

The prevailing equilibrium, notwithstanding its volatility and its drag on the administration and on the general economic well-being of the country, left little room for the minor and politically baseless crown prince. Any effort to form a reliable power base in support of the crown prince practically ceased after the death of Muhammad Khan Zangina in 1841. The Amir Nizam apparently intended to promote the crown prince as the nominal commander of the New Army. The small band of the Azarbaijan military bureau, led by Mirza Taqi Khan Vazir Nizam, held no independent status to act on their own, and the lethargic Quvanlu, the brothers of Malik Jahan, proved utterly inept at carving a home base for themselves, let alone for the crown prince. Under such circumstances, and in the absence of overt domestic backing, the precarious stance of the heir apparent depended more than ever on the goodwill of his father, his minister, and the British envoy in Tehran. As the course of the events proved, such support was slow in coming.

Five years of separation had only helped to aggravate the troublesome relationship between the shah and his young son. The cold treatment the prince received in the capital went beyond the level of tension common between the Persian shahs and their heirs. For most of his prepubescent years, Nasir al-Din was considered a nuisance by the shah and his minister. The royal father's unwelcoming attitude, no doubt, can be traced to the widening marital gap between Muhammad Shah and Malik Jahan. Mutual dislike and disputes among the families did their part in turning Nasir al-Din into a rejected child; but the rapid deterioration of the shah's health—he was suffering from severe gout—and his growing dependence on Aqasi were new factors, further complicated by the shah's affection for Nasir al-Din's younger half-brother.

By Qajar standards, Muhammad Shah's harem was significantly modest. Either because of an ascetic abstention from pleasures of the flesh or illness, by the time of his death in 1848 he had no more than seven wives and nine children: four sons and five daughters.[48] None of the shah's other wives, Turkoman, Kurdish, or Qajar, rivaled Malik Jahan in status. Yet a Kurdish woman, Khadija, the daughter of a Sunni Naqshbandi frontier chief from Chihriq (on the Ottoman border) who replaced her deceased sister in the harem, enjoyed the shah's unabated favors. The birth of a son, 'Abbas Mirza III (later entitled Mulk Ara) in October 1839, occurring almost simultaneously with Nasir al-Din's arrival in the capital, wholly diverted the royal affections. The shah was convinced that the auspicious birth was the fruit of Aqasi's miraculous blessings. To assure the good omen, and as a sign of gratitude, the child was even named after Aqasi, whose name happened to be the same as that of the shah's father.[49]

Soon after his birth the infant, like his deceased brother of the same name, was granted the title *na'ib al-saltana*, originally the official title of 'Abbas Mirza I. The shah's granting of the viceroyship to anyone but the heir apparent suggested to the observant polity of the Qajar court that the shah was clearly undermining the young Nasir al-Din's position. It was as though the shah—and probably his premier, Aqasi—was expressing disapproval of those conventions that formed the basis of his oldest son's right to succession. Moreover, it is probable that by promoting his newborn to the exalted position of viceroy, the shah was hoping to discredit any claims to regency made by his brothers, Qahraman Mirza and Bahman Mirza. Later in life, Nasir al-Din Shah himself employed the same device in an apparent effort to balance off the status of his heir apparent. Kamran Mirza, the ultimate recipient of the title, indeed served in the capacity of viceroy in the shah's absence from the capital.

Under further scrutiny it seems that the source of the shah's dislike for Nasir al-Din went even deeper. One cannot help agreeing with those accounts that traced the shah's dislike to doubts over the legitimacy of the prince's birth. Allegations against Malik Jahan not only make a general point about her unfaithfulness to the shah but are occasionally specific on the nature of her relationships.[50] The alleged incestuous relationship between Malik Jahan and her brother, 'Isa Khan Quvanlu, which led to the khan's public disgrace in Tabriz, may only have been a ploy to discredit the Quvanlu.[51] Other charges of adultery against her were more difficult to dismiss as mere fabrications. In the public eye, the distance between the alleged unfaithfulness of the mother and the illegitimacy of the son was short, and the issue occasionally was brought out in spite of the self-imposed censorship by the Qajar chroniclers. Years later, the grudging and indignant 'Abbas Mirza III (Mulk Ara), for instance, quoted (or misquoted) Nasir al-Din's premier, Mirza Husayn Khan Mushir al-Dawla, in a private conversation the two had in 1873. The angry Mushir al-Dawla went so far as to defame the capricious and ungrateful shah with an ugly remark: "You have no idea what a bastard he [i.e., Nasir al-Din Shah] is," he allegedly said. "He lacks all the virtues of the late shah. Whatever he inherited is from that bitch, his mother . . . this man is not Muhammad Shah's son. Who knows which guard of the inner quarters or which clothier's apprentice or which kitchen lad was responsible for his creation?"[52]

Even if the venomous tone of Mushir al-Dawla and the hostile pen of 'Abbas Mirza are sufficient to discredit this particular opinion, the above passage still reflects the nature of the rumors that tarnished Malik Jahan's reputation. It is not a mere stylistic nicety that the chroniclers of the Nasiri era always rhymed her official title, *mahd-i 'ulya* ("the sublime cradle"), with an additional epithet, *sitr-i kubra* ("the ultimate chaste one"), as though they were denying, albeit sarcastically, rumors that their patron's mother was unchaste.

When in 1856 Joseph Gobineau, the secretary of the French mission, first arrived in Tehran, the rumors about Malik Jahan abounded. "It was even said that [Nasir al-Din] shah himself was the fruit of her [i.e., Mahd 'Ulya's] relationship with Faridun Mirza," the shah's half-brother. The French diplomat and writer, who praised the queen mother as a "daring, sagacious woman with strong political views," also added that during Muhammad Shah's time, contrary to the reign of Nasir al-Din, she was left unperturbed to engage in her own pleasures. Her all-night parties with music, dancers, drinks, and the company of lovers—including a young Georgian merchant—later became a source of embarrassment for the morally oversensitive Mirza Taqi Khan Amir Kabir, Nasir al-Din's first premier.[53]

With such grave suspicions troubling the shah, it is not hard to see why Muhammad Shah divorced Malik Jahan (or rather demoted her from the status of a full wife to that of a temporary one), presumably in an attempt to preserve his honor.[54] It is also possible to envision the sorrowful years of Nasir al-Din's childhood within the confines of the Tehran citadel. "Lethargic and resourceless," as one source puts it, the "morose and sequestered" prince was seldom admitted to his father's presence.[55]

The bitter memories of these years never escaped Nasir al-Din Shah. Years later, in a gathering of his close companions, he drew a hurried cartoon of a frail little boy with a crooked face and frizzy hair and asked those present to identify him. He volunteered after a meaningful pause, "This is me in my childhood." "This is not true. You were always a prince," one of the courtiers flatteringly exclaimed. "Yes, of course, I was a prince but one rather like Shahzada Yusuf," replied the shah.[56] This latter remark was a reference to the ill-fated Afghan prince (son of Kamran Mirza) and claimant to the vassalage of Herat who, during the second Herat campaign of 1856, was first given shelter in Tehran, then kept hostage during a series of shifting alliances, and finally fell victim to a senseless dispute. The execution of Shazadah Yusuf in 1857 was a retaliatory gesture by Nasir al-Din for the loss of the Herat province and for the British insistence on the prince's unconditional release.[57] The plight of the helpless prince must have evoked in Nasir al-Din memories of his own childhood, when his right to the throne was the subject of endless speculations and he himself was hostage to intrigue, factional discord, and the consent of foreign powers.

The same picture of an unhappy childhood comes through in Nasir al-Din's other autobiographical anecdotes. Once he related to one of his daughters how during his youth he had been secretly assisted by Husayn Khan Mu'ayyir al-Mamalik, the influential master of the mint and an ally of his mother,[58] at a time when the "rigorous measures" imposed by Aqasi on the court finances had left Nasir al-Din "desperate for his livelihood" and needy of warm winter clothing. "Even in winter" he recalled, "I was only given cotton socks. Yet I could not part with the desire for colorful woolen socks. Mindful of Hajji [Mirza Aqasi], my father too provided me with no financial aid. Among the courtiers I was more intimate with Mu'ayyir and felt less intimidated by him. One day I revealed to him my secret and asked for woolen socks. Next morning I was expecting Mu'ayyir with much anxiety. When he finally arrived, he gestured that my desired items were ready. With caution I dragged myself to a quiet corner. In great haste Mu'ayyir pulled out from under his robe a pack of socks and handed it to me. Occasionally I also borrowed money from him. Curiously, no one ever asked me how I came by those colorful socks." The receipts Mu'ayyir kept for the small sums he had lent Nasir al-Din were tokens of his risky investment in a future shah. The investment turned out to be profitable.[59]

Even as governor of Azarbaijan, an office to which he was appointed in 1848, Nasir al-Din was not free from financial hardship. The "cash-flow" crises, caused by the customary delays in allowance payments, kept the new governor in "tattered clothes" and the members of his retinue desperate for their salaries. The allowances were to be disbursed, according to the

Figure 2. Nasir al-Din Mirza and Prince Soltykov in Tabriz in 1838. Drawing by Soltykov, *Voyage*, pl. 15.

usual practice of the state accounting department, from the revenue of Fars province, but the governor of that province apparently did not place a priority on the crown prince's needs. "We had reached ultimate poverty," recalls Nasir al-Din, "when it was relayed that our allowances had arrived from Tehran. With great enthusiasm and hope we opened the consignment. But who can imagine our disappointment when we found in the box a few dozen night caps, a candle trimmer, some china, fabrics and such like. They were all charged to us at dear prices. If we could cash them with a merchant for a small sum, we considered ourselves very lucky."[60]

The self-portrait given by Nasir al-Din partially agrees with that conveyed by other sources, at least in their descriptions of his social deprivation. Prince Soltykov, the Russian artist who visited Nasir al-Din in 1838 in Tabriz shortly before his departure for Tehran, left a brief but informative account of the young prince. He described him as an intelligent boy with attractive, though rather effeminate, features: broad woaded eyebrows, big black eyes with lashes darkened with coal, and long hair dyed with henna in the taste of his mother's female relatives.[61] The black-and-white drawing by Soltykov is one of the earliest extant pictures of Nasir al-Din. Seated on an ornamental chair amidst a few servants and his tutor, he is graciously posed for the Russian painter (see Fig. 2). He is almost drowned in an oversized ceremonial robe, and the diamond hat-pin, the gift

Figure 3. 'Abbas Mirza II, Hajji Mirza Aqasi, and Qajar officials in 1838. Drawing by Soltykov, *Voyage*, pl. 16.

of the tsar, is proudly exhibited; yet, the sense of solemn isolation to which his own cartoon alluded is not altogether missing.[62]

Nasir al-Din's loneliness is even more apparent when this drawing of him is compared with another work of Soltykov, this time of Nasir al-Din's younger brother, 'Abbas Mirza II (see Fig. 3) (not to be confused with 'Abbas Mirza III, Mulk Ara). In contrast to Nasir al-Din's insignificant company, a group of dignitaries surrounds 'Abbas, including the prime minister, Aqasi; Manuchihr Khan Mu'tamad al-Dawla; another powerful Georgian eunuch, Khusraw Khan Gurji; and the chief of protocol, Abul-Hasan Khan Shirazi, the famous Persian emissary to European courts. A symbolic undertone for this drawing, commissioned by the shah himself, is clearly implied, as the prince is positioned between the two most influential men of the realm: Aqasi and Manuchihr Khan. In a broader sense the positions in the picture make it seem as though the tutelage of the young Na'ib al-Saltana is the precious prize of their power game.[63]

Even though this 'Abbas Mirza did not live to become a useful pawn, his brother 'Abbas Mirza III (Mulk Ara) was one of several means by which Aqasi retained his sway over the shah. It was probably the shah's tacit intention to appoint 'Abbas Mirza to apparency instead of Nasir al-Din. The shah's doubts about Nasir al-Din's legitimacy may have been a strong motive, but Aqasi knew perfectly well that 'Abbas had no chance to be named heir apparent. Even if disadvantages such as not being the shah's first-born son and lacking Qajar descent on his mother's side could have been overcome, the fact that he was from a Sunni-Naqshbandi background made him wholly unacceptable in a Shi'ite country. Yet it was Aqasi who occasionally exploited the shah's fatherly sentiments for his own ends, either to deprive Nasir al-Din and his mother, with whom he was on bad terms, from any meaningful base of support or to check the growing power of Bahman Mirza, the real claimant to regency, and his Russian backers.

STRUGGLE FOR HEIR APPARENCY

The uncertainties over the choice of the heir were further complicated by Muhammad Shah's grave illness. In February 1842 this prompted the foreign powers to reassert their 1837 pledge on the order of succession. John McNeill, the British minister plenipotentiary in Tehran, was in agreement with Count Medem, his Russian counterpart, that "hereditary order of succession in the direct line from father to son was unquestionably the best calculated to insure tranquility" in a country where the right to succession had often been decided by the sword. But since Nasir al-Din Mirza was "a minor not quite thirteen years of age," and since he was of "slender frame and delicate constitution," the ministers believed some provisions had to be made should the shah die before his son reached the age of maturity. Since Qahraman Mirza's death in 1839, they held the opinion that Bahman Mirza, who was the only other surviving full brother of the shah and who had replaced his deceased brother as governor of Azarbaijan, was fit "to rule the country efficiently and well, whether as a regent or as sovereign." Fearing the disputes that might arise during his regency, the ministers felt that the right of succession should be "circumscribed as much as possible" in accordance with what has been laid down by Aqa Muhammad Khan and Fath 'Ali Shah.[64]

The arrangement proposed by the foreign envoys, colored by their simplistic assessment of Qajar domestic politics, was indecisive at best and self-serving at worst. Strong foreign endorsement of Bahman Mirza put the crown prince, in the event of his father's death, in the unenviable position of being dominated by a formidable regent. His uncle, Bahman Mirza, in whom the British and the Russians placed such faith, was by their own definition an out-and-out Davalu and would have gone to any lengths to prevent the weak Nasir al-Din from even reinstatement as the governor of Azarbaijan, let alone serve him as a faithful regent. Less than six months later, a new upsurge of the shah's gout, the first in a series of debilitating attacks, demonstrated the perils of confirming Bahman as regent. The new British minister, Col. Justin Sheil, a shrewd Irish officer of the Indian army who even more than his predecessor followed a course of bipolar diplomacy, was destined to play a decisive role in the history of modern Iran for the next twelve years. In September 1842 he reported that "the king's health, being at all times in a precarious state," had deteriorated to the extent that "reports of his death were prevalent in Tehran." Sheil, obviously critical of the earlier British support for Bahman, reckoned that the Russians had outmaneuvered them on that front. The northern neighbors exerted an overwhelming influence on Iran, and Sheil speculated that if they were able to use Bahman as a trump card, Nasir al-Din would have no choice but to appeal for Russian assistance in his bid for power. He even went so far as to ask the Foreign Office for instructions should a Russian military intervention in support of the crown prince occur.[65]

As far as the possibility of Russian backing for Nasir al-Din was concerned, Sheil's anxiety was largely misplaced, even paranoiac. If anything, the Russians attempted to promote Bahman Mirza not only as a regent but perhaps as a successor to his brother. His pro-Russian sentiments, more by expediency than choice, made him an attractive candidate. By pressing the Persian government to recognize the regency of Bahman, the Russians hoped, as a first step, to further their long-term interest in Azarbaijan. Indeed, it was these very Russian "protests and threats" that Aqasi was trying desperately to resist. In an 1843 memorandum, in his usual self-deprecating and muted style, he reported to the shah what he had told the Russian envoy on the issue of Bahman's appointment:

> I am away from such matters. I fear for my reputation and my faith. I cannot commit myself to such acts. Your threats have no effect on me. I am not permitted by His Majesty the shah . . . either to assist or to disgrace anyone. All matters, major and minor, should be presented to that blessed threshold. . . . I am a poor mulla and a subject [*ra'iyat*], not even a civil servant [*naukar*], nor am I the holder of any office, or responsible for any affair [of the state] to act on my own accord. Moreover, I am concerned that His Highness the crown prince may take offense at me.[66]

Allusions in Aqasi's disclaimer to his fear of disgracing or offending the crown prince may well be taken as evidence of Nasir al-Din's precarious position. Yet in spite of Russian intimidation, and perhaps mindful of Britain's second thoughts, Aqasi obviously could no longer afford to ignore the young crown prince and his ambitions. Even if the shah's true sympathies rested with the crown prince's brother, he too must have realized the wisdom of supporting Nasir al-Din. In the margin of Aqasi's memorandum he wrote: "May God give them [i.e., the Russians] a listening ear and us some power so that they comply with common sense."[67]

The Russian pressure, however, hardly ceased. The shah's vacillating health made the opponents of the prime minister bolder and as a consequence made the shah himself more vulnerable to domestic criticism. One wonders whether Aqasi's constant complaints and threats to resign were genuine expressions of disgust with his office or (more probably) canny ploys to exercise emotional blackmail on the shah. A combination of shrewdness, false modesty, and condescension summarized his conduct toward a sickly king hampered in the effort to rule his country by foreign intervention and domestic turbulence. "Like a corpse in the hand of his washer" is how one author defined the relation between Muhammad Shah and Aqasi—an allusion, no doubt, to their close master-disciple relationship.[68]

For all his influence over the shah and all his erratic behavior, Aqasi managed to follow a course not altogether devoid of pragmatism and common sense.[69] He felt it expedient to bring Nasir al-Din out of the pitiful oblivion into which he had fallen and present him in a light more acceptable to foreign and domestic demands. Furthermore, the events of the previous years, and more recently the shah's illness, compelled Nasir al-Din to learn the lesson of political survival. One may assume that primarily thanks to his mother he must have reached a degree of political assertiveness and begun to recognize the perils that threatened his future succession.

In spite of sharp differences rooted in an old competition for the shah's loyalties, a convergence of interests between Aqasi and Malik Jahan was evident in the first marriage of Nasir al-Din Mirza in the summer of 1845. It was thought sensible to advertise the crown prince's puberty at the age of fourteen. Such a measure was deemed necessary above all to nullify the need to appoint a regent while the heir to the throne was still legally a minor. To safeguard his own vulnerable future, and as part of the package, Aqasi also secured from the young crown prince a pledge that after the death of the present shah he would remain in charge of "the state's affairs" and be "the recipient of the royal ordinance."[70] Judging by their future conduct, it is probable that Nasir al-Din and his mother agreed to such concessions, hoping that ultimately they would renege on their commitment in the customary manner of "viziericide."

Nasir al-Din's first permanent wife, Galin (Turkish for "bride"), was every bit the generic Qajar female her name suggested. Daughter of Ahmad

'Ali Mirza, the nineteenth son of Fath 'Ali Shah, Galin possessed only one notable feature—her modest beauty, presumably inherited from her Jewish grandmother—besides her Qajar lineage that qualified her to be the bride of the crown prince.[71] It is not difficult to believe that some romance might also have played a part in this union. The fact that Nasir al-Din's French nanny, Madame Gulsaz, acted as matchmaker may have introduced an amorous element into what otherwise was a typical example of Qajar endogamy.[72]

Nasir al-Din's adolescent looks at fourteen (see Pl. 5) seem to have appealed to some women of the harem; however, he was too reserved in his behavior to convey anything of his future passion for women. "During his rides pious women wishful of a brief glance awaited from dawn to dusk on the roofs as if they were frozen on the wall. Attractive girls from every tribe employed thousands of pretexts and devices to reveal their adorned faces to him. Yet, since chastity was his guard, he showed no attraction towards them. He mixed grace with prudence and shyness with dignity. He conversed not but with the confidants in his service and smiled not but at his private attendants."[73] In his extravagant style, Hidayat implied a reticent and rather charmless boy still confined to his close-knit clique of royal companions. Such a picture is in full agreement with Sheil's impression, who remarked on the eve of the "celebration of nuptials of the Heir Apparent": "The character of the Prince Royal has not yet developed. He has not been employed in public affairs, and has hitherto lived in a degree of privacy unusual at his age for a person of his rank in this country. . . . His education has yet been altogether Persian, and he is chiefly remarkable for extreme taciturnity and bashfulness."[74]

Marriage at such an early age was customary among the Persian nobility of the time. Introducing the youth to the opposite sex was regarded as a *rite de passage* into the world of adulthood. Nasir al-Din's first experience with permanent marriage did not remove him from an adolescent fairy world entirely, for even at seventeen, during his residence in Tabriz, his childish imagination had fueled romantic fantasies. As he recalled years later: "I used to wear a robe of red velvet embroidered with pearls and hang a dagger set in diamonds. I was very proud of myself. I had recently married my first wife, Galin Khanum. Those days, when I went out for riding and hunting, I would dismount and stroll in the lush valleys away from my companions. I often fancied that the daughter of the king of fairies would fall in love with me and somehow she would contact me."[75] It is hard to ignore in such fantasies a desire for sexual awakening, hastened by his avid reading of *The Thousand and One Nights*, which had become available to him in a new Persian translation (see Pl. 6). One may conjecture that his dwelling in such a sensual world, as much as his marriage, served as a cure for what Sheil diagnosed as the crown prince's "extreme taciturnity and bashfulness" or what Hidayat emphasized as his shyness.

The nuptial celebration was exceptionally lavish and not far from the fairy world envisioned by the bridegroom himself. It went on uninterrupted for several days outside Nigaristan Palace with all the customary entertainment and festivity.[76] To ensure a perfect celebration, the shah even pledged that his minister, Aqasi, would perform a meteorological feat to make the heat of the Tehran summer subside. An unexpected cool breeze that subsequently reduced the heat was perceived, even by the skeptics, as proof of Aqasi's supernatural gifts.[77] The 50,000-tuman cost of the celebration, however, was collected by less graceful means. The gifts of money expected from the provincial governors, Sheil noted, would inevitably "press heavily on the finance of the government."[78] To match the presents worth 810 tumans offered by the Russian delegation, the British government authorized its envoy to present gifts equal to 320 tumans.[79]

The value of the gifts presented by the rival missions did not correspond to the degree of importance each of them attached to the future of Nasir al-Din Mirza. As Russian support under Count Medem and later under Prince Dolgorouki increasingly shifted toward Bahman Mirza over the next three years, the British mission under Sheil found it expedient to emphasize the legitimacy of Nasir al-Din's claim. A slight improvement in the condition of the "decrepit and feeble" shah, Sheil was happy to report, had the dual advantages of permitting the monarch to survive "in sufficient duration to allow the Heir Apparent to reach a more mature age" while preventing "indulgence of his military predilections" or "journey[ing] through his own kingdom," which most times was a "calamity to the populace."[80]

But even in September 1845, upon another attack of gout compounded by additional complications, Sheil was obliged to remain loyal to the earlier understandings. To Nasir al-Din's disappointment, both powers still held the opinion that in the event of the shah's death the crown prince, owing to his young age, was not "qualified to undertake the duties of the government"; instead, according to the understanding reached earlier, Bahman Mirza was favored to be regent. The British had cause for concern, for although Bahman Mirza's "talent for the government" could not be denied, the British envoy strongly suspected that the prince was devoted to "the interest[s] of Russia."[81] Moreover, it was public knowledge that Bahman Mirza's prospects of retaining the governorship of Azarbaijan were boosted even further by capable backing from his uncle, Asaf al-Dawla, whom Aqasi accused of having "the most traitorous designs."[82] The shah was in a "very dangerous state," for the latest attack had put him in a coma, prompting Aqasi to employ all strategies at his disposal—including a fallacious claim to the throne by his own stepson, Allah-Quli Khan Ilkhani, a libertine of notorious reputation—to try to survive the unceasing attacks of his opponents.[83] The growing antagonism of the Bahman-Asaf coalition, backed by Muhammad Shah's mother, had the effect of further jeopardizing the already precarious position of Nasir al-Din Mirza, whom the Davalus now viewed as a disposable puppet of Aqasi.

Nasir al-Din's and his mother's fear of Davalu reprisal should they overcome Aqasi added to their fears of Russian support for Bahman and were in perfect harmony with Sheil's. This served as a strong motive for them to contact the British envoy, perhaps for the first time, in search of protection. "This Lady," wrote Sheil in reference to Malik Jahan, "has expressed the utmost alarm for her son's life . . . that the prince had nowhere to look for support excepting from the British government." Responding favorably to this plea, Sheil was able to assure her that he was "forward in acknowledging the accession of her son." Owing to his formal commitment, however, the envoy had every reason to urge her to keep his advice secret and "to watch over her son's life" and convey to him "the earliest intelligence of the shah's death."[84]

Sheil's concord with Malik Jahan was the start of at least two decades of amicable relationships between the royal *andarun* and the British mission, with lasting impact on the political course of events. In spite of these assurances, the British minister had serious doubts about Nasir al-Din's legal eligibility—or ability, for that matter—to function as an independent ruler. "There is no fixed rule in Persia for deciding the age at which a sovereign is regarded competent to govern," Sheil noted; for legal transactions the age of puberty was fourteen or fifteen, but even at sixteen, he believed, "the Prince Royal is by no means qualified to assume the administration." The British envoy's characterization of the crown prince's adolescence was particularly hopeless. "He is exceedingly childish and far behind Persians, in general, of his age. His education has been neglected, he has been brought up in seclusion, and he is entirely ignorant of public life, and he would be governed by his mother who is a woman of intelligence however, and her relatives, or else he would be under the control of one or both the European missions."[85]

The prospect of a miserable boy-king, dominated by his mother, was even less appealing to Sheil when he took into account the crown prince's lack of "any influence or party." "If two missions were to remain neutral," he speculated, "his chance of succeeding to the throne would be in a high degree equivocal." This combination of ineptitude and lack of domestic backing even prompted Sheil to argue that, if necessary, Nasir al-Din and his mother should be sacrificed in favor of Bahman Mirza for the tranquility of the country.[86] Sheil's assessment would have been tantamount to a death sentence on the crown prince had it not been for the fact that the sick Muhammad Shah managed to linger for another three years.

The accuracy of Sheil's impression was somewhat blurred by his general attitude of condescension and sense of colonial omnipotence. He must have sensed the crown prince's urge for independence and his apprehension of Bahman Mirza when he commented that "if the question [of the legal age for independent sovereignty] is left to the unfitted decision of the Prince Royal, even now, he entirely would reject the control of a Regent." Such an attitude reflected Nasir al-Din's growing political instincts. It was becoming clearer to him that in order to secure his succession he must fight for it. Neither the prime minister nor the European envoys were prepared to guarantee his rights unless he proved himself worthy of them. Perhaps it was this expressed desire for independence that encouraged Sheil to arrive at his conflicting assessment of the crown prince and ask London to allow him "deviation" from the accepted policy of support for regency if necessary. If Muhammad Shah could survive a few more years, so Sheil thought, he could be induced "to bring his son more into public and active life, and give him some chance of power."[87]

These hopes were not altogether out of line with Aqasi's interests. Sheil urged the prime minister "to make the prince more prominent." He blamed Aqasi in his report for the neglect that so far had kept the crown prince in obscurity. Though on two or three occasions Aqasi had allowed the prince "to appear [in positions] of some consideration," Sheil believed that a more prominent post, such as the governorship of Tehran, should be assigned to him.[88] Nasir al-Din himself must have sensed the opportunity that the trilateral cooperation among Aqasi, his own mother, and Sheil could offer him, and when he sent a note of gratitude to Sheil, the British minister did not know to what cause he should "ascribe this mark of satisfaction" except the sympathies he had expressed in support of the desperate heir apparent.[89]

In the ensuing two years, further deterioration of the shah's health turned Nasir al-Din into the coveted prize in a highly complex charade, dramatically enhanced his prospects, and eventually brought him to the throne. The mounting pressure on Aqasi from his numerous adversaries weakened his stance and obliged him to draw closer to the crown prince as an alternative to his father. In a classic example of Qajar court intrigue, Aqasi exploited the charge of the Ilkhani conspiracy leveled against him by his opponents to set off a highly audible, though farcical, uproar that ultimately involved the crown prince. As Sheil points out, his claims of being unjustly accused by some women of the harem—probably the shah's mother—of attempting to poison the shah was of his own devising, not just to arouse the sentiments of his master, now partially recovered from his latest attack, but also to tarnish the reputation of his enemies who sought greater intimacy with Nasir al-Din in hope of future favors.[90] Employing his usual manipulative tactics, Aqasi threatened in a petition to the shah that unless a royal commission consisting of the 'ulama, the notables, and foreign envoys looked into these allegations, he would have no choice but to commit suicide.[91] The shah's passionate response in the margin of the petition only persuaded the prime minister to modify his threat from suicide to retirement in Karbala. Swearing to God, the Prophet, and the Imams that no accusation was ever brought into his presence, the shah pleaded with Aqasi to reconsider his decision. "What are we to say, what are we to commit, to prove that you are a good man? . . . I have shown a thousand times that I abhor all people to whom you take even a slight dislike. Now I am ready to do whatever you command."[92]

This end was precisely that to which Aqasi aspired. To prove the sincerity of his pledge, the shah sent into exile two of the prime minister's most formidable critics in Tehran. This "conspicuous display" of power by Aqasi was the first stage of a widespread purge that, by 1847, had put almost all of the minister's opponents out of action, turning him into a potentate who sought to function in place of the dying monarch. Under the circumstances, Nasir al-Din's sheepish compliance with Aqasi's wishes was hardly surprising, especially if it could work against the crown prince's chief enemy. In a letter addressed to the shah, presumably dictated by Aqasi himself, the crown prince was obliged to express his full adherence to the prime minister. Moreover he went so far as to parrot Aqasi's threat that unless the commission were set up and the minister's enemies purged, he too would "accompany the Hajji [Mirza Aqasi] to Karbala."[93] When a letter of similar childish content was also sent to Sheil requesting him to "institute an enquiry" into the allegations, the envoy replied with a solemn word of caution: "It would be the waste of your Royal Highness's time to enter into a lengthened discussion on this subject," which was inconsistent with "the elevated position of His Excellency."[94]

Nasir al-Din was perhaps wise enough to have listened to Sheil's sound advice had he not been swayed by the shah's response to his Karbala petition. Even more passionate than his answer to Aqasi, the shah's reply set before the young prince a macabre lesson in humility and obedience, coming from a king with a foot in the grave.

> Prince Royal! What is all this folly? Azrael [the Angel of Death] can not dissolve my affection for the Hajee [i.e., Aqasi]. By the truth of God, by the truth of the Last of the Prophets, most surely I love him a thousand times more dearly than my own life. . . . What now shall I do? A dress of honor is insignificant. Ask himself what he desires. If he thinks it neces-sary "my life itself is of no price." But what is he perpetually exclaiming "people are wicked, people are wicked?" Have these [sic] scoundrels no name? Who are they? What regiment are they? Of what consideration is the Khan my uncle [i.e., Malik Qasim Mirza]? Do I not know that the Hajee gives his life a thousand times as a sacrifice for me? Poison indeed! What abomination is this that people eat?[95]

With such a bizarre eruption of royal devotion, the crown prince must have felt grateful to be the emissary between the shah and his minister. There was no doubt that by expressing loyalty to Aqasi, he had struck the right chord in the shah's heart. It was a sad irony, though, that he who in the past was denied paternal affection should seek Aqasi's favor in the hope of receiving attention from his own father. The profound attachment exhib-ited in this letter must have stamped on Nasir al-Din's mind a paradigm of dependence on fatherly authority that he strove to cast away for the rest of his life.

If there was any doubt about Aqasi's complete hegemony, it was re-moved when his remaining competitors were put out of action and sent into exile; simultaneously, Nasir al-Din began to carry greater weight around court circles as an ally of the premier. Even the Russian envoy, without abandoning his plans for Bahman Mirza, was prepared grudgingly to acknowledge that the prince had "approached manhood" and therefore was not in need of a regent. With marked satisfaction the British envoy reported that under the auspices of the prime minister "the Prince continues to rise in consideration. He appears constantly in public and the intention of Hajji Mirza Aqasi to increase his importance does not seem to be abated."[96] The image of the dejected prince of earlier years had now faded. He had now become for other courtiers and state officials a precious token of security against forthcoming hazards.

Indeed, Aqasi was not the only one who tried to build up amicable relations with the heir apparent. Besides Malik Qasim Mirza, the exiled uncle of the shah, and Mu'ayyir al-Mamalik, another seeker of the prince's favor who suffered Aqasi's vengeance, there was Mirza Aqa Khan Nuri, the chief secretary of the army (vazir[-i] lashkar) and ambitious head of the

Nuri bureaucratic clan who later became Nasir al-Din's second prime minister. Nuri, a distant relative of Malik Jahan through marriage,[97] was even able to procure from the crown prince a written pledge (no doubt with Malik Jahan's persuasion) that once Nasir al-Din reached the throne he would reward Nuri by promoting him to a position above his present status.[98] The power base in the capital that the prince and his mother hoped to build required the support of the army secretary and his adherents. Having been on "friendly terms" with the British mission for years, Nuri was deemed by Malik Jahan an indispensable asset should the vacillating Aqasi ever deny the crown prince his backing.[99] Yet the wording of the autograph decree (*dast-khatt*) was deliberately vague, perhaps a sign that Nasir al-Din was coming of age and was alert enough not to overcommit himself. But since the prince had already given his pledge to Aqasi, the mere existence of a similar pact was enough of a pretext to turn the prime minister's wrath against Nuri. As part of the ongoing purge, and to settle old scores with the army secretary, Aqasi dismissed, arrested, and basti-nadoed Nuri and members of his clan on charges of conspiracy before sending him to exile in Kashan.[100] Nasir al-Din remained unruffled, although his mother must have felt the loss of a close ally. More than a decade later, when Nuri was dismissed from premiership, Nasir al-Din Shah inflicted the same punishments on him, but this time there would be no return from exile for the shrewd politician.

Nuri's removal was followed by further purges. Soon thereafter came the shah's recall of Aqasi's archenemy, Asaf al-Dawla, from Khurasan and his voluntary exile to the 'Atabat, the holy cities of Iraq.[101] The purge of the most prominent Davalu leader soon triggered a bloody revolt in Khurasan led by Asaf al-Dawla's son, Muhammad Khan Salar, in 1847. For the next four years the Salar revolt, the last upsurge of the Davalu drive for power, remained one of the most eminent threats to the Qajar central government. By 1847 Aqasi was confident enough to close in on Bahman Mirza, his last and most formidable adversary. He had already prepared the shah to believe that his brother was no more than a Russian puppet and conspirator ready to snatch the throne. A simple maneuver by the prime minister—sending an urgent courier to Tabriz with "a critical message"— was enough to eject the fearful prince from his seat of power in Azarbaijan. Even before the courier's arrival, Bahman fled to the capital, where he hoped to find among the European envoys a sympathetic ear. The European powers indeed demanded that Bahman be reinstated, but Aqasi resisted. Instead he ordered that his foe be put under surveillance, a move that drove Bahman to the refuge of the Russian compound in Tehran in November

1847.[102] Shortly thereafter, fearing for his life, he defected to Russia. His departure for the Caucasus marked a momentary victory for Aqasi, but it started a prolonged episode of intrigue and foreign subterfuge that cast a long shadow over Nasir al-Din's early reign.

In the short term, however, these developments were clearly beneficial to Nasir al-Din Mirza. In less than two years skillful maneuvering on the part of the prime minister and the prince's own mother removed the main obstacles from his way, though the central government under Aqasi visibly lacked the means, and the initiative, to fill the vacuum in Azarbaijan. The most coveted provincial seat in the country had been delivered from a decade of monopoly, but the government could hardly find as capable an administrator as Bahman Mirza. Nasir al-Din sensed the unique opportunity that had emerged and requested that the shah give him "a written declaration that he will now fulfill his former promises of appointing him to the Government of Azarbaijan," and Muhammad Shah, perhaps conscious of his impending death, did so. He must have realized that in view of the two powers' insistence on the rule of primogeniture, he could not deny Nasir al-Din full acknowledgment of his priority in succession, a process that took the Qajars close to fifty years to finalize. The governorship of Azarbaijan was that acknowledgment.

After receiving the written promise, Nasir al-Din declared to the British charge d'affaires, Colonel Farrant, another British officer of the Indian Army serving temporarily in Tehran in place of Sheil, that "the Russian minister had withdrawn his opposition to him, or [else] His Majesty would not have given him such a promise in writing."[103] Colonel Farrant, still unadjusted to the quick pace of events, remained skeptical. He was of the opinion that "until the Hajee gives his confirmation, the appointment will not take place." Such approval, Farrant speculated, was not forthcoming because "His Excellency at present is much inclined in favor of the shah's second son, the Na'ib al-Saltana [i.e., 'Abbas Mirza], a boy of ten years old." Moreover, he surmised that the appointment would also be curtailed by Russian objection.[104]

Some three months later, on 25 January 1848, when Nasir al-Din left the capital for Azarbaijan, he was obliged to pretend that he was going on a hunting trip. "But it soon became known that his Royal Highness' real objective was to proceed to Tabriz."[105] The secret journey was arranged in a great hurry, and the crown prince departed without the customary ceremonies and in spite of his critics. The shah, anxious to send his son off to fill the government seat in the most important province of his realm, "ordered his own mules to be furnished." The prince, being "quite alone," was instructed "to proceed slowly" toward his destination so that his aides and servants could join him en route. Not even a decree was issued to announce his governorship. Such a hurried and secretive departure was not wholly dissimilar to that of his great-granduncle, Aqa Muhammad Khan, when in 1779, after Karim Khan's death, he escaped the Zand captivity in Shiraz. In this instance, however, Nasir al-Din was escaping not the chaos that followed a ruler's death but the expected reproach of European powers.

The "clandestine affair" took both foreign envoys by surprise. Aqasi, perhaps granting the shah's wishes or, more plausibly, seeking an excuse to repeal the unwanted foreign intervention, led the envoys to believe he was supporting the apparency of the shah's younger son. But Farrant had misgivings not only because he was left out but also because he believed the inexperienced Nasir al-Din "was totally unfit to govern such a province," particularly as he was surrounded "by the worst set of dependents possible." He foresaw that this appointment, being a "severe blow to Russian influence," was bound to invite retaliation from the northern power. The Russian minister, "deeply mortified that his council has been rejected," would "create confusion in the province if the Heir Apparent" would not assent to all Russia's demands and virtually grant his "devoted dependence."[106]

Farrant's gloomy scenario was tinted as much by his outrage as by his concern for possible concessions that the Russians might exact from the crown prince. To convince him otherwise, Aqasi had to employ all his persuasive skills to elevate Nasir al-Din above what he really was. "His redoubtable talents," Aqasi insisted, were superior even to those of "the Shah and the late 'Abbas Mirza."[107] Such praise was no doubt expedited by sheer necessity, yet Nasir al-Din's progress over the previous years surely had not gone totally unnoticed by the minister.

Nasir al-Din had begun to learn the rules of the formidable contest, and the grand prize was the crown of the Qajar. The volatile political climate caused by the spasmodic illnesses of a dying shah, total dependence on an eccentric but crafty minister, the uninvited intrusions of the foreign powers, the infighting of a divided polity, and the ambivalent sentiments of an unsympathetic father finally brought the young Nasir al-Din to comprehend the realities of his personal and political life. He soon learned that in order to beat the odds he must learn to employ all his resources, to ally himself momentarily with competing rivals, to appeal to rival European envoys, and to comply with the dictates of his father's mentor in the hope of gaining his favor. Nasir al-Din could not yet be considered the master of such a stratagem at this point, but he was diligent enough to learn the rudiments of survival.

2 A Mirror for the Prince

Shortly before his death in Mashhad in November 1833, the Qajar crown prince, 'Abbas Mirza, in a farewell letter to his son, Muhammad Mirza, advised him to remain loyal to Fath 'Ali Shah and the royal family. He further reminded him to have forgiveness, justice, and compassion, respect the 'ulama and the descendants of the House of the Prophet, and reward the servants of his household. Almost certain of his impending death, he further stated:

> Whatever I wrote about the country, the [government] servants [naukar] and the subjects [ra'iyat], you should observe with utmost care. It was by the divine benevolence that Faridun removed the evil from the face of the earth. As long as the kingdom of God the Sublime endures, the evil-doers will be brought to account for their evil deeds and evil decrees un-til the Day of Resurrection. I have previously written to my daughter-in-law, Malik Jahan, that she should tell the apple of my eye, Nasir al-Din Mirza: "When you grow up, read my counsels and put them into prac-tice so that you will be blessed and enjoy pleasure [kamrani] for fifty years." I have written whatever was necessary.[1]

Indeed, in his earlier letter to Malik Jahan in reply to her correspondence, 'Abbas Mirza—then in Khurasan leading a campaign, which proved to be his last—had specified his testimonial advice for Nasir al-Din Mirza, then a child of two:

> In Khurasan, under the dome of the shrine of the Eighth Imam . . . I pray for him to be blessed and to enjoy pleasure and to rule for fifty years after his father with pride and honor provided that he follows my coun-sels [wasaya]. This is the prayer of his [grand]father, but his mother's prayer is more effective.

'Abbas Mirza proved to be prophetic in predicting for Nasir al-Din fifty years of blissful reign, at least as far as his grandson's private life was concerned. But 'Abbas Mirza's final counsel was not limited to wishes for his joy and pleasure. "He should remember God in any event, since in every instance God's benevolence will be with him if he cares for the oppressed at all times." Moreover, the crown prince reminded him of the "privilege of kinship" (*sala-yi rahim*) and of "protecting the subjects from the tyranny of governors." The servants of the state who served well should also be amply rewarded, their sons and descendants pensioned. "They should not be dismissed on the words of jealous courtiers and their rights and services should not be neglected." But above all, the dying crown prince wished that his young grandson would be "the helper [*nasir*] and the defender [*hami*] of Islam."[2]

'Abbas Mirza's counsels could not have illustrated any better the remarkable continuity in the tradition of princely education. With clarity and candor, he highlighted the same merits and values that were urged by the writers of "mirrors for princes" for centuries in the Persian tradition of government. Protecting subjects from tyranny, observing the privilege of kinship, rewarding the servants of the state, and defending the land and the faith were duties as old as the story of Faridun, the legendary king of the *Shahnama*, to which 'Abbas Mirza alluded. Only compliance with these duties, as 'Abbas Mirza noted, could secure the divine support, the charisma [*farr*], by which Faridun had vanquished the forces of Zahhak's evil.

That 'Abbas Mirza stressed the conditions for preserving the divine benevolence in his reference to Nasir al-Din, "the defender of the faith," was perhaps not accidental. It is as though he projected his unrewarded desire for the Qajar throne on his grandson's future reign even more than on the reign of his own son. He could have expressed his patriarchal wishes no more effectively, given the sad fate of his kingly paradigm; Faridun, his divided patrimony, which engendered a lasting conflict with Iran's northern neighbor; and above all the regenerating but ultimately tragic reign of his grandson Kay Khusraw. Whether consciously or not, Nasir al-Din's early education contained elements of princely counsel emphasized by his grandfather, elements that contributed not only to his intellectual development but also to his very awareness as the bearer of an ancient monarchical tradition entrusted to him by his ancestors.

FORMAL EDUCATION

In Tehran and later in Tabriz, Nasir al-Din and his younger sister, Malikzada, were exposed to some elementary education in the royal harem. Though as early as the age of seven the crown prince had been assigned a royal tutor (*mulla-bashi*) to oversee his education, Nasir al-Din must have primarily benefited from some elementary teaching by a French nanny in the service of his mother. A close companion of Malik Jahan's, she was known only as Madame Gulsaz (the flower maker), after her husband's profession. An intelligent and well-rounded native of Orleans, she had come to Iran in the mid-1830s as the wife of Hajji 'Abbas, a Persian painter who was sent to France to master the art of flower making, much admired among the Persian nobility. After marrying 'Abbas she converted to Islam, soon learned Persian, and eventually found her way to the royal harem where, in addition to her knowledge of flowermaking, her skills in European makeup, cooking, sewing, embroidery, singing, and dancing were in great demand. Madam Gulsaz's full-time supervision of the royal princes in Tehran continued for an unknown duration, but she was intimate enough with the royal offspring to call Nasir al-Din and his sister her "children" and act as a go-between for the crown prince's first marriage.[3]

The crown prince's tutor, Mulla Mahmud Nizam al-'Ulama, who since 1837 had been the Mulla-bashi, was culturally worlds apart from Madame Gulsaz. He had probably been confirmed in the position because of his ties with Aqasi, who apparently shared some of his mystical views. Although he was on the fringes of the religious establishment, his appointment as tutor to the crown prince was not without precedent. Both tutors of Muhammad Shah, Aqasi and Mulla Nasrullah Sadr al-Mamalik Ardabili, were from sufi backgrounds. To be sure, Aqasi wanted the crown prince to be brought up in the same manner as his royal father, but this did not deter Mulla Mahmud Nizam al-'Ulama from considering himself a man of many other scholarly abilities.[4] The Tabrizi mulla demonstrated some leanings toward the progressive Shaykhi school, which then was highly influential in Azarbaijan. His alignment with the tenets of Shaykhism, however, was partial. He produced works unusual by the religious standards of the time but with virtually no tangible traces of the proto-messianism or anti-Usuli dissent common to Shaykhism. His interests seemed to have been shaped mostly by the need for moral perfection. In his work on ethics (akhlaq), dedicated in 1839 to Muhammad Shah, the mulla-bashi expounded a theory of self-purification with obvious mystical traits. He argued on the grounds of "scriptural and rational evidence" that all beings, human, animal, and inanimate, share varying levels of consciousness. For a human being to dominate his "self," it is imperative to try to control his body and soul by means of "devotion and abstention."[5] Such sufi dietary techniques for achieving spiritual hygiene were not far different from Aqasi's ascetic instructions to Muhammad Shah.

The Mulla-bashi was also the author of an anti-Sunni polemic.[6] His vitriolic attacks on the personalities of early Islamic history revered by

Sunni Islam, including charges of adultery against 'Ayisha, the Prophet's favorite wife, demonstrated his strict Shi'ite worldview. His anti-Sunni criticisms were severe enough to prompt an official ban on his work. On its first publication in Tabriz in 1853, the controversial piece was quickly put out of circulation by order of the premier, Mirza Aqa Khan Nuri, who, perhaps fearing the ill effects of such inflammatory material on relations with the Ottoman neighbor, undertook one of the first cases of book censorship in Iran's history.[7]

On the personal side, too, the Mulla-bashi shared with the premier an important characteristic. He had integrated the extrapedagogical merit of self-mockery, not far different from the premier's habitual self-deprecation, which often made him the subject of ridicule in court circles. During the sufi-favoring reign of Muhammad Shah, the Tabrizi mulla-bashi claimed a government pension on grounds of his alleged descent from the celebrated mystic Shaykh Mahmud Shabastari. This prompted a sarcastic remark by Farhad Mirza, Muhammad Shah's youngest brother and an articulate essayist with an intriguing personality, who suggested that the glory-seeking Mulla-bashi might as well claim descent from another famous Shabastari, Husayn Kurd, a semifictional hero of a popular folk epic.[8] The same farcical spirit combined with cynicism and religious zeal comes through during the 1848 Tabriz trial of Sayyid 'Ali Muhammad Shirazi, the Bab, who claimed to be the Qa'im of the House of the Prophet.

The impact of the mulla-bashi's tutorship on the young crown prince was mixed. The paucity of references to his tutor in Nasir al-Din's recorded recollections may suggest the absence of long-term moral influence. The Mulla-bashi certainly failed to play a role comparable to that of Aqasi in shaping the future shah. To Aqasi's regret, Nasir al-Din never developed a pro-sufi sentiment similar to his father's, nor indeed any of the spiritual preoccupations; nor did he demonstrate any pro-Shaykhi inclination. Even the Qajar chroniclers denied the Mulla-bashi any special homage. The almanac of 1889, *al-Ma'athir wa'l-athar*, which gives the concise biography of some 370 religious scholars of the Nasiri period, summarizes the career of the Mulla-bashi in only one sentence: "He was the tutor of His Majesty the Shah."[9] But the tutor's influence brought about a more subtle result. He implanted in the mind of his pupil a deep sense of religiosity and a belief in the general tenets of Shi'ism. In later years, Nasir al-Din's understanding of Shi'ism was sharpened in some respects and mellowed in others, but he maintained a degree of suspicion, and even contempt, toward the mainstream Usuli 'ulama, an attitude originally acquired during his early training under a Shaykhi tutor.

The actual teaching record of the Mulla-bashi did not deserve any special applause. Clear gaps in the crown prince's education were a cause of concern to some observers, but the Mulla-bashi did not heed their warnings. In a humorous letter written to the Mulla-bashi upon his reinstatement to the tutorship of the crown prince (apparently after a temporary dismissal), Farhad Mirza asked him to abstain in his teaching duties, to the best of his ability, "from nonsensical talk and idle deeds . . . so that God willing, he [Nasir al-Din] shall distinguish himself in his lessons and incline toward the study of the Arabic language and attainment of literary subtleties. . . . Thus in future, your status in the royal sight might gradually supersede that of your past and your present and your critics' mouths will be shut and their reproaching tongues will seize up."[10]

The reproaching tongues of the critics continued to wag nonetheless. The report of the British envoy, Justin Sheil, must have reflected some of the common strain of criticism: "I have now found that even his [Nasir al-Din's] Persian education has been extremely neglected. Of every kind of information he is entirely ignorant, and this neglect on the part of the Shah is the more strange as His Majesty [Muhammad Shah] has an acquaintance with the rudiments at least of several branches of European knowledge. But I am in hope [that] the prime minister has discovered the error he has committed in allowing the Heir Apparent to remain in obscurity."[11]

Sheil's cautious optimism did not last long, however, for some four months later he received the report of the Persian-Armenian Mirza Ibrahim, one-time French interpreter to the Russian embassy in Tehran, who was given the formidable task of conducting a crash course in French language for the crown prince:[12]

> I regret to receive from Mirza Ibrahim the most unfavorable account of the Prince Royal, whose understanding and acquirement he represents to be equally deficient. He is even imperfectly acquainted with reading and writing in his own language, and Mirza Ibrahim is so hopeless of his instruction being of any service, from the natural want of intellect and capacity in the Prince, that it is only by my recommendation that he has consented to retain his appointment of tutor to the Royal Highness.[13]

Given Nasir al-Din's lifelong deficiency in acquiring a tolerable knowledge of French or any other European language (as attested by his future teacher, Muhammad Hasan Khan I'timad al-Saltana), it is not difficult to see the cause of Mirza Ibrahim's complaint. Yet references to "want of intellect and capacity" and lack of rudimentary knowledge of Persian point to a more serious problem. Unlike his father and his grandfather, Nasir al-Din was deprived of a systematic courtly education—a deficiency exacerbated by his shyness and introverted personality. Mirza 'Ali Khan Amin al-Dawla, his future private secretary and reform-minded minister, tended to agree with Mirza Ibrahim when he stated that "in his early youth, Nasir al-Din Mirza did not seem to be gifted with natural disposition and talent, and the means of his education was not properly provided." For this latter, Amin al-Dawla blames the "inept" tutorship of the Mulla-bashi.[14]

Judging by Nasir al-Din's later writings, his growing literary and artistic interests, and the general air of confidence he displayed on the throne, it is hard not to notice a tremendous improvement in his performance. One cannot help agreeing with Curzon that being surrounded "from youth upwards by the sycophants and flatterers who buzz around an oriental monarch, it is surprising that Naser-ed-Din Shah has turned out so well."[15] Amin al-Dawla considered the appointment of Mirza Taqi Khan Amir Kabir to premiership a timely and significant sign of the crown prince's "intelligence and instinctive perception," which was finally awakened on the eve of his accession.[16]

It is evident that much of this intellectual maturation came about once he was able to overcome his linguistic impediments. Although Azarbaijani Turkish must be considered Nasir al-Din's first vernacular, it is difficult to believe, as stated by Curzon, that up to the age of twelve he spoke solely in that language. Yet as Turkish was the language of informal conversation at the early Qajar court, even during Nasir al-Din's youth, it is probable that he had difficulty comprehending lessons in Persian or even conversing in that language. In spite of his remarkable fluency in later years, even in his earliest writings after accession, some lapses of style and occasional grammatical and spelling errors betray his entanglement with written Persian. His style reflects not the old-fashioned ornate language of the court but the straightforwardness of everyday dialogue. In 1848, shortly after Nasir al-Din's accession, Farrant, again underscoring the neglect in the education of the new shah, notices that he "is very difficult in offering an opinion on any subject; he appears good-hearted, fond of pleasure, but does not possess that requisite so very essential for a king of Persia, namely, a flow of language and a pleasing address."[17]

The fact that the Mulla-bashi was also a Turkish speaker must have added to Nasir al-Din's struggle through archaic texts of Arabic grammar and highly advanced passages of Persian literature traditionally assigned to students. The isolation of individual tutorials, the method used to educate the royal princes, deprived him of the possibility of conversing with and learning from schoolmates, although presumably he had playmates, often children of the inner-court attendants, who were fluent in Persian.

It was perhaps more by the dictates of geography than thoughtful design that a Tabrizi mulla was given priority for the crown prince's education over other potential candidates, a decision that resulted in the exclusion of topics traditionally essential to princely education. This becomes even more apparent when Nasir al-Din's education is compared to that of his favored brother. The tutorship and supervision of 'Abbas Mirza was assigned to Riza Quli Khan Hidayat (then known as Lalah-bashi), one of the most accomplished literary figures of the time. Even in the early stages of his career, this prolific court poet laureate and chronicler, literary historian, biographer, and lexicographer had far more impressive credentials than the Mulla-bashi.[18] There is enough literary proficiency and taste in the memoirs of 'Abbas Mirza to demonstrate the superior training he enjoyed under Hidayat.[19]

THE FIGHT AND THE FEAST

Notwithstanding deficiencies in Nasir al-Din's formal education, he nevertheless proved highly receptive in outlook and language to a cultural milieu that first flourished in the early decades of the nineteenth century. The literary revival patronized by Fath 'Ali Shah's court glorified the traditional values of the Persian monarchy as they reemerged during the reign of Nasir al-Din's great-grandfather. Indeed, the above-mentioned Hidayat was a typical product of this literary revival. His *Majma' al-Fusaha* (The Conference of the Eloquent), a copious literary compendium that also covered contemporary poets and writers, is an example of Qajar patronage of poetry and literary craftsmanship. Fath 'Ali Shah, himself a poet of mediocre talent, assembled a literary society known as Anjuman-i Khaqan (The Royal Society). This was part of a conscious effort to revitalize the Persian courtly tradition of classical times, a necessary component for asserting the Qajar royal legitimacy and grandeur. The Anjuman's deliberate return to the simplicity of the old Khurasan school revived the fashion of the fresh naturalist approach of the early court panegyrists as well as the works of the great Persian lyric and epic poets of pre-Mongol times. This renaissance, a reaction to the excessive symbolism of the "Indian" school of the Safavid era, had its origins in the late-eighteenth-century literary circles of Shiraz and Isfahan. The most celebrated member of this society, Fath 'Ali Khan Saba, the *malik al-shu'ara* (poet laureate), was a member of the indigenous Persian literati who, lured by the Qajars' generosity and patronage, undertook the task of glorifying the rulers of the new dynasty. In the manner of the Samanid amirs and Ghaznavid sultans of the tenth and eleventh centuries, Fath 'Ali Shah was praised in the extravagant panegyrics of Saba and 'Abd al-Wahhab Nashat. Elevating him to the status of a legendary king, Saba in his epic verse the *Shahanshahnama* ("The Book of the King of Kings"), modeled after Firdawsi's *Shahnama* ("The Book of Kings"), depicted his royal patron with an excess beyond all conventional eulogies. The shah's majestic valor and wisdom were compared to those of the kings of the mythical dynasties, and even disastrous defeats in the war with Russia were portrayed as daunting victories. Having been exposed to this body of literature, it was natural that Nasir al-Din should see his own place and relevance in the light of such monarchical glories and should take pride and confidence in the record of his ancestors' deeds.

The novelty of this flourishing school and its impact on the crown prince, however, were not confined to adulation of the ruler. A more imaginative use of language and fresh imagery in prose and poetry in the tradition of the classical masters bore greater results in the middle decades of the century. Poets such as Qa'ani, Yaghma, and Surush and the prose writers Abul-Qasim Qa'im Maqam (II), Muhammad Taqi Sipihr, and, later, 'Ali Khan Amin al-Dawla began to explore new themes and genres. Thanks to these endeavors, the gentlemanly refinements of the *adab* tradition found some continuity. Artistic families such as those of Saba, Hidayat, and Visal produced figures who for generations were accomplished not only in literature but also in calligraphy, painting, and music. As a corollary to this artistic revival, there emerged a worldview that transpired, above all, in the spheres of geography, topography, and travel but also history and philosophy. One of the outstanding features of this *weltanschauung* was greater recognition of the distinct cultural identity of Iran, which went hand in hand with the realization of Iran's material disparity and its overall decline vis-à-vis Europe. The earliest Persian travelogues, the writings of historiographers such as Jalal al-Din Mirza, and the poetry of Yaghma and Qa'im Maqam exhibit pale impressions of this awareness. Dissociated from the mainstream religious ethos of the time, the advocates of this pioneering trend anticipated the more expressed secularism of the later reformers.[20]

Nasir al-Din's writing style and literary tastes reflect some of that cultural milieu, especially after his return to Tabriz in 1848, at which point he developed a keen interest in poetry and prose and rapidly improved his Persian. Nadir Mirza, a local historian of Tabriz who saw the crown prince during his Azarbaijan governorship, remarked that "during the day his highness gave [public] audience till noon and at night he spent his time with companions and poets."[21] The Tabriz intellectual circle that Nasir al-Din inherited from his predecessor, Bahman Mirza, still echoed something of 'Abbas Mirza's age and included poets, prose writers, translators, and literati whose works and presence in one way or another shaped Nasir al-Din's intellectual progress. Not surprisingly, an early reading pastime was simple prose, such as folk tales, that first helped him break the language barrier and gradually develop a taste and appreciation for Persian literature. In this respect, the newly published Persian translation of the classic *Alf Laylat wa'l-layla* (*One Thousand and One Nights*), offered style and content very different from that of dry texts of grammar and medieval prose. Commissioned by Bahman Mirza during his governorship, the first Persian edition of this collection of tales (of Persian origin) by the talented translator 'Abd al-Latif Tasuji was published in 1845 and was one of the earliest lithographic publications in Tabriz.[22] The entertaining, and at times seductive, nature of this work (particularly as illustrated by Abu'l-Hasan Sani' al-Mulk and his students some years later in the magnificent royal manuscript sponsored by Muhammad Shah and then by Nasir al-Din Shah) must have been particularly appealing to the adolescent crown prince, who first read it in Tabriz in 1848.[23] A good example of nineteenth-century Persian literary accomplishment, Tasuji's simple yet eloquent prose was a breakthrough in the genre of storytelling. A mulla of mildly unorthodox leanings, Tasuji, who originally tutored Bahman Mirza's sons, became part of Nasir al-Din's literary ensemble and later accompanied him to Tehran.[24]

Another member of the same literary circle, Surush Isfahani, a court poet of some repute who later became the first poet laureate of Nasir al-Din Shah and received the title of Shams al-Shu'ara ("the sun of the poets"), also left his intellectual mark on the young Nasir al-Din.[25] A skillful eulogist and keen student of classical masters, he collaborated with Tasuji in his translation of *Alf laylat wa'l layla*. But he received high recognition for his numerous panegyrics in honor of 'Ali, the First Imam, and for other religious compositions on Shi'ite themes.[26] Judging by his poetry, he was a *ghali*, an excessive admirer of 'Ali with extremist beliefs concerning his divine incarnation. It is no wonder that, having been originally a protégé of Sayyid Muhammad Baqir Shafti, the powerful mujtahid of the early nineteenth century, the young Surush, son of a butcher from Sidih, was expelled from Isfahan in 1831 on charges of extremism and "ill-belief."[27] In his praise for 'Ali he only avoided open use of divine attributes: "Say! He ['Ali] is not God, but seek in him whatever you desire; No creed in the world is more venerated than this."[28] Such religious themes, saturated with allusions to 'Ali's divinity, were wholly alien to the mainstream Shi'ism of the 'ulama but still part of a popular cult of 'Ali that was deeply entrenched in the Persian psyche. The influence of this cult on Nasir al-Din Mirza was subtle and enduring. Only in the light of his early exposure to Surush's poetry can one properly assess the crown prince's lifelong devotion to 'Ali as his protector and patron saint.

Even more, the panegyrics of Surush often supplemented veneration of 'Ali with praise of the poet's royal patron. Such association between the religious and the temporal was not accidental. The sense of charismatic continuity between the first Shi'ite Imam and the future shah implied in Surush's verses gave the young prince a sense of assurance of his place in the world and predestined divine protection at a time when, for the first time, his abilities were tested in public office. In a poem composed in celebration of 'Ali soon after Nasir al-Din's accession in 1848, Surush advised the new king to remain faithful to the path of 'Ali:

> Do you know what is salvation?
> Attachment to 'Ali and his House . . .
> I would not reveal all that could be said in his veneration,
> Since I am fearful of the uproar . . .
> All the prophets, major and minor,
> Are like waves and thou ['Ali] like a sea pearl.
> Toward thee they all return,
> Since all parts return to the whole.
> Now, he, the young king, the king of Iran,
> Has sat on the throne and given an audience,
> In celebration of thy feast.
> He is generous, victorious and wise.[29]

In another passage in celebration of the Shi'ite feast of Ghadir Khum ('Ali's designation by the Prophet as his successor), the poet stressed the connection between Imam 'Ali, "the prince of the faithful," and the king Nasir al-Din, "the defender of the faith":

> Thou, the Prince of the Faithful [*Amir al-Muminin*], the lion of the desert,
> The commander of the Prophet's army!
> By thee was bolstered the back of the Prophet in the battlefield,
> On the day you succeeded the Prophet.
> The young gleeful king, the victorious Nasir al-Din, the defender of the Faith,
> Now celebrates.
> [He is] the world ruler whose limbs are enamored of your love.
> He preserves in his soul your love like a pearl in the shell,
> He entertains your affection like the angels in Paradise.[30]

The other poets of Muhammad Shah's court were no less laudatory in their adulation of the crown prince, but none seem to have had the same impact as Surush on the young Nasir al-Din. Mirza Habib Qa'ani, perhaps the greatest panegyrist of the Qajar era, was introduced to Nasir al-Din by the learned prince 'Ali Quli Mirza I'tizad al-Saltana and received Nasir al-Din's praises for an "eloquent poem" in his honor. The famous poet extolled the prince in conventional poetic forms for his dreaded wrath and his unmatched generosity but evidently found nothing more praiseworthy than Nasir al-Din's "thunder-striking stallion"—a sign, one may assume, of the poet's uncertainty about the prince's future.[31] By contrast, Fathullah Shaybani, a sufi poet from Kashan who had been assigned to the crown prince's "companionship and service," must have had more faith in Nasir al-Din's eventual accession at a time of general uncertainty.[32]

> To thy lordship [Nasir al-Din] henceforth I say openly:
> "Why so much ambiguity in speech?"
> Thou shalt [soon] become the great king of your time,
> A king to whom the rulers and sovereigns are servants and slaves,
> A king whose stature is above all kings.[33]

Beyond its immediate impact, the literary output of these poets and their exaltation of Qajar royalty served an important purpose in shaping Nasir al-Din's outlook. They helped celebrate the two complementary dimensions of traditional Persian kingly conduct—"the fight and the feast" (*razm va bazm*). A legacy with roots as ancient as the epics of the *Shahnama*, the kings of Iran were praised in song and verse—as were the Greek and Roman warriors—for these two royal pursuits. At war, it was sheer ferocity and brute force, personal valor, shrewdness and tenacity in battle, and the ability to conduct successful campaigns against formidable enemies that set the standards for majesty and glory. By extension, in times of peace the shah's skill in riding and hunting, his mastery of weapons and marksmanship, and his subtle knowledge of games and hunting grounds constituted an inseparable part of this fighting mode. At the feast, the king's merits were measured by his capacity to appreciate worldly pleasures, such as festivities, food, wine, women, poetry, music, and painting. The pomp and ceremony exhibited at court, extravagance of dress, ostentatious displays of royal insignia and ornaments, construction of elaborate royal palaces and gardens, maintenance of an extensive entourage, patronage of poets, painters, musicians, and calligraphers, and the assemblage of a large harem all illustrated the shah's prowess in the feast mode.[34]

Fath 'Ali Shah revived the Persian courtly tradition and resurrected the monarch's time-honored position at the core of an enduring polity; therefore, it is not surprising to see that the Qajar princes' education encompassed both aspects of this tradition. When the court chronicler Sipihr stated that at the outset of youth Nasir al-Din had fully mastered the arts of "fight and feast," he was consciously comparing his future patron with Persian mythical heroes: "In the court he radiated like a gold-sparking sun, and in the battlefield he was adventurous as Jamshid. On the back of the Arabian horse he was like a lion of the wilderness who mocked Rustam, and in spending sacks of golden coins he ridiculed the stories of the generosity of the Qa'an and Hatam."[35] Lavish aggrandizement as such developed an image of Nasir al-Din as a "fierce hunter" even in his youth.[36]

Nasir al-Din's lifelong passion for riding and hunting, which later turned into an obsession, symbolized the kingly traditions of ferociousness and pleasure and was transmitted to him not merely by the praiseful eulogists but also by the role models of his ancestry. No hero characterized the ultimate qualities of resolution, ferocity, and ruthlessness better than the founder of his dynasty, Aqa Muhammad Khan. His fierce campaigns against nomadic contenders and other domestic rivals, his brute sense of discipline, his kinship loyalties and disloyalties, and his vision of creating a unified empire through tact and terror were elements of the royal heritage transmitted early on to the crown prince. The legacy of the warmonger khan continued to be traceable in the later generations, though with moderation, in the military careers of 'Abbas Mirza and his brothers and sons. Seldom did Nasir al-Din remain ambivalent about this legacy of royal ferocity, though in practice he only gave in to the warlike instincts of his ancestors in opportune instances. He unfailingly praised their military might and discipline and respected war heroes of the past. But even beyond the battlefield, moments of rage in Nasir al-Din's life, when kingly wrath descended on an unlucky victim, were not infrequent.

Similarly, if Nasir al-Din looked for a role model for an extravagant lifestyle, civility, and pleasure, he could not have found a better example than Fath 'Ali Shah. The memories of the court of his great-grandfather, noted for its dazzling display of royal opulence, official patronage of art and literature, lavish spending, and extensive harem, were still fresh in the minds of the Qajar nobility. After more than a decade of austere rule under Muhammad Shah, his son showed little hesitation in adopting the same pomp and circumstance that marked the reign of Fath 'Ali. Nasir al-Din's effort to preserve a grandiose comportment, almost to the point of narcissistic vanity, and his love of ornamentation, sumptuous food, and elaborate dwellings were well in tune with this ancestor's code of feasting.

This unwritten code of gallantry and gratification needed little elaboration. Every Qajar prince of Nasir al-Din's generation was expected to know the intricate details of horse pedigree, species of domestic game, riflery, and navigation in treacherous mountains and deep ravines. It was also taken for granted that the Qajar prince was conscious of his privileged membership in a nobility for which his forefathers fought long and hard and that he would remain devoted to principles guaranteeing the supremacy of his tribe. In spite of its resplendent appearance, promoted largely by Fath 'Ali Shah, the Qajar throne still honored the bonds of nomadic loyalty as the most important warranty for its endurance even by the middle of the nineteenth century. In the long run, one may venture to say, it was these legacies of fight and feast that constituted the basis of Nasir al-Din's political conduct, more so than a thorough education or even acquaintance with indigenous or modern political thought or with the realities of government.

LESSON OF THE MIRRORS

Beyond the kingly nomadic ethos, a wide range of traditional counsels and modern writings influenced Nasir al-Din's outlook, particularly after he assumed governorship of Azarbaijan. Of the considerable collection of works produced in the Qajar period on ethics and princely conduct in the vein of the classical "mirrors for princes," he must have studied a few specifically composed for him. Besides the Mulla-bashi's book on ethics, another didactic work of practical philosophy dedicated to him in 1848 when he was still the crown prince was by a prolific, yet so far obscure, writer named Mirza Nasrullah Damavandi. Entitled al-Tuhfat al-Nasiriya fi Ma-'rafat al-Ilahiya ("The Nasirian Gift of the Divine Knowledge"), it chiefly dealt with the institution of kingship, the virtues of the king, and the administration of the kingdom.[37] Damavandi was one of several authors in the nineteenth century still producing works in this genre. Earlier, in 1819, Sayyid Ja'far Kashfi Darabi, a theologian with mystical inclinations, had composed a book of counsels to the king entitled Tuhfat al-Muluk fi'l-Sayr wa'l Suluk ("The Gift for the Kings for [Mystical] Journey and Conduct") and dedicated it to one of Fath 'Ali Shah's sons. Kashfi was one of very few in the 'ulama class, albeit an unorthodox scholar, to be conscious of the need to provide pragmatic guidance for the temporal rulers of the time.[38]

In 1839 another author, Mirza Asadullah Shahkhasti Mazandarani, under the pen name Nadir, wrote a comprehensive work, Khasa'il al-Muluk ("The Virtues of the Kings"), on the necessity of the institution of kingship and the qualities of a just ruler. He devoted a chapter to the need for consultation and another to royal education.[39] A year earlier, in 1838, a work entitled *Tuhfa-yi Nasiri* ("Nasirian Gift") by Muhammad Ja'far Marvazi (son of the renowned prose writer Muhammad Sadiq Waqayi' Nigar Marvazi) had been dedicated to Muhammad Shah, but, as the title indicates, in fact it was primarily for the education of Nasir al-Din Mirza. The book comprised seven chapters and sought to promote in the figure of the king the virtues of prudence, etiquette, justice, generosity, courage, patience, and forgiveness. Ending with dictums borrowed from *Nahja al-Balagha*, the famous collections of sayings, letters, and addresses attributed to 'Ali, the First Imam, the author acknowledged a long Shi'ite tradition of presenting 'Ali as the archetype of just such a ruler.[40]

As could be expected, 'Ali's image as a just ruler was bound to impress Nasir al-Din Mirza. Indeed, the above-mentioned Muhammad Sadiq Marvazi was only one of many Shi'ite writers since Safavid times who tested their literary skills by producing numerous exegetic translations of a famous *'Ahdnama* attributed to 'Ali ibn Abu Talib. The *'Ahdnama* (literally, "The Book of Covenant"), addressed to Malik Ashtar Nakha'i upon his appointment to the governorship of Egypt in 658–659, was probably a Shi'ite "mirror" produced in the tenth-century Buyid court. The principles advocated in it had been popular with Shi'ite writers at least since the seventeenth century, when its Persian translation, commissioned by 'Abbas I, was produced by the Safavid 'ulama. At least eight writers of the Qajar era, mostly "the men of the pen" attached to the court, produced such translations and commentaries on this document, four of them during Nasir al-Din's reign. The *'Ahdnama* represents a good exposition of the duties of the rulers prior to the introduction of Western political thought and the closest Persian equivalent to a general theory of government.[41]

With a dual emphasis on upholding high moral standards and political expediency, the *'Ahdnama*, like most medieval "mirrors," made four tasks incumbent upon the ruler: equitable collection of taxes, defense of the community (*jihad*), welfare of the people, and improvement of the cities. It required the ruler to be forthright and god-fearing, to exercise self-control, and to display affection, forgiveness, and justice toward his subjects. Further, the ruler was advised against secluding himself from the people lest he become narrow-minded and detached from reality. He was held accountable only to God but urged to explain the reasons for his actions to his subjects in order to remove any unfounded suspicions they might harbor. No blood should be shed without justification, for this would weaken the ruler's position and lower his authority. He should avoid self-admiration and exaggerated praise, have control over his sense of prestige, and prevent outbursts of anger or sharpness of tongue. He should avoid haste by delaying severe action until his anger subsides.

The government, the 'Ahdnama declared, must take into account the interests of the common people more than those of the elite. Urging continuity, maintenance of the status quo, and avoidance of innovation "in any line of action which harms the earlier ways," it reminded the ruler of his ancient duty to preserve the cycle of equity in society. The delicate balance between the main components of the government—the army, the judiciary, and the clerical and revenue-collecting agencies—should not be disturbed. Nor should the well-being of the merchants and craftsmen be compromised, "since they are sources of profit and provide society with useful articles." Similarly, the welfare of the cultivators received a high priority: "You should also keep an eye on the cultivation of the land more than on the cultivation of revenue" because revenue "cannot be had without cultivation, and whoever asks for revenue without cultivation ruins the land and brings death to the people. His rule will not last even a moment."[42]

Beyond its general moral tone, the covenant offered specific advice that could not be ignored by any candidate for the throne, least of all by ones with prospects as shaky as Nasir al-Din's. The agent of the government, it stated, should not be a miser, nor should he display exceeding praise toward his master, but above all he should not be associated with past injustices. "The worst minister for you," the ruler is warned, "is he who has been a minister for mischievous persons before you, and who joined them in sins. Therefore he should not be your close adviser, because he is an abettor of sinners and brother of the oppressors. You can find good substitutes in those who will be like them in their views and influence, while not being like them in sins and vices."[43] To be sure, this advice fully reflected Nasir al-Din's distrust in Hajji Mirza Aqasi and his choice of Mirza Taqi Khan, a relatively unknown figure, as his first premier. The executive agents, the covenant further required, should be provided with an "abundant livelihood," but their actions should be checked, and their misappropriation and corruption should be controlled with corporal punishment and public disgrace. The long list of disgraced ministers under Nasir al-Din, some of them even dying for uncommitted crimes, testifies to his uncanny diligence in complying with this counsel. But, to the future king's credit, he often provided his agents with an "abundant livelihood" before it became necessary to inflict punishment.

In dealing with his country's potential enemies, too, Nasir al-Din complied with the covenant's advice, which urged the ruler above all not to reject peace with neighbors. "Peace brings rest to your army, relief to your warriors, and safety to your country. But after concluding peace, there should be great apprehension of the enemy, because often the enemy offers peace to benefit from your negligence. Therefore, be cautious and do not act by wishfulness in this matter." Moreover, Muslims and nonbelievers alike were not to be deceived; "besides Muslims, even nonbelievers abide by agreements because they realize the danger which would come in the wake of violation."[44] One can almost recognize the broad principles of Nasir al-Din's foreign policy in the above lines as he, in later years, learned to deal with his Muslim and non-Muslim neighbors.

Aside from its ethical undertones, the advice of the *'Ahdnama* was in general accord with all classical "mirrors," from the *Letter of Tansar* to Nizam al-Mulk's *Siyasat-nama* and Ghazali's *Nasihat al-Muluk*, works that for centuries had portrayed the ideal of kingly conduct. But the fact that Nasir al-Din's political behavior was to be modeled by this essentially Shi'ite example demonstrates the ethos ingrained into every aspect of Nasir al-Din's upbringing and worldview. Compliance with the *'Ahdnama* thus complemented moral veneration for 'Ali. Even in later years, as Nasir al-Din was further exposed to modern European ideas of government, the ancient notions of rulership that he embraced early on remained largely untouched. Years later he upheld these teachings as irrevocable dictums of sound government and advised others to follow them.

DISPLAY OF THE WORLD

The traditional "mirrors" and government manuals produced under the Qajars remained limited in outlook and were never free from the cultural complacency that obscured the authors' views about the realities of the outside world. In spite of strong emphasis on "the welfare of the subjects," these "mirrors" often failed to translate the "king's duties" into modern motives of reform and the state's responsibility to the material well-being of society, although these ideas were current in the Tabriz court as early as the 1810s. This body of political writings as a whole showed little awareness of the changing international climate, with which the modern European powers were inevitably associated, nor did it recognize the perils of these powers' diplomatic and military presence. It failed to offer reliable data on geography and history, on the technological, scientific, and industrial advancements of the modern world, or on the incentives that attracted the European powers to the Middle East. For a young and increasingly curious prince such as Nasir al-Din, the answers to these enigmas of the Western world were to be found in a different genre of literature. Indeed, the description of Nasir al-Din's worldview remains incomplete without a reference to his lifelong attraction to world history and geography. Of prime importance in broadening the intellectual horizons of the peoples of the Middle East, these subjects generated a growing corpus of European translations in the nineteenth century. Compared to what was known by the Ottomans and Egyptians, the Persian understanding of modern Europe was not any less complex, though it arrived later and in haphazard fashion. Yet by the middle of the nineteenth century there was enough material to satisfy the curiosity of privileged members of the ruling elite.

Nasir al-Din's interest in history and geography started in his youth and remained strong throughout his life, constituting a considerable portion of his pastime activities. His youthful attraction for both disciplines in the following decades made him something of a gentleman scholar. He underwrote both translations from European languages and composition of a great number of popular and semischolarly works. During his heir apparency he must have been familiar with a well-known survey entitled *Jahan Nama* ("Display of the World"), whose 1845 translation from the Turkish (itself a translation of a French original) was dedicated to Aqasi. This treatise, perhaps the earliest translation of its kind, contained a general description of the human and political geography of the five continents and was initially commissioned by Mirza Taqi Khan Vazir Nizam (later Amir Kabir), then the Persian ambassador to the Erzurum conference.[45] Interest in this area prompted Nasir al-Din to commission in 1850 the composition of a work of a similar nature with the same title, by an Englishman who spent some years in Tabriz, presumably in the service of the Persian government.[46] Another work, *Jughrafiya-yi 'Alam* ("Geography of the World"), which also contained some historical accounts of modern Europe and was originally commissioned by Bahman Mirza, was presented by Edward Burgess to Muhammad Shah in 1846. Although the original text used for this translation was 100 years old, Burgess was able to update it with the help of some contemporary European gazetteers.[47]

Like Tasuji, Edward Burgess belonged to Bahman Mirza's circle in Tabriz, which Nasir al-Din inherited after the prince's defection. An English merchant turned translator and tutor, Burgess was the best the learned prince could find to satisfy his curiosity for geography, European history, and modern natural history.[48] Under Bahman, Tabriz, which was at that time the largest city in Iran, continued to enjoy a vibrant cosmopolitan character owing to its European trade, its communities of Greek,

Armenian, and European merchants, and its contacts with the neighboring Russian and Ottoman empires. From 'Abbas Mirza's time on, there were numerous publications in Persian of works reflecting such contacts with the outside world. Writing to his brother, Burgess reflected something of this change of climate: "You will perhaps be surprised to hear that we have now in Tabreez no less than sixteen printing establishments, and more in Tehran; in fact books have become so cheap in Persia that it has done much injury to the trade of the copyists. . . . You might perhaps buy a printed [copy of *Shahnama*] . . . for as many [as] sixpence."[49] European newspapers were also becoming more regularly available. Burgess could even afford to favor *Gallignani's Messenger,* an English daily published in Paris, for its fairness over the other available English papers, *Illustrated London News* and the famous satirical *Punch.* Several French papers—*Débats, Siècle,* and *National,* all published in Istanbul and Izmir—were also available.[50] Translations into Persian of the European news and current affairs made available by Burgess and others were chief sources of information for the eager Persian intelligentsia of Tabriz. Writing in May 1848 to his brother, Burgess noted that "the affairs of France have as you may suppose made a great impression in this country, and my translations of the newspapers are looked for with much eagerness." Awareness about the 1848 revolution in France was in part due to the advocacy of the American Presbyterian missionaries in Azarbaijan, who were "much pleased with the news from Europe." They hoped, reported Burgess, that all the world was going to be republican.[51]

The young Nasir al-Din Mirza and his future premier, Mirza Taqi Khan, then Vazir Nizam of Azarbaijan, were probably among the readers of Burgess' news translations. After the downfall of Bahman Mirza, the bewildered Burgess was obliged to search for a new patron in the person of the succeeding governor and his entourage. Compared to Bahman Mirza, he found Nasir al-Din at the outset "quite unfit for business," a puppet in the hand of his people, who monopolized "all the power and patronage." Since his arrival, notes Burgess, "he has done little but give away places to those about him and amuse himself."[52] Burgess's opinion quickly changed, however, as he found Nasir al-Din unvexed by the Englishman's earlier prominence under his uncle.[53] Four months later, upon Nasir al-Din's accession to the throne, Burgess was promoted to the much-needed post of chief interpreter, perhaps at Mirza Taqi Khan's recommendation.[54]

The monolithic picture presented in the atlases and almanacs translated by Burgess and others was insufficient for the acquisition of a realistic understanding of Europe and the rest of the world. Yet this flat portrayal helped shape Nasir al-Din's general worldview. The almanacs to which he had access contained dry descriptions of physical geography, with lists of countries, cities, and boundaries, topography, and climate, but were devoid of the human element of societies and social institutions. Historical accounts were no less uninspiring. They included dynastic lists, common dates of wars, conquests, and references to political upheavals, all virtually shorn of personal or intellectual content. Such an unimaginative view of the world and its past left an enduring mark on Nasir al-Din and is traceable in his long topographic passages and barren descriptions of visited localities in his travelogues, both domestic and foreign.

Some travelogues by Persian visitors to Europe may have given him a more personal and tangible picture of the outside world. *Mir'at al-Ard* ("The Mirror of the Earth") by Mirza Muhammad Lavasani, who in 1848 accompanied a Persian diplomatic mission to Russia, was dedicated jointly to Muhammad Shah and Nasir al-Din Mirza and contained some personal observations on geography and life in Russia.[55] The crown prince might have also had access to Mirza Mustafa Afshar's account of his visit to Petersburg in 1829 in the company of Khusraw Mirza, Nasir al-Din's uncle, a visit intended to convey to the tsar the shah and crown prince's apologies for the murder of Griboidov and the Russian mission in Tehran. Mirza Taqi Khan Farahani, then a minor official, was also included in this delegation. A supplementary account by yet another member of the party, Mirza Mas'ud Ansari (later Iran's minister of foreign affairs under Muhammad Shah and continuing into the first few months of Nasir al-Din's reign), may have provided Nasir al-Din with his first account of the life of 'Abbas Mirza, the two rounds of the Russo-Persian wars (1805–1813 and 1826–1828), and their causes and consequences.[56] The fascinating accounts of visits to Europe by three other Qajar princes who temporarily took refuge in England after the civil war of 1834–1835 may have given Nasir al-Din a tangible picture of public life in Europe in the early years of his reign.[57]

Of the other historical works studied by young Nasir al-Din, little is known. One suspects that he must have had some knowledge of the growing body of works on Persian, Islamic, and world history produced in the early nineteenth century both in print and in manuscript forms. There were also available in the royal collection manuscript copies of historical works of the Safavid period (such as Iskandar Bayg Munshi Turkaman's *'Alam Ara-yi 'Abbasi*) and general histories of earlier periods. He could have read a summary history of Iran and Islam compiled by the learned prince Mahmud Mirza, Nasir al-Din's uncle, for his brother Muhammad Shah in 1846. Other works about the history of his own dynasty such as

'Abd al-Razzaq Dunbuli's *Ma'athir Sultaniya,* published in Tabriz in 1825, Muhammad Sadiq Marvazi's *Tarikh-i Jahan Ara,* and Fazlullah Khavari's *Tarikh-i Dhul-Qarnayan* were also accessible to him.[58]

Beyond often dry historical accounts, there were other more visual representations for the young Nasir al-Din Mirza. He may have seen a historical album of Napoleon Bonaparte containing some ninety lithographs with French and Persian commentaries prepared for Muhammad Shah in 1844.[59] Another collection of copper plate lithographs and European illustrated books originally belonging to Bahman Mirza also might have come into Nasir al-Din's possession, giving him a chance to see European scenery, architecture, fashion, and gadgets.[60]

The crown prince's fascination with European gadgets of entertainment is evident in an account by Jules Richard, a resourceful French hanger-on in the Qajar court. In 1844 Richard had made his debut at the Tehran court by operating two early photographic cameras, gifts from Queen Victoria and Tsar Nicholas I to the shah. Officially employed, presumably as the royal photographer, he took some of the earliest photographs of the royal family and of Nasir al-Din, to whom he was introduced by the French nanny, Madame Gulsaz. It is also probable that Richard's early photographs, now lost, aroused Nasir al-Din's interest in photography, which he followed, for a while enthusiastically, in later life.[61] In October 1849 Nasir al-Din asked Richard to make him some lantern kites (or balloons), complete with the alcohol needed for the lanterns. On another occasion the young shah, disappointed by a German clock maker and European military engineers' failed attempts to operate a miniature steamship brought from Europe, turned to the innovative Frenchman. To his satisfaction, on the occasion of a public levee, Richard managed to maneuver the toy ship in the pool in front of Gulistan Palace. The demonstration was successful enough to prompt the shah and his premier, Mirza Taqi Khan Amir Kabir, to inquire about real steamships. Encouraged by Richard's performance, a few days later Nasir al-Din asked him to translate the captions on some lithographic illustrations of an old copy of the Old Testament printed in Latin, perhaps part of Bahman Mirza's collection. These services not only brought Richard a shawl worth thirty tumans but also rescued him from omission from the royal list and loss of salary during the austerity regime of Amir Kabir. The young shah had asserted: "He is necessary. Let him remain. We would need him."[62]

Nasir al-Din's early education, in spite of its shortcomings, introduced him to the parallel domains of the traditional and the modern. In later years, by means of self-education and pursuit of his artistic interests, he tried to further his knowledge of both areas. An attachment to the precepts of the past, frequently accompanied by fascination for the new, was characteristic of his entire reign and often produced curious combinations with highly individualized flavors. Nasir al-Din's familiarity with the European world, however, continued to be superficial, particularly before his first trip to Europe in 1873, and his musings on this topic of special interest hardly extended to any serious reconsideration of the basic concepts of kingship and government. Yet in Tabriz he was not untouched by the spirit of change first introduced by his grandfather. 'Abbas Mirza, with his openness toward the West and his encouragement of reform initiatives, presented Nasir al-Din with an attractive role model. In the face of European military and commercial advances, the young prince could not have remained aloof from the necessities that first prompted 'Abbas Mirza to undertake reform measures. Studying geography and history was bound to change his perceptions of the world and of his own kingdom. Moreover, the brief but important experience of administering the government of Azarbaijan exposed him to the realities of provincial rule. There he discovered that his political survival depended on the degree to which he was willing to, and able to, deal with the complex domestic and international issues that were increasingly undermining the foundation of the Qajar rule.

REHEARSAL FOR THE THRONE

The seven months' residence in Tabriz provided Nasir al-Din with his first experience of holding a government post. Unaccompanied by his mother and away from the intrigues of the Tehran court, he had his first chance to exercise some independence in making decisions and taking action. Although his appointment was largely ceremonial and in any case too brief for a meaningful exercise of power, the governorship of Azarbaijan, the most important province in the country, brought the crown prince into direct contact with some of the tangible problems he was about to inherit from his father.

For the most part the state officials who soon joined prince's retinue were charged with the actual business of the government. Besides the chief steward (*pishkar*) and provincial minister Mirza Fazlullah Nasir al-Mulk and his officials, the prince's entourage included his wife, Galin; his private supervisor, Hajji Bizhan Khan; his tutor, the Mulla-bashi; three of his maternal uncles, serving as his chiefs of protocol (*ishik-aqasi*); the keeper of the prince's seal; and his head groom. Other companions included Dr. William Cormick, a British physician whose father previously had served under 'Abbas Mirza and who himself served a long time in Tehran and Tabriz; two Persian physicians; the prince's poet laureate, Surush Isfahani; and a host of "home-born servants and aides," among them Nasir al-Din's future butler and influential confidant, Ibrahim Khan Amin al-Sultan.[63] The princely entourage also included a military chief from the Caucasian province of Qarabagh, 'Abbas Quli Khan Javanshir, who probably was selected by Aqasi, also a Caucasian, to watch over the prince and to counterbalance the influence of the three brothers of Malik Jahan. Another Caucasian, Hajji Bizhan, a Georgian slave previously in the service of 'Abbas Mirza, was apparently the best private supervisor Aqasi could find to complete his circle around Nasir al-Din. He replaced the prince's former supervisor, a totally obscure figure named Mustafa Bag Lavasani.

The Qajar practice of assigning a supervisor (*lala*) to a royal prince was an ancient Turco-Mongol one, and as a rule the supervisor exerted great control over all the affairs of the crown prince. Like many other eunuchs and servants of Georgian origin in Qajar service, he belonged to a class of white slaves who, since late Safavid times, had played a sensitive role in the inner quarters of the Persian court and in the upbringing of the royal princes. Hajji Bizhan's abilities as a confidant and troubleshooter were highlighted during the second round of Russo-Persian wars when, in 1827, he was sent by 'Abbas Mirza to open peace negotiations with the Russian commander.[64] Though characterized by Amin al-Dawla as "illiterate, simple-minded, and vulgar," it is likely that he was appointed to smooth over relations with Russians in Tabriz and to transmit to the young Nasir al-Din something of the spirit of the 'Abbas Mirza era, when Bizhan had been in the service of that crown prince in Azarbaijan.[65]

The governorship of Azarbaijan provided Nasir al-Din with a taste of what he was to encounter later on the throne—financial crises, tension with the central administration, popular discontent, religious dissent, Russian intervention, and competition among the high-ranking officials in charge of sensitive posts. By all accounts, Nasir al-Din's early performance, in spite of a number of early setbacks, was impressive. The British consul in Tabriz, Richard Stevens, commenting on the "great sedition" caused over the new appointment of the governor, gave a pessimistic assessment . He contrasted the ousted Bahman Mizra's popularity among the lower classes with the general dislike for the crown prince. Only "the people of note" whom Bahman Mizra prevented from inflicting injustices upon the public were rejoicing at the arrival of Nasir al-Din, "under whom they appear to expect a revival of the time of Abbas Mirza."[66] Stevens feared that "the young and inexperienced" Nasir al-Din—who was said to be "so obstinate when bent on attaining any object," and who arrived ahead of his officials—would commit "acts of oppression before his advisers can reach and check him." His retinue, "a most disreputable set of dependents; all poor and quite indifferent by what means they may better their conditions," en route had already "nearly ruined the villages" by extorting food, forage, and money.[67] In the vicinity of Tabriz, Hajji Bizhan Khan himself committed a breach of protocol by refusing the Ottoman consul a welcoming audience with the crown prince and later added to the insult by denying any knowledge of it.[68] The arrival of the queen mother (the Davalu widow of 'Abbas Mirza I and mother of Muhammad Shah) from the pilgrimage of the Hajj was the occasion for another embarrassment. Evidently furious over the dismissal of her favorite son, Bahman, she showed her dissatisfaction by "scarcely taking any notice" of Nasir al-Din, who had traveled two stages out of Tabriz in respect for his grandmother, only to be snubbed by her.[69]

Above all, the Russians' annoyance with Nasir al-Din's appointment promised to be a source of unwanted trouble. They were complaining of, among other things, the prince's failure to announce his arrival to the governor general of Tiflis—an act of "official politesse" they regarded as their unquestionable privilege, as though he were a vassal of the great tsar. Richard Stevens, the British consul in Tabriz, anticipated that this failure on the crown prince's part, added to his appointment in "open defiance of Russian advice," would inspire agitation and intrigue, particularly if the prince and his suite were seldom going to stay in town. "He thinks of nothing but amusement, leaving the most important business [of government] quite unattended."[70]

Stevens was not the only Englishman to observe the flaws that threatened the heir apparent's performance. Edward Burgess confirmed the excesses of Nasir al-Din's retinue and the prince's own determination not to give up his expensive habits of hunting and outdoor leisure in the face of pressure from Tehran. "In fact, things can not go on as at present, for in a short time there will not be [a] thousand pounds of available revenue in the province; all will be swallowed up by the young prince's courtiers." More specifically, Burgess was concerned with the sorry state of the Azarbaijan army, a concern that must have echoed Mirza Taqi Khan's. "Now when you consider that the Shah's great power consists in the troops drawn from this province, which troops can not do altogether without pay and clothing, and with the rebellion raging in Khurasan, in a short time you may fancy what a mess they will be in."[71]

The affairs of the army and Tehran's orders for 10,000 troops from the province to be deployed in Khurasan against the Davalu insurrection were the most urgent tasks Nasir al-Din found awaiting him. Aqasi, unwilling to assign too much power and consequence to the crown prince and wary of pro–Bahman Mirza sympathies in the Azarbaijani army, had his own trusted candidate, 'Ali Khan Maku'i, ready to take command. But Nasir al-Din was not willing to surrender entirely to the premier's wishes. He, too, was searching for a candidate. It was true, as Burgess implied, that there was a general hesitation among men of "standing and talent" to serve under him, for they viewed him as being overattached to his inner circle. Moreover, he did not want to appear hostile to Aqasi's wishes. He reflected on his understandable predicament in response to Stevens's warning regarding the political and financial hazards of calling into active service a large force. Because orders had been sent from the capital, Nasir al-Din asserted, he did not wish to appear disobedient; yet he did not have enough troops ready, and "unless [he] ruin the royat [ra'iyat, the subjects] by extraordinary taxation," he believed, he could not raise such large a force. He thus urged the Tabriz consul, according to Stevens, to inform the British envoy in Tehran of the circumstances, presumably in hopes of preventing the premier's pro-Russian Maku'i supporters from taking full control in Azarbaijan.[72] It was perhaps with this consideration in mind that Mirza Taqi Khan Farahani, the Vazir Nizam, was then promoted to acting chief of command of the Azarbaijani army after his return from the Erzurum conference. It is not clear to what extent this appointment enjoyed the initial backing of Nasir al-Din Mirza, but given the fact that Mirza Taqi Khan was known to the British for his assertiveness and political ambitions, it is probable that he emerged as the most suitable candidate. The British minister in Tehran, who detected in Mirza Taqi Khan a competent bulwark against Russian influence, must have been able to convince Aqasi and Nasir al-Din to promote the civilian army secretary to the highest military rank.

The events of the summer of 1848 proved the effectiveness of the new army appointment. Serious anti-Armenian riots in June involving the Russian and later the British consuls, the 'ulama of Tabriz, and, for the first time in action, Mirza Taqi Khan Vazir Nizam demonstrated to Nasir al-Din his vulnerability in the face of foreign intrigue and popular discontent. This episode was soon followed by another highly sensitive and potentially dangerous affair—the public trial of the messianic claimant Sayyid 'Ali Muhammad Shirazi, the Bab, in early July. The first episode allowed Nasir al-Din to face the perils of presiding over an unpopular government devoid of backing from its powerful northern neighbor. The second episode brought him firsthand experience in dealing with the ongoing confrontation between the proclaimed Mahdi and his clerical opponents.

The anti-Armenian riots of 16 June started when a crowd of Tabrizis gathered in the house of the city's chief Usuli cleric, Mirza Ahmad Mujtahid Tabrizi, to protest the alleged rape of a young Muslim boy by an Armenian servant of the Russian consulate. The suspect had been caught by the crowd but subsequently was released by the agents of Mirza Taqi Khan and duly handed over to the chief magistrate (*baglarbagi*) of the city. The chief magistrate presumably was cautioned about the servant's immunity as a Russian protégé (a commonplace nuisance for city officials), and after some hesitation he released the servant to the charge of the Russian consul. In a surprise turnabout, he then arrested six of the protesters, including a mulla, on the charge of killing the consul's dog. The incident provided all the ingredients for a sectarian riot with the undertones of foreign intrigue. A crowd of 3,000 Tabrizis, angered by the blatant impropriety on the part of the baglarbagi, possibly a pro-Russian figure, went on a rampage. Calling for all Armenians to be massacred, they attacked their quarter as well as the houses and shops of the Russians and Russian-protected Greeks in the bazaar. Some forty houses were gutted, and shops belonging to Georgians were looted. Two hundred and fifty Armenians, Greeks, and others could no longer defend themselves with brickbats against the sorties of the city brigands, the *lutis*, and took refuge in the British consulate. The Russian consul, distressed by the unexpected strength of the protest, secretly wrote to Nasir al-Din calling for him to quell the riot. Nasir al-Din's answer to the man who by insisting on the immunity of the Armenian servant had incited the riot was surprisingly blunt, even courageous: "Give up the servant who violated the boy and I will stop the row."[73] There was every indication that the riot might expand further.

The next day, 17 June, the riot reached its peak. George Stevens, in the absence of his brother, Richard, wrote to Nasir al-Din, as well as to the commander of government forces in the Tabriz citadel, asking for protection for the British consulate and foreign citizens. He simultaneously wrote to the prominent mujtahids seeking help in dispersing the crowd. But 10,000 Tabrizis, probably close to one-third of the adult male population of the city, had already gathered within the walls of the citadel in front of the government house. The crowd's fury was particularly directed against the chief magistrate who was considered responsible "for unjust punishment of Mohammedans in order to please the Russian Consul."[74] Such uncontrollable fury, however, could easily have been pointed at the crown

prince and his unpopular administration. The eyewitness account given by
Nadir Mirza, then a local official in the Tabriz government, conveyed the
utter panic Nasir al-Din experienced at his encounter with the angry crowd:

> Amidst the turmoil, I rushed to the court [of the crown prince] where, I
> heard, the mob had gathered. When I arrived, the disorderly crowd had
> occupied the entire square, the magistrate's courtyard and the registry
> office. His Majesty [i.e., Nasir al-Din] was seated in the enclosure [*ivan*].
> His face had turned pale. The crowd was busy. Some were drinking from
> the cistern, others screaming, a few sat in the shadow shouting: "Let us
> today rip all the Christians." His Majesty replied: "Wait today. Tomor-
> row I will execute all Christians who committed crimes." But where was
> the listening ear to hear him?[75]

Disturbed by the impertinent crowd and its violent demands, Mirza Taqi
Khan Vazir Nizam, alerted by George Stevens, rushed back to the city.
Accompanied by his brother and a number of his attendants, he galloped
through the streets of Tabriz, "rush[ing] away the people and [drawing]
all before him," remembered Stevens. "Well mounted," the attacking party
headed by Vazir Nizam was equipped with "thick cudgels, knocking the
fellows over by dozens." Arriving victoriously at the citadel, Vazir Nizam
"harangued" the people, cautioning them that if need be he would not
hesitate to "sweep the streets with artillery."[76] Nadir Mirza reported seeing
Vazir Nizam "with the skirt [of his robe] rolled up around his waist and
with a cudgel in his hand galloping around the town."[77]

The heavy-handed response by Vazir Nizam, an early example of what
was to come during his premiership, dispersed the crowd, but at a cost. In
the course of the sortie two or three protesters were killed, and there were
"a lot of broken heads."[78] The frightened Nasir al-Din, outmaneuvered by
the firm action of his army commander, who rescued him from a dangerous
and traumatic situation, could do little but comply. Far more agile than
other officials of the Tabriz court (including the unassuming provincial
vizier, Fazlullah 'Aliabadi), Vazir Nizam, backed by the large military force
under his command, was about to fulfill his long-awaited ambition to take
charge of the crown prince's affairs, a dream that had preoccupied him as
early as 1838.

Nasir al-Din was not the only one impressed with Vazir Nizam's swift
and forceful action. Consul Stevens was able to report to Lord Palmerston
that "nothing could possibly exceed" Vazir Nizam's "gallant conduct" and
his "anxiety and exertion to quell the disturbances, and especially to
prevent the mob from approaching this consulate and the houses of British
subjects. He visited them all several times during the day, and at night

called to satisfy himself that the guards were alert."[79] By contrast, the vexed British consul had found an opportunity to air his displeasure with Nasir al-Din. "As for the Crown Prince," he wrote with unjustifiable harshness, "he has given undeniable evidence of his total incapacity as a ruler, and I fear the people have made a discovery in this respect, of which they will some day avail to relieve themselves from the oppression under which they have been suffering ever since His Royal Highness assumed the government of the province."[80] Although that day never came for the people of Tabriz, the signs of protest did not vanish altogether. Four days after the riot, the Russian consul felt susceptible enough to write to Nasir al-Din and threaten that unless normalcy returned and the bazaars were reopened, he would leave Tabriz for Tiflis, accompanied by all Russian subjects and protégés.[81] One can hardly miss traces of a Russian grudge against the crown prince, who was deemed the instigator of the protesters.

THE PROPHET AND THE PRIESTS

Shortly after the riot subsided, the episode of the Bab's trial added to the environment of excitement and unrest. The Bab's arrival in Tabriz and his subsequent trial by the 'ulama gave the inhabitants of the city another chance to air their resentments. Growing enthusiasm for the persecuted prophet was a source of anxiety to the government as well as to the 'ulama. Never since his messianic proclamation in 1844 to the "gateship" (babiyat) of the Hidden Imam, which in practice was tantamount to the claim to Mahdihood in every way but name, had the Shirazi Sayyid and his Babi followers received as much public attention as they did in Tabriz. The Bab had been in solitary confinement in the castle of Chihriq (in the vicinity of Salmas in southwestern Azarbaijan on the Ottoman frontier) and was brought to Tabriz by Aqasi's order to stand an inquisitory trial by the 'ulama. The chief purpose of the trial was to demonstrate to the public "the heretical nature of his claims." The sensitivity of the event can be gauged by the remarks of a local mujtahid who witnessed the arrival of the Bab in Tabriz after an earlier enthusiastic welcome in the city of Urumiya:

> The ordinary people of Tabriz, too, misconstrued and began to entertain illusions about him. They were waiting for his arrival and for the gathering of the 'ulama so that if in that gathering he triumphed, or the verdict of the gathering turned out to be in his favor, then the learned and the lay, the stranger and the native, and even the government troops would pay their allegiance to him without hesitation and consider obedience to whatever he commanded a [religious] obligation. In short, such a strange spirit befell the city that a possessor of wisdom would wonder.[82]

Nasir al-Din himself presided over the tribunal, which included, among other 'ulama, Nasir al-Din's tutor, the Mulla-bashi, and the chief Shaykhi leader of the city, Mulla Muhammad Taqi Mamaqani, as well as government officials and aides to the crown prince. The non-Shaykhi 'ulama, however, turned down the government's invitation, perhaps as a gesture of their disapproval of the way the government handled the anti-Russian riot. Fear of the consequences of collaborating in any condemnation of the Bab must have kept many 'ulama away, and other mujtahids were excluded by the government for fear that their call for the execution of the heretic might create unnecessary trouble.[83]

For Nasir al-Din the trial was an event of some novelty and excitement. This was a rare occasion to observe an encounter between a messianic apostate, a young and sympathetic figure who declared the advent of a new age and called for renewal of religion, and some of the Bab's most vocal antagonists. It was clear from the start that, owing to the Bab's popularity, the government could not exercise any serious punitive measures and that the participating 'ulama, most of them close to the Tabriz court, could only hope for a collective condemnation without serious retribution. The publicity agenda for the gathering was thus decided in advance. It was to determine "with arguments, proofs, and laws of the perspicuous religion" the heretical claims of the Bab and then to publicize the outcome throughout the country.[84] Even though the position of the provincial government was clear, such clarity of purpose did not include Nasir al-Din himself. At the outset, the crown prince was visibly ambivalent about the Bab and his messianic claims. His youthful curiosity for the exotic had generated a sense of respect for a visionary ascetic who challenged the authority of the 'ulama. The mystical teachings of the Shaykhi Mulla-bashi may also have aroused some interest in the prince's mind. When the Bab was brought into the gathering, we are told by court chronicler Riza Quli Khan Hidayat, none of the participants sitting around the packed room offered him a place. After a pause, Nasir al-Din, who may have been disconcerted by this symbolic impertinence toward the claimant, offered him the seat above even his own in the room and further displayed "attention and favor" toward the indignant Bab.[85] The 'ulama would not have approved of this unanticipated display of favor, but the spectators who crowded the entrance to the hall must have seen it as a sign of the prince's fair-mindedness and even compassion; he no doubt badly needed such positive publicity in the aftermath of the riots.

The Mulla-bashi, who led the interrogation on behalf of the 'ulama, began by asking the Bab a series of questions on the exact nature of his claim and the authenticity of the writings circulated in his name. The Bab's blunt affirmation of the divine origin of his mission and the authenticity of the writings put the Mulla-bashi on the defensive and prompted a shift to a semifarcical course of disputation. "If it became certain that you are the *bab* [i.e., the "gate" to the Hidden Imam]," the Mulla-bashi asked sarcastically, "I beg you to honor me with the humble post of being your shoe attendant." Nasir al-Din must have been amused by his tutor's entertaining style but apparently missed his sarcasm altogether. In conformity with the Mulla-bashi's apparent meaning, he interjected that in case the Bab's claims proved to be valid he, too, would resign his seat of power in the Bab's favor.[86] Such an extraordinary offer, a blunder no doubt as far as the mujtahids or government officials were concerned, reveals something of the Bab's impact on Nasir al-Din's mind. The prince must have been momentarily carried away by the prophet's aura of self-confidence and candor. It is hard to believe that in a critical moment, when public opinion was swinging in the Bab's favor, he would dare to joke on so dear a subject as his own future throne, particularly one as shaky as what he was about to inherit.

The offer must have put the Mulla-bashi in an awkward position, obliging him to change course and employ all his scholastic repertoire to vanquish the Bab. A barrage of inquisitorial questions and comments by the Mulla-bashi and his colleagues followed. From Arabic grammar and syntax to textual and exegetical questions related to the Qur'an and hadith and the circumstances of their revelation, to subtle points of theology, *hikmat* (theosophy), and problems of jurisprudence (including some obscene rules of bisexual intercourse), to Hippocratic medicine and the interactions of the four elements (the Mulla-bashi's favorite subject), a wide array of questions was showered upon the indignant prophet. The Bab's sincere admission of his unfamiliarity with these sciences emboldened the inquisitors. Even when Nasir al-Din, probably annoyed by the mujtahids' line of questioning, instructed his tutor to abandon a scholastic discourse on the nature of the divine being, the Mulla-bashi was reluctant to let the Bab reiterate his extraordinary claim without having to confess to his ineptitude in conventional knowledge.[87]

The condescension and sarcasm of the 'ulama was effective enough to carry the government's agenda and prevent the public from being captivated by the charismatic sayyid of Shiraz. Adhering to the same condescending tactic, the Mulla-bashi then challenged the Bab to perform a miracle and restore the health of the ailing Muhammad Shah. Nasir al-Din, seemingly perturbed by the likelihood of such an event—an obvious hindrance to his accession to the throne—quickly reduced the stakes in this dubious bargain by requesting that, instead, the Bab should restore the Mulla-bashi's youth. He was still seemingly convinced of the Bab's miraculous powers. The answer to this sardonic demand was simple: "It is not in my capacity." Instead, as proof of his veracity, the Bab began to utter Arabic verses in the style of the Qur'an, an exercise he consistently presented as his sole miracle. Later, the Mulla-bashi related to the Qajar chronicler, Hidayat, that when the Bab began to recite, "Praise be to God who created the Heavens," Nasir al-Din interrupted him to correct his erroneous syntax by quoting a grammatical rule he must have learned as part of his religious education.[88] It is difficult to believe that young Nasir al-Din, a less-than-average student of languages with a dismal academic record, could have detected the Bab's error and much less could have recalled the relevant rule verbatim. More likely this was one of the Mulla-bashi's efforts to portray his royal pupil as wiser than he was, only to highlight his own pedagogical competence. Yet as the trial proceeded, Nasir al-Din may have deemed some kind of approbation of the 'ulama a necessary affirmation of his own religiosity. He may even have found the scolding of the claimant gratifying, though the exercise earned him a strong rebuke from a Babi chronicler, who accused him of being discourteous to the Bab. The crown prince, the Babi writer related, testing the Bab's knowledge of geography and astronomy, threw a globe at him and asked him to locate some geographical points.[89] Nasir al-Din's interest in geography and his exposure to European travelogues, a lifelong favorite pastime, probably encouraged him to flaunt his recently acquired knowledge to an applauding audience.

The Bab's repeated assertions of his unfamiliarity with conventional sciences only helped to stir the debate between the prophet and the priests at the cost of Nasir al-Din's capricious sympathy. The prince's earlier enthusiasm now turned to indifference, perhaps boredom, even when the Bab, in an angry response to the 'ulama's charges of blasphemy and fraud, for the first time publicly claimed that he was indeed the expected Imam of the Age, the Mahdi himself, whose return had been anticipated for a thousand years.[90] This dramatic announcement drew the strongest condemnations from the furious mujtahids. Their vituperative reproaches and sarcasm prompted the Bab first to ask angrily, "Am I being ridiculed?" and then in protest to observe silence for the rest of the trial.[91]

To the playful imagination of Nasir al-Din, still beguiled by fairies, the Bab and his message could only have appealed if he had passed the test of magic. As peculiar as was the Bab's demeanor, he lacked the healing touch that could turn thousands, including the crown prince himself, into his devotees. He saw himself not as a witch doctor but as a prophet, assertively putting forth his claim to Mahdihood, an almost unprecedented event in the recent history of Shi'ism. The Tabriz proclamation was a unique historical occasion because it not only made public the independence of the Babi religion from Islam but, more tangibly, symbolized the start of a messianic insurrection that was soon to ignite passions across Iran. The mujtahids of the Tabriz gathering may have sounded embarrassingly naive in their handling of the Bab, but they were canny enough to avert a situation in which Nasir al-Din became captivated by the young claimant, a fact that further dimmed the chances of any Babi reconciliation with the state.

Pressured by hard-line mujtahids who called for the Bab's execution on the charge of heresy, Nasir al-Din was faced with a dangerous dilemma. After the trial he felt he should either stand up to the powerful clergy of Tabriz or face the even more dangerous possibility of popular unrest in support of the Bab. To find a solution, he was perhaps cleverly persuaded by his advisers to send his personal physicians, including William Cormick, to examine the Bab in order to determine his sanity. Their predictable verdict of insanity, as Cormick himself acknowledged, was an expedient designed to save the Bab: "Our report to the Shah at that time," he wrote some years later, "was of a nature to spare his life."[92]

The eventual decision to go ahead with corporal punishment, with the possible aim of extracting a recantation, proved an unpopular one. As Hidayat related, even the crown prince's own servants of the outer court (farrashs), "owing to their good faith" in the Bab, "refrained from administering the punishment."[93] Thereupon the task of bastinado fell on the chief religious judge of the city, Mirza 'Ali Asghar Shaykh al-Islam, who voluntarily summoned the Bab and inflicted the punishment the mujtahid himself had called for.[94] After this public humiliation, the Bab was sent back to prison in Chihriq to await his fateful end. The Babi uprisings of the next two years against the joint forces of the 'ulama and the state eventually precipitated the Bab's execution in Tabriz in July 1850.

The gravity of the Babi revolt was to be realized by the Qajar government later in the same year. Yet for Nasir al-Din the Tabriz trial was his first taste of the revolutionary potential that impregnated the Shi'ite environment of his time. Both events of the summer of 1848, the riot and the trial, provided the inexperienced prince with critical exposure to public aspirations and resentments, to the centrality of religious passions, to the power of clerical leaders, and to the volatility of the status quo, which the government was striving to preserve at every level.

3 Ascending the Throne

The news of Muhammad Shah's impending death first reached Nasir al-Din Mirza through Anichkov, the Russian consul in Tabriz, on 8 September 1848. In response the crown prince, it was said, showed the consul the diamond ring with Tsar Nicholas's portrait on it, given to him on his visit to Iravan in 1838, a token of his amicable relations with his "grand uncle," and asked the Russian official to assist him in his departure for the capital.[1] The next day, news of the shah's death was confirmed by British special emissary Keith Edward Abbott. Letters by Aqasi and Nasir al-Din's mother, now Mahd 'Ulya, followed suit.[2] Suffering from complications brought on by his chronic gout, the forty-year-old shah died on the night of 5 September in his newly built Muhammadiya Palace north of Tehran, embracing his favored son 'Abbas Mirza in the last moments of his life.[3] Nasir al-Din's first reaction to the news was sorrow. Years later he related to one of his confidants that although his father was "very unfavorable" toward him (*khayli bi-iltifat bud*), he did not desire to see Muhammad Shah dead.[4]

A few days earlier, during the public audience for the festival of Bayram (the celebration of Fitr at the end of Ramadan), the shah's sickly appearance had alarmed spectators. The British envoy, Farrant, jointly with his Russian counterpart, Prince Dimitri Dolgorouki, suggested sending Joseph Dickson, the physician of the British legation, to aid the shah's French doctor, Ernest Cloquet. Simultaneously, they decided to dispatch emissaries to bring the heir apparent to Tehran "with utmost expedition."[5] Aqasi, who first tried to downplay the "slight indisposition of His auspicious Majesty," was obliged the next day to ask for Dickson's medical advice, only to be told, soon after, that there was "no hope" for the recovery of the "extremely sick" shah.[6]

DEPARTING FOR THE CAPITAL

The foreign envoys had every reason to call for Nasir al-Din's expeditious arrival. "Serious apprehension for the public tranquility of Tehran" was largely attributed to Aqasi's conduct. Deliberately driving away "all the influential people from the court," we are told by Farrant, Aqasi left the safety of the populace (and the envoys) to the discretion of discontented troops and "the mercy of the mob." But in reality the great fear prevailing over all classes was the predictable outcome of the uncertainties that accompanied the shah's death. "The course of things in the country has so much changed since the last illness of His Majesty in 1845," noted the British envoy, that he found it impossible to see "what steps may be advisable."[7]

In Tabriz the shah's death, predictable as it was, created similar confusion. In his first audience with Abbott, the new shah appeared "quite undecided" and altogether unwilling to listen to any suggestions to leave for Tehran immediately and without first gathering "a force of 5 to 6 thousands." The British emissary found Nasir al-Din "timid and apprehensive," surrounded by "persons who appeared to have persuaded him not to trust himself in an unprotected manner."[8] In spite of his indecision over the time of his departure, on the night of the 13 September 1848/14 Shawwal 1264, in a hasty ceremony attended by all the prominent officials, dignitaries, and military chiefs of Azarbaijan, Nasir al-Din officially declared himself shah, and soon after coins were struck in his name.[9] Among those in attendance were the two exiled sons of Fath 'Ali Shah: Hasan 'Ali Mirza Shaja' al-Saltana, the blinded pretender to the throne of Muhammad Shah, and his half-brother Muhammad Taqi Mirza Husam al-Saltana. The fallen princes must have found the accession of Nasir al-Din, son of their deceased persecutor, the final and irrevocable affirmation of the supremacy of 'Abbas Mirza's house.[10]

Resisting repeated pleas from the foreign envoys, Nasir al-Din and his aides set about to assemble a force large enough to deter any political challenge to his accession. With multiple complications—such as the ongoing controversy concerning Bahman Mirza, the Davalu revolt in Khurasan, and the disturbed state of affairs in other provinces—and with Aqasi in Tehran backed by his own Maku'i troops, Nasir al-Din was wise to calculate carefully the perils waiting for him in the capital should he arrive without a visible and large company of loyal forces. After all, it was with the aid of the Azarbaijan army, as well as the blessings of the neighboring powers, that the young shah's father had vanquished his adversaries some fourteen years ago, and Nasir al-Din could barely afford to lose either. Abbott, perturbed by further delays, was assured by Mirza Taqi Khan Vazir Nizam, a rapidly rising star in the Tabriz court and now the shah's close adviser, that some six infantry regiments, artillery, and horsemen had already assembled; but to mobilize a force of this size for a long march, the Tabriz administration faced familiar monetary obstacles. The troops had to be paid in hard cash, and promises of forthcoming rewards did not go far toward filling empty stomachs. Further, the command structure and the configuration of the troops had to be such as to prevent the infiltration of pro-Aqasi elements.

The fact that it was a "great difficulty" to procure the necessary cash for this royal venture was not surprising. Aqasi's deliberate policy of operating Azarbaijan on a deficit drove Iran's most prosperous province to such a level that it was in dire need of 50,000 tumans.[11] Knowing that any assistance from Tehran was hopeless, Nasir al-Din turned in despair to foreign consuls. To the government's great embarrassment, Stevens, the British consul, managed to persuade the Persian merchants with "much difficulty" to furnish 10,000 tumans. With the help of Anichkov, the Greek merchants provided another 10,000. The borrowed sum had to bear not only Stevens' pledge but also that of Farrant himself, a stipulation that underscored the state's poor credit.[12] The fund-raising efforts of the foreign consuls were complemented by those of the European-educated Mirza Ja'far Khan Mushir al-Dawla (I), then the agent (*karguzar*) in charge of Azarbaijan's foreign affairs, and Mirza Taqi Khan Vazir Nizam.[13] Superseding the indecisive and demoralized Nasir al-Mulk, the chief royal squire, the energetic Vazir Nizam requested that the shah issue a decree authorizing him to "sign receipts in exchange for the necessary sum to be borrowed" on behalf of the shah. Through his contacts with Tabriz merchants (who knew him probably because of their supply of goods to the Azarbaijan army), he borrowed another 30,000 tumans, to be reimbursed upon arrival in Tehran.[14]

With the money ready for the troops, Vazir Nizam swiftly assembled in Basmich, a camp outside Tabriz, a force of more than 10,000 consisting of seven infantry regiments, irregular cavalry, and artillery. The configuration of the infantry regiments (two Tabriz, one Maragha, one Qaradagh, two Shaqaqi, and the elite Qahramaniya) secured Vazir Nizam's control over the army, a measure fully supported by Abbott and Stevens, who were wary of Aqasi's machinations.[15] Deliberate exclusion of the Maku'i chiefs, the major supporters of Aqasi, and their troops was in direct defiance of the premier's wishes to place his own ally, 'Ali Khan Maku'i, in command.[16] Nasir al-Din expressed his gratitude toward Mirza Taqi Khan by promoting him to the coveted office of *amir-(i) nizam*, the commander in chief of the New Army.[17] Under the circumstances the young shah could hardly opt for any other commander. Stevens was right in depicting Mirza Taqi Khan as "the person in greatest favor" and the "leading man" in the emerging political arena, for he was able to take control of the Azarbaijan army at a time when the command was left momentarily vacant after the death of his mentor, Muhammad Khan Amir Nizam Zangina.

Some thirty years Nasir al-Din's senior, Mirza Taqi Khan Amir Nizam was something of a novelty even in the Qajar annals of meteoric rise to power. The young Taqi originally came from the village of Hazava of the Farahan district of Iraq-i 'Ajam (north-central province west of Tehran), a region with a high rate of literacy and known as a breeding ground for bureaucrats. He had benefited from the education and practical training the Qa'im Maqams offered the poor but talented son of their chief cook and co-citizen. Though the same household had involuntarily paved the way for the ascendancy of Aqasi, a Bayat from Iravan, the Qa'im Maqams preferred to recruit their bureaucratic manpower from their home base, a factor influential in Mirza Taqi's promotion within the hierarchy of the accounting department (*istifa'*) of Tabriz. Yet it was in the post of army accountant and, later, army secretary of Azarbaijan under Amir Nizam Zangina, Abul-Qasim Qa'im Maqam's chief rival before 1834, that the civilian Taqi Khan managed to complement his bureaucratic and fiscal abilities with skills in military management, logistics, and even strategy.[18]

Beyond his personal talents, the key to Mirza Taqi Khan's success was that he controlled the European-trained Azarbaijan army, the most formidable military force in the country and the most visible element of modernity yet introduced into Iran. It was a typical example of modern reformers' use of military machinery to dominate political institutions. Not unlike Muhammad 'Ali of Egypt, for whom he had admiration, Amir Nizam used his base in the army for further promotion. His efficient management and negotiating skills, and his contacts with both British and Russian representatives in Tabriz, secured him the secretariat of the New Army. Soon after, he was selected by Aqasi to replace Mirza Ja'far Khan Mushir al-Dawla as Iran's head of delegation and chief negotiator in the Erzurum conference (1843–1847). The Perso-Ottoman conference, presided over by British and Russian delegates as observers, was set up to settle, among other things, long-standing frontier disputes between the two neighbors. It put Mirza Taqi Khan on Iran's political map, but the extremely slow pace of the negotiations, which lasted nearly four years, as well as his questionable handling of an urban riot, did not make the ambitious Mirza Taqi Khan an immediate star of Persian diplomacy. It nonetheless guaranteed Aqasi's approval: "Hundred thousand praises [be upon you]. You have made me hopeful of your great competence. The faith that I had in that son [Mirza Taqi Khan] has increased many fold."[19] By 1848, Mirza Taqi Khan had returned to his position as the secretary of the New Army.

Besides Amir Nizam, who had maintained friendly relations with the British, the presence of some of Nasir al-Din's special appointees in the royal camp convinced Consul Stevens that Nasir al-Din was "decidedly a partisan of England and the English" and that "he hates the Russians and everything connected with them."[20] The royal retinue included William Cormick as the royal physician; Charles Burgess as the chief interpreter; a certain Italian artist, I. Cosolani, as the royal painter; and two other European protégés of the British as chief physician to the army and government apothecary. The fact that the shah thanked the British consul for his assistance and recommended Malik Qasim Mirza, a pro-British grand-uncle, as the next governor of Azarbaijan only confirmed Stevens's opinion. Nasir al-Din even urged Stevens through Amir Nizam to be vigilant of the governor's conduct lest it tilt toward the Russians and a repeat of the Bahman Mirza affair occur. Though in the past Nasir al-Din's administration in Azarbaijan "was not certainly distinguished for justice or a proper consideration of his ryots [ra'iyats; subjects]," concluded Stevens, "there was much to be said in palliation of his conduct." Reflecting on the new shah's troubled background, Stevens was correct in pointing out that "while at Tehran, he was deprived by the Hajee [Mirza Aqasi] of the means of living even as a private individual. He came here penniless, and was surrounded by a larger retinue as poor as himself, all anxious to improve their conditions in as short a time as possible lest the Hajee, as was his custom, should unexpectedly remove them from office." Since he became king, Stevens added, "Nesser-ad-Din Shah has taken into his councils some intelligent and honest Persians. He is fully alive to the danger of following the footsteps of his father and, unlike the late King, perfectly open to good advice."[21]

Stevens's remarks, far more optimistic than Sheil's had been some six months earlier, should be attributed primarily to Amir Nizam's counsels and his increasing influence on the young monarch. At virtually every stage of the three-week journey to Tehran, Amir Nizam registered new victories by winning the shah's support, isolating potential rivals, and limiting direct access to the impressionable monarch. His areas of concern went far beyond commander in of the Azarbaijan army. As a first step, he excluded from the royal camp all but six of Nasir al-Din's attendants of the inner court ('amala-yi khalwat), thus deliberately insulating him amidst a crowd of mostly unknown and newly employed companions.[22] To the shah's utter dismay, even childhood servants were relieved from service and returned to Tabriz on the grounds that "those people who are accustomed to serve the crown prince are unfit to attend a king. . . . They expect His Majesty to treat them like in the days of his apparency."[23] One exception, an intimate childhood playmate of Nasir al-Din, a certain Sayyid Muhammad, who had been allowed to accompany the shah to Tehran, was excused and sent back to Tabriz shortly after the entire contingent had arrived there. Some forty years later, Nasir al-Din still vividly recalled this episode. He remembered Amir Nizam sitting opposite him writing letters and issuing decrees when Sayyid Muhammad, the private servant, entered the room. Nasir al-Din recalled:

> As soon as I saw him, I smiled. Amir Nizam, while busy writing, glanced at a mirror in front of him and noticed me smile. Shortly after I ordered the Sayyid out after some business. When he left, Amir Nizam got up, closed the door, and returned saying: "Is it appropriate for the king to smile at his servants and is it [any more] possible to keep such a person in service?" I said, "What do you mean by this?" He replied: "Nothing in particular, except that I saw the presence of this man in the royal court harmful and contrary to the dignity of monarchy. I have dispatched him as a courier to Tabriz. By now, he must have reached the outskirts of the city."[24]

Amir Nizam's seemingly resolute action, though condescending and even harsh, was one way of repelling the nonsensical, and often clownish, hangers-on from clustering around the shah. Soon after arriving in Tehran he dismissed the remaining members of Nasir al-Din's retinue. His control of the shah was complemented by strict warnings against any excesses by the troops or confiscation of provisions and booty from civilians en route. Amir Nizam had already created a sense of awe, if not terror, in the royal camp when he punished severely two stable lads on charges of stealing ten pieces of Kashmir shawl from the shah's belongings. The princes of the royal family and the notables and courtiers of Tehran who came all the way to Qazvin to pay homage to the new shah must have been alarmed by these punitive measures. To impress further upon the bewildered Qajar polity his full mastery over the shah, Amir Nizam forced back into exile the first of several contenders for the office of premier who had emerged on Tehran's hazy political horizon. Mirza Nazar 'Ali Qazvini, a sufi notable and royal physician to Muhammad Shah, who earlier was a casualty of a purge by Aqasi, had rushed out to the shah's camp from his exile in Qum in pursuit of an old ambition, only to find himself outmaneuvered in his bid for premiership by a man vastly superior to him in ambition, competence, and royal favor.[25]

By the time the royal camp reached Yaftabad, seven miles south of Tehran, and awaited the auspicious hour to enter the capital, there was little doubt in the minds of the shah's retinue or the welcoming party as to the identity of the mastermind behind the throne and the future key statesman. Even as the young Nasir al-Din, a willing captive of Amir Nizam, grew unhappy over the loss of personal companions and disenchanted by Amir Nizam's severity, he was intelligent enough to appreciate his commander in chief's efforts to present the image of a strong, disciplined, and efficient monarchy—an image sharply distinct from his father's rule and Aqasi's premiership, or, for that matter, of his own governorship in Tabriz. Appreciation of the freshly transformed monarch, however, was not to be shared easily by power-hungry factions in the Tehran court.

PEOPLE'S COUNCIL AND POWER CONTEST

Ever since the death of Muhammad Shah, the situation in the capital had undergone dramatic changes. While the shah was on his deathbed, Aqasi, who was fully aware of the resentment of the Qajar ruling elite, immediately rushed to his own private summer residence, 'Abbasabad, even refusing to visit the shah in his last hour. Almost all high-ranking members of the government unified to express their collective refusal to carry out Aqasi's orders or recognize his authority. To be sure, the "eliminator of the nobles" (*hadim al-anjab*), as he was nicknamed by one polemicist for his anti-aristocratic policies, stood little chance of political survival once he lost his royal patron. The new council (*majlis*) of the "chiefs of the people" (*umara-yi jumhuri*—literally, "chiefs of the republic") that convened soon after the shah's death, declaring itself the representative of all factions of the government, was the embodiment of the same ilk of threatened nobles, and it naturally drew the support of Malik Jahan, the new *mahd-i 'ulya*. Both developments—the formation of the council and the emergence of Mahd 'Ulya as the representative of the new shah—were remarkable. Inspired by the familiar concept of *majlis*, the gathering of all statesmen to supervise the affairs of government was not entirely alien to the Qajars and their notion of tribal assembly. Yet the curious inclusion of the term *jumhuri* as part of the title, implying popular representation, was unprecedented, although the later meaning of this word—republicanism (i.e., abolishing the monarchy)—was certainly not intended.

As a first step on the night of the shah's death, two powerful representatives of the council—Mirza Yusuf Mustawfi al-Mamalik Ashtiyani, the powerful chief government accountant, and Hasan 'Ali Khan Garrusi

Ajudanbashi, a high-ranking Kurdish army officer in charge of the Tehran barracks—contacted the British chargé, Farrant, pledging their full allegiance to Nasir al-Din Shah. They emphasized their unanimous readiness to meet Aqasi's tyranny "force by force." The British envoy, taken by surprise, first only went as far as offering his cooperation to maintain order. Having already convinced Mahd 'Ulya to issue a proclamation confirming Aqasi's dismissal, the council persuaded Farrant, jointly with Dolgorouki, the Russian minister plenipotentiary, to send a note to Aqasi recommending that he stay in his summer residence and refrain from governmental activities until the shah's arrival.

The next day, however, Aqasi decided to make his final bid for survival. Leading a dwindling band of his Maku'i-Iravani guards, he unexpectedly arrived at the Tehran citadel (the Arg), took residence in his ministerial headquarters, and shut the gates. To preempt open dissension, he even ordered the arrest of the Davalu mayor (baglarbagi) of Tehran. His desperate attempt was of no avail; the open revolt of the "council of the people," drawing on Mahd 'Ulya's support and the envoy's repeated warnings, soon forced Aqasi out of the citadel. Desperate and dejected, escaping the Shahsavan troops who came to arrest him, he headed for his own estate, Yaftabad, but even there he met with resistance from the local villagers. He wandered over the plain south of Tehran in search of protection before eventually taking refuge in the sanctuary of 'Abd al-'Azim and waiting for the arrival of the royal retinue. In the ensuing confusion in the capital, further exacerbated by public hatred of the Maku'i troops, all supporters of the fallen premier were routed.[26] "A few of the street people set out to get at them," wrote Sipihr, who himself witnessed the event. Every twenty or thirty of the Maku'i troops were chased out by ordinary people, who took the soldiers' swords and sabers and, after disarming them and extracting their wealth from them, "subjected them to all kinds of misery and disgrace and clubbed them out of the city gates naked and injured. In less than one or two hours, not even one of them remained in the entire city."[27]

The ignominious collapse of the Aqasi regime and the emerging political vacuum brought to an end the fragile truce between diverse factions of the council. "Under the guidance of Queen Mother," observed Farrant with some cynicism, the government, which was "composed of some of the servants of the late shah, had taken the form of a sort of republic" whereby "everybody appeared to order and command" but "all aspir[ed] to the premiership on the arrival of the shah."[28] Yet there was a semblance of consultation and collective action. "In reality," as Hidayat puts it, the council, which consisted of "notables of the people," the "chiefs of the army," and the "trustees of the immortal state," adopted the "republican regime" (*tariqa-yi jumhuriya*). "Day by day their power was in ascendancy, and in the absence of the victorious cavalcade of the imperial star, they, in consultation, debate, and unanimity with one another, handled the affairs [of the state,] and after arriving at a consensus their decrees bearing the stamps of the chiefs of the republic were brought to Mahd 'Ulya to be ratified by her."[29]

In spite of factional divisions within the council, the temporary arrangement would have worked reasonably well had it not been for unexpected challenges the council faced from the minister of foreign affairs, Mas'ud Khan Ansari Garmrudi, and a few other high-ranking officials who organized themselves into an opposition party (*anjuman*) relying primarily on the support of the city folk. "As the notables [of the council] dominated the citadel, they [i.e., the opposition party] dominated the city." The city party challenged the council's legitimacy as well as its aims. "For five thousand years," it argued, "the Persian monarchy has remained uninterrupted. Now the notables [of the council] are about to inflict an injury [upon it] and intend to lay the foundation of the state on the rule of the people and pose themselves as members of the consultative house [*mashwarat-khana*]."[30] Petty rivalries between the two groups aside, references to "the rule of the people" and "the consultative house" are all the more remarkable when seen against the sociopolitical backdrop of the time. The urban unrest and religious revolt then on the rise throughout the country had, in fact, challenged the arbitrary but rather weak and inefficient Qajar state, particularly under the management of Aqasi. Although unarticulated, aspirations of the council were bound to cause anxiety among those who were left out of the new arrangement. With developments in the shah's camp still unknown in Tehran, and with the ascendancy of the council in the capital, both Mahd 'Ulya and the British envoy had lost the political initiative, and it was expected that they would seek out a trusted candidate for membership to balance off both the council and the emerging opposition.

The arrival of Mirza Aqa Khan Nuri, the influential *vazir-i lashkar* (secretary of the [old] army), from his Kashan exile, to which he was banished following his unsuccessful bid to oppose Aqasi in 1846, added a new challenge to the council and almost immediately became a formidable factor in the ongoing power struggle in the capital. He was closely associated with Mahd 'Ulya and "for years" was on "friendly terms" with the British mission and "personally known" to Farrant. Nuri relied on both sources to further his influence, though it is wrong to believe that he lacked any other support. He wrote from outside the capital to the British envoy seeking assistance and even presented as his credentials Nasir al-Din's "very complimentary autograph," which was written after Nuri's disgrace. Farrant clearly saw Nuri's worth as a British sympathizer and a viable candidate for premier with considerable influence in the army, and he had no hesitation recommending him to Mahd 'Ulya. "The presence of a person like Mirza Aqa Khan [Nuri] is very essential to the Persian Government," he wrote.[31] In reply, Mahd 'Ulya, who was delighted with Farrant's endorsement, praised Nuri and asked the envoy to "send him here to remain at the palace until the arrival of the shah whose favor he will no doubt enjoy."[32] The "kind and affable manner" by which this "great favorite" of Mahd 'Ulya was received in Tehran convinced Farrant that Nuri's "return to power," with British support, would help the young shah acquire popular backing.

Nuri's steady rise in popularity may not have been merely wishful thinking on Farrant's part. The public desire for an end to the unrest caused by the clashes between pro- and anti-council forces may have stimulated support for him. Characterizing him as a man of "talent, great weight and *mayanderah*," Farrant took Nuri's "reception by the people in passing through the public bazaar, on his way to the palace," as visible evidence of "how much he is esteemed by all classes."[33] He was also received by Mahd 'Ulya "with great distinction" and was lodged in a royal building inside the citadel. These were ominous signs for the notables of the council, who saw Nuri's dual backing as "a heavy blow" to their authority.[34] They could not help but notice that the British were also able to secure cooperation for their own candidate from the two "chief priests of the capital." Farrant was delighted by the mujtahids' "sentiments" and "feeling of Good will" toward Britain. Soon after, Mahd 'Ulya also assured Farrant that she would impress upon her son to attend the good counsel of the British.[35]

Serious opposition to Nuri came from an unexpected quarter. Objecting to his unauthorized return to the capital, the newly appointed Amir Nizam, in his first real show of force, advised the shah to order Nuri's return to Kashan. Nuri and his advocates must have been rudely surprised by the assertiveness of the new commander in chief. In response to the shah's order, Nuri tried to explain his action in a meeting of the council held in the Mahd 'Ulya's presence. He argued that his quick arrival in Tehran was calculated to preempt the imminent rebellion of Mazandaran chiefs.[36] This excuse must have been so unacceptable to Amir Nizam, who was still outside the capital, as to require Farrant's mediation. As one contemporary historian explains, "since for some time owing to the interruption and weakening of the office of premiership, the adventurous representatives of foreign states grossly interfered in internal affairs [of the state]," on this occasion, too, "owing to their intercession and protection," Nuri was only obliged to leave his lodging in the citadel and instead take up residence in his own house in the city.[37] It was clear that Farrant did not wish to allow Amir Nizam, whom he considered another British sympathizer, to carry the day. Upon further insistence from the shah's camp, he opted for a familiar ploy long used by his predecessors. To nullify the royal decree, he extended diplomatic protection to Nuri and his relatives.

Nuri's wishes to receive British protection no doubt originated in his habitual opportunism. He was clever enough to grasp the benefits of diplomatic immunity in the face of Amir Nizam's retribution. The sense of fear and insecurity, offered as a justification for Nuri's seeking protection in the memoirs of his brother, Mirza Fazlullah Nuri, must have been shared by Amir Nizam's other contenders:

> Like a sudden calamity Mirza Taqi Khan Farahani, who by the appoint-
> ment of His Blessed Majesty was assigned to be the supervisor of the
> affairs of the people (*jumhur-i khala'iq*), with his twisted mind and his
> obstinate manner set out . . . to remove us, the servants [of the shah]
> from our home ground. As the dignitaries and leaders of the notables
> tried to dissuade him of such intentions, not only was it of no avail,
> but it added more to his determination. He was oblivious of the fact
> that whoever sows the seed of alienation will not harvest loyalty, and
> whoever plants the tree of conflict should not expect the fruit of coop-
> eration. . . . Putting an injured serpent in your pocket, unmindful of its
> venom, is not the way of the cunning. It is obvious that once the cap-
> tive falcon opens [its wings of] aggression and domination, the desperate
> sparrow has no shelter but [to hide behind] the bush. Every wilderness
> has a path [to safety] and every refugee a shelter. Thus, to [escape] that
> ill-intentioned tyrant we were obliged to make the British government
> our intimate shelter and seek protection in the most desperate conditions
> and therefrom remove from the tablet of our mind the image of security.
> [Later] it was only because of the compassion of the king of the time
> [Nasir al-Din] that we were given safe conduct and returned to the
> path of salvation.[38]

There was little doubt that Amir Nizam had planted deep anxiety in the hearts of many of Tehran's statesmen and alienated them even before entering the capital. Having sought British protection, Nuri was obliged to shelve his plans temporarily, but he did not leave the political arena altogether. Farrant, for his part, viewed the reversal of fortune of his favorite candidate as a personal challenge. Some two weeks later, report-ing on the situation in Tehran, he made no mention of his granting of protection to Nuri. Instead, playing up the confusion and intrigue in the capital, he blamed the members of the council for "reaping personal benefits for themselves and friends." Counting on Nasir al-Din's "best intentions," he hoped the shah's arrival would put an end to the power struggle, yet he foresaw problems in forming a viable government. There were "numerous aspirants" for the premiership but few with "talent and experience." With Nuri forced out of the picture, the most likely candidate, Farrant believed, was Sadr al-Mamalik Ardabili, "a priest endowed with some of the ex-minister's crude ideas of sanctity." Growing support for Ardabili, whose voice was "paramount in the assembly," had already dissuaded Mirza Mas'ud Ansari, the city party's candidate, from pursuing his earlier ambitions, thus leaving Amir Nizam as the only other contender for the office. Farrant concluded that Amir Nizam, too, would be ruled out, thus leaving the stage free for the council's candidate.[39] As it turned out, he was too hasty in this assumption.

WEARING THE KAYANID CROWN

Nasir al-Din's coronation took place with all the pomp and ceremony symbolic of the shah's official assumption of power. Entering the capital on 20 October 1848 at the most auspicious hour, as determined by the royal astrologer, he was received by "the princes of the royal family, the notables, the chiefs of departments and nearly the whole population of Tehran." Seven hours and twenty minutes past sunset (in the early hours of 21 October 1848/22 Dhu al-Qa'da 1264), in his first public levee, he "sat in state for a short time" on the marble throne in the open veranda of the Gulistan hall of audience, "wearing his crown and all the insignias of royalty."[40] These symbols—the Kayanid crown, a twenty-four-pound, bejeweled creation of Aqa Muhammad Khan; the two armlets holding the legendary diamonds, Darya-yi Nur and Taj Mah (originally the spoils of Nadir's 1739 Indian campaign and once worn by Lutf 'Ali Khan, the last of the Zand rulers); and the diamond-studded sword known as the sword of the Twelfth Imam (worn by Aqa Muhammad Khan on his 1795 visit to the shrine of Riza, the Seventh Imam)—all were timely reminders to the "princes, notables and mullahs" present in the coronation ceremony of the continuity of the Persian kingly traditions in the Qajar dynasty.[41] With understandable satisfaction, Farrant could even claim that "thus far no shah of Persia ever succeeded to his right so peaceably as His Majesty has done."[42] Though unmindful of the troubles in the making, the envoy's comments reflected the success of the rule of primogeniture in the house of 'Abbas Mirza. Thanks to Fath 'Ali Shah's decision in 1833, and through the consistent blessings of the European powers, the highly disruptive wars of succession that had accompanied royal accession in the past were effectively prevented. In his panegyric composed for the occasion, Hidayat hoped with a guarded optimism that "the ancient state that had turned decrepit and weak" would become under Nasir al-Din "young, powerful and sound."[43]

On the same night, 21 October, Amir Nizam, wearing a pearl-ornamented robe of honor reserved for the premier (*sadr-i a'zam*), was appointed to the status of First Person (*shakhs-i awwal*) and the office of premier (*sidarat*) and was granted the honorary title of *atabak-i a'zam* (grand tutor or guardian).[44] The shah's decree, issued a few days later, declared: "I have delivered all affairs of Persia into your hands and hold you responsible for the good, or bad, that may ensue. We have this day made you the First Person in Persia. We have every trust and confidence in your justice, and treatment of our people; and in no one else do we put any faith except in you; and to this effect we have written this note."[45] Never before in Qajar history had so much power rested with one official. To the Tehran political elite the further promotion of Amir Nizam to the premiership came as a shock. His powers were even more all-embracing than Aqasi's, from under whose yoke they had just managed to free themselves. To delegate to Amir Nizam "all the affairs" of the country, both civilian and military, underlined the young shah's exclusive "faith" and "confidence" in this relatively minor army administrator from Tabriz. By appointing Amir Nizam the *atabak-i a'zam*, Nasir al-Din intended to imply that in conducting the complex task of rulership he would benefit from the guidance of a "guardian," thereby removing any doubt regarding the need for a regent. Implicitly, Amir Nizam was that regent. Though the shah was not officially a minor, such a precaution was necessary to protect him against possible imposition of pretenders such as Bahman Mirza.[46]

There was already a precedent in Qajar times for the office of *atabak-i a'zam*. In 1828 Fath 'Ali Shah had appointed Mirza Abul-Qasim Qa'im Maqam to be the *atabak-i a'zam* for one of his favorite sons, Farrukh-Siyar Mirza,[47] but even prior to that the office of *ataliq*, an identical Safavid office, was granted to the Qajar chiefs. Upon 'Abbas Mirza's nomination as heir apparent in 1799, Sulayman Khan I'tizad al-Dawla Quvanlu, Mahd 'Ulya's grandfather, was appointed *ataliq* to the crown prince.[48] As Turkomans, the Qajars of Astarabad would have been familiar with the office of *atabak* (or *ataliq*), but it was probably the Qa'im Maqams and like-minded statesmen of Safavid-Zand background who reintroduced it into the Qajar prince-governorate system. Considering some references in his works, it is likely that the erudite Abul-Qasim Qa'im Maqam looked to Abu 'Ali Hasan Tusi, the Nizam al-Mulk, the classical archetype of Persian states-manship, as his role model when he was promoted to the office of *atabak-i a'zam* and later to premiership. Amir Nizam was trained in the Qa'im Maqam school of statecraft as well and may have also entertained the same notion of *atabak* and looked to the same role model.[49] Similarly, tracing an intellectual trend through the Qa'im Maqams and their lasting sym-pathies for the Zands, it is possible to see in the political career of Amir Nizam faint vestiges of Karim Khan Zand, the celebrated ruler of the eighteenth century who proclaimed himself the *vakil al-dawla* (deputy of the state) and who theoretically ruled on behalf of the Safavid puppet Isma'il III. Further still, Mirza Taqi Khan may have looked upon Nadir's regency of Tahmasp II as a precedent.[50]

By his own account, Amir Nizam was able to demonstrate his unrivaled value to the shah as an instrument of consolidation. While still waiting outside the capital for the auspicious hour, Amir Nizam had managed to remove potential hurdles in the way not only of his royal master's accession but also of his own premiership. The New Army that he brought from Azarbaijan proved, after all, to be a weapon more vital to his own as-sumption of power than to Nasir al-Din's so-far unchallenged accession to the crown. It is not surprising, therefore, that on the occasion of his coronation, or soon after, the shah even conferred upon his prime minister the title of *amir(-i) kabir*, a title by which he came to be known to posterity. This was an unprecedented honor for a non-Qajar and entitled him to be not only the commander in chief of the New Army of Azarbaijan but also the supreme commander of the entire Persian army.[51]

The office of *amir(-i) kabir* was a Qajar modification of a military rank of the Safavid and pre-Safavid periods.[52] It was first conferred in 1799 to Sulayman Khan Quvanlu, presumably as an incentive for his hard-to-acquire loyalty to Fath 'Ali Shah and even before he was appointed to the post of *ataliq*.[53] By 1833 it had become hereditary in Sulayman Khan's house after it was bestowed on his son Amir Muhammad Qasim Khan Quvanlu, Nasir al-Din's maternal grandfather.[54] To the disapprobation of the old-school Qajar chiefs and Mahd 'Ulya, who could not save the office for her brother 'Isa Khan, the title of *amir kabir* had now gone to the commander of the New Army, a clear sign of the decline of the old tribal army of the early Qajar era. The new Amir Kabir now concurrently controlled the regular army and the irregular tribal forces, served as the guardian of the king himself, and as the First Person monopolized the Qajar

administration. Concentration of power of this magnitude went even beyond the unspoken safety limits set by the timid Aqasi. Upon his rejection
of the title *sadr a'zam,* which Aqasi apparently avoided for fear of falling
victim to its fatal possibilities (as had happened to Qa'im Maqam), he chose
to be addressed as the "First Person." Owing to Aqasi's predominance,
however, in reality this title came to represent a concept transcending the
standard idea of premiership but still far from the powers accumulated by
the new Amir Kabir.

With the army finally in Amir Kabir's hands, the young shah had little
choice but to comply with the former's demand for total power. The
general state of crisis in the country lent greater legitimacy to such a
contingency. Thirteen years of Aqasi's administration had left the government with a larger-than-usual budget deficit, a treasury depleted by a
failure to collect taxes and repeated military expeditions, and an inefficient
civil service ready to compensate itself for the lack of government payments with bribery and extortion. The "indescribable confusion" in the
administration, no less than Aqasi's "grasping cupidity and love of power"
and the "folly of his proceeding, wildness of his language, and absurdity
of his reasoning," not only created an immense distrust "among the
inferior classes of the government servants" but also provoked popular
discontent to a dangerous level. Aqasi had assured the dying Muhammad
Shah of the tranquility of his kingdom "whilst the whole of Europe had
been convulsed by revolution."[55] Yet only two months later the spirit of
popular rebellion had gathered such momentum that even the optimistic
Farrant, now highly anxious about the ongoing revolt in the provinces,
was compelled to predict that in the event of Amir Nizam's failure to quell
the uprisings, the ensuing anarchy and foreign intervention "may probably lead to the overthrow of the present dynasty" and disintegration of
Iran.[56]

The threat of this overwhelming anti-Qajar revolution was too conspicuous not to capture Nasir al-Din's Shah's attention given the strength
of the Davalu revolt in Khurasan, the claims of the defected Bahman
Mirza, and the dim prospects of the messianic Babi uprising, then in the
making. Critical of Nasir al-Din's education, Farrant still subscribed to the
opinion that the shah was "incapable of directing any department" and
was "very difficult in offering an opinion on any subject" but could not
fail to acknowledge that he had "a great degree of obstinacy of character
of the late shah and [was] most jealous of any interference with his
authority," an opinion probably inspired by the shah's resistance to complying with the envoy's wishes on his choice of premier.[57] No matter how

unavoidable the appointment of Amir Kabir was, to the outside world this appeared to be Nasir al-Din's first occasion to prove his independence.

The appointment of Amir Kabir once again confirmed the supremacy of the Azarbaijan administration. Over the past half-century it had been Tabriz, rather than Tehran, that produced men of outstanding statesmanship, though few of them were originally from that province. The men of the Tabriz government often fused features of traditional Persian statesmanship with a reformist outlook influenced by trends in the neighboring Ottoman and Russian empires. Four years' residence in the far-reaching frontier province of the Turkish empire was enough to confirm Mirza Taqi Khan's commitment to change, a conviction originally inspired by earlier visits to St. Petersburg in 1829 in the company of Khusraw Mirza and to Iravan in the company of Nasir al-Din in 1838. Even if Mirza Taqi Khan had only an indirect exposure to Western-style reforms, he definitely felt an urgency to undertake sweeping changes encompassing bureaucracy, military, finance, judiciary, and education. He envisioned that these measures would be immediately beneficial to the performance of the central government. The Ottoman and Russian models of reform had been implemented from above and required vision and power. Though in the past 'Abbas Mirza, and after him Qa'im Maqam and even Aqasi, had attempted some reforms with varying degrees of success, it was Mirza Taqi Khan who came closest to combining a monopoly of power with a consistent plan of reform, primarily catering to the needs of the army. It was precisely this conjunction of power and reform that for a time received the blessing of the Qajar throne and heralded a brief though important period of change.

The nascent council of the republic was the first victim of this conjunction. Upon his arrival in the capital, Amir Kabir immediately sent Sadr al-Mamalik Ardabili, the head of the council, into exile in nearby Qum.[58] The idea of a consultative council, which had already come under attack by critics even before Nasir al-Din's arrival, had even less of a chance to receive the shah's blessing. Thanks to Amir Kabir's swift action, nothing more was heard of the "consultative house" for another decade. Actual fulfillment of the dream of creating an effective consultative body had to wait for another half-century, until the time of the Constitutional Revolution of 1906–1911. The notables of the fragile "people's council" ignominiously disappeared from the pages of all correspondence and chronicles.

The dissolution of the council could well have been related to a diplomatic incident involving Amir Kabir and Comte de Sartige, the French envoy in Tehran, that finally led to the break in relations with France. On the surface, this was a quarrel over an easily offended diplomatic pride. The premier's refusal to bestow on the French envoy the decoration of the royal portrait (created for Nasir al-Din's coronation and already given to both the Russian and British envoys) outraged the status-conscious Sartige to the extent that, to repay the insult, he returned to the Persian government the decoration he had received five years earlier from Muhammad Shah. Yet Amir Kabir's refusal to decorate the French envoy may have been related to reasons other than the Persian government's prerogative to determine who merited its decoration.[59] Nor was it a sheer blunder resulting from inexperience. Rather, Mirza Mas'ud Ansari, an early critic of the council who had since been reinstated as the minister of foreign affairs, convinced Amir Kabir that the French envoy was the person responsible for introducing the idea of the consultative council, and the republic, to the Persian polity. With the 1848 revolutions sweeping across Europe, and with the French role as the center of radical republicanism, Amir Kabir had good reason to be wary of the French minister and the government he represented.[60] In January of the same year, the French Second Republic had replaced the monarchy of Louis Philippe, and by November a new constitution was declared.

It was perhaps with the same considerations in mind that the Persian government, in spite of the French envoy's anxious pleas, refused to recognize the French Republic or to officially declare to that government the accession of Nasir al-Din Shah before October 1848, some ten months after proclamation of the Second Republic.[61] Soon Franco-Persian relations took another downturn over the ratification of a commercial treaty that Aqasi had already negotiated. Sartige's quarrelsome conduct and Amir Kabir's desire to renegotiate a new treaty with better terms for Iran contributed to the dispute. Yet the premier's conduct was a clear departure from Aqasi's sound policy of befriending France as a balancing force against the dual Anglo-Russian pressure. One may attribute Amir Kabir's anti-French attitude to his desire to demonstrate to the neighboring powers, particularly the British, his recognition of their inviolable supremacy in the sphere of Persian foreign affairs. The ultimate break in relations with France in 1850 was one of Amir Kabir's obvious policy errors, one that helped inadvertently to further intensify the Anglo-Russian rivalry in Iran.[62]

As a product of the Tabriz administration, Amir Kabir had learned that to harness the ambitions of the northern neighbors it was necessary to heed to the demands of the southern neighbor. It is not surprising, therefore, that "having been for many years on terms of private friendship" with Amir Kabir, the British chargé d'affaires should feel exhilarated that the new premier had fully acknowledged the vitality of British friendship and would promise that "he would constantly instill into the royal mind" the value of such friendship. No doubt the enmity of those "jealous of the high station to which he had been so suddenly elevated" obligated the premier to Farrant, not only because of the envoy's efforts to facilitate the ascension of Nasir al-Din Shah at a time when "in general the popular feeling was against him" but also because Farrant gave his consent to the shah's choice of premier. Amir Kabir could further enlist Farrant's cooperation by assuring him that Nasir al-Din's sympathies lay with England precisely because the shah abhorred any Russian interference with his right of succession, an obvious reference to the prolonged Russian support for Bahman Mirza's regency. Farrant, clearly impressed with the premier's "wishes to do well" and his "courage to carry out his plans," saw credible reasons to give his support to the new administration but could not help noticing that although Amir Kabir was neither "wanting in ability" nor "avaricious," he was nonetheless "slow, very obstinate, and easily alarmed, and not well acquainted with the court." Assessing the general political setup, he observed that the premier had a "powerful party" against him and thus "must be liberal and not attempt to grasp the whole executive power," which, as Farrant aptly pointed out, had "caused the downfall of his predecessor."[63] Farrant's reservations concerning Amir Kabir's monopoly of power no doubt encouraged him to continue backing his own protégé, Aqa Khan Nuri. In spite of earlier setbacks, Nuri, who unlike other contestants could not be easily brushed aside, was now confirmed by Amir Kabir in his old position as the secretary of the army (vazir-(i) lashkar), no doubt because of Farrant's persuasion. Reinstating the shrewd and experienced Nuri no doubt benefited the premier in finding his way through the capital.

Engaging Nuri as a partner, though little power was delegated to him at first, was a strategy that would also appease Mahd 'Ulya at the court. From the very start Mahd 'Ulya viewed Amir Kabir as a dangerous threat to her own power and an intruder into an otherwise manageable political scene. She must have found it particularly difficult that in a short time at a critical juncture—the few months during Nasir al-Din's governorship—an army secretary had managed to win her son's full confidence. She must also have found his appropriation of her father's title, amir kabir, a humiliating affront. All the more unacceptable to her was Amir Kabir's unflattering aloofness, for he did not express the recognition to which the queen mother was accustomed, let alone the tributes that she, as a partner in Nasir al-Din's reign, expected to receive. The fact that Amir Kabir was "enjoying the unbounded confidence of the shah who [wa]s entirely guided by his advice," however, did not discourage Mahd 'Ulya from trying, though with no immediate success, "to shake the shah's confidence in his premier." His Majesty, Farrant observed, had "the same firm belief in the talent and capacity of the Ameer [Nizam], as his late father had in those of Hajee Mirza Aqasi."[64] Such a striking resemblance only deepened Mahd 'Ulya's resentment.

The growing tension between Amir Kabir and Mahd 'Ulya troubled the shah's mind as much as it disturbed his emotional peace. At the very outset of his reign the young king was caught between two conflicting poles of loyalty. In Amir Kabir, his Atabak, he vested his hopes for overcoming the perils threatening his throne; in Mahd 'Ulya he sought not only motherly care but also a refuge from which he could control the discontented Qajar elite. To reconcile the two parties of the divan and the harem, both indispensable to the welfare of his throne, the shah in February 1849, some four months after his accession, ordered thirteen-year-old Malikzada (later 'Izzat al-Dawla), his only full sibling, to marry Amir Kabir, then in his early fifties. The shah's initiative did not have Mahd 'Ulya's blessings; nor did Amir Kabir accept it with enthusiasm. The premier agreed to the marriage largely to escape criticism concerning his humble origins. In a private note in response to the shah's instruction for marriage, and presumably after having divorced his first wife (who was his cousin and living in Tabriz), as was the custom in any marriage with members of the royal family, Amir Kabir reluctantly complied with the shah's wishes: "[T]his slave has no wife. Whatever the terms on which the royal wishes rest would be of utmost expediency to this slave."[65] Later, in another private note to the shah, he was brave enough to mention the marriage of convenience forced upon him without naming Malikzada. "It is apparent to that pivot of the universe [*qibla-yi 'alam,* the common honorific for Qajar monarchs] that from the start this humble servant was unwilling to convene a household and a wife in this city. Later, obeying the royal command and to augment [my] service to you, I acted upon such an undertaking."[66]

The "long talked of" marriage aroused the "strongest opposition on the part of the Queen Mother, who dread[ed] the increased power and influence such a step w[ould] naturally bring into the hands of the Prime Minister." As Farrant noted: "The Shah, however, was not to be turned aside from his intention, insisting that his own welfare depends on the Amir [Kabir]." Nasir al-Din's justification, self-serving as it was, could not convince "the members of the royal family, [who] also attempted to ridicule the idea that the son of a servant of the late Kaim Makaum [Qa'im Maqam] . . . should aspire to the hand of the daughter of the late and sister of the present Shah."[67]

Yet Nasir al-Din was acting within the traditional code of Perso-Turkish kingship. The *atabaks* of the Saljuq and Safavid eras sometimes married the widowed mother of the minor prince or the king, primarily to comply with Islamic requirements for familial privacy (*mahramiyat*).[68] The shah may also have considered a marriage with an immediate member of the royal family an effective means of surveillance on his premier's private life. In this case, substituting the sister for the mother may have at least partly been due to Amir Kabir's concern with Mahd 'Ulya's infamous reputation. Such concern, one suspects, must have added to the queen mother's resentment toward the ignoble usurper of her family title. The choice of Malikzada thus seemed to be a compromise undesirable to all but the shah. Beyond political purposes, one may detect in his action a desire, unconscious though it was, to adopt Amir Kabir as a father and humanize such adoption in the setting of a congenial family, which was denied him in childhood.

MACHINATION AND MUTINY

The relationship between the shah and his premier was based on mutual dependency, both political and moral. Nasir al-Din realized the need for a capable administrator outside Tehran's faction-ridden administration, and he found in Amir Kabir the ferocity of an army commander, the meticulousness of a divan accountant, and the political skills of a statesman. The devotion of a caring, though on occasion admonishing, Atabak gave the shah comfort and confidence. Amir Kabir, for his part, relied on the good wishes of the shah as the key to realizing his vision of reforms—although the young shah did not seem at the outset to share his premier's vision. For a man devoid of aristocratic privileges and an independent base of support, such a blessing was even more critical. He needed a royal mandate immune from the checks and balances that often undermined the office of premier. Creating a centralized state with an effective army, efficient bureaucracy, regulated finance, and well-defined foreign policy required above all that the old ties between the court and the government be regulated if not severed altogether. In practice this meant that the young shah had to opt for the full delegation of authority to his premier, what the classical theory of government defined as "delegatory vizierate" (*vizarat-i tafwiz*). This concept of premiership was in contrast to "executive vizierate" (*vizarat-i tanfidh*), whereby the premier merely acted as an enforcing agent for the shah. Eventually, the clash between these two concepts precipitated the downfall of Amir Kabir, but it took some time before this duality of vision became fully apparent. The three crucial years that followed Nasir al-Din's coronation (1848–1851) were enough to lay a viable foundation for the next forty-five years of his reign and gave him a much-needed chance to learn the art of government from his premier. Only four months after Nasir al-Din's accession, Farrant observed: "His Majesty has in a great measure thrown off that timidity which he possessed on his accession; he converses more freely and has acquired of late much greater self-possession in public."[69]

From the outset two challenges threatened the very survival of the Qajar throne. By 1848 the Babi movement, in open defiance of the religious and, ultimately, secular establishments, had evolved into a revolutionary current that over the next two years erupted in successive insurrections in Mazandaran, Fars, and Zanjan. In addition, the Khurasan revolt (1847–1850) of the Davalu chief Hasan Khan Salar, Asaf al-Dawla's son, and his Turkoman and Kurdish allies brought to the surface the last outburst of internecine conflict within the Qajar tribe. Besides minor insubordinations in other provinces, soon pacified, the concurrent challenges of the Babis and Salar engaged the financial and military resources of the Qajar government. "The attention of the whole country," noted Farrant, was devoted to Khurasan and then to Mazandaran and Zanjan, where the two major Babi uprisings unfolded. Unless the government could restore order, the premier told the British envoy, he could not hope for regular collection of taxes or the acceptance of other reform measures.[70]

The premier's wishes for security and order, however, were seriously undermined by a new phase of intrigue in the capital. The fact that the tsar's request for the return of Bahman Mirza to Iran had been rejected was perceived by the Russians as a sign of strong pro-British leanings in Tehran. To retaliate, the Russian government had refused to accept a Persian mission dispatched to St. Petersburg to announce Nasir al-Din's accession. Nicholas I was particularly displeased with Amir Kabir, as it appeared to him that the premier was "following the footsteps of his predecessor" in filling "the royal mind with the dislike . . . for his uncle [i.e., Bahman Mirza]." The premier was assisted in this task, so the tsar believed, by "the Queen Mother and her party."[71] The tsar's real concern, however, was to counterbalance Amir Kabir's pro-British tendency by reinstating the pro-Russian Bahman Mirza as the viceroy of Azarbaijan. In a private petition to the shah, Bahman Mirza had appealed to his "former friendship" with Nasir al-Din and declared his readiness to serve him faithfully. "If the answer to this petition is unfavorable," he declared, "I will write again and walk on foot to St. Petersburg. Except for Azarbaijan, I deserve nothing. Finish my business speedily and when I come to Tabriz, I will send the necessary presents." Given such explicit demands, Nasir al-Din was right to reserve "great suspicion" about Bahman's scheme, not forgetting "the treatment he received [during his heir apparency] at his hand"—a reference, no doubt, to Bahman's refusal to allow Nasir al-Din to take up his seat in Azarbaijan. "Azarbaijan would soon become an independent province," argued Amir Kabir, and the old Russian dream of Iran's disintegration would come true. He insisted that the British foreign secretary, Lord Palmerston, be duly informed. Allowing Bahman Mirza to return, Amir Kabir concluded bluntly, would require that the same favor be extended to the Anglophile Asaf al-Dawla, who was then in exile in Iraq. Because both men were popular (in Azarbaijan and Khurasan, respectively), "the Shah would be a mere puppet in their hands."

In Amir Kabir's argument there was a clear desire to stress the vitality of a powerful and centralized monarchy for Iran. The British envoy felt obliged to support Amir Kabir in his report to Lord Palmerston by further highlighting the premier's "good intentions" and his "devotion to the sovereign." Characterizing him as the "best servant" of the shah, a man who is neither "avaricious" and cruel nor "incumbered with family connections," he stressed that Iran needed support from both powers to provide Amir Kabir with a chance to carry out his reforms.[72] Yet the premier's determination to prevent Bahman Mirza's return deeply enraged the Russians. "The Shah is a kind [and] well disposed young man," declared the Russian envoy in an angry conversation with the premier, "but you wish to corrupt his heart." Alluding to Aqasi's exile to the 'Atabat, Dolgorouki even went so far as to threaten Amir Kabir with his habitual condescension: "Karbela is a very large place, there is plenty of room left there."[73] The insolent Russian envoy was not capable of making good on his threat immediately, but in a classic example of diplomatic intrigue and rivalry he was able to incite some serious trouble for the premier and cause great embarrassment to Nasir al-Din himself.

Dolgorouki chose to target the same Azarbaijan army that was at the center of Amir Kabir's power base. There was enough loyalty to Bahman Mirza among the troops and enough resentment toward Amir Kabir to make subversion possible. A rapidly spreading mutiny among Azarbaijani regiments stationed in Tehran soon reached such grave dimensions that even "the stability of the Shah's throne" was at risk. On 11 March 1849 three regiments, among them the elite Qahramaniya created by Qahraman

Mirza and long patronized by Bahman, expelled their officers from the barracks in the citadel and proceeded toward Amir Kabir's residence in an uproar about arrears in pay and supplies. The mutineers declared that "they were the servants of the Emperor [i.e., tsar] and Prince Bahman Mirza and that they would proceed to Azarbaijan." They also complained about the repressive treatment under Amir Kabir's brother, the notorious Mirza Hasan Khan, the new secretary of the Azarbaijan army. Mirza Hasan's "haughtiness and violent conduct had injured the troops who were [so far] fearful to present their grievances" to the premier.[74] They were persuaded to return to their quarters "on the promise that their alleged grievances would be inquired into on the following morning, and redressed if proved to be real."[75] For a moment it seemed the mutiny had subsided, but next morning, when the clamorous but unarmed troops tried to force their way into Amir Kabir's house, they were confronted by the prime minister's guards, who, presumably carrying out instructions, opened fire on them. Two soldiers were killed, and soon the rebellious troops, in full arms, returned to the premier's residence inside the citadel, demanding his dismissal and threatening to kill him in revenge if their demands were not met immediately.

In distress, Nasir al-Din and Amir Kabir, as well as the chief clerical personage in the capital, the Imam Jum'a of Tehran, implored Farrant to use his influence with the troops. A one-time instructor in the Azarbaijan army (where he first met Amir Kabir), Farrant went to the barracks in military uniform, only to hear the unanimous demand by 2,500 troops for the premier's dismissal. They were "evidently acting," Farrant observed, "on the instigation of [a] high authority."[76] The shah, "much alarmed" but wisely aware of his limits, declared, against the advice of Amir Kabir, that he had not the means for putting down the mutiny, that he "disliked the shedding of blood, and had made offers to pardon mutineers."[77] Yet Nasir al-Din resisted repeated suggestions by Amir Kabir's opponents in the court that the premier be immediately dismissed. He argued: "Today, if I submit to the demands of the troops and dismiss Mirza Taqi Khan from his post, I have brought myself down from the summit of kingship. Therefrom all the dismissals and appointments of my officials would be at the mercy of the army."[78] Instead, he found the alternative suggestion of the British envoy—that Amir Kabir be temporarily removed from the citadel—a sensible maneuver. In his meeting with the "depressed" and "bewildered" premier, now "deserted by nobles of the court," Farrant tried to persuade him to retire to the city, arguing that if the revolt was not put down that very day, "the sovereignty of the Shah is threatened." Amir

Kabir reluctantly agreed only when he realized, in a subsequent royal audience, that he could not "counsel the Shah to shed blood." For Amir Kabir this was an open admission of defeat.[79] That very night, writing a private note in reply to the shah in a subdued but confident tone, Amir Kabir tried to console Nasir al-Din yet stressed the need for punitive action. "Yes, tonight the soldiers were excessively loathsome. This slave will endure. May the soul of this slave be a sacrifice to the dust of His Majesty's feet. These will all elapse and, God willing, in the shadow of that Majesty . . . they will be properly punished. The concern of this slave is that tonight your blessed soul was disenchanted."[80]

Dolgorouki could have celebrated his victory had it not been for the fact that Farrant's successful intervention had enhanced the British position and allowed Mirza Aqa Khan Nuri to take full advantage of the situation. With Amir Kabir taking residence in the city at Nuri's house while the pro-Russian notables pledged loyalty to Nasir al-Din, prospects for Nuri's promotion seemed eminent. Nuri's house, enjoying British immunity, had now become "the rallying point of the supporters of the government." In spite of a "coolness" in his relations with Amir Kabir, the Imam Jum'a, an ally of Farrant, was also persuaded by the envoy to visit the barracks. Farrant upheld Nuri's conduct "above all praise" but reserved his best words for Amir Kabir's growing popularity in the city. "Such a demonstration in favor of a minister had never been witnessed in this country," he observed.[81] Boosted by the British backing, Amir Kabir, in another private note, assured the shah that "although the soldiers committed excessive maleficence, now they are quiet and will gradually disperse." He further expressed disbelief that the shah, in distress, might have authorized an order that the soldiers be paid 50,000 tumans to settle their arrears.[82]

The next day "greatest commotion prevailed" over the city. "The whole of the Bazaar was closed, the populace armed and determined, if necessary, to force the soldiers to obedience." Later, when Farrant visited Amir Kabir in Nuri's house, he saw "the dense crowd which lined the streets from the citadel to the Ameer's house." He was of the opinion that the bulk of this popular support, particularly among the guilds, was mobilized by the Imam Jum'a, who "possessed greatest influence over the citizens," and by Nuri's followers. Yet it was evident that the backing of the rival 'Iraq 'Ajam regiments, coming from the same region as Amir Kabir, also played a part.[83] The unanimous desire "to defend the rights of their Sovereign," as Farrant saw it, paralyzed the rebellious forces.[84] Demoralized and leaderless, the regiments gradually returned to their barracks, and the mutiny subsided. "The excited townsmen, backed as they were by the approval of the shah and his minister, by the exhortations and blessings of the Imam-i-Jum'a, and by the full moral support of the British legation, were more than a match for the tumultuous crowd of soldiers without their officers."[85] The suppression of the mutiny with support of the civilian population, "an armed assemblage" never before seen at the capital, upheld the "dignity and authority of the young Shah." Three days later, the whole city accompanied Amir Kabir to the shah's palace. Sheep were slaughtered as he passed, and it was "a day of rejoicing for the young sovereign of Persia."[86]

There was little doubt that the grievances of the troops were genuine. Arrears in soldiers' salaries was an endemic cause of discontent throughout the Nasiri period, and Amir Nizam's vast mobilization further exacerbated the treasury's constraints. Nor was there much doubt as to the oppressive conduct of officials such as Mirza Hasan Khan Vazir Nizam toward the miserable and desperate troops. Discontent so near the surface could easily have been manipulated by opponents of the government, most likely disgruntled allies of Bahman Mirza, who were in cahoots with Dolgorouki. It was the strength of this alliance that obliged Nasir al-Din and his premier, contrary to their wishes, to disregard the widespread rumors in the bazaar and over the pulpit implicating the Russian mission in the mutiny. Anti-Russian sentiments were indeed on the rise in the capital. In a joint visit with Farrant to Amir Kabir, the Russian envoy was told that on 13 March 10,000 persons "cursed Bahman Mirza and his mother [i.e., ex-queen mother and Nasir al-Din's grandmother]" for their betrayal of the shah.[87] In response, the offended Dolgorouki, who held the remark as a sign of anti-Russian feeling, refused to receive a return visit from the premier and further demanded that the shah himself publicly acknowledge "the falsity of [such] rumors." For fear of serious repercussions, an announcement was duly issued in which Nasir al-Din openly and in the presence of all notables "assured the Prince [Dolgorouki] that he had not for a moment believed these wicked rumors." Yet Amir Kabir did not miss this opportunity to punish some of his numerous court opponents who possibly were in contact with Bahman or with the exiled Sadr al-Mamalik Ardabili.[88] The Qahr-imaniya regiment, after reaffirming absolute loyalty to the shah, was dispatched to Kirmanshah, only to be sent later to Tabriz for reasons of insubordination, and there the regiment suffered terrible punitive action in 1851 at the hands of Amir Kabir's brother, the Vazir Nizam.[89]

The Tehran mutiny was an important test of Nasir al-Din's authority and his commitment to Amir Kabir. In spite of his obvious distress, the shah maintained some degree of consistency. He did not bow to pressures to dismiss his premier, nor did he resort to any drastic course of punitive action. Nevertheless, the mutiny plainly demonstrated the vulnerability of the Persian government in the face of unceasing foreign intrigue. The shah's and the premier's reluctance to budge against the Russian demand obliged them to accept the pro-British Nuri as a partner in the government, thereby distancing themselves further from the Russians and increasing their reliance on the British. Promoted to the position of de facto lieutenant to the premier, Nuri received the highly venerated title of *i'timad al-dawla* (the trustee of the state), a title traditionally reserved for the prime minister. Yet by granting this title, vacant since the violent downfall of the influential early Qajar premier Hajji Ibrahim Khan Shirazi in 1800, the shah seemed to be trying to strike a balance. If not "an allusion to [the forthcoming] premiership" of Nuri, as interpreted by one observer,[90] his promotion was at least a reminder to Amir Kabir to relax his grip over the government. It is hard to believe that Nuri's promotion could have taken place without Farrant's persuasion. The British envoy hoped that Amir Kabir would learn his lesson "to conciliate all classes and put aside the haughty demeanor which has caused so much offense to the higher functionaries of the court." He stressed in his conversation with Amir Kabir "the necessity of dividing the labor of office and not usurp[ing] the whole executive power" while advocating the benefits of cooperation with Farrant's favorite protégé.[91]

The Tehran mutiny occurred while Iran was in the grip of a secessionist insurrection. The Khurasan revolt, which had been renewed following the death of Muhammad Shah and had spread rapidly throughout the province, was another test of the new premier's statesmanship and the soundness of the shah's judgment. By late 1848 most of Khurasan was in the hands of the rebellious Hasan Khan Salar and his allies. Salar himself reportedly did not advance claims to the throne but rather sought to promote Bahman Mirza's cause. The revolt also reflected the centrifugal tendencies prevailing in the Khurasan province, where Amir Kabir's centralizing policies met with even greater resistance. Salar benefited greatly from the support of the frontier Turkomans of Astarabad and the dislocated Kurds of Buzanjan (Bujnurd) and Khabushan (Quchan), all of whom shared a long history of insubordination to the Qajars. The urban population, particularly in the provincial capital, Mashhad, was distrustful of the central government's expanding control and also backed Salar. By March 1849, in spite of some setbacks, the government forces were able to reclaim several cities in Khurasan from Salar, mostly through negotiation and an occasional show of force. Mashhad, however, was resisting. It was no accident that at the conclusion of the Tehran mutiny, Amir Kabir, more conscious of his vulnerability, resumed negotiations with Salar. He certainly tried to minimize the ill effects of the mutiny while troops were laying siege to Mashhad. He instructed Nasir al-Din Shah that in his letter to Hamza Mirza, the shah's paternal uncle and the governor general of Khurasan, he should downplay the mutiny in Tehran. "Some of the riffraff from two Azarbaijani regiments," he advised the shah to write, "committed acts of wickedness and maleficence at the instigation of a few thugs and scum in Tehran. For one day and night they misbehaved and raised their voices. Although they have been and will be punished, nevertheless we are writing to that distinguished uncle in order to assure the chiefs of the army and the rest of the victorious army of our utmost blessing."[92]

Through his negotiator and troubleshooter, Chiragh 'Ali Khan Zangina, Amir Kabir at the same time sent a mixed message of conciliation and warning to Salar, promising royal pardon, restoration of 95,000 tumans' worth of assignments and pensions, and even the governorship of Hamadan, Zanjan, and Qazvin. "Do not let the honor of your forefathers, who for long were proud of their service to this state, be punished. . . . Come to the presence of the king of the age so you may receive blessings and rest in safety. . . . If, on the other hand, you pride yourself in the company of riffraff and base people and set your mind on the ambition of kingship, which never rested with your house, [be sure] that you will never succeed."[93]

Neither the promise nor the threat produced the desired effect. Salar expressed some willingness to come to terms with the government but refused to surrender unconditionally, demanding instead that the siege of Mashhad be lifted as a sign of goodwill. The atrocities committed by government troops in the earlier siege of Sabzivar, however, checked any inclination the people of Mashhad may have entertained of surrendering. A breakdown in negotiations thus seemed inevitable. For eleven more months, until April 1850, the new governor general, Sultan Murad Mirza (Husam al-Saltana), and his forces were stranded behind Mashhad's walls, fighting a war of attrition with Salar's remaining supporters.[94]

The stalemate once again gave the foreign envoys a chance to offer themselves as mediators, but Amir Kabir, apprehensive that interference of this sort would ultimately compromise the shah's authority and result in the government's acquiescence in some form of autonomy for Khurasan, adamantly resisted. No doubt with the Tehran mutiny in mind, he reminded Sheil, now back in his post as British minister plenipotentiary, that "foreign intervention in the affairs of Persia had been stretched to the utmost limit which were compatible with the dignity of government, and he therefore would not avail himself of this mode of bringing the rebellion to an end." It would be "better for Persia," he was even reported to have said, "that the inhabitants of Meshed [Mashhad] should be brought back to their duty through the loss of twenty thousand men, than that city should be won for the shah through foreign interference."[95] To Dolgorouki, the premier's message was even more lucid: "We would not allow Khurasan to turn into a second Egypt," he wrote, hence comparing Salar with Muhammad 'Ali Pasha and particularly alluding to joint mediation during the crisis of 1839–1841, which ended with Muhammad 'Ali's being recognized as hereditary viceroyalty of Egypt.[96] Steadfastly holding to his anti-interventionist position, Amir Kabir was able, by the early 1850s, to turn Salar's revolt into a pocket of desperate resistance. "From Khurasan," he wrote to Nasir al-Din, "excellent news and reports have arrived, all confirming the advances of the victorious army."[97]

It is a small wonder that Sheil, acutely aware of Amir Kabir's success, should present the shah as a nonentity entirely under his premier's thumb. "The king may be passed over as a cipher in the administration," wrote Sheil with the subtle aim of highlighting Amir Kabir's power. "He is twenty years of age, and though perhaps not altogether destitute of intelligence, his education has been wholly neglected and he seems to have no desire to take a share in the government of his kingdom (see Pl. 7). The prime minister apparently encourages this disposition as a means of rendering the shah dependent on himself and of perpetuating the power he now engrosses." With a note of sarcastic optimism, Sheil appeared to sneer at the shah's blissful isolation: "The king has the merit of endeavoring to remedy his defective education by acquiring a conversational knowledge of history and geography."[98]

With the same double-edged tone he also portrayed Amir Kabir as a "man of talent," not avaricious of "material passion," who desired the "good of the country" and, if given time, would "carry out reforms" but who nonetheless was "short tempered" and "full of prejudice," suspicion, and obstinacy. Although he was "anti-Russian," Sheil remarked with sincere irritation, he was "scarcely favorable to England" either and altogether aimed "at diminishing the influence of [foreign] missions." Moreover, because of his "pride and overbearing and most injurious manner," he "scarcely possesses [a] single friend or supporter"; "discontent, if not dissatisfaction, pervades all classes." Complaints of the upper ranks and clergy, he pointed out, were "mainly selfish" and were made to thwart reduction of salaries and pensions, the thrust of Amir Kabir's financial reforms. But the commercial classes and the lower ranks were also unhappy, and in fact every class questioned the prime minister's policies. "Not only is there no amelioration, but [there is a sense] that Persia is in a much worse condition than when the Ameer assumed the government."[99]

No doubt there was much truth in the British envoy's assessment. Aqasi's prediction that he would throw the affairs of the government into "such confusion and disorder, rendering it an impossibility for his successor ever to reclaim them," seemed, at least for the moment, to have come true.[100] Turmoil in the provinces, the growing peril of the Babi uprisings in Zanjan and Mazandaran, insecurity along the trade routes, declining commerce, noncollection of taxes and nonpayment of salaries, and the 'ulama's resentment of checks imposed on them even prompted Sheil to ask why the government did not "dissolve and at once fall to pieces?" The fact that the capital was still under the precarious control of a centralized government, he suggested, was one explanation. In such bleak circumstances, Sheil concluded with a note of pessimism, the reign of the shah is "dependent on the support of England and Russia." But the latter's support could only be secured effectively, Sheil believed, if the Persian government would rehabilitate its two powerful contenders, Bahman and Asaf al-Dawla. Because Bahman was "an excellent governor" for his time, if ever returned, Sheil predicted, his prime ministership would be unavoidable "with or without the consent of the Shah."[101]

There could have been no more ominous prospect for Nasir al-Din and Amir Kabir than this concluding sentiment. True, both neighbors were in broad agreement about the necessity of preserving the Qajar dynasty, and their collaboration during Nasir al-Din's accession once more proved this commitment. But, locked in the game of imperial rivalry, both powers resorted to complex means to further their influence through the court, the army, and the administration, thus hindering the monarchy's consolidation. The quarreling factions within the government were prone to court intrigue and foreign manipulation. In these circumstances, the ascendancy of a powerful and visionary premier such as Amir Kabir, who relied on the army and on the shah's favor, was bound to alarm both the Qajar elite and the foreign powers and in due course draw them closer to each other.

4   The Shah and His Atabak

On 11 November 1851 Nasir al-Din Shah dismissed Amir Kabir from his position as premier of Iran. He was retained, however, in his other post as commander in chief of the army (*amarat-i nizam*). "Since the office of prime minister and grand vizierate involves too much labor," the shah wrote to him, "and the burden of such toil is difficult for you, we relieved you from this duty. You must continue in [the post of] commander in chief with full confidence."[1] Only two months later, on 10 January 1852, Amir Kabir was executed on orders from Nasir al-Din Shah in the bathhouse of the Fin royal garden in the vicinity of Kashan, where he had spent his last days in exile.

Amir Kabir's murder was a turning point in the life of Nasir al-Din Shah and one of the darkest moments of his reign. It also marked the end of a brief but crucial phase of the Qajar era that began with Amir Kabir's premiership. In the collective psyche of Iranians, Amir Kabir's death approximates the familiar moment when mortals enter the pantheon of martyred heroes. Yet in spite of a general preoccupation with this, the murder most bemoaned in Iran's modern history, and in spite of several primary and secondary accounts, many questions were left unanswered. Nasir al-Din's motives for dismissing and destroying his first premier and Atabak still need to be fully explored, as do the complex roles played by Amir Kabir's successor, Mirza Aqa Khan Nuri; the shah's mother, Mahd 'Ulya; and the foreign legations. The intensity of the drama of Amir Kabir helped sharpen the contrast between the heroes and villains, but it also blurred the circumstances of his decline and downfall. Similarly, public idealization of Amir Kabir has glossed over some flaws in his character and helped obscure the underlying causes of his differences with the shah.[2]

LEARNING TO RULE

Amir Kabir's efforts to remedy many of the ills of the Qajar state had one important personal component—to recast Nasir al-Din in the public eye as a powerful monarch supportive of the premier's program of reforms, to educate him in the art of government, and to make him conform within the boundaries Amir Kabir set for the court and the government. This remolding of a temperate boy king with a neglected education required as much devotion as astuteness. At first the shah willingly complied with his assigned role as an eager pupil ready to learn the intricacies of government. But gradually, as he acquired an aura of self-confidence, the challenge became too demanding and the limits to what he learned to call his royal prerogatives (*huquq-i saltanat*) too restrictive to be accepted unconditionally. The underlying theme of private correspondence between the shah and Amir Kabir demonstrates on both sides tension as well as stubbornness and devotion. Servile and courteous though a traditional minister ought to be, the premier's tone occasionally lent itself to a blend of condescension and fatherly rebuke. Nasir al-Din's attitude, or at least that which is apparent from their correspondence, remains that of an affectionate and grateful pupil who occasionally, under the thin guise of holding childish grudges, demonstrates a growing urge for self-assertion and even independence.[3]

In their correspondence it was above all the dereliction of royal duties that elicited repeated warnings from Amir Kabir, always delivered in a patronizing tone. He blamed the shah, for example, for canceling a military parade (under the pretext of the premier's being ill) and used the occasion to advise him on the duties of the ruler:

> With these excuses and postponements and escaping from duties it is absolutely impossible to rule over such an unruly [country] as Iran. Suppose I was ill or dying—may my soul be Your Majesty's sacrifice—do you intend to rule or not? If you must rule, then carry on with it. Why are you evading? It was not a universal principle for all kings of the past to reach the throne at the age of thirty or forty. Some ascended at the age of ten and ruled with utmost fortitude for thirty to forty years. Why don't you inquire every day about the happenings in the town? And after inquiring, what rulings would you pass with reference to the affairs of the court, the people, and the current reports from the provinces? Have you found out about the army arsenal and the artillery due to be sent to Astarabad? Of all the troops stationed in this city, have you ever inquired from their chiefs of their well-being and their good and bad? Suppose I am ill and do not recover soon, you should not suspend your duties or remain constantly dependent on a servant [*naukar*]. Although [it] sounds contemptuous, I was obliged to bring it to your attention. The rest is Your Majesty's command.[4]

Amir Kabir's call for the shah's greater involvement in the affairs of the state was evidently at odds with Sheil's portrayal of the premier as monopolistic and domineering. To be sure, the historical example alluded to in the premier's note was a prime model of monarchical self-assertion. The ten-year-old king was a reference to the great Safavid ruler 'Abbas I (1588–1629). Though in the early period of his reign he was far more constrained than Nasir al-Din, a powerless cipher in the hands of the Qizilbash chiefs who brought him to power, he later established himself— ironically, after executing his tutor—as one of the greatest rulers in Iranian history.[5] Amir Kabir's inadvertent allusion, however, aimed at royal efficiency rather than at inviting royal wrath against himself.

Nasir al-Din's gradual refocusing nevertheless from the world of pleasure, the harem, riding, and the hunt to the realm of ruling and administration must have been encouraging enough to prompt Amir Kabir to commend the shah on his persistence and severity, albeit at the expense of his own authority. In another private note he promoted the same values of royal discipline he had attributed to Shah 'Abbas:

> If Your Majesty would be willing to set your mind for two months on your duties, all the corrupt assumptions would depart from people's minds. The affairs would be in such order [*nazm*] as to make the entire world envious. Then the existence of servants like myself would be nonessential. By God's grace, the sole existence of that blessed soul will remedy every defect and [Your Majesty] would become so predominant over all affairs that without anyone's counsel major undertakings would be achieved by a mere show of imperial intent. That is because all the affairs of the world, good and bad, would depend on their initial unfolding and prearrangement so that every one would see [for himself] how, owing to the fear of the throne [*vahimah-yi saltanat*], all matters would automatically fall into order.[6]

Here again the general perception of Amir Kabir as a manipulative premier aiming to cut off altogether Nasir al-Din's involvement in running the government certainly does not withstand the test of historical evidence. His wishes that the shah actively participate in running the country were real and detectable in many of his private notes. His insistence on consistency and discipline was often complemented by calls for the shah to be constantly present in the political arena. And for good reason: The shah's vigorous presence was essential to legitimize Amir Kabir's reform program and give a perpetual, albeit symbolic, backing to any drastic measures the premier undertook against his opponents. A strong monarchy was vital to the success of his premiership. Emphasis on the "fear of the throne" and constant concern with the "dignity of the monarchy" (*shawkat-i saltanat*) were indicative of his desire to enhance Nasir al-Din's public image as the symbol of state.

Constant warnings and exhortations from Amir Kabir were bound to bring Nasir al-Din to his senses and make him more attentive to state affairs and conscious of his absolute powers. Many of Amir Kabir's notes were indeed responses to the shah's inquiries on matters of government, issues of both domestic and foreign concern, from the army to security to appointments, salaries, and occasionally details of the premier's conduct and policies. These inquiries may suggest that Amir Kabir's criticism at the outset of the shah's reign did not fall on deaf ears. Constant requests to be informed of all details and demands that the premier regularly report his daily actions further reveal the awakening of Nasir al-Din's mind. With greater frequency he now asked about the arrangement of troops, supplies, and ammunition, the dispatch of reinforcements to quell insurgencies, and appointments of military chiefs.[7] He demanded action on finances, taxation, and pensions, sometimes with the hurried enthusiasm of a naive beginner. Even more remarkable, in issuing decrees and instructions he was not always in agreement with Amir Kabir and certainly not slavish to the premier's dictates. Increasingly, sometimes excessively, he found fault with some of Amir Kabir's actions and forced the premier to explain his reasons and justify his conduct. Yet he was seldom irrational or stubborn. On many occasions he accepted the premier's decisions, though he was never content with the role of a ceremonial monarch. The prime minister, wishing to involve the shah in government, increasingly found himself asking for instructions rather than giving advice and still more frequently having to explain his actions. During negotiations with the foreign envoys regarding the issue of abolishing physical torture, for instance, he urged the shah "to look into the matter . . . since the wits of the pivot of the universe are more composed than those of this slave. Whatever you instruct will be written." Yet he was daring enough to ask the shah not to elaborate any further on that issue before hearing all the details from him.[8] At times he was even asked to explain to the shah changes in his work routine. For instance, on one occasion he had to clarify that he did not start late; on the contrary, accompanied by other officials, he had been busy preparing correspondence for the Azarbaijan courier since four hours after sunrise.[9]

But it was still predominantly Amir Kabir who was setting the direction for matters of state and royal conduct. When a foreign envoy asked for a royal audience, Amir Kabir, who was concerned that the shah might possibly blunder, felt it necessary to remind him: "Be careful tomorrow not to utter a reply that would be contrary to the best interests of your state."[10] Unhappy with a phrase in a letter addressed to the envoys of the two European powers, he insisted that "before His Majesty alters a word in the royal script, the same [draft] should be returned to this humble servant for revision."[11] Pessimistic that negotiating with the Russian representative, Dolgorouki, over an unspecified issue would lead to success, he noted: "In the humble opinion of this servant, it seems that this affair was not good from the start and will not be good until the end. But even if you do not commit yourself to any arrangement, you have no way out. Presumably, they would not give up. This is like a loss. As much as one reduces the loss, it will count as profit."[12]

Beyond setting directions, the premier also handled the majority of the appointments, instructions, assignment of missions, budget allocations, and negotiations with foreign envoys. At times, consulting with Nasir al-Din and requesting his oral or written approval in the form of autographs and marginal notes were no more than formalities. "It is appropriate," he wrote to the shah on one occasion, that edicts appointing the governors to Simnan and Damghan "be issued by your own blessed hand."[13] On another occasion, when the shah merely signed a decree (*farman*), Amir Kabir meticulously insisted that the royal seal, a symbol of the monarchy rather than the shah's signature, be added, for a signature "does not replace the royal seal."[14] Aware of the shah's concerns that he might be deprived of overall supervision of the government, Amir Kabir was careful not to appear autonomous or arrogant. "Needless to say," he wrote with reference to instructions for the Khurasan command, directives "without being reviewed by that blessed sight will not be dispatched to their destinations."[15]

What concerned the premier most in his official dealings with the shah, however, was the apparent lack of efficiency and swift responses to his inquiries. Repeatedly he urged him to certify a large volume of official correspondence on short notice. "As soon as possible," the shah should read and approve letters to Sultan Murad Mirza (now Husam al-Saltana), the new governor general of Khurasan, "so that they can be dispatched with the forthcoming courier."[16] Again requesting that the royal orders for Khurasan and Azarbaijan be issued quickly, he reminded the shah that the correspondence must be ready for the "regular state postal service on the fifteenth of this month." Presumably alluding to earlier instances of the shah's inaction, he concluded with a mild rebuke: "God willing, there will be no delays and postponements."[17] Urging speedy ratification of an official note to the foreign missions, he warned: "Any delay may result in the renewed demand for compensation."[18] A letter from the Russian minister, too, required instant attention, as "he definitely request[ed] an answer by noon tomorrow."[19]

Negotiations with foreign envoys, sometimes on petty points of protocol and prestige and other times on matters of policy and imperial pursuits, occupied a significant, and at times bitter, part of the royal exchanges with the premier. Reporting a stormy meeting with Dolgorouki, the dejected Amir Kabir, utterly displeased with the outcome, quoted for the shah a statement attributed to 'Ali ibn Abu Talib: "I like this world only because its good and evil are both in passing."[20] His stoicism was almost inevitable, given the frequency of hostile and quarrelsome letters from both the Russian and British ministers which were, as he put it, "from top to bottom full of incrimination."[21] In another instance, his complaint to the shah that the Russian envoy was pressuring him to extend protection to members of the Armenian community captured his spirit of resistance. "I fail to see where the dictates of these Excellencies would end," he wrote. "Since compliance with their request is beyond the state's best interests, I am bewildered as to how to respond to them. Nevertheless, so long as there are prospects, the struggle should continue."[22] After a particularly acrimonious session with the two envoys in the royal camp, Amir Kabir was even more confirmed in his negative opinion of the aggressive Europeans. "To sum up, to [our] logical argument they have no answer, and they never had. But they have an attitude which is called Ottoman aggression [*zur-i 'Usmani*]." He then turned his criticism to the shah, referring to unpleasant circumstances presumably caused by his indiscretion. "In the middle of our discussion, a few bullets were shot in the direction of the envoys' tent. It was said that they were shot from the shah's rifle. It was not a pleasant moment and did not appear so."[23]

On domestic issues, besides routinely reporting, the premier occasionally took issue with the shah, especially concerning favored relatives who were granted official appointments merely because of their royal ties. Overhauling government appointments was one the key reforms under Amir Kabir, and, predictably, his policy clashed with the wishes of the court and the nobility. The case of one of the shah's maternal uncles, Sulayman Khan Quvanlu, Khan-i Khanan (literally, "chief of chiefs," presumably the ceremonial *ilkhan* of the Qajar tribe), who was notorious for his corrupt conduct, demonstrates this point. Obviously displeased with Sulayman's forced appointment to the governorship of Isfahan, Amir Kabir wrote boldly in an undated note: "Your Majesty inquired about the news. What is more newsworthy than the fact that today, thanks to the deeds of your relatives, the Isfahanis have staged a villainy [*luti-bazi*] and put up a spectacle of rascality in the Shah mosque? Gathering about one thousand protesting men and women and five thousand spectators, they were shouting [in distress], Allah, Allah. God knows its origin and its outcome but thanks to God and to His Majesty's good fortune, it subsided. Yet you cannot know what I have been through."[24] This same uncle's conduct was the subject of four other angry remarks by the premier: "Hajji Mirza Yusuf [Ashtiyani, the Mustawfi al-Mamalik] is here, demanding [repayment] of the twelve thousand tumans, the balance of Khan-i Khanan's debt, but the lady [navvab—i.e., Mahd 'Ulya] has put up a guarantee," he reported to the shah with scarcely hidden anger. "For me there is neither death nor release from these sorts of dealings."[25] Again pressing the shah on the subject of his uncle's debt to the treasury and his elaborate scheme to avoid paying it—an issue which eventually led to Khan-i Khanan's dismissal and even detention—Amir Kabir remarked: "I do not know what to do with a man whose word, from start to end, is unworthy."[26] He was careful, however, not to implicate the shah's mother in the swindle, fearing that it might exacerbate the animosity already present in his strained relations with her.

> This slave takes pity with her excellency Mahd 'Ulya, as with myself about the [evil] deeds of these people. She knows their wickedness. They do not even listen to her advice. Except for being distressed there is nothing that she can do. Swear to Ali's head, I am totally bewildered as to how to deal with this Khan-i Khanan of yours. If he remains in detention, it would be a cause for the lady's annoyance. If he will be released, frankly, it does not go well with the stature and dignity of the monarchy. . . . Still it is advisable that he should [be obliged to] behave in accordance with the lady's wishes.[27]

The premier was obviously succumbing to the wishes of Mahd 'Ulya, who was now emerging as the most powerful personality in Nasir al-Din's court. The revision of state expenditure undertaken by Amir Kabir, which included reduction or even omission of pensions and salaries, had caused unprecedented dissatisfaction in court circles. The support of the shah's mother at the head of the harem was thus crucial, for she held great influence over the Qajar nobility. In spite of the acute financial crisis and the burdens of inadequate revenue, Amir Kabir was willing not only to make occasional concessions to Mahd 'Ulya—as, for instance, allowing a grace period during which Sulayman could repay his overdue debt—but also to persuade Nasir al-Din to behave more compassionately in his often strained relations with his mother.[28]

The financial restrictions imposed on the court and on the shah's private purse generated other notes of warning from the premier. In reply to the shah's inquiry on the lack of progress in the construction of royal buildings, the newly founded polytechnic, the Dar al-Funun, and the army barracks, the indignant Amir Kabir explained:

> The reason is clear. It is due to lack of funds. The reports that are brought daily . . . to your notice complain about [shortage of] money and that four thousand tumans has been borrowed so far. Here too, if funds are available, Mu'ayyir [al-Mamalik, the master of the mint and head of the treasury] would bring them to your attention. This slave is not dishonest in his opinion, if he draws your attention to the fact that the expenses for [Nawruz] celebration, the two [military ?] companies to Gurgan and Khurasan, and the supply and pay of the troops and camp were provided with great trouble.[29]

Construction of new buildings and renovation of the royal palaces, two of Nasir al-Din's lifelong pursuits, were not the only areas in the shah's life affected by Amir Kabir's austerity measures. There were even concerns with the cost of gold coins, ancient symbols of Persian sovereignty, awarded by the shah to the audience during the annual Nawruz levee. "About the sum of Ashrafi *shahi* [coins]," wrote the premier in reply to an unflattering remark made by the shah,

> Your Majesty had stated: "A certain person [i.e., Amir Kabir himself] would not leave us in peace." It must be clear to Your Majesty that at all times this devotee had no hesitation or reservation to reimburse the occasional expenses of that pivot of the universe. In your royal wisdom, it must be apparent that by God, I wished the [blessings of] the entire world for the tranquility of that blessed imperial soul. If occasionally, however, I dare to caution, it is by way of service to you so that funds for necessary expenses would not be delayed. Otherwise, the entire treasury is yours. What is the status of this devotee to obstruct the fulfillment of Your Majesty's blessed wishes? But as far as this devotee is concerned, he would not give even one *dinar* to anyone and the sum that I am supposed to distribute among people will be spent instead on necessary expenses of the royal army. But Your Majesty, of course, would, by God's grace, distribute the new year gifts.[30]

Although conciliatory in tone, Amir Kabir did not hesitate to spell out his priorities; nor was he willing to comply unconditionally with the shah's desire to control the treasury. Once, when the shah expressed his desire to use some of the diamonds in the treasury to make an ornamental piece—an early example of royal obsession with jewelry—the premier felt obliged to remind him that "regarding a visit to the treasury and removal of diamonds, no doubt whatever you have planned is correct. Of course, prior to that occasion we would discuss as to what you have in mind to make [with the diamonds] since it should not happen that no unmounted diamonds remain in the treasury. This is not right."[31] The premier persuaded the shah to act with circumspection even when granting the traditional robes of honor (*khil'at*), usually quite a lavish occasion. "If sometimes on . . . [the need] for reducing expenditure, I dare to bring the matter to your attention, it is because the sum [borrowed] from the merchants should be repaid and the state treasury of this government should not resemble that of the previous government." Implicit in Amir Kabir's remark was a preference for the government's needs over those of the shah and the court. Stressing that it was absolutely necessary to reimburse subjects for services performed, he added that unless officials were paid, "how could they carry on with their duties? [Indeed,] twice as much money should be spent in order to expect [proper] service."[32]

With the same resilience, he again cautioned the shah of the excesses of granting new land tenures, pensions, and rewards. He objected to upgrading the pension of a greedy official, alluding in a humorous tone to the ever-expanding appetite of the civil service and the courtiers. "If once I say that this straw [i.e., available funds] is a pot of yogurt, he, like others, assumes that this is nothing but a sacrificial lamb of which there is a share for him." He continued, "It is not this slave's business, but [Your Majesty is] bestowing too many grants. I hope it is clear to your blessed wisdom annually how much these would add up for each individual." He even forewarned that because of increases in the number of pensions, the shah might not be able to honor his royal promises.[33] Further dissuading the shah from granting his own robe to a sycophant as a sign of honor, he expressed utter disgust at the sight of dishonest flattery. "If the intention of these people for requesting your personal robe is honor and prestige, that is correct and auspicious. But if it is for togging themselves up for extortion," he warned with characteristic bluntness, "that is another matter. At any rate, by God's grace, it will not be granted."[34]

The shah's personal expenses were subject to the new economic measures, and he was urged to modify his entertainments. "If more than one hundred tumans are issued," Amir Kabir warned, "I doubt I will be able to honor it. That is because of paucity of cash." The pain of admitting that the government treasury was empty was compounded by having to caution the shah to restrain his expensive habits. "I swear to God, even the [betting] money for the day after the horse race, which was close to five hundred tumans, was provided with enormous trouble."[35] Even the personal gifts presented to the shah at royal banquets were not excluded from the premier's scrutiny. "All [of the gifts] should be considered as state property," he wrote to the shah. "During the time of the deceased Khaqan [Fath

'Ali Shah], there were many such celebrations, and all [gifts] were to be recorded and documented."[36] As late as 1851, on the eve of the royal visit to Isfahan, the anxious premier reminded Nasir al-Din he needed a cash sum of 50,000 tumans to pay the accompanying troops. "How could a monarch of such grandeur set out on a journey without taking with him in the royal chest twenty to thirty thousand tumans for necessary and unforeseen expenses?" After listing the many pressing needs that would require financial remuneration, he continued: "No matter how stringently this slave acts, without money these affairs will not be resolved, and God is my witness that I am not even able to provide five hundred tumans."[37]

There was little, if any, discussion in these written exchanges with Nasir al-Din of a preconceived program of political or other reforms. Amir Kabir's objective (as far as Nasir al-Din was concerned) was to create a centralized, well-financed, and efficient government with a strong army, expanding bureaucracy, and independent foreign policy but also intolerant of the autonomy of peripheral powers and of political dissent at home. These objectives were the basis for improvements in the organization of the state judiciary; a reduction of clerical influence in the judicial process; foundation of the Dar al-Funun, the first modern educational institution in Iran (initially perceived as a military academy); agricultural, industrial, and construction projects; and adaptation of a system of conscription (*bunicha*). But for the most part they remained beyond the reach of the shah and independent of his initiative.

Instead there was a fair amount of indulging the shah's malleable ego. Frequently, in reply to childish complaints and requests, Amir Kabir was obliged to assure the shah in the most flattering language of his utmost loyalty and servitude: "I desire life and time and glory and greatness only for the sake of Your Majesty's pleasure and that you will be happy in heart. Whatever toil I shoulder day and night [is] all for that blessed soul." All this humility was necessary to explain to the offended shah that the assigned budget for the royal kitchen had not been reduced. To further console the royal gastronome, he was obliged to praise the "majestic compassion" in the shah's intention to feed the poor out of court expenses.[38] In response to another unspecified complaint by the shah he stressed: "This servant in his few days of this worldly life would not lose faith in you. God is my witness that if I had a hundred thousand souls, I would have sacrificed them all for that Majesty. But it is true that even with all this faith in my own servitude, of course grievous words would cause me despair." Then, blaming his own adversaries for prompting the shah's bad temper, he added: "By God's blessing, I hope that [such harsh words] are not those of Your Majesty but those of the evildoers who intend to offend me . . . [anyway] these are not important. This servant is not going to be disappointed at your service."[39] One can almost sense the rising tensions between the shah and his premier.

On another occasion Amir Kabir's displeasure at the shah's criticism behind his back is more clearly audible: "Today, I heard certain words," he remarked sarcastically, "concerning His Majesty's sympathies toward myself which caused this slave utter grief."[40] It is conceivable that the disenchanted premier was reminding the shah that he had access to an intelligence network in the palace; yet he knew well that his very political survival depended on the shah's favor. "I always expected, and will expect from you, that for the rest of [my] life you never change your opinion about this slave" on the ground of "people's baseless words." He thus hoped that in exchange for "special servitude and obedience," the shah would extend to him his favorable sentiments.[41]

Exchanging sympathies, part of the everyday lives of both men, had the effect of moderating the tensions on both sides. Besides, the shah's health was of immediate concern to the premier. He approved of simple medications: "It is a blessing that today Your Majesty has taken a dose of fruit-salt." He cautioned him, however, not to fall victim to physicians overprescribing medication: "Within the sphere of servitude," he wrote humorously, but with a hypochondriac's zeal, "informing this slave [of future medication] is one of the principles of the faith."[42] Having in mind the chronic illness of Nasir al-Din's father, which had caused so many crises in the past, and aware of Nasir al-Din's own "weak constitution" in childhood, Amir Kabir had good reason to hope that the shah would observe his diet (parhiz) thoroughly, "since the soundness of your sacred constitution is essential for the well being of eighteen kurur souls."[43] The shah was even more anxious about the failing health of his prime minister, who often wrestled with a range of real and imaginary illnesses. In numerous replies to the shah's inquiries, Amir Kabir complained of illnesses and deteriorating health. Headaches, chest pain, recurring flu, exhaustion, insomnia, failing eyesight, and diarrhea routinely put him out of action and subjected him to a variety of treatments: doses of fruit salt, bleeding, and a variety of diets and fasting. "This devotee has been fasting for the past two days. It is neither good nor bad, I manage to walk about, but not like before. Neither am I pursuing work, nor can I sit idle."[44]

The extent of intimacy between the shah and Amir Kabir could also be gauged by the details of their daily routines. Long hours of intense work and supervision of all details of the administration, army, and court left the exhausted premier little time to keep up with the young shah's hectic recreation schedule and frequent riding excursions in the vicinity of the capital. "From dawn to seven hours past sunset this devotee is incessantly engaged in royal service," he wrote in an early note in 1848, urging the shah to reconsider his decision to remove the domestic eunuch in Amir Kabir's inner quarters. "Hoping that the affairs of my household are in order, I stay out and serve . . . otherwise this devotee . . . in this unfamiliar land [i.e., Tehran] and in the absence of my mother and brother cannot afford having a wife. Either tomorrow I must dispatch my wife to Tabriz or else from dawn to dusk I should retire in my house next to my wife and her maid. In that case it is clear what sort of service I would be able to render."[45] This was probably a reference to his first wife, who indeed was divorced and sent back to Tabriz before the marriage of convenience with the shah's sister. Yet he seemed to have accepted his fate and even developed great affection for his second wife, in spite of the circumstances of their marriage and their age difference. His concern for the welfare of Malikzada surfaced in another amusing note, in which Amir Kabir complained to the shah that he did not keep his promise to take her for an outing because he was waiting in the rain for an audience with the shah. Now I am "left out from one place and driven away from another. What do you say and what do you give to compensate for this double loss? Tomorrow this devotee cannot come over [to the court]. He intends to move to Shamiran both for pleasure and to do business, that is, to look at the new[ly constructed] qanats [the subterranean irrigation systems native to Iran]."[46]

Excessive work, however, did not prevent Amir Kabir from commenting on details of the shah's affairs. On the eve of the new lunar year he wrote: "That you have mentioned your intent to pay a visit to the bathhouse, that is certainly necessary."[47] On other occasions he commented on the shah's attending Muharram mourning ceremonies, or setting up fireworks in the palace, or taking daily riding excursions. "I was about to write in my note that by God's grace you should go riding [but] there was a pause [i.e., that a sneeze cautioned him to pause temporarily to avoid a bad omen]. To this devotee, this is not free from discouragement."[48] Superstitious warnings such as this appeared in other notes: "Tomorrow there is a conjunction of the moon and Scorpio that falls on the first of the month; caution around the house is advisable."[49] Exchanges of gifts provided other occasions for affable expressions. At one point Amir Kabir thanked the shah for sending him a few partridges from a recent shooting trip and took the opportunity to express gratitude for the shah's appreciation of his own recent present: "That His Majesty indicated his pleasure with the Arabian horse presented by this devotee makes me proud that I have been able to find something suitable to the royal taste."[50]

Occasionally, however, the exchange of gifts went beyond expensive toys. The shah's interest in reading historical, biographical, and geographical accounts was encouraged by the premier, who tried to create intellectual incentives toward furthering the shah's education. "Regarding the translation of the two-volume book on Napoleon that Your Majesty had commissioned," he wrote, "now the translation of one volume is complete, but since Mirza Shafi' Munshi [the scribe], who was supposed to make a fair copy, was in royal attendance, it has not yet been rendered. . . . The other volume is in the process of being translated."[51] For Amir Kabir, as for other Middle Eastern statesmen of his time, the story of the French conqueror held great fascination and pedagogical value. The emperor with humble origins, whose military genius brought him victory on the battlefield and glory on the throne, who created a new sociolegal order, and who fought against Britain and Russia held a lofty stature in the conquest-conscious Qajar era. Even his blunders and defeats, and his ignominious end in exile, must have prompted Amir Kabir and Nasir al-Din to draw lessons in caution and circumspection. There is perhaps a kernel of truth in Amir Kabir's allegedly dissuading Nasir al-Din from commissioning a translation of Malcolm's *A History of Persia*. The premier warned that "for Persians reading such a book is fatally poisonous," because Malcolm's portrayal of the Qajar government at the end of his second volume was one of a fading empire about to be subdued by its imperial neighbor. Instead, the premier preferred that the young shah read the Persian national epic, *Shahnama*, and the histories of powerful rulers such as Isma'il I and Nadir, both of whom had reputations for military conquest and ruthlessness.[52]

The question thus remains: What kind of influence did Amir Kabir exert in shaping Nasir al-Din Shah's personality? More accurately, what kind of monarch did he aspire to see on the throne, and to what extent did the young Nasir al-Din measure up to his expectations? To be sure, the image of Amir Kabir as a farsighted and devout reformer who tried avidly to hammer out an effective and responsible ruler from the raw material of an inexperienced, volatile, and at times stubborn boy-king holds true only to a degree. As much evidence as one will find of Amir Kabir's sincerity and vision—and of Nasir al-Din's shortcomings—such a picture is not complete. Looking beyond the popular image we see a premier sharing many characteristics with his predecessors and successors not only in his policies but also in his desire to create a more disciplined, cost-efficient, and effective monarchy. Perhaps Amir Kabir envisaged Nasir al-Din as a ruler in the mold of his Ottoman contemporary, Sultan 'Abd al-Majid (1839–1861), a supporter of reforms and an arbiter in determining crucial matters of the state. Yet in attempting to infuse some sort of rationality into the conduct of the crown, Amir Kabir did not wish to sever the arbitrary power embedded in that institution. Moreover, his measures aimed to address the old defects inherent in the Qajar political order. But whatever the premier's intent in creating a strong and all-embracing state, such a vision had the potential to manifest itself as an even more absolutist monarchy, significantly free from all the old restraints.

It may be argued that Amir Kabir could probably have prevented monarchical intervention had he been willing and able to exclude Nasir al-Din from the governmental process altogether. He could have allowed the shah merely to play the role of a feeble nonentity busy with his own artistic and recreational activities without disturbing his extravagant but harmless slumber and his never-ending frequenting of the harem and the hunting ground. By giving Nasir al-Din the chance to envisage a different role for himself—that of a statesman responsible for the survival of his throne and for the integrity of his realm—Amir Kabir helped the shah launch a career of royal assertiveness that not only contributed to the premier's own downfall but also set a standard of behavior for the rest of Nasir al-Din's long reign. Such an argument seems less convincing, however, when the intricacies of the relationship between Nasir al-Din and Amir Kabir are brought to mind. Nasir al-Din was not a Muhammad Shah, nor was Amir Kabir an Aqasi.

In spite of his reliance on Amir Kabir, Nasir al-Din now began to seek other channels through which to assert his independence. The young shah acquired a semblance of active statesmanship with all its trappings. He issued directives and decrees, demanded swift action, exercised symbolic justice, and even learned to maneuver his way through a labyrinth of court intrigue and diplomatic impasses. As early as February 1849, for instance, he informed Farrant, through the minister of foreign affairs, Mirza Muhammad 'Ali Shirazi, that on the question of complying with prohibition on the slave trade, an ongoing source of friction with Britain (which sought direct inspection of the Persian ports), he, out of "respect for friendship with the august government of England," would confirm his father's earlier assurances. "Yet," he continued, "we would not make another agreement. If our subjects did not honor our ordinance, we would punish them in whatever way we see fit, since the authority for such apprehensions and punishments is ours and not that of any other government."[53] The shah's tone in reply to the British chargé d'affaires was blunt and confident but apparently not forceful enough to convince Amir Kabir of the shah's effectiveness. Some months later, shortly before an audience requested by the Russian envoy, Amir Kabir referred to the exchange of notes with Farrant and cautioned the shah of the need for discretion and prudence. "The humble servant," he wrote,

> hopes that if this is a mere visit [by the Russian envoy], His Majesty converse in such manner that if in future there would be a need for exchange of notes, the claim of this devotee, that I act according to an imperial command, would hold credence. If [on the other hand] he [i.e., Dolgorouki] raises a [specific] issue, I hope Your Majesty would provide such sound answers with calm and gentleness as would be worthy of praise. Hence the story of the black [slaves] and the British envoy would not repeat itself; as a result of which over the past six months they [i.e., the British] have been constantly charging: "His Imperial Majesty had given his consent, but you interfered and disturbed [the understanding]."[54]

There is little doubt that the young Nasir al-Din did benefit from his premier's administrative, negotiating, and military expertise. Amir Kabir's attention to detail, his policy of symbolic punishment and reward, elimination of dissent, his method of terrorizing the populace at times and at others reconciling and compromising with them, and his firm grip over appointments provided the shah with a picture, albeit a hazy one, of how the affairs of the state should be conducted. The premier's exhortations were bound to awaken the shah's desire for greater involvement to an extent that even Amir Kabir himself could not foresee. In a note probably written toward the end of Amir Kabir's time in office, he was clearly annoyed by the shah's increasing interferences. The note also revealed Nasir al-Din's misgivings about what he believed was a deliberate attempt to exclude him from the executive process. The stern tone and contents of the note justify its full citation:

> May my soul be a sacrifice at your blessed imperial threshold. I read your majestical rescript. You have commanded that all civilian petitions be presented to Your Majesty. This slave was of the opinion that indeed all petitions are brought to Your Majesty's attention. Whatever petitions and complaints [are submitted] by the people are no business of this devotee. They are referred to the *divan-khana* [the government judicial bureau dealing with civilian litigation] as I have repeatedly pointed out [to you] and advised them [i.e., the officials of the *divan-khana*] to present petitions to Your Majesty. If they failed to do so it is not this devotee's responsibility. As for the city's daily reports, as soon as the news is brought to me, I immediately draft the report and send it to your pres-

ence. All budgetary reports, too, are brought to Your Majesty's attention. As for settlement of outstanding accounts, I have informed the [accountant] office that as soon as the bills of expenditure are complete and ready to be cleared, they should be brought to your presence. As for the reports concerning the state of the army, you are witness that repeatedly I have asked Mahmud Khan [Mukri] and [Hasan 'Ali Khan Garrusi] the Ajudanbashi [the adjutant general] to report all matters to Your Majesty. There is not even one *farman* or a money draft issued without royal approval. All correspondences from the provinces, mostly unread, and the rest after being read, are brought to your presence, and all replies meet the royal sight, and only after they received your approval will they be dispatched. Of the correspondence with foreign envoys, which one, whether the original letter or the reply, has not been brought to your attention? The same is [true] of all provincial and administrative affairs. What [matter] has been settled without the royal consent? At the end, what remains [for me] is the nuisance and the noise of [settling] accounts that if it occurs in the royal presence, is contrary to the dignity of the crown. But if His Majesty ordains, this devotee would refrain [from that duty,] too. All these sufferings, outward and inward, that this devotee endeavors and all the grief and irremediable pains that I brought upon myself, let God and his messenger be my witness, are for the sake of that blessed soul. Although it may sound impudent, this is the truth of the matter. If in reality, however, Your Majesty has other intentions he is unwilling to divulge or, God forbid, considers this servant's intervention [in the affairs] obstructive to your service, I urge you, by your blessed crown, to utter your desire. Needless to say that this servant was not, and is not, desirous for such services and can not see for himself any benefit except suffering and waste of life. Whatever is your inner intention, by God, I submit to it with full consent.[55]

If there was any doubt as to the nature of the shah's "inner intentions," the events that soon followed made them tragically clear—intentions dreadful enough in their consequences to fit the premier's portrayal of his services as nothing but "suffering and a waste of life."

THE SUBLIME CRADLE

By the middle of 1851 Nasir al-Din and the Qajar establishment felt considerably safer than they had in 1848, at the shaky beginning of the new shah's reign. Thanks to Amir Kabir's perseverance, the most pressing menaces to the throne had abated. The Salar revolt, the last of the Qajar intertribal conflicts, was crushed and the Davalu claim to the throne severely weakened. The Babi insurrections, too, had been forcefully suppressed and many of the movement's leaders, including the Bab himself, arrested and destroyed. Its last belligerent outburst came when the remnants of a previously decimated militant wing of the movement re-organized and carried out an unsuccessful assassination attempt against Nasir al-Din Shah in August 1852. Yet signs of Babi military exhaustion were eminently apparent by the end of the bloody Zanjan resistance in January 1851. Amir Kabir's pacification policy had its effects on peripheral sources of power. The 'ulama were restrained from political intervention even at local level, and insubordinate tribal lords were punished severely enough to serve as examples to others.

The growing power of the central government under Amir Kabir, how-ever, was a two-edged sword for the Qajar ruling elite; although it helped to buttress the precarious existence of the dynasty, it did so at a cost. The government's limited funds were diverted to subsidize urgent military expenditures, but revenue through taxation was barely sufficient to cover these burdens. This was bound to reduce the financial benefits of the Qajar nobility. The court clique, royal harem, and princes in military service were invariably incensed by the drop in their pensions and privileges. Royal spending, too, was affected. Contrary to high expectations the court, par-ticularly the small but influential Quvanlu circle surrounding Mahd 'Ulya, did not receive the full range of material rewards they yearned for. The premier's long arm of monetary control had now reached the inner court, the harem, and even the royal purse.

Moreover, Amir Kabir's desire for joint control of the army and the administration, combined with his near total supervision over the shah, mobilized a common front against him with the determined aim of putting him out of office and, if necessary, destroying him. Indeed, the three major figures involved in the downfall of the premier represented the most disgruntled groups within the Qajar elite. Even as early as 1848, there were latent signs of court intrigue and defamation, but by 1850 they had turned into open hostility. Mahd 'Ulya led the Qajar nobility in its resistance to Amir Kabir's dual policy of reducing privileges and, more unacceptable, distancing the shah from his relatives. She was joined in her opposition by the royal chamberlain, Hajji 'Ali Khan Hajib al-Dawla (later I'timad al-Saltana I), and Mirza Aqa Khan Nuri, Amir Kabir's lieutenant and partner in the government. Nuri's loosening grip over the inherited office of secretary of the army may have prompted him to reinvoke his old alliances with Mahd 'Ulya. The same motive may have inspired him to utilize his close association with the British mission for the purpose of toppling Amir Kabir. Loosely attached to this small but powerful core of opposition were a number of government officials, courtiers, army chiefs, and members of the royal family. Among them, Mirza Yusuf Ashtiyani, Mustawfi al-

Mamalik, the chief government accountant and future premier, must be mentioned (see Pl. 11). Like Nuri he came from an established bureaucratic family and regarded the premier's monopoly as dangerous to his inherited tenure.[56] Also involved were the maternal uncles of the shah, whom Amir Kabir deprived of the customary misuses of power associated with the royal family.

Mahd 'Ulya's grievances with Amir Kabir were profound and complex. She regarded him as the chief cause of Nasir al-Din's growing repulsion for her. Having no intention of retiring to the seclusion of the harem, she believed the shah's favor toward her could not be restored as long as Amir Kabir mastered his temper. The tension between the shah and his mother was in part due to the rumors about her promiscuous lifestyle, rumors that had already resulted in her divorce from Muhammad Shah. Amir Kabir's appearance as the shah's impenetrable guardian was an additional source of contention. It is even possible that Mahd 'Ulya held Amir Kabir responsible for besmirching her reputation in her son's eye. This accusation Amir Kabir apparently tried to avoid. "Yesterday I observed Her Highness your mother being very upset," Amir Kabir at one point wrote to the shah in an obviously conciliatory tone. "Please do not take offense if I suggest that His Majesty should duly express towards her his bounteous affection and hearty consolation."[57] On an earlier occasion, soon after his marriage with Malikzada, Amir Kabir tried to convince Nasir al-Din of Mahd 'Ulya's good wishes: "[It is very doubtful] that during the first six months [of your rule] she would wish to see the infringement of your royal authority since she desires the throne for your blessed soul and for the strength of your authority. By God, I saw her more obedient for the execution of your imperial will than anyone in this world."[58] Amir Kabir deemed such assurance necessary in order to avoid an open collision with the most influential figure in the court. Nevertheless, the contest for the shah's deference is well evident in Mahd 'Ulya's correspondence.

A woman of some literary refinement, she complained to Nasir al-Din about the obvious disfavor to which she had been subjected lately: "When are you going to know me?" she wrote to the shah. "I am behaving more cautiously than all others, and yet you treat me with less trust than anyone." Rejecting rumors of manipulation and contact with government officials such as Nuri, she added: "God bears witness that I am neither acquainted with your minister, nor do your servants know me or I them."[59] Such disclaimers, however, did not save her from temporary exile to Qum, a customary place for disfavored royalty. A far stronger outcry was audible in a letter to her brother, Shir Khan 'Ayn al-Mulk. Written around 1850, at the height of Amir Kabir's power, it reflected some intricate details of the crises in her relations with Nasir al-Din:

> If His Majesty was impartial enough to acknowledge my prerogative and recognized my motherly right and, by now, realized how I have always acted as a vigilant and conscientious mother, and that I never desired his grief even for one day or the slightest drawback in his reign, then it would never have been necessary for you [i.e. Mahd 'Ulya's brother], or anyone else, to take my message to the shah's presence.... I myself should have acted as intermediary for everybody and delivered other people's messages [to the shah]. Now, because of the words of slanderers, His Majesty forcefully passed the verdict of guilty on his mother and thus scandalized himself in front of other states and on the face of the globe.[60]

Mahd 'Ulya's veiled reference to scandalous rumors concerning her conduct was followed by further exhortations. "I reckon that from the dawn of the universe until now no mother loved her child, or toiled for him, as I did. Now matters have been portrayed as though I do not like the shah but other people do. Alas, His Majesty does not realize the reason for other people's [apparent] affection for him and the reason for my love for him."[61]

Such complaints of the shah's conduct, competition for his favor, and her limited access to him, as well as her expressions of the sincerity of her affection, were poignant symptoms of Mahd 'Ulya's misgivings toward the premier. "Like the King of the Martyrs [i.e., Husayn ibn 'Ali, the Third Imam] in the plain of Karbala," she wrote,

> I remained here alone and on my own. Looking in all directions, I see neither a friend nor a supporter. Now in the position of queen motherhood [madar padishahi] no one is as defenseless as I am. I thus take refuge with the same King of the Martyrs so that if anybody desires to turn the king against me, drive me away from here, and scandalize the shah, that person himself will become the victim of the shah's wrath. This is the pledge I made in the shrine of Ma'suma [sister of 'Ali ibn Musa al-Riza, the Eighth Imam, buried in Qum] for Mirza Taqi Khan [Amir Kabir]. Let him not harass me. If at God's threshold I am blameworthy, still He has done many great works for me. Here, too, He will not let a mother be so severely parted from her son.[62]

The passionate tone of Mahd 'Ulya's letter betrayed her desperate defiance. Whether the allegations against Amir Kabir were true it is difficult to know. Amir Kabir's above-cited note to the shah sincerely called for Nasir al-Din to reconcile with his mother. Yet it is conceivable that the premier was behind her exile. Her appeal in the Qum shrine to a female saint to help her reclaim her "queen motherhood" was a telling example of how the Qajar harem still held matriarchal claims to power. In a culture that adhered firmly to the values of honor and shame, even more so to women's modesty and concealment, such public disclosures concerning royal household members could not have been easily ignored.[63]

Maligned and scandalized, Mahd 'Ulya saw her political survival and her reputation held ransom in a relentless power struggle in which the cost might even be a deadly confrontation with her own son-in-law. "Up to now," wrote Mahd 'Ulya, "it was women's gossip and the affair of the harem. Now it is a matter of government and the outer court." Fiercely denying the accusations, she rebuked Amir Kabir for fostering the Shah's hatred toward her. "Hajji Mirza Aqasi, too, used to tell the late shah [Muhammad Shah] that his mother did not love him. At the end the mother burned out, but Hajji, too, was forced to flee the middle of the road. . . . I am sick of hearing such rumors. This affair has gone too far. . . . If it was only a matter of throwing me out or disgracing my reputation, and had not caused the shah disrepute, by God I still would have been content . . . [but] for God's sake you are making me impatient. Kill me at once and set me free."[64]

Indeed, before he sent her into exile, the thought of killing his mother may very well have crossed Nasir al-Din Shah's mind. Infuriated by reports of her illicit contacts, the shah allegedly intended to shoot her in the gardens adjacent to the royal palace.[65] Whatever the truth of the charges of promiscuity, it is plausible that the queen mother's contacts with princes of the Qajar family and other elements in search of a united front against Amir Kabir were conveniently presented to the shah as evidence of licentiousness. Mahd 'Ulya's pledge to Nasir al-Din at a later date that she would no longer permit the Qajar princes to visit her "without [royal] permission and order" was made on the grounds that after the fall of Amir Kabir the contingency for such contacts had been removed. Referring to the time of Amir Kabir, she wrote:

> Those days it was another story. They [i.e., the princes] were not permitted into your service. Mirza Taqi had reduced this party [i.e., the Qajar nobility] and the helpless princes to less than dogs. They were cut off from the heavens and the earth. Thus in order not to be humiliated, and to communicate their grievances and pleas, in desperation they used to turn to me. Now, thank God, because of this favor that the king conferred upon Iran, everybody understands his business and presents his request to the king. What business do I have any longer? Thank God I, too, am relieved.[66]

The growing sphere of the premier's opponents reflected his increasing political isolation. Amir Kabir's exacting attitude, particularly toward the lower ranks, made his premiership seem a reign of terror, complete with a secret service, public executions, and censorship. Nor did his honest and uncompromising dealings with foreign envoys win him allies in either the Russian or the British camp. Much of what has been preserved in official accounts, and even in popular ones, confirms his lack of flexibility in a system founded on negotiation and compromise. Moreover, in spite of the royal union, his humble origins could not provide him with a kinship network as strong as his opponents'. The little loyalty that his background and training experience could effectively draw from the remnants of the Farahani party was nullified by factionalism among the officials and by Mahd 'Ulya and her allies, who painted Amir Kabir as another Qa'im Maqam.

More than an average prime minister in the traditional Perso-Islamic system could afford, Amir Kabir had left his battle lines recklessly unguarded. His sole reliance on the shah was beginning to crumble and make him susceptible to palace intrigue. He began his drive for power by mastering the shah's temper, playing to his favor, and keeping him away from rival sources of influence. A miraculous mixture of flattery, fatherly advice, and admonition, he thought, could keep Nasir al-Din in a state of blissful contentment. Clinging to the shah's favor and trusting in his sympathies, however, was effective only as long as the shah was willing to place his trust and loyalty solely in the premier's hands. But the dual role assigned to the shah had already made the process of sustaining such loyalty a formidable one. On the one hand, Nasir al-Din was expected to participate in the affairs of the government and present to the public the appearance of a mighty and responsible monarch. On the other, he was required to remain obedient to the line of policy dictated by the premier. Such a dichotomy in function showed visible signs of strain during the royal visit to Isfahan in the summer of 1851, when Nasir al-Din's almost paranoiac concerns for the security of his throne clashed openly with Amir Kabir's efforts to sustain predominance over the government.

It was perhaps out of fear of foreign intervention and mischief on the part of his enemies in his absence from the capital that Amir Kabir requested the inclusion of 'Abbas Mirza (III), the shah's younger half-brother, and his mother, Khadija, in the royal company. Since the death of Muhammad Shah, the young prince, then thirteen years of age, and his mother had been the subjects of recurring harassment by the Quvanlus and their allies, who had loathed the special favor Muhammad Shah showed toward his son. Nasir al-Din himself was no less spiteful of his younger brother and barely tolerated his presence in the capital. Death threats, confiscation, and the torturing of some servants in her household had already persuaded Khadija to seek British protection through the good offices of Farhad Mirza, 'Abbas's uncle, who had now emerged as a virtual British protégé. As in similar cases, the British responded favorably, not solely out of humanitarian concern but also because they saw in 'Abbas Mirza a potential alternative to Nasir al-Din, should there be a need for it. Mindful of foreign and domestic manipulation, Amir Kabir consistently advised Nasir al-Din Shah to act with leniency and benevolence toward his half-brother—advice that was interpreted by his enemies as a sign of the premier's interest in the shah's hated brother.[67] It is not unlikely that the premier found in 'Abbas Mirza a useful tool in checking Nasir al-Din's temper. By parading a one-time candidate for the throne in front of the king, Amir Kabir may have intended to remind Nasir al-Din of his vulnerability and underscore the premier's centrality to the throne (see Fig. 4).

Added to the shah's dislike for his brother was Mahd 'Ulya's repulsion for her old rival, Khadija. Although in 1848 the queen mother had assured the British chargé d'affaires of the other wife's safety, there was no way that three years later she would tolerate Khadija's presence in the royal camp. Her concern was relayed to Amir Kabir and received a harsh response reflecting his growing impatience with the queen mother. "For two reasons," he wrote back to the shah,

> her highness is obviously not justified in her wishes. Firstly, the mother of the shah of shahs, may God sacrifice my soul for him, is unique and has no comparison, be it a Kurdish [i.e., Khadija] or a Turkish girl. No one in this kingdom competes with her. Let her not needlessly carve out rivals for herself [*bi-jihat baray-i khudishan ham-chasm natarashand*]. Second, Khadija's residence in Tehran, in the absence of the shah, is not expedient. Her highness should wish what is acceptable to you and expedient for your kingdom. In the traveling camp beside the royal tents there are ten other tents and camping enclosures. It is obvious that they [i.e., their residents] are all servants of the king. Women, too, in their servitude to the queen mother are like slaves. It is not [therefore] out of custom if her highness would regard Khadija's presence as part of my household. His Majesty, however, will bear witness that I have not been aware of this matter. His Majesty must silence Mahd 'Ulya so that in this journey she does not utter such words.[68]

Amir Kabir's closer association with 'Abbas Mirza and his obsequious conduct toward Khadija during the Isfahan visit only helped shake the shah's trust in Amir Kabir further. This was bound to aggravate the shah's suspicion to an almost paranoid level.

Figure 4.   The Abbasid caliph, Harun al-Rashid (786–809), conversing with his ill-fated minister, Ja'far Barmaki. Oil painting from an illustrated manuscript of *One Thousand and One Nights* commissioned by Nasir al-Din Shah. The talented painter Abul-Hasan Ghaffari, Sani' al-Mulk, utilizes the historical theme to portray Nasir al-Din Shah and Amir Kabir in Qajar attire, presumably during the Isfahan royal tour of 1851, when the premier quarreled with the shah over 'Abbas Mirza III, who probably is the figure standing to the right of the minister. *Hizar u Yak Shab* (Persian trans. of *The One Thousand and One Nights*), completed 1276 Q./ 1859, Gulistan Library. Reprinted in Atabay, *Fihrist-i Divanha-yi Khatti va Kitab-i Hizar u Yak Shab-i Kikabkhana-yi Saltanati*, II, no. 50.

On the way back to the capital in September 1848, the tension between the shah and the premier came to the surface. While the royal party was in Qum, the shah went ahead and appointed 'Abbas Mirza to nominal governorship of the city, an appointment synonymous with exile. Caught by surprise, the premier swiftly challenged the shah's order and instead instructed 'Abbas and his mother to depart immediately for Tehran ahead of the royal camp. Infuriated by the premier's action, Nasir al-Din then ordered their return to Qum and reaffirmed 'Abbas Mirza's appointment. This was, as Sipihr puts it, "the first confrontation in the concluding pages of Mirza Taqi Khan's dealings with the shah."[69]

Amir Kabir's response to the shah's self-asserting move came in a blunt note, betraying his anxiety for the apparent loss of control over the monarch:

> About 'Abbas Mirza and his mother, whom you have instructed to remain for a while in Qum, there are two dimensions to this slave's reaction. The first is absolute obedience out of servitude. In this case whatever Your Majesty commands is his own choice and this slave is prepared to notify them in the morning that according to royal command they should stay here. The second, if I understand something with my own inferior wisdom, I would most definitely present [to you] so as to preempt future repercussions. In that I am not infallible either. At times I may understand it correctly; at other times I may be wrong. Now it is up to His Majesty's judgment. Whichever course you opt for, I will obey.

He then went on to remind the shah in clear terms of his own loyalty and the shah's need to respect his ministerial authority:

> You have said that without the permission of this slave Your Majesty would not act on the slightest matters. God and his Prophet are witness that I have spent, and will spend, the whole world and whatever is in it in the way of your satisfaction and service and am content with your outward and inward favors. If on occasion by way of appellation and desperation I have presented a word, it was, and will be, out of the care and servitude that I reserve for you, since so long as I am alive and in your service I cannot see or hear people criticizing you and am aware myself of my own personal and statuary limits. In this instance you have no right [*shuma dar in surat haqq nadarid*] to be upset with such a servant or to conceal the current affairs from this slave.[70]

It is remarkable that Amir Kabir, in spite of his mastery of Nasir al-Din's temper, misjudged his sensitivity on the issue of his half-brother—and this at a time when the death, in 1849, of Nasir al-Din's first heir to the throne, Sultan Mahmud Mirza, once again left the question of succession up to palace intrigue and foreign speculation. Some decades later, describing the Isfahan episode, Qajar historian Muhammad Hasan Khan I'timad al-Saltana remarked that Amir Kabir wished to have 'Abbas Mirza nominated heir apparent. Regardless of its veracity, such news echoed the anxiety that must have vexed the shah's troubled mind.[71] In an imaginary confessional monologue, the same source cited Amir Kabir's supposed words: "With this intention and aim [in mind] I prepared for his journey to Isfahan and took him and his mother with myself with utmost splendor. In Burujird, I instructed Hajji 'Ali Khan Farrashbashi [Hajib al-Dawla, the author's father] to notify the local governors en route that the same protocol and decorum that were observed for the shah should be observed for 'Abbas

Mirza." Even if there had been no other reason, the report of such instructions from Amir Kabir was enough to make Nasir al-Din determined
to remove the premier.[72]

CASTLE OF MIRRORS, CANNONBALLS
OF SEDITION

The 'Abbas Mirza affair was a serious blow to Amir Kabir. Upon returning
to Tehran, he found that his influence on the shah had eroded substantially.
Royal suspicion had now superseded devotion to the Atabak, and courage
had overcome awe. The prospect that the British might offer full diplomatic
asylum to his brother haunted Nasir al-Din and raised his fears that, with
the consent of the British, Amir Kabir might try to replace him with his
minor half-brother and subsequently take hold of the reins of power as
regent. Such a thought might have been suggested to the shah by the
attendants of the inner court and reinforced by Mahd 'Ulya's allegations.[73]
The chief reason for the delay in Amir Kabir's complete dismissal, however,
was Nasir al-Din's fear of the military repercussions that would follow. "It
was presented" to the shah, says one source, that since Amir Kabir was in
"collaboration with the army chiefs and governors of Iraq [-i 'Ajam], it was
probable that his instant dismissal might lead to mutiny."[74]

Uncertain of the extent of the premier's popularity with the troops in
the capital, the shah thus decided to retain Amir Kabir in the post of
commander in chief. But days before his dismissal, Amir Kabir seems to
have been practically deprived of the command. Homebound and with no
access to the shah, on 6 November 1851/10 Muharram 1268 he wrote
anxiously, though sardonically, to Nasir al-Din: "As for the post of *amir-(i)
nizam*, that too, like royal letters, has gradually [disappeared]. The king is
amidst the troops, but the intensity of His Majesty's favor towards the
Amir Nizam is so great, and so willing is he to receive him, that the Amir
Nizam is now sitting in his house reading the prayer of the day of 'Ashura
[day of ritual mourning for the martyrdom of Husayn, the Third Imam].
This, of course, is the reward for the hardship he endured to bring discipline
[*nazm*] to the royal army."[75] The shah was not making his presence felt
among the troops without reason. By way of precaution he stationed 400
royal guards around his palace. One may assume that by retaining Amir
Kabir in the military command, he may have been motivated by the nobler
cause of division of labor in the government. Yet his future action leaves
little doubt as to his real intention to deceive his premier.

Despite his apprehension, Nasir al-Din still seemed to be feeling deeply
toward Amir Kabir, and his dismissal came after an apparent emotional

agony in which gratitude and devotion conflicted in the shah's anguished mind with a strong desire for self-assertion. Perhaps for the first time the two sides of the young shah's complex personality came into open conflict here. Nasir al-Din's letter of 15 November to Amir Kabir is replete with remorseful expressions of guilt. It is as though he was apologizing to the premier for the fate that was about to descend upon him.

> Your excellency the Ameer Nezam! I swear by God, I swear by God, and I now write to you with the utmost truth, that I love you passionately, and may the Almighty deprive me of life if I attempt to desert you as long as I live, or if I should wish to lessen your dignity by a hairbreadth. I will treat you and behave to[ward] you in a way that not a single soul shall know what has been the matter; it will look as if you were wearied with the multiplicity of affairs, and had thrown two or three of the departments on my shoulders. All the orders and fermans, both military and civil, which formerly had to be sealed and signed by you must still continue to be sealed by you in the same manner; the only difference will be that people will now see for a short time that I myself transact the business not connected with the army. I shall not interfere in any way with the affairs of the army, but will do whatever you deem proper. Don't imagine that I will permit any person to present improper petitions to me, or that I will grant salaries and pensions, or allow the money to be squandered, as in the late shah's time. Heaven forbid it, that I should grant one farthing more than you yourself allowed, or that anyone should dare to alter a word.[76]

The shah's passionate promises seemed sincere enough to Amir Kabir to prompt a request for an audience. He hoped to mend fences with Nasir al-Din and retain his old post by appealing to the same sentiments that were expressed so affectionately in the shah's letter, by convincing the shah of his sincerity and his opponents' evil intentions, and by arousing feelings of awe and gratitude. This latter, however, was exactly the shah's reason for avoiding the intimidating presence of Amir Kabir, and his request was rejected.

Writing in a subdued tone, Amir Kabir once again tried to appeal to the shah's best intentions, this time by stressing the vital importance of the "orderly system" he had created, the very "discipline" that was the cornerstone of his reform program. "My intention was not to present to you matters that make you regret what you have intended, . . . since this slave, with or without a petition [i.e., request to see the shah], from the start was obliged by your orders and your consent. . . . Appointment, dismissal, holding an official post or not, whatever you order, as a subject I would see in it my own expediency." Not failing to allude to the "mischievous soul" (possibly a reference to Mahd 'Ulya) who advised Nasir al-Din to refuse the audience, he added, "He [or she] has not done so out of the best motives. The reason I insisted, and still do, to be received by Your Majesty is to humbly present to you a few words in person since I am familiar with the mischief, calumny, and malevolence of the people of this land. Once they fix on a pretext, they will not give up before spoiling and bringing to ruin this orderly system [*kar-i munazzam*], which is the envy of the entire world. They will ruin me, too. Not only will they ruin me, but they will undo whatever has been accomplished." It was remarkable how clearly, and tragically, Amir Kabir detected in his opponents' intentions not only his own destruction but also the demise of his discipline. Concluding on this ominous note, he pressed once more for an interview: "Rest assured, I will not for a moment insist on [altering] your edict, but it is obvious that in spite of my persistence there is no chance of an audience."[77]

Amir Kabir's moving pleas only aggravated Nasir al-Din's emotional dilemma. It was perhaps in response to the above note that through his sister, Malikzada, Nasir al-Din reaffirmed his affection for Amir Kabir, her husband, and reiterated his promises of unconditional support, though still denying the request for an audience. In conversation with Malikzada he may also have revealed some of his considerations for the dismissal. This is apparent in Amir Kabir's answer to this message, possibly written on 15 November. Here he was even more malleable and persuasive than in the first note but at the same time responsive to criticism leveled against him. Repeating his wholehearted dedication and attachment to the shah and his complete submission to the royal will, he went on to say: "You have cautioned that I should not harass people. By God, I do not know when I ever bothered, let alone oppressed or persecuted, [people]." Appealing to Nasir al-Din's devotion to him, he repeated: "Do not refrain from giving an audience to this slave. You are refraining because, from the start, I intended and still intend to [achieve] your contentment. Let me come to an audience for an hour, if you like, where the lady [Malikzada] stays. All this talk will come to an end." He then went on to stress the fallacy of his enemies' charges. "These words were presented to you to provoke you and cloud the issue. Otherwise, by God's will, I do not behave such in your service as to cause you, heaven forbid, humiliation in this world."[78]

There was as much paternal rebuke in Amir Kabir's assurance as there was filial remorse in Nasir al-Din's reply:

> I swear it by God I was ashamed to admit you today. What am I to do? Would to God I had never been [the] Shah and that it had not been in my power also to commit such an act. I swear it by God that while I

write this I weep. By the Lord, my heart yearns for you. I love you. If
you believe me not you are unjust. The Mayor [presumably Mahmud
Khan Kalantar] came and I gathered from what he said that you were
afraid how this would end. Who is the whore's son who could for an
instant speak before me in disparagement of you? I swear it by God also,
if any one should speak a disrespectful word of you, either before me, or
before others, I am a bastard if I don't throw him before the cannon's
mouth. By the Lord, I have no other intention than that you and I
should be one and both of us manage affairs. By my own head, by my
own head, if you should grieve, by the Lord, I cannot bear to see you
grieved. While you live and I live I should never forsake you.

Asserting that Amir Kabir's appointees would continue to serve and that
"all the affairs of the army" were in Amir Kabir's hands, the shah urged
that if he would not accept the new arrangement,

God and the Prophet will call you to account. As a mark of my favor I
beg to present you with a diamond-mounted sword of high value and
also the decoration I wear on my own neck. By God's will, you will accept them and come to me tomorrow. By your own orders and injunc-
tions the rations and the pay of the regiments must be issued. From
the first I wrote that I should not in any a manner interfere in the affairs
of the army. The revenue, too, will not vary in the slightest degree from
regulations which you established for it.[79]

Amir Kabir failed to sense the extent of Nasir al-Din's predicament,
which even made him wish he were not the shah. Was it that he doubted
the sincerity of the shah's effusive sentiments and felt that compliance with
the suggested demotion would seal his impending removal from office and,
possibly, his eventual destruction? Perhaps. But he may simply have found
the division of labor unacceptable and, as he indicated in his note, ruinous
to the order he had brought to the army and the administration. The
appointment on Friday, 17 November, of Mirza Aqa Khan Nuri, I'timad
al-Dawla, to the post of prime minister with the title *sadr-i a'zam*, helped
to harden attitudes on both sides. Indignant about his dismissal, which was
now definite, Amir Kabir committed the grave error of refusing to attend
the royal levee on the same day, thus giving credence to the shah's darkest
suspicions. He may even have dared to inquire about the reasons for his
dismissal, which would only have confirmed the shah's paranoid fears.[80]

Nuri's appointment was a remarkable victory for Mahd 'Ulya and, in
effect, for all the Qajar nobility. It was also a victory for Nuri and his British
protector, Justin Sheil. The queen mother managed to convince the shah
that this appointee, as opposed to any of the other candidates, would not
only guarantee the loyalty of the army (or at least large sections of it

subordinate to the ex-secretary of the army) but, more important, would provide the administrative skill necessary to replace Amir Kabir. Through Nuri, Mahd 'Ulya hoped to recover her lost hold over her son and thus safeguard her privileges as the queen mother and the brains behind the throne. As for Nasir al-Din, one may assume that Nuri's appointment was an effort above all to close the widening gap between a persuasive mother and a devoted premier. The shah may have speculated further that Nuri's strong ties with the British secured their backing for his reign, in effect nullifying any possible designs for 'Abbas Mirza. This was a definite gain for Sheil. Though there is little direct evidence to implicate him in the shah's choice of the new premier, it is quite conceivable that he welcomed the replacement of the stubborn Amir Kabir with the flexible and friendly Nuri.

All the same, the shah was cautious enough not to appoint to premiership a man with the status of a British protégé. In spite of rumors of the impending appointment circulating in Tehran, Nuri's nomination did not come before he renounced unequivocally his British protection. Under duress, kept in detention for four days, and after consultation with Sheil, who reluctantly and conditionally agreed, Nuri gave written assurances that he was "under the protection of no state but that of the shadow of the Majesty the shah of Iran may God immortalize his reign." He made this pledge, however, after asserting in the same document that: "Heaven forbid, if from this old devotee a betrayal will appear in the affairs of the state, I would be the subject of the shah's interrogation. But the humble plea of this obedient servant is that if a report is presented [against me,] it should be first investigated and after it is proven, the [appropriate punishment] be inflicted."[81] Implicit demands in this pledge for future immunity against execution (an ominous hint at what might befall the deposed Amir Kabir) met with the shah's written assurances that after his dismissal Nuri's life would never be in danger.[82]

Only after the public acknowledgment of Nuri as premier, and perhaps with his persuasion, was Amir Kabir asked to make a pledge in the same vein as Nuri's but more poignant in its terms. Securing such a pledge was meant to bind Amir Kabir, particularly in view of his past conduct, to greater compliance with the wishes of the shah, though in reality it was little more than a stratagem to extract from him an admission of guilt. He acceded to twelve demands in writing—most important, that he would be content with the position of commander in chief, would not treat court functionaries antagonistically, would recognize that Nuri and Mustawfi al-Mamalik were responsible for government accounts, would renounce all authority to appoint and dismiss or interfere in salary raises, would not interfere in foreign affairs or in the affairs of the capital, would not bar public petitions from being presented daily and directly to the shah, would not abuse or intimidate people or demand homage or some elaborate show of respect from them, and would respond quickly to the shah's autographed notes.[83]

The contents of Amir Kabir's pledge revealed the nature of the grievances voiced against the ex-premier by the growing circle of his opponents, grievances that Nuri had every reason to highlight and bring to the attention of the monarch. Notwithstanding the vengeful tone of this document, at least on the surface the new arrangement contemplated by the shah seemed rational and workable except for the peculiarity of the circumstances and the sharp differences in the attitudes of the actors involved. The triple division of the government—with domestic affairs in the care of Nuri (with some degree of autonomy for the chief accountant, Mirza Yusuf Mustawfi al-Mamalik), foreign affairs in the hands of a new minister and under the direct supervision of the shah, and the army under the control of Amir Kabir—should be seen as the first of Nasir al-Din's many attempts to restructure the machinery of the state. His intention was to prevent concentration of power in any one office and to end the destructive factional quarrels in the administration, the traditional malaise of Persian statecraft. Monarchical control of foreign affairs in particular reflected Nasir al-Din's understanding of the importance of dealing directly with powers. "As far as the affairs of the foreign states are concerned," read the Persian minister of foreign affairs' official communiqué announcing the premiership of Nuri, "His Majesty's august command asserts that all matters, great and small, should be communicated to this officeholder so that they could be presented to His Majesty the king and upon receiving replies the royal edicts be relayed. Under no circumstances shall his excellency the prime minister interfere in foreign affairs."[84]

The viability of the above arrangement was questioned by Sheil, and for good reason.[85] The gaps separating the ambitious new premier, the dismissed Amir Kabir, and the erratic shah, argued Sheil, with all appearances of a benign but pessimistic well-wisher, were too great to be bridged with official communiqués. Yet it is not hard to see the envoy's other concerns. Not only had he no wish to deal with the shah directly, but the new arrangement put Nuri beyond his direct reach. Furthermore, as far as Nuri was concerned, easy access to foreign representatives—and, by extension, the envoys' ability to make unsolicited interventions in domestic affairs—was equally compromised. All these factors were destined to play an

unfortunate role in the fate of Amir Kabir. The clashes of interest between
Nuri's party, lionized by Sheil and impatient to take over the entire
government (including the army), and the indignant Amir Kabir made the
arrangement unworkable. Witnessing the rapid decline of his authority in
the army and the swift appointment of pro-Nuri elements instead, often
through bribery or favoritism, Amir Kabir had little choice but to complain
bitterly to the shah almost immediately. "About Sadr A'zam's presentation," he wrote to Nasir al-Din in response to Nuri's criticism that as
amir-(i) nizam the deposed premier had exceeded the limits to which he
had agreed, "this humble servant has not acted without his permission, but
[Nuri's] relatives increasingly intercede on behalf of unworthy people
whom they wish to appoint to army ranks." Again reasserting "his utmost
modesty toward his excellency the Sadr A'zam," he registered his profound
indignation. "This slave is incapable of maintaining order and without
order affairs will not progress. . . . The royal decree issued yesterday must
be canceled. Otherwise everybody will get the wrong impression. The pain
kills this slave that people say: 'That order of Mirza Taqi Khan is past [an
nazm-i Mirza Taqi Khani guzasht].' I prefer death to such words."[86]

Indeed, death was not too far from the minds of conspirators lurking
around the private quarters of Gulistan Palace. The final interview between
Nasir al-Din and Amir Kabir, after several written communications and
only after Nuri's appointment, furnished the opponents of the fallen
premier with new ammunition. Even Sipihr's exaggerated version of the
interview, in which he praised the shah's sagacious replies to Amir Kabir's
proud presentation of his services, was not altogether devoid of reality.
Contrary to his earlier assurances of subdued behavior, Amir Kabir surprised the shah with reproaches. "Is it fair that instead of rewarding me the
king now prosecutes me as a criminal?" he asked. The fallen premier's
question only ignited "flames of rage" in the shah's mind. He replied: "You
are a plebeian of humble origin who took pride in the high position that
I conferred on you. Having been in power for seven generations, the Qajars
are in no need of a ra'iyat like you to put into order the foundations of their
monarchy." He further blamed his ex-atabak for what, after all, was an
effort to increase the power of the government. "And your claim that you
have removed all places of refuge [i.e., basts: sanctuaries], both religious
and royal, is indeed a major treason to religion and the state."[87] In sharp
contrast to his passionate note a few days earlier, Nasir al-Din's defiance
signified a major shift in attitude. "Mirza Taqi Khan was stunned by these
words," wrote Sipihr. "He realized that from now [on] his pretensions were

unacceptable to the king and his spell ineffective upon him. Tears ran across his face. He took the way out and returned to his own quarters."[88]

The stormy interview had grave repercussions. It gave credence to Nuri and others in the court who were advocating that Amir Kabir be removed from the army command in exchange for a provincial governorship. His removal would have allowed Nuri and his party the chance to control the sizeable force of some 100,000 regular troops and 36,000 irregulars already reorganized by Amir Kabir.[89] Moreover, it drove Amir Kabir further away from the shah and in the direction of alternative sources of protection. The circulation of rumors from the shah's quarters of a threat to Amir Kabir's life was worrisome enough to the desperate Amir Kabir to oblige him to send a message to Sheil on or about 18 November expressing his "earnest hope" that the British envoy would forget their past contentions and "allow him to take refuge in the mission should he apprehend danger from the Shah." Sheil's reply, as he reported to London, "contained an intimation of these doors being open to him whenever he thought fit to enter."[90] Needless to say, in such a petition from an erstwhile opponent Sheil saw new opportunities. The shah and his new premier, wary of these approaches, had offered Amir Kabir governorships of Fars, Isfahan, and Qum (to which 'Abbas Mirza had recently been appointed but not sent), but these offers were rejected outright. Amir Kabir refused not only because he was reluctant to quit a post that had given him power and prestige but more urgently because of his "fear of deceit and that his life might be in danger if he left Tehran."[91] In seeking assistance to resolve his "dilemma," Nuri, too, turned to the British legation. There he encountered little trouble convincing Sheil of the advisability of removing Amir Kabir from the capital. For whatever reason, Sheil failed to secure in this meeting written guarantees from Nuri for the safety of Amir Kabir should the latter opt for the provincial post.

Such assurances of safety seemed all the more necessary given the unexpected turn of events against Amir Kabir. Only a few days earlier, on 15 November, upon hearing the news of his brother's dismissal, Mirza Hasan Khan Vazir Nizam hastily took refuge in the English mission, but at the urgent request of Amir Kabir Sheil was obliged to let the frightened brother leave the premises. Still hoping to resolve his differences with the shah and stay in the capital, Amir Kabir had tried to vindicate himself and apologized in a note to the shah for his brother's action. Alluding to fickle fate as a capricious horse, he wrote, "'When it comes your way, it can be harnessed with a hair; when it rears up, it breaks all chains.'" It seemed that he was beginning to lose all hopes of his own safety. "Well!" he wrote. "It is obvious that the dictates of destiny are set on the destruction of this slave. 'The catapult of the heavens rains down cannonballs of sedition' [zi manjaniq-i falak sang-i fitna mibarad]." Explaining his urgent actions by fear of the "slanderous tongues" of his enemies, he ended on an even gloomier note: "I pray God to give me death not to see these dark redundant days. But Judgment belongs to God. I am prepared for the dictates of the heavens and the royal command." These were the outcries of a wounded soul who foresaw all too well the outcome of an extraordinary combination of intrigue, suspicion, and his own misjudgment that in the next few days was destined to end his career and soon afterward his very life. The second hemistich of the above verse, though not quoted, is equally telling, given Amir Kabir's futile attempts to take refuge in foreign missions: "How foolishly I retreat into a castle of mirrors" (man ablahana gurizam dar abgina hisar).[92]

At Nuri's request and with the shah's approval, Sheil agreed to intervene. Thus, the appointment of Amir Kabir to the governorship of Kashan, a provincial seat sometimes reserved for high-ranking statesmen and notables who had fallen from favor, was guaranteed by the British minister. Sheil's assurances to Amir Kabir that the safety of his, and his family's, life and property would be safeguarded by the British mission and that he would govern respectfully and unmolested provided an acceptable alternative to Amir Kabir's request for asylum. For a moment it seemed that the tragic course of events could be averted. The guarantee of safe passage to ousted premiers, usually a joint endeavor by the European envoys, was not unfamiliar in Qajar Iran. In 1834 Mirza 'Abdullah Amin al-Dawla, the last premier under Fath 'Ali Shah, and in 1848 Hajji Mirza Aqasi were safely sent into exile in Iraq after they pleaded with the European powers for assistance.[93] Princes of the royal family, Qajar dignitaries, and high-ranking bureaucrats, endangered by power rivalries or otherwise imperiled, had received safe passage, or sometimes full protection, from one or both missions over the years. In the case of Amir Kabir, however, his appeal for protection highlighted a sad irony, not only because he consistently fought against the missions' misuse of diplomatic privileges but also because of his policy of abolishing the institution of bast. The traditional places of refuge—the religious shrines, the royal stable and palace gates, and houses of mujtahids—had been repeatedly invaded as a result of his own orders. The foreign missions were thus the only shelter available to Amir Kabir if he wished to escape the shah's whims. The suggestion of Mirza Ya'qub, the Persian first secretary of the Russian mission, that he take refuge "in some shrine or under the roof of some [religious] dignitary" must have been a discomfiting reminder to Amir Kabir.[94]

Sheil's mediation, however, did not stem merely from humanitarian concerns, nor from his sense of self-gratification. It was vital that Amir Kabir be absent from the capital during the consolidation of Nuri's government. Moreover, protecting a deposed statesman such as Amir Kabir was desirable. It secured his future gratitude should he ever be restored to favor. It also preempted a Russian move to grant diplomatic immunity to Amir Kabir, a possibility too enticing to be missed by Sheil's Russian counterpart, Prince Dolgorouki. Sheil even received a word of encouragement from Mahd 'Ulya, who, apparently as a result of an overnight change of heart, urged the envoy "to watch over the Ameer's safety." The request probably sprang from her anxiety that if Amir Kabir were refused British shelter he might go over to the Russian side.[95] On the morning of 20 November, therefore, Joseph Dickson, the British mission's physician, was sent to Amir Kabir "to acquaint him with the arrangement which had been formed" whereby in exchange for accepting the governorship of Kashan he was given British assurances for the safety of himself and his family. "He received the announcement with joy," reported Sheil, "and I considered the matter terminated [i.e., accomplished]." As an additional precaution, Amir Kabir sent his eldest son and brother to stay in the British legation.[96]

But as Amir Kabir himself had predicted, the "cannonballs of sedition" were destined to rain on his "castle of mirrors." Merely half an hour later on the same day, the situation changed dramatically. Upon hearing the news of Amir Kabir's imminent acceptance of the British offer, Dolgorouki instructed the entire seven-member Russian legation in Tehran, "all attired in uniform" and accompanied by Cossack guards, to appear in Amir Kabir's residence and make him a counteroffer of full and unconditional diplomatic immunity, "the emperor's protection." While the Persian first secretary of the British mission, Husayn Quli Khan Navvab, was still waiting in the room, presumably for Amir Kabir's written acceptance of Sheil's arrangements, the ex-premier decided to opt for the Russian bid instead. He told the secretary, as Sheil recounted, that "he defied the Shah, that he would not go to Cashan [Kashan], that he had never intended to do so, and that he was resolved not to quit Tehran." Whether or not this was an accurate recording of Amir Kabir's words, Sheil's reaction to this news was swift: "I then intimated to the Sadr [i.e., Nuri] again that I had no more concern with the Ameer Nizam's affairs."[97] Shortly thereafter, in an exchange of notes with Dolgorouki, he asserted again that because Amir Kabir had "declared he would not proceed to Cashan, and would not quit Tehran, according to the engagement concluded, the arrangement was of course at once annulled."[98]

It is hard not to see Sheil's deep annoyance at Amir Kabir's change of heart and his apparent effort to take advantage of the Russian offer. The indignant envoy must have seen fit to call the Russian bet in the game of diplomatic prestige. In response to Nuri, who sought his advice regarding Dolgorouki's offer of protection, Sheil said "[T]he Russian minister had not the slightest title to act in this violent manner, or to confer a protection unless in his own house." He must have been particularly annoyed with the Russian envoy to advise the new premier that even "if the Persian Ministers seized the Ameer Nizam notwithstanding the presence of the Russian attaches," though Prince Dolgorouki might quit Tehran, his government would not support him.[99] Indeed, for whatever it was worth, the arrival of the entire mission, including the Cossacks, was intended to strengthen the claim that Amir Kabir's house was an extension of the adjacent Russian legation, an arrangement, thought Dolgorouki, that would preempt the shah's predictable protest. Sheil was at a loss to explain Dolgorouki's conduct, "whether to attribute it to earnest solicitation" of Amir Kabir or to the prince's "irritation in not being invited to take a share in the transaction." Detecting the motives should not have been as puzzling as Sheil suggested. Only a few days earlier the Russian envoy had complained to the shah through the minister of foreign affairs that the Sadr A'zam (i.e., Nuri), who was "a partisan of the English," never took him into consultation.[100]

Dolgorouki's erratic and often turbulent behavior, which in the past had occasionally provoked severe crises in Russo-Persian relations, stood in sharp contrast to Sheil's cool and calculating tactics. The Russian envoy's "sentiments d'humanité," to which he ascribed his altruistic motives for offering Amir Kabir protection, manifested themselves in provocative opportunism and had the effect of stirring Nasir al-Din's all too easily incitable rage. Whether he was moved by rage or by design, the shah regarded Dolgorouki's actions as a symbolic violation of royal honor. Russian Cossacks had surrounded the royal premises in the Arg (where his sister and, he claimed, his mother were in residence) while the Russian officials were offering diplomatic immunity to his own brother-in-law and ousted premier; the combination of insults was enough to outrage any Qajar who cared for royal honor, an honor particularly associated with strict preservation of the privacy of the harem. Yet the shah, who was terrified by the grave prospect of Amir Kabir's taking sanctuary in the Russian mission, must also have entertained other, less lofty, motives.

Some time later, in response to Count Nesselrode (the Russian minister of foreign affairs, who protested the murder of Amir Kabir), Nuri gave an interesting account of Nasir al-Din's gradual change of attitude toward the ex-premier and the circumstances that, in Nuri's self-serving version, led to Amir Kabir's total fall from favor:

> It was more than a year that Mirza Taqi Khan had been irking His Majesty with his exceeding arrogance and his discourteous conduct. The royal intention rested on some reduction of his authority and thus on obliging him to retain the position of the commander in chief. It is public knowledge, however, that because of intense pride he refused the post. His Majesty then offered him the governorship of Kashan so that he might stay there with his wife for a while in order to cast off his pride and accept the position of commander in chief. He again made some excuses and demonstrated hesitation in obeying the royal command. . . . The notables of this state, who were extremely incensed with Mirza Taqi Khan, went to His Majesty and presented to him that the stationing of the [Russian] attaches and Cossacks around a house in which Her Highness Mahd 'Ulya and Her Highness the shah's sister resided was totally contrary to the dignity of the state and that all the civil servants and citizens of the capital were aggravated and were about to launch a major uproar and riot. His Majesty was so infuriated that he intended at that very moment to put an end to the whole tumult by ordering Mirza Taqi Khan's punishment [*siyasat*]. I begged with His Majesty, however, and pleaded with him that I would undertake to put an end to the entire affair in a peaceful manner. His Majesty's mind thus was gradually relieved.[101]

Even though mention of Nuri's role in orchestrating the notables' honor-conscious protest was conveniently omitted, there was no exaggeration in his remark to Sheil that "if the Russian attaches had not been removed, the Shah had resolved to go in person at the head of his attachments to the Ameer's residence and cut off his head on the spot."[102]

The shah's threat of reprisal forced Dolgorouki to retreat temporarily. He ordered the Cossacks removed from Amir Kabir's residence, but not before receiving verbal assurances from Muhammad Hasan Khan Sardar Iravani, a Russian protégé in the shah's service, of the safety of the ex-premier. No doubt Sheil's advice to Nuri, laying bare Dolgorouki's improper conduct, went a long way toward discrediting his rival and in turn jeopardizing the future of Amir Kabir. "The Russian Minister's reputation has suffered by this affair," wrote Sheil with secret relish.[103]

Three hours into the evening of the same day, 20 November, Amir Kabir was arrested by the royal guards and removed from his residence. To be sure, his vacillation between the two foreign missions was a grave error of judgment. He must have thought he could maximize his gains out of the existing rivalry between the two envoys, much as he sought to do as premier in the conduct of foreign policy. He failed to realize that by declining the terms set by Sheil and opting instead for Russian protection, he not only antagonized Sheil but, far more fatally, gave the appearance of open insubordination to the shah. "Misled by promises from other sources," stated Mary Sheil, wife of the British envoy, in her memoirs, "the Ameer cast off his English protection at the very last hour and refused to depart at the time and to the place arranged. The sources [he] relied on failed him at the need, and abandoned him in a position worse than before."[104]

Next day, 21 November, Amir Kabir was stripped of all his positions, titles, and privileges. Tehran's official gazette, *Vaqayi'-i Ittifaqiya*, of the same day found this "world-embellishing royal decision expedient for the welfare of the country and the state and best for the well-being of the throne." The same publication also announced for the first time Mirza Aqa Khan Nuri's appointment as premier.[105] A note from the Persian minister of foreign affairs to the European missions quoted Nasir al-Din directly and was less ambivalent. It attributed Amir Kabir's complete disgrace to his "personal pride and erroneous conduct" and "signs of bad faith and malice that in the past, and at present, have been observed in him." Thus, "presently, no position has been assigned to him, nor is he involved in governmental affairs. He is merely one of the subjects (*ra'iyat*) of Iran."[106] The last assertion was made to remove any chance for the Russians to claim that as a member of the royal family Amir Kabir was entitled to the "emperor's protection." A few days later, the post of *amir-i nizam* was abolished altogether. The affairs of the army were to be reported by the adjutant general (*ajudan-bashi*) to Nuri, who in turn would inform the shah. Contrary to Nasir al-Din's earlier wishes, this new arrangement returned virtual control of the military to the new prime minister and made a mockery of the shah's lofty designs for division of power in the government.[107]

Dismissal and disgrace of the fallen premier could not secure his complete subordination, it appeared to the shah and his advisers, if it was not accompanied by his renunciation of all foreign protection. On the night of 21 November Sheil received a person he described as "a most confidential attendant" of Amir Kabir. The visitor brought along a curious document presumably written by the detained ex-premier "renouncing for the future all right and desire to avail himself of sanctuary in the English mission, or any English consulate."[108] Even more curious than the document was Sheil's reaction. He had no trouble believing the attendant's claim that this was "the real and anxious desire" of Amir Kabir and "most essential to his interests" and that "it had not been extorted by force or by threat."

Without hesitation the experienced diplomat signed and sealed the document, thus in effect bringing Amir Kabir a step closer to his "doomed destiny."

A similar document, when presented to Dolgorouki for his approval, met with the envoy's total refusal. Unlike Sheil, the infuriated prince, humiliated by his own earlier retreat, suspected that in all probability the ex-premier had signed the document under duress. Instead, he made it known that he had every intention of pursuing Amir Kabir's case. Although the ex-premier "was ill disposed toward Russia," Dolgorouki was reported to have written to St. Petersburg, "yet for the internal administration of the country he possessed superior qualifications." With Nuri, "an almost Englishman," in power and with "a worthless crew" surrounding the shah, he anticipated great danger ahead and even hinted at a suspension of relations with Iran. Sheil's sarcastic remark at the conclusion of his report that "this is the first time the Russian Minister has been able to discover any good quality" in Amir Kabir underscored a standard of diplomatic opportunism matched by the British minister himself.[109] Sheil, however, made an additional attempt to cover up his role in the whole affair—a role, as it turned out, in which he was blundering at best and deceitful at worst.

As a consequence of Dolgorouki's refusal to renounce any offer of protection to Amir Kabir, reported Sheil on 26 November, "no resource was left to the shah but to retain the Ameer Nizam as a prisoner." He further informed London that the ex-premier had been "conveyed as a prisoner to Cashan, where he is to live in confinement."[110] In the same dispatch to the Foreign Office, however, he enclosed for the first time an important document, which he called the "Translation of a letter the late Ameer wrote to me *before* the Russian attaches occupied his house" (emphasis added). Sheil enclosed this document in defense of measures he had undertaken in Amir Kabir's case. Yet the letter, requesting British protection, bears the date of 22 November, two days *after* the Russian offer of protection was made and a day after Sheil himself had ratified the note in which Amir Kabir renounced under duress any desire to seek British protection. This letter deserves to be quoted in full:

> Your excellency has often said that you were specially directed by the
> English government to protect the weak and oppressed. I know not this
> day in Persia a person more oppressed or more forlorn than myself. In writing these two lines to you I am at my last gasp. Not only have I been deprived of my rank and office without any crime, but from hour to hour
> I am subjected to fresh threats. The interested people who surrounded

the Shah are not content that His Majesty's anger only should fall
on me; they have so instigated the chief people of the court against me
that I have no longer any hope of the lives of myself, my family and
my brother.

I therefore throw myself, my dependents, and my brother on the protection of the British Government. I trust that you will hasten to my aid,
and that you will act toward me and my family and my brother according to the dictates of humanity and generosity and in the manner that
benefits the crown and the throne of Great Britain, and the honor of the
British Nation.

The absence of any crime on my part is distinguishable in the official
notification from the Minister of Foreign Affairs to the Foreign Minister
at this Court. I have not power to write more.[111]

Amir Kabir's desperate tone, his declaration that he was at his "last gasp,"
"forlorn," and "oppressed," that he had been "deprived of [his] rank and
office," and that he had "no longer hope" for his safety removes any
possible doubt that, contrary to Sheil's claim, this petition was sent to him
on 22 November.

One can only speculate on the circumstances behind Amir Kabir's
apparently erratic behavior or on Sheil's reasons for inaction. While under
arrest, one can conjecture, with "neither time" nor "in the condition to
write,"[112] Amir Kabir pleaded with Sheil for protection for the second time,
only to be ignored completely by the British envoy. By 22 November it was
painfully clear to the ex-premier that Dolgorouki's refusal to certify the
document had increased the shah's suspicion, and therefore he was even
more susceptible to denunciation by his enemies yet still had no guarantees
for asylum. Dolgorouki's appeal to St. Petersburg for authority to extend
diplomatic immunity to Amir Kabir further aggravated the situation,
removing any doubt in the shah's mind that if Amir Kabir were left on his
own he would defect to the Russian legation. The experience of such intense
stress upon Amir Kabir and extreme fear for his own safety brought about
a remarkable change of character, turning the powerful commander in chief
of a few weeks earlier into a meek and vulnerable man prone to obvious
errors of judgment and hasty, almost impulsive, moves. Not yet recovered
from the shock of his political and personal decline, he was confused enough
to overestimate the extent of British friendship for him. If the best of
intentions could be attributed to Sheil's refusal to give asylum, it could be
reasoned that since he had already approved of Amir Kabir's renunciation
of foreign protection, there were no grounds on which to reconsider the
case, nor would reconsideration be acceptable to the shah. No matter how
solidly such an argument could have been made in so fluid a circumstance

as the dismissal of Amir Kabir, however, there was perhaps a deeper trace of disdain, even personal vengeance, in the envoy's conduct. His motivation went beyond expediency or observation of correct diplomatic protocol. Rivalry with Dolgorouki, annoyance with Amir Kabir's vacillation, support for Nuri's government, and even the importance of preserving diplomatic prestige do not in themselves explain Sheil's failure to help Amir Kabir. But sole reliance on Sheil's account leaves much of the real story in the dark. More puzzling is the fact that his rather clumsy attempt to cover up his inaction by passing off Amir Kabir's petition of 22 November as his initial request was not noticed, or acknowledged, in London. Throughout his reports on the fall of Amir Kabir, Sheil consistently refrained from presenting the whole picture, a course of action out of character for such a seasoned diplomat. His selective treatment, under the pretext of not wishing to "fatigue" Lord Palmerston with details, points at a cover-up either to conceal a course of action reprehensible to London or, even worse, a serious blunder contrary to London's instructions.[113]

One cannot help concluding that the moving and gloomy picture depicted by Mary Sheil of the "melancholic" scene of Amir Kabir's departure for exile in Kashan was somewhat the result of a bad conscience for what her husband had failed to accomplish. Nor was her approach "within a few yards" of Amir Kabir's party while she was horseback riding outside Tehran's city walls quite as "unexpected" as she made it seem. Sheil's decision to ignore Amir Kabir's request must have been known to his wife, and her description leaves little doubt as to the real sentiments of this Victorian woman or her silent rebuke for her husband's deed. "It was the Ameer and the princess," recalls Mary Sheil with an obviously tormented tone. "They were both in a *takhterewan* [horse-mounted palanquin], surrounded by guards. It seemed to me like a funeral procession, and I have seldom beheld a more melancholy sight. I longed to open the carefully closed *takhterewan*, and to take the doomed Ameer and his poor young wife with their two infant children into the carriage, and to drive off with them to Mission-house."[114]

KILLING THE ATABAK

"I may as well anticipate his fate," wrote Mary Sheil when she last saw Amir Kabir on his way into an exile that lasted only forty days.[115] The shah's *farman* gave detailed instructions to the accompanying guards on the treatment of the prisoner and his family. To prevent an attempt to defect to the Russian mission, strict security measures were applied, but "at all times" the guards were cautioned "to behave with courtesy and dignity." Wherever the roads were impassable to the royal coach, Amir Kabir was permitted to ride "a tame, slow-going horse with gold-trimmed bridle and good quality saddle but without [wearing] a pistol, a sword, or [other] weapons." In Kashan, the prisoner was permitted to stroll in the garden and in the surrounding countryside, but only on foot and accompanied by guards, who were to behave "with utmost respect." All necessary servants were to be employed, provided their numbers did not exceed 100, and all were warned that should they ever convey messages or other communications from the exiles, they would be punished and imprisoned. Amir Kabir was permitted no correspondence except with the new premier, and then only in emergency cases. The decree specifically and repeatedly warned off the guards from intruding into Amir Kabir's inner house, stressing the family's isolation and the severing of all communications. "Whatever riding horses are available should be under the charge of the head groom. Neither themselves nor their servants are permitted to ride."[116]

Such precautionary measures reflected Nasir al-Din's anxiety but, at least on the surface, did not betray any designs to destroy or even mistreat Amir Kabir. Although the shah was ambivalent toward his *atabak*, the presence of his own sister obliged Nasir al-Din to behave with civility and moderation. Malikzada's remarkable loyalty to her husband and her determination to accompany him into exile despite apparent pressure from Mahd 'Ulya must have put her brother into an uneasy moral predicament. Yet neither Amir Kabir nor his young wife felt secure in their exile, and for good reason. Soon after their arrival they became the targets of harassment by the guards and other vengeful officials who found an occasion to square old accounts. During forty days in Kashan Amir Kabir seldom ventured out of his house, except once a day in order to report to the guards.[117] Moreover, "as a security against poison, that exemplary lady [i.e., Malikzada] made it a rule to partake first all the food presented to Ameer."[118]

In Tehran the question of Amir Kabir's future was yet to be settled. His shadow loomed large across the court and over the government. Nuri's government, less than a month in power, had performed dismally. There was rampant corruption and nepotism from the start, governmental positions were sold, and the overall mismanagement stood in sharp contrast with Amir Kabir's "orderly system," perhaps even in the mind of Nasir al-Din himself. The idea that Amir Kabir might be restored to power looked realistic enough to Sheil that he reported it to London.[119] It is unlikely that

Nasir al-Din ever shared the British envoy's projection. On the contrary, conscious of Nuri's difficulties and of the Russian hostility toward him, the shah tried to consolidate his administration by delegating to the premier more extensive powers; subsequently he was allowed to dismiss and appoint officials and provincial governors, even banish troublesome elements in the palace, including the shah's own mother. With Nuri in power, the anti–Amir Kabir alliance was about to crumble. Evidently the new premier was too busy monopolizing all positions of power for himself and his clan to be able to gratify Mahd 'Ulya's ambitions for power. The shah's fear of failure without Amir Kabir was clear in a cautionary note to Nuri: "With such authorities, should [you] fail to perform properly, [you] should be replaced by a more competent person."[120]

Yet even the remote possibility that Amir Kabir would be restored to power was enough to keep alive the scheme for his total elimination. Dolgorouki's boastful pronouncements that soon he would grant protection to the ex-premier and secure his freedom magnified, in the shah's already poisoned mind, as well as in the minds of Nuri and other conspirators, the dangers of clemency. Displaying his usual frantic temperament, Dolgorouki impatiently awaited the arrival of the tsar's request for a royal pardon, which he hoped would be viewed in Tehran as the ultimate success on the part of the Russian envoy. Nuri observed in his abovementioned response to Nesselrode the excitement caused by Dolgorouki's promises:

> Every day he [Dolgorouki] spreads rumors that soon His Majesty the emperor [tsar] will take Mirza Taqi Khan under his own shelter. The enemies of Mirza Taqi Khan took advantage of the [Russian] minister's words and every day placed new apprehensions in His Majesty's mind. The young shah was anxious that Mirza Taqi Khan's affairs may turn out to be similar to [the affairs of] Prince Bahman Mirza and he, too, would take refuge with that government [i.e., Russia]. Then the Russian authorities would insist that he should take the shah's only sister, together with all the property and jewels, with him and defect to Russian territory and delegate all the [crown] properties of Azarbaijan to the authority of the Russian consul. . . . Thenceforth, to put his own mind, and the mind of all the notables of this state, at rest His Majesty completely gave up on him [*bi-kulli az u chashm pushidand*].[121]

Nuri's interpretation of Nasir al-Din's motive was as far-fetched as his euphemism for Amir Kabir's execution. Had it not been for Dolgorouki's intrusion, he concluded with blatant hypocrisy, Amir Kabir "would have ruled as governor of Kashan for a few months and by now he would have been restored in his post and never would the affair have reached such an end. God forgive Knaiz [Russian for Count] Dolgorouki who over the past seven years ruined most notables of this country either by way of friendship or enmity."[122]

It is true that the envoy's action considerably dimmed Amir Kabir's chances for survival. But Dolgorouki's mishandling of the sensitive diplomatic situation and the courtiers' machinations aside, the shah's decision to eliminate his *atabak* was rooted at a deeper level. There is little doubt that his emotional insecurities and suspicions persuaded him eventually to side with his mother and eliminate his fatherly minister and guardian. "Although the shah's companions only aimed to remove the Amir from office and send him away," believes one observer, "the shah was so scared that he could not stop there, and until he murdered him he could not sleep well at night."[123]

Killing the first premier, who in this case was very much the kingmaker and the *atabak*, was not out of character within the tradition of kingship inherited by most Islamic dynasties since early Abbasid times. There were enough examples of executed ministers to establish a pattern sanctioned by the political culture. The sacrifice of the guardian-vizier, brutal though it was, served for many young rulers as a rite of passage for entry into the world of political adulthood, an action to reassert the king's independence. All through the history of Islamic Iran, as well as in the Ottoman Empire, recurring struggles between the kings and their ministers for a greater share of power were intensified by rivalry among bureaucratic factions and caused numerous casualties among the vizier ranks. One can trace striking parallels in the circumstances that led to the fall and destruction of numerous ministers and their parties. Among the most well known are the celebrated house of Barmak (between 799–803) in the early Abbasid era; Abu-'Ali Hasan Mikail, better known as Hasanak (d. 1031), under the Ghaznavids; 'Amid al-Mulk Kunduri (d. 1063) under the Saljuqs; Shams al-Din Sahib Divan Juvayni (d. 1284) and Rashid al-Din Fazlullah Hamadani (d. 1318) under the Ilkhanids; and, later, Murshid Quli Ustajlu (d. 1588) and Mirza Muhammad Taqi I'timad al-Dawla, better known as Saru Taqi (d. 1645), under the Safavids. The case of Murshid Quli Khan, executed at the start of 'Abbas I's reign (1588–1629), was typical of the fate of guardians (*lalas*) who reared their royal pupils as puppets on the throne, only to become their ultimate victims.[124] One cannot help speculating that Nasir al-Din's knowledge of the life of the Safavid ruler, the most celebrated shah in Persian history since Khusraw I, Anushiravan (531–579), may have contributed to his determination to end Amir Kabir's domination as mentor. Ironically, Amir Kabir exhorted Nasir al-Din to act confidently, like young Safavid shahs at the outset of their reigns. Nasir al-Din's own interest in the history of past dynasties may very well have contributed to his emulation of assertive, though ruthless, role models.[125]

Aside from early historical examples, in the Qajar period there were two striking cases of execution of ministers. Hajji Ibrahim Khan I'timad al-Dawla Shirazi, one-time mayor (*kalantar*) of Shiraz and later the powerful premier under Aqa Muhammad Khan and during the early years of Fath 'Ali Shah, was brutally put to death, together with most of his ranking relatives, in 1800 at the outset of the latter's reign. I'timad al-Dawla's contribution to the consolidation of the Qajar throne was as great as was his monopoly over the Qajar administration.[126] Like Amir Kabir, he fell victim to the shah's sensitivity on the question of succession, a fate that came to be shared with Muhammad Shah's first prime minister, Mirza Abul-Qasim Qa'im Maqam. The cruel method by which I'timad al-Dawla was executed—he was blinded and had his tongue cut off before being sent to the executioner a few weeks later—demonstrated not only the depth of Fath 'Ali's fears but also his intention to demonstrate his total command over the life of his vizier and the institution of the vizierate. Though Mirza Abul Qasim Qa'im Maqam, the first *atabak-i a'zam* and Amir Kabir's patron, was murdered in secret, his family was subjected to the same ruination as I'timad al-Dawla's. Unlike the case of Fath 'Ali Shah, however, Muhammad Shah's elimination of Qa'im Maqam did not result in the creation of a more assertive shah; rather, it led to a long period of paraministership by another guardian-minister, Hajji Mirza Aqasi. In this respect, Nuri's seven-year term of office after Amir Kabir resembled Aqasi's tenure. Like several ministers under Fath 'Ali Shah, Aqasi preferred never to assume the title of premiership (*sidarat*) lest he ultimately fall victim to it. Nasir al-Din, like his predecessors, replaced his capable but independent-minded prime minister with one who was more flexible and, he thought, more easily governable. Yet Nuri's seven-year term proved even more stormy than those of his predecessors.

The fact that there was precedent from both the remote and recent Persian past for executing ministers was not a sufficient motive to carry out a "viziercide," but such precedent was necessary to justify it somewhat for the shah and his like-minded courtiers. The order to execute Amir Kabir finally came at a time when the shah was fully embroiled in anxiety over the future of his throne. Interested parties of the court provoked memories of his childhood, when his very survival was almost compromised by the choice of Bahman Mirza, and they further aroused his antipathy for his half-brother, 'Abbas Mirza. That Nasir al-Din ultimately sided with his mother—that is, for the court, the harem, and the nobility and against the government administration—accentuates his emotional desperation in an environment of intrigue and betrayal. Amir Kabir was no longer a soothing fatherly figure to him once the disturbing shadow of foreign protection was cast over the dismissed premier, threatening, Nasir al-Din thought, his very throne. His siding with his mother after much inner struggling may indicate an Oedipal bent in his personality. If, however, this was a political patricide meant to liberate Nasir al-Din from the tutelage of a father-guardian, it only made him the captive of another father figure in the person of Nuri.

No doubt the shah was under great pressure from his mother and others to put an end to the affair of Amir Kabir. Although he had already twice issued, then canceled, Amir Kabir's death warrant, by 13 January 1852 he was ready to act. The shah's autograph note informed 'Ali Khan, the chief of the royal outer servant (farrash-bashi) and Amir Kabir's old protégé turned enemy, that he had been "designated to go to Fin of Kashan and relieve Mirza Taqi Khan." In accomplishing this mission, promised the royal command, "he shall be honored among [his] peers" and should be confident of the shah's "imperial benevolence."[127] The order was carried out with exceptional speed, for Amir Kabir's enemies in the court feared the shah might change his mind. Heading a small contingent of royal farrashes, 'Ali Khan arrived in Fin in great haste to play fate's last trick on the fallen Atabak. Amir Kabir was reportedly led to believe that 'Ali Khan was carrying the royal autograph announcing the end of his exile and even his reinstatement in office. It was apparently in anticipation of the good tidings that he entered the bathhouse of the Fin royal garden to prepare himself, as was customary, for the receipt of the royal robe of honor (khil'at). Instead, a prolonged and agonizing death awaited him. He was suffocated with a bath towel thrust into his throat after he had bled for several hours from opened veins in his hands and feet. The stratagem was apparently a precaution against any last-minute resistance, but Amir Kabir seems to have accepted his cruel end with dignity. His wife was only informed afterward.[128]

The "letter of remonstrance" prepared by Sheil arrived too late to save Amir Kabir's life. He blamed Nuri for the fatal delay. Though the new prime minister had promised the envoy to give timely notice of any danger, he did not do so until some hours after the executioner's departure from the capital. Strenuously denying his involvement, Nuri maintained that had he "expostulated with the shah," his own life would have been threatened. The British minister could not "exonerate" the prime minister from "connivance in the tragedy," but its principal instigator he considered to be Mahd 'Ulya. He did not regard the shah as equally blameworthy. "His youth, and the pernicious influence of his mother, [w]ere considered an extenuation of his unworthy treatment of a man who had conferred so many benefits on him."[129]

Sheil's explanation did not satisfy Lord Malmesbury, the foreign secretary of the new Liberal government, which came to power shortly before the news reached London. Nor did Sheil's earlier letter of remonstrance reflect adequately the new British government's repugnance with Nasir al-Din's senseless act. Malmesbury's own letter, addressed to Sheil but meant for the shah through his minister of foreign affairs, was perhaps one of the harshest ever written in the history of Anglo-Persian relations and laid the blame squarely on the shah. To ensure that the contents of the letter would be delivered verbatim to the shah, the British foreign minister went to the trouble of having it translated and transliterated into Persian in London. Such a practice reflected not only Malmesbury's indignation toward the shah but also his lack of confidence in the dependability of the British envoy. "Her Majesty's Government," he wrote, "have learnt the particulars of that shameful and barbarous transaction with feelings of the utmost horror and indignation, and those feelings are increased by the consideration that at the very time when the Ameer-i-Nizam was so treacherously put to death, he was in possession of the most solemn assurances under the Shah's own hand that no violence whatever should be inflicted on his person." Choosing not to elaborate on "the dishonour which must attach to the Shah in the estimation of all civilized governments on account of the perfidy and cruelty of which the Ameer has been the victim," Malmesbury continued, he felt obliged to point out that the shah "will form a very erroneous estimate of the sentiments of the British Government if he supposes that the commission of this enormous crime will not tend most essentially to weaken the sentiments of good will which the British Government has hitherto entertained for that of Persia." Sheil was instructed to "warn the Persian Government that if this cruel murder of the late Prime Minister should be followed up by other crimes of the like nature, the British Government will have seriously to consider whether it is compatible with the honour of the British crown or consistent with the duties of England as a civilized nation, that a British minister should reside in a country where he may be exposed to witness the commission of acts so revolting to humanity."[130] It is difficult to sense from the tone of the letter whether the new British foreign minister was aware of the extent of Sheil's involvement in "acts so revolting to humanity."

The Russian protest, relayed by Nesselrode himself to the Persian minister in St. Petersburg, was not as acerbic, but it was potent enough to generate a written defense from Nuri. In a conversation with Sir Hamilton Seymour, the British ambassador to St. Petersburg, the tsar himself commented on Amir Kabir's execution. He assured Seymour that he had expressed to the Persian envoy to his court "the indignation and horror" with which he heard of "the murder of the Shah's late minister." He further stressed that this was not "favorable" to his government; quite the contrary, the murder was "an act of despotiocity [sic]," and he had asked the Persian envoy to convey to his master these feelings, which "must be shared by every honest man." The tsar then garnished his remonstrance with a disdainful remark about the Persian character. "After all," he told Seymour, "the Persians are such a people who have neither faith nor law" (*Enfin, Les Persans ce sont des Gens qui n'ont ni foi ni Loi*).[131]

Nasir al-Din probably did not expect the British protest. He must have been led to believe by Nuri that once he secured the consent of the British envoy to prohibit Amir Kabir from taking refuge in the British legation he could do as he saw fit with his deposed minister if the security of his crown were threatened. Even less did he, or Nuri, anticipate the publicity the murder of the minister received in the European press. The Persian chargé d'affaires in London, Mirza Shafi' Khan, reporting on the condemnation of the execution in the British papers as an act contrary to the norms of civilization, found its impact on the public "difficult to combat."[132] The fate of Amir Kabir, as R. G. Watson observed, excited "greatest horror throughout Europe" and "indignant protests and remonstrances" directed toward the shah.[133] Neither official condemnation nor negative publicity seemed to have affected the unremorseful Nasir al-Din, who regarded it a divinely bestowed prerogative to execute his plebeian servant on suspicion of treason. Yet the official reply to Malmesbury reflected slight apprehension, if not embarrassment, while laying the blame on Russian mischief-making. The shah's response to Mirza Shafi''s report to the Foreign Office, however, was more open in admitting responsibility for the execution. The report switches to the first person as the Persian minister of foreign affairs quotes the shah directly on his reasons for the execution:

Mirza Taqi Khan was of ignoble birth [*gada-zada bud*]. His Majesty the late shah favored him and cast his affection upon him and appointed him to the post of secretary of the army of the government of Iran. After we departed from Azarbaijan for the capital we promoted him to the First Person and invested in him all the responsibilities and authorities [of the state] to the extent that never before had there emerged in Iran a minister and a guardian of such power. So long as traces of servitude were apparent in his conduct, we, too, multiplied our royal favor, until the intensity of his pride and arrogance gradually made him disregard the royal decrees. He had such fallacious intentions in his mind—intentions that no one was aware of but myself and are not fit to be recorded here—that I had no choice but to dismiss him.

After giving an account of Amir Kabir's dismissal, his refusal to cooperate in spite of having been granted "a decoration and an ornamented sword" while out of favor, and his being placed in the royal levee next to the prime minister, the report then refers to the deposed minister's intention to seek Russian protection. "This move, that in spite of royal favor he [Amir Kabir] should feel content to betray the dignity of the state and to call for Russian Cossacks to enter a place where the mother and sister of the shah resided, left an extremely unfavorable impression on the royal mind. [It was thus ordered] that at any cost, it should be stopped." He was exiled to Kashan because of his "evil intentions." "There," the report concludes with an innocent understatement, "with God's blessing he departed from this world. Under such circumstances and with the mischief that he committed—known to Colonel Sheil from beginning to end—no future criticism can be made concerning the civility [literally, *sivilizasiun*, from French "civilisation"] of this state."[134]

For domestic consumption, however, the execution of Amir Kabir was denied altogether. The *Vaqayi'-i Ittifaqiya* of 16 January, six days after his death, notified readers that "Mirza Taqi Khan does not feel well. His face and his feet, up to his knees, are swollen."[135] Two issues later, on 30 January 1852, the same official gazette announced in a small notice: "On Saturday, 18 Rabi' al-Awwal, Mirza Taqi Khan, who previously was the commander in chief and the First Person of this government, died in Kashan."[136] Following the example set by the official gazette, all through the Nasiri period the Qajar chroniclers, with few exceptions, diagnosed imaginary ailments as causes of Amir Kabir's death, perhaps in part based on his actual deteriorating health, to cover up an open secret.[137] Yet in spite of the official denial, even prior to his execution rumors about Amir Kabir's impending death were in circulation.

After his death, the immediate deterioration in the affairs of the government under Nuri was too conspicuous to be missed by the watchful public hoping to see a change for the better after Amir Kabir's harsh rule.

"The Ameer's measures," according to one source, "were distrustful to so many persons, that the Shah was compelled to listen to the cry of discontent." Yet soon after his elimination the country's return to familiar disarray was so swift that "the Persian king, as well as many of his subjects, became sensible to the irreplaceable loss their country had sustained." Watson, an early admirer of Amir Kabir (with access to the British correspondence as secretary of the British mission), found it gratifying to record a popular belief, in circulation as early as the 1860s, that the remorseful shah, "in his grief [over the execution of Amir Kabir], resolves to observe each anniversary of the Ameer's death as a day of fasting and humiliation."[138] Other early European accounts by Richard and Mary Sheil, Gobineau, and Polak, all praising Amir Kabir, were also influenced by memories of the slain minister. A blend of fact and fiction soon created a halo of sanctity around his image, paying full tribute to his qualities of statesmanship and patriotism.

It is difficult to gauge the long-term impact of Amir Kabir's murder on Nasir al-Din. Little hard evidence can be found purporting any serious change of opinion on the part of the shah either concerning the man of "ignoble birth" or the fairness of the treatment he received. Brief moments of nostalgia, even bouts of remorse, for the Atabak surfaced in the shah's travelogue or were depicted in a hurried sketch. In his 1892 tour of the central provinces, for instance, when Nasir al-Din reached Hazava in the Farahan district, the birthplace of Amir Kabir, he ordered surviving relatives of his old Atabak to be brought into his presence, perhaps more from curiosity than gratitude.[139] On another occasion he drew a sketch of Amir Kabir for publication in I'timad al-Saltana's Mir'at al-Buldan (see Pl. 9).[140] It has also been reported that in order to make friends with Amir Kabir's two young daughters, his own nieces, Nasir al-Din used to bring them toys. The children, who were brought up hating their uncle, returned the kindness by calling him the murderer of their father.[141]

The more permanent impact on Nasir al-Din, however, may be traced in the manner of Nuri's dismissal seven years later and the treatment he received from the shah afterwards. Moreover, the sense of distrust he reserved for high-ranking statesmen with reform programs restrictive of the shah's authority haunted him for the rest of his life. Perhaps the greatest long-term effect of the execution on Nasir al-Din's reign was that it removed the chance of establishing a strong state with an efficient bureaucracy and a strong military. Yearning for a strong government was no doubt rooted in the earlier Qajar administrations and the premiers' common desire to curb the shah's powers in favor of a strong vizierate.

Amir Kabir's vision of government, however, was far more conscious of such modern notions as state-sponsored reforms, material improvement, and institutional discipline (*nazm*), characteristics peculiar to all modernizing regimes of the Middle East in the late nineteenth and early twentieth centuries. Though Persian society and state differed from the Ottoman Empire and Egypt—indeed, Amir Kabir's intended reforms were peculiar to himself—in principle he stood in the same league with the men of the Tanzimat in the Ottoman Empire and even closer in his modernizing aspirations with Muhammad 'Ali in Egypt. Middle Eastern parallels notwithstanding, Amir Kabir's vision of reform was also not untouched by changes in Russia. His 1829 visit to St. Petersburg must have given the intelligent and receptive Amir Kabir a fair picture of administrative and military reforms on the European model first undertaken by Peter the Great.

Yet neither Peter nor Muhammad 'Ali was restrained by the limitations imposed on reformers in Iran. Amir Kabir was not a ruler but a minister in charge of the shah's government. During his term in office he suffered from the most common weakness of the ministers vis-à-vis the rulers—lack of an independent and reliable power base. In the case of Amir Kabir, his plebeian origin made him even more dependent on the shah's favor and vulnerable to his whims. The relative ease with which he was removed from office and then eliminated proved the dangers of reliance on the good wishes of the shah and against the interests of the ruling elite. The removal of Amir Kabir above all secured the survival of the imperiled Qajar establishment and continuity of the status quo for the coming decades. Not only did the court and the nobility remain intact with their status and privileges preserved, but the associated urban groups—the high-ranking 'ulama, the tribal khans, and the conservative bureaucratic class—did as well. Nasir al-Din opted for the old establishment against the strong man of the New Army not only because he was pressured to do so but also because the conventional wisdom of government ingrained in his political upbringing made him wary of the hazards of change.

As much as Amir Kabir was able to implement his policies, it may be argued, he did create a momentum that secured the survival of the Qajar political system for another half a century, above all by reorganizing and expanding the army and reforming some aspects of government finance and fiscal practices. Both of these policies continued under Nuri and later, but with modifications. His successor lacked the discipline and organization Amir Kabir so avidly cared to preserve. Nuri's foreign policy proved to be even a greater failure than Amir Kabir's had been. Amir Kabir's two other major contributions, the Dar al-Funun polytechnic and the official government gazette, *Vaqayi' Ittifaqiya,* survived him, but with the same haphazardness with which most European innovations were treated during the Nasiri period.

In his own time, Amir Kabir's heavy-handed treatment of religious and political dissent eliminated avenues of change other than the ones he introduced himself. The Babi movement, a religious current with a conscious message of renewal and a broad grassroots basis, was isolated as a heretical revolt threatening the very foundations of the state and the established religion. With its political defeat, it may be argued, chances for an indigenous movement of change ceased to exist for decades to come, and Amir Kabir inadvertently cleared the way for the consolidation of the high 'ulama for the rest of the century and beyond. The embryonic experimentation with the council of the republic could not last under the weight of Amir Kabir's regime either. He probably looked upon such innovations with the same suspicion with which he viewed the Babi heretics: as deviations from the norms of correct and assertive authority.

Finally, the role of the foreign powers, and especially their representatives, in the downfall of Amir Kabir was highly questionable. Their actions on both sides, British and Russian, were determined by a jealous yet often senseless rivalry. Sheil's role was particularly puzzling.

With the collapse of the reform-minded statesman, and in the absence of any other viable organ of fundamental change, the traditional components of the status quo were reasserted. As far as the Qajar establishment was concerned, the powerful Atabak had outlived his purpose once the pillars of the throne were sufficiently strengthened. Yet even a Qajar prince such as Farhad Mirza, a potential beneficiary of Amir Kabir's downfall, was not altogether ignorant of the magnitude of the premier's loss to the future of Iran. As early as 1852/1268 he composed an epigram on the occasion of Amir Kabir's death that read: "He served" (*khidmat kard*). He also quoted two other epigrams perhaps reflective of the desolate mood of some unknown admirers: "Where is Amir Nizam?" (*ku amir-i nizam*) asked one. The second one echoed an answer: "A great man perished" (*mard-i buzurgi tamam shud*).[142]

Plate 1. Aqa Muhammad Khan Qajar in 1210 Q./1794–1795. Painting by a contemporary Persian artist. (M. 'A. Karimzada Tabrizi, *Ahval va Athar-i Naqqashan-i Qadim-i Iran va Barkhi az Mashahir-i Nigargar-i Hind va 'Us-mani*, II, 1029, pl. 119.)

Plate 2. Fath 'Ali Shah Qajar in 1800s. Painting by Mihr 'Ali Isfahani. (Averey, Hambly, and Melville, eds., *Cambridge History of
Iran*, VII, pl. 65 [B. Robinson].)

Plate 3.   Muhammad Shah Qajar in early 1840s. Watercolor by Colonel F. Colombari. (L. Thornton, *Images de Perse: Le Voyage du Colonel F. Colombari a la cour du Chah de Perse de 1833 a 1848*, 10, pl. 6.)

Plate 4.   Malik Jahan Mahd ʿUlya in a late 1860s photograph. (I. Afshar, *Ganjina-yi ʿAksha-yi Iran* [Tehran, 1992], 202.)

Though to the end of her life she maintained a rarely disputed sway over the shah's harem, her influence over the shah himself waned in later years. Her death in 1873 nonetheless was a turning point in Nasir al-Din's life, liberating him from the entanglements of a complex relationship with his dominant mother. No woman of the Qajar era demonstrated more fully than she a desire for empowerment, and to her the Qajar nobility was indebted for its sustenance through the early years of Nasir al-Din's reign. An accomplished and cunning woman of some political gifts, strong personality, and family pride, she best characterized the undercurrent of matriarchy in the Qajar elite.

Plate 5.   Nasir al-Din Mirza in 1844 in Tehran. Drawing by Mme. Labat.
(Thornton, *Images*, 18, pl. 23.)

Plate 6. Janshah flying on the back of a fabulous bird. True to the fairy-tale imagination of Nasir al-Din's adolescence, the artist depicted the young crown prince in the garb of an adventurous and amorous prince from *One Thousand and One Nights*. (Watercolor by Abul-Hasan Ghaffari, Sani' al-Mulk. *Hizar u Yak Shab* in Atabay, *Fihrist* II, no. 65.)

Other illustrations from this magnificent seven-volume manuscript—perhaps the most important example of book illumination in the Qajar era—allude to scenes from Nasir al-Din's early life and to personalities and places of his time. Sani' al-Mulk's effort to present the ancient tales in contemporary garb may have been influenced by Nasir al-Din's keen interest in painting and possibly his supervision. Under Sani' al-Mulk's directorship the royal workshops (Dar al-Sanayi'), where this manuscript was produced, thrived as a center for Persian artistic continuity and innovation.

Plate 7. Nasir al-Din Shah, 1266 Q./1850. The painting in the background
probably depicts a Napoleonic battle. Painting by Mubarak ibn Mahmud Mirza.
(Habsburg and Feldman, *Islamic Works of Art*, no. 112.)

Plate 8. In full regalia and wearing the Kayanid crown, Nasir al-Din Shah, in this 1277 Q./1860 drawing by Sani' al-Mulk in the official gazette, conveys to the public an image of power and splendor, attesting to his taking the reins of power.

The account of "the conditions pertaining to His Majesty's blessed person, may God immortalize his kingdom and his reign," which heads the "domestic reports of the Guarded Domains" is typical of the prosaic court news reported in the government gazette. It is also a specimen of the ornate style of the time: "The firmness and health of His Majesty's glowing temper—which is the chief desire of all peoples and the ultimate wish of all his servants and chattels— praise be to God, is in order. Since these days because of the exceeding cold a sojourn in the summer resorts was no longer advisable, the white ray of the majestic opinion was inclined toward royal return to the seat of the grand caliphate [i.e. Tehran]. Yet taking into account that it was the end of the month of Safar, His Majesty preferred to stay until the beginning of the month of Rabi' al-Awwal in the outskirts of the capital, in a place more temperate in climate than the summer resorts'. Thus, on the 23rd of this month His Majesty descended upon the village of Kan which, because of its sunken location in the midst of surrounding mountains, has a warm climate, and His Majesty will stay in that aforementioned village for a few days. Here the courier who had arrived from Marv to convey the news and good tidings of the victorious armies received the honor of visiting the dust of His Majesty's feet [i.e., he was granted an audience]. In the morning His Majesty spent his blessed time reading reports and uttering their responses, and it was here too that the conclusive commands were issued and the bonus and robe of honor were granted [to the courier for the chiefs of the Marv campaign] and he was sent back." (Government of Iran, *Ruznama-yi Dawlat-i 'Alliya-yi Iran* no. 473, 26 Safar 1277 Q./ 25 Aug. 1860.)

Plate 9.   Mirza Taqi Khan Amin Kabir, based on a sketch by Nasir al-Din Shah for the centennial history of the Qajar dynasty. The caption reads: "Portrait of the late grand Atabak Mirza Taqi Khan Farahani, the prime minister of the sublime state of Iran." The entry on the opposite page reads: "Also in 18 Rabi' al-Awwal of this year, which is 1268 [Q./ 10 January 1852], Mirza Taqi Khan, who previously was the Amir Nizam and the First Person of this eternally ordered state, died in Kashan." Muhammad Hasan Khan I'timad al-Saltana. (*Mir'at al-Buldan-i Nasiri*, II [Tehran, 1294 Q./1877], 99–100.)

The brief entry is typical of the Qajar chroniclers' attempts to discount the gravity of Amir Kabir's downfall and to cover up his secret execution. "Eternally ordered state" (*dawlat-i abad intizam*) may be an allusion to Amir Kabir's endeavor to institute "order" (*nazm*) in the affairs of state. The author must have felt it necessary to add the phrase to underscore the endurance of the shah's reign without denying (albeit implicitly) Amir Kabir's contributions. The sketch, made some twenty-five years after the fall of the premier, may have relied less on the shah's memory than on the oil portrait by Muhammad Ibrahim Naqqash-bashi commissioned by the shah in 1849 (now in the Tehran Museum of Decorative Arts). He is wearing the pearl-tasseled, mink-bordered kashmir robe (*jubba*) of a premier and a medallion adorned with Nasir al-Din Shah's portrait, a symbol of his elevated position but also of his ultimate subservience to the crown. (Princeton University Libraries, Department of Special Collections.)

Plate 10.   Mirza Aqa Khan Nuri in 1850s. Watercolor by Sani' al-Mulk. (British Library Or. 4938, F11.)

Plate 11.   Mirza Yusuf Ashtiyani, Mustawfi al-Mamalik (ca. early 1880s). Watercolor. (Habsburg and Feldman, *Islamic Works of Art*, 20.)

Plate 12.   Farrukh Khan Amin al-Dawla in 1860s. Watercolor by Sani' al-Mulk. (Isfahaniyan and Rushani, *Majmu'a-yi Asnad*, I, 6.)

Plate 13.   Mirza Malkum Khan Nazim al-Dawla in 1303 Q./1885. Watercolor.
(Government of Iran, *Sharaf* no. 53, Dhul-Hijja 1304 Q./August 1887.)

Plate 14.   A royal hunt scene in Jajrud near the capital, 1278 Q./1861. (Government of Iran, *Ruznama* no. 516, 5 Ramadan 1278 Q./14 April 1861. I, 357.)

Plate 15.   A scene of execution in Shiraz in 1861 reminiscent of the killing of
the Babis in 1852. Public scenes of retaliation (*qisas*) such as this one were
common throughout the Nasiri period, though their visual depiction in the
newspaper was rare. The condemned, a low-ranking mulla and private tutor in
Shiraz, is accused of poisoning his young pupil in retaliation for having revealed his homosexual advances. Interrogated by the prince-governor, he is
then handed to the victim's uncle before being beheaded. The fact that the condemned is a mulla attests to the Qajar's willingness to punish, when necessary,
members of the clerical class, though rarely the mujtahids. The artist's realistic
portrayal of the scene added to its public impact. (Government of Iran, *Ruznama* no. 504, 10 Jamada I 1278/19 November 1860, I, 269.)

Plate 16.   Women and the miracle of the shrine in Gilan. The event coincided
with the bread riots in the provinces during the famine of 1860–1861. (Government of Iran, *Ruznama* no. 485, 24 Sha'ban 1277 Q./March 1861, I, 132.)

The accompanying report informs the reader that shortages in the central
provinces and impassible roads during the harsh winter of 1861 caused high
prices in Rasht and other cities of Gilan. To remedy the ensuing famine the
prince governor, his minister, and the chief mujtahid of Rasht requested that
each of the city's notables provide two months' provisions and expenses for one
assigned group of starving citizens. While the relief effort was in progress, the
paper relates, a blind peasant girl miraculously regained her sight after a night
vigil in the local shrine of a female saint, a sister of the Eight Imam. This illus-
tration reveals more than mere euphoria over the miracle, however. The artist's
realistic portrayal offsets the paper's restrained tone in reporting the women's
protest against hoarding and high prices.

Plate 17. Royal levee (*salam*) in 1277 Q./1860 on the occasion of Nasir al-Din Shah's birthday. A similar levee was held for the conquest of Herat in 1856. Celebration of the shah's birthday was Nasir al-Din's innovation, probably borrowed from Europe (together with the much cherished fireworks display on that occasion). The outdoor public levees were usually held in the veranda of the Gulistan palace (though the ceremony shown is in the Niyavaran summer palace, north of Tehran). The levee was attended by the princes of the blood in royal attendance, some senior members of the 'ulama class, ministers and officials of the court and government, military chiefs, and foreign envoys. The court's chief of protocol, dressed in a ceremonial robe, stood in front of the veranda and read a customary sermon and was followed by the poet laureate who recited a panegyric in praise of the shah. Gold and silver coins, minted for the occasion, were then dispensed in small bags. In the ceremony shown Surush Isfahani's panegyric extolled the shah in the usual laudatory terms and promised him the arrival of good tidings from the Marv campaign. Yet contrary to the poet's forecast, the gloomy reports of the Persian army's dissipation in the Marv desert caused the shah much distress and humiliation. (Government of Iran, *Ruznama* no. 472, 19 Safar 1277/ 9 September 1860, I, 3–4.)

Plate 18.   Nasir al-Din Shah reviewing troops outside Tehran in November 1860. A similar review was held in Sultaniya in 1853. (Government of Iran, *Ruznama* no. 474, 18 Rabi' I 1277 Q./ 10 November 1860, I, 27.)

Plate 19.   Jacob Eduard Polak in Tehran in 1857, by Nasir al-Din Shah. The Persian caption in the shah's hand reads: "Portrait of the chief physician, Hakim Polak, the Austrian, in Tehran, Monday, 20th Dhul-Hijjat al-Haram of the year 1273 [Q./ 2 Aug. 1857], Sichqan 'Il [Turko-Mongolian calendar]." The erroneous date in the German caption—1854—was apparently added later. Drawing by Nasir al-Din Shah. (Slaby, *Bindenschild und Sonnenlowe*, pl. 6b.)

Plate 20.   Sir Charles Augustus Murray in 1850. Drawing. Maxwell. (*Murray*, facing p. 289.)

Plate 21. Sir Henry Rawlinson in 1865. (G. Rawlinson, *A Memoir*, facing p. 246.)

A renowned archaeologist, philologist, and explorer (and later president of the Royal Geographical Society) as well as a military officer, diplomat, Member of Parliament, and political observer, Rawlinson was an orientalist in the true sense of the term. His ties with Iran and his expertise in Near Eastern and Central Asian affairs gave him an unequaled authority, though his advocacy of greater cooperation with Iran periodically put him at odds with the Foreign Office. His vision of British imperial presence in the region, nonetheless, was no less intrusive. In his old age he served as the official host appointed by the British government during Nasir al-Din Shah's first visit to England in 1873.

Plate 22.   Nasir al-Din Shah on the Peacock Throne surrounded by his sons, ca. 1855, the centerpiece of the wall painting in Nizamiya (Nuri's mansion in Tehran). The first prince to the right of the shah, toward whom the royal gaze is directed, is Amir Qasim Khan, son of the shah's favorite, Jayran. First to the left of the shah is Mu'in al-Din Mirza, then the crown prince. Next to Mu'in al-Din are Muzaffar al-Din Mirza and Mas'ud Mirza (later Zill al-Sultan). The composition of the painting, the ranking and depiction of the sons, and the verses in praise of Nasir al-Din (added to the base of the throne by the painter) were reminiscent of Fath 'Ali Shah's court, which was revered by Nuri. It is probably Amir Qasim's prominent position in this painting that convinced Jayran of Nuri's support for her son's heir apparency when she was invited by the premier to visit Nizamiya in 1858. Lithograph by Sani' al-Mulk. (Iran Bastan Museum. From E. Bosworth, et al [eds.], *Qajar Iran*, 310, pl. 10 [B. Robinson], detail from the wall painting in the Iran Bastan Museum, Tehran.)

Plate 23. Muzaffar al-Din Mirza (left) and Kamran Mirza receiving robes of honor. Lithograph. (Government of Iran, *Ruznama* no. 491, 10 Dhul-Qa'da 1277 Q./ 20 June 1861, I, 172.)

Plate 24.   Mas'ud Mirza Yamin al-Dawla (later Zill al-Sultan) in 1861.
Lithograph. (Government of Iran, *Ruznama* no. 489, 10 Shawwal 1277 Q./
2 March 1861, I, 158.)

Plate 25. Gulistan palace, *andarun* quarters in 1880s. Painting. (Benjamin, *Persia*, 203.)

Plate 26. Shams al-'Imara in 1285 Q./1868. Painting by Mahmud Khan Malik al-Shu'ara. (Gulistan Museum, Tehran.)

Plate 27. Hall of Audience (Talar-i Salam) with the Peacock Throne (top left). Initially named the Sun Throne (*Takht-i Khurshid*), it later came to be known as the Peacock Throne (*Takht-i Tavus*) in vague memory of the throne of India's Mughal rulers (though it may have been named after a favorite of Fath 'Ali Shah). The original Peacock Throne, part of the spoils of Nadir Shah's Indian campaign in 1739, was destroyed in the chaos following his assassination. The Sun Throne was commissioned by Mirza Husayn Khan Sadr Isfahani for Fath 'Ali Shah and was built in Isfahan. Covered with gold and heavily studded with precious stones, it came to symbolize, especially for Western visitors, the Qajar monarchy and the opulence of its court. During Nasir al-Din's time it was the formal throne on which he often held indoor public and private levees. Painting by Mahmud Khan Malik al-Shu'ara in the 1860s. (Gulistan Museum, Tehran.)

Plate 28.   Interior of Takkiya Dawlat in 1880s. Oil painting by Kamal al-Mulk. (Gulistan Museum, Tehran.)

Plate 29.   Nasir al-Din Shah received by Queen Victoria at Windsor in 1873.
(*The Graphic, an Illustrated Weekly Newspaper*, vol. VIII, no. 187, 28 June
1873, p. 604.)

Plate 30. Nasir al-Din Shah and Malijak. (Photograph, 1880s. Postcard, c. 1910.)

Plate 31. Nasir al-Din Shah visiting Dar al-Funun in 1896. He is accompanied by Kamran Mirza. (Photograph, Khurumi collection.)

میرزا رضای کرمان که مرحوم ناصرالدین شاه طبیب بقره شهید کرد

Plate 32.   Mirza Riza Kirmani, Nasir al-Din Shah's assassin, in confinement before his execution in 1896. (Postcard, c. 1910.)

Plate 33.   Nasir al-Din Shah's casket, May 1896. The shah's public funeral, replacing the festivities arranged for his jubilee, inspired a baffling sense of destiny among his subjects. Yet the critics of his autocratic rule saw in his demise a new beginning. The "Martyr King" was mourned in the Shi'ite passion plays sponsored by the government, although Muzaffar al-Din Shah's coterie could hardly disguise their delight, having long cherished the dream of a speedy windfall. They soon found the state treasuries nearly empty, however. The funeral expenses were paid for out of the last trifles in Nasir al-Din's private chest. A royal mausoleum was constructed in 1897 adjacent to the shrine of Shah 'Abd al-'Azim, where Nasir al-Din's beloved wife Jayran was buried. (Postcard, c. 1910.)

5   A Narrow Escape

The story of Amir Kabir did not end with his death. The collapse of his regime represented something greater than the tragic fall of a grand vizier. His political legacy survived in more ways than one and was personified in none other than Nasir al-Din himself, albeit selectively. From his Atabak the young shah learned, above all, how to rule. His method of controlling the state's machinery, his treatment of political dissent, and his militaristic ethos owed as much to the Qajar political culture as to Amir Kabir's vision of a centralized state with a powerful monarch at its head. His foreign policy, too, was patterned on Amir Kabir's brinksmanship, but with important adjustments that came with age and experience. As much of a positive attitude toward modernity as is visible in Nasir al-Din may also be traced back to the early influence of Amir Kabir, but Nasir al-Din remained ambivalent and at times cynical when it came to any serious commitment to reform and development. Never in his long reign did Nasir al-Din demonstrate the vigor and commitment to change that his premier displayed in only a brief span of time. Nor did he remain above the corruption that polluted his court and government at every level. Giving way too easily to a policy of appeasement toward the Qajar elite, Nasir al-Din almost consciously invited nepotism and inefficiency. The age of Mirza Aqa Khan Nuri best characterized these ailments.

RETURN TO THE OLD WAYS

Nuri's seven-year term of office (November 1851 to August 1858) constitutes a distinct phase of the Nasiri era accentuated by an uneasy interplay among the monarch, his court, and his premier. In the same period, the development of Nasir al-Din's personality and political career also took a new turn. More conspicuously than before, the shah's restless mind and abrupt yet calculated conduct rose to the surface, breeding resentment among those who contrasted Nuri's laxity and the corruption in his government with the consistency and solemnity of Amir Kabir's. Writing on 18 January 1852, two months after Amir Kabir's dismissal and a week after his execution, Jules Richard, a Frenchman in the Persian service, noted that "government affairs have reverted to the situation of Hajji's [i.e., Aqasi's] time. Buying and selling of government bonds [*barat*] reinstituted, the payment of salaries is a struggle, [unprovided] payment orders were assigned to all provinces, and all the chaos that existed previously has now returned." With bitterness he noted the employment of unqualified teachers in the recently established polytechnic (Dar al-Funun). "If the Amir were alive, he would not have condoned this deplorable situation and prevented such improper arrangement."[1]

The report of the British envoy only confirmed Richard's pessimism. In spite of "the continuance of tranquility," Sheil observed, "the Sadr Azam appears to be unable to obtain any control over the Shah, or even to exert a proper degree of influence over his colleagues and the other officers of the court." Responding to this criticism, Nuri blamed the shah. He confided to Sheil that he was "entirely devoid of power; his recommendations to the Shah are constantly threatened by His Majesty's maternal relations, or even by the obscure officers of his household, and the Shah may be said to rule his kingdom directly, in his own power." Fearful of "severe financial embarrassments" and of "the revenue not being equal to the expenditure," the premier attributed his problems to the shah's "personal extravagance, and his propensity for wantonly augmenting the salaries of the persons who have access to his presence."[2] With Nuri failing to measure up to Sheil's expectations, the British envoy could only regret Amir Kabir's loss. "He has not displayed the ability which was anticipated, and there is a general conviction that valuable as he was, as second in authority to the late Amir Nizam, yet, that he does not possess capacity sufficient to undertake the charge and the responsibility of the First Minister." In the noticeable absence of Amir Kabir, it was clear that the shah was trying to consolidate his gains.

Mirza Nasrullah Nuri, better known as Aqa Khan (1807–1865), was a man with a personality very different from the late premier's. He stood for much that Amir Kabir had tried to change and for the same reason appealed to Nasir al-Din and his court. Though relatively young when he came to power, he represented the old school of statesmanship at its most pragmatic. A conservative-minded and shrewd maneuverer, he was heir to a family of bureaucrats who had long served the Qajars as army accountants and secretaries. His lofty demeanor, long, old-style dyed beard, ornamented robes, lavish lifestyle, and extensive household and entourage were deliberate reminders of the glorious days of Fath 'Ali Shah, when Persian statesmen were less conscious of their disadvantages and prouder of their magnificence (see Pl. 10). For Nuri, Fath 'Ali Shah was a model king to whose era he had a nostalgic attachment and yearned to return, as he sometimes revealed in his correspondence. His love of luxury, flattery, titles, decorations, and other symbolic implements of power and his elaborate ways of addressing himself and others were rooted in the same royal environment in which he had been brought up. But his special care to preserve protocol and observe hierarchical order represented the formal side. His personal charm and persuasion, his humor, his deceptive congeniality and scheming mind, and above all his unforsaken opportunism constituted the informal side of his personality.

Years of bureaucratic service and close attachment to the Qajar house had bred in Nuri a curious mixture of servitude, intimacy, and mild assertion of authority.[3] A man of "talent and spirit," as Comte de Gobineau, the first secretary of the French legation in Tehran, described him, Nuri prided himself on his "profound knowledge" of his country and the character of his countrymen. "He sleeps only for a few hours in the early hours of the morning and works all day and almost throughout the night," wrote Gobineau in 1855. "He wants to monitor everything: interior, exterior, finance, commerce, and trials. Other ministers are only nominal and of no consequence; and the Sadr 'Azam discharges their duties. He is constantly surrounded by secretaries; he issues orders, they write them in front of him, he stamps his seal, and himself hands them to couriers." To add to his busy schedule, Nuri also personally supervised his enormous wealth, partly amassed during his premiership. "He sells his own rice, silk, and wheat, and engages passionately in the business of letting his houses and collecting their rents." Finally, added Gobineau, "there is no domestic affair in Tehran or elsewhere that he does not relate an anecdote about and since he possesses a prodigious memory, and a gay spirit, and that he knows every family in the country and their adherence and relationships, he is one of the most agreeable and spirited storytellers that one can listen to."[4]

Yet such monopoly remained ransom to the shah's "extreme" favor. Nuri's charm and humor amused Nasir al-Din and boosted his self-confidence. This was the key to the premier's success. He carefully nurtured a spectacle of subservience to the shah and care for his well-being and carefully sustained it over the years with emotional and material rewards. Learning from Amir Kabir's mistake of trying to engage Nasir al-Din in earnest in the affairs of government while checking his excesses, Nuri chose a different course. He came to recognize, at the outset of his premiership, that to maintain a safe relationship with the shah, he had to gratify his master's sense of power and of pleasure. Reluctantly, he relinquished to

Nasir al-Din the conspicuous luxury of making broad decisions, hoping that he would be left alone to control the day-to-day affairs of the government. "Thank God Mirza Taqi Khan [Amir Kabir], the unblessed one, has been despatched to Hell," wrote Nuri to Nasir al-Din Shah with an exaggerated show of allegiance. "May God sacrifice the life of this devotee and the entire human race for one word of His Majesty's autograph. This slave is not Mirza Taqi Khan, having power of his own or the ambition [of having power]. Control of this devotee rests on the authority of the shah."[5] Such was the understanding between the shah and Nuri from the very beginning of his premiership. But it was obvious from the very start that such an arrangement was in trouble.

In February 1852, for instance, when the largely ceremonial minister for foreign affairs died, it was decided that Nuri's nineteen-year-old son, Davud, would be appointed to replace him. Sheil commented drily: "What the Shah's object could be, I cannot imagine, but from His Majesty's duplicity of character, it is difficult to attribute the proposal to a good motive." What appeared puzzling to Sheil was indeed an example of how, by appointing a stooge from the Nuri family, Nasir al-Din augmented the premier's power yet himself benefited because the arrangement allowed him to supervise foreign affairs directly. Even Sheil resisted so "preposterous a nomination." A compromise choice was found in Mirza Sa'id Khan Ansari (later Mu'tamin al-Mulk), "a person of intelligence, and respectability of character, without tendency either towards England or Russia." Previously an aide to Amir Kabir, Sa'id Khan had little diplomatic experience, a fact that made him a fitting complement, in his role as acting minister of foreign affairs, to Nasir al-Din and his premier.[6]

The shah's own erratic conduct and his growing sensitivity toward the British after 1852 alarmed Sheil, who on another occasion observed: "The character of the shah appears much changed of late. More than one prince of his family has told me that since the dismissal from office of the Ameer Nizam, his arrogance, and above all his deceit, are incalculable."[7] Whatever justification can be found for the envoy's criticism, the truth was that there had indeed been a change in the shah's character since Amir Kabir's time, but it was of a different nature. Over the years, distractions of all sorts—women, entertainments, outdoor excursions, and hunting—were encouraged and occasionally even sponsored by the lenient premier in hopes of keeping Nasir al-Din regularly indulged. "It is cold today. Your sacred body may get harmed," wrote Nuri with the obvious intent of dissuading the shah from attending one of the all-too-frequent military parades. "Take a couple of ladies with you to Arghuniya and have some fun ['aysh kunid]."

The premier's private summer garden north of Tehran soon became Nasir al-Din's love nest and the venue of numerous liaisons. "That place is beyond Mount Qaf. Have fun for three consecutive nights."[8] At times, Nasir al-Din was obliged even to allow his mother and sister to participate in the more benign forms of entertainment arranged by Nuri. The shah once wrote to Nuri: "Tonight the Navvab [Mahd 'Ulya] and Malikzada insisted so much that I was obliged to write. I know that it is exceedingly unscrupulous, but they say: 'Those two nights we were not present. We too want to have fun and [listen to the] tar.' Whatever way you deem fit will be done."[9]

By arranging the shah's entertainment and leisure activities Nuri functioned very much as his atabak, albeit a less exacting one than Amir Kabir. Astrologers were employed to determine the auspicious hour for every detail of the shah's daily life, even his amorous adventures. The premier could inform the shah, in response to his query, that on Friday, "the best of nights, when the moon is in conjunction with Pisces and is close to the honorable Venus which is the planet of happiness and pleasure," the auspicious royal wedding would be in order. Further, he could report to the shah that at an ominous hour he should not visit the army arsenal or order the royal tailor to make a new dress; he would instruct him to fast for a day "without anyone knowing it, even the staff of the private quarter."[10] It is no wonder, therefore, that in response to the premier's frequent complaints about possibly losing favor with the shah, he should assure Nuri: "You are my tutor [lala] and the tutor of all my children. So long as you are alive yourself and after you, your children . . . God willing, for years to come you will carry on your tutorship and premiership and never get ill."[11]

Neither the assurances of the shah nor his intimacy with Nuri should be seen as signs that there was a continual rapport between the two men. On the contrary, the familiar tensions were beginning to build up. The royal appetite for pleasure only slightly diverted the shah's attention from power, and the life of pleasure and romance in which he took such great delight was only one side of his character. A more rigorous side, that of ferocity and self-assertion, began to emerge during the same period, and the momentum created by a series of dramatic events only helped its development.

THE ASSASSINATION ATTEMPT

In the early morning of 15 August 1852 a group of Babi militants, perhaps as many as six, attacked Nasir al-Din Shah just outside the Niyavaran summer residence as he was about to set out for a shooting excursion in the valleys of northern Tehran. A few days earlier *Vaqayi'-i Ittifaqiya* had announced the royal intent: "Since the weather in Rudbar is cool and there are plenty of partridges in Ushan, His Majesty's intention is to depart during the next few days for these locations."[12] Briefly riding ahead of the royal guards and his entourage of several hundred, the shah was accompanied only by a few attendants when he was approached by some men, who while handing him a petition "loudly and with menacing gestures demanded redress for the insult done to their religion by having put their chief [i.e., the Bab] to death."[13] One of the assassins, Mirza Muhammad Nayrizi, dressed as a Lur tribesman, fired the first shot while struggling to grab the reins of the shah's horse. Another accomplice, Muhammad Sadiq Tabrizi, fired the second shot, taking the guards totally by surprise and injuring the shah. He fell off his horse, or probably was pulled off for his own protection by Mirza Yusuf Ashtiyani, the Mustawfi al-Mamalik, who happened to be close at hand. Another assassin, Mirza Fathullah Qumi, fired a third shot but was intercepted by another attendant. In the struggle that broke out with the guards now rushing to the scene, one of the attackers was killed and two others captured. "So intent was the assassin [Tabrizi] on effecting his object that he immediately drew a formidable dagger, and in spite of several desperate wounds, persisted in assailing the Shah, ripping up the entrails of one of the attendants, nor did he cease his efforts until he was slain."[14]

The shah escaped the attempt with little physical harm. One shot entered in his loins as he fell from his horse, "but the pistol being loaded with only partridge shot and a few slugs," it merely created a skin-deep wound. He may have also received slight wounds in his mouth and his thigh.[15] The shah's physician, Ernest Cloquet, assured the British envoy that there were not the slightest grounds for alarm.[16] Yet the emotional impact upon Nasir al-Din was profound and enduring. He had displayed "calmness and firmness" during the trying scene, but the intensity of the attack, which for a few agonizing moments brought him very close to death, aggravated by the political repercussions of the event, left a psychological scar that lasted for decades.[17]

The first intelligence of the assault to reach the capital declared the shah dead. Typical of contingencies on such occasions, the royal summer camp was temporarily disbanded. "No one thought himself safe unless within the walls of Tehran. Every bush was a Babee [Babi], or concealed one. . . . Ministers, meerzas, soldiers, priests, merchants, all went pell-mell into Tehran." Fear of a popular attack against the British mission was compelling enough to oblige Sheil to seek the protection of Afghan horsemen under the command of an Afghan pensioner of the East India Company then residing in Tehran.[18] In the capital the shops were immediately shut, bread became scarce, and even the troops were in disarray, all in anticipation of a Babi onslaught. The crisis was severe enough for the government to take immediate action. To inform the public of the shah's safety, not only was a special issue of *Vaqayi'-i Ittifaqiya* printed, but a large body of troops as well as the 'ulama and the civic authorities were brought to the palace to view the shah. In spite of his injuries, Nasir al-Din received Sheil and Dolgorouki jointly on the afternoon of the very day of the attack. Unexpectedly, perhaps, they found him seated as usual and presenting "no appearance of alarm or agitation." He was pale but looked more angry than alarmed. In the course of conversation he insisted that an attack such as the one he had gone through was without precedent. He also repeated, "often with fierceness," that this attempt had had instigators.[19]

The shah's assertions were not far from the truth. In spite of the frequency of regicide in Persian history, this was the first assassination attempt by members of the public, the first with features comparable in some respects to contemporary European examples.[20] Thus, the two foreign envoys were justified when they paralleled the incident with attempts on the lives of royalty in St. Petersburg and London. "The shah did not, however, seem to derive any consolation from companionship in his danger."[21] Beyond the initial and obvious horror, what was particularly terrifying to the shah was the possibility of a conspiracy, one organized and directed by remnants of the Babi leadership, possibly with the cooperation or encouragement of some elements within the government. The memory of engaging for some minutes with the assassins while receiving hardly any protection from the royal guards added to his suspicions. At the outset, Nasir al-Din seems to have suspected a plot hatched by an ambitious Russian protégé, Muhammad Hasan Khan Sardar Iravani. His involvement in the murder of Amir Kabir had already earned the Sardar infamy, but it was his later intimidations and intrigue, with the clear aim of acquiring the post of commander in chief of the army, that put him at odds with the shah.[22] Even more ominously, the premier himself was not unblemished. Nuri's opponents, now including Mahd 'Ulya, implicated him in the plot, first jointly with the Sardar, then as a collaborator with the Babi leaders. "The affair was so complicated," wrote Sipihr, "that their misrepresentation darkened the purity of the shah's heart, and because of their calumny the premier's crime was confirmed in his mind."[23]

From the outset there was no doubt as to the accomplices' Babi commitment or their motives. Two assassins were captured on the spot, but the remaining three (or more) managed to escape. "The two survivors declared themselves to belong to this faith, that they were ready to die, and that they had come to seek death in paradise, or rather annihilation." Only "religious fanatics" would so unabashedly devote themselves to certain death, Sheil believed.[24] Thousands of Babi devotees, added Sheil, continued to hold Nasir al-Din responsible for the execution of the Bab, and there were many who, like the culprits, were prepared to die for their cause. Such a thought, no doubt, was extremely distressing to the shah.

After disastrous military defeats in the fortress of Tabarsi and the towns of Nayriz and Zanjan, followed by the execution of the Bab in July 1850, the Babis were badly demoralized, but they saw a chance to reorganize and recover some of their network after the collapse of Amir Kabir's regime. Given the messianic epiphany that characterized the movement and the centrality of its charismatic founder to its very existence, it is not surprising that retaliation for the death of the Bab should preoccupy the minds of many Babi activists. It is wrong to believe, however, that this was a sporadic attempt by isolated members. The assassination was inspired and planned by the remnants of the Babi leadership. Shaykh 'Ali Turshizi, better known by his Babi epithet, 'Azim (Great), one of the last surviving members of the early Babi nucleus and the recognized vicar (*na'ib*) of the Bab, may not have been alone.[25] Muhammad Sadiq Tabrizi, the slain assassin, was 'Azim's personal attendant and no doubt under his influence.[26] In an effort to form a united front, 'Azim may have also discussed his assassination plan with other Babi leaders, including Sulayman Khan Tabrizi, son of an army official with court connections, and the few remaining prominent Babis. Contrary to the pacifist view that prevailed much later among most Babis in exile, at this stage Babi activists were still dedicated to the apocalyptic struggle against the Qajar state and the 'ulama. What had changed were the tactics involved, not the motives. Frustrated by the outcome of earlier efforts, political assassination rather than peaceful debate or armed resistance seemed to them the most viable shortcut. It is likely that the leaders envisaged the death of Nasir al-Din as a prelude to a popular revolution and ultimately the triumph of a new Babi order. The millenarian idealism that prevailed over such a scheme was not devoid of anger and desperation. The inadequate weapons chosen—pistols loaded with slugs rather than bullets—and the haphazard though daring method of assault revealed something of the assassins' aggravated state of mind. They were no more "wild and feeble-minded fanatics" than they were "obscure and irresponsible young men," as they often have been portrayed.[27]

Mulla Muhammad 'Ali Nayrizi, the first assassin to shoot, was a calligraphy artist from a family of petty landowners in Fars province. His close ties to Sayyid Yahya Darabi (otherwise known as Vahid, the leader of the Nayriz resistance), the wounds he received in that uprising, and the fact that his family fortune had been confiscated by the governor of Nayriz only sharpened his revolutionary zeal.[28] Fathullah Qumi, another of the assassins, was the master bookbinder of the library of the shrine of Ma'suma in Qum and possibly close to the trustee of the shrine, Mirza Husayn Qumi, who was himself a Babi and was implicated in the conspiracy.[29] Not much is known about Muhammad Sadiq Tabrizi except that at one stage, presumably prior to his service under 'Azim, he was a confectioner. The assassins' determination was further evidenced by the self-sacrifice they endured under horrendous torture. Aside from their Babi beliefs they revealed nothing—no names of accomplices or instigators, nothing of the existence of a network. Nothing could have added more to the shah's frustration or the premier's growing fear of implication. Mahd 'Ulya and others had enough circumstantial evidence to put Nuri in grave danger.

One leading Babi figure, Mirza Husayn 'Ali Nuri, the Baha' (later Baha'ullah), whose family was from the same region as the premier's, had long been in contact with the premier and his family. After his return from exile in the 'Atabat (to which he was sent by Amir Kabir in 1850), he was the guest of the premier for months preceding the assassination attempt and was residing in the house of Ja'far Quli Khan, one of the premier's brothers, in Shimiran. There he had managed not only to establish contacts with the "notables and dignitaries" in the capital but also to meet the Babi leader, 'Azim, at which time he had acquainted Baha'ullah with his assassination plan. Baha'ullah reportedly advised him "in the most emphatic terms to abandon the plan he had conceived . . . condemned his design, [and] dissociated himself entirely from the act it was his intention to commit." Such an attempt, Baha'ullah reportedly warned, "would precipitate fresh disasters of unprecedented magnitude."[30]

There is no evidence to confirm that the premier knew of the plot, yet Baha'ullah's continued residence at Nuri's summer resort in Afja at the time of the attack was enough to raise questions. Mahd 'Ulya openly denounced Baha'ullah as the "would-be murderer" of her son and tried to incriminate Mirza Aqa Khan Nuri as an accomplice. Baha'ullah's hasty flight to the safety of the summer compound of the Russian legation in Zarkanda, no doubt with the intention of seeking protection from his brother-in-law, Mirza Majid Ahi, a Persian secretary of the Russian mission, only lent further credence to accusations of his guilt and thus aggravated the premier's position.[31]

Under the circumstances, Nuri had to come up with a solution. He either devised a plan himself or submitted to the shah's decision to crack down on the Babis, on the one hand to alleviate the shah's fear of another Babi outrage but on the other to clear himself of collaboration charges. He appointed the shah's chief of royal servants, 'Ali Khan Farrash-bashi, a tactical ally of the premier and Amir Kabir's killer, as the primary investigator and henchman, to be assisted by the adjutant general, 'Aziz Khan Mukri (later Sardar Kull), who after Amir Kabir rose to become the de facto commander in chief of the army, and Mahmud Khan Kalantar, the mayor of Tehran and a relative of Nuri.

Two days after the incident, having extracted nothing from the assassins, 'Ali Khan, apparently acting on intelligence from the chief of the Sarchishma city ward, raided the house of Sulayman Khan Tabrizi. His house, a gathering place of the Babis, was an obvious choice.[32] Thirteen Babis, allegedly part of a larger group of seventy conspirators, were captured there, "all ready and well-armed" to come out en masse and foment an urban uprising. They remained active in spite of the failure of the attempt against the shah. Under torture, members of this group revealed more names, and more arrests were made. By whatever manner the suspects were apprehended, in almost all cases without any evidence of a connection to the assassination attempt, the number of detainees grew and soon exceeded thirty, including most leading Babis.[33]

Before the end of the week about ten Babis were executed, "some with circumstances of great cruelty." Fathullah Qumi, Sulayman Khan Tabrizi, and another Babi leader from Nayriz were killed in different locations by the exceptionally barbaric method of *sham'ajin* (candle decoration). "Lighted candles have been stuck into the bodies of two or three, and after being allowed to linger, they have been halved with a hatchet while still alive." The long and painful death, with deep holes made in the breasts and shoulders of the victims as signs of celebration for the shah's safety, was accompanied by gaiety and music and colorful decorations in the bazaar. They were taken in a long procession around the bazaar, where people were encouraged to insult and molest the victims or to reward the executioners as a sign of their loyalty to the shah. Then 'Ali Khan himself, acting as the shah's representative, carried out the "retaliation of blood" (*qisas*) by shooting Fathullah Qumi on the same spot in Niavaran that the failed assassin shot the shah, first with a pistol loaded with slugs; then he blew out his brains with his own hand. "As soon as he fell on the ground he was immediately cut to pieces by the agents of the Farrash-khanih." Mirza Muhammad Nayrizi, too, was shot and cut to pieces by Muhammad Khan Qajar, the chief of the royal guards (later prime minister), and his officers, troops, and servants. Others were blown from the mortar or killed in other terrifying fashions improvised by the executioners and their masters.[34]

The arrests and subsequent killings seem to have partially vindicated the premier but did not lessen the shah's anger or remove his increased anxiety of a Babi resurgence. In response to Russian objections to the mass killings Nuri admitted to Dolgorouki that he was having difficulties resisting the shah's "irritation" and the "provocations of those who imbue the Shah with the desire for vengeance," namely his mother and 'Ali Khan Farrash-bashi. Dolgorouki observed that in the court they talked about the executions "with a joyful air, trying to make people think that all this slaughter is a most common and natural thing."[35] The shah's sentiments are well apparent from this important note addressed to Nuri on the subject of the Babi arrests:

> Your excellency the Sadr 'Azam! The Adjutant General ['Aziz Khan Mukri] submitted a report [in which] some names were mentioned. I could not understand whether they were captured or they ought to be captured. Two letters of Hajji Sulayman [Khan Tabrizi] were also attached. If the names [on the list] have not yet been detained let them be captured. Also instruct that, God willing, these damned [literally, "those whose corpses were moved from grave to grave" (gur bi gur)] Hazrat Basir and Subh Azal be handcuffed and brought [to us]. [Also] let the prayer book and the Qur'an to be brought to us. Each time that I recall this affair [i.e., the assassination attempt], by God, I wish to leave Iran and go to London.[36]

The shah's wish to go to London, odd as it may sound, reflected his frustration over his volatile situation at home, leading him to fantasize about England as a place of refuge. Yet further harsh measures against the Babis proved to be a more viable alternative to royal disenchantment. The above-mentioned Hazrat Basir was the Babi name of a blind Indian disciple of the Bab and one of the claimants to his succession. He was killed in 1852 in Luristan by order of Khanlar Mirza, the shah's uncle and the governor of the province, apparently in compliance with the shah's order. Subh Azal was the Babi name of Mirza Yahya Nuri, the younger brother of Baha'ullah and the claimed successor to the Bab. He was then in hiding in Takur, his family's estate in the Nur region. Takur was attacked, presumably in an attempt to find Azal, and a number of Babis were killed. The shah's mention of a prayer book and Qur'an no doubt was a reference to the Bab's writings. His *Qayyum al-asma'*, a commentary on the *sura* Yusuf of the Qur'an, and his major work, *Bayan*, were often referred to as the Babi Qur'an. They must have been recovered from the raid on Sulayman Khan's house.

THE BABI BLOODBATH

The arrest of the Babi leader, 'Azim, a few days after the shah's directive was hailed as a major breakthrough. It took place largely thanks to cooperation by the Russian mission, whose involvement turned the assassination affair into an issue with some diplomatic consequences. A note from the ministry of foreign affairs provided Dolgorouki with the same list of Babi suspects as the one submitted to the shah, a list probably based on information extracted from the Babis under torture. Moreover, the note informed the Russian envoy that four of the suspects had taken refuge in Zarkanda, presumably in the hope of receiving Russian protection.[37] A search through the Russian-controlled village, Dolgorouki reported, led to the arrest of one unnamed Babi, who in turn, probably under duress, revealed 'Azim's hiding place in the village of Ivin, some four miles away. The Russian search party also discovered Baha'ullah hiding in the house of his relative in Zarkanda. His name was on the same government list. Equipped with the information drawn from the Zarkanda detainees, the team then conducted a raid on Ivin. 'Azim was taken by surprise at his hiding place and brought to the mission, but the royal farrashes refused to escort him to the royal camp, apparently for fear of being attacked by Babis along the road. Dolgorouki was probably unwilling to grant protection to the mastermind behind the assassination and cautious not to be associated with the affair altogether. It was only at his insistence and because of remuneration paid out later by Nuri that some Persian guards of the mission were induced to escort 'Azim to the city, where he was handed over to government agents.[38]

'Azim's testimony, produced under duress, provided the main grounds for exonerating the premier. In the interrogation, conducted by Nuri himself, 'Azim was said to have admitted that he was "the chief instigator and leader" of the conspiracy and that Muhammad Sadiq acted on his orders. Furthermore, as Nuri told Sheil, 'Azim confessed that even after the failure of the attempt against the shah he had exhorted his followers that "the work must be completed; that when the Shah entered the town he ['Azim] would bare his arm, and advance with his sword on the Shah; that if they saw him ['Azim] lying as if dead, they were not to believe it, as it would be only a semblance; that they were to fight and that he would rise and be among them." Given the belief in symbolic reincarnation (*raj'at*) among the Babis and the level of militancy that had been triggered by earlier confrontations with the state, such a statement was not atypical even if Nuri used it to absolve himself or to justify the executions.[39]

It is not surprising that in response to the European envoys' warning against acts of brutality Nuri pretended he had opposed some of these acts, but it was "the Shah's anger and vindictiveness" that prevented him from paying attention to their advice. Whether or not 'Azim had really admitted sole responsibility for the plot, Nuri used the occasion to save himself by diverting royal wrath toward the taking of dispensable Babi lives. With a sinister ingenuity peculiar to Nuri, he saw the benefit of staging a collective frenzy of killings, spectacular even by Qajar standards. The decision to allow the remaining Babi detainees to be lynched by government and court officials and other related groups was supported not only by the shah's mother and the courtiers but also by some of the 'ulama. Involving the entire ruling elite as partners in eradicating the Babi menace, it was argued, would prevent the possibility that the Babis would retaliate against the shah, his premier, or any one individual or group. The more subtle reason was to foster, through collective killings, a sense of solidarity with the throne against a common threat and to preserve an order symbolized by the shah. At least twice in the past, mass killings of heretics had borne the same result. The massacre of Mazdakites in 629, at the outset of Khusraw Anushiravan's reign, and that of the Nuqtawis in 1593, on the occasion of 'Abbas I's consolidation of the throne, may have been in the minds of Nasir al-Din and his premier.

Reports of recent attacks and even assassinations of other anti-Babi elements in the capital, regardless of their veracity (some reports were simply fabricated by Nuri), further helped unnerve the entire government and encourage a harsh reaction to the Babis. Indeed, fear of a Babi backlash and potential public support for it was terrifying enough to persuade the government not to reveal the Babi association of the attackers even two weeks after the attempt. The earlier persecution of the Babis, noted Alfred von Gumoens, an Austrian instructor in the Dar al-Funun and a witness to the events of 1852, "produced exactly the opposite of the effects intended. The Bab's teaching gained more and more ground, and is at the moment diffused through the whole country."[40] It is not hard to see Nasir al-Din, his court and his government petrified by the general tumult and excitement that had overtaken the capital at the time of the assassination attempt. The killings, and the gruesome fashion in which they were conducted, were thus to remind the populace, whether sympathetic to the Babis or not, of the consequences of challenging the existing order—a spectacle to remind as well as to avenge.

The legal justification, if any was needed, was based on a rather self-serving interpretation of the Islamic rule of *qisas* (punishment inflicted in retaliation for an injury; see Pl. 15). The attempt to take the shah's life was considered a public crime. Had the Babis been successful, they would have indulged in "injury to all people because of bloodshed, the rape of the women, and violation of other prohibitions," declared the Tehran gazette, *Vaqayi'-i Ittifaqiya*. These were hazards that must be combated at the level of the general public, an obligation considered not only an individual duty but also a "great crusade" with otherworldly rewards.[41] The Qajar court was thus required to present, as Sheil put it, "the extraordinary and disgraceful spectacle of all the chief officers of the state being converted into executioners."

> Each department of the government has had a victim among the conspir-
> ators, or supposed conspirators, against the King's life. The minister of
> foreign affairs [Mirza Sa'id Khan], the minister of finance [Mirza Yusuf
> Mustawfi al-Mamalik], the son of the prime minister [Nizam al-Mulk],
> the adjutant general of the army ['Aziz Khan], the master of the mint
> [Dust 'Ali Khan Mu'ayyir al-Mamalik], each fired the first shot, or made
> the first cut with a sabre, at the culprit delivered to them, who was then
> despatched by the subordinates. The artillery, the infantry, the cavalry,
> the camel artillery, each had a victim, and I believe the priesthood is also
> to be allotted a share in these transactions.[42]

Indeed the 'ulama cunningly stayed out of the collective *qisas* they were asked to endorse, as did the shah and Nuri. In response to Sheil's remon-strances against "the disgrace which he was heaping on the reputation of the Persian government and nation," Nuri asked rhetorically if Sheil wanted "to place the responsibility of so many executions on him alone and bring down Babee vengeance on himself and his family."[43] The prime minister's brothers and sons could not avoid participating in the frenzy, however, and they were obliged to kill a few Babis of their own. In addition the princes of the Qajar family, the royal servants, stewards, table and private attendants, guards, porters, grooms, farrashes, the royal herald, the master of the ceremony, and other court functionaries also took part in the mass slaughter. Furthermore, the "instructors and the students" of Dar al-Funun were not spared from the compulsory role of executioners. Mirza Nabi Damavandi, a Babi from Tehran, was their victim, killed with sabers and bayonets. Even the merchants, the least politically involved group and exceptionally proud of their piety and group solidarity, were obliged to kill one of their own. The chief of the merchants of Tehran, Aqa Mahdi Malik al-Tujjar, took the lead in slaughtering the Babi merchant and chronicler of early Babi history Hajji Mirza Jani Kashani. First he was dragged out of the sanctuary of the shrine of Shah 'Abd al-'Azim, where he had taken refuge, and then was put to death with "all sorts of weapons."[44] That the sanctuary of 'Abd al-'Azim was broken into was in direct violation of the government's earlier reinstatement of the right to take refuge (bast) in the shrines, a practice whose beneficiaries were the merchants themselves.

Besides the three assassins' deaths, twenty-three other executions were announced, with more killings probably unacknowledged. The Babis exhibited their determination and messianic certitude as they encountered death. It is highly unlikely that they were all collaborators or had any knowledge of the plot at all, though a few had been involved in previous Babi uprisings. The victims represented a cross-section of Babi converts, both geographically and socially.[45] Regardless of their involvement, what they shared was a common hatred of the Qajar monarchy, not only for its murder of their prophet and most of his early disciples but also for its maintaining and promoting a regime they considered illegitimate and in collaboration with the equally illegitimate 'ulama. The attempt on Nasir al-Din Shah's life thus symbolized an open defiance against the whole sociopolitical system, which relied on monarchy. The victims "cursed the shah and expressed joy at dying," reported Dolgorouki, "because such a death assured them the crown of martyrdom."[46]

Two other Babi figures were also slain. Zarrin Taj Baraghani, better known as Qurrat al-'Ayn (and Tahira), one of the most celebrated leaders of the movement, was secretly put the death. Since her arrest in Mazandaran and subsequent transfer to the capital in 1850, she had been in detention in the upper chamber of the mayor's house. She had escaped death under Amir Kabir, apparently because of the shah's intervention. On that occasion, after she was interviewed by the shah, he reportedly had ordered his premier: "I like her looks, leave her, and let her be (az hay'atash khusham miayad, bugzar bimanad)." Beyond her physical attractiveness, her personality and noted eloquence, or even her lineage—coming as she did from a family of influential 'ulama—what temporarily saved her may have been the Islamic injunction restricting the execution of a female apostate. Yet she was too much of a symbol of the Babi resistance to be spared for the second time, even though the chances of her being an accomplice in the assassination were remote. Less than a week after the assassination attempt she was interrogated, apparently for several days, by two senior mujtahids of Tehran. Though she was apparently offered clemency in exchange for recanting her beliefs, she remained unrepentant. After some hesitation the mujtahids issued the death sentence, presumably when they were sufficiently intimidated or otherwise induced by Nuri. In addition to her association with Baha'ullah, the reports that Nuri's own wife, sister, and other women of his harem were sympathizers of Qurrat al-'Ayn may have hastened her execution. She was strangled less than a week after the incident by some low-ranking attendants of 'Aziz Khan, the adjutant general, and her body was dumped in a garden outside the city walls. All the roads leading to the site of execution were blocked for fear of a Babi rescue attempt that never came.[47]

'Azim, the confessed leader of the Babi circle, was put to death nearly two months after he was captured and a full three weeks after the news of his impending execution had already been reported in the government gazette. "Since the most learned 'ulama were hesitant about the nature of his beliefs," declared the correction note in *Vaqayi'-i Ittifaqiya*, "for a few days they have postponed his execution until his erroneous beliefs are investigated." The fact that he was a qualified mujtahid capable of legally defending himself may have had some bearing on the 'ulama's hesitation. Understandably, they may have also waited to see if chances of a Babi retaliation would subside.[48]

Several Babis escaped certain death, among them the trustee of the shrine of Qum. He may have reminded his captors, surely with sufficient material inducement, that he had already repented his Babi association three years before, at the close of the Tabarsi uprising. More significant, Mirza Husayn 'Ali Baha'ullah was spared, although his name had appeared on the government's "wanted" list. Upon receiving the foreign ministry's above-mentioned note, Dolgorouki ordered Baha'ullah (who had taken refuge in the house of his relative Mirza Majid Ahi, the Persian secretary of the Russian mission) to be delivered to the authorities, as he was "a Babi and a Persian subject, and was not one of our official employees."[49] He was sent to the city independently, not in the company of 'Azim and other captured Babis. Ahi himself accompanied him to the royal camp in Niyavaran "in order to explain the innocence of his brother-in-law."[50] Nevertheless, together with other Babis awaiting their fate, he was relegated to the dreaded dungeon (*anbar*) of the Tehran citadel. Four months later he was released and sent to Ottoman Iraq, a punishment of exile from which he never returned.

It is hard to imagine that Baha'ullah was released because it was recognized that he was innocent. Many other Babis died, or were imprisoned, because of guilt by association. In the eyes of the government, Baha'ullah's high status among the Babis and his association with 'Azim were reason enough to implicate him. Yet the Nuri connection, and possibly the support offered by Dolgorouki, must have helped to procure his escape from execution. Once it was generally accepted at the court that 'Azim was solely responsible for masterminding the assassination, it was essential for Nuri to vindicate Baha'ullah so as to protect himself against charges of collaboration. Moreover, in response to repeated warnings from the foreign envoys concerning the savagery committed against the Babis, the premier could hold up the release of Baha'ullah as proof of the government's fair treatment.[51]

The premier's puzzling stand vis-à-vis the assassination affair deserves further explanation. It is possible that on the eve of his premiership Nuri welcomed Baha'ullah's overtures to bring about a reconciliation with the Babis, thereby avoiding a recurrence of the ruinous confrontation between the government and the persecuted movement.[52] During his exile in Kashan before he was appointed premier, Nuri had contacted the Babis, hoping to trade their backing, in his bid for power, for promises of future immunity to their followers. Under Amir Kabir he also cautioned the shah and Amir Kabir against the repercussions of the Bab's execution. It is not unimaginable, therefore, that he should look on the Babi rehabilitation as a viable option against the excesses of the 'ulama, an alternative Aqasi had toyed with previously. Further advantage lay, one may speculate, in the assumption that the Babis could also provide Nuri with additional insurance against royal wrath. Amir Kabir's hapless fate would have led any premier to seek contingency assurances, not only in the shah's written guarantees but also by soliciting the support of an opposition force, especially as he found himself increasingly at odds with Mahd 'Ulya.

Mutual hopes for such understanding were shattered once the attack against the shah had occurred. By its very definition it was an act diametrically, and perhaps deliberately, opposed to any conciliatory move. If 'Azim was the chief instigator in the assassination affair, it may be argued that his action was the outcome of an ideological difference with the movement's moderate wing, led by Baha'ullah. Before his execution, when he was questioned in prison about Baha'ullah's leadership, he reportedly said the leader of the Babi community was none other than the Bab himself,[53] a statement that may have sprung from differences over strategy and leadership within the Babi community. He paid with his own life, perhaps unfairly shouldering all the responsibility for the assassination attempt.

The short- and long-term consequences of the assassination attempt were significant both for the shah and for the country; for the Babis they were disastrous. The incident further subjected the Babi community, still in its infancy, to a clandestine existence from which it never really recovered. If any further confirmation was needed, the events of 1852 ranked the Babis as religion's and the state's most dangerous enemies. This reputation deprived the more moderate elements within the movement of even a slim chance of arriving at an understanding with the government. The disastrous events did, however, provide some grounds for reconsidering the Babi tenets at a later date. Under Baha'ullah the revisionist wing of the movement began to seek peace with the state while opting for milder opposition to the religious establishment. This strategy ultimately crystallized in the Baha'i doctrine of political nonintervention. The rival tendency, symbolized by loyalty to the tenets of Babi activism, remained a potential force of political dissent that, under the nominal leadership of Subh Azal, survived in exile, though it was barely actualized before the Constitutional Revolution. The idea of assassinating the shah was occasionally revived among the Babis but was never attempted again.

Nasir al-Din never again felt safe from the Babi threat. The differences between the two tendencies within the movement—moderate and radical—were almost nonexistent for Nasir al-Din Shah; Babis were all his sworn enemies, ready to destroy him if they could. The assassination attempt impressed upon his mind a deep-seated hatred not only of the Babis but of any force of political opposition and above all popular dissent. Inevitably, in the post–Amir Kabir era, the entire episode, and particularly the symbolic atrocities committed against the Babis, served to strengthen the monarchy's "defense of true religion" and hence forged a closer association with its representatives, the 'ulama. Thereupon, as prescribed by traditional manuals of government, the state and religion, the twines that maintained the balance of society, remained in tacit alliance, combating sedition and heresy.

Decades later, endorsing his son's suppression of the Babis of Isfahan and Abada, Nasir al-Din Shah recommended to Zill al-Sultan that "punishment, isolation, and intimidation of this despicable sect is one of the necessities of kingship and the state. That you have punished the Isfahani [Babis] is very good. Of course, the father of the Babis of Abada must be also burnt but after proper investigation. Punishment and chastisement of the Babis must be carried out properly."[54] The emphasis on "proper investigation," no doubt to avoid mistreating others under the Babi pretext, ironically confirmed his irreconcilable enmity toward the Babis. Nasir al-Din's cold tone as he singled out Babis as the only ones deserving punishment was rooted, one senses, in an older grudge and was upheld in other instances of Babi-Baha'i persecution.

AN INADVERTENT VICTIM

Coming only seven months after the murder of Amir Kabir, the assassination attempt convinced Nasir al-Din even more strongly of the suffocating confines of his lonesome world, surrounded by conspirators and assassins within and outside the palace walls. Beyond its immediate effect, the Babi attempt had one other unexpected casualty in the person of the shah's half-brother, 'Abbas Mirza, posing again as the chief threat to the throne. Rampant accusations by Mahd 'Ulya and others concerning his involvement in the attempt were pure fiction yet credible enough to persuade the shah to try to fulfill his long-standing desire for 'Abbas's elimination.

The unresolved question of heir apparency intensified the shah's desire. In 1851 he had not yet officially nominated a new heir following the death of the infant Mahmud Mirza, his first choice. Of the two infant sons born to him recently only one, Sultan Mu'in al-Din Mirza, the child of a permanent marriage with a Qajar woman, was eligible for succession. Had the shah been killed by the Babis before naming an heir, the right of his infant son to the throne would have been contested either by 'Abbas Mirza or, more likely, by claim to regency of his uncle Bahman Mirza. Both potential contenders were given shelter and immunity by rival powers with an eye to their political prospects. Speculating on the circumstances of Nasir al-Din's death, Sheil asserted, in agreement with Dolgorouki, that after the shah's son 'Abbas Mirza was next in line, though he believed that Bahman Mirza, in spite of his Russian support, deserved to be the regent. He knew of no other person of equal "commanding power, talent, or character in Tehran, or any other part of Persia." This was the best alternative for Iran, Sheil believed, even if Bahman would kill the minor king and declare himself the shah. "It may be hoped that the Shah's life will be prolonged, but Babeeism is not extinct nor does His Majesty possess a good constitution." Sheil never abandoned his opinion on Nasir al-Din's weak constitution nor did he ever reveal to the Foreign Office his diagnoses.[55]

Even if Nasir al-Din had not been informed through Nuri of the intricate details of Sheil's speculations, he was canny enough to see the overall implications for himself. Not surprisingly, two weeks after the attempt he officially nominated Mu'in al-Din Mirza as his heir, but only after he was assured that the British would approve his choice. The shah was delighted with the British approbation, but the "embarrassing question of regency" that made Sheil speculate on 'Abbas Mirza's and Bahman Mirza's chances remained very troubling to the shah. Mahd 'Ulya's outrage seemed equally inevitable then as later, not only because of the danger to her son's crown but also because of her own enmity toward her ex-rival, Khadija. For all the suspicion with which he had earlier looked on Amir Kabir's attention to 'Abbas Mirza, not to mention his own deep-seated hatred for the young prince, the shah now found a new, and even more dangerous, Babi dimension. The possibility that 'Abbas had collaborated with Mirza Husayn Qumi and other Babis, however far-fetched, seemed highly plausible in the eyes of the frightened shah. One of the assassins, a well-known Babi accomplice, came from Qum, where 'Abbas resided as the nominal governor, and this coincidence was enough for Mahd 'Ulya and her willing son to try to implicate the prince. Rumors that the shah intended to blind 'Abbas and Khadija abounded shortly after the assassination attempt. The rumors were worrisome enough to Sheil that he warned the shah through Nuri against the repetition of committing "barbarous deeds." Dolgorouki was less perturbed. He was willing to intercede, jointly with Sheil, on behalf of 'Abbas but not of his mother—"a woman of an intriguing temper" to whose fate the Russian prince was indifferent.[56]

These warnings seem not to have immediately altered the shah's mind in his decision to have 'Abbas Mirza blinded or killed. "Apart from the fact that in my own heart there is a conviction," he wrote to Nuri in response to Sheil, "all the chief servants and nobles of the kingdom are also united in the opinion that the instigator of the late event [i.e., the assassination attempt] is 'Abbas Mirza and the people about him." The shah's tone, insisting on the urgent need for exemplary punishment, betrayed his insecurity as well as his fear of not having his authority recognized by his subjects in the aftermath of the assassination attempt:

> People seem not to care either for the united endorsement of the two powers for us nor for the support [*dawlat-khwahi*] and presence of the two [foreign] ministers. They pay no regard to my benevolence and clemency, nor have they any fear of your [i.e., Nuri's] loyalty and that of my other devoted servants. Therefore, when all the above circumstances, together with the means and measures on which I depended for security in evil days, prove to be unavailing, it is necessary that for the protection of my own person, and to give tranquility to my own heart, I should carry into execution that which seems to me expedient. At the moment the solution that occurs to me is that I must remove the danger and the conspiracy proceeding from 'Abbas Mirza and his adherents in so

effectual a manner that quiet and tranquility may be acquired, so that seditious persons may not be able to make use of him as an instrument for my harm and disquiet.[57]

In support of his decision, as he had done to enhance his case for Amir Kabir's dismissal, the shah provided testimony of chief notables of the court, a consensus the shah deemed necessary to buttress his shaken authority and to persuade the envoys of the veracity of the rumors. Declaring to the two foreign representatives their readiness to sacrifice their lives on behalf of "the illustrious and resplendent jewel of royalty," the forty-eight signatories among the notables of the court regarded 'Abbas Mirza and his mother as "not free from having instigated and prompted this nefarious outrage." Zealous in guarding the crown and the government, they urged the shah "to put an end to the latent depravity" of 'Abbas Mirza, his mother, and his defenders by removing him from Qum, where "people of all descriptions not only pass through but congregate together." The notables deftly avoided endorsing any further, more serious punishment, at least in writing.[58] Nuri's cover letter was even more noncommittal, insisting repeatedly that, as the shah's servant and subject, he merely carried out royal orders.[59]

The reasons for this noncommittal tone were clear, at least to some of the signatories. Mahd 'Ulya was undoubtedly behind the whole scheme. Years later, Mirza Husayn Qumi, the trustee of the shrine of Qum and one of the Babi accomplices, stated in exile in Baghdad that in 1852 he was forced under torture to sign a confession prepared by 'Ali Khan Farrashbashi and doctored by Mahd 'Ulya with the intention of implicating 'Abbas Mirza and his mother.[60] It was not an exaggeration, therefore, when Sheil diagnosed Mahd 'Ulya as the chief instigator, "owing to the unbounded hatred" she bore for Khadija, her old adversary.[61] With Amir Kabir dead and Nuri sufficiently intimidated by suspicions of his Babi involvement, it was Mahd 'Ulya that now ruled supreme and posed as savior to her son.

The envoys' joint reply was predictably blunt. As there was nothing that could prove the involvement of the thirteen-year-old prince "with utmost conviction," they urged the shah not to physically harm or imprison him but to allow him instead "to reside somewhere with dignity."[62] Sheil's motives for intervention were not solely humanitarian. Because Bahman Mirza was under Russian protection, it was logical that Sheil would try to balance the scales with 'Abbas. Moreover, as they had learned in the civil war of 1834, protecting contesting princes of the royal family provided the British with an inexpensive, though not easily redeemable, insurance against the shah's unfriendly behavior. The same considerations encouraged Sheil at the same time to offer asylum to Farhad Mirza, the pro-British uncle of the shah, who was under suspicion not only for helping 'Abbas Mirza but also for collaborating in the Babi plot.

Typically, Nuri opted for a middle-of-the-road position. Once he had sufficiently cautioned the shah of the consequences of alienating the envoys, he felt it safe to propose an alternative without further exposing himself to Mahd 'Ulya's accusations. Recalling ample precedent for fratricide under earlier Qajar rulers, he argued in his response to the European envoys: "The condition of our country, Iran, necessitates prudence and caution, though an outrage such as the attempt on the shah had never happened [before]. . . . In such circumstances if His Majesty undertakes every precaution, he cannot be faulted." The prime minister's "precautions," a euphemism borrowed from the shah's autograph, implied in diplomatic language a penalty milder than gouging the prince's eyes. In this case it meant that 'Abbas should be incarcerated in a fortress in Simnan. Anticipating the envoys' objections, he then added: "Whoever is a trustworthy supporter of this government and friendly to that blessed being not only must he be happy with our concern but indeed encourage such cautionary measures." It was probably this timely assertion that prompted the shah to applaud his premier's performance in the margin of the original copy: "Well done a thousand times Your Excellency the Sadr A'zam. By God, if Nizam al-Mulk himself [the celebrated minister of the Saljuq era] would come alive he would not be able to write one such line. Never did I see a letter so perfect and powerful. Immediately dispatch it."[63]

Nuri wisely omitted the royal remark from his official reply; yet, unimpressed with his ministerial marvels, Sheil was adamant that external exile only, perhaps to Mecca or Karbala, would save the prince. He noted that 'Abbas's household had already been looted by the royal guards and that he was already under arrest. The intelligence regarding 'Abbas Mirza's miserable state had been smuggled to Sheil in a letter by the prince's loyal tutor, Riza Quli Khan Hidayat, who safely crossed the checkposts outside the city gates.[64]

The prospect of deteriorating relations with the foreign powers was compelling enough to bring the shah to his senses. After much negotiation, the Persian government agreed to the prince's "pilgrimage" to Iraq, provided that the envoys guaranteed his future conduct and with the stipulation that he would not be able to return to Iran without royal permission. But Sheil only went so far as promising to dissuade 'Abbas in the unlikely event he desired to return to Iran. Dolgorouki had "remained aloof" all through the negotiations. With an annual pension of 2,400 tumans

(£1,100) secured by Sheil, the prince was then immediately escorted to the border. Stripped of his valuables by the shah's orders, the despairing prince was abandoned in a frontier town, only to find himself barred from entry into Iraq by the Ottoman authorities. The governor (*vali*) of Baghdad, fearing unpredictable political repercussions, protested the use of the Ottoman province as Iran's prison camp. "Not allowed to enter the mosque for being a skeptic; nor into the tavern for being an unseasoned drunkard," wrote 'Abbas Mirza in his memoirs.[65] After lengthy negotiations, 'Abbas was eventually admitted to the Ottoman territory with an English passport issued by Sheil, "as if His Highness were under English protection." Acting in contravention of his agreement with the Persian government, which had refused to allow Sheil's representative to accompany the prince all the way to the frontier lest this be mistaken as a sign of diplomatic immunity, the British minister justified his measures in his usual self-righteous style. With an apparent lapse of memory that safely disregarded his own initiative in sending 'Abbas into "pilgrimage," he wrote: "The conduct of the Persian ministers has been criticized in severity in allowing the Prince to proceed to Baghdad, where there are so many elements of discontent and disloyalty collected. Should an insinuation of this nature reach the Shah, the life or the eyes of the Prince would be in immediate jeopardy."[66] Although the "elements of discontent," an allusion to the exiled Babis, abounded in Baghdad, no negative "insinuations" of any significance originated from 'Abbas's quarters. He settled in Baghdad for the next two decades, leading a largely uneventful life of exile.

For the shah the victory against his brother, curtailed though it was, was the only bit of comfort he gained out of a harrowing affair. 'Abbas Mirza's expulsion ended any speculations on the succession question for some time and was a turning point in Nasir al-Din's reign. The crown's definitive actions asserted its control over the mode of succession. For Mahd 'Ulya, too, the affair was a victory, though not complete as yet. Once 'Abbas Mirza and Khadija were out of the picture and in exile, clinging to their English passports, she turned against Nuri for having convinced the shah to go along with his plans. The premier's moderation, combined with the circumstantial evidence implicating him in the assassination attempt, gave her enough to undermine the shah's trust in Nuri in spite of his apparent vindication.

Once again the shah was feeling threatened by his prime minister, though he praised his Sadr A'zam in the highest terms. The semblance of a Babi resistance stirring in Mazandaran, this time in Nur, further darkened the horizons. Coinciding with the planned assassination in Tehran, 100

Babis took up arms in the village of Takur, apparently under Mirza Yahya Subh Azal, Baha'ullah's brother. Although easily crushed by a small detachment of local forces, the uprising was enough to rekindle the shah's suspicions.[67] It is not surprising, therefore, that on 18 October, coinciding with the execution of 'Azim, the premier secretly complained to Sheil in writing that, given the shah's "deceit and caprice, he found it impossible to conduct the government with any hope of success and credit." He further predicted in an ominous tone that he would "inevitably be murdered in the same manner that the late prime minister, the Amir Nizam, had been murdered." He must have been sufficiently alarmed to consider retirement his safest option with at least "some chance of preserving his life," but this option would have been greatly augmented had he acted "in such manner as would force either the English or Russian minister to demand his dismissal." Even after dismissal, he believed, his life would remain threatened by "the band of intriguers who surround the Shah," an obvious reference to Mahd 'Ulya and her allies, who, fearing Nuri's retaliation, would "insist on his death" to save themselves from his vengeance.[68]

Nuri's apprehensions clearly demonstrated the insecurity of the office of the prime minister, an insecurity rooted in the shah's unpredictable mood. Sheil, for reasons of his own, could not have agreed more with Nuri on the issue of the shah's "duplicity and capricious temper," which vacillated with the level of tension between the divan and the harem. Yet Sheil was shrewd enough to detect "some mark of intelligence" in his conversation with the shah after the 'Abbas Mirza affair: "It is not easy to discriminate what share of his discourse is a lesson learned by heart and what portion is the result of his own reflections." The shah's emerging maturity, however, appeared to the British envoy as being subverted by a sense of inner insecurity and confusion. "He is perpetually ordering and counter-ordering, and again repeating the same acts of administration, so that it is impossible for his minister to trust a single day to the stability of his conduct."

Notwithstanding the capriciousness that would characterize his entire reign, the shah's conduct may be attributed to Mahd 'Ulya's predominance. "His Majesty is constantly seeking advice from other people in secret," observed Sheil, "and unfortunately his chief confidants, particularly his mother and Farrash Bashee, the murderer of Ameer Nizam, are persons toward whom no terms of obloquy would be misapplied." Sheil was outraged to see that the premier, his own ex-protégé, had been virtually isolated in the court thanks to Mahd 'Ulya's machinations. In addition to making other charges, she now accused Nuri of collaborating with the

British against the shah. Nuri thus sounded convincing when he made the excuse that "under compulsion of speaking slightingly of the English Mission and . . . to preserve himself from the imputation of disloyalty with which his enemies were constantly filling the Shah's mind," he was forced on occasions to use stronger language than usual against the British minister.[69] This was a clear sign of tension between Nuri and Sheil.

6 Playing the Power Game

The bloody end to the Babi affair weakened Nuri's position and increased the shah's power. Though he still relied on Nuri's abilities as agent and executor of the royal wishes, the shah increasingly saw himself as the ultimate decision maker and initiator of policies. The underlying battle with the premier for control of the government, a primary theme in the history of the period, was further complicated by the intense rivalry between the two European powers, the other major theme in the history of Qajar Iran. The shah's earliest experiences of international diplomacy, and its domestic consequences, opened a chapter in his political career that left its mark on his foreign policy for the rest of his reign. Coinciding with an episode of European imperial reassertion, which soon turned the Eastern Question into the Crimean War (1853–1855), the shah's efforts to benefit from the unfolding European conflict brought few successes and major losses.

THE HERAT DEBACLE

After the victory over Salar in Khurasan, it was to be expected that Nasir al-Din would rely on military power to reassert Persian territorial claims over neighboring Herat province (in western Afghanistan). With Khurasan under his control, he could not resist the urge to fulfill a historical ambition that had eluded both his father and his grandfather. In 1838 Muhammad Shah had suffered a humiliating setback when he was forced to lift the siege of Herat under British pressure. The desire to reclaim Herat was also accorded legitimacy in Nasir al-Din's perspective by general concern over the political turmoil in that province and its impact on Khurasan. The prospect of a united Afghanistan, conceived and contrived by the British and about to be realized by the ruler of Kabul, Dust Muhammad Khan, was not welcomed in Tehran. Iran's historical claims on Herat went back at least to the Safavid era, when the ancient city served as the empire's second capital after its conquest by Isma'il I in 1510. Even before the Safavid conquest, under the Timurids, Herat was the cultural capital of the eastern Iranian world and an integral part of greater Khurasan. With a large Shi'ite urban population often at odds with the Sunni tribal warlords who came to dominate the region and with internecine conflicts among the chiefs of Herat, the role of the Persian suzerain as protector and mediator became ever more important in the early nineteenth century.

At least on paper the Persian army, on which the shah rested his hopes, consisted of 137,168 men and required an annual expenditure of 1,618,000 tumans (£ 735,758).[1] This force was formidable enough to worry the British, who had long resisted Iran's control over western Afghanistan and as early as January 1852 had warned the shah that the intention of proceeding to Herat "will not be regarded with indifference."[2] The British reaction was essentially tied up with its concerns for the security of India and the Russian threat to the northwest frontier if Iran was allowed to secure Herat and gain access to Khyber Pass. The Anglo-Persian diplomatic quarrel that broke out over Herat and ultimately resulted in the 1852 Sheil-Nuri agreement was rooted in such concern at a time when Russia's ambitions were becoming apparent to other European powers.

After the fall of Amir Kabir the British government set its hope on Nuri to commit Iran to a course of nonintervention in Herat as a first step toward creating a united Afghanistan. Yet these hopes encountered resistance from Nasir al-Din Shah's quarter. In early 1852 he pressed the premier to highlight the problem of security in Khurasan in negotiations with Sheil. Should the frontier Afghan-Turkoman tribes continue to attack Persian towns and villages and should the chiefs of Kandahar and Kabul move to Herat, the Persian premier warned Sheil, Iran would be compelled to respond to any plea for assistance from the inhabitants of Herat unless assurances were given that no foreign power would interfere in the internal affairs of that region.[3] Nuri further emphasized that the Persian government could not ignore the alarming increase in Turkoman raids on the towns and villages of Khurasan, carried out with the collaboration of the Afghans, in which innocent inhabitants were killed and thousands of slaves captured, causing damage to the trade and agriculture of the region and, in turn, to the shah's prestige.[4]

Sheil naturally found this argument "unsatisfactory," for it virtually excluded Britain from intervention in Afghanistan. In his response to Nuri he threatened that "for maintenance of the English interest" Britain would "carry out her own policy regardless of Persia." In an unusually harsh tone (perhaps resulting from Sheil's frustration over Amir Kabir's execution a few days earlier), he then informed the prime minister: "If Your Excellency desires to have any conversation on this subject, I am ready to receive you."[5] Appealing to the shah's wisdom to place "a check on the unreasonable ambitions of his ministers," Sheil then used all his diplomatic eloquence to warn the "Persian ministers" not to delude themselves "in pursuit of a phantom" and to avoid risking the substantial advantage of English friendship "for the merest illusion."[6]

The shah's response to Sheil's protests came in an autograph note to Nuri. It was prompt but equivocal, somewhat reflecting the shah's improving diplomatic skills. Reiterating Persian claims of sovereignty over Herat and the "homage and obedience" of its loyal chiefs, the shah insisted that refusing to help them in their struggle against their rivals was not only "contrary to proper government and the duty of protecting our servants, but it will also give us a bad reputation among foreign governments, and diminish the confidence of the people of Persia and Afghanistan in us." With several tribes "desirous of exciting disturbance, and those headstrong Afghans, this will give rise to trouble, bad conduct, and lawlessness, and create disorder in the province of Khurasan." It seemed as if his duty as the defender of the Guarded Domains of Iran impelled the shah to treat the warlords of the eastern frontier in the same manner as his predecessors had done for centuries. In order to minimize the danger they posed and to preserve tranquility, it was necessary to balance them off against one another and, if that did not work, to intervene militarily. But the shah had British friendship to worry about. To moderate his proposed course, he added that "by the soul of the late Shah, I am heartily desirous that the friendship of the two governments should daily become more firm." Nor, he declared, did he intend to withhold "giving satisfaction to the British government," especially in any matter having connections, though slight, with the "honour and dignity of that government." But in this matter of Herat, he continued, "I am bewildered; let him [Sheil] show us what course to pursue, so that our reputation may not suffer in this government and in others, and in a country which hopes to receive favors and aid from us." The shah's desire for friendship was real, as was his bewilderment. It was evident that he was offended by Sheil's disregard of protocol toward his premier: "You must either put the British minister to the trouble of seeing you at your own house," wrote the shah, "or send this autograph so that he may be acquainted with its contents."[7] For obvious reasons, Nuri preferred the latter.

Sheil refused to give in or to take Nasir al-Din's comments seriously. In his indirect reply he warned the shah that he was jeopardizing friendship with Britain for "worthless murderers" and "slave sellers" and reminded him of Muhammad Shah's "pledge" of never marching against Herat.[8] In a report to Lord Palmerston, the British foreign minister, Sheil put all the blame on the premier's shoulders. He characterized Nuri as the chief culprit who wished "to make a demonstration towards Herat, to ingratiate himself with the shah, display his zeal and thus prop up his waning influence." Although Nuri had promised Sheil that he would be able to reverse the shah's decision, the British envoy was not convinced. "He is so full of duplicity," wrote Sheil to Palmerston, "that his promises are not always to be relied upon."[9] Even an unusual show of loyalty by five frontier chiefs from the vicinity of Herat who came to the capital to pay homage to the shah failed to impress Sheil. His diagnosis, after an interview with one of them, was that they came in pursuit of money, presents, and land.[10]

The shah's impression of the delegation and the chiefs' appeal for Persian protection was very different. He saw their entreaties as a legitimate reason to send reinforcements to Khurasan. Writing to Nuri, he replied to Sheil's new warnings and criticisms in an angry tone. "Our debt to a foreign state and the want of discipline in our [own] army are quite foreign to the present question. Even if our army be without discipline, it is not requisite that we should lose sight of the honor of the government, and the protection of our subjects on the frontier, or make Khorassan the plain of the combat [i.e., a battlefield] for our enemies. Doubtless, the minister ought to make an arrangement, so that neither the British government shall be dissatisfied with us, nor that we shall be liable to the taunts of foreigners and the people of the country."[11] This firm statement was beyond what Sheil expected from a boy-king.

Soon, however, in an audience with Sheil the shah revealed his concerns for security. "Deep anxiety" for Iran's "welfare and independence" encouraged him to complain that although the political existence of his country depended on the "friendship of England," such friendship had not saved his country from the severest losses. "Nor would it protect it from the aggressive design which Russia too clearly had in contemplation." Only "relations more intimate and definite" with England, the shah believed, would save Iran "from the fate which, otherwise, inevitably awaited her." But since Iran's "complete subjugation to Russia would certainly be injurious to England," the shah argued, he was willing to accede to a proposal that would avert the catastrophe. He left it to the wisdom of the British government to determine the exact nature of such an engagement and to regulate its details "whether by means of a treaty, or by taking Persia under its protection, or by the promise of aid to Persia, in the event of an aggression by a European power." Should Britain acquiesce in his wishes, the shah concluded, there could be no doubt that the Persian government would listen to all her wishes. "Herat and Afghanistan would then be as nothing in the estimation of the Persian ministers [i.e. government], who would be guided by the opinions of Great Britain in external policy."[12]

What the shah was proposing, no doubt under the influence of his premier and as transmitted by Sheil, was little less than a voluntary resignation to the status of a protectorate such as had been offered by the British to the defenseless principalities of India before they were fully annexed by the Empire. The kingdoms of Audh, Kashmir and Sind were the most recent examples. In principal, the idea of a defense treaty with a provision for financial aid was not contrary to the earlier Persian stance vis-à-vis Britain. Sheil claimed that a year earlier Amir Kabir "had made a proposition somewhat similar" to that currently put forth by the shah. The most striking aspect of Nasir al-Din's proposal, however, was that he was not only willing to allow the British to determine the terms of agreement but also prepared to demote himself, and his country, to the status of a protectorate whose external policies would be "guided" by Britain. Even if such a proposal were to be explained as a political maneuver, the tactless and uncanny approach adopted by Nasir al-Din and Nuri was indefensible.

After such a performance, it is a small wonder that Sheil felt justified in adopting an unusually sarcastic stance when trying to see through the shah's proposal. "With a nation so faithless and fickle as the Persians," he wrote, "it appears to me a hazardous measure to enter into [an] engagement which would be permanently binding on Her Majesty's government." Therefore, he gave the shah the same answer Palmerston had previously given to Amir Kabir. Britain preferred "to keep itself free, and to act according as the exigencies of each case" might require. Only at the shah's insistence was Sheil induced to suggest to the Earl of Granville, the new British foreign secretary, that a treaty with limited duration, perhaps as short as five years, might be advisable. As a zealous supporter of Russian containment, Sheil regarded "the junction of Russia and Persia" as the "most formidable coalition" that could threaten India from the west. A limited Anglo-Persian treaty, therefore, would reduce the likelihood of such an alliance and operate "as a curb on the fickle temper" of the Persian government.[13]

Outrageous as the shah's proposal might have been, there was reason for his "deep anxiety." After Dolgorouki's failure to save Amir Kabir, the Russian minister was conspicuously searching for pretexts on which to avenge his country's loss of prestige. Flagrant breaches of diplomatic conduct by the Russian consul in Rasht constituted one such provocation. In the same interview with Sheil, the despairing Nasir al-Din went so far as to suggest that Britain immediately appoint consuls to Rasht and As-tarabad as counterbalances to the even less tractable power of the Russian consuls. The shah described the Russian consul in Rasht as "a sort of a king, grasping at, and exercising, more authority than the Persian government." The day after the shah made his surprise offer, Sheil was told by Nuri that British consulates were not needed.[14] Indeed, the experienced Sheil did not take seriously the generous offer, which in the past had been consistently resisted by the Qajar government. A few days later, in another audience, when the envoy pursued the offer long sought by his government, the embarrassed Nasir al-Din left the matter to Nuri to resolve. "A very amusing altercation ensued between the shah and his minister," reported Sheil. Such a sudden change of plans was most probably the result of renewed Russian threats rather than any restored wisdom on the part of the shah.

Embarrassed or not, however, the shah could not remain aloof from the British, even if it meant swallowing his royal pride. Less than three months after tabling his proposal for a defense treaty and, ironically, on the very day he acknowledged the "deep impression" Malmesbury's fierce note regarding Amir Kabir's murder had left on him, the desperate shah had to ask Sheil for his advice concerning another matter. The Russian demand to introduce their ships into the Anzali lagoon in the Caspian Sea was considered by the Qajar shahs a long-standing territorial threat "highly injurious to [Iran's] interests." Sheil's reaction was noncommittal. With Palmerston's earlier instructions in mind, he cautioned the shah that there was not much Iran could do because, according to the code of international law between friendly countries, ships of both nations could reciprocally visit each other's ports. "The shah remarked, jestingly," reported Sheil, "that he had no doubt that the opinion of the British government was not formed on any consideration of their own ships in the Persian Gulf; and that even if it were, they were welcome to the use of all waters of Persia, for England was the friend of Persia, and, that for his part, he sincerely regretted that English ships could not come to Tehran."[15] Whether this was an impulsive gesture by the nervous shah to accommodate the angry British or a masterfully sarcastic remark springing from his feelings of desperation cannot be determined. What was clear to Sheil, however, was that the shah could not be trusted in spite of his effusive pro-British pronouncements. Nor should his claim over Herat, historical or otherwise, be of much value to the British government. Such an attitude was formed, at least in part, out of Sheil's personal biases rather than out of a realistic assessment of Iran's potential and territorial concerns. As matters stood,

Sheil was bound to react negatively to the opinion the Foreign Office received from Henry Rawlinson, a well-known observer of Persian affairs, concerning Nasir al-Din's stand on Herat. The British consul general in Baghdad and Sheil's ex-colleague in the Indian Army was of the opinion that a "boy king" in Tehran was less of a threat to the security of India than the unreliable Kuhandil Khan of Kandahar, a petty Afghan warlord who chronically entertained pro-Russian sentiments. Sheil argued in response that the twenty-three-year-old Nasir al-Din was not only no longer a boy-king but also that "he may march to India, in which case Russians will be at his heels."[16]

Predictions such as this were characteristic of British suspicions toward the Qajar crown. Throughout the nineteenth century the British government often opted for the more easily manipulated nomadic khans, coastal sheikhs, and petty warlords over the Persian sovereign. Such attitudes, supplemented by aggressive diplomatic measures, carried the day in London even when Sheil's mentor, Lord Palmerston, was no longer in office. Sheil's stance that Iran should be kept out of Herat was further intensified once it was concluded that the new Anglo-Persian treaty of friendship proposed by the shah was untenable. By October 1852 Sheil was convinced that the shah was determined to annex Herat. He thus concentrated all his efforts to try to extract from Nuri an agreement that would stop the shah from any intervention. Whether by persuasion, indirect pressure, or sheer coercion, the prime minister, and the shah himself, were forced, step by step, to comply with British wishes.[17] This was a personal victory for Sheil as the hour approached for his departure from Iran. The hawkish advocate of Persian noninterference was in the end able to compel Iran to allow an agreement that for two decades it had consistently refused to contract. The agreement was a disheartening setback for the shah, who started with a demand for an ambitious alliance with England and ended up acquiescing in the loss of influence over a vassalage on his eastern flank.

According to the terms of the 1852 agreement, the shah was obliged to write to the chief of Herat, informing him that the Persian government "at no time have had or will have any idea of taking possession of, or annexing, or governing Herat or claiming the subjection of the people of Herat." Not only would Iran not interfere in the internal affairs of Herat, it would recognize the province's independence and consent to the discontinuation of the two practical symbols of Persian sovereignty: the reading of a sermon (*khutba*) and the striking of coins in the shah's name. The one concession the Persian government could draw out of the agreement was as meager as it was ineffective: "[I]f an army from abroad should attack Herat, the

Persian government will appoint an army to aid," but the Persian force was to remain outside the city and, having expelled the foreign army, "will immediately return to the Persian territory."[18] After intense negotiations, Nuri, in an astute move symbolic of his—or possibly the shah's—improving diplomatic skills, was able to add one important provision to the final version: The Persian obligation was to be binding only as long as there was no British interference in the internal affairs of Herat; "otherwise these engagements will be null and void."[19]

In a special levee (*salam*) held to receive the Herat chiefs a few days after the royal announcement required by the treaty was issued, the shah tried to put the best face on a sad occasion. He received "in great form and pomp" the offering sent by the chief of Herat—500 tumans coined in the shah's name, some shawls, and some horses. "After much display of exultation," wrote Sheil, with a hint of sarcasm betraying the bitter aftertaste of his still unfinished triumph, "the Shah then passed a large share of encomium on his own magnanimity in having recognized the independence of Herat, dwelling at the same time with great emphasis on his determination to march an army against any power whatever that might interfere with that state."[20] The royal gestures—receiving the Herat coinage struck in his name and declaring that he would march on Herat to defend it—were conscious moves in defiance of the spirit of the agreement. Perhaps it would have been possible to avoid such an agreement with a more experienced shah and a less intimidated premier. The final objective, however—control of Herat—was ultimately untenable, given the British concern for the security of India and Iran's precarious resources. It took a full-scale war three years later for Nasir al-Din to recognize this unpalatable fact. Though he swiftly and impatiently shifted his emphasis from Herat to other areas, the shah's resentment remained deep. As a "defender of the land," he had seen his prestige and self-esteem tarnished. His historical extraterritorial rights as the only Shi'ite sovereign to "protect" the Shi'ite subjects were to be denied in another episode that soon followed the conclusion of the agreement.

THE KING OF THE SHI'ITES

It is not surprising that immediately after the Herat agreement the question of maltreatment of the Shi'ites of Iraq, who like the Shi'ites of Herat looked to the rulers of Iran for protection, became a priority for the shah. He looked to his western frontiers in search of a remedy for his injured pride. Persecution of the Shi'ites of Iraq was a matter that could not be overlooked

by a ruler whose dynasty built its legitimacy around the theme of upholding Shi'ism. These periodic persecutions were often ignored by the
Ottoman authorities, if not officially sponsored by them. Frontier raids by
the Sunni Kurdish tribes against mostly Shi'ite populations in towns and
villages in western Azarbaijan and Kurdistan also remained unpunished as
rebellious Kurds sought refuge in the Ottoman territory. Problems that had
overshadowed Perso-Ottoman relations for decades were particularly compelling to Nasir al-Din, who saw himself as increasingly embittered and
humiliated in the face of British support for his Ottoman neighbor. Simultaneously with the signing of the Herat agreement, the shah ordered
30,000 to 40,000 troops to be gathered in Sultaniya, near Zanjan, for a
military review in the style of Fath 'Ali Shah's annual summoning of the
troops.[21]

Whether the Sultaniya review was intended to demonstrate the shah's
military might or to dissuade Ottomans from persecution of the Persian
population of Baghdad province, it was bound to incur British displeasure.
Considering the forthcoming review a potential threat to the Ottomans, the
British envoy tried to dissuade the shah by pointing out that the 200,000-
tuman cost of the review would be a major drain on the government
resources. Given the state of animosity between the shah and Sheil, the
envoy's advice met with little success. The shah "distinctly and officially"
announced that the purpose of the review was a military exercise and that
his troops would not go a single step beyond the district of Sultaniya or
in any other direction. At the same time, he expressed to the *vali* of Baghdad
his willingness to join forces to pacify Kurdish frontier disturbances in the
Sulaymaniya region. Yet neither his assurance nor his proposal prevented
the British envoy from speculating on the shah's ulterior motives, nor did
they prevent him from bombarding Nuri with a round of protest notes.[22]

In reply to the third protest note submitted by the British, and pointing
out on behalf of the shah the precedence for the Sultaniya exercise since
Fath 'Ali Shah's time, Nuri went on to say in a blunt tone indicative of Nasir
al-Din's aggravation: "But that which annoys me is that whenever, in
matters like the present, the real sentiments of the government are stated . . . no faith or credit is given to their real intentions; and you still insist
on your own views." When Turks gathered troops in the Van district, Nuri
observed, no one took notice; but "when His Majesty proceeds for the
organization of the internal affairs of the country to Sultaniya, which is
the spacious place of summer residence . . . your excellency protests."[23]
The shah's own autograph followed, "repeating in the strongest terms" his
resolution to carry on with the Sultaniya plan in spite of foreign objections.

Insisting on his benign intentions "to make a circuit in the interiors of the country, to inspect and review the troops and to take recreation," he assured Sheil: "We have also limited our journey to a short time. Please Heaven, we shall return with great speed at an early date." It must have only added to the shah's irritation to feel compelled to give undertakings to foreign envoys not only concerning his nonintervention in his vassalage of Herat but also on what, after all, was purely an internal affair of his country. Moreover, these undertakings had to be put in such degrading terms where they concerned the short duration of his journey and his speedy return to the capital. Evident behind the subdued tone of the shah's note there was a suppressed outrage, and the premier bore the brunt of royal rage. In a private note to Nuri the shah complained bitterly of the Ottoman conduct. Evidently angry that they allowed 'Abbas Mirza, his exiled brother, to receive British protection, he broadened his criticism to say:

> Neither their words, their actions, nor their promises have any validity. What sort of creatures are they? . . . I wonder how much these damned people [literally, "father-burnt," *pidar-sukhta*], this worthless [Wandering] Jew, these Persians ['*ajam*] must suffer in this world? When will they be relieved? Ten years ago they [i.e., Ottoman authorities] repeatedly killed and plundered and gradually laid down a precedent [literally, an "innovation"]. In whatever way they could they have offended and degraded the *shari'at*. But on the Last Day we will be held responsible. No doubt we will pay for it. Certainly God disapproves that thirty thousand Shi'ite human beings can be violated so much in that province [i.e., Baghdad]. What is the purpose of this life? To hell with [political] expediency [*bar pidar-i mulahiza la'nat*]. I am not the sultan of the Shi'ite nation! I am not! I am not! That is all.[24]

The inability to act as "the sultan of the Shi'ites," the "defender of the faith," in lands beyond his recognized sovereignty was the source of the shah's frustration. His sense of pious liability and disavowal of his traditional duty was aroused because he was denied extraterritorial authority not only by the Christian powers in the Russian-annexed Caucasus and British-dominated Afghanistan but also by the Sunni Ottoman sultan and his Turkish agents in Iraq. One can almost hear the agonizing pain of readjustment in Nasir al-Din's desperate exclamations. The "sultan of the Shi'ites" had encountered serious challenges to his authority in lands that were demarcated by European ambitions in the north and the south and sectarian division in the east and the west.

Changing international circumstances, however, blew this apparently insignificant Sultaniya affair beyond all proportion into a subject of great

British concern, even to the point of obsession. In his audience with the shah in April 1853, on the eve of the Crimean War, William Taylour Thomson, the British chargé d'affaires after Sheil, noticed "a considerable culmination in the shah's desire for military spectacle." The shah insisted that although the review would cost some money, he felt "forced to carry it out to save himself from accusation of being feeble of purpose," particularly because of the publicity that had surrounded the whole affair.[25] An outbreak of cholera convinced the British that the Sultaniya issue had been shelved for good; but it was brought out again by the shah after Sheil's departure in the summer of 1853 with even greater vigor. The incursions of the Kurdish tribes at the frontiers provided "ample cause of serious alarm," to the extent that Thomson believed the Persians might retaliate, and then war in the northwest frontier would be inevitable. With the shah "full of resentment" at the treatment he had experienced from Ottomans in Iraq, and with Nuri now developing intimate relations with the Russians at the shah's behest, it was only to be expected that the British felt threatened.[26] Dolgorouki's advice concerning Iran's need to take precautionary steps against the possible amassing of Ottoman forces in Erzerum on the Perso-Ottoman frontier, no matter how self-serving for the Russians in their upcoming conflict with the Ottomans in the Crimean War, was taken up enthusiastically by the shah.

Yet Thomson dismissed the rumors that the Russians were the prime movers behind Nasir al-Din in his renewed calls for a military review. To Lord Clarendon, the new British foreign secretary, he wrote: "But your lordship is aware with what tenacity, from the first moment when this military review was mentioned, the Shah has addressed to his resolution, even when Russia and Turkey were apparently in the most friendly terms." Any further interference, Thomson warned, might cause Nuri's political collapse "for having pushed with too much warmth his opposition to the Shah's wishes." It was clear that the shah had remained resolute against all odds on grounds of prestige. If it had no other result, the review could free him "in the eyes of his people from the imputation of being infirm of purpose." Moreover, his presence in Sultaniya with an army at such a time would—in his own country, in any event—"give him the imposing attitude of holding the balance between the two powers." Yet Thomson was quick to point out that although the shah's religious feelings may have been enlisted on the side of his Muslim neighbor (i.e., the Ottomans), his "fears and venality" might be worked in so many ways by Russia that, unless by the "same means as strong counter-influence" were exerted by England, "Russia would not experience much difficulty, if the moment of action should arrive, in inducing him to side with her and disregard all arrangements in favor of the expediency of his preserving a strict neutrality."[27] Whatever the reality of these speculations might have been, it was clear that by 1853 the new European anti-Russian alliances in the wake of the Crimean War had alerted Nasir al-Din to new possibilities.

The moment of military glory had arrived, but unexpected calamities intervened. Receiving the troops who were about to depart for Sultaniya, the shah was exposed to the rays of the Tehran sun until midday in the August heat (see Pl. 18). But his enthusiasm was no match for the ravages of cholera or the chaos in the camp, all exacerbated by shortages of cash and logistical problems. Even before the troops left Tehran, three soldiers had died of cholera. Others soon deserted, rushing back home unswayed by the pathetic equivalent of one shilling offered by the army to induce them to continue to Sultaniya.[28] The situation in the camp had worsened by the time the shah arrived. Thomson assiduously shadowed the shah to the Sultaniya camp. Reporting on his movements with a religious zeal befitting an up-and-coming chargé d'affaires in search of commendation, he still found ample occasion to subject Nuri to an inquisitorial examination on the veracity of the shah's intentions. Declining to give written guarantees lest he offend the Russian representative, Nuri resorted to oral assurances concerning the shah's brief stay in the camp with a dash of the wit for which he was known. "I swear by the Messiah, in whom you believe and in whom I believe," declared the irked but still humorous premier, "I swear by Mohammad in whom I believe and in whom you do not believe; I swear by the head of the shah; by your own death [i.e., soul]; by the death of every member of my family; by the Koran and by everything I hold sacred" that the shah would not stay in the camp one day beyond the previously declared date and would immediately return to Tehran.[29]

Far sooner than expected, the chief actor in the unglamorous spectacle was forced to leave the stage. Only one day after the shah's arrival, the already chaotic camp began to break up because of another outbreak of cholera. Full of fear and indignation, the disenchanted shah ordered the cancellation of the review and rushed back to Tehran, only to realize that Dolgorouki had found the cancellation "very unpalatable." It was only accidental that on his return trip the shah had avoided encountering the secretary of the Russian mission, who was instructed by Dolgorouki "to use every exertion to detain the shah at Sultaniya, or at any other station on the road." Overnight the prospect of war with the Ottoman Empire had turned the Russian minister into a sincere advocate of Iran's military strength.[30] Thus, under the most miserable circumstances, ended the shah's grand review and his hopes for its political advantages. To lessen the impact on Tehran's population, which was aware of the royal initiative through reports in *Vaqayi'-i Ittifaqiya*, the shah intended to enter his capital with "great ostentation and ceremony." That pleasure, too, was denied him. Neither the Russian nor the Ottoman representatives would agree to attend, leaving the desperate shah with Thomson as the only symbol of foreign support. To keep him in public view as long as possible, the shah conversed with the British chargé d'affaires all the way to the city gate. Thomson decided to appear in informal dress, however, anxious to make the public understand that the Sultaniya review was not "with the concurrence of Her Majesty's government."[31] Soon, however, other incidents obliged him to express his government's displeasure less discreetly.

THE CURSE OF THE PROTECTED

Thomson's reference to British "strong counter-influence" to combat Russian advances was an ominous euphemism for an even more intense round of diplomatic quarrels with the Persian government, this time over British protégés—quarrels that were most humiliating for the shah and intrusive in the activities of his government. Perhaps at no time in the diplomatic history of Qajar Iran other than the turbulent period between 1852 and 1857 did the two European powers use their capitulatory rights so unreservedly to try to force the host government to submit to their vengeful and often opposing wishes.

Ever since Nasir al-Din's attention was directed to Herat in 1852, the number of cases of diplomatic protection issues increased radically. Sheil and his colleagues, in conjunction with the Palmerston doctrine, systematically used arbitrary offers of protection to Persians of status and influence—a practice often justified as a privilege for the "most favored nations" but in reality little more than a symbolic means of upholding the prestige of the British mission. Amir Kabir's abolition of the traditional right of seeking refuge (*bast*) in the religious sanctuaries further increased the number of those seeking shelter in foreign missions as the only safe haven outside the pale of the Persian government. But even when *bast* in the sanctuaries of Qum and Shah 'Abd al-'Azim was restored for noncriminals—a move Sheil believed was influenced by Nuri's "personal motives, to secure an asylum for himself in his day of need"—the surge in the number of disputed cases did not decrease. Under the particular conditions of Iran, Sheil further remarked with an air of paternalism, "human life and suffering are counted as nothing in comparison to the gratification of the national passion for gain." He favored the move initiated by Nuri, therefore, on the account of "the number of people who in spite of discouragement from me were inclined to seek [British] protection."[32] Commenting on the circumstances of a Khurasani khan seeking British protection, Sheil again reasserted "the spirit of disgust or dissatisfaction" as the motive among the higher classes for taking refuge with foreign missions.[33] Notwithstanding the truth of Sheil's observation, the British minister sought maximum benefit from this situation, much to the annoyance and anxiety of the shah and his premier.

The Russian involvement in protégé patronage, though not as frequent, was no less annoying to the shah nor less demeaning to the dignity of his throne. A dispute with Dolgorouki over Muhammad Hasan Khan Sardar, the influential member of the Iravani party in the capital, serves as one example.[34] The old Sardar, who was forced out of his homeland by the invading Russians in 1827 but allowed to adopt Russian citizenship and even hold the rank of major in the Russian army, had no reservation in airing his desires to succeed Amir Kabir as the commander in chief of the Persian army. The Russian envoy was happy to offer his warmest support, regardless of the fact that Sardar was involved in the murder of a man against whose execution Dolgorouki had protested so passionately. With the position of *amir nizam* still vacant, Sardar threatened that unless he was appointed to the post, he would go to Russia and press a claim for 200,000 tumans against the Persian government. He further threatened to hand over his lands in the frontier of Iranian Azerbaijan to Russia. Even though he was backed by powerful allies, the shah opposed his demand. Hesitant to assign a sensitive post to a man of dubious loyalty, the shah, in a private audience, assured Sheil that he would not appoint Sardar even to command "one soldier unless under the compulsion and pressure of the above claim." Indeed, Dolgorouki's pressure, combined with that of Nuri and Mahd 'Ulya, who both now supported Sardar against the wishes of the British, was sufficient to result in an announcement in *Vaqayi'-i Ittifaqiya* of Sardar's appointment to the far less important position of commander of the light regiments of Azerbaijan. But even this promotion the shah was unwilling to ratify, much to Sheil's delight. Clearly anxious that the appointment not go through, the British envoy lectured the shah on the virtues of resisting blackmail and foreign pressure and "thus render[ing] himself an independent monarch, which he certainly was not so long as he was held in the present thraldom." He heartily urged the shah to "resist to the last" and managed to bring him fully into the spirit of his observations. "But this inexperienced young monarch is alone," Sheil was compassionate enough to write when it was in his interest to be sanctimonious. "His mother, his prime minister and various other influential persons about the court are bent on sacrificing the shah's interests in favor of the worthless foreigner."[35]

Sheil nevertheless was right to sense imminent danger. With Bahman Mirza near the frontier and four of the best regiments of Azarbaijan in the hands of Sardar, "the helplessness of the shah excite[d] commiseration." The shah fully shared Sheil's concern that even if the Sardar was not a Russian subject, it was advisable to curb his power. Indeed, only a fool could fail to comprehend the danger of appointing to the office of the commander in chief of the army a well-connected chief who claimed Russian citizenship, a base in Azarbaijan, and an annual income of 40,000 tumans that he had amassed for several years as the absentee governor of Yazd.[36] In the end, Nasir al-Din had little choice but to bribe Sardar out of his way by adding the provinces of Kirman and Baluchistan to his highly profitable Yazd governorship. The offer was substantial enough to divert the old Sardar from military ambitions in Azarbaijan to financial greed in southeastern Iran. Some weeks later, while Nuri was complaining of "the instability of the shah's temper," presumably because he had refused to go along with the premier's wishes, Sheil found the shah surprisingly "indifferent to Sardar's problem."[37] Yet the shah was forced to promise an angry Dolgorouki in writing that he would never dismiss Sardar from his post unless the Russian protégé were convicted of an offense. He must have taken into account Sardar's old age when he made such a guarantee. Though Dolgorouki made it clear in his reply that he would always protect Sardar from any false accusations, he never again had that chance. Sardar died at his post in 1854.[38]

The Russian support for Sardar was bound to motivate an almost identical claim by a British protégé, 'Abbas Quli Khan Larijani, which in turn triggered a new dispute, this time with the British envoy. Sardar's reappointment to the governorship of Yazd led to Larijani's ejection from that office. Larijani—a military chief who served the Qajars on many occasions, including the campaign against the Babis in Tabarsi in 1848–1849—initially was appointed military governor of Yazd to mop up the last remnants of another Babi urban uprising. But when he was driven from his post by Sardar's agents on charges of financial misappropriation, he duly took refuge in the British legation in Tehran, having long nurtured friendly relations with the British envoy. Sheil had no trouble offering Larijani protection, nor did he have any compunctions in stating his real motive, which was to retain influence in the army and if possible to push Larijani's appointment as commander in chief.

Sheil's action touched off animosity. A note addressed to Nuri demonstrated the shahs's helpless position vis-à-vis the wishes of the British envoy. "If we take no notice of the matter," wrote the shah, "the whole nation will by degree become Englishmen. We have guilty persons (in Persia), we have traitors on the frontiers, in Tehran, in fact everywhere." The effects of such slights on his royal authority were painfully obvious to him: "Some will lose all confidence in us, others will become dejected, and the people will end by becoming English, and then of what value will my kingdom be? What sort of mission is this of England, and what does such protection mean? Why should they protect people who have offended?" The shah's tone then turned fearlessly blunt. With a sarcastic undertone aimed at Sheil's habit of issuing ultimatums, he warned Nuri: "Don't you consider this autograph as one of the usual description. . . . The matter must, to use an expression which is English, be settled within twenty-four hours." Still not losing sight of reality, he offered a compromise on the Larijani case but warned that if Sheil were going to act as he had in earlier cases, "I have ordered Hajee Alee Khan (the Ferrash-bashee) to go and drag him from Colonel Sheil's house, and bring him to my presence, and most assuredly after such conduct, I shall have him hacked to pieces, as an example to the people."[39]

Even though the shah had warned his premier in the strongest terms that he should not make any promises, whether in writing or verbally, and if he did he would not confirm them, the affair was settled on Sheil's terms. Producing a copy of an earlier note by the shah sanctioning Larijani's British protection in 1848, Sheil compelled the Persian government to promise that no harm would come to his protégé. In his search for security against the constant threat of dismissal and even execution, the premier was prepared to go to great lengths to save his own skin. Larijani's case proved a prelude to further collisions.

Facing the shah's growing anti-British feelings, Nuri tried to demonstrate his value as a skillful mediator capable of taming the defiant monarch. Over the course of the next few years this became a prominent pattern in the tripartite relations among the shah, his minister, and the European envoys. Nuri's efforts were largely devoted to the task of remaining the sole channel of contact between the court and the envoys. Such an objective inevitably required him to eliminate any rival among the British protégés that might threaten his monopoly. Meanwhile, the British representative was consistently using alternative channels to undermine Nuri. The case of a peripheral court parasite, Mir 'Ali Naqi, demonstrates this point. 'Ali Naqi enjoyed the protection of the British crown and at the same time received from the Persian government a pension of 1,000 tumans a year "for absolutely nothing" except spending his time "gossiping" on sensitive court issues and government scandals dear to Sheil. In simpler terms, 'Ali Naqi's main function was to spy for the British legation. With a checkered career that stretched dangerously close to the court of Bahman Mirza, he had earlier been punished by Muhammad Shah, to whom he served as a confidential secretary (*katib-i asrar*), for revealing state secrets to the British government during the siege of Herat in 1838. For this betrayal he received the promise of protection from the British.[40] In spite of an earlier friendship, 'Ali Naqi was thus a potential hazard to Nuri for knowing too much, including, one may surmise, the premier's secret dealings with Sheil, which could be used, if need be, to taint him with scandal before the shah. A dispute between the prime minister's servants and those of 'Ali Naqi soon turned into a full-scale battle. In the process, the premier's threat that he would "burn the father of 'Ali Naqi" provided an excellent pretext for Sheil to press successfully not only for a cash reparation but also for a personal apology from Nuri.[41]

The controversy, nevertheless, triggered a complaint from the shah to the Foreign Office. On royal instructions, the not-yet-accredited Persian representative in London, Mirza Shafi' Khan, made a representation concerning Sheil's misconduct, his support for troublemakers, and his refusal to allow 'Ali Naqi's expulsion from the capital.[42] Sheil's reply—that if protection were lifted he feared for 'Ali Naqi's life—created an even greater uproar. In an autograph to Nuri that was meant to be distributed to all foreign ministers in Tehran, the shah questioned the very principle of foreign envoys' offering protection. "There is too much of this mediation and interception," he wrote in a diplomatic language that barely concealed his frustration. Spelling out his deep fears that his authority was being undermined, the shah repeated bluntly: "If it be the intention of the (foreign) ministers [i.e., envoys] to give protection in this way, many of our subjects and servants will eagerly seek such protection, and we necessarily must become suspicious of our subjects." He thus resolutely concluded: "We shall not accept the interference and intervention of the ministers with reference to our subjects."[43]

Sheil must have felt somewhat embarrassed for insisting on a case that had little purpose but to uphold the prestige of the British legation. In his reasoning with Malmesbury he admitted: "I consider any extremity preferable to being accusing [sic] to this state of things; for it is only by its reputation that the English mission can maintain its ground against the substantial power of Russia." Sheil no doubt was trying hard to hide his excesses behind the customary smoke screen of prestige, the old but still quite effective rhetoric of the Palmerston school. Any doubts regarding the virtue of his conduct, Sheil cautioned the disenchanted Malmesbury, would give the wrong impression to the Russians, who would conclude that he had exceeded his limits. The occasional diplomatic storm in the Persian tea cup should be allowed to continue, Sheil seemed to be recommending to the British foreign secretary.

Yet the shah saw in the Foreign Office's hesitation a chance to condemn 'Ali Naqi and recover some of the lost ground. Based on Shafi' Khan's report, he wrote again to Nuri that "in truth, the minister of foreign affairs of the British government conducted himself very well. I do not know this being the case, why you are still irresolute in regard to that son of burnt father, Meer Ali Nakkee [Mir 'Ali Naqi] and Farhad [Mirza] and the others. Please God, you will by degrees serve them both out, and for that matter, the rest of them [i.e., the protégés] too."[44] The shah did not know that behind the solemn appearance of official correspondence, his unscrupulous premier would duly hand over his private note to the British envoy. There was a rancorous tone of retreat in Sheil's comment when he wrote: "All this was done to annoy my resistance to the arbitrary conduct of the government, and to lower me in the public estimation."[45]

Temporarily restraining the two foreign envoys was a small victory for the young shah, achieved in part against the wishes of his premier. Yet by no means did the British pressure on the issue of protégés ease. As the shah gradually leaned toward the Russian camp, dragging Nuri along with him, the British resorted to even more retaliatory tactics. Even after Sheil's departure, the four cases of protection disputes—those of the shah's grand-uncle, Malik Qasim Mirza; Hajji 'Abd al-Karim, a wealthy Kandahari money lender whose false claims to British citizenship and dubious character led to temporary suspension of Anglo-Persian relations in November 1854; the shah's uncle, Farhad Mirza, whose intermittent asylum in the British mission created two severe crises; and, finally, Hashim Khan Nuri, whose case ultimately led to the break in Anglo-Persian relations and contributed to the war of 1856—were all used by the British government to arrest the shah's obvious tilt toward the Russians.

There was also an element of personal distrust between the foreign envoys and the shah. Thomson, the new chargé d'affaires, had many reasons for manipulating the protégé issue, not the least of which was his well-nursed grudge against the shah for his strong language in his private notes to Nuri—notes that were made available far too freely by the deceitful premier to Thomson's old superior. On one occasion, Sheil sent one of the shah's private notes to the Foreign Office, a note received through "a confidential source," hoping to present "an insight into the character of the sovereign of this country." In a suspiciously pious tone, oblivious of his own illicit interception, Sheil noted: "Not a day passes without several communications of the same kind" between the shah and his premier. Among other items addressed, the note in question gave approval to Nuri's stand in his heated discussion with Thomson (then the secretary of the mission) and Mirza Husayn Quli, the Persian secretary of the British mission. The shah commented: "They have completely prevented us from engaging in our own internal affairs. A curse on both their fathers. You will, as far as you can, not give up the internal affairs; please God."[46] One can assume that Sheil considered himself, along with his secretaries, included in this royal damnation. Not surprisingly, after his departure for England, he refused to accept the shah's portrait, which was sent to him as a sign of gratitude for his long service in Iran.[47]

In the long and tedious case of Hajji 'Abd al-Karim, Thomson found ample chances to put into practice the "strong counter-influence" he had advocated against Russia. Under instructions from Clarendon and, later, Sheil in London, for obvious political reasons, and in the face of consistent Persian denial, he pushed for a bogus claim to British citizenship for the Afghan money lender. There was little doubt that 'Abd al-Karim's insisted he had been born in Shikarpur in India, rather than in Kandahar—a claim that entitled him to British protection—so that he could collect large, unpaid debts he had amassed by lending money to Qajar dignitaries and princes at earlier dates. By bringing up one of 'Abd al-Karim's many claims—the one against Fathullah Mirza Shu'a' al-Saltana (son of Fath 'Ali Shah and father of Shukuh al-Saltana, one of the shah's principal wives and mother of his future heir apparent, Muzaffar al-Din Mirza)—Thomson hoped to strike a blow at the shah's vulnerability. His timing suggests that his action was calculated to prohibit the Persian government from making deals with Russia. To this end Thomson was prepared to use all his resources, even making available to 'Abd al-Karim the servants of the British mission for the purpose of evicting Fathullah Mirza from the house he had rented from 'Abd al-Karim. To give this action the semblance of legality, he concurrently wrote to Nuri informing him of the course he was about to take, knowing full well that his action would be perceived as deliberate contempt for the royal authority and was bound to incite a strong reaction from the shah. Nuri's bold but measured reply to the chargé d'affaires denied not only 'Abd al-Karim's claim of citizenship but also condemned Thomson's offense.[48]

The episode brought into action the harem and the court, as agents of the shah, and helped him keep the rather unreliable premier on course. Beyond all its farcical wrangling, the case demonstrated the underlying reason for the shah's leaning toward Russia. The shah considered it an outrage that Fathullah Mirza's people were evicted and servants of the mission were stationed on the prince's property. In a private note to his premier he wrote: "[I]n short, Thomson has chosen a wrong course. Today they petitioned me in the andarun, and we will never tolerate that [women] in the andarun would plead and petition about the actions of the British representative. If I hear again that their servants [i.e., the British] have gone to his [i.e., Fathullah's] house, I will order their servants to be beheaded."[49] It was clear that Shukuh al-Saltana's complaint, particularly in the presence of other woman in the harem, greatly injured the shah's sense of honor. His temper is well evident in another angry note to Nuri. "If Thomson does not abandon his action of tonight," he wrote, "I swear to God the Almighty that tomorrow morning I will set fire to the British embassy and I would not be afraid of the consequences."[50]

The shah's threat materialized the next morning, not in an act of incineration but in a popular backlash, possibly orchestrated by Mahmud Khan Nuri Kalantar, the mayor of Tehran.[51] A crowd of 300 women, "assembled from various andaruns," armed with sticks, stones, and bricks, and accompanied by the Kalantar's and Fathullah Mirza's men, rushed into the prince's garden and, bolstered by 2,000 citizens, beat the much-hated mission servants and turned them out from the disputed property. Responding to Thomson's demand for an apology and reparations from the Persian government, the shah's angry outburst was even more dramatic. In a private note to Nuri he wrote:

> Even if he [i.e., Thomson] could prove Hajji 'Abd al-Karim's citizenship and that indeed he was born in London, still he could not on his own initiative send [his men] even to the humblest Persian subject in order to resolve disputes, let alone the house of the monarch's father[-in-law]. Thomson himself is at fault vis-à-vis the government. He is desperately trying to do something [*mikhwahad dast va pa'i karda bashad*]. . . . Absolutely refuse to abide by his unjustified demands. What is this? Is he trying to rule in this country? And so conspicuously? If he asks for satisfactory answers [i.e., satisfaction], you write back satisfactory answers: these demands cannot be met.[52]

The shah's refusal brought from the British chargé d'affaires further threats of suspension of diplomatic relations, which in turn engendered an even stronger reaction from the shah. Incensed by the "very discourteous tone"[53] of the chargé d'affaires' letter, the shah warned Nuri once more: "I am not possibly going to give up on the case of the house [of 'Abd al-Karim] and Thomson. Do whatever is in your power. Once you have proved yourself incapable leave it to me. I will burn their father. Do not delay in this matter."[54] The emerging royal self-confidence, boosted by minor successes in earlier protection disputes, is evident in the hint, perhaps the first, of the possibility of direct rule, independent of a premier. His bitter anger and desperation reached its climax in a note on the margin of Nuri's cover letter seeking approval for the official answers to Thomson's demands:

> I will abdicate from this kind of rule with utmost pleasure but will not possibly accept such blatant and acute dishonor [bi-ghayrati ba in shiddat va vuzuh]. . . . If you too have honor you will respect our right of sovereignty [haqq-i saltanat] upon yourself and generations of your forefathers and particularly the favors that we have bestowed on you, you will then not abandon us. Our destiny is in the hand of the Lord of the Universe.[55]

The shah's allusion to abdication was not a mere figure of speech to demonstrate his anger. His throne, he believed, was about to be seriously subverted by the British. To withstand the pressure of the neighboring powers, the shah could appeal to no one but the Lord of the Universe. More than ever, the momentum in this confrontation convinced him that divine destiny would preserve the Persian monarchy, and himself as its embodiment, from outside threats, and this conviction gave him some strength and resolve. In response to Nuri's inquiry as to how Thomson's threatening note should be answered, he instructed again: "His excellency should reply that London is completely at fault [Landara bisyar ghalat mikunad] to require anything coercively from us, the monarchy of Iran."[56]

In such a state of mind the shah saw any British gesture as evidence of denial. Anxious about the possible manipulation of 'Abbas Mirza, now under British protection, he was even prepared to meet 'Abd al-Karim's claim, provided he could regain custody over his half-brother. When this proposal was rejected, the shah resigned himself to the possibility of a break in relations. Thomson's next note to the shah—bearing no addressee, a deliberate sign of disrespect to the sovereign—turned this possibility into a certainty. "I am utterly bewildered and surprised by his unaddressed letter," wrote the shah to Nuri. "You should only reply that he should seek an answer to his unaddressed letter from whomever he had sent it to. . . . [Moreover] because of an unaddressed letter one should not clear the stage. If he intends to leave in protest, let him go to hell, to the very bottom of hell. Every day one hundred thousand times the government of Iran dies and is resurrected. Let it for once liberate its soul from the yoke of these 'sons of burned fathers.'"[57]

Emotional outbursts and cries of indignation reflected the shah's desperation in coping with British threats. Yet such a state of mind could easily change, in a matter of days, into a conciliatory course, even at the expense of humiliation. Accompanied by the renewed threats of war and of occupation of the Khark Island and Bushihr (a favorite British tactic of resorting to "gunboat diplomacy" first tested successfully in 1838), the prospects of a break in relations were enough to make the shah think twice. His premier's assessment on the brink of the suspension in relations provides a rare insight into the Persian predicament: "Not to undertake any [of Thomson's conditions for] satisfaction is not practical," he wrote. "War with the British is not expedient." He recommended that the shah comply with the conditions set by Thomson—to bastinado the mayor's and Fathullah Mirza's servants, accept Hajji 'Abd al-Karim's claim to British citizenship, and send an official apology from the Persian minister for foreign affairs. He further argued that not accepting these terms would provide the British with a pretext "so that it could be said to other governments: 'We demanded satisfaction and they refused.' Then they will declare war on us and in the eyes of all governments they will be proven right. Of course, if it can be settled without embarrassment, it is fine, [that is] we are not humiliated [*zalil nabashim*] and there would not be a war but there would be friendship." The argument was compelling enough to persuade the now fearful shah to reply anxiously: "Definitely you are permitted tonight to erase my lines from the despatch, certainly, certainly!" Not fully satisfied, he again added in a second marginal comment to Nuri's note: "We too wrote an account. [Tomorrow] morning let it be brought to our presence so that I will erase my lines."[58] It was not clear what lines he meant to erase, but if they were written in the same angry tone as his previous remarks, the shah's anxiety concerning possible British retaliation was not misplaced, to say the least.

The shah's autograph note, written in the last hour before the suspension of relations, betrayed his muted feelings—tempered by outrage but tamed with apprehension. Speaking of "friendship and cordiality" with England now, he wished that "the desire of ill-disposed people" will not make it appear "in a different light to the eyes of the British government." Summing up Thomson's demands, he pointed out that although the Persian government was not responsible, it was his "royal desire" to treat the foreign representatives with respect, and he instructed his minister for foreign affairs to go to Mr. Thomson's house and on the part of the Persian ministers "express to him their regret for the indignity to his servants." He further agreed that the warden [*kadkhuda*] of the city ward in which the incident occurred should entertain the servants of the mission for one full night in the garden of the disputed house. But he refused to allow the servants of the mayor or the prince to be punished on the grounds that "their innocence is known to the prime minister" and "it is at variance with justice and equity to punish without rhyme or reason the guiltless slaves of God." He further proposed that the 'Abd al-Karim's affair be brought to "the direct knowledge of Her Majesty the Queen of England, and whatever her justice may dictate, the ministers of our government will not dispute." Not agreeing with these terms, he warned Thomson, was evidence that the chargé d'affaires was "seeking a pretext and that he is endeavoring to make the friendly feelings existing between the governments appear doubtful and questionable in the eyes of the world. It is evident that he will be responsible for the consequences of the proceedings."[59]

The shah's conciliatory tone went a long way toward meeting the British conditions, yet despite an appeal to Queen Victoria for justice against the mischiefs of Her Majesty's agent, his compromise was not enough. After all, the implicit demand to abandon rapprochement with Russia, for which the whole episode had been staged, had not yet been met. On 8 November, therefore, twenty-three days after the incident and after exchanging twenty-three fierce notes on the subject with the Persian government, Thomson declared suspension of diplomatic relations with Iran. Less than a week later, upon returning from his summer camp, he lowered the British flag. His action, he proudly announced, created a "sensation" in the capital and a "general feeling of regret" by the people of all classes.[60] He himself had no remorse, nor did he have any intention of leaving the capital or terminating communications with private Persian subjects or with the Persian government on other pertinent issues. It was clear to Thomson that the right dose of coercion, backed by full approval from his government, sooner than later would remove the last of the shah's crumbling resistance. For an up-and-coming chargé d'affaires who was trying to advance his diplomatic career on the much-cherished sport of "humbling the natives," nothing seemed inaccessible. If the chief agent of the host government, in this case Nuri, had too many embarrassing skeletons in his closet, and if the shah himself was clearly at odds with his premier, a scheme such as the one devised by Thomson was bound to render the desirable result.

ALLIANCE WITH RUSSIA

The diplomatic tension with Britain reduced the prospects of Anglo-Persian relations in Nasir al-Din's eyes to little more than open war and persuaded the shah to look seriously at the proposed military alliance with Russia. On the international scene, the Russo-Turkish war that broke out in October 1853 polarized Europe and soon brought France and Britain decidedly to the side of the Ottomans. This meant that the Ottoman Empire and Britain would employ all their resources to dissuade Iran from any involvement against its Ottoman neighbor. The shah's frustration with the British over protégé cases was bound up with his lack of authority in controlling his home affairs. The Herat and Sultaniya episodes, meanwhile, clearly showed the limits of British tolerance for any military ambitions aimed at reasserting control over the peripheries. At home the shah was faced with Nuri, who in spite of his negotiating strength and other skills was on the side of reconciliation with Britain. Nuri favored this course as long as he could maintain the Russians at arm's length for necessary bargaining and as long as he could stay in power and amass a fortune for himself and his clan. For him brinksmanship, elaborate stratagems, intrigue, and betrayal were thus in order against his formidable adversaries, both in the court and in the foreign missions. The shah, perhaps unaware of the extent of his premier's Machiavellian devices, was prepared to overlook the flaws for the positive qualities—his capacity to outmaneuver the British in the war of words and diplomatic notes and his reassuring, fatherly character, which was soothing to the monarch's battered psyche.

In the course of the international bickering and realignments prior to the Crimean War, the advantages of ensuring a new Russo-Persian rapprochement became increasingly clear to both sides. Naturally the Russians did not look with approval at Britain's efforts or those of its allies. Nor did they condone the notoriously pro-British Nuri's appointment to the office of prime minister, particularly as their efforts to appoint a pro-Russian—or, rather, Russian—commander in chief of the army had failed earlier because of the shah's resistance. Recognizing the advantages of Iran's support for Russia in the prospective war with the Ottomans, Dolgorouki reversed his initial pose. He went as far as making conciliatory gestures over the final Persian payment of 473,000 tumans in war retribution from 1828. Such gestures were enough to convince Nasir al-Din of the advantages of coming to terms with the Russians. Giving Mirza Sa'id Khan Ansari prominence by appointing him to the office of minister for foreign affairs (since the previous year he had been acting minister for foreign affairs) was the shah's positive answer to the Russian move. It was as though in Sa'id Khan he was purposefully nurturing a reputation for pro-Russian proclivities to balance off, one may surmise, Nuri's reputation for pro-British tendencies. The assigned pro-Russian role for Sa'id Khan as antagonist to Nuri came with little practical power and thus did not particularly alarm the British. "A man without any capacity, whose mind is absorbed in devotional exercises and in the study of the traditions of his prophet," is how he was defined by Sheil, who nevertheless admitted that he was "less corrupt" than others and not "wholly destitute of national feeling."[61]

Signs of increasing Russian rapport with the shah were evidently worrisome to the British. In early November 1853 Dolgorouki, accompanied by the tsar's special envoy, Bebitove, received a private audience with the shah that lasted nearly two hours. All the officers of the court usually in attendance were excluded, but "a person employed by the Persian government" (a euphemism for a British spy) communicated the substance of the discussion indirectly to Thomson. Announcing the declaration of the war between Russia and the Ottomans, the Russian envoy resorted to his usual tactics by declaring that "the emperor would consider the shah his enemy if he withheld the cooperation which present circumstances demanded." This was a threat in line with Dolgorouki's diplomacy, a mixture of coercion and concession, as well as with the tsar's recent rejection of Iran's request to reschedule the 1828 war indemnity to be paid in ten rather than five installments.[62] In the aftermath of the abortive Sultaniya plan, the envoy requested that "a strong military demonstration" be made by Iran against Turkey in Azarbaijan and Kirmanshah, assuring at the same time that the war would soon end in Russia's favor. Then the emperor would be at liberty, Dolgorouki assured him, to implement his plans for an eastern policy. A force of at least 60,000 would be sent to Khiva, and eventually Afghanistan and Kandahar would be handed over to Iran as its share. "Military munitions and money would be supplied by Russia, corn and straw being all that would be demanded from Persia." To convince the young and still politically naive shah of his sincerity, Dolgorouki offered what seemed the only real incentive: "The debt due from Persia to Russia [i.e., the war indemnity] would [then] be canceled."[63]

The Russian proposals received the shah's enthusiastic, almost impulsive, assent, though he was sober enough to ask, among his conditions, for the return to Iran of Qutur, the disputed Perso-Ottoman frontier territory in western Azarbaijan, which he hoped he would be able to acquire with Russian cooperation. As the "sultan of the Shi'ites," he might even have let loose the bird of his imagination around the golden domes of the Shi'ite holy shrines in Iraq. The offer was not "forced upon the shah" but readily accepted by him, believed the Russian envoy. Given his deep impression of Russia's military predominance—a fact that Iran's bitter experiences in two rounds of wars with that empire must have stamped on his political consciousness—the shah's positive response was not unexpected. He did not want to appear as an enemy of the tsar. The outbreak of the Russo-Ottoman war, a conflict still confined to two parties, encouraged the young monarch to seek consolation for his earlier foreign policy setbacks. This was the first time since the Napoleonic wars that an unfolding European conflict had loosened the dual Anglo-Russian yoke on Iran, though Nasir al-Din was not so simpleminded as to believe that he could lift it altogether. He hoped Iran would benefit, as it had in the Russo-Ottoman war of 1829, from such conflicts enough to rectify what he could not achieve by peaceful means. The war likely would enable the shah to force the Ottomans to take a more tolerable course in Shi'ite Iraq, ideally without alarming Britain; he might also have found the prospects of Russian assistance over Herat encouraging. In "high spirits" he thus immediately ordered an assembly of troops to be sent to the Turkish frontiers under the command of the Kurdish officer, 'Aziz Khan Mukri, now the commander of the army (*sardar-i kull*), and Muhammad Khan Qajar, the chief of the royal body-guards (*sar-kishikchi-bashi*).

The shah's high hopes, however, proved to be premature. His ambitions were soon dampened by Nuri's more sober reasoning. News of the shah's decision rapidly traveled through the corridors of intrigue connecting Gulistan Palace to the foreign embassies until it reached the anxious Ottoman ambassador, no doubt through Thomson, and caused a new diplomatic uproar. Threatening the shah with a break in relations and his immediate departure, the Ottoman ambassador demanded the cancellation of the planned troop movements. The shah obviously miscalculated British penetration into his court and government no less than he misjudged the depth of his country's political isolation. Suspension of relations with Britain and the impending threat of a break with the Ottomans now counterbalanced Russia's compelling demands for a dangerous alliance, which were sweetened only with far-fetched rewards. It is hard not to sympathize with the shah's plight or his effort, adventurous as it might have been, to benefit from the emerging international realignment. Even Nuri was taken by surprise, to his disgust, by the shah's undertaking and its potential consequences. He pointed out to the shah, after being summoned to resolve the Ottoman crisis, that an alliance with Russia was not in Iran's best interests. He correctly predicted four months prior to the European powers' entry into the war that an Anglo-French military involvement on the side of the Ottomans would isolate Russia and cause her eventual defeat. Alliance with Russia, he believed, was a highly dangerous prospect for a weak country like Iran. His further advocacy of an alliance with the Ottomans and their allies instead was not altogether altruistic. Such reasoning appealed to the shah's common sense, though he condoned a complete reversal of his course with reluctance. Nuri's remedy for the crisis required an embarrassing change of the shah's word. It also necessitated a full acceptance of the British demands on the 'Abd al-Karim affair in exchange for British mediation with the Ottomans in order to avoid a break in diplomatic relations. It must have been with extreme aversion that he agreed to cancel the troop movements and drop his last resistance to British demands.

Nuri's successful initiative aroused Dolgorouki's strongest opposition. In his view Nuri's conciliatory initiative was too perfectly staged not to have been preconceived in horse trading with Thomson. Accusing Nuri of being the "enemy of the tsar" and responsible for changing the shah's mind, he caused the premier "deepest mortification" when he declared that he had in his possession two royal decrees confirming the shah's pledges to Russia. This claim was solemnly rejected by the shah, who was now moving away from his pro-Russian stance. "At the present," reported Thomson triumphantly, "the influence of the Russian minister has almost totally disappeared, and if it were not for the uncertainty and the want of stability in the policy of Persia, there would be room to fear that this government would adopt a more defined course of opposition to Russia than appears to be judicious."[64] Thomson's enigmatic remark suggested that after he disengaged from Russia, the shah renewed his earlier demand for a British commitment to defend Iran, a demand that in the past the British had denied him. Three weeks after relations were officially suspended, Thomson, having forced the shah to accept his terms and to plead with him for assistance, recommended to the Foreign Office that relations with Iran resume.[65]

Iran's refusal to conclude a defense treaty with Russia created an outrage in St. Petersburg. The thrust of the criticism regarding Russia's weakened position in Iran thus fell on Dolgorouki's diplomatic conduct. In what proved to be his last diplomatic battle before departure, Dolgorouki "struck back" in more than a metaphorical sense against Nuri in revenge for a failure that he believed had blemished his reputation. In his last interview with Nuri, the Russian envoy again insisted on the shah's written commitment to an alliance with Russia and warned the premier of the consequences if he refused to ratify a proposed treaty to which the shah had already given his assent. As R. G. Watson, the secretary of the British mission, recorded, "In his eagerness, the prince [Dolgorouki] rose from his seat and approached the Vazeer [Nuri] flourishing his cane in the air to give emphasis to his argument and words, and it unluckily happened that the cane came down somewhat heavily on the Vazeer's leg." Containing himself in the presence of others, the prime minister reacted calmly to the envoy's violent act and, throwing the cane to the far end of the room, he requested Dolgorouki leave.[66] Whether it was an embarrassing accident or a purposeful act to humiliate the premier, the incident worked in Nuri's favor. Dolgorouki was soon recalled, and the premier boasted that it was his doing that brought about the recall.

Dolgorouki's debacle was not the end of Russian efforts to subscribe Iran as a silent partner for its war effort. Nor was the shah's search for an alliance with Russia at its end. Both these required a new envoy in Tehran with greater patience and less contempt. By March 1854 it was only to be expected that when an Anglo-French defense treaty was signed with the Ottoman Empire and the two European powers subsequently entered the war, Nasir al-Din Shah would revert to his previous policy of alliance with their opponent. He interpreted the two powers' defense guarantees for the Ottoman Empire, backed by the thunder of their guns in Sevastopol, as a sign of British willingness to allow the Ottomans to take territorial advantage of Iran's imposed neutrality. In the early days of the Crimean War the remarkable Russian advances against the Ottomans in the Caucasus, including the capture of Kars (Qaras) and the near blockage of the Trabizon-Tabriz trade route, was bound to impress the shah and again make him see the advantages of siding with the Russians, if not for territorial gains or the security of his own frontier then at least to please his northern neighbor and to gratify his anti-British sentiments.

Criticizing Nuri for having submitted to British wishes, the shah wrote in March 1855: "I will, by my own intent and with contentment and utmost enthusiasm, give away to Russia the entire Kingdom of Iran, not to mention Azarbaijan, Gilan, and Mazandaran, in spite of Britain but will not succumb to her strenuous demands." A rhetorical question in the margin complemented his gloomy mood: "Are we [puppets] made of wax (*[aya] ma ra az mum sakhta-and*)?" he asked with a strain of self-contempt. "In this world there are no human beings like us."[67]

The premier's refusal to resume negotiations with the Russians, a position reinforced by Thomson's threat of reprisal, was an obstacle in the shah's way and required some royal persuasion. Once more the chronic rumors of Nuri's dismissal were in circulation, providing his opponents within the court with new ammunition. One may assume that the shah utilized the rumors, initiated by Mahd 'Ulya's allies, to bring the premier back into the royal fold. The fact that the shah negotiated directly with the new Russian charge d'affaires, Nicholai Anichkov, and tentatively accepted his proposed terms further obliged Nuri to rethink his position. To make his point even more emphatically, the shah instructed his closest ally in the court, 'Ali Khan Farrash-bashi, to stand within hearing distance of the premier during an interview with Thomson on the subject of the Russo-Persian alliance. This symbolic gesture was sufficient to remind Nuri of the fate that might befall uncompromising premiers, especially if they were to seek foreign assistance.[68] But the shah still needed his premier. In a private note, mixing assurances with promises of violent reprisal, the shah's tone was unmistakably confident. "What words are these?" he wrote in response to Nuri's apparent gloom with the rumors of his impending fall.

> What are these doubts you entertain? God willing with your support in a short time we intend to make in this world a name for ourselves that no one has ever made and we regard your role essential in [achieving] it. With people's tasteless nonsense [*jafang*] I will never give up my intent. I write candidly and you repeat it candidly: "I swear by God! I swear by Murtaza 'Ali [the First Imam]! I swear by the soul of the late shah! If anyone entertains any assumption of wrongdoing or dishonesty about you, I will behead him with my own hand and give his wife to a muleteer. Certainly! Definitely! It is of course necessary to make everybody understand this so that they will not be subjected to such a fate.[69]

Intense emotions and vulgar outbursts aside, the shah's emphasis on fulfilling his ambitions, on making a great name for himself, lay at the very heart of his emerging self-image. Great as were his ambitions, though, the shah still relied on a premier possessing a distinct capacity for maneuverability and political agility. If he was denied the military power to reassert his authority on his own frontiers and lacked the machinery to stop foreign proxies from pestering his government, it was only to be expected that he would resort to deceptive tactics, machinations, and secret deals using Nuri's proficiency. He was prepared to ignore the charges of "wrongdoing and dishonesty" brought against his premier, charges of which he himself must have seen examples, in order to use Nuri's British connections to beat his formidable adversaries on their own terms.

The course that remained for Iran in the volatile international situation was to aim at maximizing its gains by bargaining with both sides and maintaining its neutrality. This was the rationale behind the secret treaty with Russia that was finally exchanged between Nuri and Anichkov in September 1854 under the shah's personal auspices. Under the terms of the treaty, Iran was to halt the movement of arms, namely British consignments via Azarbaijan, to the Ottoman side, as well as prevent the transport of food and provisions to the Ottoman Empire. Russian gains against the Turks on the Caucasian front during the summer must have encouraged the shah to undertake such a commitment. Iran's reward, the only benefit to the Persian side for the duration of the war, was relief from paying nearly 500,000 tumans, the last of the 1828 war indemnity. The shah must have found such a reward particularly gratifying and a sign of goodwill on the Russian side for future support, a good start toward the great ambitions outlined in his note. His premier, however, put his oval Lion-and-Sun seal of approval on the treaty with trembling fingers. Some days later he dispatched a copy of the treaty in great secrecy to his own agent and relative, Mirza Sadiq Qa'im Maqam Nuri, the minister of Azarbaijan. Fearing its discovery by the ever-present British agents, Nuri instructed one of his trusted agents to sew the document into the lining of his coat and travel incognito to Tabriz. He also attached a note to the treaty alerting Mirza Sadiq to the grave consequences of any leak. With deep fear he wrote: "If there are any faults and shortcomings [in the treaty] it will result in a scandal. If it is uncovered, we will be confronted by Britain, France, and the Ottoman Empire." Naming the few who were aware of the treaty's existence, including the shah, he then added in his own hand: "If it is discovered it will be a major blunder for the state. I will be finished, and so will you and the Dabir Muham [the provincial officer in charge of foreign affairs]."[70] Nuri's fears were not unwarranted, given his pronounced British loyalties. The dramatic events of the next three years, which eventually ended with his downfall, proved their accuracy.

ROYAL RIGHTS RIDICULED

Nasir al-Din's new political assertiveness could hardly go unnoticed or fail to invite British retaliation. With the shah now leaning decidedly toward the Russians and dragging along his pro-British premier, and with the Qajar court infested with spies and treachery, the "secret treaty" could not have remained a secret for long, if at all. And the British had ample means to show their dissatisfaction. The battle over protégés was far from over. In confronting foreign legations, the shah had to deal not only with defecting military chiefs, intriguing courtiers, and greedy money lenders but also with the more hazardous cases of princes of blood with shaky loyalties. Their refuge at the British mission discredited the shah in the eyes of the public, which was still uncertain of his political survival.

As early as August 1853, the case of Malik Qasim Mirza, a grand uncle of Nasir al-Din, demonstrated the shah's sensitivity on the point of granting protégé status to princes of the royal family. Richard Stevens, the British consul in Tabriz, gave protection to Malik Qasim, the learned pro-European son of Fath 'Ali Shah, who had been accused of making secret contact with Bahman Mirza. He had already been dismissed from the governorship of Azarbaijan and was about to be arrested on the charge of treason. Facing objection from Tehran, Stevens complained to the acting chargé d'affaires, Thomson, that the Persian government was "trying to destroy his influence in Tabriz." Nasir al-Din's reaction to Stevens's complaint was exceptionally angry: "Frankly, his action bears no interpretation beyond stupidity," commented the shah, who was anxious to consolidate his authority in the province. "Most definitely cut off Malik Qasim's salary and take back his *tuyuls* [land tenures]." He then reaffirmed his previous order: "Of course send orders that all his private villages, too, should be confiscated. Let him eat from a certain place of the British." Dismissive of Nuri's concern over the possible worsening of relations with the British, he went so far as to declare: "If it leads to a break in relations, to hell, I will do it so that they would not [in future] interfere so much with my internal [affairs] and allow me to put into order my own country. A curse on these busybodies."[71]

The shah's candid expression of dismay with foreign intervention and his willingness to go so far as to break off relations was the first sign of his growing impatience. Almost immediately after rumors of the Russo-Persian secret dealings reached the British in September 1854, the old affair of Farhad Mirza resurfaced. An articulate uncle of the shah and a close member of the royal family, Farhad had consistently used his well-cultivated British connections for almost fourteen years as a security shield. In the aftermath of the Babi assassination attempt he was accused of collaborating with 'Abbas Mirza, with whom he had developed amicable relations ever since the time of Amir Kabir. He may have entertained some affection for Khadija, 'Abbas's mother, for whom he acted as a go-between with the British mission. For the shah this was an even greater villainy than having alleged Babi leanings. After Amir Kabir's downfall Farhad was removed from his post as governor of the strategic province of Fars and was threatened with confiscation of his properties.

Seeking refuge in the British legation soon after 'Abbas Mirza's exile, Farhad had avoided the worst of the shah's rage but was obliged to opt for internal exile rather than protégé status in order to preserve his substantial wealth. He spent two years at his estate in the mountainous resort of Taliqan before returning to Tehran, without royal permission but possibly with Thomson's encouragement. Writing to Faridun Mirza from Taliqan, he complained of the lack of support for him and the false accusations that had landed him in a lonesome and cold exile. "There is as much snow here as there is chatter in Tehran [*harcha dar Tihran harf ast, inja barf ast*]," he wrote.[72] As it turned out, studying Arabic literature, his lifelong favorite pastime, could not keep him away from the gossip and the excitement of Tehran's circles, particularly when called upon by his English protector.

Farhad's return to the capital in December 1854 prompted a diplomatic stir. After he was reprimanded by Nuri for the consequences of his unwarranted return, he again sought refuge in the British legation. Of course this was a perfect pretext on which Thomson could embarrass the shah and his premier in the wake of their secret negotiations with the Russians. Seeking "satisfaction" for the "great dishonor" that was committed "deliberately" toward the British mission, Thomson repeatedly asserted in his correspondence that Farhad Mirza's enthusiasm for "European philosophies" [*hikmatha-yi Yurup*] and his desire to advance in those philosophies was the only reason for his attraction to the British mission.[73] In response, Nuri blamed Thomson for his provocative conduct and accused him of "insignificant pretenses and bellicose pretexts."[74]

In December 1854 the shah issued a memorandum concerning Farhad's case. The document was one of the most assertive of his early career, demonstrating a sharp awareness of the dilemmas of the monarchy in encountering the foreign powers. Highlighting the harm that the foreign missions' support for renegade state servants brought to his royal authority, he bluntly stated:

> If it becomes a practice that every culprit and rebel seeks refuge in the British embassy and remains immune from any kind of punishment, not only my servants from now on will not bow to my authority but I would have no peace of mind from the mischief of the villains. I say it candidly and without hesitation that my confidence in the people of Iran, great and small, lies in my prerogatives [*huquq*] and my ability [*dastrasi; literally, "access"*] to punish, discipline, and intimidate them. Without such right, it is wholly unwise to remain undisturbed, even for one hour, among the rebellious [*ashub-talab*] people of Iran.

Criticizing the utilization of the British embassy as a sanctuary beyond royal access and, unlike traditional sanctuaries, immune to material losses, the shah concluded: "This kind of refuge that Thomson Sahib intends to establish in my capital never existed in Iran and is incompatible with the rights required for the security of the monarchy [*itminan-i sultani*]."[75]

This was a remarkable recognition of the challenge that Europe had brought to traditional kingship. The shah unapologetically considered coercion and punitive action the very source of his political control, and intervention by the European powers was a dangerous impediment to its realization. For the Qajar shah the symbolic display of kingly wrath, like any display of royal favor, was an essential element for upholding sovereignty, and Nasir al-Din was as acutely aware of it as any legendary king of the *Shahnama* or ruler of medieval Islam. It was rooted in the ancient practice of power and was sanctioned by classical manuals of government, which considered reward (*iltifat*) and punishment (*siyasat*) the two pillars of sound kingship.[76] Yet there was something new in the shah's self-conscious recognition of his "prerogatives," of the "security of the monarchy" and of the "dignity of the throne" (*sha'n-i saltanat*). His assertion of such rights vis-à-vis the "rebellious" people of Iran, a reference not out of character with the shah's perpetual fear of a popular revolt, may be interpreted as a royal effort to articulate the Persian tradition of monarchy. He seemed to be contrasting his rationale for absolute power with Farhad Mirza's study of "European philosophies" in the British embassy. Whether this was an interest in modern thought or in old intrigue is not known. What is known is that the shah was eager to go beyond Thomson and appeal directly to London, where he was hoping to find among the British conservatives a sympathetic listener. Questioning Thomson's motives, he stated: "I do not know that such elaborate support for the rebels and such blatant provocation and misdirection of the people is Thomson Sahib's own doing or that he acts on his government's instruction. . . . This neither corresponds to the dignity of the throne nor to the requirements of discretion and prudence." In what sounded like an open plea for support, he then ordered that copies of his memorandum be sent not only to Thomson but also to the British foreign minister and to Stratford Canning (later Lord Stratford de Redcliffe), the British ambassador to Istanbul.

If the shah was seeking understanding from higher British authorities, he seemed not to have received any.[77] Farhad Mirza was only persuaded by his brothers to come out of his sanctuary in the British embassy once he received further royal assurances of safety and immunity for his property. Yet the shah had no reservation about speaking his mind, even if it meant a breach of Victorian sensitivities or a deviation from the reserved language commonly used with the Foreign Office. The prime minister's official notification to Thomson regarding Farhad Mirza's return to the fold contained a direct quote from the shah that combined, in a sardonic tone, indignation with self-mockery and formality with sarcasm:

> His blessed Imperial Majesty, our souls be his sacrifice, has ordained me to declare to Your Excellency that this time this tragic incident and this extraordinary turmoil that was ignited by Your Excellency's disrespect and lack of expediency for this state eventually receded in a certain fashion. Yet the authorities of the Persian government would expect from the friendship between the two states that in the future that mission would not use the notables, the servants, and the subjects of this state as a means of causing such vexation for both parties and in effect diminish the prestige of this kingship in the eyes of the alien and the native. It can be trusted that the embassy of that state by the way of utmost expediency and support for this state from now on would not engage in renewing a conduct similar to the above-mentioned and avoid taking such cases that, owing to its infirmity, ridiculed [literally, "broke wind at"] the dignity of our throne [*bi sha'n-i saltanat-i ma guzid*] and aroused evil intentions among the rebellious people of Iran and gave pretext for [unwarranted] actions of emissaries of other neighboring states.[78]

Acknowledging that the "dignity of his throne" had been ridiculed was a sad admission on the shah's part. His venture into high politics, the first initiated and conducted by himself, brought about mixed results. Materially, it paid off only to the extent that his financially strapped government was relieved from the burden of a war indemnity—the last installment of Turkmanchay. In his frontiers and at home he nonetheless felt pressured by his neighbors. This uneasy interplay between aggressive European diplomacy and threatened royal authority generated in Nasir al-Din a spirit of defiance that became more apparent in the next episode of Anglo-Persian confrontation.

7   Youthful Ambitions

The secret treaty with Russia infused the shah with a much-needed sense of achievement. Not only had he secured a bargain from his northern neighbor in exchange for maintaining his imposed neutrality, but he had also obliged his premier to comply with it. Encounters with the European powers engendered in him a sense of defiance that, though primarily motivated by a desire to protect his own crown and nurtured by visions of military glory, was not devoid of a pristine patriotism. Guarding the realm, after all, was the duty traditionally assigned to the Persian shah. These high hopes for maximizing royal gains from the Crimean War was incompatible with the shah's meager resources. The shah's "war-like inclinations," in the words of R. G. Watson, had engendered in him a sense of confidence that overcame Nuri's meek expediency, hence the former's restlessness to descend on Herat, Karbala, or Iravan (Erevan).

The events of this period also demonstrated Britain's central role in Iran's political orientation. To set limits on the shah's power, at the center and on the periphery, and to habituate the royal mind to the realities of the foreign presence, a military showdown seemed unavoidable. Perhaps no one could have brought out in the shah the combination of resentment, patriotism, and military adventure more than Charles Murray, the new British minister plenipotentiary.

BULLY-BOY DIPLOMACY

Over the years, the British attitude toward Nasir al-Din and his prime minister had reverted to a scathing impatience. Rumors of the Russo-Persian secret treaty that surfaced in the British press, though probably already known to the Foreign Office, precipitated further criticism for the absence of a British minister in Tehran. The choice of Murray, therefore, was intended to retrieve the supposedly lost ground and, as hoped for by the London *Times*, "to bring the shah to his knees."[1] He "would soon bring His Majesty's nose to the grindstone," the English paper hoped. Having read the Persian translation of the *Times* article, the shah could not possibly have been unaffected by this renewed gesture of goodwill. "Conceive the effect," wrote Murray with an air of imperial contempt, "of such a phrase upon a monarch who has been a spoilt child from infancy and has never heard himself styled otherwise than 'center of the universe,' 'king of kings,' etc. etc."[2] The effect on the shah, as indeed Murray's own subordinate in the British mission noted, was to bring out his "firmness and independence" in the face of what quickly came to be a grotesque diplomatic exercise in insolence and folly.[3]

Charles Murray (see Pl. 20) was the first British representative to Tehran with no previous Indian experience since Gore Ouseley in 1809. Nevertheless, he had learned his fair share of colonial hauteur in Egypt, where he had served as British consul general. A member of the nobility, Murray switched to a diplomatic career after having served for seven years as the head of Queen Victoria's imperial household. His family contacts as well as his handsome looks and eloquence served him well in the early Victorian court. Had it not been for Prince Albert's puritanical purges, Murray might have clung for the rest of his career to his court duties rather than feeling obliged to accept posts clearly unworthy of the son of the fifth Earl of Dunmore, impoverished as he may have become. Though on good terms with "Old Pam," as Palmerston was nicknamed in high circles, Murray was reluctant to accept the Tehran post, a reluctance perhaps related to his earlier quarrels with Stratford Canning, the influential British ambassador to Istanbul, which had kept Murray out of active service since 1850. Given his brash Palmerstonian style and troublesome career, Murray's appointment to the Tehran post could only be explained by Lord Clarendon's vengeful attitude toward Iran.

Murray had a long attachment to Oxford; for a number of years he was a fellow at All Souls College. As an undergraduate, he had a reputation as a bully, earned by playing dreadful tricks on no less a figure than John Henry Newman (later Cardinal Newman), then his tutor at Oriel.[4] Not unlike Griboidov, the Russian poet and literary figure sent as minister to Tehran in 1829, only to be killed by the Tehran mob for his lack of diplomatic discretion, Murray combined literary refinement and sophistication with an acute sense of cultural superiority and diplomatic adventure. His *Bird of the Prairie*, a commercially successful tale of innocent love in an American Indian setting (in which he had spent some time), was a revamping of the familiar themes of the "noble savage" and the purity of love, produced in the nineteenth century to boost the spirit of imperial adventure.[5]

Murray's romantic orientalism ran aground, however, once he entered the treacherous waters of Anglo-Persian diplomacy. Like many other diplomats of his time, Murray entertained an almost fetishistic devotion to the imperial ethos as promoted by Britain. His honor-shame morality was well divorced from the realities of his new surroundings. His biased view of the Persians, possibly based on statements rampant in the works of Morier, Fraser, and others with which he was familiar and tainted by his somewhat friendlier attitude toward the Arab Imam (sultan) of Masqat (Muscat)—then in the midst of a quarrel with the Persian government over the port of Bandar 'Abbas—set the pace for his diplomacy from the start. The lingering disputes with the Persian government left over from the times of Thomson, Sheil, and others before them provided the necessary framework.

Aware of the British resolve, the Persian government was willing to indulge Murray's sense of self-importance. Measured by the number of horses provided from the royal stable upon his arrival in Tehran in April 1855, Murray's reception was intended "to convey an impression of more than the usual compliment and courtesy." In his first interview with Nuri he was also impressed with the premier, judging him to be "a man of fluent and agreeable conversation" who was "disposed to cultivate friendly re-lations" with him and who was quite obviously "in need of British sup-port."[6] Soon, however, the envoy's diplomatic honeymoon came to an end, as he began to discover that Nuri was no longer a reliable ally of his country. Indeed, access to the shah was the crux of the growing conflict between Murray and Nuri that was soon to develop into one of the most serious crises in Anglo-Persian relations. Murray admitted it was his refusal to work through Nuri's channels, as well as the premier's desire to obtain assurances for continued British protection, that resulted in the deterio-ration of their relationship.[7]

Above all, however, it was the shah's attitude that set the uneasy diplomatic course. Bruised by the repeated setbacks, from the Herat agree-ment to the Sultaniya affair to the endless disputes over protégés, he nursed a deep sense of indignation toward the British. He was wise enough, nevertheless, to recognize that his country's precarious position with re-gard to Russia required, instead, accommodation of the British at all costs. He even hoped—or at least pretended he did—to sign a defensive alliance with Britain once the fortunes of the war began to shift in its favor. Along the same lines, under Nuri's auspices a new diplomatic initiative was made toward the French, who, after nearly seven years, reappeared on the Persian horizon. It was hoped their presence would serve as a modifying force against the background of Anglo-Russian bipolarity. Obviously, neither of the two powers welcomed it.

The mutual misgivings between the shah and the British government were further complicated by the renewed struggle between the premier and Mahd 'Ulya. With Farhad Mirza as the British minister's eyes and ears within the royal harem, an alliance began to emerge in the early months of Murray's residence in Tehran intended to counterbalance the prime minister's influence over the shah. Murray was drawn into the dispute willingly. "It is difficult to ascertain with accuracy what passes within the walls of the harem," he wrote with an air of mystery reminiscent of oriental novels. What was certain, he believed, was that "many of the state projects and bloodiest tragedies are hatched" there, an allusion perhaps to Amir Kabir's murder. That is what made Farhad Mirza's intelligence all the more valuable.

Farhad's case, as Murray admitted, was one of "considerable delicacy and difficulty" because it had given, and would continue to give, "umbrage to persons so suspicious and self-willed" as the shah and his premier. Though Farhad was "a well conducted and well educated gentleman," Murray could not accord to him "the merit of prudence and discretion in the use of his tongue." When, in a public audience, the prince was insulted by Nuri in the "most offensive and apprehensive terms" for an alleged insult to the shah's messenger, he immediately rushed to Mahd 'Ulya's caring bosom. "Very jealous" of the premier, the influential queen mother forced Nuri to apologize. The premier kissed the prince's knee and his cheeks in the presence of Mahd 'Ulya and went through all the ceremonial atonement of a Persian apology. The dual backing of the British and Mahd 'Ulya emboldened the prince, who lost no time in paying back the premier's earlier offense by insulting Nuri in the shah's presence and "in a language so unmeasured that he put the Shah in a passion." This miscalculated outburst reversed his fortune, shifting the shah's support firmly behind Nuri and against Farhad. Neither asylum in Mahd 'Ulya's quarters nor Murray's mediation could change the shah's mind. Farhad was given the choice of remaining obedient to Nuri, as were all other princes of the royal family, or going into internal exile. If he decided to seek British protection, he was warned, he must leave Iran and risk having all his properties confiscated. Having the shah's support, at least for the time being, Nuri consistently tried to isolate any stooge propped up by the British to challenge his own access to the shah.

Murray's angry exclamation was proof of his inability to outmaneuver Nuri as much as it was a symptom of his troublemaking diplomacy. "Armed with your lordship's last dispatch," he wrote optimistically to Clarendon, "I would give the Sadr such a lesson as would ensure the prince

[Farhad Mirza] a twelvemonth's immunity of annoyance." He nevertheless admitted that the shah and Nuri were "too cunning to commit themselves on paper."[8] As it turned out, it was Murray himself who was not immune from annoyance. He was infuriated by Nuri's boastful promise to the shah that soon he would make both Farhad Mirza and the British mission "eat dirt." Murray, seeking further approval from Clarendon, had no hesitation in taking part in the slurring contest. He predicted that "it is more than probable that before Your Lordship's reply reaches me, the Sadr will himself have partaken of that Persian meal."[9] He was wrong. Seeking French mediation, now represented by the energetic envoy Nicolas Bourre, Nuri was able to persuade the prince to renounce in writing his British association in exchange for a guarantee of security.[10]

The Farhad Mirza affair, settled for the time being in Nuri's favor, set the tone for future confrontations. It was obvious that the British envoy was longing for trouble and missed no opportunity to spot it. A few weeks later, during the mourning month of Muharram, an occasion of great sensitivity and expression of religious passion, he protested to Nuri about the exclusion of European missions from the annual royal *ta'ziya* performance (passion plays reenacting the tragedies of Husayn's martyrdom in Karbala and the sufferings of his house), which Murray predicted would be a "clumsy and ridiculous" drama anyway. He was not satisfied by Nuri's explanation that, because the *ta'ziya* was considered "an amusing spectacle" by Europeans but a very serious occasion by the Shi'ites, the 'ulama found the European presence disagreeable. Murray was convinced that this was another device used by the premier to lower "the influence and the prestige" of his mission.[11]

Against the background of growing animosity between the premier and the British legation, Nasir al-Din was nevertheless willing to reopen negotiations with Murray for the long-desired defense treaty with Britain. For a brief time in October he was able to cut through mutual distrust and convinced Murray that a defensive alliance with Iran was in both parties' best interests. In what he considered to be an expedient shift of policy, he further revealed to Murray the terms of the secret treaty with Russia, a revelation no doubt rooted much in the Franco-British victory at Sevastopol.[12]

A memorandum, the greater part of it written by Nasir al-Din himself, further elaborated the shah's concerns and his awareness of international contingencies. Ever since "that never-to-be-named day" that Turkmanchay was concluded, the memorandum declared, Iran had been "sick," and its daily thoughts were to prepare the means for its own remedy in order to liberate itself from the domination of Russia and to reoccupy its lost provinces. Iran's signing a treaty in "utmost secrecy" secured a "windfall," in the shape of a remission of the country's war indemnity, without violating its neutrality. But under the new circumstances Iran could "no longer be silent and remain neutral." What the memorandum demanded for Iran's remaining in the British fold was a guarantee of Iran's territorial integrity, participation in the peace conference at the close of the Crimean War, and three-quarters of a million pounds in financial aid in the event of a Russian attack. The memorandum also called for the return to Iran of the provinces in the Caucasus lost to Russia a quarter of a century earlier. If these conditions could not be met, the document warned, Iran might be forced to take a different course; without such support Russia was bound to attack Iran in order to silence the Caucasian provinces.[13]

In his interview with Murray, the shah went even further. He was evidently moved by extravagant dreams of recovering the Caucasus. "The war is coming to our doors," he reminded Murray with a touch of exaggeration. The Muslim inhabitants of Nakhjavan (Nakhichevan) and Iravan "are writing to my ministers that they want to rise up and come again under our banner." The shah was "so highly excited" with such a prospect that Murray "hardly knew how to curb his impatience" until Clarendon's answer to the Persian proposal arrived. "Fretting with anxiety and vexation at the bands of the neutrality" in which he was tied, the shah could only share with Murray his bold dream. If Georgia (Gurjistan), the weakest point of the Russian empire, was to be liberated, the shah believed, Iran "on the score of religious and ancient possession . . . holds her title best." Reading the French newspapers published in Istanbul and Beirut, the shah was seemingly impressed with the French performance in the war and was hoping, as was Nuri, to employ its newly acquired influence to maneuver the British into an alliance. In this regard the shah was not far from the target. Murray was impressed enough with the shah's argument on the expediency of an Anglo-Persian alliance to write to Clarendon, "Fas est et ab hoste decori" (It is right to learn even from an enemy), adding that Iran's offer of cooperation should be taken seriously.[14]

Clarendon had not been moved previously by the shah's more modest proposals, and at present there was nothing in Tehran's overall attitude to require a change of mind. The British feelings were that the shah could again be snubbed at no cost. After six months of negative answers and uneven dealings from the envoy, the shah and his premier were bound to lose hope in Murray, too. "A hyena at hand is more to be feared than a lion afar," was what Nuri would again advise his master on Iran's position vis-à-vis the two powers, one in the vicinity of its northern frontiers and another beyond the distant seas.[15] Even if there had been a glimmer of hope for an eventual accord with the lion of the British empire, that was extinguished in the forthcoming diplomatic storm that was destined to end in a war. Once the shah was disappointed with the prospects of an alliance with Britain, he was ready to break away completely from his southern neighbor in the hope of greater collaboration with Russia.

UPROOTING THE VICTORIAN TREE

On 28 November 1855 Nasir al-Din Shah wrote to Nuri in a private note:

> Last night, that is the night of Sunday 17 Rabi' al-Awwal [1272/27 November 1855], was the night of the birthday of the Prophet, praise be to him and his family. In a dream I saw a garden with a tall, massive pine tree in the middle. I was viewing it from a distance and the name of the tree was Victoria. Indeed, that tree was the country and the monarchy of England. I ordered the pine tree called Victoria to be uprooted and replanted in another location and said: "Call it Muhammad. Victoria is bad."[16]

What was remarkable about the shah's dream was not only its naked symbolism, almost too perfect to be subliminal, but also its timing. On 27 November, after three weeks of vehement quarreling with Murray, the break in Anglo-Persian diplomatic relations was finalized. The shah's dream, for all its spontaneity, fit well into a course that was destined to be one of the most critical in Nasir al-Din's reign. In the Hashim Khan affair, as the episode leading to the break in relations came to be known, all the various themes from the early life of the shah seemed to converge. They culminated in its aftermath, the Anglo-Persian war.

The episode started with the shah's blunt opposition to a seemingly innocuous appointment. When Murray informed Nuri that he had employed Mirza Hashim Khan Nuri as the new British agent in Shiraz, he hardly expected to receive on the same day a negative response from the shah. Nuri was instructed by the shah to communicate "word by word and without a dot missing or added" that Hashim, being the "salaried servant of the Persian government" and "hereditary slave" of the royal household, could not be employed by the British mission. Blaming Murray for throwing the internal affairs of his country into confusion and creating bad examples for the others, the shah cautioned that if he proceeded with the appointment "and does not comply with the honor [*namus*] and reputation of the monarchy and the government, any consequences arising from this will rest with that person who takes the initiative in this affair."[17]

Coming at a critical stage in negotiations over the proposed defense treaty, and given the delicacy of Hashim's case, both Murray's move and the shah's sharp response were puzzling. Hashim, a member of the Is-fandiyari clan of Nur (in Mazandaran), a rival of the premier's clan, was a childhood companion of Nasir al-Din and later served among his royal attendants during Amir Kabir's term. It was perhaps his close association with the fallen premier—who three days before his exile to Kashan apparently proposed to him an alliance (possibly against Aqa Khan Nuri and 'Ali Khan Farrash-bashi)—that cost him his transfer to the army. It also made him a target of Nuri's hostility. As a brother-in-law of the shah, Hashim could have been a potential menace to the premier, particularly when, out of fear and ambition, he cultivated amicable relations with the British mission. Thomson, who in June 1854 offered him the recently vacated and highly sensitive post of Persian secretary of the British mission, must have prized in Hashim his court and harem connections and inside influence rather than his secretarial abilities. The premier strongly resisted his appointment for the same reason he resisted British protection for 'Ali Naqi and Farhad Mirza. Encountering another Nuri in the British service, he must have experienced a strange sense of deja vu. Whether because of Nuri's intimidation or Thomson's enticement, shortly afterward Hashim took refuge in the British embassy, where he stayed idle for more than a year before his reassignment. His young wife, Parvin, daughter of Say-fullah Mirza and sister of the shah's second permanent wife, Khujasta Khanum Taj al-Dawla (mother of his heir apparent), accompanied her husband to the embassy. Hashim, her third husband, may have been married to her at the shah's command in order to put a guise of respect-ability on Parvin's allegedly promiscuous lifestyle.[18]

If Nuri wanted Hashim far from the political center, he should have welcomed his posting to Shiraz by Murray as a fair compromise. Not so. Nuri felt an element of personal animosity toward Murray, perhaps because the premier felt he was deliberately being left out of the envoy's intimate discussions with the shah. But this could not have been the sole reason for the Persian government's strong opposition. The shah's resolve to oppose Hashim's appointment from the start went far beyond Nuri's petty wishes, a fact that Murray was never capable of understanding. He believed Nuri was merely using the shah's name "just as it suits his convenience." Viewing the situation through the lens of British interests, he did not see in the premier's actions anything but oriental intrigue. Five days into the crisis, Murray informed Clarendon—perhaps preparing him for the bad news—that "when it answers his [Nuri's] purpose to act on his own responsibility and at his own pleasure he makes no scruple of saying that His Majesty has nothing to do with such matters and that he himself is the organ of the Persian government. When on the contrary it suits his purpose to clothe his own personal views under the pretence of zeal for the shah, however, then he excites and initiates His Majesty and draws him personally into the discussion that may be going on."[19] Whatever the truth of Murray's diagnosis, the circumstances he described point to the complex—at times complimentary, at others tense—relationship between the crown and the premier, deeply rooted in the history of the Persian political order.

From the lofty summit of his mission house, Murray went on to pontificate on a home-brewed political psychology of his. "Persians," he declared confidently, "especially those high in office, know no law but force. They will talk or write at interminable length about justice, humanity and the truth etc. etc. but wherever their interest or inclination leads to oppress . . . they do so without scruple . . . combat every argument with subterfuge until they see their opponent is about to employ angry deeds in place of angry words; then they would give way saying that they had only yielded to superior force: Destiny would have it so, they could do no more." There was an element of personal truth in Murray's remark, a curious Freudian slip, perhaps, reflecting the paradoxes that tainted the conduct of most British envoys and policy makers of the period. It was he, rather than the shah or Nuri, who was resorting to "no law but force" and writing, as his dispatches attest, at "interminable length" about high human values but with a decided political agenda.

With these explanations in mind, Murray continued his crusade for Hashim's appointment, a matter of "most trifling importance" in itself, he admitted, but serious in its consequences because of "the perverse obstinacy of the Sadr Azam."[20] Wholly unconvinced by the shah's reply, Murray wrote back criticizing Nuri above all for what he believed was an "innovation of causing the shah to take part in the official correspondence"—an act, he was quick to point out, which tended to lower "the dignity of the shah" and was against "the established customs of diplomacy."[21]

Murray's protest, though it was secondary to the actual quarrel, triggered an important exchange on the growing authority of the shah and his involvement as the sole architect of Iran's foreign affairs. "I believe I have frequently informed you," replied Nuri, "that in all matters of business, especially in affairs connected with the foreign department, I am charged to submit the entire question to the shah." Contrasting such a practice with procedures prevalent in Europe, he further stressed that the shah's attentions to the administration of his country were not "derogatory to his royal dignity, nor is the obedience and submission which I practice unsuitable to the position and office which I hold."[22] Nuri was especially correct about the shah's behavior on the Hashim Khan question. Yet the premier's allusion to his own limited authority was entirely missed by Murray. In response, after insisting that diplomatic procedures in Iran and England were "exactly the same," he reminded the premier that failing to explain Hashim's appointment to the shah "in few amiable words," he had jeopardized the good relations that so lately the premier "pretended a desire to cement by a still closer alliance." Murray's unqualified contempt for the premier and his patronizing attitude toward the shah—treating him as an idiot who could be deceived by a few amiable words—were accompanied by threats if Hashim were harassed.[23]

Stressing the shah's total and arbitrary power, Nuri punctiliously emphasized in a subsequent note to Murray: "In this country the source from which originate all commands, both trifling and of great importance, is the person of His Majesty the Shahanshah [King of Kings]. That is how it always was and will be in this country." It was as though the premier was anxious to exaggerate the extent of the shah's authority beyond its historical reality when he argued that "all subjects and servants" (naukar va ra'iyat) were to the shah as slaves to a master. "No one in the face of the shah's wishes can assume to himself any liberty of action." If Hashim were liberated from this bondage by means of British protection, as Farhad Mirza and others had been, Nuri insisted, such an action would undermine "the chain of authority" in the country. By order of the shah, he ominously cautioned, Hashim would be arrested should he be sent to any mission as a British employee.[24]

The shah's uncompromising behavior from the outset may be explained in part by his disgust with repeated intrusions into his private surroundings. The Hashim Khan case was the second in recent months in which the British proved willing to meddle with his court and the royal family. As much as prestige and a symbolic show of power were essential to maintain the British presence and overall viability in Iran, so were they essential to the shah's very survival. In an ancient monarchy such as Iran, the ruler's sovereignty and control over his people largely depended on symbolic spectacles of power, including the manner in which he was treated by the representatives of his mighty neighbors. Nasir al-Din's repeated references to the dignity and honor of the monarchy and charges that the British totally disregarded his public status were not mere pretensions contrived to excuse his political follies, as Murray and most British representatives before him wanted to believe.

With Hashim Khan's case the shah's indignation reached its peak, and there were clear reasons for it. Not only was Hashim the shah's intimate childhood companion and now his brother-in-law, both sufficient reasons for the shah's frustration with his seeking sanctuary, but Parvin's dubious reputation had become the talk of the town. Thomson and Murray, both bachelors, were allegedly being offered her sexual favors in exchange for protecting Hashim. The couple's prolonged stay in the British embassy, as well as their position in tents adjacent to Murray's at the British summer camp in Qulhak and, later, in a house next to the embassy in the city, all were taken as compelling evidence that there was truth to the rumors of adultery. In a society governed by strict rules of female discretion, allowing such behavior, notwithstanding any invidious intentions, was enough to invite trouble. Murray's fierce denials of the charges as sheer calumny generated by Nuri and his newfound ally, Bouree, carried little weight. Whether or not Hashim's wife was "old, ugly, and married to her 3rd husband," as Murray claimed in his dispatch to London, was immaterial. Regardless of their veracity, the rumors were bound to incite the shah once they reached the level of a court scandal. "How easily dirt sticks if enough of it is thrown," grieved Murray's official biographer.[25]

Attacks upon the honor of the throne, once it had been publicly associated with the harem, as in the case of Parvin, could not have been ignored, even if in practice the alleged promiscuity of the shah's own mother was well known. The least the shah could do in the face of such serious accusations was to press for Parvin's removal from Hashim's house. Armed with some mujtahids' legal opinions (*fatwas*), the shah ordered Parvin to be detained in her brother's house, presumably on grounds of protecting her from prostitution. Even if, besides preserving the shah's public reputation, this move was calculated by Nuri to check Murray—a supposition hard to prove—the envoy was foolish enough to play into the premier's hand. By producing counter-*fatwas* from other mujtahids who were on good terms with the British mission and subsequently dispatching the embassy's servants along with Hashim to retrieve Parvin, Murray gave further substance to the rumors. This move was destined to fail, however, for it obliged the shah and his government to act more forcefully. The preservation of a symbolic facade of chastity, this *sanctum sanctimonium* of the monarchy, to the point of a fetishistic isolation was further amplified because the scandal involved the European infidels. At a time when even watching the royal harem's cavalcade pass through the streets was strictly prohibited—requiring all males, regardless of their class and status, to turn their backs or face the clubs of royal bodyguards and eunuchs—it was to be expected that the shah would not act according to the norms of the eighteenth-century French court or those of early Victorian England to which Murray was accustomed.

Regardless of his pompous homily on the vices of the "Persian character," the envoy seems to have been so intoxicated by the sensuality of his own idea of the royal harem that he had lost sight of the diplomatic principle of nonintervention in the host country's domestic affairs. It was "justice, equity, and restoration of the rules of the shari'at," he claimed, that had motivated him to make such a heroic effort to return Parvin to her own household.[26] Thus, when Murray officially requested that Hashim's wife be immediately restored to her husband, Nuri refused even to consider the subject. He declared in a solemn but respectful tone that discussing the relatives of the royal harem, let alone determining their conduct, was completely out of his power. "So tender and delicate a subject unprecedented in this kingdom and among this nation" was best left alone, as if it had never been approached.[27] To this refusal Murray responded in the fashion long cherished by his predecessors, with an official ultimatum stating that he would suspend friendly relations between the two countries if his request were not met immediately.[28]

It seemed both sides, British and Persian, were ready for a showdown. The premier's harsh reply to Murray's ultimatum, no doubt produced under pressure from the shah, only added to the envoy's indignation, as it threatened to disclose "the true reason" for Murray's behavior. Thus, neither intense mediation by the French and Ottoman representatives nor Nuri's subsequent conciliatory letter to the English envoy could change Murray's mind. The next day he officially declared the break in relations with Iran and struck down the Union Jack from the embassy's gate. Nevertheless, both Murray and Nuri were still hopeful. As Murray had pointed out earlier, he regarded the whole episode as another maneuver to enable him to humble the Persian government.[29] As for Nuri, he saw Hashim's case as a trial to initiate Murray into the informal side of Anglo-Persian politics.

To the shah the break in relations and Murray's departure was a *fait accompli*. Three days later, a royal memorandum confirmed his uncompromising stand: "If the advantages which are to accrue to us from the residence of a British minister here are those which we see, it is for the benefit of both governments that he should quarrel and depart." The shah was "drowned in a sea of amazement" when he compared his own good-will and friendly intentions with the ill conduct of the British mission, always protecting the "perverse and obstinate, and the simpletons" of his household. "The rights of the guest now exceeded those of the masters and of the host," he wrote. Urging whoever was "the true servant" of his government not to submit to pressure (a reference, no doubt, to Nuri), he declared: "If the British minister desires the humiliation of this government, of course we, so long as we have power, will not submit to any indignity."[30]

Considering the shah's age and temperament and the fact that he was "totally inexperienced in affairs and accustomed to have his word or his nod considered as law," Murray believed, his behavior was not surprising. To save face—in an affair that was rapidly becoming a notorious scandal in London as well as in Tehran—it was only natural that Murray again blame Nuri for the "unbecoming" contents of the shah's letter. There was a faint hint of regret in Murray's response to the shah, however. It was only the "ill-will and the ill-advised proceeding of the Sadr Azam," he complained, that caused him "to allude in public dispatches to subjects that ought not to appear in official correspondence." Yet his hint regarding the Parvin incident was buried under heaps of incrimination, slurs, and abusive statements about the premier. But if Murray's two-edged strategy, to condemn and to console, was meant to motivate the shah against Nuri, he misjudged in his diagnosis both that the shah was immature and that he would fail to back his premier.[31]

The shah's next memorandum was even more implacable. He found the envoy's "insulting expressions" toward the premier annoying, for all his conduct had been guided by royal commands. "We do not require any foreigner to give us information regarding the administration of our own country," wrote the shah in answer to Murray's criticism. Murray's letter, the shah was convinced, only confirmed the "threatening reports" circulating in the town that the envoy intended to incite anti-government turmoil and trouble. As Murray himself had declared at the time of the break in relations, the shah cautioned, he should stop corresponding with the Persian government unless he were to hoist his flag again. Further, the envoy's recent letters should be returned to him because "Mr. Murray exceeded his limits of courtesy, and has out-stepped the privileges of the mission." Striking at the heart of the quarrel, the shah then rhetorically questioned Murray's assertions: "How wonderfully the British representatives are desirous to maintain our independence! They wish to take from us our power and authority, even over our own family and special wife ['ayal-i makhsus]." After Farhad Mirza and Hashim Khan, "our home-born servants," the shah avowed, "today they demand forcibly our wife's sister." Calling upon his own ministers, he then thundered:

> We can't understand why you have all allowed the argument of the case to escape you? Mr Murray's object is forcibly to take [away] our wife's sister. Our command is that we will not submit to this indignity, and we will not give her [up]. If His Excellency the Sadr Azam should still continue to show moderation and forbearance to the mission as formerly, we shall be obliged to do what is necessary for giving preference to the preservation of the dignity of the throne.[32]

It is a small wonder that the shah was subconsciously so aware of the "tree called Victoria" and had a full interpretation for his timely dream. Not only he was indignant and angry, but he feared that Murray's insistence on retrieving Parvin might bring about a tragic end similar to that of the Griboidov affair. In 1829, following a similar attempt by the Russian envoy to remove forcefully (under the pretext of Russian protection) from the harem the Armenian wives of Allahyar Khan Asaf al-Dawla, the influential Davalu dignitary and 'Abbas Mirza's brother-in-law, a mob incited by the Tehran mujtahid attacked and massacred the entire Russian legation. If the 'ulama had already passed opinions, and the public, the same "unruly mischief-making" people, were longing for "turmoil and trouble," then the shah's wishes to replace the English tree with a Muhammadan one were not misplaced. For the same reason both Nuri and Sa'id Khan, the foreign minister, were determined not to drag out the affair any further.

The exchange of angry notes continued for one more round. A compulsive writer and a master of double-talk, Murray could hardly allow the brutish Nasir al-Din the pleasure of having the final insult. In his own defense against the royal charges, he stressed, with a touch of sarcasm, that in his previous correspondence he merely adopted the shah's example of using "most improper terms" and unjustified complaints. In open defiance of the shah's instructions, he further insisted that having said "nothing disrespectful" toward His Majesty, he would not withdraw his earlier notes unless the shah's memoranda were withdrawn as well. Finally, on the charge of the envoy's romantic inclination toward Parvin, Murray pronounced that the shah had merely "signed and sealed" the unfounded calumnies his ministers had circulated earlier.[33] Even after delivering such a note, Murray was hopeful enough, though embarrassed, to report to London that he still expected "they will concede" to his demand.[34]

A few days later Murray was obliged to pack and leave Tehran in the company of the staff of the mission. He even took with him all the records of the mission.[35] On his way to Tabriz, reflecting on the whole affair, he concluded that perhaps relations could not be restored until Nuri was removed. Still squarely placing the blame on the premier for the break in relations, he charged that although Nuri was reputed to be "one of the ablest men in Persia," he in fact was "a most consummate hypocrite" whose talent was to estrange his best allies and to degrade the royal family "to be the common talk of the town." He concluded, with a sardonic tone, that he preferred a pro-Russian, straightforward man to "a false and treacherous intriguer" such as Nuri.[36]

Nothing in Murray's vast vocabulary of pungent affronts could have hurt Nasir al-Din more than an allusion to his passivity. The implication that he was merely a stooge in Nuri's hands, rubber-stamping his malicious designs, profoundly annoyed the shah. It was a sore point from his background, reminding him of the years during which he was undermined and cold-shouldered and the dreadful lengths to which he had gone to assert his independence. His reply, addressed to Nuri and perhaps the harshest he ever penned on the subject of foreign affairs, sincerely expressed his disdain, even to the point of transgressing all norms of diplomacy. Murray's "rude, unmeaning, disgusting, and insolent tone and purport" had only confirmed for the shah in written form the reports he had previously heard about the envoy. The shah pointed out that even in his own house the envoy was "constantly speaking disrespectfully" of him, an allusion, no doubt, to Murray's frequently verbalized opinion of him as a nonentity. "We are therefore convinced that this man, Mister Murray, is stupid, ignorant and insane, who has the audacity and impudence to insult even kings." Most remarkable, the shah then made a historical comparison between himself and the last Safavid ruler, Shah Sultan Husayn (1694–1722), a ruler infamous in Persian history for his ineptitude and lack of political willpower. "From the time of Shah Sultan Hossein (when Persia was in its most disorganized state and [especially] during the last fourteen years of his life, when by serious illness he was incapacitated from business) up to the present time," wrote the shah with bookish accuracy, "no disrespect toward the sovereign has been tolerated, either from the government or its agents. What has happened now that [this] foolish minister plenipotentiary acts with such temerity?"

The shah's rhetorical question, much like his dream, was rooted in a bitter reality in which he found himself, his monarchy, and his country hammered into submission. He evidently must have given thought to the comparison with Shah Sultan Husayn, and he deplored the similarities. If he failed to resist British pressure, then he would be just as impotent and miserable as the ignominious terminator of the Safavid dynasty, who in 1722 was forced to come out of his besieged capital, Isfahan, and hand over his crown to Ashraf, the Afghan chief of the Ghalza'i nomads, only to be incarcerated and later decapitated by the vicious frontier warlord. With a peculiar transparency, Nasir al-Din thus expressed his desire to end un-equal relations that required submission and restraint on the part of Iran in the face of its southeastern neighbor—the same region from which the Afghan invaders had put an end to the Safavid dynasty 133 years earlier. "From last night until now our time has been passed in vexation," wrote the shah of the night of his dream. Uprooting the Victorian tree now came to be verbalized in a poignant reference to the British sovereign: "We now command you, in order that you yourself may know, and also acquaint the [foreign] missions, that until the Queen of England [*malaka-yi Ingilistan*] herself makes us a suitable apology for the insolence of her envoy, we will never receive back this, her foolish minister, who is a simpleton, nor from her government any other minister."[37]

The reference to the "Queen of England" instead of the customary "Her Majesty the Queen of England" (translated into Persian as *a'lahazrat padshah-i Ingilistan* and always religiously observed by the British envoys to emphasize her sovereignty vis-à-vis a patrimonial monarchy such as Iran's) was deliberate and bound to be interpreted as an affront. Moreover, such an irreconcilable demand for an apology from the Queen herself contradicted the shah's repeated assurances earlier that Iran would main-tain friendship with England in spite of Murray's obnoxious behavior.

The shah's determination to resist the British had now found other motives as well. The shift from negotiation to confrontation was too explicit to be explained solely by the shah's offended pride or his heightened irritation. In spite of the sensitivity of the Hashim Khan affair and the angry exchanges about it, Nasir al-Din was not entirely moved by erratic outbursts of emotion. Rather, one can trace in his responses to the British provocation a calculated political course that, taken together with his previous and future actions, fit a distinct political pattern. Though he did not invent or invite the confrontation with the British, it was obvious that he tried to exploit the occasion to the best of his ability. By trial and error he had learned that only through utilizing the same course of diplomacy as his adversaries could he increase his chances of survival and possibly even achieve glory and military success.

Beyond his own experience, however, there were other, outside currents that shaped the shah's political outlook at this time. In this respect, the influence on the shah of the celebrated Persian reform-minded statesman

Mirza Malkum Khan (see Pl. 13), even as early as 1855, was crucial. It was not accidental that immediately before the Hashim Khan affair, Murray had expressed to the Foreign Office his concern regarding young Mirza Malkum Khan's employment as official interpreter during the sensitive negotiations with the Persian government over the defense treaty. A son of the Armenian Ya'qub Khan (the Persian secretary and chief interpreter for the Russian mission), Malkum was the "last person in the city of Tehran" to whom Murray could entrust "a secret of this important and dangerous character." He remonstrated with Nuri over "the inconsistency of keeping this man as a confidential Mirza [secretary]."[38] One may even surmise that Hashim Khan's appointment by Murray a few days later as the British agent in Shiraz came in retaliation for Malkum's official appointment as the royal dragoman.

Malkum Khan, an Armenian convert to Islam, was one of Nuri's discoveries. Almost the same age as the shah, he was educated in France for some years before his return to Iran in 1852 and subsequent employment in Dar al-Funun. A man of talent and political insight, Malkum, as interpreter and political adviser to Nuri and, soon after, to the shah himself, expounded on both of the themes most dear to Nasir al-Din Shah: greater monarchical authority at home and bolder diplomatic initiatives in foreign policy. He first impressed the shah—who was always fascinated with modern technological gadgets—with the simple scientific experiments he performed during royal visits to Dar al-Funun, where Malkum was employed as an assistant to French teachers. It appears he created the first experimental telegraph line in Iran in 1854, between Dar al-Funun and the shah's summer palace in Niavaran, north of Tehran. We may assume the shah also took special interest in Malkum's knowledge of European politics and liked the simple, unobtrusive Persian in which he expressed his views. As the royal dragoman (*mutarjim-(i) humayun*), translating French papers, Malkum would have had direct and regular access to the shah.

At this stage of his career Malkum subscribed to a political outlook not too remote from the shah's. Having been in France during the 1848 revolution and Napoleon III's rise to power, Malkum had formed an ideal of monarchy, as expressed in his early writings, modeled on the notion of a benevolent but authoritarian monarch who could repel imperial intrusion from his doorstep and undertake domestic reforms as a way of preserving his independence. With France's growing prominence in Europe and its presence as a balancing force on the Middle Eastern scene, Malkum's French orientation made perfect sense. So did his advice to Nuri and the shah to resist British intervention. Murray was not wrong to suspect that Bouree, the French minister plenipotentiary in Tehran, was supporting Malkum, "the intriguing Armenian." Nor was he too far off course to assume that through Ya'qub Khan, Malkum's father, Nuri was informing the Russian envoy, Anichkov, of what transpired between his government and the British mission. Moreover, the shah's instructions (in the above-mentioned memorandum) that Malkum Khan bring to the attention of the French mission the contents of Murray's insulting letter could also be taken as evidence of his growing influence. There is no truth to the fantastic claims Malkum made later in life that he was the shah's foster-brother and that upon Nasir al-Din's accession he was made the prime minister of Iran. Yet one can detect a faint resonance of his rapidly growing presence in the court from his enigmatic boast to Wilfred Blunt—an English aristocrat well known for his support of Middle Eastern anti-colonial causes—that at the age of twenty he was "practically despotic in Persia."[39] Charges of expansionist ambitions leveled against Malkum by his early critics should also be seen in light of his early impression on Nasir al-Din, the shah's desire to repossess Herat, and the consequent military engagement with the British that resulted from this expedition.[40]

Malkum's influence aside, the shah's political sentiments were also remarkable for their close affinity with Islam. Renaming the Victorian tree Muhammad in a dream that occurred on the night of the break in relations with England may be seen as a sign of religious awakening, a conscious desire to employ Islam as a source of resistance to foreign intrusion. Earlier on he emphasized his duty as the "sultan of the Shi'ites"—a ruler on par with the Sunni Ottoman sultan—with the same anger with which he was now resisting the British infidels. Recording his dream and interpreting its symbolism reflected a self-awareness that must have been heightened by recent developments such as the Hashim Khan affair or the uproar over the 'ulamas' opposition to invitation of foreign representatives to the ta'ziya performances. The shah could not have remained insensitive to the 'ulamas' generally anti-European sentiments. Moreover, the course of events starting with the shah's refusal to condone Murray's wishes corresponded closely with his long-standing ambition for Herat. It was as though the quarrel over royal honor set in motion a chain reaction that eventually was bound to reignite the shah's territorial reassertion and dreams of expansion under the rubric of defending the land of Islam. Justified by religious and patriotic duties and embellished by a desire for self-assertion, the shah could not pass up his chance for military glory.

CONQUEST OF HERAT

On 24 October 1856, after a long stalemate in a campaign that took more than a year, the news of the Persian conquest of Herat finally reached the capital. Reports of this military victory, after months of anxious anticipation, were brought to the shah at an unfortunate moment coinciding with the death of his son, Mu'in al-Din Mirza, the second heir apparent to die in childhood. A week later, reading a biography of Napoleon by Louis de Bourrienne in Persian translation, the shah wrote a brief note in the margin that captured his mixed emotions:

> Monday, 4 Rabi' al-Awwal, Luy 'Il, 1273 [2 November 1856]. Four in the afternoon. I was in the outer court. I had just finished my lunch. His Excellency the Sadr A'zam was present. It was rainy. I was sitting in the Mirror Hall [Talar-i A'ina] next to the Crystal Fountain [Hawz-i Bulur]. Suddenly Yadullah Khan, servant in waiting, entered and presented the good tidings of the Herat conquest. I stood up. Ghulam Husayn Khan Yuz-bashi Shahsavan, the official news writer [*vaqayi'-nigar*] of the campaign, who had traversed [from Herat] in nine days, reported that the city had surrendered to the victorious army. Thanks to Murtaza 'Ali's blessings, peace be upon him, this was a praiseworthy victory and the eyes of the enemy, particularly the British, turned blind [with jealousy]. Hundred and ten gun salutes were fired in honor of his holiness 'Ali. The Naqara-khana, too, performed. One thousand tumans was awarded to Yadullah Khan for the good news. By a fateful coincidence, at that very hour the crown prince who was six years of age departed from this world in a coma caused by chronic fever. We didn't know whether to be merry or to mourn. "Surely we belong to God and to Him we return."[41]

It is as though Nasir al-Din meant to preserve this moment for posterity. Buried symbolically in the margin of Napoleon's biography, the lucid description of himself and his premier in the lavish surroundings of the Mirror Hall, which held in its center a crystal fountain presented to the shah by Tsar Alexander II, the sound of gunfire mingling with the kettledrums and huge trumpets of the Naqara-khana (the ancient Persian music house) above the gateway to the royal citadel, suggests that the convergence of events must have left a deep impression on the shah (see Fig. 5). Kamal al-Mulk's masterpiece, *Talar-i A'ina*, executed years later under close royal supervision, perhaps meant to capture something of this dramatic moment. The shah sits in solitude in the Mirror Hall looking out onto the garden of Gulistan Palace, conveying the image of a sorrowful yet confident man whose character is reflected in the above passage. The Napoleonic inspirations are not far from the surface.[42]

Figure 5.   The Mirror Hall (Talar-i A'ina) in 1313 Q./1896. Painting by Muhammad Ghaffari, Kamal al-Mulk. Though the Mirror Hall was rebuilt in the
1880s, the royal painter of the late Nasiri period (who worked under the shah's
supervision) captured the spirit of the shah's solitude in the splendor of his
surroundings. Gulistan Museum.

The conquest of Herat was the locus of such inspirations. If Nasir al-Din
Shah needed additional incentives to feel reassured about the break in
relations with Britain, they were provided in two areas: by upheavals in
Afghanistan and by the illusive prospect of a Russian victory in the
Crimean War. On 28 November 1855, simultaneous with Iran's break in
relations with England and a week before Murray's departure from Tehran
(on 6 December 1855), Russia captured the strategically important Ottoman fortress town of Qaras (Kars) in the western Caucasus, about 100 miles
northwest of the Persian frontier. This last desperate effort by Russia
before finally accepting conditions of peace on 1 February 1856 seemed
valiant enough to convince the wishful Nasir al-Din momentarily that
Russia would eventually achieve victory. His failure at first to conclude a
defense treaty with England and then his disappointment over the eventual
break in relations convinced the shah that he could take advantage of the
British preoccupation with the war and aim at a military target long desired
by his dynasty.

Events in Afghanistan only confirmed his impression. The long-standing Qajar ambition to assert direct control over Herat seemed to Nasir al-Din not a luxury but a necessity. Ever since the death in 1851 of the semiautonomous ruler of Herat, Yar Muhammad Khan Zahir al-Dawla—originally the vizier to the local Saduza'i dynasty of Herat—and the subsequent accession of his inept son Sayd Muhammad, the troubled province had been in a state of flux. The 1853 Anglo-Persian agreement, "the most unpalatable to the shah," only promoted British hegemony in the region while barring Iran from any meaningful say in the affairs of its eastern vassal.[43] By 1854, as part of an overall scheme to secure India's northwestern frontier, the British actively sought to create a united Afghanistan, illusory though it was, out of the three principalities of Kabul, Herat, and Kandahar, which were at odds with each other historically, ethnically, and politically. To achieve their objective the British sought to collaborate with Dust Muhammad Khan, the ambitious emir of Kabul and one-time British foe now turned friend. The signing of the first Peshawar treaty on 30 March 1855 was a turning point, as the terms of the treaty condoned not only Dust Muhammad's annexation of Kandahar, the third province of the divided Afghanistan, but also gave to his territorial designs for Herat the implicit blessings of the British. The British envisaged a Herat under Dust Muhammad's united Afghanistan as being much more predisposed to their influence and control than had been (or could ever have been) the case under the Persian shah. As the strategists of British India saw it, such an arrangement was aimed at making Afghanistan "an effectual barrier against Russian aggression" at a time when the British suspected Iran of falling under the Russian yoke. The Peshawar treaty thus recognized Dust Muhammad's control over Kabul "and of those countries of Affghanistan now in his possession," a veiled reference to his recent annexation of Kandahar, and required of the emir "to be the friend of the friends and enemy of the enemies of the Honorable East India Company."[44]

The conclusion of the Peshawar treaty seemed all the more ominous to Nasir al-Din Shah, to whom the term "enemy" seemingly referred. Dust Muhammad's annexation of Kandahar coincided with yet another episode of unrest in Herat—the assassination of its governor, Sayd Muhammad Khan, by his political rivals and the accession of the young Saduza'i prince Muhammad Yusuf, son of the previous ruler of Herat, Kamran Mirza. Nasir al-Din surely saw both a threat and an opportunity in this violent shift of power from Sayd Muhammad, a callous usurper with doubtful loyalties to Iran, to Muhammad Yusuf, a helpless puppet susceptible to manipulation. The shah concluded that if he did not assume control over Herat, Dust Muhammad and his British backers would. The growing prospect of a united Afghanistan under the wing of the British was too grave to be ignored, especially when Persian relations with Britain were at their lowest ebb.

In Nasir al-Din's mind, the threat of another Afghan invasion and possible annexation of Khurasan province were inevitable corollaries closely associated with the memories of earlier upheavals in Persian history. Historical paradigms die hard, and the shah knew enough about them to see the contrast between Shah Sultan Husayn, who miserably lost the Safavid empire in 1722 to a Ghalza'i Afghan chief not unlike Dust Muhammad, and Nadir Shah Afshar, the fierce military genius and conqueror who, only eight years later, crushed the Afghan invaders, ended their occupation of Iran, and soon afterward overran the whole of Afghanistan, Central Asia, northern India as far east as Delhi, southern Iraq, the Persian Gulf coasts, and the eastern Caucasus. Reference to Sultan Husayn in Nasir al-Din's note (cited earlier) showed the extent to which he was apprehensive of the impending Afghan danger. His Nadir-like self image, by contrast, could only be reinforced by confronting a world power such as Britain, much as the underdog Napoleon had done.

Beyond the lessons of history, the shah's fears were not altogether misplaced. It was only in 1843 that the annexation of Sind brought the British directly to the Persian frontiers, and the policy of annexing principalities actively pursued by Dalhousie (including the acquisition of Kashmir in 1849, a province with long cultural and family ties with Iran, and the virtual annexation of the Awdh kingdom in the early 1850s) could easily be extended to the northwestern frontier and beyond to vulnerable Khurasan. As in similar cases elsewhere, here too the great powers' advances on the southeastern and the northeastern peripheries of Iran had provoked an understandable reaction in the Iranian center, a martial spirit of defiance in the shah, who was anxious to lay claim to and verify possession of all territories that constituted his Guarded Domains before they were annexed or declared independent by one or another of the neighboring powers.

Herat thus occupied a symbolic place in the mind of the Qajar monarch: He wished to be a Nadir and not a Sultan Husayn. Murray's observation, after the Persians had captured Herat, that "the King . . . already considers himself a second Nadir Shah," was more than a condescending remark.[45] The conquest of Herat was deemed necessary not only as a preemptive attempt to safeguard Khurasan but also to reassert the Persian claim long held by the Qajars, from Aqa Muhammad Khan onward. Although Nasir al-Din was reacting to the threat of Dust Muhammad by taking advantage of the chaos in Herat, he also desired to succeed where his father, Muhammad Shah, and grandfather, 'Abbas Mirza, had failed. An article in the *Vaqayi'-i Ittifaqiya*, translated (possibly by Mirza Malkum Khan) from a Belgian weekly, summed up the shah's feelings toward Herat. The shah's "disenchantment" and "annoyance" with the British and his "disgust with his present condition" is such, the article claimed, "that he highly prefers the headship of a village to his kingdom as long as it would be free from [foreign] coercion." No longer keeping his resentment confined to angry private notes to his premier, Nasir al-Din was now prepared to admit publicly that although "from the outset of his reign he kept quiet about all the difficulties, now his honor and dignity have overcome his forbearance so much that he seems to have no desire to keep his throne but for vengeance."[46] The "change of attitude" could "even be observed in the shah's mood," the *Vaqayi'-i Ittifaqiya* informed its readers:

> Whoever has seen him once could ascertain that such a course of conduct and treatment could not agree with his nature. He is a proud and fierce young man who is ambitious, highly autocratic, combative, and extremely warlike. The English departure [from Iran] was a cause for celebration for him. Since then, his spirits, which for a long time had been depressed because of the intimidation of the foreign powers, have begun to turn to joy and jubilation and his melancholy and subdued mood indoors has changed into pride and self-esteem.[47]

The shah's attitude aptly fit the Qajar political culture, in which glory and chivalry were judged in the battlefield and greatness measured by territorial conquest. He aspired to a victory that had been denied both his father and grandfather. "The continual preoccupation of Nasir al-Din Shah is to achieve deeds that his father failed to accomplish," wrote Joseph Gobineau, the astute French chargé d'affaires, who arrived in Tehran shortly after the end of the Herat affair to replace Bourre. Two decades earlier, in 1838, Muhammad Shah had been forced to lift the siege of Herat and return from the costly campaign empty-handed largely because of British threats and retaliatory occupation of the port of Bushihr in the Persian Gulf. What could give the young shah greater satisfaction and better soothe his troubled pride than coming out of his ancestors' shadow with a successful campaign in Herat? This was one chance to live up to the warlike Qajar legacy and to prove to the world, and the memory of his father, his merits as a king and a conqueror.[48]

The last sentence in the article in *Vaqayi'-i Ittifaqiya* clearly hinted at a disagreement, even a power struggle, within the inner circles of the court. Whether by his own initiative or with Malkum's help, the shah forced Nuri to comply with his desired course of action. "Although the premier is pro-British," declared the article, "he was obliged to abandon his support for them because of their conduct." While praising Nuri as "a peace lover" whose "instinctive talents would come out better at times of crisis" and as "the most courageous and venturing of all the Persians," it nevertheless admitted that "after putting forth much effort to prevent a conflict," Nuri realized that "without the British departure from Tehran [even] his own position would be endangered."[49]

This was not how Murray viewed the situation. Assessing in retrospect the causes of the break in relations and the Herat campaign, Murray believed it was his attempt to bypass Nuri and arrange confidential communications and a "tete-a-tete audience with the shah" that prompted the "jealous" premier to be "more than ever resolved" to estrange the British envoy from his master. Murray thought himself "in error in supposing that the Shah [was] capable of keeping a secret even for his own interest."[50] Obviously dismissive of the shah's political agenda, Murray continued to hold Nuri the chief culpable for the anti-British policy of the Persian government. Faced with the shah's pressure and concerned with his own precarious position, Nuri had little choice but to try to advance a two-track strategy in collaboration with the young Mirza Malkum Khan. Murray was perhaps not exaggerating Malkum's role when he identified him as the "chief instigator" behind the Herat enterprise, this despite the harsh censure heaped upon Nuri. Reconciling step by step the shah's ambitions for conquest with Nuri's pragmatic approach, Mirza Malkum Khan was instrumental in shaping a strategy that also involved Mirza Sa'id Khan, the minister for foreign affairs, Farrukh Khan Ghaffari, Amin al-Mulk (later Amin al-Dawla; see Pl. 12), a rising court official chosen to represent Iran's case in Europe, and Nicolas Bourre, the French envoy in Tehran.

IN SEARCH OF FRIENDS:
FRANCE AND THE UNITED STATES

The purpose of the Persian strategy was twofold. It intended to use Herat, and the Persian territorial claim to it, to negotiate with the British a fair settlement conducive to the safety of Iran's eastern frontiers; and it aimed to register greater international recognition for Iran to help reverse the dominant pattern in its diplomatic relations and to deter further humiliation and loss of face. It was believed that expanding diplomatic relations with the West, taking advantage of the democratic institutions and the free press in Europe to voice Iran's grievances, and seeking closer contacts with political figures, among them heads of state such as Napoleon III and, later, Prince Bismarck, would enhance Iran's standing in the world community and protect it from becoming the prey of its neighbors and their diplomats.

In theory the two-track policy sounded realistic, befitting Iran's political interests and limited resources. Yet the shah's confidence in his country's military capabilities was no doubt exaggerated. The military obstacles and diplomatic stalemate soon turned Herat into a risky enterprise. To set in motion the military side of the plan, the royal order for troop mobilization went out to five provinces as early as December 1855. The shah's uncle, Sultan Murad Mirza, Husam al-Saltana ("the Sword of the Kingdom"), was instructed to proceed with full speed toward Herat as the commander of the Persian army.[51] The first signs of trouble appeared when the hapless Persian forces were stranded outside the formidable walls of Herat. The siege went on for close to nine months; the shah's high hopes for rapid conquest, raised by the promises of Husam al-Saltana, were soon dashed.

No doubt Husam al-Saltana's exhortations encouraged Nasir al-Din to appoint him in January 1856 as the commander of the expedition to Herat.[52] A cultivated yet rambunctious prince, he was known for his Qajar pride and outspoken anti-British sentiments. His valor in the battlefield was tested when he fought Salar in Khurasan. He was tested in the royal council as well. During the Farhad Mirza affair, he threatened forcibly to remove his younger brother from the sanctuary of the British legation for the disgrace he had caused the royal family.[53] During the Hashim Khan scandal he allegedly used "most grossly indecent language about Her Majesty the Queen," conduct for which Murray promised he would procure reparation once relations were restored.[54]

After four months of suspense in anticipation of a breakthrough, Nuri was nervous enough to remind Husam al-Saltana that "you engaged, with 10,000 troops and 10,000 tumans, to occupy Herat. I have sent you 80,000 tumans, and you have 15,000 troops, and what have you done? We will admit of no further excuse. Herat must be taken."[55] Five months later the premier had almost given up hope when he cautioned his emissary to Europe, Amin al-Mulk, of the "empty courage and pride of His Highness the prince. Frankly, it is now more than four months he has been promising that any day soon Herat is ours, and yet he is right where he began."[56]

With troops behind the high walls of Herat, there was every reason to concentrate on the diplomatic front. Simultaneous with his issuing the admonishing note to Husam al-Saltana, Nuri was delighted to learn through the Persian chargé d'affaires in London that the British ambassador to Istanbul, Lord Stratford de Redcliffe, was willing to negotiate the restoration of diplomatic relations with Iran. This was an opportunity not to be missed. Highly optimistic about the political wizardry of Malkum Khan, the premier convinced the shah to dispatch the young diplomat to Istanbul. "If we want to give satisfaction," he reasoned with the shah, "why should we bother with him [i.e., Murray]? Let us give it [directly] to his government."[57] Given the existing animosity between Redcliffe and Murray, Nuri's argument seemed reasonable.

Malkum's appointment, however, was viewed with deepest suspicion by Richard Stevens, the acting British counsel in Tehran, who, having been left behind to take care of the legation, wasted no chance to spy on the host government. The shah had questioned the suitability of Consul Stevens's remaining in Tehran in charge of the mission—this man's "proceedings and mischief-making," the shah believed, "fill ten books." Reminding the shah of Stevens's good services on the occasion of his accession to the throne, Murray cautioned sarcastically that it was only the consul's honest reporting from Azarbaijan that made him a "moofsid" (mischief-maker) in the eyes of the shah. Stevens informed Redcliffe that Malkum's "intrigues and counsels contributed in no small degree towards the rupture between this government and Mr. Murray. That his language about our government, our mission, and in fact, everything English, is invariably hostile and offensive." He believed that Malkum's "connections, his position, or his conduct [did not] entitle him to the least consideration." The fact that he was "a great admirer of the French," and as such "very intimate with M. Bourre," was all the more reason for the British ambassador to avoid Malkum; as Stevens surmised, the Russian mission had turned Malkum's position to its own advantage.[58] It is no wonder that Redcliffe's negotiations with Malkum in Istanbul were doomed from the beginning. The young emissary, though intellectually impressive, was snubbed for not wielding sufficient clout.

Further dimming the prospects of a peaceful settlement was the tough line advocated by Murray toward the shah and his dynasty. Furious with Clarendon for denying him the Foreign Office's blessing over the break in relations, the grudging envoy called not only for a British expeditionary force to be sent to the Persian Gulf to occupy vital Persian ports and islands but also for the stirring up of an anti-government rebellion in southern Iran. He observed that the shah, who was "studiously kept in ignorance of the disorganized state of his army, and of the spirit of disaffection prevalent in the mass of Persian population, is dreaming of conquest of Afghanistan, while the incidents of a week might suffice to drive him from his palace at Tehran." Speculating on Nasir al-Din's fate in the event of a British attack, he did not hesitate to hint at the possibility of a British-staged coup d'etat. "The unpopularity of the Kajar dynasty is so great in the provinces," he argued, "that it is far from impossible that a hostile demonstration, made for the purpose of exacting the dismissal of the Sadr [A'zam], might end in the dethronement of the Shah; indeed I have no hesitation in saying that if the young prince Abbas Meerza, from Bagdad, were to accompany the invading forces, the result above alluded to would be more than probable; this eventuality demands the serious attention of Her Majesty's Government." The Russian reaction to such a move, Murray believed, would be hostile and the consequences unpredictable, but he was assured by his Persian contacts that "if Abbas Meerza were to enter Persia from the south, supported by a British force, a rising in his favour would take place even in the northern and populous provinces."[59]

The envoy's predictable enmity aside, the proposed scheme to dethrone Nasir al-Din and replace him with his half-brother raised important questions for the British policy makers. Clarendon was obviously dismayed by the outcome of Murray's scandal and was cautious not to overplay the British demands for satisfaction. Five months after the break in relations, when he eventually replied to Murray's terse inquires, he rebuked him not only for the unwise choice of Hashim Khan and the even more unwise decision to confront the Persian government but furthermore for the "impolicy of risking a rupture with Persia at a moment when such rupture might have the effect of giving her a pretext for throwing herself into the arms of Russia, and of thereby adding to the difficulties with which the Allies [of the Crimean War] had to contend."[60] London's approach was obviously pragmatic, even conciliatory, for it rejected Murray's viewpoint entirely, but it was not outright forthcoming. To persuade the shah to lift the Herat siege—a matter of cardinal importance to Palmerston's power politics and his Russophobic perspective—the British premier and his foreign minister gave their first warning on 24 May 1856, hoping that compliance with it would open the doors for further negotiation.[61]

This was not the way the shah interpreted London's message, however. For five months he had witnessed how the Foreign Office had rebuffed Murray while the envoy was inching his way through Iran to Baghdad. The wishful shah was naturally inclined to believe that London would offer favorable terms if Iran displayed a steadfast facade in Herat. Earlier, in response to Bourre's concern over a possible British reprisal over Herat,

Nuri had pointed out that the shah was "determined" to seize Herat and that "nothing could divert him from the idea."[62] The conclusion of the Paris peace treaty at the end of Crimean War no doubt caused "undisguised disappointment" for the shah and his ministers,[63] as did the setbacks in the siege of Herat. Yet, faced with the prospect of defeat and humiliation if his troops retreated empty-handed, Nasir al-Din did not give up immediately. If need be, he was prepared to assume command of the military himself; he even toyed with the idea of departing for Khurasan but was dissuaded by Nuri. He contented himself with warning Husam al-Saltana from the comfort of Gulistan Palace. "At all costs," he wrote to the prince in one of many dispatches, "the Persian troops must hold out their positions" around Herat's outer rampart, a hazardous task that cost high casualties in the face of stiff Afghan resistance.[64]

With Malkum rebuffed on the diplomatic front, a new envoy was to be sent with all the proper credentials. Amin al-Mulk's mission, first to Istanbul and then to France, was intended to achieve a settlement by high-level diplomatic negotiations. The France of Louis Napoleon had now emerged as a worthy ally and an influential advocate on Iran's diplomatic horizon. The shah's private letter to the emperor, his "august and compassionate brother," displayed all the signs of Malkum's influence. It pointed out that permanent relations between the two countries had been the source of "envy among friends, let alone foes," and that Amin al-Mulk, one of the shah's "confidants aware of his master's secret thoughts and inner intents," would personally present the royal wishes to the emperor. Besides pleading for assistance in settling the ongoing crisis with England, the letter assured Napoleon that "if in the domestic affairs of this state he would have advice conducive to the progress [tarraqi] of the Persian state," the shah would put them into practice without hesitation. "God willing," Nasir al-Din concluded, the emperor "would wield a policy that would bring some tranquility and a sense of security to the people and government of this country."[65]

The shah's affinity for the French monarch and his possible assistance was not merely a matter of expediency. Nasir al-Din viewed the emperor as a role model and his rise to prominence in defiance of bipolar Anglo-Russian Europe as an example to be followed. The shah's interest in France was further enhanced by his fascination with the image of Napoleon I and his military feats against the British. Reading about Bonaparte, the shah seems to have associated the valor and grandeur of the grandfather with the political skill and extravagance of the grandson. Gobineau accurately noted the shah's "fantasies of being likened to Napoleon I. He wants to be independent of all the European supremacy and furthermore to be a conqueror."[66]

The shah's newfound pro-French sentiments and his hopes to build up, through France, a broader base of international support are well evident in an "instruction booklet" (*kitabcha-yi dastur al-'amal*) evidently written by Sa'id Khan, the minister for foreign affairs, under Nuri's supervision and probably with Malkum's help. The booklet set guidelines for Amin al-Mulk's mission. Iran's entry into the "Concert of Europe" (*mizan-i Urup*), declared this early statement of Iran's foreign policy, was deemed necessary to preserve the country's security against foreign aggression. It observed that "if the ambitions of the French emperor are comparable to those of Napoleon the Great . . . then he surely knows that the two powers [Russia and Britain] will soon quarrel and at such an opportune moment Iran, because of its proximity to India, will be instrumental in bringing greatness to her ally." In a tone clearly inviting and even encouraging French support in the dispute with England, the author of the booklet tried to capitalize on the shah's French connection. He argued that "if the objective of the French government is other than that of the great Napoleon, then the Persian government confesses that under such circumstances the necessary benefit would not materialize, since the only way Iran could truly cooperate with France and attack the British government [in India] is through Afghanistan." The veiled invitation, naive as it sounded, no doubt coincided with shah's desire to utilize the growing anti-British feelings in India.[67]

The royal gifts sent to Louis Napoleon certainly demonstrated the high diplomatic stakes. In addition to the Order of the Lion and the Sun, set in diamonds and worth 3,000 tumans, the Persian ambassador also took with him four pedigreed Turkoman horses, a string of valuable pearls for the empress, a jeweled saber for the crown prince, and the shah's portrait set in diamonds for the French foreign minister. The pearls, valued at 5,000 tumans, were given by the shah with great reluctance. He only consented to part with them when Nuri convinced him that "such a handsome present would enable him to attain important objectives through the French Government."[68]

The shah's search in the international forum for new security alliances against the powers stretched beyond France to Austria and Prussia and over the Atlantic to the United States. Nasir al-Din and his premier, acquiring more knowledge about international affairs, were quick to grasp the growing importance of the United States as a world power. In the face of Britain's sensitivities and in spite of its resistance, the shah's government hoped to explore the prospect of concluding a treaty of friendship with the United

States, if for no other reason than to gain a bargaining lever in negotiations with England. In addition to a mutual trade agreement, as early as 1856 the shah was willing to offer the United States some military and commercial bases in the Persian Gulf "to remain permanently in the hands of the agents of that state on lease or license in order to build residences and offices for their representatives and harbor for their ships."[69] Given Iran's precarious circumstances, such a generous invitation to the warm waters of the Persian Gulf was not altogether unwarranted. Article 15 of the draft of the treaty with the United States, which the British envoy obtained through his spies in the Persian government, went on to demand that because the Persian government did not have "vessels of war," the U.S. government was thus committed "not to neglect the protection of the Persian merchants carrying the flag of that country, nor allow any violence or irregularity toward them." Article 16 went even further, engaging the United States in protection of "all the Persian islands and ports in the Persian Gulf against the violence and attack of the enemies, weak or strong, Christian or non-Christian." In exchange for the Persian government's help and "full honor" to U.S. vessels of war, the United States, in the event Iran wanted to establish territorial claims over its islands (including Bahrain) in the Persian Gulf, would provide vessels for Iran "on the rate of the day." It is no wonder that Murray viewed the Persian initiative as a move "aimed so directly at the destruction of our maritime influence in the Persian Gulf" and warned London to block the agreement.[70]

Wishful as the Persian terms may have seemed, involvement of the United States in the Persian Gulf reflected some diplomatic ingenuity toward relieving Iran in its most vulnerable area. Soon after Amin al-Mulk opened negotiations with the U.S. minister plenipotentiary in Istanbul, on the eve of the war with England, Nuri even looked optimistically on the prospects of borrowing one-half to one million tumans from the United States. But his hopes were soon to be dashed. Anxious to conclude a treaty before Britain could impose its own restrictions, in December 1856 Amin al-Mulk and Charles Spence, brother of the U.S. minister in Istanbul, hurriedly signed a much modified protocol treaty of friendship between Iran and the United States, pending ratification in both capitals. Persian approval came along with a royal decree and a second-degree Order of the Lion and Sun issued in Spence's honor. Yet, in spite of apparent ratification of the treaty by the U.S. Congress, the shah's eagerness to receive a high-level U.S. representative in Tehran was not fulfilled, possibly because of British pressure on the United States. Direct diplomatic relations between Iran and the United States were delayed for another quarter of a century, only to be established in 1882.[71]

Consideration for British interests in the Persian Gulf may have dampened the United States' enthusiasm to involve its newly expanded navy and send fleets to the remote waters of the Persian Gulf. No U.S. businessman was willing to lend financial support to the Persian government either. Yet all of these queries and negotiations came at a time when the United States sought to increase its international presence. One can surmise that the news of Commodore Perry's momentous attempt in 1854 to open up Japanese ports to U.S. commerce using the threat of a naval attack and the ensuing treaties signed by Japan with the United States and soon thereafter with England and Russia caught Nasir al-Din's attention.[72]

British reaction to the shah's diplomatic initiative was far less amicable. From the start Amin al-Mulk's mission was riddled with uncertainties rooted in the tensions between the shah and his premier. As an ex-treasurer in the royal private quarters (*'amala-yi khalwat*) and an old ally of Nuri, Amin al-Mulk was accustomed to palace intrigue and fully aware of the pitfalls in the treacherous path ahead of him. A man of intelligence and tact, he knew how easily he could be blamed for all the problems that, under the circumstances, a peace treaty with England would entail, and he was determined not to be such a victim. Though the premier exhorted him to rush to Istanbul without delay to resume negotiations with Redcliffe, the shah, in the margin of the same correspondence, instructed him to procrastinate until 15 Safar 1273 (15 October 1856), presumably in anticipation of the capture of Herat, recently prognosticated by the royal astrologer.[73] When he eventually reached the Ottoman capital, Amin al-Mulk was repeatedly crippled by the equivocal, even contradictory, messages that came for him from Tehran reflecting panic and confusion at court. His natural discretion and his obsessive concern with authorization, which he repeatedly acquired from the shah, contributed to the ultimate failure of the negotiations with the British ambassador, which lasted several months.

The shah's differences with Nuri, though mostly tactical rather than substantive, were deepening. Nuri had employed his remarkable persuasive abilities, embellished with anecdotes and didactic tales in the style of sagacious ministers of the books of mirrors, to bring some sense to Nasir al-Din's defiant mind. With little deviation, he argued that to the Persian government Herat was nothing more than a negotiating tool through which to establish an enduring peace on the eastern frontier and a less menacing British presence in Iran. He knew too well that his government was in no position to wage a successful war against Britain and was alert to the dire consequences of such an action. "At any rate the policy of the Sublime Government [of Iran] is to avoid further complications with the British government," he wrote to his emissary in Istanbul. He surely had in mind the naval attack by Britain and its allies upon Muhammad 'Ali's forces during the Syrian crisis of September 1840 and the 1855 engagements against Russia in the ongoing Crimean War when he observed that "a government that in five hours can fire one hundred and fifty thousands shells at 'Akka, flout a fleet of four to five thousand battleships and fight with a [mighty] government such as Russia, obviously has no trepidation about sending ten to twenty ships to Bushihr and Shatt al-'Arab or dispatching some twenty regiments from Punjab to Afghanistan and Khurasan to collaborate with Dust Muhammad Khan or [sending] some ten regiments to Kirman." His concerns were realistic. "If one cannon is fired in the Persian Gulf or in the Shatt al-'Arab or in Kirman," he asked rhetorically, "do we have that kind of strength to remain engaged in the siege of Herat and yet encounter the British at those locations? Where do we find the troops?" His argument made perfect sense, given the hazards of a two-front war for a vulnerable country such as Iran. "Our army is confined to the one engagement in Herat. Suppose we managed to put together the troops, how can we procure the money? All of a sudden we will wake up to the fact that we are overcome by the British and are obliged to comply with whatever terms they may dictate, even to surrender a port or two in the Persian Gulf and thus keep for ourselves an enemy in the sleeve." Nasir al-Din could only go as far as adding to Nuri's letter the expediency of insisting on a British guarantee for the security of Iran's eastern frontiers in return for a Persian troop withdrawal.[74]

Soon afterward, however, encouraged by the prospects of victory in Herat, Nuri felt compelled to blend his own caution with the shah's more adventurous designs. To Amin al-Mulk he wrote that the shah's "ultimate wish" was that the affair should not precipitate a war with Britain. "If, however, the British are dragging their feet, trust in God, we too, are ready," wrote Nuri on behalf of the shah. "Why should we bear the shame of relinquishing Herat and yet every year be exposed to the terror of the Afghan [attacks]?"[75] The shah fully approved of Nuri's strong language but insisted, in a separate note, that he would like to see Afghanistan remain divided and the three emirs not interfere in one anothers' affairs in the future, nor have Britain interfere in their affairs, terms that reflected his sharpened political insight and were legally grounded in the 1814 Anglo-Persian agreement.[76]

With the capture of Herat, the tone of the shah and his minister turned decidedly more assertive. Even Nuri, carried away by the occasion, seems to have forgotten his earlier tact when he exhorted Amin al-Mulk not to succumb to excessive British demands, to avoid cowardliness, and to speak out on the subject of Persian counterdemands in an almost Lilliputian spirit. "Suppose they declare an unjust war against us," he wrote. "Let us even imagine that they occupy Bushihr. There is no cause for alarm. We then capture Kandahar. If they advance further, then we capture Kabul. If they come further, we capture Punjab. This is no grave hassle." He was careful, nevertheless, to balance his pipe-dream remarks by reminding Amin al-Mulk to do his best to maintain friendship between Iran and England.[77] Yet the pride of the conquest, achieved as much by Husam al-Saltana's valor as by the introduction of modern siege techniques by M. Buhler, a French army engineer in the service of the Persian government, thrilled the court, at least for the moment. "This is the same Herat that did not succumb even to Timur," wrote Nuri, "the same Herat that resisted two attempts by Nadir Shah. . . . The Blessed Khaqan [Fath 'Ali Shah] repeatedly sent expeditions without success. So did the Viceregent ['Abbas Mirza] and the Deceased [Muhammad] Shah."[78]

The shah and Nuri tried to make the loudest possible public noise over the conquest of Herat, casting it as the most substantial Persian victory since Aqa Muhammad Khan's time. The celebration was too important to be spoiled even by the death of the crown prince. The worrisome prospect of an heirless shah could be put aside for the time being. Though the loss had "caused great grief for the servants of the state," Nuri convinced the shah that, given his health, soon new sons would be born to him worthy of heir apparency.[79] At the public levee (*salam*) announced for the occasion, the court chronicler, Sipihr, read the epinicium (*fath-nama*) composed by Husam al-Saltana and sent over by a special courier (see Pl. 17). It began with a verse from Hafiz: "This is that stage in the remote desert; Where the armies of Salm and Tur were lost." In florid language it then praised the prince's accomplishment. "I built trenches and was hit by boulders. I fought battles and employed devices. I blocked the city gates with repeated sorties and massive artillery. I positioned the victorious army around the city walls." The height of his achievement, the epinicium continued, was the mention of the shah's name in the Friday sermon (*khutba*), an ancient rite symbolizing sovereignty, and the public call to prayer (*adhan*) that was amended with insertion of the Shi'ite salute: "'Ali is God's vicegerent."[80] In celebration the capital was illuminated and a public holiday declared. A "national booklet" (*kitabcha-yi millati*), written by a certain Badayi'-nigar, was also published at the request of the "people of the nation" (*ahl-i millat*) to describe the conquest.[81]

The sweet taste of victory, brief though it was, rekindled the shah's youthful ambitions to expand eastward toward India, his idealization of Nadir's Indian campaigns and Napoleon's designs for it. The appearance on the scene of an Indian prince from Delhi, a certain Muhammad Najaf Mirza, who claimed to be a cousin of Bahadur Shah, the last Mughal ruler of India, provided further encouragement. He had taken refuge in the Persian court, seeking assistance against English "infidels" who had dominated his land and were about to put an end to even the nominal existence of his dynasty. He had pleaded with the shah that "all the people of India are desperate because of maltreatment of British agents and all complain about the ills [inflicted] on their religion." On the eve of the Indian revolt he was confident enough to promise, on behalf of his people, that "once the shah's army passes beyond Kandahar, his people [i.e., the people of India] will provide one million tumans for military expenses and they themselves will start the rebellion against the British troops and will kill them wherever they find them." To assure the shah of success in such a dramatic venture, he reminded him that "the Indian Army [*qushun-i Hindi*], too, is in alliance with the people of India." Muhammad Najaf was anticipating the "Indian Mutiny" when he said that "all diverse nationalities [of India] are united and seek refuge, but they are awaiting a pretext and need a motive." The shah was also assured that the chiefs of Kandahar, one of three principalities of divided Afghanistan adjacent to India's northeastern frontier, were ready to rebel against Dust Muhammad's shaky hold over the city. Muhammad Najaf was careful, however, not to invite the shah to India: "As soon as the victorious [Persian] army reaches Girishg, all the people of India will take it upon themselves to eradicate the Christian nation from all the provinces of India." Underlining British military exhaustion after the Crimean War and the inexperience of the Indian Army's new recruits, he believed that the shah "not only will be redeemed before God and the Imams, but in this world will make a good name for himself and expand his own empire."[82]

There was little time, if any at all, for the shah to contemplate conquest in remote lands. Soon he was to awaken to dangers much closer to home. He may have decided not to fight the British, but the British had come to fight him.

WAR IN THE PERSIAN GULF

Reverence for 'Ali was not limited to 110 gunshots in the Tehran citadel and the call to prayer in his name in Herat's mosques. As part of an ingenious policy to capitalize on public sentiments, a second public levee was held on 25 November 1856, a year after the shah's dream in which he renamed the Victorian tree. The auspicious date, although determined by the royal astrologer (who was earlier rewarded for his prognostication of Herat's capture), suspiciously coincided with the arrival of the British declaration of war, a development the shah and prime minister claimed took them by surprise. In perilous times of war and foreign invasion, a closer association with the sacred symbols of Shi'ism was a clever way to boost the monarchy's image. As the "defender of the faith," Nasir al-Din had to demonstrate in public his devotion to 'Ali, the most valiant of the Shi'ite saints, and exhort his subjects to render, if need be, their religious duty to protect their land and participate in a holy war. The gold coins that were stuck in Nasir al-Din's name in Herat just after it was captured were rushed to Tehran to be distributed among the 'ulama and the dignitaries of the state.

The ancient symbols of royal authority, reading Friday sermons and striking coins in the name of the sovereign, in this case were complemented by an improvised dedication ceremony, perhaps the closest a Muslim ruler could come to the Christian cult of St. George. This was perhaps the first conscious effort by Nasir al-Din Shah to promote what may be defined as a royal cult of 'Ali. Distinct from the reverence for Husayn, the Third Imam, the cult of 'Ali represented sovereignty and political authority as well as military valor and victory. As a sign of his devotion to 'Ali, the shah, whose "essence of existence was ingrained with the love of 'Ali" and who from his youth "had not ever slept but by remembrance of 'Ali," decorated himself with a pictorial medallion specially created for the occasion. The portrait of 'Ali painted on the medallion by the renowned court painter Abul-Hasan Ghaffari, Sani' al-Mulk, was copied from an old icon preserved in the royal treasury. This was the very same icon (*timsal*), Sipihr informs us, to which the shah paid homage every morning.

The ceremony was designed to enhance both the shah's and his prime minister's stature. As soon as the medal was brought forward by Nuri, the shah descended from the veranda (*ivan*) of Gulistan Palace. "Then, helped by His Excellency the prime minister, the Imam Jum'a, Shaykh Riza, who enjoyed full seniority among the 'ulama, hung the medallion on His Majesty's blessed frame." The shah then returned to the veranda and took his seat on the four-pillowed throne. Once again the sound of a 110-gun salute rang out. By dedicating himself to the Commander of the Faithful (*amir al-mu'minin*), for whom he would risk his head and his very soul, he would stand proudly among all the kings of Islam. "On the day of

Resurrection I will be saved by the intercession of the lord of this medallion," the shah assured his audience. Nuri's response to the royal
sentiments was predictable. "Obedience to the sovereign equals devotion
to God," he declared, calling upon the shah's subjects "not to be sparing
of their lives on the path of the crusade [*ghaza*] and the holy war [*jihad*]."[83]

Reference to holy war was not accidental. Clarendon's second ultimatum, dated 10 October (two weeks before the fall of Herat), reached Tehran
on 19 November, causing outrage and anxiety. Ominously, it informed the
Persian government that an expedition had been dispatched to the Persian
Gulf and threatened that "whatever may result to Persia from this measure,
which her government has wantonly provoked, the responsibility thereof
will rest on the evil counsellors of the Shah, who have led his Majesty to
countenance insult and injury towards Great Britain, and to violate the
solemn engagements of an international pact."[84] The obvious reference to
Nuri, "the evil counsellor," reflected Clarendon's anger over the premier's
cool reply to his first warning in July. Dodging any firm commitment, in
his answer the Persian premier waited until September in order to give
himself time to find a settlement to the Herat dispute while Amin al-Mulk
was negotiating with Redcliffe. But the Persian emissary's arrival in Istanbul was delayed. By the shah's instructions he was to pause on the road
long enough for Herat to be captured. Finally, heartened by the news of
the Persian success in the capture of Herat, Amin al-Mulk immediately
entered into negotiations with the British ambassador, hoping to reach a
quick settlement on all disputed issues.

Incensed with the Persian delaying tactics, the British government could
only be appeased now by the removal of the premier from office. This was
one of six demands, based on a list prepared by Murray and handed to Amin
al-Mulk on 28 October 1856. Among other conditions, the envoy's letter
unceremoniously called for the surrender of the port of Bandar 'Abbas to
the sultan (Imam) of Masqat, a Persian vassal and friend of Murray who
had changed sides by pledging allegiance to the British and was wreaking
havoc in that southern Persian port in the hope of turning his temporary
lease into a permanent possession. This particular dispute was an additional
sore spot in Anglo-Persian relations. Bandar 'Abbas had long been coveted
by British representatives in Tehran and Bushihr who wished to turn the
Persian Gulf into a British lake. Withdrawal from Herat, a commitment not
to intervene in Afghanistan, a new commercial treaty to facilitate British
imports to Iran at a preferential ad valorem rate entirely favorable to British
subjects, and settlement of disputes with British subjects and protégés
constituted the other items in the list of British demands. But it was certain

that such demands would be accompanied by the thunder of the guns that soon were to bombard the besieged port of Bushihr.[85]

The shah's downfall, however, was not part of the plan. Murray's incessant schemes to overthrow the shah did not interest the Foreign Office. Clarendon had read Murray's proposal "with interest" but reminded him that if the object of the British government was "to break up the Persian monarchy" and make "a permanent settlement in the southern provinces of Persia it would [then] be useful to encourage the tribes to revolt, and to march to Ispahan; but if, as is the case, they only seek to bring the Persian Government to terms, it would hardly be fair to excite the people of the southern provinces to revolt, in which they would not afterwards be supported, and then leave them to the vengeance of the Shah." He reiterated his position to the expeditionary force about to depart from Bombay. "Her Majesty's Government do not seek to subvert the dynasty of the Shah; they do not intend to encourage insurrection on the part of his subjects, or to put forward any pretender to his throne."

Shortly afterward the same undertaking was relayed to the Russian foreign minister, Prince Gortchakoff, whose concerns about possible British territorial gains had been fanned by the Persian chargé d'affaires in St. Petersburg. "I hope I might be excused for saying," added Clarendon with hardly concealed rancor, "that a lecture upon moderation and forbearance from Russia to England in dealing with Persia was amusing." Reminding his counterpart of the harsh terms Russia had imposed on Iran in the Gulistan and Turkmanchay treaties of 1813 and 1828, respectively, he conceded with condescension that Britain had no wish for a "change of dynasty" and no intention to "create revolution" or to "humble the shah" in the eyes of his people. Ironically, at no time previously in the history of Anglo-Persian relations had the survival of the Qajar dynasty been so expressly guaranteed by the British government. Some room was left for maneuvering, however. "It must be understood," continued Clarendon with a tacitly threatening tone, "that if the Shah would not yield, and [if] the war continued, Her Majesty's government would not be answerable for the consequences, nor would they engage to adhere to the conditions they had now proposed."[86]

There was little chance for the shah to take comfort in the British assurances had they ever become known to him. The contents of Clarendon's letter and Amin al-Mulk's reports were threatening enough to eventually make him abandon his hopes for keeping Herat. The request for the removal of Nuri seemed to him as humiliating as the demand to surrender Bandar 'Abbas. As late as October Nuri had repeatedly assured him that the British government would never resort to "coercive measures" and "would not move a soldier or a ship in connection with Herat." No wonder that in an interview with Bourre the shah appeared "incredulous" when he was cautioned by the French minister that the British might soon occupy Persian Gulf ports, if indeed they had not already done so. Even exaggerated reports of the appearance of forty British warships in the Persian Gulf and the occupation of Khark Island less than two weeks before the fall of Herat, though a cause of alarm for the shah, were viewed as sheer tactical maneuvers.[87]

In the "council of princes and nobles" convened on 15 October to decide on the steps necessary to face the British threat, the shah again repeated his "fixed determination" not to relinquish Herat; moreover, he declared he would persist "even if it should entail the loss of his Throne." In addition to recruiting troops and carrying out military preparations in Bushihr and Muhammara, the council decided, the government should send a circular to all the 'ulama of the provinces calling upon them to prepare for the jihad. The shah even volunteered to go to Mashhad himself to "rally his forces for a march to Afghanistan and India" and to send his second son, Amir Qasim Khan, the six-year-old Amir Nizam, to assume nominal military command in the south.[88]

Whether or not the shah was emulating Napoleon in his encounter with the British, he certainly felt his was a historic mission, evident in his encouragement and moral support for Nuri. Worried that the Istanbul negotiations might result in a degrading compromise, he warned the premier: "Remain firm at heart and do not lose ground. Reconciliation is fine. So long as it is possible we will observe it. But if the Lord of this world were to kill us, it would be preferable to bearing humiliation and disgrace." This was perhaps the shah's finest hour of patriotism and military honor, but even then his vision of history, from which he drew strength, betrayed early signs of resignation. "These affairs will pass, but you must have read the histories. What king and country have spent all their time in tranquility and have never experienced toil and suffering? God has created both the trouble and the tranquility. Both should be tasted. Of trouble we should not complain, nor become arrogant and reckless in tranquillity." The shah's religious preoccupation was evident. Trust in the will of God at the hour of peril was not unconnected in his mind with the dream of the Muhammadan tree and his reverence for its most noble branch, the house of 'Ali. If God's will was against his intent, the shah could only be resigned to it.[89]

Yet the British threat did not destroy his youthful hopes all at once. "I would keep it a secret, but he has greatly insulted you," he wrote in a private note to Nuri acknowledging the receipt of Clarendon's ultimatum. "He accused you of mischief and yet there is no one more amicable than you. Of course, for the sake of the faith and the state you are courageous and valiant in facing the enemy." As for himself, the shah was prepared to make extraordinary personal sacrifices. "Surely this is not the time for relaxation, not even for nightly rest or eating, let alone riding. We must plan." He still hoped, though with a touch of incredulity, that Nuri would make good on his claims to recruit 150,000 irregular partisans (*charik*) to confront the British. "If this is true, what a great blessing. It is not far from your poignant thoughts, though. God willing you would be able to do it. All depends upon God." The shah's increased reliance on divine intervention was still focused in the direction of war. "God willing everything will go well so that the British will realize and understand that they can not slight you."[90]

Almost at the same time as he bitterly rejected the newly imposed British demand for reparations (for the harm that the Persian army had supposedly inflicted on the people of Herat), there was still in his tone an implicit sense of defiance. "Providing for such demands is a penalty so bitter and dangerously unpalatable to the people [*millat*] and government of Iran that it runs contrary to an enduring friendship between the two countries." This was a veiled reference to the demand for Nuri's dismissal. He further insisted that this "unprecedented request" was clearly contrary to the friendship between the two states. "How could the people and state of Iran either now or later tolerate it?" he asked. In the same letter, however, the shah personally acknowledged to Amin al-Mulk his acceptance of the 1853 Sheil-Nuri agreement over Herat as the basis for settlement.[91]

As much as their voices were audible, the people of Iran initially regarded the whole affair as a dispute between Nasir al-Din Shah and the British government. Although the conquest of Herat was cheered by all, there was little desire to wage a war for it, let alone a war with a world power that promised nothing but new taxes, shortages, insecurity, and popular unrest; later protests only confirmed such reluctance. But the call to jihad, not unlike an earlier attempt in 1826 against Russia, proved to have some effect in invoking public sentiment. The gathering of 9 November in the Shah mosque was attended with enthusiasm by the Tehran populace, who had been invited by the governor of Tehran, Ardishir Mirza, an uncle of the shah. The 'ulama of the capital, who, following the official line, hoped to use the occasion for a display of religious devotion, invited Nuri to attend the gathering. The shah's public address, read over the pulpit by the chief orator (*khatib-bashi*), insisted that the shah and the people of Iran would not tolerate the excesses of the British representatives and their evil designs to "humiliate the Islamic nation." It called upon the people to comply with their religious duty and join the shah in "removing the air of arrogance from the enemy's head" and prove that the people of Islam and the government of Iran would not be humbled by British "deception and duplicity." Most certainly, the royal address proclaimed, "the people of Iran and our co-religionists will not leave us alone."[92]

If the Qajar chronicles can be trusted, only the premier's call for calm and patience mellowed the public fervor. Whether because of his pro-British sentiments or his memory of the disastrous outcome of the 1826 declaration of jihad against Russia, Nuri was unwilling to endorse such an enterprise. He probably realized that public involvement would be ineffective against a modern army and possibly dangerous to his survival and that of the Qajar throne. What he sought to achieve, under the circumstances, was public approval for the war, a gesture of public support, in order to preempt the possibility of an anti-government rebellion or a tribal insurrection. "In the path of expansion of the faith," declared Nuri, "there is no need for men or money."

The premier's position was not shared by the 'ulama. Shortly thereafter, more than thirty of the highest ranking mujtahids from eleven provinces responded positively to the shah's appeal by each pledging to recruit 10,000 to 20,000 men from their own regions. Even as late as March 1857, Hajji Muhammad Karim Khan Kirmani, the celebrated leader of the Kirmani Shaykhis and himself of Qajar bloodlines, wrote a treatise at the shah's request on jihad entitled *Nasiriya*, encouraging the believers to defend the land of Islam against the infidels and warning them against the secular and religious harms that would befall Muslims from domination by infidels. In spite of the mujtahids' efforts, however, "they were not permitted to engage in jihad." Evidently against the shah's wishes, Nuri reminded the 'ulama that their task was to pray (*du'a-gu'i*) for the endurance of the throne.[93]

Soon, however, the realities of the war made it clear that there was neither sufficient manpower nor enough money or morale to repel the British. When the British naval expedition occupied the port of Bushihr and its surroundings in early December, it encountered little resistance by the local Persian troops. After a brief engagement, the port surrendered quietly. No one, not even the shah himself, entertained the illusion that Bushihr could withstand the firepower of the mightiest navy in the world. Yet the speed of the surrender came as quite a shock. Soon a large force, probably as large as 15,000 British and Indian troops, was gathered in Bushihr under the command of the celebrated warrior of the Indian Army, Lt. Gen. James Outram. Fresh from Awdh, where he had just completed the task of annexing that waning Shi'ite kingdom for the British crown and the Honorable Company, the British commander, who enjoyed a reputation for severity and resolve, was ready to teach the Persians a lesson.

As in most other colonial conflicts, from the British point of view the purpose of the Persian campaign was punitive. It was meant to restore British prestige, to bring home to the shah the vulnerability of his defense and force him to abide by British conditions. If there was any logic behind Outram's seemingly futile advance into the interiors of Fars province in early February 1857, it was to reaffirm that awesome message. Encountering British forces in Khushab in the vicinity of Burazjan, the regular and irregular Persian troops suffered a serious defeat. In spite of valiant resistance by the Dashtistani irregular detachments, which resulted in some British losses, the tactical and technological superiority of the British forces and general lack of coordination in the Persian forces resulted in high casualties and a complete breakup of the Persian camp. Nothing could have more forcefully enhanced the image of British invincibility in the eyes of the demoralized Persian government.[94]

The shah's initial reaction to news of the invasion was one of defiance and injured honor but also a pensive resignation to Providence. Such feelings were colored more by the image of his patron saint, 'Ali, than by the resolve of his military role models or by the pragmatic compromises of his prime minister. In early December, on the eve of the British invasion, he wrote Nuri one of the most moving statements of his political life:

> "Man," as people say, "is born one day and will die one day." This verse, too, is very well-known: "Dying with honor is better than living two hundred lives in disgrace" [*yek[i] murda bi-nam bih du-sad zinda bi-nang*]. Surely the creator of this world and the founder of the faith [*sahib-i shari'at*] will not accede in the humiliation of the Persian state. God knows that from the outset we were not, and still are not, desirous to fight with England. I wished to make them recognize a limit to their mischief and arrogance. [But] I did not want to behave like a loose woman who gives in as soon as she is asked to remove her underwear. The honor of the founder of the faith certainly would not consent that the government of Iran be ruined in vain. I as the king and you as the prime minister and a state's servant have not behaved contrary to the

honor of our faith and our nation or against reason and fortitude. If the
Lord of this world approves, this is our ideal. If not, there is no fault
upon us. What else can be done?[95]

Here again the shah's desire to defend his land and throne against an
imperial power was linked, almost consciously, to the two complementary
themes of religion and patriotism. His appeal to a providential will and,
more specifically, to the "founder of the faith" (apparently a reference to
'Ali, the first Shi'ite Imam, rather than Muhammad the Prophet) to save
the "Persian state," the symbol of the "saved nation" of Iran, reflected a
novel view of Shi'ite Islam as a source of common identity and national
cohesion. His reference to "death with honor" and the "honor of the
nation" versus disgrace and a whorish submission to unjust demands
hinted at a sense of modern patriotism with a romantic tinge. Whether such
pristine Shi'ite nationalism came to him by way of reading history or was
the outcome of historical circumstances, it was a remarkable element in
redefining his self-image as a modern ruler, a king with a mission to save
his nation by means of "reason and fortitude."

The realities of Iran's limited resources and the hazards of confronting
a world power, however, soon began to sink in. Under the bright sun of
the Persian Gulf, Iran's most vulnerable spot, the financial and military
restraints of a helpless army became even more evident. Soon the obstacles
to raising a sizeable army, beyond what had already been mobilized and
sent to Herat, turned the young shah's resolve into bitter indignation. In
1838 Nasir al-Din's father had been forced to give in to the British threat
and lift the siege of Herat as soon as the port of Bushihr and Khark Island
were occupied. As Gobineau observed, the shah was determined, almost to
the point of obsession, to achieve what his father had never accomplished.[96]
The shah instructed Nuri in a private note. "Summon Aqa Muhammad
Hasan and ask him immediately to hand over to you all the money available
in the [royal] treasury for whatever expenses you might have. When that
is gone, mortgage all the crown lands, mortgage the Darya-yi Nur [sea of
light]." What made Nasir al-Din so generous with the coveted royal
treasury, with the crown property and the crown jewels, and even the
legendary diamond that sat on the royal armlet worn by the Qajar kings
was the painful reality of his plight.[97] Insufficiency of funds was at the heart
of his government's inability to mobilize troops. "It was God who finished
up the treasury, not me," he announced in an agitated tone tinged equally
with despair and sarcasm. "When we became the king," he recalled un-
remittingly, "there was one *kurur* [i.e., 500,000 tumans] in the treasury.
Then some 200,000 went for Salar's [revolt]. We, too, added one hundred

[thousand] per annum but only by borrowing. That, too, was often gone for the [running] expenses. Most years we could not even put that one hundred [thousand] down." But if in the shah's view divine forces were partially responsible for the empty treasury and the crown's bankruptcy, so were his predecessors. "What is my fault?" he asked rhetorically. "They put the filth of Iran's mess on our shoulders and left. I wish it had gone to someone else rather than being inherited by me."[98]

For the moment he seemed disgusted even with the burdens of his crown. The crisis brought out into the open the shortcomings of his government, first on the battlefield, where his army was unable to repel the invaders, and then at the negotiating table, where his emissary, futilely begging at the doors of the European courts, had no choice but to accept the humiliating terms imposed by his enemy. "From now on till the Day of Resurrection I will burn," the shah wrote, fearing that a large reparation similar to that in the Turkmanchay treaty would be imposed on Iran in addition to the loss of Herat and defeat on the home front. Since his father's time, he believed, Herat had cost Iran close to 2.5 million tumans, and yet he was required to pay for the supposed damage to the city itself.

If only on paper and in the privacy of the royal palace, he was not yet devoid of vengeance. "May God preserve for us a servant like you and the heavens not envy us even for this," he assured Nuri with obvious reference to the British demand for his dismissal. Like an indignant child, he seemed to be seeking approval from his premier for his heroic fantasy. "God willing, I would not be a man if I do not drive the British out all the way to Calcutta. By God! Tonight if you put me in charge I would assume the military command and throw these people into the sea rather than tolerate the presumptuousness of Lord Redcliffe of Istanbul who wants to order me around."[99]

Nuri had little difficulty persuading his master to modify his ambitions. The enemy's superior power as well as the shah's troubles at home spoke for themselves. He consoled the shah, no doubt using the same argument with which he had reminded Amin al-Mulk that defeat at the hands of England was not a dishonor. "Napoleon, too, was defeated by the British," he wrote. Although Nuri was in a hurry to borrow from the "merchants and subjects of the United States" to the tune of one million tumans to finance the war, he was in an even greater hurry to settle with the British. "Settle! Settle! Here comes the sound of the cannons," he wrote to Amin al-Mulk on 21 December. By 22 December, almost simultaneous with the shah's harsh words for the British, Nuri managed to persuade Nasir al-Din to abandon his fantasy and instead insist in writing that he was "very anxious for the friendship of England," and that he "never thought and will never think of deviating even one step from the path of friendship." The pain of uttering such words, in fear and frustration, must have been great—and enduring. Even more painful, he forced himself to add, "To satisfy the wishes of that government we will comply with whatever obligation that is within the capacity of our state." Such satisfaction, he nevertheless stated boldly, could only be given if his "status and honor" were preserved. Almost in a state of panic, the shah's insistence on haste is evident from his note in the margin of a decree authorizing Amin al-Mulk to negotiate the terms of settlement. "Of course! Of course! Swiftly settle the matter in whatever way you deem advisable. Do not allow it to come to severe hostility."[100]

In another rescript written on the same day, the shah gave his reasons for approving the negotiated terms even more explicitly. "Although compliance with any such terms entails obvious harm to the Persian state, the massive British preparations [for the war] and their obvious desire to proceed with the present conflict make it inexpedient for the Persian government to prolong this affair." It was left to the emissary's "mastery" to reduce the burden of the British demands, which included the prime minister's dismissal. "If untenable," the shah wrote on the margin, "there is no way out. Accept them."[101] It was as though the shah had submitted to the very checkmate he had been so anxious to avoid earlier.

A short lull in the British advance in the Persian Gulf in January 1857 reduced the initial panic in the Persian capital and raised new hopes, naive though they were. The shah even felt secure enough to resume his never-ending hunting excursions in the vicinity of Tehran, and he spent no less than two weeks in the middle of the winter in the Jajrud Valley shooting partridges.[102] For the premier, anxious about his survival, the priorities were different. Nuri persuaded the shah to capitalize on the breakdown of the Istanbul negotiations, which had been suspended when hostilities commenced, and order Amin al-Mulk to proceed to France, his original destination. By utilizing the good offices of the French emperor, the shah's new ally, it was hoped that Iran could lessen the burden of peace with Britain. Moreover, he argued that by taking Bushihr and even Muhammara on the westernmost corner of the Persian Gulf, the British could achieve little, as their forces could not penetrate into the interior. Following Amin al-Mulk's caution, Nuri decided not to negotiate with Outram under the shadow of the British guns, which Clarendon initially mandated the British general to do. The Persian emissary, heartened by Malkum Khan, hoped to make Iran's case audible not only in the French court and the European press but in the British Parliament as well.

The two-track strategy was not yet entirely dead. Taking heart in reassurances of his minister and emissary, the shah was persuaded to look to post-Crimean Europe to seek guarantees for his country's territorial integrity and the security of his throne. Although geographically remote from Europe, the shah proclaimed, "We, the Imperial Majesty, would not regard our kingship and country separate from" European kingdoms. The government of Iran, he urged with some innocence, like the great countries of Europe, was seeking to achieve its "rights" (*huquq*) so that peace and tranquility, security for its cities, and prosperity for its subjects could be maintained by means of "justice and wisdom." He hoped that Europe would not deprive him of such privileges and would not ignore his pleas.[103]

The British demands for Nuri's dismissal nevertheless persisted, and nothing could have disturbed the premier more. He had threatened that if the British did not drop their demand, "by the shah's order" he or his son would gallop all the way to Russia to mortgage some Persian provinces in exchange for Russian money and assistance in order to "remove the dishonor inflicted by the British." But his gallop to St. Petersburg, though good for morale, was no more feasible than the shah's sortie to Calcutta or the call for jihad in the Tehran mosques—so loud, the premier claimed, that "no church bell could match it." The conclusion of the friendship treaty with the United States, Tehran came to believe, and faint hopes of igniting a "mild sedition" in India kept the capital's morale afloat. Even by mid-March, after the engagement in Khushab, Nuri was smug enough to claim that soon the Herat army would proceed to Kandahar.[104] He knew well, however, that his government was bankrupt and that the Persian forces, hungry, ill-equipped, and unpaid for months, were in no position even to resist an Afghan attack on Herat, let alone open a new offensive. "Worst of all is the lack of funds," he wrote only a day earlier. Even the 8,000 to 9,000 tumans' worth of *ashrafi* gold coins of the Aqa Muhammad Khan era were brought out of the treasury, re-struck, and put into circulation. The premier's empty maneuvers, like his empty treasury, had little effect on the outcome of the war or the peace negotiations. They did, however, keep him in the shah's favor.

PEACE WITH ENGLAND

On 5 April the draft of the Paris peace treaty that ended Anglo-Persian hostilities reached Tehran. Just before it was ratified, Gobineau, the French chargé d'affaires in Tehran, rushed to Gulistan Palace to offer his congratulations. "It seemed to me that His Majesty was in a cheerful and positive mood," he wrote with some puzzlement.

> His Majesty honored me by saying that although the terms of the treaty are not quite certain, for the sake of the Emperor [Napoleon III] he is prepared to sign it blindfolded since he believes whatever the Emperor wishes is definitely good for his [Nasir al-Din's] people and for him the value of the Emperor's friendship is more than all consequences of the treaty. As he was talking, the shah was laughing and jostling on his throne, and when I asked to be discharged the shah forgot to throw the usual stern look upon me which is typical of the Persian kings in their public audience. He dismissed me with a smile.[105]

What seems to have brought smiles to the shah's otherwise grim days was probably the fact that he was still on his throne with his country virtually intact, a phenomenon not to be taken lightly in the age of high imperialism.

In Paris Amin al-Mulk negotiated with Lord Cowley, the British ambassador to France, in a more favorable climate. The sympathetic treatment of Iran's case in the European press—in part thanks to the energetic Malkum Khan and criticism of Clarendon's Persian policy and Murray's conduct by, among others, Henry Rawlinson, the well-known soldier, strategist, archaeologist, and then member of parliament—strengthened the hand of the Persian mission. Napoleon's ambitions to compete with Britain in the East also helped Amin al-Mulk. Moreover, after occupying the port of Bushihr for four months, Palmerston's government was willing to drop its harshest demands, thus allowing Nuri and the shah to compromise without themselves becoming casualties of the war. As a sign of appreciation for Napoleon's good offices, Nariman Khan, the Persian emissary who had brought the draft of the treaty to Tehran, took back with him some more royal gifts. An engraved sword belonging to Shah 'Abbas the Great (I), the celebrated ruler of the Safavid dynasty, was sent to Napoleon complete with a document charting its history. Presented to Napoleon as a choice treasure from the royal armory, the sword, known as Qara Khurasani, had an interesting life after leaving its original owner. At one time belonging to Nadir and then to Aqa Muhammad Khan, it was treated as a symbol of kingly valor and imperial power before finally being worn on official occasions by no more charismatic a warrior than Hajji Mirza Aqasi, who took it with him to the 'Atabat after his fall. Ironically, it was bought back by Nuri from a jewel merchant in Tehran for 150 tumans to be given to Nasir al-Din, who, now presented it to his French "royal brother" together with his "heartiest gratitude." Mahd 'Ulya, for her part, sent as a gift to the wife of the French foreign minister, Count Walewski, a Persian women's wardrobe, complete with underwear.[106]

As Nuri masterfully managed to link his own survival to the shah's prestige and future credibility, his removal proved less desirable. "About prime ministership," he cautioned Palmerston in a message to Amin al-Mulk, "if we comply [with dismissal], in a couple of days the Russians, in spite of you, would favor another prime minister, and a couple of days later the French would ask [for their favorite], then of course the United States (*Yangi Dunya*), which has lately found her way to Iran, would desire her own [favorite], and thereafter the Ottomans and others respectively. All this would write off the Persian government." Iran's situation, he insisted, was different from England's: "Prime ministership in Iran is not like Europe and cannot be changed every two to three years." His office, he added, was "highly prestigious" and "after kingship the most essential."[107] Self-aggrandizement aside, Nuri's warning convinced the British not to treat him as an expendable item, at least for the time being.

Aware of the negotiations in Paris but impatient with what he perceived as his own virtual irrelevance, Outram tried to remind the Persian government of its vulnerability and the ease with which his forces could move into the interiors of Iran. Completely unprovoked, the assault on Muhammara in late March 1857 and its bombardment was quickly followed by landings in the city of Ahvaz in early April. The collapse of the Persian defense and piecemeal surrender of the troops was another moral blow to the shah and a testimony to the government's military feebleness. Nuri confessed that his correspondence with Khanlar Mirza Ihtisham al-Dawla, the governor of Khuzistan province, assuring him of the bright prospects for peace with England had softened the prince commander's resolve and contributed to the fiasco. It was a small wonder that after the war he stopped just short of condemning the prince for his ineptitude.[108] Ironically, the attack on Muhammara occurred three weeks after the peace treaty was concluded in Paris on 4 March 1857. The earliest news of the assault reached Tehran on 7 April, two days after the draft of the peace treaty reached Tehran. Though the full impact of the assault was not known before 24 April, the fact that such an attack had happened at all must have encouraged Nasir al-Din to hurry and ratify the treaty on 15 April. Outram was already notified of the peace by 4 April. Save for further intimidating the Persian government and inflicting useless casualties upon miserable Persian troops, the operation was of little value. Murray's presence at the scene added a vengeful twist to the assault.

All through the crisis, slow communication proved to be a major obstacle. Average travel time for a letter between Tehran and London was forty days, and an exchange of correspondence often took longer than three months. Between London and Bombay such exchanges took no less than eight months. Although by 1856 the telegraph line had just connected Istanbul to Europe, and brief messages were dispatched almost instantly to and from London, it still took a month for a letter to travel between Tehran and Istanbul. Decisions were thus often based on outdated information. Clarendon ordered Outram to set off for the Persian Gulf five days before the capture of Herat. The battle of Khushab, waged on 8 February, was not known in Paris on 4 March and thus had no bearing on the actual negotiations.[109]

The peace treaty was designed to put a definite end to Iran's territorial claims over Herat and Afghanistan as a whole. It specifically demanded that "His Majesty the Shah of Persia" not only withdraw from Herat immediately but also "relinquish all claims to sovereignty" over the territory and "abstain from all interference with the internal affairs of Afghanistan." Holding the shah, rather than the Persian government, responsible for administering the most vital articles of the treaty, it required that in case of disputes the Persian government was obliged to "refer them for adjustment to the friendly offices of the British Government, and not to take up arms unless those friendly offices fail to effect." Yet the treaty was not as unfavorable as it could have been, nor was the popular view of Nuri's betrayal and Amin al-Mulk's ineptitude justified. In spite of obvious flaws in Tehran's conduct of the war, the two-track policy envisaged by the shah and elaborated by Nuri and others had some notable successes. The British government, for its part, promised "to prevent any cause of umbrage" being given by the Afghan principalities and agreed to use its "best endeavors" to resolve disputes "in a manner just and honorable to Persia." To satisfy genuine Persian concerns for the security of the eastern frontiers, the treaty further stipulated that in case of any violation of the frontier the Persian government "shall have the right, if due satisfaction is not given, to undertake military operations for the repression and punishment of the aggressor." The exercise of such a right, the treaty specified, was not to be made a pretext for annexation or permanent occupation. In the same spirit as all British colonial treaties, the Paris treaty also stipulated the establishment of new consulates in Iran and reasserted for Britain the capitulatory rights of Most Favored Nation. In spite of inevitable disadvantages, perhaps the greatest victory for the Persian government was on the issue of the protégés. The treaty clearly required the British government to "renounce the right of protecting hereafter any Persian subject not actually in the employment of the British mission," provided that no such right was accorded to or exercised by any other foreign powers, an unmistakable reference to Russia. Given the long and irksome history of the protégés, the embattled shah at least could uphold this accomplishment and present it to his people. The treaty also required that all hostilities cease immediately and that the British forces be evacuated from all Persian territories as soon as the British minister returned to Tehran.[110]

The credit for the treaty's relative leniency went above all to Amin al-Mulk. He was a man of caution and common sense who sustained his consistency and composure in spite of the premier's vacillations, the shah's sunken morale, and British intransigence.[111] Credit was also due to Malkum Khan, Amin al-Mulk's chief adviser, who at quite a young age was instrumental in placing Iran on Europe's diplomatic map. As he received endorsements from both Tehran and Paris, it is no surprise that he was frowned upon in London and scorned by Murray and Stevens. The Persian mission was also indebted to the French emperor, his minister of foreign affairs, Count Walewski, and various French diplomats who assisted with mediation and advice. Altruistic or not, Napoleon's counsel encouraged the Persian ambassador to settle without delay, arguing that the British would persevere in their objectives in Afghanistan at any price. "Under the circumstances," he remarked, "one should not think of the loss of Afghanistan but consider preservation of Persian territory itself." If Iran "gives up on Afghanistan," the French emperor proposed, "there is another country to be occupied and annexed, more prosperous than Afghanistan and its people less capable than Afghans. Its name, too, is much greater than Afghanistan." Projecting his own dreams of expansion, Napoleon was alluding no doubt to Ottoman Iraq. Given the long-term Anglo-French rivalry in the Ottoman Empire and the latter's precarious position after the Crimean War, the aspirations of the French emperor were transparent enough.[112]

With the Herat fiasco behind him, Nasir al-Din Shah was sensible enough not to take the French proposition seriously. Yet he was effusively grateful to Napoleon. "The people of Iran," he wrote, would never forget the emperor's "kindness, honor, and good intentions." Anxious to secure a long-term French interest in his throne, he concluded, "I beg Your Majesty not to forget under any circumstance this noble people, your ally, and expect you to be sure that my friendship and brotherhood toward you is at its highest." This time Napoleon reciprocated the shah's sympathies with more sensible advice about domestic reforms and guidelines for foreign policies.[113]

The British government, too, was anxious to put an end to the whole affair. With the Indian Mutiny about to break out, the task of restoring friendly relations with Britain proved less formidable than expected. Despite misgivings about Nuri, the British were becoming more accommodating, perhaps sending a message to the shah to drop his premier. "From now on," promised Palmerston to Amin al-Mulk during his visit to London, "our representatives will not interfere in your domestic affairs"—an attitude very different from the harsh words uttered by the same British statesman to Husayn Khan Ajudanbashi, Muhammad Shah's envoy to London in 1838. His foreign minister, Clarendon, even went so far as expressing his regret for the past hostilities between the two countries and admitting that without amicable relations with Iran it would be impossible to defend India, an admission no doubt encouraged by the ominous news of the earliest disturbances in India. Even more remarkable, with all due pomp and circumstance Amin al-Mulk was received by Queen Victoria.[114]

The shah, on his own, had changed course and warmly welcomed the British gesture. "I have now pledged myself [*bar khud mukhammir kardam*] to preserve this friendship for ever and ever," he wrote to Nuri, a promise he kept with greater consistency than any long-term policy throughout his reign. He further confided to Amin al-Mulk that even from the start he had "utter repulsion" for the "ominous occurrences" and that for him and his country there was no better "well-intentioned and sincere friend" than England. Such royal sentiments were far different from the angry words uttered only a few weeks earlier in his private notes.

The shah was not entirely unaware of the domestic repercussions of the war. With some despair he urged the Persian emissary to plead personally with the queen of England to accept his "friendly request" and return thirty cannons that were taken from the Persian army in Bushihr and Muhammara as spoils of war—as though the monarch's public image at home hinged on having these cannons returned. He argued that although the Russian tsar had given Iran several cannons as restitution for those taken by Russia during the 1826–1827 war, "never in the eyes of the nation and people of Iran did it seem as welcoming, since our own guns were taken and others were given instead. This always remained an agony in the heart of this nation." In a passionate tone he thus called on the queen: "It is a pity that for thirty cannons an ill feeling should remain in my heart."[115] Pleas for the queen to restore the plundered cannons revealed the shah's concern for royal prestige. Amin al-Mulk had no qualms about rejecting this request of the shah's. Not only did he regard it as highly inappropriate and contrary to the practices of all nations, he even had some harsh words for his master. "Power and discipline," he wrote back, was what the shah needed, "so that all nations will see how far the government of Iran cares for the organization of its army, the development of the country, the tranquility of its subjects, and the fortification of its ports."[116] The ambassador's apt rebuke, a sad reflection of the contrast between the world the shah knew and the world his envoy had come to know, could only be taken by His Majesty with a mixture of remorse and concealed dismay.

SAVING FACE

The shah did not inquire about the cannons again. Closer to home there were other unscrupulous means of restoring his sway over the populace than the lost cannons. He could not guarantee the "tranquility of its subjects," as Amin al-Mulk advised him to do, but could certainly terrify them into submission. One day before ratifying the peace treaty with England, which obliged him immediately to release all prisoners of war, the shah ordered the execution of the helpless prince Muhammad Yusuf. This Saduza'i claimant to the principality of Herat, who had been ousted by his own minister, 'Isa Khan, was living in exile in Tehran under nominal Persian surveillance. The gruesome blood reprisal (*qisas*) was carried out with obvious disregard for British sensitivities. Muhammad Yusuf was dragged out of town to a mound in front of the shah's palace of Qasr Qajar, then clumsily hacked to pieces by the sabers of his feudal enemies. The shah himself was present at the scene.[117] Although by removing the prince Nuri hoped to safeguard the survival of a puppet in Herat after the Persian evacuation, the killing reflected the shah's frustrations over the Herat episode, now aggravated by popular unrest at home.

A variety of other incidents demonstrated the shah's recourse to severe punishments. In January 1856 Nasir al-Din had personally supervised the execution of a murderer, the brother of a servant (*ghulam*) of the British mission, who had committed five murders. The method of execution, according to Stevens, was "barbarous to the extreme." First his hands were cut off, then knife wounds were inflicted on his head, and finally his throat was cut and his body dragged through the bazaar. In October two other offenders, an Armenian and a Muslim, fell victim to the shah's wrath on charges of adultery. The pimp and the adulterer had already been given one hundred lashes each, while the "woman of loose character" involved in the case was given the luxury of choosing her own death. She was dumped in a sewage well, where she died of "foul air." Not so the unfortunate men. Upon returning from a hunting excursion, the shah had them brought to

Nigaristan Palace, where, if Stevens was to believed, the shah himself "assisted at the execution." Again the bodies were dragged through the streets of the capital.[118]

It was the unrest in the provinces, rather than an instinctive inner brutishness, that triggered such severe acts. In spite of such punishments held up as examples, the defeat in the war had brought out the dormant popular discontent. In Tabriz, in late March, 30,000 armed citizens, starving and outraged, sacked the government house and forced the governor, Mirza Sadiq Qa'im Maqam Nuri, out of the city. A relative of the premier's, the greedy governor had hoarded the city's supply of wheat and sold it at a profit of 700 percent. The crowd also expelled the mayor. Prisoners were freed from the jail, and a stray dog labeled "His Excellency Sadr Azam" was carried around the city. Most ominous of all, some 300 lutis, probably the city's entire stock of street gangs, went to the Russian consulate and called for Russian troops to take over the province. Quick to place the blame on the dismissed governor, Nuri admitted that the people were "desperate with hunger and high prices."[119]

In Qazvin government agents harshly forced members of the public out of the Friday mosque, where they had gathered to protest the shortages, and publicly assaulted the protesting mujtahid of the city. By May 1857 popular discontent was clearly visible in Isfahan and Tehran. As in similar instances in time of trouble, Jewish communities, as in Mashhad and Kashan, became targets of renewed persecutions. Earlier on, an unpopular attempt to raise new revenue, to the tune of 500,000 to 750,000 tumans to finance the war effort was called off in the face of vigorous public protest. Instead the government hoped to lean on the big merchants of the bazaar for monetary assistance.[120] But in spite of such unrest, the prospect of a "popular revolution" temporarily disappeared thanks to the all too familiar methods of terror. Soon Nuri could reassure his emissary in London that "God willing there was and there will be no rebellion. There is no bad news. Opponents of the state and shameless Persians were predicting uprising and sedition in Iran . . . but not a single individual dared to utter a word."[121]

The turmoil at home had subsided by the time the British minister arrived. For months the shah and his premier tolerated the pompous extravaganza that London, out of pure vainglory and self-gratification, had imposed upon them by attaching to the treaty a set of specific demands regarding Murray's reception in Iran. The British minister plenipotentiary had negotiated every possible detail: the rank of the official host (mih-mandar) and those in the entourage that would accompany him from Baghdad to Tehran; the number and ranks of the dignitaries who would receive him at every stage of his journey; those who would come out of the capital and the distance they would traverse to receive him; the letter of apology to be written by the premier; the time, number, and order of visits that would be paid to him by the premier; the size and composition of the procession that would take him to the capital and to and from the royal palace; and the specifics of his audience with the shah and the dignitaries present. Murray insisted that the premier personally usher him into the shah's presence. The entire spectacle was calculated to impose on the vanquished shah, his prime minister, and his annoyed subjects the ultimate humiliation of a triumphant return. Nothing less would gratify Murray's vengeful obsessions.

Further to undermine the host government, the English minister brought along with him one of the most despised British protégés, Mirza Aqa Shirazi, as the mission's Persian secretary. He also demanded that Stevens be admitted again to Iran as the British consul. The even more hated Hajji Sayf al-Dawla, a Qajar prince descended from Fath 'Ali Shah under British protection, and the infamous Mir 'Ali Naqi, who for quite some time had spied for the British mission, were to be allowed to return to Iran against the strong protests of the shah. Even Farhad Mirza, who earlier had repented all the way to the palace, only to spy for the British with more convenience, was allowed to return to the British fold to provide vital contacts inside the court and the government. Never before in the six decades of Anglo-Persian relations, perhaps not since the arrival of Antony Jenkinson to the court of Tahmasp I in 1558, had the Persian government been degraded so meticulously by the whims and wishes of one fierce adversary.

The *Vaqayi'-i Ittifaqiya* covered the minister's arrival in full. Accompanied by six ranking officers and an escort of fifty cavalry, Murray entered the capital on 18 July 1857, riding a horse with a gold harness from the royal stable. From the city gates ten royal runners (*shatirs*) at the front of the procession, twenty royal farrashes, and two hundred soldiers accompanied the British minister to his embassy, where four ranking government accountants (*mustawfis*) and two hundred cadets officially welcomed him.[122]

At least this was the official version of the reception. Gobineau, an acute observer of the event, noticed that, unable to come to terms with Murray on protocol, the government arranged the reception in a fashion that could "save face in the eyes of the population of the capital without jeopardizing its own position." Although "ostensibly" orders were given to exhibit great gaiety for the reception of the minister, "underneath it had been made known to those in charge that they were not expected to be overenthusiastic." There were not more than thirty regular cavalry of the royal guard, an incomplete battalion of infantry, a few untidy ghulams, and hardly any superior officers. "People of the bazaar, too, who on such occasions are sent before the guests of honor, were quite sparse if not totally absent."[123]

On the same day Nuri paid a visit to Murray. In contrast, his cavalcade was "extremely ostentatious," reported Gobineau. The cunning premier began his conversation with the most tasteful device of Persian parlance, a verse from Sa'di: "Come, now is the time of peace, friendship, and warmth/Provided we do not speak of what went between us." He ended it with another verse by the great poet of Shiraz: "Two friends value each other's company/Who had parted for a while and then reunited." Later, recounting his visit, Nuri was not as eloquent or as welcoming, though conscious of etiquette all the same. "According to the terms of the treaty," he wrote, "I preceded in paying my visit to the minister plenipotentiary. I wish I had died. Anticipating death was better than anticipating this visit, coming down from Niyavaran, passing through the Tehran bazaar, and going to the embassy."[124]

The next day Murray was received by the shah. After much bargaining in advance, the British minister was persuaded to have his audience in Niyavaran, the shah's summer residence. This was a small victory for the shah because it was contrary to Murray's wishes to be received in Gulistan Palace in Tehran, which would have obliged the shah to come to the capital for the purpose. The agreement also demanded that the premier usher the British minister into the royal presence and remain there throughout the audience. Not only was the requirement of ushering Murray humiliating to Nuri, so was the premier's extended presence during the audience, since Persian court etiquette required that the premier never be seated in the shah's presence, at least in public, whereas for decades the European envoys had been privileged to sit in the royal presence. To avoid diminishing their dignity and status, premiers were thus never received together with foreign envoys. Although earlier Murray had knowingly insisted on this condition, he was now prepared to drop it in compliance with London's wishes for reconciliation. But Nuri insisted on accompanying the minister. If not on the battlefield, at least in the war of protocol the shah and his prime minister hoped to make a victory out of defeat. Gobineau, who was consulted by Nuri on the issue of protocol, recommended that the shah, like the French emperor, would be better off receiving Murray standing, but Nuri had a better idea. When Murray was seated, the shah asked the prime minister to be seated as well, opposite the shah and in a position higher than that of the British minister, where three of the shah's senior uncles stood. "His Excellency the Prime Minister, not only in private but in such a lofty gathering was honored with the permission to be seated," declared the *Vaqayi'-i Ittifaqiya*. Although Murray claimed that according to the treaty he was "ushered into the royal presence by the Sadr Azam," even he admitted that Nuri "turned what [might] have been a humiliation into an unprecedented honor paid to himself."

Murray found the shah's reply to his address "friendly and energetic" but delivered with great rapidity, and it was rendered even more indistinct by the consenting and approving comments of the Sadr A'zam. The shah was determined to maintain friendship with England but did not fail to point out that this friendship had been "interrupted by mischievous and designing persons."[125] Under the circumstances, Murray decided to swallow his pride and not to treat the shah's remark as an insult. His sensitive "honor" could not afford to be offended again at so delicate a time. He would wait for a more opportune moment. In the same spirit, he even accepted Nuri's word when he denied the very existence of the note written by the shah in December 1855 in which Murray was called "foolish" and a "simpleton." He even dropped his demand that Nuri make a second visit to the embassy. With the rising anti-British sentiments in the government and among the populace, Murray must have found prudence more effective than his usual haughtiness.[126]

The alarming news of the revolt now spreading across India attracted much enthusiasm in the court and among the people of Iran. In late June, just before Murray's arrival, the earliest news of the Indian Mutiny reached Tehran. After all, the prophecies of the Mughal prince Muhammad Najaf Mirza had come true; Mirza Sadiq Khan Kashani, the Persian consul in Bombay, had also warned against the changing political climate in India. Throughout the Indian Mutiny, starting in earnest on 10 May, reaching its peak in June, and largely contained after the three-month long siege of Delhi in September 1857, he sent reports to Tehran before his arrest by the British and his subsequent temporary exile. Writing aboard a British steamer on 15 May, he reported to Nuri accounts of the mutiny in Delhi, Lucknow, and elsewhere, the massacre of the English officers, and the British dispatch of ships from Bombay to bring back the British troops from Bushihr, who were suddenly in great demand. Unaware of the conclusion of the peace treaty on 4 March and its ratification by the shah on 15 April, he warned Tehran not to make peace with the British. "May God bestow support on the King of Islam, this is not the time for peace."[127]

Strategically not much could be invested in the Indian Mutiny, but it did provide an opportunity to clip Murray's grossly overgrown wings. By mid-July 1857, when he received the British minister, the shah was probably hoping to capitalize on British susceptibilities. By late August the mutiny had became Tehran's preoccupation. "All the news, true or false," noted Gobineau, "is commented on passionately, in particular among the shah's entourage, who allow themselves the reverie of the most hostile dreams against England." Gobineau dismissed as false the European press reports that insisted the shah's forces were on high alert. He emphasized that the shah had no intention of interfering in that affair. Yet in October he again observed that Persians had no sympathy for the British plight, were against British interests in India, and were supportive of the rebels. All details of the mutiny in the London *Times* and the *Morning Post*, he noted, were read enthusiastically, and the news from Kandahar and Bombay was given full and immediate publicity.[128] Perhaps it was the impact of these reports that prompted the premier to go to dangerously great lengths and instruct Mirza Sadiq Kashani to despatch "a few able and skillful Persians" to trouble spots in India to incite "flames of dissatisfaction" among the people. The Persian agents, who were to be disguised as merchants, Nuri advised the Persian consul in Bombay, should make the rebels understand that "Persia is still unchanged in her policy." Murray, who later acquired a copy of the premier's secret correspondence through his spies in the government, believed that "a more highly distilled essence of duplicity and treachery is not to be found in any document" that had come under his observation.[129]

Renewed Persian aspirations were soon curtailed, however. By December reports of the suppression of the mutiny dampened the shah's hopes and brought an anticipated change to Tehran's political climate. Apparently war in the Persian Gulf was not enough to bring home the message of British supremacy, but the conclusion of the Indian Mutiny to Her Majesty's advantage was. The British minister found his chance to retaliate and did so with his familiar cynicism. Demanding nothing less than a royal gesture of goodwill toward Britain, his request had all the elements of blackmail except the name. The shah was virtually compelled to contribute £ 500 (1,125 tumans) in his own name and £ 250 on behalf of the prime minister to the Indian Relief Fund established for the British victims of the revolt. "His Majesty," Murray reported to Clarendon with a sneer barely disguised behind his formal tone, "offered his deep sympathy" toward English "orphans and widows who have been sufferers by the late Mutiny in India." As a further slap in the shah's face, Murray demanded that a full report of the royal and ministerial charity be made public in the *Vaqayi'-i Ittifaqiya.* Commending the compassion of His Majesty and His Excellency, the published article resorted cleverly to the "pure faith of Islam" to legitimize the act of royal charity to those "helpless women who are exempt from the rules imposed on men" and to "innocent children" who have not yet attained obligatory age.[130]

The Victorian tree was still firmly in place.

8   Abolishing the Sidarat

The resumption of peaceful relations with England concluded one of the most tormenting episodes in the shah's political career. If not by personal preference, then at least for reasons of expediency, he resigned himself to the fact that the endurance of his throne depended on his ability to secure the consent of both of his powerful neighbors in foreign and to some extent in domestic affairs. He quietly accepted this reality. The shah's effort to choose a new heir apparent, the third since his accession in 1848, demonstrated the degree of foreign involvement in the Persian court. The new heir apparent (vali'ahd—literally, vali-yi 'ahd, "the guardian of the age"), Amir Qasim Khan, a five-year-old son of the shah's new favorite, Jayran, had no maternal Qajar lineage to qualify him for succession. The royal wish to nominate him as the heir resulted in a new entanglement in the labyrinth of Qajar court politics. In a classic example of a showdown between the prime minister and the harem—now momentarily dominated by Jayran—even the shah was at times overshadowed. The shrewd premier tried hard to preserve his position and for a while even gained full executive power, but his efforts proved ineffective in the end largely in the face of an alliance among the members of the harem, the British representative, and his opponents.

THE FLYING GAZELLE
AND THE ABSOLUTE POTENTATE

The daughter of a villager from Tajrish in the north of Tehran, Jayran (Turkish for gazelle; so nicknamed for her charming eyes) was the first of the women of humble origins among Nasir al-Din's wives who because of the shah's affection managed to wield great influence over the affairs of the court. Brought to the royal harem to be trained as a female musician and singer, she must have first caught the shah's attention in 1851 while in Mahd 'Ulya's retinue, perhaps just after the Amir Kabir affair. With a style reminiscent of the stories of The Thousand and One Nights, of which the shah was so fond, the young singer found her way into the shah's heart as much with her own charms as with Mahd 'Ulya's blessing. Not long before this, Mahd 'Ulya had reportedly used another dancing girl, Sultan Khanum, as her secret weapon to poison the shah's mind against Amir Kabir. She probably felt the need for a similar weapon against Nuri when their relations turned sour in the aftermath of the Babi assassination attempt. But Jayran proved far more formidable than an ephemeral debutante.

Attractive and outspoken, she was fond of riding and hunting. In the saddle, complete with boots and a man's outfit and wrapping her facial cover around her forehead, she was a total anomaly next to the grave, often overweight and timid ladies of the harem and in her behavior exhibited a sharp contrast to their mute mannerisms. It was almost inevitable that she became "the locus of the shah's infatuation" and hence the most influential woman of the andarun, even overshadowing Mahd 'Ulya herself. During a royal hunt, accompanied by a large retinue of gamekeepers, falconers, and servants, with her own falcon (called Ghazal, Persian for *gazelle*) on her wrist, and riding her bay horse Ahu (Persian for *gazelle*), Jayran daringly took the lead, galloping in a direction opposite that of the shah. Whether because of the novelty of a woman hunter, possibly with her facial veil removed, or the lure of Russian golden imperial coins with which she awarded gamekeepers who found prey for her, she captivated the royal entourage. His Majesty was not perturbed in the slightest when he noticed that he was all but deserted. His favorite's popularity was pleasing to him.[1]

The shah's affection for Jayran was fashioned after a modern romance, individualized and private, in contrast to the collective life of the harem. It was further highlighted in the shah's eyes by her association with nature and wildlife. She seemed an evasive prey, hard to catch and difficult to tame, a rare gazelle that the shah had so feverishly searched for in the ravines and gorges of Alburz and found in a village on its outskirts—the stuff of fairy tales almost—striving to part with the world of the harem and the crowd of women in their pigeonholed living quarters. For the shah, affection for Jayran symbolized a search for an alternative family perhaps, a wife and a child who could offer him a human touch behind the royal facade.

The shah's affection only increased after Amir Qasim Mirza's birth in 1852, when Jayran was still only a temporary wife, but reached its height after the death of the previous heir from another wife. Jayran came into the political limelight at a critical juncture, when a crisis of succession coincided with war with Britain. Apart from his touching note on the margin of Napoleon's biography, the shah did not seem to have particularly mourned the loss of his heir, Mu'in al-Din. Soon he had become so "intensely affectionate" toward Jayran's son that he viewed him as his only true heir. Joseph Polak, the Austrian physician in the service of the Persian government, noticed the shah's infatuation for Amir Qasim in contrast to royal indifference toward his other sons. Nasir al-Din even confided to Polak his wish to abdicate voluntarily in favor of Amir Qasim "as soon as the crown prince reaches his adolescence" and make a tour of Europe.[2]

The urgency in appointing a new heir could not have been overlooked. Nasir al-Din had reason to fear that the British, in the midst of the war, would resuscitate 'Abbas Mirza's pretensions to his throne. Murray, in 1856, had already delineated before his superior the vices and virtues of such claims. He did not "promise much good" for his "bigotry and duplicity," wrote Murray about 'Abbas Mirza with his usual tone of condescension. "Politically uncultivated," the nineteen-year old prince had not yet "tasted blood and power," and it was impossible to say whether he would "show himself a true Kajar in his relish for those sweets." Murray was nevertheless prepared, if Clarendon permitted him, "to place him at the head of the invading force now about to enter the [Persian] Gulf" and was confident that "the present shah would not remain six months on the throne."[3]

For a long time, ever since Nasir al-Din's childhood, Russia had had its own candidate up its sleeve. Bahman Mirza, now living in Russian-occupied Qarabaq (Karabak) on a hefty pension from the tsar, could always be thrown in as a regent for a shah's minor heir. Nuri revealed during a confidential discussion with Gobineau in June 1857 that the Russian minister in Tehran constantly pestered him with the possibility of Bahman's becoming the heir while 'Abbas, through his mother, Khadija, was negotiating with Murray to go to London himself in hopes of steering British support his way. To neutralize Murray's designs and consolidate the shah's shaky throne, the premier had even tried to lure 'Abbas Mirza back to Tehran with promises of security, money, and office, a measure that not long afterward was to be exploited by the premier's opponents to charge him with arranging secret deals and even treason.[4]

Against such a troubling pattern of foreign rivalry, Jayran tried hard on the shah's affections and pressed for her son's appointment in spite of seemingly insurmountable obstacles. Indeed, the appointment of Amir Qasim—who was named after the shah's maternal grandfather—was a flagrant breach of preconditions for succession and flew in the face of the very principle that brought Nasir al-Din to the throne. In effect, the shah was repeating the same favoritism toward Amir Qasim that his father had extended to Nasir al-Din's half-brother, 'Abbas Mirza. In addition to Amir Qasim and eight-year-old Mas'ud Mirza (later Zill al-Sultan) from a temporary wife (*sigha*), the shah had another son, four-year-old Muzaffar al-Din Mirza, from a Qajar wife, a sickly boy who, according to the condition of required maternal Qajar lineage, was the son entitled to succession.

To prove her worth and that her love equaled the shah's "subservience," observed 'Ali Khan Amin al-Dawla, Jayran "intervened in critical affairs [of the state] and her mediation would never fail." Small wonder that Nuri found in her a formidable rival. The shah not only granted her the title of Furugh al-Saltana (the light of the monarchy) but also made her son the Amir(-i) Nizam, a lofty title fallen into disuse since the execution of Amir Kabir.[5] Given the stature of the earlier holder of that office, there was an ironic twist in nominating a five-year-old as the commander in chief of the army, an irony the shah was prepared to ignore provided the boy's symbolic appointment safeguarded for the shah control of the army and averted the rise of another overly powerful military potentate. The shah was also willing to invest all administrative powers in Nuri in order to quell all potential opponents, both foreign and domestic, standing in the way of Amir Qasim's succession.

Among Nuri's domestic adversaries, 'Aziz Khan Mukri, Amir Qasim's chief of staff and the acting commander in chief of the army (*sardar-(i) kull*), was Jayran's closest ally. A protégé of Amir Kabir, 'Aziz Khan gained prominence through his military prowess in the campaigns of the early Nasiri period (as much as his part in the execution of the Babi heroin, Qurrat al-'Ayn in 1852, earned him notoriety). He had earlier parted with Nuri because of the premier's expanding control over the army. 'Aziz Khan was not the only person willing to throw in his lot with Jayran. In the early months of 1857, even after the British dropped their demand for Nuri's dismissal, there was some expectation within government circles that Nuri would soon be removed from office. In the aftermath of the conflict, when the shah hoped to mend fences with Britain, such an expectation was not entirely wrong, for Nuri seemed more of a liability than an asset. But the premier's hold over the administration and his skillful politicking weighed against a hurried decision. The shah was torn by conflicting concerns, and the uneasy equilibrium that emerged in the government contained an even greater degree of mistrust and machination than the Qajar court had witnessed for some time.

As always, Nuri was quick to discern the shah's wishes to nominate Amir Qasim, and like any good grand vizier he tried to gratify them once he found there was no way to change the royal mind. Pleading first with the French and then the Russian envoys, Nuri hoped to neutralize London's possible opposition, a course that inevitably gave his actions a Russian slant. He even reasoned with Gobineau that article seven of the Turk-manchay treaty did not state a requirement of maternal Qajar lineage, and he managed to persuade the French envoy to write, with his personal assistance, a memorandum in Persian acknowledging that the matter would be favorably examined by the French government. Even a note in the "most general terms," supporting Amir Qasim's nomination in conformity with Persian laws and interests was sufficient to allow Nuri to present it to the other foreign envoys as proof of French approval. Gobineau convinced his superior in Paris that because Nuri's survival was at stake it was important to prolong his gratitude by consenting, for it was obvious that he would use all at his disposal to obtain the other two powers' approval with or without France.[6]

Gobineau was right. The Russian reaction to the shah's nomination was surprisingly mellow. This was curious, because only a short while before the Russian legation had seriously raised the issue of Bahman Mirza's regency. With tacit support obtained for the time being from the French and the Russians, Nuri decided to keep the British out of the picture. He deliberately kept Amin al-Mulk, then in Paris, uninformed of the forth-coming nomination, fearing that by amplifying the possibility of British disapproval of the new heir, the Persian envoy might try to undermine him in the hope of enhancing his own chances for premiership. Yet already in January 1857 the British had given their consent to Bahman's regency in the event that a minor heir were to reach the Persian throne. They even agreed to Bahman's succession in the event that Nasir al-Din were to die without an heir. In contrast to previous British support for 'Abbas Mirza (as late as November 1856), this new British position seemed suspiciously like a bribe to obtain Russian cooperation, or rather nonintervention, in the war with Iran. The two powers also agreed on their preference for Qajar lineage on both sides, hoping for a son to be born in future to the mother of the deceased Mu'in al-Din. Yet, to avoid provoking "the jealousy of the shah against his [putative] son," the Russian envoy in Tehran, Anichkov, was instructed, with British approval, "to abstain at present from taking any direct step to promote" what the powers believed to be the shah's "legitimate" heir apparent.[7] Even when in June 1857 Lagovski, the Russian chargé d'affaires, discovered a prince of double Qajar lineage in the person of Muzaffar al-Din and an even older one with "servile" maternal lineage in Mas'ud Mirza, he preferred not to contest the shah's choice of Amir Qasim.[8]

The premier's efforts to secure the new heir apparency for Amir Qasim did not save him from the intrigue of his opponents. As early as April 1857 'Aziz Khan, with Jayran's blessing, had tried to organize a coup against the premier, with all the familiar characteristics of a factional court intrigue. He had at least some Kurdish regiments behind him and enjoyed the backing of some powerful figures in the court and the government. Mirza Yusuf Mustawfi al-Mamalik, the redoubtable accountant general who for decades had jealously guarded his domain against the incursions of monopolizing premiers, was an obvious accomplice, for he had been virtually replaced in office by Nuri's older son, Kazim Khan Nizam al-Mulk. Other supporters were the shah's private secretary, Nasrullah Khan Dabir al-Mulk; Mirza Sadiq Qa'im Maqam Nuri, the ambitious nephew of the premier and ex-governor of Azarbaijan, who had turned against his uncle; and finally Hajji 'Ali Khan Hajib al-Dawla, the royal chamberlain and chief of the *khalwat*, who in the past had carried out the shah's dirty work. His wife was a close companion of Jayran.

In June 1857 the premier's opponents drew up a list of Nuri's "misdeeds" (*taqsirat*)—like the one made for Amir Kabir—on the basis of revelations made by the defecting Sadiq Khan. This list was to be presented by Jayran to the shah as evidence of Nuri's treason. It contained revelations concerning Nuri's embezzlements, lucrative monopolies, and an unprecedented accumulation of wealth. But at the last moment Jayran decided to drop the most damaging items from the list. She revealed enough of the indictments to arouse the shah's suspicion but left out the more embarrassing parts, presumably in the hope of negotiating a deal with the premier on final approval of her son's nomination.

Nuri no doubt must have sensed the danger and thus was more than willing to gratify Jayran's wishes. To work out a deal, he invited the shah's favorite to visit his newly built Nizamiya residence, itself a conspicuous testimony to his and his family's recently accumulated wealth. Built at an enormous cost with a tasteful mix of Persian and European styles and named after his son, Nizam al-Mulk, the mansion at the western edge of the capital was quite a spectacle, its reception halls painted with magnificent royal and ministerial scenes and adorned with portraits of the Qajar royalty, officials, and dignitaries. Jayran must have been sufficiently bedazzled by the way the skillful painter, Sani' al-Mulk, depicted in the centerpiece the direction of the royal gaze toward Amir Qasim (see Pl. 22). She was further enchanted, no doubt, by Nuri's persuasive tone and fatherly mannerisms. The premier reaffirmed his promise to finalize Amir Qasim's nomination. In return, he persuaded Jayran to promise not only to conceal the damaging evidence in the list of misdeeds but also to reveal to him the names of its producers. Offered "rich presents of jewels and money," Jayran must have found the premier's offer more worthwhile than any alliance with his opponents. 'Ali Khan's wife, a royal attendant of Jayran's, only found enough time to rush out and alert her husband to the latest change in the palace climate.[9]

Equipped with Jayran's deal and with 'Ali Khan's loyalty, newly acquired in exchange for a French decoration promised to him, Nuri launched a successful counterattack that temporarily saved his *sidarat*. In response to the modified allegations brought against him by his opponents, he produced a rejoinder listing both his deeds and his misdeeds, complete with entertaining anecdotes for the royal amusement. Predictably, he boasted of his critical role in the capture of Herat, the peace treaty, and Amin al-Mulk's mission. He was hoping that Jayran would use a fair dose of her charms to make the ministerial response more viable.

The pact proved to be a great success for Nuri, even beyond Jayran's expectations. As early as the next day the shah honored Nuri with a privilege perhaps never before granted to any prime minister, even in Iran's turbulent ministerial history. He was made, by royal decree, the "irrevocable grand vizier" (*sadr-i a'zam-i bila-'azl*), which meant, if it meant anything, that the shah himself could not dismiss the prime minister. The royal decree announced that because it was "necessary that the splendor, discipline, and glory should increase day by day, and hour by hour" and that His Majesty's "mind on his blessed head should be perfectly at ease, and quiet," the premier should take charge of "all affairs whatever, whether military or non-military."[10] It was as though the shah was following his father's footsteps. He left the job of amassing "splendor and glory" to his Aqasi-like minister so that he himself could find "perfect ease and quiet" in the refuge of his beloved Jayran. This was not the first of the shah's seemingly unpredictable shifts, and it certainly was not the last. If seriously applied, the heightened power of the prime minister could have relegated Nasir al-Din to the position of a figurehead, a monarch with no executive power.

But there were other motivations behind the otherwise puzzling royal generosity. The "irrevocable premiership" more specifically was aimed at the question of regency and was prescribed by Nuri as a remedy to the threat of Bahman Mirza's claim. If Amir Qasim was to be confirmed as the heir, Nuri reasoned with the shah, it was necessary that he, the irrevocable premier, rather than an outside pretender or a member of the Qajar house imposed upon the heir by foreign powers, should act as regent. Nothing could have been more soothing for the shah, who had lived in fear of foreign proxies all his life, than Nuri's reassuring proposal. If the foreign powers insisted on a regent, Nuri could declare that "the trustees of the state, the notables, the heads of the nation [ru'asa-yi millat], and people of the country [ahl-i mamlikat] would not condone that a regent or a deputy or a guardian be chosen from the [Qajar] princes or from the royal family." Only the irrevocable premier was able to fill that role more than adequately and at the express request of both the shah and the people. The emphasis on the wishes of the people was not a mere ploy. Nuri may have also warned the shah of the public's displays of anger over Iran's general state of affairs, a national mood exacerbated by the war. By investing full authority in the premier, the shah may have been induced to believe that he had erected a safety barrier in front of his throne. Perhaps in all sincerity the shah believed that Nuri had done as much good in five years to preserve his throne as other premiers had in fifty.[11]

It was this same concern with security that Nuri immediately exploited to remove 'Aziz Khan from his command post. Predictably, Nuri accused the military commander of harboring more sinister designs than the mere removal of the Sadr A'zam, including even a plot to replace the shah with the minor Amir Qasim. He further accused him of "delinquency in matters of the arsenal and the military." Once he was convinced of 'Aziz Khan's designs, the shah even wanted to execute him, but through the premier's mediation his sentence was reduced to exile. In spite of 'Aziz Khan's "wrongdoing," Nuri claimed that he "never condoned his disgrace," and whatever happened to him was "of his own making."[12] On 13 June 'Aziz Khan was stripped of his decorations and his title and subjected to the usual ordeal of settling his accounts before being sent in exile to his estate in Savujbulagh on the Ottoman frontier. In a trial-like gathering of state dignitaries Nuri proposed that, once free of his financial burdens, the condemned 'Aziz Khan should make a pilgrimage to Mecca at least to save a title of *hajji* for himself, perhaps a sarcastic allusion to Aziz's failure to take over the office and the title of *amir(-i) nizam* in the fashion of his ex-patron, Mirza Taqi Khan Amir Kabir.

The title remained Amir Qasim's, but the actual office of commander in chief went to Nuri's younger son, Davud, who replaced 'Aziz Khan as the minister (*vazir*) of the new heir apparent. Mirza Sadiq Qa'im Maqam temporarily escaped punishment by taking sanctuary in the shrine of Shah

'Abd al-'Azim, near the capital, and his other allies remained unmolested. Standing by his side of the bargain, Nuri arranged to change the Jayran's status from that of a temporary (*munqati'a*) to a permanent (*da'ima*) wife, a necessary step toward legitimizing Amir Qasim's succession. It was necessary for the shah to divorce one of his four permanent wives, and in this case the affected woman was Sitara Khanum, the shah's second wife from a humble Tabrizi background. Though divorce had been routine in the Qajar court, this one created something of a controversy and was carried out in spite of evident resistance in the shah's harem to Jayran's ascendancy. The mujtahids who were invited to resolve the legal obstacles refused to sanction it, claiming that sufficient grounds for such a divorce were nonexistent. Nuri nevertheless managed to direct enough pressure on one mujtahid so that he finally sanctioned the divorce.

But Nuri could not easily quell the harem's opposition, particularly when led by as formidable a figure as Mahd 'Ulya. Though Sitara's objections to her divorce were finally resolved through her expulsion from the andarun, there was a more powerful source of protest. Representing the Qajar princes and nobility, Mahd 'Ulya voiced the "disgust of the whole Kajar family and tribe . . . down to the remotest clansman" over the choice of an heir in violation of the recognized privilege of the Qajar house.[13] It was no accident that the invitation notes sent out for Jayran's wedding ceremony on 24 June, when she would become the shah's permanent wife, were not signed by Mahd 'Ulya, as was customary for the head of the harem. They were signed instead by the shah's sister, Malikzada, the ex-wife of Amir Kabir, who in 1852 was forced for the second time to marry an unwanted husband, this time Nuri's son, Nizam al-Mulk.

It was no doubt in response to "general ridicule" of the marriage with Jayran that the "chief of the royal historiographers" (presumably Riza Quli Khan Hidayat) was commissioned to make out a title of royal descent for the father of the bride, "an obscene rustic," as Murray called him. The royal chronicler did his best to please his master. The pedigree that was made up traced the descent of the Tajrishi peasant back to the Sasanian monarchy and through them to the legendary Kayanid kings. Genghis Khan, too, may have been brought into the genealogical tree to make it sufficiently Turco-Mongolian, and thus Qajar, to make Jayran's son an heir and to ensure her father and brother a place among the court dignitaries.[14]

Other pretexts were also made for domestic and foreign consumption regarding ineligibility of Amir Qasim's other brothers. To the Russian chargé d'affaires Nuri pointed out that although Mas'ud Mirza was slightly older than Amir Qasim, he was "very very ill, undergrown, and witless."

What wiser precedent to be found for Nasir al-Din's choice than that of Fath 'Ali Shah—Nuri's ideal of kingship—who preferred the younger 'Abbas Mirza (I) over three senior sons, one of them of maternal Qajar descent? In an open allusion to Bahman Mirza, Nuri also cautioned the Russians of "major flaws" in the choice of a Qajar regent, who in reality would "seek partnership with the crown and thus the affairs of kingship and discipline in Iran would come into disrepute and anarchy." That was why, Nuri continued, he had been appointed "absolute potentate" (*mukhtar-i kull*) and also why the shah would never nominate an heir whose mother was a princess.[15]

To his potential rival, Farrukh Khan Amin al-Mulk, whose star was rising, the premier broke the news of his own promotion only in a passing reference. "Incidentally," he wrote on the margin of a letter about the heir apparent's nomination, "keep in mind that, since according to a blessed autograph this embarrassed servant has been called the absolute irrevocable deputy [*vakil-i mutlaq-i bila-'azl*], hence [Amir Qasim's] deputation and tutorship also was assigned to me as was his vizierate to Nizam al-Mulk." Amin al-Mulk may have shared other officials' annoyance over Nuri's promotion, but he could not disagree with the premier's predicament. "I myself am puzzled by what happened. His Majesty, may my soul be his sacrifice, in spite of numerous wives has no other sound [male] child except His Highness the Amir [Qasim]. For example, prince Muzaffar al-Din Mirza, from the daughter of Shu'a' al-Saltana, is invalid and ailing and for some time has been suffering from seizures."[16]

There was some truth to Nuri's claims, no matter how conveniently they fit his purpose. Since his first marriage in 1845 at the age of fourteen, most of the shah's children had died at an early age, and those who survived mostly suffered from what appear to be hereditary ailments. Excluding the temporary ones, by 1858, at the age of twenty-seven, the shah's five permanent wives had borne him eighteen children, of whom fourteen died in early age. Even considering the ongoing high child mortality rate, mostly due to epidemics, the rate of 80 percent in the royal family was unusual and especially problematic given the fact that after 1858 the shah became, for some decades, infertile. With hundreds of permanent and temporary wives over the course of his life, the shah produced a distressingly low rate of surviving offspring. Jayran's four children all died before the age of five. Muzaffar al-Din, although from maternal Qajar descent, was a sickly child disliked by his father and relegated to the invisibility of the harem. Mas'ud Mirza, from a temporary wife, was not exactly "witless" and may not have suffered from a defect in his leg, as Nuri claimed, but he certainly qualified as maladjusted. Once caught in the palace garden gouging the eyes of sparrows he had captured, he was punished by the shah, and Muzaffar al-Din was forbidden to play with him.[17]

The shah sought happiness in Jayran's affections, hope in her son, and comfort in the fatherly advice of his premier. These were perhaps the principal ingredients of the "perfect ease and quiet" he was after. On no less propitious a day than the *salam* of the feast of Ghadir Khum—when according to the Shi'ite calendar on 18 Dhul-Hijja 632 Muhammad nominated 'Ali as his successor—the shah announced his intention to nominate Amir Qasim as heir apparent. As on other occasions, the shah and his premier intended to utilize religious symbolism to boost the monarchy at home. The *Vaqayi'-i Ittifaqiya* of 23 Dhul-Hijja/14 August, which carried the news of the heir apparent's nomination ("the lustrous Amir-i Kabir, the Amir Nizam"), also informed its readers of a new robe of honor given to the premier for the occasion, as well as the news of Murray's first audience with the shah since his return.[18] Moreover, the report in the same issue of the review of the troops by Nuri's young son, Davud, the new acting commander of the army, was complemented by a curious (and otherwise misplaced) account of the office of "deputy of the subjects" (*vakil al-ru'aya*), a veiled reference to the historical precedence for Nuri's deputation (*vikalat*) traceable all the way back to Zand and Safavid times. The entire newspaper that day emitted a suspicious unanimity of purpose to glorify Nuri and play down Britain's victorious return.[19]

The use of the title Amir Kabir for the first time since Mirza Taqi Khan's death underlined, in the eyes of the public, the royal prerogative assigned to the heir apparent and deputized by the premier. Yet it must have annoyed the status-conscious Mahd 'Ulya tremendously. Not only was her father's name given to the son of a humble village girl, but his title, too, was undeservedly abused for the second time. Even prior to the festivities surrounding the nomination in September 1857, criticism continued to be voiced by the Qajar princes supportive of Mahd 'Ulya. Nuri's blunt denunciation of such criticism betrayed a sense of defiance. "No one but the most obtrusive has the audacity to question," he warned. If the heir apparent's mother were a Qajar princess, repeating what he had said earlier, the "people could not afford the arrogance of his uncles," a clear reference to Mahd 'Ulya's obnoxious brothers. Even if the senior princes were not content, Nuri dared to add, "let them remain discontent, let them turn blind with jealousy."[20] With the shah's enthusiasm at its height, there was little that either Mahd 'Ulya or the princes could do but wait for their chance. This was not Mahd 'Ulya's first clash with her son's prime minister.

Murray, who read the nomination in the *Vaqayi'-i Ittifaqiya*, must have felt the same way. With the revolt in India at its height during the summer of 1857, London was in no mood for another quarrel with Tehran, a fact that Nuri knew well. Although Murray could see "dissatisfaction through-out the country" and forecast "confusions and anarchy" in the event of the shah's death, he was resigned to the reality that under the circumstances neither Britain nor Russia (which after the Crimean episode was in no mood for confrontation) could seriously interfere with the choice of successor. At the best they could anticipate for Amir Qasim a fate similar to that of his deceased brothers. Having seen "how complete is the control" exercised over the shah and over his harem by the mother of the heir apparent, Murray was convinced that "opposition would have a negative effect." Thus, in September, when on the occasion of the shah's birthday the French and the Russians gave their consent, Murray, too, was obliged to con-gratulate the shah on the choice of his heir apparent. When he approached the shah in the *salam* and in an "undertone" pronounced London's consent, he noticed that "His Majesty's face brightened exceedingly."[21]

With great annoyance Murray also observed the ongoing consolidation of Nuri's power in "foreign, as well as internal, financial, military, and religious" affairs. The *"bee-azl"* prime minister, of whom "the shah him-self can not dispose," had told him that not only was he the "sole guardian" of the shah's successor, in effect "the regent," but that on the occasion of his own death "the high charge was to descend to his son, Nizam al-Mulk." Murray was right to observe that the "unexpected development of His Highness' ambition and nepotism" had ruined Bahman Mirza's chances forever, but it did not entirely dim the envoy's sincere hope to see the house of Nuri in ruins. What could not be done in the galleries of the Tuileries during the peace treaty negotiations earlier in the year perhaps could now be done behind closed doors in the women's quarters of Gulistan Palace.[22]

DELEGATING POWER

By the beginning of 1858 Nuri seemed to have fully recovered from his earlier crises. Foreign affairs, finance, and the army were under his control and assigned variously to his sons and subordinates, the shah and the heir apparent were under his wings, the French sympathetic to his government, the Russians conciliatory, and the British apparently harmless. Finally, after seven eventful years, he seemed for a short period to have reached the apex of his premiership. His authoritarian sway, what the classical manuals of government would have defined as "delegatory vizierate" (*vizarat-i tafwiz*), or the full mandate given by the shah to his minister, was almost identical with that of his predecessor, Amir Kabir. Nuri's authority, however, proved illusory. The seed of adversity that had been sown throughout the winter had only come to blossom in the spring of 1858. Mahd 'Ulya and the senior princes of the Qajar house, anti-Nuri officialdom, and Murray were all at work to bring about the end of the Nuri-Jayran pact and anxious to lure the shah away from the hated "potentate."

Murray was at first too happy to return to his old adversarial role when in January 1858, relying on his voluntary spies in high places (among them the incorrigible Farhad Mirza), he began to receive from Nuri's opponents most damaging reports about His Excellency's secret correspondence on the Indian revolt. Nuri's correspondence could not have touched a sorer spot in the British colonial consciousness, particularly if it enabled Murray, as it did, directly to link the premier's designs for India with Russia's courtship of Nuri. "Little dependence" could be placed upon Nuri's "most solemn assurances of sincerity and friendship," diagnosed Murray, who after receiving the reports tried to portray him as a tool of Russian territorial ambitions. More damaging even than association with Russia in the eyes of Murray was the sin of seeking "mechanical aid" from Europe and inviting the United States to become Britain's "maritime rival in the Persian Gulf." He ridiculed the premier for setting his heart on "the most distant power on earth from Persia," the one in which military instructors, skilled labor, and hardware were "the most scarce and extravagantly paid."[23] The Persian premier's geopolitical horizon, perhaps inspired by Malkum Khan, was surely broader than that of the complacent envoy, although realistically there was little at that time that could make viable the U.S. presence in Iran and the Persian Gulf.

Hostile reporting to the Foreign Office was a symptom of Murray's frustration. He complained to London of the "humiliating condition" to which he had been reduced because of the "conciliation and forbearance" he was asked to demonstrate toward the Persian government. His efforts to keep a close watch on new palace alliances against the premier were made obsolete when contacts between Persian citizens and the mission were restricted by Nuri. Not only were British friends and agents targeted and persecuted, he claimed, but even Dickson, the physician of the British mission, was banned from treating members of the royal harem, whereas Russian and Austrian physicians were given "free entree." This denial of access was not merely a sign of disrespect but a matter of vital importance, for communicating with the shah's andarun, and especially with Mahd

'Ulya, was one of the most productive ways of getting information about court matters and coordinating necessary action. Murray was not deprived of all his spies, however. Farhad Mirza, who had sent him "secret information of what was passing in Tehran" throughout the war, secretly contacted Murray through a third party in peacetime, too. This he did under the oath of being "obedient and submissive" to the shah and under the threat of "total ruination," a condition that obliged Murray, in disrespect for the terms of the peace treaty, to ask London for permission to extend British protection to the prince.[24]

A portrayal of Nuri's "real sentiment" as nothing but "personal animosity" and "treachery" toward England was not without substance. In April 1858 with a new air of confidence Murray admitted to the new British foreign minister, the Earl of Malmesbury, that he could either choose "to submit to repeated humiliations," or "recourse to measures tending to the renewal of the rupture" that took place in 1855. "To the latter course," he assured Malmesbury, "they shall not drive me; whatever be the amount of provocation." The envoy's tone of resolve suggests that a countermeasure was in the works and about to be put into practice.[25]

It was to be expected that by late May 1858 there would be another concerted effort to topple the Nuri regime. The opposition party, made up of those whom the premier had injured, conspired to gain access to the shah and lay before him a statement concerning the "miserably disorganized state of the army, the revenue, and all other branches of the public service" brought about by the prime minister's corruption. Murray must have had reason to believe, through his contacts, that the "present storm [was] more dangerous." The revelations made by Mirza Sadiq Qa'im Maqam Nuri, the main source of information, about his uncle's shady finances and about his secret dealings behind the shah's back were too scandalous to be left unpunished for long. Nuri's agents arrested the family defector and extracted under torture both cash and the names of his contacts. But the premier could not easily deflect Jayran's renewed hostility and her "powerful support" for the malcontents. To her displeasure, Nuri had managed to turn Amir Qasim's nomination to his own advantage and, in effect, to undermine Jayran's position. She even had the temerity to press the shah to "choose between her and his minister as both can not remain in the palace together." Besides Jayran, the revived opposition party represented "some leading personages of the city, the court, and the royal harem" whose object was to expose to the shah "the disorganized state of the army" and to open "His Majesty's eyes to the proceedings of the all powerful minister and to procure his dismissal."

Contrary to the shah's earlier support for the premier and his hope that a balance would be achieved between the divan and the harem, the new round of anti-Nuri activities propelled him increasingly in the direction of Jayran. She had managed to convince the shah's drifting mind of the advantages of dismissing his all-powerful and irreversible premier. In a bold move Jayran's brother, Asadullah Khan, who was now beginning to make his presence felt around the capital, approached the Ottoman embassy in Tehran in the hope of persuading the chargé d'affaires, Tawfiq Pasha, to help him gain the consent of other foreign missions against Nuri. There is little doubt that the ambitious Asadullah enjoyed the shah's discreet blessing.[26] Perhaps not quite accidentally this appeal to the Ottoman embassy coincided with Tawfiq's attempt to grant protection to an adventurous mujtahid, Sayyid Salih 'Arab (also known as Damad for being the son-in-law of Sayyid 'Ali Tabataba'i, the renowned jurist of the early nineteenth century). The mujtahid's appearance on the Tehran horizon and claim to Ottoman citizenship had provoked a brief but acute diplomatic crisis between the two neighbors. Sayyid Salih, who was exiled to Istanbul after the 1843 Karbala massacre (in which he had played a leading role inciting the Shi'ite population to revolt against the Ottoman authorities), appeared in Tehran on the eve of the Herat campaign. "Vigorous in enjoining the good and prohibiting the evil," as Aqa Buzurg Tihrani described him, Sayyid Salih threw his combativeness, a faded version of his father-in-law's crusading penchant a generation earlier, behind the anti-Nuri party, possibly with Murray's implicit blessing.[27]

Watching his opponents' intrigues through his spy in the Ottoman embassy, Nuri obtained a copy of Sayyid Salih's disparaging letter to the Ottoman chargé d'affaires in which the mujtahid criticized the premier and called for sympathy and support for his opponents. It was not entirely unexpected, therefore, when he was declared persona non grata by Nuri on charges of anti-government "subversion" (*fasad*). The premier threatened Tawfiq that unless Sayyid Salih were immediately sent back to Ottoman Iraq, he would have no choice but to expel him. The scandal that followed Tawfiq's foolhardy insistence on keeping the troublesome mujtahid in the capital, which included an assault on the chief gatekeeper of the capital by the Ottoman guards, gave Nuri further justification to act swiftly against his conspirators.

The shah's "vacillating mind" provided all the more reason for Nuri to act urgently. Any hopes for rapprochement with Jayran were obviously at an end when her supporters approached the foreign envoys. Not only Tawfiq but Murray also was barraged "with an abundance of secret messages." Even the shah wanted to know where Murray stood—whether he was in favor of the Sadr A'zam's dismissal or, alternatively, whether he was "personally disinclined" toward the new heir apparent. Murray's pious reply that he did not wish "to interfere in the internal affairs of the kingdom" and that the shah should choose whomever he desired was expedient but not entirely innocuous given Murray's troublemaking role in the past. Neither the shah nor Jayran could have misinterpreted his reply, particularly when it was topped by an "ornamental French pastry" for the young heir apparent and accompanied by Murray's friendly letter for Jayran. The symbolic gesture was unmistakably heartening. The shah was "exceedingly pleased" to know that his son's appointment was not in question. "The Harem, or the opposition party," observed Murray with secret relish, "construed it of course in a manner favorable to their own wishes."

The fate of the premier would have been sealed had it not been for his extraordinary capacity to maneuver, compromise, and intimidate. Knowing the central role Murray would play in the shah's decision, Nuri approached him at the last hour to obtain his support in exchange for honoring a series of British demands. These ranged from officially acknowledging the hated Aqa Khan Shirazi, the new Persian secretary of the mission, whom Murray wished to set up against the premier as he had previously tried to set up Hashim Khan, to receiving Dickson "with every mark of confidence and esteem," which in reality meant allowing restoration of the English physician's access to the harem. He also requested the establishment of a consulate in Tehran, promises of friendship with England, and a solemn declaration that his government would discontinue holding the Friday sermon (*khutba*) and striking coins in Herat in the name of the shah. Quoting Milton—"Ease will recant vows made in pain as vacant and void"—Murray scoffed quietly in his dispatch to London at the prime minister's promises, only to highlight his own righteousness. "Had he ever weathered the storm and regained his place in the shah's favor, he should not be able to say that I slighted him in the hour of danger and difficulty."[28] Murray did not elaborate on what he gave in exchange for the premier's promises, but it was not hard for all parties, including Nasir al-Din, to notice that at least temporarily the British envoy had decided to remain equivocal in his blessing for the anti-Nuri party. The apparent favor was hardly more than a momentary truce extracted at what he believed to be the premier's last hour. In spite of a facade of amicability, inside there were layers of burning grudges waiting to erupt when the time was ripe.

Murray's assurances thus were barely sufficient to calm the premier. There was an element of desperation in his conduct when he engaged in a new "coup d'etat" against his opponents, aiming either to "break his fall or crush his enemies." He first started with a threat of resignation. In a private interview with the shah, the contents of which were relayed to Murray by Nuri, the premier presented himself with "expressions of profoundest humility and loyalty" only to alert the "royal ear" that it had been "assailed by the calumny of his enemies," a situation that, the premier claimed, left him with no choice but to offer his resignation. The shah was "confused," no doubt realizing that Nuri had succeeded in outmaneuvering the conspirators and winning over the British envoy. He scarcely knew how to reply to Nuri. His "countenance was troubled" so much that for a moment Nuri even expected "to hear the fiat of his disgrace come forth." But the "feeble character" of the shah, reported Murray, could not "assume resolution" sufficient to overcome "his habit of submission to the will of his minister."

With displeasure Murray diagnosed the shah's "feeble and vacillating character" as the prime cause of Nuri's "complete victory" against the opposition party. This was achieved primarily because, as Murray believed, Nuri was "thoroughly acquainted with the weak points in his sovereign's character." As before, appealing to the shah's moral sense of duty and his gratitude worked. As always, the shah was touched by the grand vizier's captivating tongue, his wit and demeanor, and his remarkable ability to persuade the shah to see his own interests as aligned with those of his fatherly minister. The premier's manner—like Amir Kabir's before him, treating the shah as if he were a young son, giving him unsolicited advice, cautioning him of the perils along his way, voicing decisions on his behalf, sitting at his feet, near his chair, and interjecting comments—his confidence in his own rectitude and the honor of his family, and his veiled references to dire consequences upon his removal from office all gave him formidable power. He would not easily be crushed even if the shah had the entire harem and all the foreign embassies pressing him to do exactly that.

Nuri's gamble paid off. The discussion about his resignation ended with the shah giving the premier "a renewed *dast khatt*" (autograph note) in which he conferred upon Nuri "the powers of life and death, of exiling, imprisoning, appointing and dismissing any Persian subject from the highest to the lowest based on delegating to him the supreme authority over every branch of the administration, religious, civil, and military."[29] On the face of it, the sweeping monopoly of executive power, even greater than the shah had previously assigned to Amir Kabir, was a testimony to the shah's temporary setback. Yet the chemistry of the shah's interaction with his premier was more complex. One suspects that the shah decided to grant sweeping powers to Nuri only to make the premier's position more viable and hence more vulnerable, knowing that Nuri had no real military or foreign backing to make use of his newly granted authority. At best, it was a final effort made on the part of the shah before breaking off with his premier when alternative avenues of dismissal were impassable, and at the worst a premeditated scheme to destroy Nuri by placing on his shoulders an irredeemable burden.

Reassuring Amin al-Mulk of his unshaken power, Nuri, confident of his own victory, employed his usual sarcasm to laugh at his opponents as "a bunch of riffraff" who were stupid enough to follow Asadullah, Jayran's brother. "A group of idiots thus went around to embassies saying that the job is finished from within [the andarun]. The Russian embassy, as well as the French, conducted themselves with honor and friendship and paid absolutely no attention. The British played it shrewdly and waited for the end. The crazy Ottoman kid began dancing around but was caught red-handed." Mustawfi al-Mamalik, whom Nuri recognized as the central figure in the conspiracy, had even sent signals to the shah that he was "ready to take over the government in full confidence." His immediate exile thus was meant, as Murray stated, to "strike terror into all others." With pleasure Nuri recorded that upon hearing of the conspiracy, the shah ordered Mustawfi al-Mamalik "to be put on a mule and be sent off to Ashtiyan," his hometown. Jayran's brother only escaped the bastinado because of Nuri's intercession. Nizam al-Mulk, Nuri's son, received a new robe of honor—a sequenced *tirma* robe with emerald buttons that had belonged to Fath 'Ali Shah. "All the crows were dispersed with one throw of His Majesty's stone of blessing and benevolence," Nuri was proud to announce.[30]

The decision to give the minister greater power, in effect power over the shah's own court, was welcomed least of all by Jayran, "the only one remaining who venture[d] still to offer any resistance." She threatened again that if Nuri or any of his family were allowed any authority over her or her son, "she would fly from the royal harem." Perhaps an allusion to the Persian proverb "runaway gazelle" (*ahu-yi gurizpa*), this was an apt reflection of Jayran's desire for independence. Murray believed the grand vizier would find "some scheme either for running away or perpetrating the angry lady," but the gazelle of Gulistan Palace could not be easily chased off.[31] The prime minister was clearly puzzled by Jayran's antagonism. In a letter to Amin al-Mulk he "opened his heart" to relate "stories of [his] sorrow," for after all his labor to persuade the foreign missions to endorse Amir Qasim's nomination and the heavy cost he bore of more than 10,000 tumans, he was paid back by Jayran with "antagonism and suspicion."

Deceived by "the temptation of devils" such as his brother, Nuri believed, she was "determined to the best of her ability to hurt and degrade" him.[32]

Jayran's outspoken rejection of Nuri's authority over herself and her son must have incensed not only the premier but the shah's mother as well. The fact that Jayran exchanged gifts with Murray and later with Madame Gobineau may be taken as one sign of her desire to replace Mahd 'Ulya as the head of the harem. The shah's extreme fondness for Jayran further strengthened her hand. It was as though the shah was trying, albeit unconsciously, to break away from his mother's sway and seek independence and maturity in a favorite wife who combined some of Mahd 'Ulya's qualities with artistic and athletic features he greatly admired. Temporarily eclipsed by Jayran, the queen mother once again had to rely on the support of the Qajar nobility, much as she had during the time of Amir Kabir, to remove Jayran, but at a time when she was largely isolated. Both the shah and the prime minister were basically inconsiderate of her and of the princes' wishes. Even her devoted Qajar prince-minister, 'Ali-Quli Mirza I'tizad al-Saltana, kept a safe distance from her.[33] Deprived of her usual outside contacts, she must have welcomed the renewed contact with the British embassy through the English physician, Dickson.

To this complex pattern of rivalry and intrigue was appended an element of royal concern for the well-being of the army. Soon after Nuri's promotion to total authority, the shah became increasingly critical of the premier's performance. A royal autograph note reminding Nuri of his duties was almost hostile in tone. The shah seemed particularly reticent to part with his executive powers over the army when he wrote: "From the day we demanded that you conduct all affairs of the state—and we do not recognize anyone but yourself in governmental affairs—we held and will hold you responsible for its good and its evil, particularly the army and arsenal and artillery which are paramount in government and the source of all concerns. Unquestionably and without any excuse we require discipline from you. You have tried, but it was not compatible either with our taste or yours." The shah no doubt was reflecting on the recent war and the hazards of defeat when he urged nervously, "I pledge by my own head" that "the survival of the state and the survival of the name and the tradition [ism va rasm] and everything in this world depends on the army. If that is well and orderly, everything else is well. If that is disorderly everything else is disorderly. Frankly, if you, too, intend to ignore it, there is no excuse."[34] Only military might could safeguard the throne at a time when loss of face in the battlefield had brought open criticism from the anti-Nuri opposition. Nasir al-Din fully understood the vitality of military "discipline" (*nazm*) to the survival of "the name and the tradition" of monarchy, and he was persuaded to believe that any show of military might was about to be spoiled under Nuri.

RUINOUS FEVER

If harem opposition and the deteriorating state of the army were not enough to break the back of Nuri's regime, there was other unpredictable trouble in the making. Only two weeks after his reaffirmation on 29 June 1858, Amir Qasim Khan, the six-year-old heir apparent, died of what was diagnosed as "brain fever," an illness most likely to have been meningitis. His death, after a short illness, was a terrible shock to the shah, to Jayran, and, ironically, to Nuri. This was a "very severe blow" to the shah, noted Murray. He "certainly had more affection for it [sic.] than for any other member of his family." Joseph Polak observed that in sorrow the shah was helpless, "hitting his forehead against the wall," and would not eat for days.[35] The sense of loss was profound, leaving a permanent mark on the shah's sentiments and on his ability to forge emotional attachments for decades to come, particularly after having lost two other heirs since 1849. The loss plunged the court into yet another political crisis even before it had recovered from the previous one.

Under the mournful air of the royal loss there were darker currents of allegations and counterallegations. The heir apparent's sudden death at a time of heightened factional hostility in the court was too striking to be accepted easily as a coincidence. Even before Amir Qasim's death, Jayran had viewed her son's illness as the outcome of a conspiracy hatched by Nuri and his agents to destroy the new heir apparent. To prevent their evil influence from taking its full effect, she thus refused to allow the prime minister or any of his people, including physicians she perceived to be his subordinates, to come close to the dying boy. Her behavior provoked bitter complaints from the premier, which reflected the extent of animosity between the rival camps. "This slave cannot bear not to present his humble opinion," he wrote in a passionate private note to the shah complaining in animated language of the restriction imposed on him.

> May God sacrifice my life and the life of my children for the blessed soul of His Majesty and his children. The wise among my children and my friends advise me: "Take it easy and do not offer [counsel] since His Majesty will be upset with your counsel." But what can I do? I cannot ignore the expediency and the good of the government and the shah. . . . I amply alerted you to the death of Russian emperors at the hands of their

physicians, but it was all in vain. Again I warn: How long [will you re-
main] captive of [your] infatuation [i.e., for Jayran] [*khatir-khwahi ta kay*]?
Your beloved son who was the apple of Iran's eye is about to perish because of the obstinacy of the womenfolk [*lijajat-i zanana*] and [your] infatuation for them. May God strike me blind so I do not see his defect . . . but
there is no effect in my counsel and no fruit on my tree. At last I am to
be ruined because of [your] son. Why, in His Majesty's best judgment,
should the words of women [*harf-i zanana*] take precedence over mine? Even
for the son of a village grain merchant, physicians will be brought. For Heav-
en's sake, this is the king's son! I do not even dare to come close [to him].
No one listens to me. All my life I toiled and gained experience. The fruit
of all my labor is that someone would take pride in my wisdom and learn
from my experiences. [Otherwise] dust be upon my vizierate and upon
my wisdom [*khak bar sar-i vizarat-i man va 'aql-i man*]. On the word
of two good-for-nothing maids you sold out a prince to a Jew. May God
kill me and set me free so I do not hear anyone's order. Now everyone but
myself is informed about the condition of my master's son. I only hear
it from the people.

The shah's reply to this plea was reserved and even distant. "His Excellency
the prime minister!" he replied. "Today I summoned Hajji Mirza Mahmud
and other physicians. Upon examination they assured me that God willing
he will recover. Again this afternoon the same physicians will come and
make a proper examination. Of course we will summon all physicians here
and will not leave the matter to the womenfolk."[36] In spite of assurances
one gets the impression that the shah had already lost hope.

Nuri's note showed clear signs of tension. The premier interpreted his
exclusion not only as a personal insult but also as a symptom of his
loosening grip over Nasir al-Din. His rebuke of the shah's infatuation for
Jayran was indeed an admission of defeat. In the battle with the harem, Nuri
realized, not only he was a possible casualty but the very office of the prime
minister, the symbol of the government's independence from the palace,
was about to be buried under the weight of the shah's personal fixations.
What he probably could not foresee at the time was that from the "dust"
he had symbolically cast upon the office of vizierate soon would arise the
phoenix of monarchical autocracy.

Beyond the raw indignation of the note, Nuri's allusive reference to
selling out the prince to a Jew deserves attention. It certainly corroborated
Murray's statement that Amir Qasim's death had "been probably accelerated, if not caused, by the attendance of conflicting remedies of a half a
dozen Persian and two Jewish doctors."[37] The Jewish physicians in question
were Hakim Haqq Nazar and his brother Hakim Musa, sons of a Khwansari
family of physicians who had served the Qajar court for some time. Haqq

Nazar, handsome and well connected, had a close relationship with Mahd 'Ulya and presumably through her was acquainted with Jayran, a fact that may have had some bearing on the conflicting treatment prescribed by the various physicians. As was typical of all court physicians, Haqq Nazar and his brother functioned as contacts between women of the harem and the outside world. By contrast, Hajji Mirza Mahmud, the Muslim physician invited by the shah to attend his son, was a wealthy and influential confidant of the prime minister.[38] With a Qajar high society almost unanimously suffering from hypochondria, there could have been few professions more lucrative and influential than the physician's. Polak informs us that in addition to Persian physicians, Jewish and Muslim, he too was called upon, albeit reluctantly, to participate in the treatment (see Pl. 19).

It is likely that all the physicians summoned to cure the prince realized very quickly that Amir Qasim's case was hopeless. In the mid-nineteenth century there was almost no cure for meningitis or any other infectious inflammation of the brain membrane.[39] Seeing no other options, Haqq Nazar restored to simple home remedies. Once Amir Qasim had died, however, the physicians of rival parties and their patrons used the occasion to capitalize on the shah's agony and accuse the opposite camp of criminal malpractice. In reality the chances that Amir Qasim had been poisoned or maltreated were slim, given the extraordinary perils involved. Yet the medical culture of the time greatly emphasized the physician's role and often held him responsible for the condition of the patient, regardless of the type and severity of the illness or the causes of death. Murray's comment that the conflicting treatments had accelerated or caused the death should be seen as a reflection of just such a belief, and under the circumstances it was not difficult to point hostile fingers in opposite directions. The Jewish physician, Haqq Nazar, was the first to be accused of ill intent, presumably because of his close ties with Mahd 'Ulya, which made him the target of Hajji Mirza Mahmud's insinuations. In the heat of anger aroused by Nuri's accusations, the shah ordered Haqq Nazar arrested with the intention of having him blinded. Only when Jayran, alerted by Haqq Nazar, interceded was he saved from a cruel punishment, but once she had the upper hand it was inevitable that she should arrange to have Hajji Mirza Mahmud accused and arrested on the charge of having poisoned the heir apparent. Other physicians closer to Nuri were also punished. The tent of one physician collapsed when its ropes were deliberately cut. He managed to escape with his life to a sanctuary, but all his belongings were appropriated. Even Polak was told that his services were terminated, only to have this order rescinded after three days.[40]

THE VALLEY OF DISMISSAL

In spite of all his loyal exhortations, Nuri was "ruined" by the death of the heir apparent. Although, as he noted to Farrukh Khan Amin al-Mulk, he may have wept so much at the loss of Amir Qasim that the "elements of his being and the foundation of his existence were dissipated," he could not have stopped the innuendos generated by "a pack of bastardly ungrateful villains" who "day and night wandered around foreign embassies" scandalizing "the government and the nation." Their connivance, Nuri reckoned, might cause his fall for power, but he assured his emissary that they could not prevent him from service to his "patron and the state."[41]

Rumors of the premier's involvement in the death of the heir apparent circulated by the anti-Nuri party, although completely unfounded, severely diminished the premier's stature and left the desired ill effect on the shah's perception. Although the shah was sensible enough not to believe that Nuri had killed his favorite son, under the circumstances it was not difficult for Jayran to persuade the impressionable royal mind that with Amir Qasim dead the premier would use all means at his disposal to remove the target of the shah's "infatuation." Besides the shah's favorite, an important sector of the princes, courtiers, and ranking officials headed by Mahd 'Ulya were remobilized in severing the shah's last emotional tie to his grand vizier.

An incident involving the murder of one of the proxies of Jayran's brother provided a final opportunity. The victim was beaten to death in secret by agents of Mirza 'Isa, son of the influential chief accountant of Tehran, Mirza Musa Mustawfi Tafrishi, a close ally of the then exiled Mustawfi al-Mamalik. Mirza 'Isa capitalized on the murder to implicate Nuri as the man who ordered the killing. On the morning of 30 August the victim's mutilated body was carried by his relatives to the roadside, where the shah was passing on his way to a hunting ground in the vicinity of the capital. The sight of the slain man and his lamenting relatives overwhelmed the shah. Reminiscent of popular folktales and accounts abounding in Persian didactic literature with kings encountering wronged subjects, often in the wilderness of a hunting ground, the scene presumably generated in Nasir al-Din Shah an impulsive surge of conscience against his sinister minister.[42]

A little before sunset of the same day, while passing across a valley in Sauhanak not far from Niyavaran Palace, the shah issued a decree that ended the seven years of Nuri's prime ministership. What was finally uttered in the "valley of dismissal" (*darra-yi 'azl*), as the place came to be

known, was "unexpected," according to Murray, an indication that up to
the last minute the shah had not yet made up his mind about his "all-
powerful" minister.[43] The dismissal contrasted markedly with the shah's
reaffirmation of Nuri's power monopoly only six weeks earlier. The premier was blamed for taking upon himself "all the state affairs" and not
taking a "single person as partner and associate." It became obvious to the
shah that "one person would not be capable of rendering all the state
services, and in the process many failures and flaws had occurred," to the
extent that "all the affairs of the state remained redundant."

> Of course, your loyalty to the state [*dawlat-khwahi*] would not be con-
> tent that we remain obliged to cast our blessed sight on such disorga-
> nized affairs. Thus today, that is, the twentieth of Muharram, we dismiss
> you from the premiership and Nizam al-Mulk and Vazir Lashkar [Nuri's
> first and second son, Davud] from their posts. Retire to your house with
> utmost confidence and security. On our part we will certainly display
> absolutely nothing but benevolence. Our oral goodwill and assurances, as
> necessary, and our intimate sentiments we have instructed ['Ali Khan
> Farrash-bashi] Hajib al-Dawla to convey to you.[44]

The "disorganized affairs" he mentioned were the main reason for four
months of "trepidation and ill-feelings" that had clouded the shah's relations with his premier. In his reply to the shah, Nuri acknowledged the
shortcomings of his final months of service, ever since his countercoup in
May 1858. After sacking Mustawfi al-Mamalik he was evidently crippled
by financial troubles that rendered him incapable of fulfilling one of his
vital duties toward the shah, providing a steady flow of money to cover
royal expenses. He was proud of his seven years of "honest service,"
however. "If after me impartial people come to power," he wrote with an
air of aloofness, "and if all correspondence would be brought to the royal
sight as before, then the efforts of this humble servant will become apparent." Although he was ashamed of his shortcomings, and although, as
a slave companion, he was no more than "a night-watch servant of the
shah" who lost the "path of servitude," yet he had managed for seven years,
"within his capacity," to "conduct the affairs of Iran properly. It was not
perfect, but it was not very imperfect either." Pleading with the shah for
compassion, he cautioned him that "morally and religiously" it was incumbent upon the royal master to secure Nuri's and his children's dignity
and financial well-being.[45]

At least on paper the shah was obliged to acknowledge Nuri's services.
Not only would the ex-premier's children remain in the shah's service, but
Nuri himself would not be completely expelled. Whatever he found to be

expedient he should report to the shah. Nasir al-Din did not hesitate to pledge repeatedly, and in the name of 'Ali, that he would try his best to comply with his ex-minister's request for compassion. Though he deprived the minister of a last interview, a ban that stretched throughout the unhappy remainder of Nuri's life, he assured him in writing that he did not have any thoughts but "goodwill and compassion" toward him. "Do not assume, since your opponents now have found some access to me, that they will be able to reverse my resolute benevolence toward you. By Murtaza 'Ali [the Imam 'Ali], our concern toward you will absolutely never turn adverse."[46]

The definition of goodwill would have to be stretched very far to embrace the treatment extended to Nuri after his dismissal. Indeed, if any feeling was prominent in the shah's heart it was fear that the ex-premier would make a comeback and retaliate for his disgraceful dismissal. Polak was correct in noting that although the shah regarded Nuri as his "father and guardian," deep down he feared and hated him. "Yet the premier knew well how to keep him firm on the belief that no one but himself could administer the country and that his dismissal would result in chaos and popular unrest." The Austrian physician himself witnessed that the shah, accompanied by a large detachment of guards and retinue, issued the warrant for Nuri's arrest "with great anxiety," and only after he was informed that Nuri was under house arrest did he return from a hunting excursion to Niyavaran. "Even in the Niyavaran palace he was looking out of the window with alarm, fearing that the crowd gathered underneath might take possession of his horses by force." When nothing happened, the exhilarated monarch shouted: "I never thought that my minister's dismissal would be carried out with such ease, or I would have removed him several years earlier."[47] It is hard to believe that Nasir al-Din had forgotten completely about his experience with Amir Kabir.

On the night before Nuri's dismissal, Nasir al-Din seemed to have come close to a final decision. Nuri himself left a record for posterity on the margin of the shah's note addressed to him. "The night before [my] dismissal," he wrote, "I learned about it and submitted a petition. [This] reply was granted." The shah's reply indeed had an ominously familiar ring to it. It could have been written seven years earlier in reply to Amir Kabir, not only in its deceptively reassuring tone but on the very date of its issuance, 20 Muharram 1275, exactly seven lunar years after the dismissal of Amir Kabir, on 20 Muharram 1268. Nuri must have shuddered not only at the chronological coincidence but at the resemblance in the shah's reassuring tone. Seven years earlier he himself had probably made a copy of the shah's note to Amir Kabir available to Sheil. The shah's resorting to his fatalistic beliefs could hardly soothe the frantic prime minister.

His Excellency the Sadr A'zam! Except for heavenly destiny [*muqaddar-i asimani*] to what else can we attribute it, since it is four months now that without any reason you and I are in [the state of] trepidation and ill-feeling. I swear to God Almighty that as long as I live nothing but benevolence will come forth from me under any condition—whether [I am] the prince or the pauper [*khwah darvish, khwah padishah*]. In this world I believe, and in the other world it is obvious, that neither benefit nor harm is intended from my side toward you or from your side toward me. God has created you for my service and me for compassion toward you. It is obvious that these rumors and nonsense, whether too much or too little, will not affect, God willing, our relations. May God be my witness that you will not see any misdeeds on my side. Do not consider me as frivolous and ignorant, and hence from my quarter you remain unmolested. People are intriguing and talk nonsense.[48]

The shah's reference to "heavenly destiny"—that which eventually brought the shah and his premier at odds with each other—only confirms that he consciously chose the dismissal date. According to Baron de Pichon, the new French envoy in Tehran, the shah even promised, in an earlier private note to Jayran, the downfall of Nuri on that date.[49] It is not unlikely that the dismissal was seen by the shah not only as a rational decision based on the merits of the case but also as an end to a predestined seven-year cycle, a concern further insinuated in his reference to the prince and the pauper, a popular imagery recurring in Persian folk legends as well as in high literature on monarchical fortune. It was as though the shah, not confident of his own future, sought support in the old concept of the king's fortune (*dawlat*, or *bakht*), which specified that the survival of the throne was dependent upon the downfall of the minister once his natural cycle of administration came to an end. Even for a Persian ruler in the second half of the nineteenth century, the celestial cycles, with their propitious and ominous moments, were to be observed and complied with. In such a scheme the dismissal of a premier was more than a political decision; it signalled entry into a new cycle that required Nasir al-Din to withstand the world independently.

The symbolism of terminating Nuri's premiership on the seventh anniversary of Amir Kabir's dismissal reveals even more fascinating dimensions of the shah's personality. One can speculate that, tormented by the memory of the slain Amir Kabir, the shah's bad conscience caused him to punish the man who was partially responsible for the earlier premier's dismissal, if not for his death. Could it be that he was symbolically eliminating a second fatherly figure with the same intensity and inner grudges with which he had destroyed the first? His assurances to the trembling premier that he was not "frivolous and ignorant" but mature and wise were clearly made with the fate of Amir Kabir in mind.

Yet beneath the shah's expressions of loyalty and Learian engagements with fateful forces that shaped his reign, one can discern a certain Machiavellian cold-bloodedness. Despite the exchange of notes the night before, he received Nuri in the morning with exceptional warmth, and he even laid his hand on the premier's Kashmir cummerbund shawl as a sign of ultimate intimacy, then mounted his horse for the customary ride to Niyavaran. Moreover, the resemblance between his assurances in the above note to Nuri and his last private notes to Amir Kabir are striking. "I swear by God, I swear by God," he wrote to Amir Kabir, "I now write to you with the utmost truth, that I love you passionately, and may the Almighty deprive me of life if I attempt to desert you as long as I live, or if I should wish to lessen your dignity by a hair's breadth. I will treat you and behave to[ward] you in a way that not a single soul shall know what has been the matter."[50]

The revealing expressions in the shah's notes, a strange blend of fatalism and duplicity, were touched up with sarcasm in two remarkable sketches he drew shortly before Nuri's dismissal, serving as a therapeutic release of sentiments, one may assume, for what proved to be one of the most critical decisions of his political life. Playful in their motivation, these caricatures added a convivial dimension to an otherwise grim affair. One could see him sketching them in the privacy of the andarun and sharing them with his beloved Jayran, a fanciful rehearsal for what was to come. If in reality he could not bring himself to remove his premier and his entrenched clan, he could at least symbolically strike back and take courage in his own artistic imagination.

As the shah himself captioned it—oddly enough, some twenty-five years later—one sketch illustrated the prime minister's council (majlis) upon receiving the "good news," and all are "in the state of dancing and joy" (see Fig. 6). One can assume that this is a depiction of Nuri's "countercoup" in June 1858, when the shah delegated full power to him. Nuri, dancing wildly in the center, is watched by a fantastic bird with horselike hoofs, branched tail, and an elongated beak that almost touches the joyous premier and is perhaps a satirical depiction of the "bird of fortune [or state]" (tayir-i dawlat), the symbol of fortuitous political power in Persian literature. Surrounding Nuri are his sons, relatives, and retinue, all carefully identified in captions and in a state of ecstasy. His beloved sons, all four

Figures 6 and 7.   Two caricatures from 1858 by Nasir al-Din Shah depicting
the circumstances of Nuri's dismissal. "Naqqashiha-yi Nasir al-Din Shah,"
Nashriya-yi Vizarat-i Umur-i Kharija, 3, no. 3, pl. 3, 4.

of them, are circumambulating around their father, while another Nuri aide carries an ornamental chair, a subtle hint at Nuri's desire to usurp the royal position. Another figure, Mirza Hashim Aqa Qazi, possibly the chief state judge in Nuri's administration, wearing an enormous turban and with equally enormous buttocks, is graciously walking into the scene. Lying on the floor is yet another assistant with an exaggerated penis, captioned underneath: "Mirza Shafi' who has passed out of euphoria." The whole scene was viewed with a humorous eye, far from the reality of the shah's anxious looks through the window of Niyavaran Palace as observed by Polak.

The second sketch depicted the premier's assembly when, as the shah captioned it, "he has heard the news of his own dismissal (see Fig. 7). He is mournful and depressed together with his subordinates." "I drew it about the time of his premiership," the shah noted. Here Nuri, his sons and aides, separated by a partition line from his minor subordinates and servants, are all in a miserable state, some squatting, others scattered over the floor, others raising their hands in grief. Mirza Hashim Aqa Qazi is in great pain, almost weeping, as are others, at the terrible fate that awaits them. In front of Nuri lies an open scroll, his dismissal warrant. In contrast to the fantastic bird of the first sketch, here a turtle is approaching the prime minister, perhaps a playful symbol of the slowness and inefficiency of Nuri's administration in its last months, for which he was rebuked in the royal decree.[51]

Twenty-five years later, in 1300 Q./1883, the shah still remembered all the personalities. Perhaps even then he took some comfort in the pictorial parody and pondered the event that set in motion a new cycle in his political life. Although Nuri's sons, after years in exile, were readmitted to government service, the shah could only resolve his ambivalence toward their father by sentencing him to a symbolic execution. Nuri's exile for the rest of his life was "worse than death." One may assume that he escaped real execution not only because the shah was no longer "frivolous and ignorant" but because of the international repercussions of Amir Kabir's murder. Yet if the British posthumously repudiated the execution of Amir Kabir, they had sanctioned his dismissal at the time; and they certainly did the same in Nuri's case. The fact that Murray was not willing to support Nuri, let alone give him shelter and protection, no doubt was a decisive factor in the shah's decision to go ahead with the dismissal.

At the time of Nuri's appointment in January 1852, Lord Granville, the British foreign secretary, had given specific instruction to Sheil regarding Nuri's protection. In a lengthy dispatch he had advised Sheil that although

Nuri was compelled by the threat of the shah to renounce British protection, "that renunciation is to be considered by you as precluding you from interfering in behalf of the Ittimad ood-Dawleh [I'timad al-Dawla], in the event of his being seized or exiled, or his property having confiscated." He had further stressed that the British envoy no longer could allow Nuri "to resume his dependence on British protection, if circumstance should render it expedient for him to seek refuge from the persecution of his own government." Sheil had even been warned by his superior that he has "no right to inquire into the motives" of Nuri for the course he had adopted, namely his acceptance of premiership under duress. Yet in the same dispatch Granville had rendered a very significant exception that almost reversed his noninterventionist approach. "Of course if in the vicissitudes which attend official employment in Persia," he added, "the Ittemad ood-Dawla should hereafter incur the displeasure of the Shah, and seek refuge in the premises of the British mission from violence or death, you would be warranted in extending to him under such circumstances, and as long as he remained under the shelter of your roof, the same degree of protection as by long-established and long-recognized custom you have habitually extended to persons seeking an asylum from tyranny and oppression."[52] With the long history of animosity between Murray and Nuri and all that had happened between the fall of Amir Kabir and the Hashim Khan affair, it is hard to believe that the British envoy would have welcomed the fallen premier's refuge in the British mission. Moreover, the shah was anxious not to give the impression that Nuri's life was in any danger. His grounds for dismissing Nuri, the shah wished to relay, were purely political.

Indeed if more reasons than bureaucratic opposition and chaos in the administration were needed to justify Nuri's removal, the shah could always point to his ex-premier's failure in foreign policy. On the day after the premier's fall, when Murray rushed to Niyavaran to "pay respects" to His Majesty, to congratulate him "beyond hearing distance" of all courtiers "upon the emancipation from the thraldom in which not only the royal dignity but the whole country had been so long and so unfortunately held," and to urge the shah and his kingdom into a "new era of prosperity," he found the shah "evidently much gratified." Oblivious of his own anti-British sentiments earlier, Nasir al-Din assured Murray that he was now well aware that "all differences, coldness, and, subsequently, the hostilities which had been aroused between the two countries had been owing to the intrigue and misconduct of the late minister." He further declared "in the most emphatic manner" his desire for friendship with Britain and his "personal regard for the Queen" and avowed plainly that one of the reasons, "if not the chief reason," that had induced him to dismiss Nuri was that he was "the principal obstacle to that cordiality of relations" between the two countries. "Everything disagreeable that may have passed between us," added the shah, was brought about by "evil machinations and intrigues of others." The minister plenipotentiary could not have agreed more, given the deep and dwindling contempt in which he held the ex-minister. He offered his altruistic recommendations for the purge of all pro-Nuri elements from the administration—those who "rendered the shah and his government most unpopular especially in the important cities of Tehran and Tabriz." He further suggested a series of proposals for crucial government reforms, which the shah promised to follow, adding that a "new epoch of friendship and cordiality" had begun.[53]

Murray's delight turned to ecstasy when the next day Dr. Dickson visited Mahd 'Ulya to hear from her the shah's "gratification at the frankness and sincere friendliness" of Murray's advice. But more important than the shah's gratification, it was Mahd 'Ulya's blessing for Murray that indicated her return to the center of the political arena once a united anti-Nuri front in the harem had been formed after the death of Amir Qasim. Again, as in the case of Amir Kabir, the Russian minister, fearful of losing the initiative to his British counterpart for the second time, reacted belatedly but predictably to the news of Nuri's dismissal with a blunt warning to the shah. The premier that the shah had just dismissed for his "acts of extortion, peculation, and mal-administration," declared the Russian memorandum in a painfully plain tone, was a man who not long ago was hailed in the European press for having "full power" conferred upon him and for his devotion in sparing "no exertion in discharge of his duty to his government." Shedding tears at the premier's dismissal, the Russian minister also informed His Majesty that in consideration of the respect due to the holder of a Russian decoration and the friendly attention accorded to Nuri by the tsar, the envoy's "August Master," it was out of his power to cooperate with any measures supportive of Nuri's fall, and thus it was his duty to report them to his government. But Anichkov's warning, accompanied by a similar one from the French minister, was more an angry response to what had happened behind their backs rather than a serious demand for Nuri's restoration. At the most he and the French envoy wanted the shah to guarantee the safety of the ex-premier and his family and to observe "the dictates of prudence." Soon afterward, Murray, in his last correspondence before his departure from Tehran, in veiled language also stressed the security of the dismissed minister.[54] Yet in spite of his professed "astonishment" at Nuri's dismissal, the British minister could hardly hide his delight. One cannot help but wonder whether his departure from Tehran only a month after Nuri's fall was a mere coincidence. Suffering from amoebic dysentery for months, he had been expected to quit Tehran, but no time was ever firmly set before the dismissal.

FATE OF A FALLEN MINISTER

For the shah and Nuri's opponents, the "dictates of prudence" meant something quite different from what the Russians or the French had in mind. Under strict house arrest, Nuri's contact with the outside was completely cut off. He gave written guarantees that he would not interfere, "secretly or openly," in the affairs of the state or correspond with "conspirators," a guarantee deemed necessary because of his foreign and domestic sympathizers. Soon thereafter he was obliged to "present" as gifts some of his personal belongings for the auspicious anniversary of the shah's birthday. His Majesty, with typical largess, asked for a diamond-studded snuff box he had previously given to his minister, but Nuri himself gave him an emerald ring as well, a valuable calligraphed Qur'an, and a Parisian gold coffee set the ex-premier had ordered with great care via Amin al-Mulk at no less critical a time than the height of the war with England. But this goodwill gesture backfired. On the shah's orders, a careful inventory was made of the rest of Nuri's family possessions.

The shah's appetite for the wealth his ex-minister had accumulated over the years must have harshened his treatment. This was perhaps the first instance in which Nasir al-Din attempted to confiscate the personal wealth of a high-ranking official after his dismissal in order to settle the score for arrears and embezzlement. Efforts were made to recover from Nuri huge sums of six to seven *kurur* tumans, equivalent to £ 1.5 million sterling, which he had allegedly misappropriated during his term. By all accounts the intimidation techniques employed by the royal agents bore good results. Two hundred and twenty thousand tumans (equivalent to £ 100,000 at the current rate of 2.2 tumans per pound) were recovered from Nuri. The sum total was possibly reimbursed to the shah's private purse to replenish his war expenditures. An even larger penalty was fixed on the Nuri clan to the tune of 390,000 tumans (£ 170,000). Furthermore, all their land and property were confiscated, only to be partially returned to them after Nuri's death. The kitchen utensils of his household, the only items left over from the royal plunder, were thrown into the street.[55]

Once the customary humiliations were exercised upon the fallen minister and the full extent of his monetary value was extracted from him, it remained for the shah to decide what to do with Nuri himself. It was only to be expected that he would be sent away to a location inaccessible to his potential allies. Together with his entire family he was thrown out of his Nizamiya mansion, first to his estate in Adiran in the vicinity of the capital, and therefrom to Sultanabad, Kirman, and finally Yazd, where he spent five years in agony and isolation before being transferred to Isfahan.

Nuri's downfall put an end to a quarter-century of ministerial power, starting with Qa'im Maqam in 1834 and continuing under Aqasi and Amir Kabir. A succession of powerful premiers since Qa'im Maqam helped strengthen the hand of the central government. During this period internecine revolts, such as the Davalus', were brought to an end, tribal warlords and provincial potentates were reduced, pretenders to the throne were crushed or exiled, the power of the clergy was reduced, and popular movements were brought to an end. In spite of their shortcomings, the central government under these powerful ministers had succeeded in enforcing greater direct control over the "Guarded Domains" than the princely states of Fath 'Ali Shah's era had been able to do. Yet, even as late as 1858, the nature of ministerial authority, and its enduring symbolic dependence upon the sovereign, had not essentially changed since the outset of the Qajar state a half-century earlier. Nor was it much different from the old model of vizierate delineated in the Perso-Islamic manuals of government and manifested in the careers of famous ministers. An institution as old and as essential to the Perso-Islamic system of government as kingship itself, the vizierate represented not only an organic interdependence with kingship but an almost unavoidable tension with it as well. Small wonder that in the course of Persian history a larger number of ministers were executed or disgraced by order of their royal masters than lived in dignified retirement or died a natural death.

Even up to Nasir al-Din's time the minister's political survival, his very life and security, was still held ransom to his ability to maintain control over an unpredictable, at times cruel, master and keep him amused in the isolated world of women, hunting, weapons, gadgets, artistic impulses, and the palace private quarters. Nuri's attempt to control the government by reducing the shah's executive power, even though it was a less efficient and less ethical method than that of Amir Kabir, was in essence not much different. Nuri lacked Amir Kabir's vision and his commitment to reform. Nor was he anxious to awaken the shah to the full responsibility of government. But like Amir Kabir he tried to restrict monarchical intrusions in the affairs of state. Although Nuri had a somewhat better hold over the shah and, like Aqasi, was capable of playing on his personal sentiments and fears, at the same time he was more servile to the shah's capricious and self-centered wishes. He had a more independent constituency than Amir Kabir, based not entirely on the shah's favor but also on family loyalty and for a while on British support.

What ultimately brought him down, however, was not only his loosening grip over a politically maturing shah with a distinct drive for independence; there were other domestic and foreign concerns working toward his overthrow. If Amir Kabir alienated the bureaucracy, the court, and the harem by monopolizing access to the shah or by his austerity measures, Nuri managed to do so, albeit over a longer duration, through clan nepotism, palace intrigue, accumulation of enormous wealth, and excessive diplomatic acrobatics. Though he began his political ascendancy with the blessing of the British, he was ultimately forced to distance himself from them as Amir Kabir, Aqasi, and Qa'im Maqam had done before him. In attempts to safeguard the state, the monarchy, and their own credibility and political standing, all the premiers were obliged to balance off the demands of the rival Russian and British diplomatic camps on critical issues concerning the viability of the Persian state, issues to which all reacted almost identically. As on previous occasions, the lessening of British support for Nuri brought about a closer coordination between the opposing elements in the Qajar polity, which were desperate to secure foreign blessing against their common enemy. But recurring conspiracies by the premier's opponents helped reinforce even greater ministerial autocracy over the affairs of the government and eroded the very foundation of the shah's trust for his premier. Once the ministerial monopoly went beyond the accepted limits, the gathering strength of the opposition camp encouraged the monarch to shift his favor away from his fatherly minister toward the opposition, fearing that by remaining loyal to the minister he might jeopardize his own throne. Save for a muted affirmative signal from the British envoy, no catalyst could have precipitated the royal reorientation more effectively than the wild gazelle of the andarun.

Whether through Qa'im Maqam's and Amir Kabir's firm approaches or Aqasi's and Nuri's latitude, the ministers failed to eradicate sovereign autocratic intervention and rescue the state from the yoke of a capricious monarchy that was willing neither to part with executive power nor to shoulder the full burden of its weight. Not only did the person holding the ministerial position remain vulnerable to the shah's whim, his vested interests, and his opportunism, but the parameters of ministerial authority remained poorly defined and often indistinguishable from the shah's. In spite of his manipulative designs and nepotism and in spite of his dishonorable involvement in the fall of Amir Kabir, Nuri should be seen as a remarkable statesman who, like his predecessors, was in search of ministerial independence. He was a capable tactician and dogged negotiator, a patron with a sense for political talent, and a man with an extraordinary capacity to convince by charm, humor, deception, and rapport. Yet at no time during his term of office did he make an effort to establish a viable division of labor within his own administration, let alone a division of authority with the monarch. In spite of his distinct position in the Qajar political arena, Nuri is often undeservedly condemned by modern "hell-fire" historians to the abyss of treachery and treason. In that respect his career resembles that of his predecessor in office some half a century earlier, Hajji Ibrahim Khan Kalantar Shirazi, the first I'timad al-Dawla, to whose method of government Nuri looked with admiration.

Nuri did not lose his sight or his life, but his fate in exile was no less painful than Hajji Ibrahim's. When he indirectly addressed the shah in a letter to one of his confidants in 1863, after five years of confinement and disgrace in front of some sixty people of his household and his numerous young sons and daughters, he was "fed up" with his life.

> I have neither a Shahsavan tribe nor an Afshar, nor am I a tribal chief [*ilkhani*] with a hundred thousand men at my disposal. I was a humble man. My pride was in hereditary service. When commanded to be, I was. When ordered to die, I died. Who am I to require imprisonment? Besides, five years of confinement is unheard of in any era. If you are a butcher, kill me; if a [slave] merchant, sell me; and if a king, forgive me and let me return to my niche and settle my debts and pay attention to the affairs of my son and daughter.[56]

Complaints such as the above, and intercessions by remnants of Nuri's allies, only brought him from Yazd to Isfahan in 1863 and, later, to Qum, in the vicinity of Tehran, but they were not effective enough to reverse the shah's initial verdict. For years after his downfall, even though dramatic changes had occurred in the organization of the government, Nuri's reinstatement was still an option for a possible revival of ministerial office. But the shah was unwilling to revive the old-fashioned sidarat, an institution he had taken much trouble to abolish. He rightly recognized Nuri's inability to fit into the new system, in which the shah held the executive power. "Mirza Aqa Khan [Nuri's] options are limited to two," the shah reportedly said. "Either he should wear the pearl-edged robe of sidarat or die in his present condition." Citing the shah's words in a letter, with reference to the ministerial robe, Nuri retorted: "I wish from the outset that it would have become my shroud."[57]

9 Balancing the Old and the New

Ten years into his reign Nasir al-Din Shah was finally beginning to emerge as a ruler much more formidable than the impulsive boy-king with a flair for women and hunting. Leaving aside his many weaknesses, he was confident enough to contemplate direct monarchical rule as an alternative to the ministerial system. But, ironically, his perception of direct rule was indebted as much to the institution of the vizierate as it was to the tradition of monarchical absolutism. From Nuri he had learned "the art of the possible," the politics of expediency as it had been played out for centuries on the Persian scene by means of negotiation, intrigue, coercion, and factional loyalty and disloyalty. From Amir Kabir he had learned the importance of a centralized state with a strong military to quell peripheral dissent and preserve the country's territorial integrity. The shah became even more conscious of this dual legacy in the 1860s, when he encountered a new phase of the Great Game, the Anglo-Russian competition for supremacy over Central Asia. The frailties and squabbles within his own domestic institutions also drew upon his skills as an administrator. After much persuasion, he began hesitantly to appreciate not only the advantages of a European-style government machinery but the very need for it. Direct rule, he was led to believe, was the only way safely to incorporate new ideas and institutions. Although Amir Kabir was unsuccessful in convincing the shah of the vitality of his own ill-fated reforms as he was of his political sincerity, some vague memory of his perceived order (*nazm*) had survived in the shah's mind and resurfaced in later times. As also happened in the Ottoman Empire, for the Persian shah and his advisers the very term *tanzim* (to put into order) came to represent the entire modernization process and the European outlook that accompanied it.

HOLDING THE REINS OF POWER

Even before Nuri's fall the shah had begun to toy with the idea of Western-style reforms. The military confrontation and defeat in the war with Britain sufficiently aroused in the shah a consciousness of the need for change. As early as 1856 he sought advice from Napoleon III (1852–1870), his most obvious model for enlightened absolutism. Napoleon advised the shah to maintain a balance between modernity and tradition. The French emperor, who viewed himself as "Iran's most disinterested friend," recommended to Farrukh Khan Amin al-Mulk that the government of Iran "preserve firmly its own customs and traditions and unlike the Ottomans not become an imitator of Europe." By abandoning their national dress in favor of European fashions, he cautioned the shah, the Ottomans "not only were demeaned in the eyes of their own people but lost prestige in Europe."[1]

Napoleon believed the path to "civilisation" was not contrary to preservation of the past heritage. In a letter to the shah written in his own hand, he outlined his vision of a progressive yet traditional Iran. In dealing with the expansionist neighboring powers, he advised, the shah should adopt a conciliatory but nonaligned course, one that would guarantee Iran's independence and would be backed by its military strength. On domestic policy his thoughts reflected the populism of the Second Empire—the need to "capture the spirit" and "patronize the interests" of all classes as the key to sound government founded on a strong military, thorough administrative, fiscal, and judicial systems, and religion.

If Napoleon's secular counsel was based on his own experience of defining authoritarian government before the liberalization of 1860, his image of accommodating Islam was probably a projection of his largely unsuccessful effort at the close of the Crimean War to bring the Sunni Ottoman Empire into the French sphere of influence. (In Algeria, too, his attempt to reconcile French colonial objectives with the indigenous Islamic resistance was frustrated.) He was thus persuaded to view Shi'ite Iran as "the refuge of true Islam." By contrast, the emperor saw the neighboring Ottoman Empire as "shaken" by the Tanzimat concessions to the Christian minorities. He urged Nasir al-Din that by preserving Persian traditions he could "prove to the world that Islam is not against the progress of civilization." Under the aegis of a benevolent monarch, and by undertaking material reforms in communications and in the army, Iran could become the best country in the East and the focal point of all pilgrims to Mecca.[2]

French imperial interests were not altogether neglected in the emperor's promotion of Shi'ite Iran. For one thing, the Ottomans, the leaders of the

Sunni world, declined to lift Turkish suzerainty over North Africa and hence facilitate total French domination over Algeria and neighboring lands. Moreover, Napoleon saw the weakening of the Ottomans as a gain for France against Great Britain, its traditional rival in the eastern Mediterranean. He advised the shah to look favorably on the British proposal for constructing a railway from the Levant to the head of the Persian Gulf, a section of which was to cross Persian territory. He assured Nasir al-Din that he, too, would have a share of the Ottoman territory. Once the sick man of Europe collapsed and died, Iran could dominate Iraq, control the British lifeline to the Persian Gulf, and hence gain an enormous advantage on the western frontier. Fanciful as it sounded, such a proposal was in harmony with Napoleon III's simultaneous, but confidential, proposal to Iran to contemplate capturing Ottoman Iraq as compensation for the loss of Herat. To achieve it, the emperor recommended, a combination of regular and irregular forces, similar to the army created by the French in North Africa, should be created. After the Herat experience, Nasir al-Din was careful not to take the emperor's expansionist dreams seriously, though he must have been impressed by Napoleon's concern for a strong army, for balancing tradition and change, and for preserving Islam—themes that would remain essential throughout his rule. In response to Napoleon's advice, the shah asked him "not to forget the proud and united" Persian nation or the shah's "friendship and fraternity."[3]

Yet Europe of the late 1850s also had other models for the shah's nascent propensity for direct rule. The initiative of the modernizing tsar Alexander II (1855–1881) to abolish serfdom was eventually carried through in 1861 in spite of resistance from the Russian landed aristocracy. Other reform measures in Russia, constitutional, educational, and religious, may have further caught the shah's attention. Beyond Russia, toward the west, the accession of Wilhelm I of Prussia (1861–1888) initiated, under Prince Bismarck, a new era of authoritarianism in the guise of a parliamentary system that was a prelude to the unification of Germany. Closer to home, in the Ottoman Empire, there were more applicable examples of reformed monarchy for the shah's exploring mind. Widespread reforms under Mahmud II (1808–1839) and then 'Abd-al Majid I (1839–1861) during the first phase of the Tanzimat (1838–1856) were no doubt in Nasir al-Din's mind when he introduced his new institutional initiatives. Moreover, the 1856 Imperial Rescript (*khatt-i humayun*) opened a new era with far-reaching consequences for Ottoman society and the state. Judging by his political outlook, Nasir al-Din may not have been impressed with 'Abd al-Majid's somewhat hands-off approach to government, nor by the relative constancy with which the "Men of the Tanzimat" presided over their administrative, legal, and military reforms. But the spirit of reforms and their feasibility in a Muslim society comparable to his own undoubtedly left an impression on the shah.

Even more important from a diplomatic viewpoint, it was perhaps the change of government in Britain that provided the real impetus for reform. The collapse of Palmerston's government in February 1858, which kept in power a coalition of the Tories and their conservative allies for more than a year, ended a phase of imperial assertiveness in favor of a more cautious course under Malmesbury as the new foreign minister. Though a thorough suppression of the Indian revolt by December 1858 removed all hope of a restoration of the Mughal Empire in India, the transition of the Indian government from the East India Company to the British crown promised a more tolerable approach, less exploitative and more committed to good relations with India's neighboring countries. A reflection of change in London appeared in Murray's interview with the shah in August 1858, just after Nuri's fall and before the envoy's own departure. This was a shift in Britain's long-standing contentment with the status quo in Iran, in contrast to its support for reforms in the Ottoman Empire. Murray's conversion to the cause of Persian reform prompted him to recommend to the shah not to entrust "uncontrolled and unlimited power over all departments of the state to one individual" and to avoid "submitting himself and the royal prerogative to similar inconvenience by delegating to any other hand whatsoever the vast and uncontrolled charges held by the late Sadr A'zam." He pointed out that the kingdoms of Europe, whether great or small, "formed and recognized a cabinet, a council, or in short a ministry of some kind composed of a certain number of persons who, although one of them was acknowledged chief, were all responsible to the sovereign." No matter how "humble, faithful and devoted might be the language and the bearing" of the candidates for premiership, Murray asserted, it was only consistent with human nature that once a minister attained the same height of uncontrolled power, he would subject the shah to the same "inconveniences" as Nuri had. To prevent such a recurrence, Murray specifically urged the shah to hold the "reins in his own hand." Although Murray thought it fitting that a sadr a'zam should be named, he believed the shah should appoint ministers separately responsible for the "Home Office, another for Foreign Office, a third for Finance, and a Fourth for War," together with any others the shah might think fit to entrust to a separate administration.

The shah's positive response to these recommendations was not a mere formality. "The king smiled and said that my advice was very prudent, and that it was his full determination to follow it," reported Murray. The shah was adamant that no minister of his, even were he so inclined, should have the power to estrange him from Britain, "the ancient ally of his dynasty." Such assurances, the shah insisted, were not "matters of mere form and ceremony."[4]

The shah's conversion to the idea of ministerial responsibility and the division of labor under his direct supervision was a turning point in his reign. Subsequently—at least, for the next thirty-five years, up to the appointment of 'Ali Asghar Khan Amin al-Sultan to the sidarat in 1886— with very few exceptions (most notably Husayn Khan Mushir al-Dawla's premiership between 1871 and 1873), the shah kept his promise to hold "the reins in his own hand." The way he understood Murray's suggestion did not lead either to a constitutional or representative model of government nor even to the opening of new sociopolitical horizons, as had happened in the Ottoman Empire; rather, it only facilitated an arbitrary rule under the shah devoid of the traditional intermediary function of the premier. In spite of numerous shifts in the government in the following years and confusion caused by the shah's erratic conduct, this feature remained more or less unperturbed for the rest of the Nasiri period.

The royal decree, issued immediately after the interview with Murray and published in the 3 September issue of *Vaqayi'-i Ittifaqiya*, declared the royal wishes to "promote the mores of monarchy" (*a'in-i saltanat*) by dividing up the responsibilities of the government among ministries of the interior, foreign affairs, war, finance, justice, and pensions. Acknowledging the problems of concentrating "all important affairs" in the hands of one person, the decree then designated six independent ministers with specially defined duties who would be directly answerable to the shah. They were loosely organized in a cabinet-like body called the Council of the State (*shawra-yi dawlat*), which would meet only in contingencies to deliberate (*shawr*) on affairs of government. But, declared the royal decree, neither the ministers nor the council could enforce their decisions without royal approval. The next issue of the *Vaqayi'-i Ittifaqiya* emphatically stressed the royal decision to "abolish the office of sidarat and its requisites."[5]

The shah's first reformist initiative thus aimed to reconcile the European model of government with domestic constraints. At the outset, the shah's choice of conservative figures such as the formidable Yusuf Khan Mustawfi al-Mamalik, the accountant general (who had returned from exile) as finance minister, Sa'id Khan Mu'taman al-Mulk as minister of foreign affairs, Sadiq Khan Qa'im Maqam Nuri as minister of the interior (who would oversee the others and to whom the shah addressed his speech during the salam), and Muhammad Khan Qajar, the chief of the royal guards, as war minister (with the new title of *sipahsalar*, commander of the army) reflected the shah's concern with striking a balance within the administration rather than appointing men with progressive outlooks. The first priority for him, and for his ministers as well, was to block the rise of another overarching sadr a'zam, a fact further stressed by the dismissal of Sadiq Khan Nuri and his subsequent disappearance altogether from the political scene once it became clear to the shah that this nephew of Mirza Aqa Khan Nuri may have conspired with the exiled ex-premier to facilitate his return to power.

In addition to the Council of the State, the shah also introduced another advisory body, the Assembly of the House of Consultation (*majlis-i maslahat-khana*) or, for short, the Consultative Council. Headed by an elderly statesman, Mirza Ja'far Khan Mushir al-Dawla, the English-educated diplomat and statesman (who no doubt was chosen because of his familiarity with the British parliamentary system), this council was the closest thing to a legislative body that the shah created at the outset of this ephemeral reform period. It was mandated to deliberate on all domestic issues that were "expedient to the state and promote development of the country." For the first time since the ill-fated 1848 Council of the People (*majlis-i jumhuri*), the idea of consulting and representing the "nation" had resurfaced. All "sages of the nation" (*'uqala-yi millat*) were invited to present their worthwhile ideas to the twenty-five-member assembly of "experienced" notables and civil servants, though the council was prohibited, without royal permission, from discussing "political affairs" (*umur-i pulitikiya*), a synonym for foreign affairs in the parlance of the Qajar era. Not only could the council hear from members of the public and deliberate on matters related to the "growth of trade" and "agricultural development," this council was also empowered with "legislating estimable laws" (*vaz'-i qawanin mamduha*) to lift undesirable customs, disseminate sciences, establish industries, construct channels and streams, plant gardens, explore mines, build roads, increase revenue, reduce expenditure, promote means of justice and equity, remove causes of oppression and coercion, encourage the growth of the population and improve sanitation." Even more remarkable, a majority vote was to determine the Consultative Council's decisions, which later were to be presented to the shah for approval and implemented by the State Council.[6]

The shah's accompanying rescript expressed his "virtuous intention" to "preserve and accomplish" the implementation of this lofty institution and appealed to the "innate honor and inherent integrity of the nation" to follow the shah's "revered example" and avoid any ills caused by the "ignorance and incompetence of predecessors," ills that in "the eyes of the wise ['uqala] would entail no benefit but to generate trouble and encroach upon affairs of this world and the next." The royal rescript, no doubt inspired by Ja'far Khan's program, hoped the Consultative Council would "undertake measures that are desirable to the possessors of reason, would facilitate the prescribed duties, and rectify [islah] the affairs of all the people."[7] A spectrum of notables, ranging from conservative Qajar nobles to ranking bureaucrats and officers to diplomats with European experience to men of letters with reformist tendencies, were appointed to the Consultative Council. However, the distinct absence of two groups, the Qajar princes and members of the 'ulama class (except for Hajji Mahmud Mulla-bashi, the shah's ex-tutor), reflected a desire to keep the Council a secular institution free of princely or clerical privileges. The resemblance to the French Estates-General, the British House of Lords, and the Ottoman Majlis-i Tanzimat was not accidental.[8]

Nasir al-Din's concept of reform was no doubt influenced by a burgeoning reformist debate taking place during this period and advocated by a handful of European-educated statesmen and diplomats in the Persian service. It is difficult to identify any one individual as the architect of the new arrangement. The shah, no doubt, valued the counsel of Ja'far Khan, who, though old, was viewed as a capable and trusted statesman. His advocacy of reform was echoed by Farrukh Khan Amin al-Mulk, who, after his hasty return from Istanbul in late 1858, was now promoted to the position of court minister and soon after to interior minister with a new title, Amin al-Dawla. Other critics of the old system, with no direct European exposure, were also instrumental. But of all the early advisers, perhaps the greatest modernizing influence on the shah came from Malkum Khan. After returning from his European mission in July 1858, he had managed to reestablish his rapport with the shah. In his capacity as adviser behind the scenes, he also tried to nurture the shah's pristine concept of reform, either by means of his political writings or by organizing a political body that could press the need for change.

The shah's enthusiasm for implementing the new measures may also have been precipitated by new developments in the harem. Jayran's death in January 1860 after a long illness (possibly tuberculosis, which had first surfaced in April 1859) had a profound and yet liberating effect on the shah.

It engendered a deep sense of loss, coming so soon after the death of his favorite son, Amir Qasim. In spite of these emotional blows, the shah maintained a peculiarly detached facade. As soon as the "consumptive symptoms" of Jayran's illness first showed themselves, wrote the new British envoy to Tehran, Henry Rawlinson, she lost "her hold upon the affection of her royal husband." Though aware of his ex-favorite's impending death, the shah set out on a long hunting excursion and was absent from the capital during Jayran's burial and mourning period (see Pl. 14).[9] Once again, Mahd 'Ulya emerged as the chief of the harem and the most influential person in the shah's private life. Her ascendancy, however, did not acquire explicit political expression. The shah seemed to have succeeded in severing the most obvious links between the harem and the outside world, hence preventing alliances from being forged between the harem and high-ranking officials of his government. Mahd 'Ulya continued to exert influence by proxy, but she could never again muster the same emotional hold over the shah as before. With the shadow of a fatherly premier removed from the shah's life, he seemed better able to resist the demands of the harem.

IN THE HOUSE OF OBLIVION

Malkum Khan's early political writings were designed to impress on the shah the need for constitutional reforms. They were rough drafts for a political program meant to strengthen the shah's hand, increase the efficiency of his government, improve the material state of the country, and make Malkum himself the mastermind of the new order. His French education and exposure to the eighteenth-century Enlightenment (and in particular Montesquieu) set the framework for this program, whereas the ongoing Tanzimat in the Ottoman Empire provided the setting and terminology. The shah was not unfamiliar with Western political institutions, nor was he a stranger to the values and principles on which they were built. But Malkum's significance lay in his astute presentation of Western ideas and institutions in the familiar context of Iran and in contrast to the realities of the Iranian state and the society.

His *Kitabcha-yi Ghaybi* (literally, "the manual from the invisible"), subtitled *Daftar-i Tanzimat* ("the book of restructuring"), written in 1858 and reputedly the first proposal for state modernization, stopped well short of advocating a political order with democratic foundations. Nevertheless, in this work and in three supplements he wrote shortly afterwards, Malkum advocated for the first time the rule of law (*qanun*) as the social contract that would hold the shah and his people responsible to each other. Condemning the traditional arbitrary rule of the sovereign, he encouraged the shah to withstand the growing tide of conservative opposition by implementing what he defined as "constitutional absolutism." With his words wrapped safely in the language of a fantasy dream narrated anonymously (hence the name), Malkum called directly upon the shah to reorganize the government, legislate laws for the security and welfare of his subjects, and eradicate the entrenched conservatism of the Qajar polity without losing his own predominance and privileges. Such reforms, Malkum promised, would effectively increase the power of the shah in his position as the supreme head of the legislative and executive branches of the government.[10]

In Malkum's view, the preconditions for royal reforms were highly encouraging. He could see neither resistance similar to that of the Ottoman Janissaries against Mahmud II nor hostility such as that of Europe's ancien régime employed against Bonaparte. With an "insightful," "competent," and "persevering" monarch and with internal tranquility, foreign security, loyal 'ulama, and a nation of king-adulators (*shah-parast*), he perceived all the means of reform to be present. Nasir al-Din's reformist intentions, which he considered "amazing" and "worthy of much congratulation," were, in Malkum's eyes, so promising as to qualify him as Iran's Peter the Great.

The image set forth by Malkum put all the blame on the shoulders of ignorant and obscurantist statesmen whose self-interests and ambitions were against the shah's lofty initiatives. They had caused Iran's defeat in the war, precipitated famine and popular malcontent, fostered corruption and tyranny, and remained entirely alien to Western material and political advances. Defects at the ministerial level provided Malkum with his prime reason to argue in favor of "monarchical absolutism [*saltanat-i mutlaqa*] similar to [that of] the Russian, Austrian, and Ottoman Empires." He judged the "constitutional monarchy" (*saltanat-i mu'tadila*) of Britain and France untimely and impractical, but the absolutism—the "autocratic monarchy" (*saltanat-i mustaqilla*), as Nasir al-Din's rule came to be known—he proposed was nevertheless "orderly" (*munazzam*) and sought to rationalize the machinery of the state. "The authority to legislate and execute laws are both the monarch's prerogatives," declared Malkum in article five, part one, of his proposed program, but he made it clear that "the royal will" should "guarantee the public welfare" and entitle all subjects to equal rights before the law. He defined the law, for the first time in Persian reformist literature, as "every ordinance that emanates from the government for the welfare of the entire nation, and its equal obedience would therefore become necessary by all." Success in implementing an extensive program of 180 articles, as Malkum proposed, depended on the shah's ability to create a powerful state, check ministerial opposition, and suppress the conservative backlash. The shah could only defeat the opposition, he advised Nasir al-Din in a manner reminiscent of traditional Persian manuals of government, if he dismissed in succession several ministers, so that for every minister in office there would be even more ministers out of office, a device he hoped would constantly remind officeholders that unless they abided fully by the reform program, they would be immediately replaced.[11]

Malkum was equally mindful of the need for reforms as a way to cope with the growing danger of European domination. The major fault with Nuri's premiership, Malkum warned the shah, was that he had considered the Fath 'Ali Shah era the standard of statesmanship and was not aware that in the 30 years since Fath 'Ali Shah's death in 1834 the world had changed the equivalent of 500 years.

> Put the map of Asia in front of yourself and read the history of the past one hundred years and examine carefully the course of the two bursting deluges that were propelled in the direction of Iran from Calcutta [the first administrative capital of British India] and St. Petersburg and see how these two streams which in the beginning were not noticeable in a short time became so great. . . . Then after examination you can lift yourself up from popular beliefs and see from the height the speed of the two deluges that from one side reached Tabriz and Astarabad and from the other side entered Herat and Sistan. Then you can tell how many minutes remain of the life of this state.

The grim picture depicted by Malkum must have been particularly alarming to Nasir al-Din, who was acquainted with both the geography and history of European expansion. Alluding to the blatant complacency of the old-fashioned statesmen who had begun to take over the government, Malkum mocked their knowledge of "Arabic verses" and their pride in "hereditary bones." Of what effect could they be, he asked, against the designs of a few English merchants (i.e., the Board of Directors of the East India Company), who sit in their homes and run a country (i.e., India) ten times the size of the land of Anushiravan (i.e., Khusraw I, the Sasanian ruler of Iran [531–579]) from 5,000 *farsakhs* [20,000 miles] away? What could they do against those who 3,000 *farsakhs* [12,000 miles] away from Iran could build a floating "steel fortress" and destroy the port of Muhammara in two hours? The "knowledge" (*'ilm*), which Malkum regarded as complementary to wisdom (*'aql*), necessary for maintaining a modern government against the ills of domestic ignorance and imperial appetite was, he believed, completely lacking among the old school. "Nowadays wisdom is not entirely sufficient for the vizierate. Mirza Aqa Khan [Nuri] was no doubt wiser than most European premiers, but if at any time he was replaced by a minor secretary of any of the European ministries the latter could have discharged his duties a thousand times better."

Malkum placed great hopes in the shah's enthusiasm for knowledge in order to avoid the pitfall of which Nuri had been a victim. In an imaginary dialogue, he had a pro-reform "friend" telling an old-fashioned and cynical "minister": "You have not yet comprehended the shah. He has a certain bent to his character that makes you gullible. It is the shah's habit to behave as though he believes whatever [advice] he was given. You believe you can deceive him, but you ignore the fact that for seven years he deceived someone like Mirza Aqa Khan [Nuri]. As European philosophers say: 'Which one is more canny, the one who deceives or the one who pretends to be deceived?'" Malkum's psychological breakdown of the shah's political behavior was intended to bring home to the class of officialdom the futility of their intransigence. He called upon them to learn their lesson from Nuri's fall and accept the inevitability of royal reforms. "Even if the shah decides to reject the reforms, the Western-style changes will be implemented in Iran. Yet the shah is no doubt committed to the [new] order and the more he knows about the reforms of the foreign states the more he will crave."

Not only the content but also the style and presentation of Malkum's treatises were novel for their time. His dream-like vision in the "manual from the invisible" and the allegorical dialogue were vehicles by which to convey open criticism of the conservative outlook and norms. He skillfully employed the old genre from Persian literature of fantasy dreams (*khwab-nama*) to voice otherwise prohibited criticism (an ingenious device that has caused some myopic modern writers to accuse him of charlatanism). The element of the unreal throughout his writings of this period, almost approaching the level of mystery, was indeed deliberate, not only to protect him against charges of sedition and disbelief but also to allow the pro-reform elements, including the shah himself, to identify with his views and adhere to them without fear of retaliation.

The same spirit of secrecy also dominated Malkum's semiclandestine society, which he and his father, Mirza Ya'qub Khan, the secretary of the Russian legation in Tehran, organized to advance similar objectives shortly after the publication of *Kitabcha-yi Ghaybi*. Named Faramush-khana (literally, "the house of oblivion"), the society was meant to transmit a sense of mystery and magic, to serve as an invisible source of "knowledge" and to acquaint "initiates" with the "secrets of progress." In reality Faramush-khana was a political club with a semisecret membership striving to broaden its popular base by advocating a message of liberal secularism embellished with quasi-masonic rites and loyalties. The "oblivion" in the title probably implied a shedding of social, religious, and hereditary loyalties. The followers were to ignore whatever status the initiates maintained on the outside and strike a new bond of loyalty within to further the cause of progress and the rule of law. Malkum had probably been acquainted with European secret societies since his time in Paris during the volatile years leading to the revolution of 1848, in which such societies played a crucial role. On a more recent visit to France in 1857 he was even initiated into a masonic lodge. Even the name *faramush-khana*, as Gobineau pointed out, was a mimic rendering of the French *francmaconnerie* and, presumably, had been in use in Iran even before Malkum. But Malkum did not seem to have any authorization from the Grand Orient, the lodge to which he was attached, nor any other lodge to establish a masonic organization in Iran.

One cannot overlook the importance of the long tradition of Persian esoterism (*batiniya*) in Malkum's conception of his Faramush-khana nor in its attraction for the initiates. The acceptance of free thought inherent in this tradition made Malkum's Faramush-khana a viable forum within which to exhibit cultural skepticism. Malkum's own heterogeneous background and upbringing, particularly his conversion to Islam as an adult, no doubt greatly enhanced his fascination with the idea of an all-embracing creed similar to that of the masonic brotherhood, one that could bring about national assimilation and a universal political objective beyond the pale of religion and hereditary privileges.

The aura of mystery that surrounded the society soon attracted a small group of initiates from among the Persian literati and fringe statesmen. Jalal al-Din Mirza, perhaps Iran's first nationalist historian in the modern sense and an enlightened Qajar prince (son of Fath 'Ali Shah) with a fascination for Zoroastrianism and pre-Islamic Iran, served as host to the society's meetings and was identified as its head. Malkum's "confession" years later in London to Wilfred Blunt that he had mobilized 30,000 adherents for the Faramush-khana should be safely dismissed as an exaggeration or, at best, merely a reference to the potential membership. Yet he did manage to attract many of the students of Dar al-Funun, some literary and intellectual figures, probably a few students of philosophy (such as the renowned Sadra'ian philosophers of his time, Mirza Abul-Hasan Jilva and Mirza Ja'far Hakim Ilahi) and a few mujtahids (including

Shaykh Hadi Najmabadi, a revisionist with liberal Babi leanings). The report from the French envoy, Blonnet, that "the house of oblivion" attracted all honorable people in the country from among the civilian and religious classes corroborates closely with the figure of 500 initiates in Tehran given by another source. Even the membership of Sayyid Muhammad Sadiq Tabataba'i, a mujtahid from a prominent clerical family, and Sayyid Zayn al-'Abidin, the Imam Jum'a of Tehran and a member of the influential Khatunabadi family of Isfahan, do not seem implausible. We have no record, however, of their having pro-reform views either before or after Faramush-khana. Toward the end of its short life, the society may also have attracted membership from among "commoners," including merchants, guildsmen, and others.[12]

The shah could not have remained uninterested in Faramush-khana. Malkum's later assertion to Husayn Khan Mushir al-Dawla in 1862, then the Persian ambassador at the Sublime Porte, that he had established Faramush-khana on explicit instructions from the shah and submitted to him a daily report of his activities, may not be dismissed altogether as boastful imagination. Malkum made this remark in exile, probably while awaiting for the shah to exonerate him. When Husayn Khan relayed this claim to Tehran, the shah stated through his minister of foreign affairs that he did not regard Malkum guilty of any offense and that he would not overlook the services he had rendered. This implicit admission on the part of the shah only confirmed the view of the new British envoy, Charles Alison, who in his report of November 1861 regarded the establishment of "Freemasonry," as he put it, an initiative that had received royal sanction.[13] According to Ibrahim Badayi'-Nigar, Malkum had managed to captivate the royal imagination with "the brilliance of his intelligence and shrewdness," an impression no doubt reinforced by the latter's display of modern scientific experimentation and magical illusions.[14] Gobineau's citation of Malkum's warning to Nasir al-Din that "the shah no longer in this age could content himself to reign like his predecessors by relying on the two elements of domination and force" captures the spirit of his aforementioned warnings in his *Kitabcha*. Malkum must have encouraged the shah to sanction his masonic society so that he would be able, as Gobineau has pointed out, to put into practice what he had advocated in the "manual from the invisible":

> It is desirable that he [the shah] preserve a moral guarantee through the loyalty of his subjects. By establishing in Tehran a lodge to which he would be the grand master [*grand maitre*], he will have the advantage of securing the loyalty of everybody . . . because such a masonic pledge will

never be broken, and provided that he ensures that all people of consequence enroll, by this device he would find himself at the top of all the
forces of his nation and as such no one would ever have the power to
dispossess him of it.[15]

Gobineau further stated that the shah "looked with interest upon this
overture and showed himself sensitive to the brilliant perspective that was
promised to him." What Malkum offered, it appeared, was to create a
popular base of support for the shah's throne to complement his domination by the sword. The national loyalty Malkum sought to forge among
the notables by means of a masonic-like pledge promised to withstand not
only the foreign powers but also the conservative challenge within the
shah's own government. At least six members of the Consultative Council
were alleged initiates of Faramush-khana. Moreover, a number of the
shah's appointees to the Consultative Council corroborated with Malkum's
list of twenty-four candidates, who he proposed would sit on a "council of
reforms" (majlis-i tanzimat), as elaborated in his treatise Tanzim-i Lashkar va Majlis-i Idara ("Reform of the army and the administrative council"). The above treatise was produced in response to a royal request for a
comprehensive reform program and apparently was transmitted through
Farrukh Khan Amin al-Dawla.[16]

Malkum's concept of enlightened absolutism was fashioned out of Pet-
rine and Napoleonic models of "benevolent despotism." Even though the
concept may be viewed as a contradiction in terms, most European monarchies of the mid-nineteenth century, particularly after the failure of the
1848 revolutions, were variations on the same theme. It was thus expected
that the shah would conveniently resort to the same pattern of monarchical
authority to legitimize his direct rule. But Malkum's objectives, particularly his advocacy of the rule of law, in theory went beyond rendering
legitimacy and support to a despot with a sanguine notion of reform. The
charges made against Malkum—that he was conspiring in his "house of
oblivion" to establish a republic (jumhuri)—though perhaps exaggerated
in their claim that he was fostering subversion, were true in that he called
for a constitutional government, possibly even with popular representation, in what would amount to the conversion of the royal subjects into a
political society far better defined than anything Malkum had explicated in
the Kitabcha-yi Ghaybi and other works.

AN HONEST GOODWILL MISSION

In spite of his early enthusiasm, the shah's commitment to administrative
reforms was compromised primarily by his desire to preserve a balance of

power in his government. He was not adamant about disarming the conservatives altogether as long as they were prepared to comply with his direct rule and as long as they did not interfere with his royal prerogative, of which he was becoming highly conscious. Officials such as Mustawfi al-Mamalik and Mu'ayyir al-Mamalik, the latter being the director of the royal mint and the minister of the treasury, were essentially hostile to reform because they recognized correctly that modern practices of government would destroy their private monopolies, most notably their control over the ancient fiscal and monetary systems. These were the "hereditary bones," as Malkum had put it, that had been preserved against the wishes of Amir Kabir and now were to be preserved against those of the new reformers. Even though the shah first dismissed the conservatives' resistance, he soon became a prisoner to their entrenched power because he was neither willing nor able to replace them with a younger generation of officials whose true intentions he could hardly trust.

Moreover, in the shah's political culture, reforms were synonymous with restrictions upon what he called his "prerogative," and such a sacrifice to the altar of progress could be made only if a substantial reward were to be gained. He sought the approval of the British government, for example, because he hoped that, like the Tanzimat in the Ottoman Empire, his reform program could help make his throne more secure during a hazardous period of Russian expansion. Moreover, like his counterparts in Istanbul and Cairo, Nasir al-Din looked to Britain with the hope of finding his way through the perplexing maze of reform and acquiring skills he had difficulty mastering. William Doria (the chargé d'affaires from October 1858 until December 1859 who took over after Murray's departure on sick leave), displayed an initial interest in the changes in the government. Yet his circumspection reflected London's ambivalence.

In the absence of a premier, an increasingly obvious deterioration in domestic affairs only added to British ambivalence. In April 1859 growing popular unrest—possibly incited by Nuri and his allies—obliged the shah to make the first amendments to his new cabinet. Sadiq Khan Nuri, who may have been in contact with his exiled relative, was sacked as interior minister and replaced with Farrukh Khan Amin al-Dawla, who also served as acting first minister with limited responsibility to the cabinet. On the surface this was a gain for the reformist camp; it was thought that the new appointment might compensate for the shah's lack of a "steady hand and head" in directing the government, and thus the move was supported by the British, who set their hopes on the new minister's eventual premiership. But neither Amin al-Dawla's appointment nor the shah's promises of broad-based improvements could redirect the marked deterioration in the affairs of the country, a downward trend increasingly affected by economic factors beyond the government's control. The shah's own behavior clearly illustrated his difficulty in coping with the burden of direct rule, which he tried to enforce by the traditional methods of coercion and consent.

In September 1859, while the shah was in the Sultaniya summer camp to review the troops, the false reports that he had been assassinated, the first of many in this period, caused bakeries and other shops in Tehran to close "as if a general riot and insurrection would ensue." The prince governor of Tehran, Firuz Mirza, and the provincial minister responsible, Mirza Musa Vazir, "acted with energy and decision," cutting off several ears and beating two or three others to death. Their brutal measures "installed terror into the minds of the delinquent" and temporarily restored order. Yet "public opinion" at once attributed the desire "to cause a general insurrection in the town" to the Babis. According to Doria, who must have been briefed by anti-Nuri elements in the capital, the Babis were "extremely numerous throughout Persia" and "counted among their most strenuous adherents members of the priesthood, persons of wealth and influence, connections and relatives of the late Sadr A'zam Mirza Agha Khan." The report mentioned two of Nuri's relatives by name, Mirza Musa and Mirza Husayn 'Ali Nuri, Baha'ullah, both residents of Baghdad, as "being continually in receipt of money from Nuri's munificence during his premiership." Moreover, from among the "considerable" number of Babis in Tehran, Doria continued, a person of repute was seized and sent to the royal camp on the charge of disseminating rumors about the assassination.[17]

The British representative's reference to the Babis reflected the innuendos and hearsay that routinely pointed to the Babis as being responsible for urban unrest and popular protests throughout the Nasiri era. The shah's experience with the Babis in 1852 was, no doubt, compelling enough to make such allegations seem realistic. They were certainly worrisome enough to bring him back to the capital immediately. During his five-month stay outside the capital—most of it on horseback and in hunting grounds—the shah seemed in "excellent health and spirits," but he was clearly oblivious to the kinds of problems that were aggravated by his long absence, during which he pretended to be in direct charge of his government. He was equally unperturbed by the hardship that the military review, the greatest joy and source of pride in his life, had caused to villagers in the area throughout the country or by the enormous cost that it incurred.

Even after his apparent conversion to the cause of reform, the shah obstinately tried to maintain this hollow image as a forceful ruler primarily to compensate for his defeat in war. Despite the pleas of his ministers, who did not want him to stay away from the capital for long, and contrary to a deputation by the Tehran 'ulama, who urged him to cancel the review, as many as 30,000 troops were ordered to gather in Sultaniya. This review was no less of a fiasco, as it turned out, than the one commanded by the shah in 1853.[18]

The interview with Doria just after the shah's return from the royal tour was a good specimen of his delinquency. He was "led to believe," he confessed with debatable sincerity, that all the provisions and mules confiscated from impoverished peasants by his agents all along the way from Tehran to the Sultaniya camp and throughout his tours to Qum, Zanjan, and Hamadan were paid for in cash, a claim that could not be supported by facts. According to Doria, he seemed equally unmoved by reports that peasants were robbed of their small grain stores and their means of subsistence and in many instances were beaten in "the most barbarious and unmerciful manner." Even the uncommonly high degree of general discontent among the starving troops and the numerous instances of arrest and imprisonment did not move the shah. Some of the troops were beaten so severely that they died under the lash.[19] Nor were the royal sentiments aroused by the sight of stable lads attached to his own military bands dying of starvation and fatigue on the roadside. "Such has been the effect of the royal progress through the country," Doria complained, "to spread terror and desolation wherever it approached."

Not all the fault belonged to the shah. Doria believed the shah was "misled" about the conditions of the "unpaid troops, the miserable state of the peasants, and the daily increasing dearness of provisions in the large towns owing to the venality of the authorities." Throughout the country "the distress and misery of the people [was] universal." Amin al-Dawla's promotion to first minister did not ameliorate the chaos in the government, as had been hoped. He could not advance "in the confidence of his royal master," nor did he wield any more influence than the rest of his colleagues in the council. Instead, the shah increasingly fortified himself with a circle of conservative court advisers such as Mu'ayyir al-Mamalik, who only recently had been brought into the limelight.[20]

When Henry Rawlinson (see Pl. 21) arrived in Tehran in December 1859, seven months after his appointment to the post of minister plenipotentiary under the newly created India Office, his presence was perceived in Tehran as a sign affirming London's friendly attitude. In the past

Rawlinson had always been an advocate of closer ties between Britain and Iran and development of the latter's military and economic potentials to the level of a regional power. But unlike Stratford Canning in the Ottoman Empire, Rawlinson did not view political modernization as an essential element for creating an efficient and stable bulwark against Russian expansionism. Instead he called for recognition of Iran's sovereignty (particularly over Herat and elsewhere along its eastern frontiers) and argued, contrary to the prevailing thesis advanced by the Foreign Office, that it would be advantageous for Britain actively to support Iran's territorial integrity rather than to lionize peripheral warlords on its frontiers.

A man of many talents, Rawlinson combined the mind of a scholar with the discipline of a soldier and the vision of a strategist. He was the ablest British India had produced in the area of Persian affairs since John Malcolm early in the century. While still a young officer of the Indian Army serving in western Iran in the 1830s and early 1840s, he had deciphered the famous rock inscription of Bisutun (before being assigned as the British consul general to Baghdad, where his Babylonian explorations distinguished him as "the father of Assyriology"). Regarded as one of the greatest archaeological breakthroughs of the century, the translation into Persian of the text of the Achaemenian inscription of Bisutun, which was presented by Rawlinson to Muhammad Shah, was an important step in Iran's rediscovery of its pre-Islamic heritage.[21]

Like Farrant and Sheil before him, Rawlinson had an Indian colonial training and thus was noticeably different in both outlook and approach from other Foreign Office diplomats such as Murray. He was appointed during the short episode when Palmerston was out of office, two months before the latter's return to power as the prime minister, and with John Russell as foreign secretary. Rawlinson must have been known to Nasir al-Din from earlier years. His good command of Persian, which allowed for long private conversations with the monarch and other Persians, his appreciation of Persian history and culture, which he shared with Nasir al-Din, and his sympathetic mannerisms and tact immediately placed him in contrast to Murray and brought him into the shah's confidence. As Rawlinson himself described it, the "elastic usage of Indian diplomacy, unfettered by strict rule or precedence, and thus permitting a large liberty of action," ran counter to the "inexorable tradition of the Foreign Office" and helped him to appreciate the "temper and feeling of a court as irregularly constituted as Tehran, where a free interchange of presents, personal tact and address, a nice appreciation of Oriental character, and numberless matters of language, conduct, and even of dress, unheard of in Europe" were indispensable to his "acquisition and retention of influence."[22]

It is not surprising, therefore, that in their first private discussion in January 1860 the shah confided to Rawlinson his long-standing offer of a comprehensive alliance with Britain, a request he had made indefatigably to all British representatives since Sheil with little result. With no apparent compunction he declared that Iran, by which he meant himself, was "ready to place herself completely and unreservedly under the tuition of England and hold exclusively to the English alliance as had been the case in the reign of Fath 'Ali Shah."[23] The shah's concern was primarily strategic—hence the comparison with the reign of Fath 'Ali Shah—as he ultimately hoped to secure a protective shield against the Russian danger.

To impress on the British minister the seriousness of his search for security, in the next private interview with Rawlinson in February the shah tried to sound out the British position on the questions of reform and overhauling the state institutions. The shah expressed his gratitude for Palmerston's advice to Hasan 'Ali Khan Garrusi, the new Persian minister to the European courts, on matters of "home administration" and for the British statesman's expressed wish for Iran's "gradual advancement in the path of civilization." He then proposed a sweeping seven-point plan of reform, for which he sought Rawlinson's comments and criticisms. Though Rawlinson did not mention it, the proposed plan was drawn up at least in part by the Consultative Council, perhaps in collaboration with the shah, and was inspired by the current debates on the nature of and approach to reforms. The plan called for a census of the population; a survey of the country's natural wealth and resources, aiming at a "more equal distribution of the burden of taxation"; reduction of the standing military forces and creation of a conscript militia force (*radif*); a new currency, "with a view to prevent[ing] further drainage of precious metals from Iran's economy"; promotion of irrigation; encouragement of European capital investment in railroads, telegraph, mines, and industry; and, finally, reform in the provincial government structure, financial, and administrative departments and a division of their functions at all levels.[24] The proposed program was remarkable in that it sought to collect the much-needed data for planning an overhaul of taxation and looked to the West for technology and capital, an early sign of what was to become a predominant theme in the forthcoming age of concessions.

Rawlinson's vision was far less ambitious and reflected Britain's overall desire not to introduce drastic innovations into Iran's traditional state and society. Furthermore, his four-month stay in Iran made him conscious of more urgent problems. He prudently pointed out that engaging in such widespread reforms was beyond Iran's current capacity because of administrative limitations and because of the persistence of traditional ways. "Reforms should be introduced one by one," pronounced Rawlinson. With concern for "insecurity of life and property," he recognized corruption, favoritism, indifference to merits, and intrigue in all government departments as the root causes of Iran's regression. He further stressed the need for a communications network and agreed that the army should be reduced in size but felt a conscription system would be detrimental to the agricultural economy of the country. Pointing out the "evil resulting from an oligarchy" of the ministers, Rawlinson perceived the most urgent matter to be the need for a prime minister. No doubt with the shah's recent five-month absence from Tehran in mind, Rawlinson stressed that the "want of a directing hand at the Capital" had paralyzed the government in dealing with famine in Azarbaijan, the growing Russian threat in Gilan, Turkoman encroachments in northern Khurasan, and misgovernment in Khurasan, Fars, and Kirman.[25] Reference to the "oligarchy" of ministers was no doubt Rawlinson's way of criticizing the shah's poor performance, which had brought the government to a standstill. The instability of the Qajar throne was naturally of concern to him. The shah's insistence on direct rule increasingly exposed him, rather than his premier, to the rising tide of public discontent that was triggered by economic hardship, commodities shortages, famine, and political intrigue. Moreover, dealing directly with the shah, rather than a premier, was understandably less desirable for the foreign envoys, who in the past had always found it easier to achieve their objectives by either influencing or intimidating the prime ministers.

Rawlinson's blunt criticism almost completely disarmed the shah. Though he called the British envoy's observation an "exaggeration," he surprisingly admitted that he was "sufficiently aware" of the need to "revert to the old form of government through a prime minister" but could not find the proper candidate. At this juncture, only eighteen months after the fall of Nuri, he confessed that direct government was "beyond his strength"; his eyesight had already suffered, and his general health was failing. He was "wearied beyond endurance" with the "jealousies of his ministers, and he knew not whom to trust." If he could find a minister to act as an "alter ego," someone who was as honest and impartial as the shah himself "in forwarding the interests of the country," who would release him from the "intolerable load of examining every question that arises either of policy, or administration, or finance" and of "mastering the details before coming to a decision," he would be "too glad" to confine himself to what he considered to be strictly his "royal functions." Yet every candidate, the shah observed, served his own self-interests and had "a following of needy relatives and dependents" and enemies and rivals that allowed "personal considerations [to] become his main principle of action."[26]

With remarkable clarity the shah then demonstrated that he appreciated the essence of the political dilemma his government encountered in dealing with ministerial authority.

> If a prime minister is appointed either he must be paramount and no one could take the office without thus aiming at supremacy—in which case he will be in the same position as myself, obliged to look into the affairs of each department, overwhelmed with details and thus, while striving to do everything, doing in fact nothing—or he must be held in check like the other ministers . . . [in which case] he will only add one more wheel to the complicated machinery which I have already in hand.

Thus it was "against my will," continued Nasir al-Din shah, "to act as my own prime minister, doing the work, no doubt, imperfectly enough, but still avoiding greater evil."[27]

Few rulers in the course of Iran's modern history have had the courage to face the problem that invariably complicated their reigns. What the shah consistently failed to grasp, however, was the lack of an organizational framework within which his prime minister and other officers of the government could function, with clear duties and responsibilities they could not exceed. Such an organizational framework was at the heart of the reforms for which Malkum, and no doubt others, had already proposed models. Rawlinson pointed in the same direction when he reminded the shah that the authority of the premier "depends entirely" on the shah's decision. He even felt it appropriate to suggest a list of potential candidates for the premiership, only to have them conveniently rejected one by one by the shah. The list included Mustawfi al-Mamalik, who was regarded as having "the highest character" but was suitable only for finance; Ja'far Khan Mushir al-Dawla, who was old and of failing health; Amin al-Dawla, who was able but of "low extraction"; and the shah's maternal uncle 'Isa Khan, a man Rawlinson oddly believed to be blessed with a "fair share of knowledge and talent" but too near to the shah.

Perhaps it was not an accident that the shah found all of Rawlinson's candidates inappropriate. When the shah set forth Nuri as a possible candidate and pointed out his unquestionable "ability and thorough knowledge of statesmanship," Rawlinson was only too delighted to agree. In the minister's view Nuri was "the only person who could, under the present circumstance, efficiently administer Persia," in spite of the fact that he was responsible for the war with England. Clearly distressed with Rawlinson's positive reaction, the shah tried desperately to adhere to his original position, stressing the "embarrassment" that Nuri's reappointment would cause. He would "assuredly ruin every individual of the present cabinet," the shah believed. Speculating on Nuri's future conduct, the shah portrayed a realistic picture of ministerial intrigue:

> He might again weave a network of intrigue around me which could place me completely at his mercy; he might involve Persia in hostilities with England, or Russia, or Turkey, to suit his personal policy. I could not feel assured of peace, or security or independence, so long as he had the supreme direction of affairs in his hand. . . . So long as I *can* carry on the administration, I will endeavour to do my duty honestly to the country, whatever may be the sacrifice of health or comfort or even efficiency, for I do not pretend to be as experienced a financier or administrator as the statesmen who have proceeded me.

Once he reached a state where he could not take it any longer, the shah assured Rawlinson, he would call a prime minister to his assistance and consult Rawlinson again. Moreover, the shah warned, the "slightest whisper of the return to power of the Sadr A'zam [i.e., Nuri] at the present moment could convulse the kingdom."[28] The shah's concerns for the peace and security of his kingdom were not unreal. They demonstrated the tightrope on which the shah had to walk in order to preserve the political balance. Without Nuri he was helplessly impotent, and with him he risked his own independence and the revolt of Nuri's opponents.

The purpose of Rawlinson's maneuver, no doubt, was to examine the chances of Nuri's being restored to power. He believed under proper control the ex-premier was of "inestimable advantage to Persia." Rawlinson predicted that if Nuri could survive for a few more months, his return to power would become an absolute necessity. In the event of Nuri's return, "the present ministers with all their unsubstantial pageantry of councils and mimic parliament will be scattered like chafes before the wind." There was little doubt as to Rawlinson's preference. The great scholar was gracious enough, however, to promise that he would save Amin al-Dawla from Nuri's rage by giving him protection. The resemblance between his own offer and Murray's protection for Hashim Khan must have escaped Rawlinson. He informed London that in fact he had already "invited and received" from the Nuri "an explanation of his previous conduct." The communication in question, written on Nuri's behalf by his wife, predictably exonerated him from being a warmonger and instead held the shah fully responsible for any belligerence. But Nuri's letter to Rawlinson went far beyond simple explanation when it promised that if returned to power he would "make up for the past services and will show what the word 'service' implies." He would "gather around him [men] well disposed to the English and will carry out the objectives which England has in mind for Persia and its inhabitant without causing them [i.e., the British] any expense or embarrassment or trouble so that they may reap great advantage from the arrangement." To emphasize his loyalty, he enclosed with the letter a ring given to him by Palmerston or Clarendon (he was not sure which) for his earlier services in the first Herat crisis of 1839, a gesture perhaps inspired by the practice of dispatching signet rings in folk stories. If he could not be restored to office, Nuri proposed, perhaps at least his British protection could be returned to him so as to save for him his life, dignity, and property.[29]

If Rawlinson was not yet fully alert to the dangers of restoring Nuri to power, the shah certainly was. Under pressure from Nuri's opponents and fear of agitation, he had already forced into exile the rest of Nuri's family. To Rawlinson's disappointment, after the February interview the shah, whose great weakness was "exaggerated finesse"—a euphemism perhaps for the shah's extreme impressionability—further gave in to pressures from the anti-Nuri camp and forced Mirza Kazim Nizam al-Mulk, Nuri's son, to divorce the shah's sister, 'Izzat al-Dawla, presumably to have her ready to be bartered for the loyalty of the next prime minister. She later came to be known in the elite circles as "the furniture of premiership" (*asasiya-i sidarat*) for her four forced marriages with candidates of high offices.

Rawlinson seems to have gone too far, even for Palmerston, in his enthusiasm for interfering in Iran's domestic affairs. It was the above report that presumably caused him to be recalled from Tehran in early April, only four months after his arrival. Although disagreements between the India Office and the Foreign Office no doubt provided the root cause, the immediate reason was Rawlinson's slightly naive attempt to restore a premier who only three years earlier had been at the center of a military confrontation with Britain. Palmerston and his foreign secretary feared that Rawlinson's preoccupation with Iran's domestic affairs might result in yet another entanglement. But even before his angry resignation and immediate departure from Tehran in mid-May, Rawlinson himself became aware of the difficulties of restoring Nuri and returning to the old system when Nuri, despairing of British intercession, threw himself to the Russians who, according to Rawlinson, made "every possible effort" to restore him. The subsequent joint protest by Russia and France calling for Nuri's restoration to help combat the "state of anarchy" and insure the "safety of the empire" could not persuade the shah. "He would rather abdicate than submit to the dictation of foreign governments on a point that so nearly touched his prerogative and even his life." Rawlinson agreed that unfortunately "too much ground" existed for the Russian complaints, but he preferred not to cooperate with his diplomatic counterparts.[30] The shah's victory on the Nuri issue was remarkable but not complete. He made it plain that he would not restore Nuri under foreign pressure, but in order to resist he was forced to rely even further on the anti-Nuri conservatives and hence gradually to abandon the most significant aspects of the reforms.

Any ability on the shah's part to act as his own prime minister was curtailed by the inertia within the Qajar polity. His abortive effort to prohibit what Rawlinson called the "ruinous system of official corruption" was typical of his disheartening failures. In this, his first attempt since Amir Kabir to prevent the provincial governors from raising illicit revenue (madakhil), the shah decided to separate on an experimental basis the governorship of Gilan from the financial functions of that province. His plan encountered serious resistance when Ahmad Khan Nava'i, the candidate for the Gilan governorship, turned down the shah's offer because the fixed salary set for the office removed the incentive for exacting madakhil. Even the shah's personal insistence could not change Nava'i's "somewhat peremptory and insubordinate" behavior. In a surge of royal rage the shah ordered him bastinadoed immediately and fined him 3,000 tumans. Rawlinson concluded:

> Thus ended the first attempt to introduce administrative reforms, showing that for the abuses that existed in Persia the Shah is not so much himself responsible as is the vicious state of society over which he presides. "What is the use," as His Majesty said to me on a late occasion, "of asking me to forego presents, and practice purism, when bribery and corruption is the universal rule of Persian society through every grade, and in reference to every individual?"[31]

Even before Rawlinson's hasty departure from Tehran the shah seems to have lost faith in substantial reforms, but if further discouragement were needed it came with the change of the British minister. Rawlinson's assurances that his recall should not be interpreted as a sign of a British change of heart were hardly convincing. Rawlinson almost agreed with the shah's doubts when, fifteen years later, he reflected in his book on the return of the responsibility for the Persian mission to the Foreign Office.

> As the change in 1859 had been understood at Tehran to indicate a more lively interest on our part in the welfare of Persia, so the return of Foreign Office control in 1860 was interpreted to mean a resumption of the old policy of indifference; and certainly the experience of the next few years immediately following the appointment of Mr. Alison [Rawlinson's successor] to Tehran, so far from disabusing the Shah of this impression, must have tended rather to confirm it. The distinguishing feature, indeed, of our Persian policy at this period seems to have been a desire to reduce our expenditure to a minimum and to withdraw as far as possible from all interference with the internal or external affairs of the country.[32]

It is not hard to see why after Rawlinson's departure the shah praised him for his "honest goodwill" and characterized him as "one of his best personal friends," whose departure was a source of "real and great sorrow."[33] Reportedly he even shed a few tears at the news of the representative's retirement. A Qajar prince who expressed dismay when he found the shah guided more by the advice of the English minister than by that of his own ministers was right to observe how absolutely the government of Iran could "depend upon the personal influence of a foreign representative."[34]

OMINOUS CONJUNCTION

Advocates of reform within the government were too few and their constituency too small to withstand the entrenched conservative opposition or to maintain their rapidly evaporating influence on the shah. The most senior among them, Mirza Ja'far Khan, the head of the Consultative Council, was the first to be removed. In May 1860 he was temporarily relieved of his post in the council and despite his advanced age and "physical infirmities" was appointed Persian ambassador to London. Some doubted he would ever reach his destination, but he survived the trip, returning to Tehran in September 1862, only to be reassigned as trustee of the shrine of Imam Riza in Mashhad, a respectful exile reserved for statesmen out of favor with the shah. He died there in December of the same year.[35]

Ja'far Khan's departure, occurring simultaneously with Rawlinson's recall, emboldened conservatives to close their circle around the shah. Capitalizing on the shah's dark fears for his life and his superstitious beliefs, Mustawfi al-Mamalik—who because of his interest in alchemy, the "esoteric sciences" (*'ulum-i ghariba*), and astrology wielded "great influence on the shah"—found an effective device with which to ward off his opponents, above all Nuri. Backed by the chief astrologer, he renewed an earlier forecast that an "ominous conjunction" (*qaran-i nahs*) of heavenly bodies was inimical to the life of the shah. Appraising the shah's fortune at various astrological conjunctions in order to determine its ominous (*nahs*) or fortuitous (*sa'd*) disposition was a normal practice in all Persian courts, often affecting the outcome of any given political situation. In 1857 an astrological forecast had contributed to Nuri's downfall, and in late January 1860, when Nuri's return was being contemplated, a similar prognostication caused "marked disquietude" in Tehran among the notables and princes of the blood. Because of such prognostications, the public was alarmed at "any trifling indisposition" of the shah.[36]

The date of the fatal conjunction this time was determined to be 1 Muharram 1277/20 July 1860 or thereabouts, leading to rumors of the shah's approaching death. Fixing an ominous conjunction at the beginning of the year under either the solar or the lunar calendar in anticipation of some sedition or popular uprising was not unprecedented.[37] Not only was the shah "destined for early death, but . . . His Majesty [wa]s to be murdered." The British acting chargé d'affaires, Pelly, found "valid grounds" for the possibility of the shah's murder. He believed that the grounds for such an "act of high treason" lay nowhere more obvious than "in the disorder of the government, in the general mal-administration of justice, and in the common insecurity of the private rights." As in all despotic regimes, Pelly added, "the resource against real or fancied tyranny lies in the death of the king," and thus it was "impossible not to feel that these silly forecasts of astrologers may cover some plot of a treasonable character." Inevitably in an oblique reference, the Babis, "a sect implacably hostile to the sovereign power," were identified as the greatest potential threat, and Pelly did not hesitate to trace the root of the widespread rumor to Nuri's doorstep.[38]

Nasir al-Din Shah responded with typical hedonistic fatalism, though deep down the forecast only added to his distress and emotional insecurity. "Providence preserved him once from an attempt like that now apprehended, and will doubtless preserve him a second time," reported Pelly. "Anyway, His Majesty will enjoy life while he can."[39] It was this trust in providential protection, one may surmise, that earned him the title of "lord of the [fortuitous] conjunction" (*sahib-qaran*).[40] Nevertheless, his fear of assassination was so real that in mid-July he took refuge in an isolated Alburz mountain resort (see Pl. 8). There the callous execution of a helpless petitioner demonstrated the shah's frenzied state of mind. The victim, a menial servant who had been "tyrannized" by his master, a minister of the government, had fled for justice to the shah's stable—a customary place of refuge—but having received no attention he committed the fatal error of trying personally to submit a petition to the shah on the royal hunting ground. When the shah arrived almost unattended, the petitioner rose up and advanced toward him. "Recalling to mind the circumstances of the former Babee [Babi] attempt," Pelly suggested, the shah became "intensely alarmed" and shouted for his guards, assuring the petitioner that all he desired should be immediately granted provided he would only stand still. "Upon the king's cortege coming up, His Majesty at once ordered the petitioner to be strangled."[41]

The only real outcome of the conjunction of heavenly bodies, however, was the arrival on 19 July 1860 of Charles Alison, the new British minister plenipotentiary, who seems to have been destined by the dictates of Lord Russell to cling stubbornly to the Tehran mission for the next twelve years. In the end only death parted him from his post. An anomaly even by the standards of English eccentricity, Alison so far had served in no higher post than that of dragoman of the British embassy in Istanbul under Stratford Canning. His curious appointment can best be defined as the revenge of the Foreign Office, which under Russell and his undersecretary, Henry Layard, had decided to go the way of Stratford Canning and relegate Iran to diplomatic oblivion, a policy that contrasted with the Indian government's general diplomatic outlook and excessive preoccupation with its buffer states. He was sent to Tehran not so much to humiliate the shah and his government as to give the Foreign Office an excuse to forget about them. Alison's famous beard, which had defeated all laws of gravity to create a hazy barrier in front of his face, and his Orientalized mannerisms and lifestyle, which he originally picked up in Istanbul and in which he became fully accomplished in Tehran, must have generated a very curious portrait of the British character in the Persian capital. If he had ever been sober enough to go about his duties, as Edward Eastwick later testified, he would have had a better sense of Tehran's prostitutes than the affairs of the Persian government or the British mission. His brutally brief and inarticulate reports to London (embellished with his enormous signature, mockingly shaped like a dog's head) conveyed only the bare minimum of information necessary to satisfy the Foreign Office without arousing its curiosity. As it turned out, however, Alison's term of office was neither a fortuitous nor an ominous one. The new minister's hands-off approach, devoid of the previously utilized network of protégés and spies, lessened the traditional British influence in governmental circles, creating a period of stability and relative calm in Anglo-Persian relations that contrasted with the rancor of the three preceding decades.[42]

For the shah and his government, the hurried change of envoys with such contrasting qualities carried the clear message that Britain was keen neither to involve itself in domestic reforms (perhaps with the noticeable exception of establishing a telegraphic service) nor to provide moral support for it. This impression left by the British was a further blow to any fundamental reform initiative some statesmen around the shah might have conceived. Instead, it encouraged Nasir al-Din to continue the improvised and erratic method of government he had confided to Rawlinson earlier. That which can be gleaned from Alison's brief and uninformative reporting indicates that he was unwilling to propose a line of political reforms or even to question the conduct of the shah's domestic policies.

The shah's candid admission to Rawlinson of his incompetence and the self-serving resistance of the bureaucracy to basic reforms thus helped aggravate a phenomenal growth in the country's social and economic problems. The disastrous Marv campaign against the Turkomans of the northeastern frontier in early 1860, which resulted in enormous troop casualties and a total loss of face, only added to the public discontent. The shah's grave concern with Russian territorial ambitions and his fear of losing the newly acquired British friendship left little room in his mind for domestic concerns. The seven-point memorandum drawn up by the shah on the occasion of Rawlinson's departure clearly reflected his anxieties. Among other items he renewed the call for British guarantees of Iran's territorial integrity, asked for military assistance, stressed continuous separation of the three Afghan principalities as a guarantee of security along Iran's eastern frontier, and even invited a British naval presence in the Caspian Sea with sufficient force to match that of the Russians.[43]

Domestic troubles hardly left the shah with time to ponder these foreign policy issues. Early outrage in Tehran and Tabriz in the summer of 1860 over "continued high prices of provisions" was soon followed by famine throughout the central provinces, occurring for the first time in the Qajar era on a massive scale. Not only in the capital but also in Khurasan, acute shortages brought high prices, up to 300 percent higher in some cases, and led to extensive hoarding and speculation. During a bread riot in Mashhad in 1859, the wealthy Imam Jum'a of the city, "who possessed large stores of grains, was attacked by the low men while in the mosque, dragged from his pulpit and otherwise maltreated." Although a royal decree immediately banned the export of any provisions to Russia, the chief cause for the shortages in the northeast, and called for the corrupt officials to be punished, it had limited effect in inhibiting similar instances in other provinces.[44]

By February 1861 public discontent led to serious bread riots, threatening the very stability of the shah's rule. In Tehran, as soon as a European showed himself in the streets "he was surrounded by starving women supplicating assistance." On the shah's return from hunting on 28 February, he was surrounded by 5,000 to 6,000 women with their veils removed and with mud rubbed on their heads as a sign of misfortune, "yelling for bread." Responding to the sticks and lashes of the royal guards with pellets and rocks, the women clutched at the shah's carriage, and only with great difficulty did the royal cavalcade manage to bull its way through the crowd and slip into the royal citadel. The hungry demonstrators nevertheless gutted the bakers' shops "under the very eyes of the king," and the minister of war, Muhammad Khan Qajar, who accompanied the shah, was apprehended by the crowd. His reputation as a major speculator with massive sealed granaries was well known to the women, who dragged him out of his saddle and beat him up. As always, the presence of women in the riots was highly conspicuous, not only because of their supposed immunity from harm (which created a human shield for the men) but also because it was nothing less than the weight of household burdens that brought them out into the streets.[45] This was not the first time, nor was it the last, that women appeared at the forefront of popular protests, in clear defiance of the flawed image of timidity and domestic confinement associated with them.

Next day the starving crowds surrounded the royal palace in even greater numbers. Climbing the closed gates, "thousands of women made their way into the citadel and began to assail the guards with large stones [while] being urged on by their male relatives, who under cover of their attack, were looking out for an opportunity to effect a more serious rise." In facing a far more dangerous riot than that he had encountered in 1848 in Tabriz, the shah seemed utterly helpless. An emergency meeting of the Council of the State convened in the shah's presence could do little but summon the influential mayor of the city, Mahmud Khan Kalantar Nuri. A seventy-year-old official with three decades of service as mayor, he was a public figure known to the entire Tehran populace. Firmly in control of a network of city wardens (*kadkhudas*), he had kept his constituency even after the fall of his ally and clansman, Mirza Aqa Khan Nuri, mastering a semiautonomous urban power base dreaded even by the shah himself. While watching the crowd from the citadel's tower with his monocle, the shah received the frightened mayor, who on the way to the palace had also been attacked and beaten up by the rioters. He could only promise the reproachful shah that he would soon put down the riot, but when he returned to the crowd the second time in the company of his servants and furiously beat several women with large sticks, it was inevitable that his action would only further incite the crowd. One of the assaulted women even ran as far as the British legation calling out for help. Experiencing some "trepidation" upon the appearance of the tumultuous mob, the shah immediately summoned the mayor back into his presence. "If you are thus cruel to my subjects before my eyes," he reportedly said, "what must be your secret misdeeds?" He then ordered the mayor bastinadoed and his beard cut off. But while his orders were being carried out, in a moment of rage the shah "uttered the terrible word *tanab* [rope]." The executioners immediately "placed a cord round the unhappy man's neck and in an instant more their feet were on his chest, trampling out the last sign of life." Following the execution of the mayor, the wardens of all the city quarters who served under him were punished by bastinado. As Edward Eastwick witnessed, "at the sight of these punishments, the frenzy of the populace was for that day disappeared, and Tehran was saved by the hair's breadth from a revolution."[46]

The speedy execution of the powerful mayor of Tehran, one of very few ranking notables to be publicly executed under Nasir al-Din Shah, came in a moment of royal wrath. Yet it was not an entirely spontaneous act. The mayor was notorious for his collaboration with the Tehran brigands (*lutis*) in controlling the supply of provisions to the capital and was one of those responsible for hoarding and for the soaring prices. No ruler of a traditional monarchy, least of all Nasir al-Din Shah, could afford bread riots in his capital, the place where he was most vulnerable to naked public rage. No doubt the deteriorating economic conditions and poor roads and communication were far more responsible for the widespread famine in the capital than the conduct of the mayor and his associated *lutis*. But the mayor, an influential public figure with a checkered record, provided a visible culprit, a sacrificial lamb, to divert public blame away from the shah; this was a course of action Nasir al-Din consistently pursued in times of crisis. When as the result of abolishing the office of premier the shah was exposed even more directly to his subjects' anger, the extreme measure of sacrificing a high-ranking city official with a certain civil status and constituency seemed to Nasir al-Din unavoidable. "In reality the mayor of Tehran became a casualty of the shah," wrote Brugsch, the Prussian envoy in Tehran, "and with his execution the course of the revolution was halted."[47]

Mahmud Khan's execution may also have been triggered by the shah's suspicion that the mayor, who came from the Nuri clan, was an ally of the ex-premier. The fear of the mayor's "secret misdeeds" no doubt was augmented in the shah's mind by Mirza Aqa Khan Nuri's opponents. Partly to whitewash the shah's unmerciful verdict, no doubt, the State Council, dominated by Mustawfi al-Mamalik and his allies, resolved that Mahmud Khan had instigated a popular revolution with the ultimate aim of over-throwing the shah and the Qajar dynasty. The vizier of Tehran, Mirza Musa Ashtiyani, a crafty and Machiavellian ally and agent of Mustawfi al-Mamalik and a part of the network of Ashtiyani accountants (*mustawfis*) who, far more than Mahmud Khan and his *lutis*, were responsible for the shortages and disruption of supplies, was saved by his patron. Moreover, his brother, Mirza 'Isa (the man who earlier had put the murder scene of Jayran's relative in the shah's view), was appointed the new mayor of the capital, giving full control of the city to the Ashtiyani party. One can surmise that although the popular riots were genuine and even sponta-neous, they were fueled by factionalism between the weakening Nuris and the ascending Ashtiyanis.[48]

The mayor's execution only temporarily ameliorated the public pro-test—a "hair's breadth from a revolution"—and only when Mahmud Khan's naked body was dragged through the streets "amid the execration of the multitude" and hung up by the heels at one of the city gates. To complete the spectacle of ferocity and intimidation, the next day the shah wore a "suit of red clothing," an ancient symbol of royal rage and further bloodshed. Brugsch perhaps was correct in observing that the shah followed the example of his father, who, when facing a bread riot in 1833 in Tabriz just before his accession, ordered the execution of three representatives of the city population against the advice of his minister, Mirza Abul-Qasim Qa'im Maqam.

Nasir al-Din's retributive justice promised the public that he planned to "proceed vigorously on their behalf," but even when he reverted to the red garb of rough justice his orders had little effect. The famine continued to ravage the population until the next harvest, but the large granaries of the "ministers and high authorities" remained intact, despite repeated royal commands that all supplies should be brought to the market.[49] In early April Tehran witnessed another "great discontent" targeted against the shah and the speculators in high office. This time a crowd of women forced their way into a mosque, found the Imam Jum'a of the city, Sayyid Zayn al-'Abidin, at prayer, and dragged him out into the street. "Nearly thronged to death," the Imam Jum'a was forced by the attackers to call upon the shah and seek assurances that there would be immediate bread distribution. Other gangs of women forced their way into the British and Russian legations and demanded that the envoys bring their distressing condition to the shah's attention. They were so excited that "the law of the veil was quite disregarded." The minister of war, Muhammad Khan Qajar, the rising star of the conservative camp emerged with his troops in a show of force but was hooted and abused in the streets for the second time. Women of Qazvin also broke into the government house and did "a good deal of mischief." The government's efforts seemed hopelessly inadequate. The shah's initiative to import large quantities of wheat and other provisions from Azarbaijan and Gilan, where there was a "superabundance" of agricultural products, was thwarted by bad roads. With provisions unable to come in, the starving multitudes desperately fled to the northern provinces in search of food.[50]

For the next few years the government encountered further public disturbances in Yazd, Astarabad, Hamadan, Shiraz, Zanjan, and even Rasht (see Pl. 16). Though more often exhibited through indigenous tensions, in clashes with European consuls and protégés, and in outright protests against local governments, the rampant urban instability that swept Iran throughout the 1860s and 1870s was primarily caused by high prices and shortages of supplies. In Tehran at one time during the years 1860–1861, the price of bread soared fourfold, and the government's draconian measures to improve the situation had only limited effect. Between 1856 and 1861 the prices of all other essential provisions showed sharp increases ranging from 70 to 400 percent. The shortages and visible misgovernment caused the people to aim their anger directly toward the shah. He was openly abused and insulted in the streets of the capital, and "major harm was inflicted on the shah's reputation," as Brugsch noticed, without the shah's ever realizing it.[51]

Instances of mutiny among the troops were not rare, either, particularly after the disastrous Marv expedition. They were motivated in most instances by long delays in the payment of the soldiers' minuscule salaries and dismal provisions; at other times they were the outcome of abuse and brutality by the officers. In December 1860 a regiment returning from Khurasan in the aftermath of Marv took refuge en masse in the shrine of Shah 'Abd al-'Azim near Tehran, complaining of the "extortion and cruel conduct of their colonel." Though they were persuaded by the shah and his war minister to withdraw in exchange for their commander's dismissal, the mutiny continued. A few days later they even waylaid the royal procession on its return from the races. At last they were "eluded" by the shah to surrender their arms, leaving them defenseless and at the mercy of the war minister. One-third of the troops were subjected to a cruel bastinado, and fifty were sent back to the barracks with their ears cut off.

The harsh disciplinary measures hardly stopped future mutinies. In July 1864 two regiments stationed in Tehran and consisting of 5,000 troops altogether staged another mutiny because they had not been paid for three years. Some other regiments in Tehran refused to obey their Italian instructors, who required them to march "double," on the grounds that it would wear out their boots. A more serious mutiny in Tehran in July 1865 over the misappropriation of salaries by corrupt officers once more brought out the royal rage. The shah reportedly ordered Muhammad Khan Qajar to shoot all the soldiers, an order the war minister ventured not to obey, fearing mutiny among the troops under his own command.[52]

The shift to the politics of coercion was the only resort left open to the shah in his effort to preserve his otherwise waning authority. This political approach was in total contradiction to his ephemeral desire for lofty reform. He became more tyrannical during the times when he was less in control, a position that adhered quite well to the traditional model of insecure kingship. His insistence on direct rule made him alone the subject of public scrutiny, and as a consequence he was held responsible for every unfortunate fault of his ministers.[53]

FEARING HIM WHO FEARS

The growing discontent exhibited in the riots and mutinies and the government's failure to deal with routine shortages, soaring prices, and epidemics dampened even further the shah's enthusiasm for political change. He looked with suspicion at the remaining advocates of reform and above all at Malkum's Faramush-khana, which since its establishment three years earlier had adopted a more independent position, even attracting some elements of dissent. Another rumor of the shah's death in July 1861 "greatly disturbed" the capital and its surroundings, causing a further shortage of provisions and exorbitant price increases. Probably disseminated by Mustawfi al-Mamalik and his allies, the rumor lead the shah to suspect that members of Faramush-khana were involved. Even the shah's immediate return from a hunting expedition in the hills of northern Tehran and the fact that he held a levee to "satisfy his subjects that he was alive" had only a limited effect in alleviating the insecurity in the city. Tehran remained "unsettled."[54] It was as though the inhabitants of the House of the Caliphate (*dar al-khilafa*), as the Persian capital was known in the grandiose nomenclature of the Qajar era, wished the "shadow of God" to be lifted from among them.

Whether or not Faramush-khana subverted against the shah is not clear, but a report from the French chargé d'affaires in Tehran, M. Blonnet (who had replaced Baron de Pichon in April 1861), sheds some light on Malkum's efforts to broaden his popular base. His first step toward reform, Blonnet pointed out with an obvious touch of naive exaggeration, was to combat the moral corruption, decadence, and open and continuous theft that was completely destroying the machinery of the state. But "public opinion was against Malkum, who had tried to rescue the shah. Thus, in order to join the people, he had moved away from the shah and henceforth introduced to Iran the concept and practice of freemasonry. Whoever in today's Iran believes to an extent in honorable principles has joined this society."[55] Most notably, the report indicated, it was the rampant anti-monarchical sentiments in the capital that encouraged Malkum to adopt a more critical stance toward the government and advocate some form of constitutionalism, at least within the confines of his secret society. Gobineau believed that even debates on such benign subjects as "humanity" and "civilization" were enough to arouse the shah's suspicions and gave Malkum's opponents a chance to alert Nasir al-Din to the dangers of the extremism that lay behind such activities. Bolder allegations labeled Faramush-khana nothing but "a place of rallying for the Babis."[56] Muhammad Khan Qajar, the commander in chief of the army, seems to have been particularly zealous in suppressing the Faramush-khana, having been criticized by Malkum for his scandalous role in the Marv expedition.

The "unfavorable impression" that such reports left on the shah prompted him to close the Faramush-khana. Malkum, "by whom the new practices were chiefly propagated," was accused of convening secret meetings in a house that allegedly had been "the rendezvous for the Babi conspirators who attempted the shah's life in 1852." This no doubt was a reference to Jalal al-Din Mirza's house in the Masjid-i Hawz quarter where the society held its meetings.[57] The announcement attached to the *Ruz-nama-yi Dawlat-i 'Alliya-yi Iran* of 18 October conveniently denied that the shah had any previous knowledge of the organization. It declared that the "riffraff in the city are speaking of arrangement and organization of European Faramush-khanas and are desirous of establishing one. Therefore a plain royal decree is issued that henceforth if anyone utters the word and expression Faramush-khana, let alone tries to establish one, he will be the subject of the government's utmost wrath and chastisement. Let the use of this word be completely abandoned and let no one conjure such absurdities, for undoubtedly he shall face thorough punishment."[58] Encouraged by the shah's ban on the Faramush-khana and probably instructed by him to do so, the 'ulama issued a *fatwa* denouncing the secret society for disseminating disbelief. Subsequently, the house in which Faramush-khana met was razed to the ground by a mob. Malkum took refuge in the shrine of Shah 'Abd al-'Azim, but Jalal al-Din Mirza, together with some other members, was put under arrest.[59] Soon afterward, perhaps a month later, Malkum himself was exiled to Baghdad, and others of the group were pursued and punished on charges of subversion. Although Mahd 'Ulya's intercession may have spared the life of one member, others may even have been put to death.[60]

The extent of Babi involvement in Faramush-khana cannot be easily determined, but Malkum's own admission of conflict with the shah may provide a clue for his exile. Some decades later, in his discussion with Wilfred Blunt, he reminisced, no doubt with a dash of the embellishment typical of his inventive mind, that the shah, having become alarmed of Malkum's power, "which in truth became superior to his own," sought to kill the reformer in spite of their friendship. "For two months, we both lived in great fear of assassination, and then we came to an explanation. I loved and revered the shah, and I asked permission to travel. My followers took leave of me with tears, even the Mullahs kissing my feet."[61] It is plausible that Malkum was alluding to the rumors of the shah's death in late July, which led to the closure of the secret society and his own expulsion. Yet the clandestine circle in Tehran did not disappear altogether.

The Consultative Council, though never officially dissolved, lost all its significance after 1861 partly, because of the crackdown on Faramush-khana and the members of the reformist wing who had been appointed to the council. It was gradually pushed aside and its decisions ignored because even in its short life it demonstrated some independence and was at times critical of the Council of the State and the excesses of the individual ministers. Its proceedings made the body seem more assertive than the shah's government was willing to tolerate.[62] Malkum's criticism that the Consultative Council was denied the ability to act upon its main legislative task may have aggravated the shah's antagonism. In 1860, in his Daftar-i Qanun ("manual of law"), an early prototype of his 1880s periodical, *Qanun*, Malkum had criticized the "ministers of the state" for not distinguishing between the legislative and the executive powers. After thousands of years of confusion, he wrote, "at last the shah of Iran understood this crucial point and decided to separate the two functions of the state."

Now, "instead of separating the legislative function from the executive function, they mixed them up even worse than before." In Malkum's view this was the reason the ministers of the state had become "the subject of national hatred." He implicitly blamed the shah's arbitrary power when he wrote, "now the control of Iran and its twenty *kurur* [ten million] population is in the hands of one individual and that individual, because he holds such great power, considers himself as omnipotent over the life and property of twenty *kurur* people and uses the resources of the land in whatever way he wishes. My mind is incapable of understanding the basis for such power." He went on to add, "If we want to keep the authority of the government devoid of order and employ it merely to destroy Iran, then the government administration should be kept in its present shape."[63]

The shah must have been blind not to see the sharp edge of criticism raised against him, even though Malkum tried to balance off his criticism against the ministers by benign advice for the shah. In the same Daftar-i Qanun he asked rhetorically, "Why should the ministers in Iran be 'undismissable'? Why should there not be twenty dismissed ministers in the Persian government? Why should any individual who has no distinction over the rest of the subjects stay in office more than six months? What would have been wrong if every year among these ten ministers two new ones would have emerged? How do we know that all the wise men of Iran are limited to these few men? How do we know that the generation of Amir Nizam [i.e., Amir Kabir] is extinct?"[64]

Indeed, the shah followed Malkum's advice diligently so far as it recommended the swift change of ministers, although he never did look for another Amir Kabir. Malkum probably hoped the shah would find one in him. The ministerial changes, however, were determined not by merit but for quite different reasons: the shah's desire to balance off rival parties, his rather capricious moods, his growing appetite for presents in cash and kind offered in exchange for appointments, and finally his haphazard attempts to reorganize his government. Amir Kabir was dead and at any rate undesirable for the royal taste, but the shah could still follow Malkum's advice and hold a Damoclean sword over his ministers' heads by threatening them with the return of Nuri. For example, using Nuri as a deterrent to control his exceedingly powerful conservative camp in May 1862, the shah made a favorable gesture toward the dismissed grand vizier and his son, Nizam al-Mulk, who was appointed governor of Yazd. But the shah's initiative was faced immediately with the revolt of the "whole body of ministers," and he was forced to recall the appointment. "This change of purpose," Alison pointed out, "has not raised the shah in popular estimation."[65] An evidence of the unpopularity of the shah's move was also supplied by the British envoy.

On 18 May 1862 an anonymous pamphlet (*kitabcha*) was delivered to the shah, and the author claimed that 500 more copies of it had been prepared and were about to be distributed throughout Iran.[66] Though Ya'qub Khan, Malkum's father and the secretary of the Russian mission in Tehran, was soon identified as the author, the letter was representative of a broader body of opinion originating in the Faramush-khana environment. Though noteworthy for the immediate motives of the author or authors and the circumstances of its publication, the pamphlet was even more important for being the first extant anti–Nasir al-Din critique save for disparaging references in Babi literature. Three decades prior to the Regie protest of 1891–1892 and nearly half a century before the Constitutional Revolution, the pamphlet was already dabbling in themes that would become common in the "night letters" and clandestine literature at the turn of the twentieth century. The letter presented an assessment not only of the shah's performance during his fourteen years on the throne but also of the changing image of monarchy in Persian political culture.

Beginning with the familiar subject of obedience to rulers, the author invoked the classical Perso-Islamic theory of government in order to stress the conditions essential to the survival of the monarchy. "A king deserving to be obeyed is he who devotes all his faculties to the internal prosperity of his dominions, and to the credit and reputation of his country abroad," declared the pamphlet. As though hinting at the theory of the "cycle of equity," preservation of which was always regarded as the key to the kingdom's welfare and endurance, the pamphlet warned that "the prosperity of a country depends upon agriculture and commerce, and for a long time past there has been no protection for the cattle of the cultivator nor for the capital of the merchant." This no doubt was a reference to the chronic famine and shortages of commodities that had caused widespread popular unrest. It was as though the author had the *Siyasat-nama* of Nizam al-Mulk in mind (or the *'Ahd-nama* of 'Ali for Malik Ashtar) when he said that "the protection of a realm and the maintenance of its credit are dependent on the soldiery and the civil officers; and these are reduced to such utter distress as to have become objects of ridicule."

The open letter then went on to specify some naked cases of injustice and oppression under Nasir al-Din. "What happened to the two regiments of Khamsa on their return from Astarabad is not forgotten," declared the author angrily, referring to the aforementioned mutiny of February 1861. In an allusion to the fateful Marv expedition and the deaths of thousands of Persian troops in the desert because of shortages of provisions and logistical problems, the pamphlet chided, "Our leaders have no horses to mount on the day of battle. Instead of that, through the excellent justice and favor of the King of the Kings, the Mustawfi al-Mamalik has in his stables in 'Iraq ['Ajam] 300 famous horses, each of which has been procured by dispossessing a hundred proprietors of their possessions." The misery of the troops and the insecurity of the frontiers were contrasted with the opulent lifestyle of high-ranking officials, along with their newly acquired taste for European luxuries and their accumulated wealth under the new order: "The troops in garrisons on the frontiers are so starved that they are thinking of running away. Owing to royal favor, the palace of His Highness the Mu'ayyir al-Mamalik surpasses that of the King Bahram, while men like the Sarim al-Dawla die of poverty and disappointment. But through the refulgent favor of the Vicegerent of God, the musicians and dancers drive away slumber in the houses of —— in the —— quarter of the city."

The mansion built by Dust 'Ali Khan Mu'ayyir al-Mamalik in a lavish European neoclassical style in the Sangilaj quarter gained notoriety for competing with the shah's palace in luxury even more than Nuri's Nizamiya did. The son of Husayn 'Ali Khan, the master of the mint and the shah's childhood confidant who had died in 1857, Dust 'Ali (who gained the title Nizam al-Mulk after its previous holder, Muhammad Kazim Nuri, the ex-premier's son, was stripped of it) had succeeded his father in all his offices. A member of the old bureaucratic nobility and one of Mustawfi al-Mamalik's closest allies, he made an enormous fortune by extending monopolies over the state treasury and the royal mint during the 1860s. Comparing Dust 'Ali's mansion with the legendary seven palaces of the Sasanian ruler Bahram V (A.D. 420–438), immortalized in Nizami's twelfth-century lyrical masterpiece, Haft Paykar, the author alluded to the innovative design introduced by the Frenchman Jules Richard and imitated by the shah when he built his new inner quarters.[67] The impoverished 'Abdullah Khan Sarim al-Dawla, by contrast, was a Qaraguzlu chief who led the Persian forces in one of the very few successful military operations of Nasir al-Din's reign against the British-backed occupation of Bandar 'Abbas by the sultan of Masqat in 1854.[68] Both references were veiled criticisms of the shah's extravagance and his dismal military record. The charge of partaking too much of the "feast" and achieving too little success in the "fight" was unmistakable.

The author employed the analogy of Bahram's seven palaces, where the ruler held nocturnal feasts with dancers and musicians in the company of his seven wives, as a symbol of the kingly bazm life to contrast Nasir al-Din

Shah's pleasure-seeking life in the harem with his highly publicized claims of enjoying the "favor" of his patron saint 'Ali ibn Abu Talib, the Vicegerent of God (*Waliullah*). Even in an anonymous letter, the allusions did not need to go beyond two blanks. Filling in the blanks, the first with the name of the shah and second with Gulistan Palace, was not difficult for educated readers.

The author of the pamphlet was also critical of the 'ulama's general ineffectiveness and loss of status. "The doctors of the faith, who always used to be mediators between the sovereign and his people and objects of great respect and reverence to foreign powers on account of the honor and respect shown to them in their own country, can now do nothing but express regret, and hope for the advent of the Prophet." By referring to the reverence of foreign powers toward the mujtahids (the "doctors of faith," as Edward Eastwick translated the term), the author had in mind the heyday of the 'ulama's political power under Fath 'Ali Shah and Muhammad Shah, during whose reigns the mujtahids on a few occasions came into contact with foreign envoys. For example, Sayyid Muhammad Baqir Shafti mediated between Muhammad Shah and the British envoy, John McNeill, during the first Herat crisis of 1838–1839. Their effective restraint under Nasir al-Din, the author regretted, left little for the 'ulama to do but harbor messianic expectations for the advent of the "Prophet." Although not spelled out (possibly due to the vagaries of the translation), the author probably meant to contrast the futility of the Shi'ite messianic hopes with the harsh realities that necessitated more than ever the return of the Hidden Imam. There was probably a Babi vein still throbbing.[69]

The admonishing tone of the pamphlet then turned pointedly toward the "*shah-i kamran*," a kingly epithet with the double meaning of "pleasure-seeking" or "fortuitous" king.[70]

> Thou hast passed thy thirtieth year, and it is time that thou didst learn wisdom, and were thoughtful of the welfare of thy subjects. Know that ruling well is something different from setting up a few puppets, mirrors to be stared at. The state has been ruined by want of good faith in the government, which has brought ill enough on the people. Every man acts now as he pleases owing to thy vacillating counsels. One man is desperate, another rendered confident in his evil deeds, another plots treason, another meditates flight, another is on the look out for an insurrection.

Setting up puppets and staring at mirrors, activities that prevented the shah from recognizing the welfare of his own subjects, probably should be taken as references to the shah's ministerial puppeteering and his appointment of individuals who mirrored his own selfish wishes. These symbols also were hints at Nasir al-Din's growing appetite for building new palaces, in particular his much-adored Mirror Hall in Gulistan Palace, and for displaying statutes, jewels, and other objets d'art from the royal collection in a private museum hall (see Pl. 27). The responsibility for the country's ruination and the people's misery was thus placed squarely on the shah's shoulders and regarded as the outcome of his "vacillating counsels," which in turn nurtured among the ministers loss of faith, cynicism, and insecurity. It was no doubt this royal incursion on statesmanship and the erosion of ministerial independence that inspired the author's boldest criticism.

> Why didst thou slay Mirza Taqi Khan [Amir Kabir], the innocent? Wilt thou say that he was a Babi? Why didst thou ruin Mirza Agha Khan [Nuri]? Wilt thou pretend that he was a Freemason? Why hast thou exalted and the next day abased Mirza Sadiq [Nuri]? Thy blunders have destroyed Persia. Thy faithlessness and broken promises rendered Persia contemptible. What mean these appointments made in the morning and unmade in the evening? Hast thou no shame for thy condition? Mirza Taqi Khan, notwithstanding all his power, still left thee so far authority that when thou didst utter the word "Let him cease to be," he ceased to exist. Now they have not even left thee power to show favor to any one thou wouldest.

Sympathy for the "innocent" Amir Kabir, who "ceased to exist" only by the shah's wishes, presents a striking example of his enduring memory. The author sneered at the shah's labeling of his opponents as Babis, given that Amir Kabir himself was the Babis' archenemy. Lamenting Nuri's ruination, the same rhetorical sarcasm was evident with reference to Faramushkhana. But most remarkable perhaps was the realization, as the author pointed out, of a historical process. The shah's monarchical authority, mastered by Amir Kabir, had allowed the shah to destroy the institution of sidarat, only to have that authority itself fall victim to other usurping forces made up of the same officials who only a few days earlier had forced the shah to reverse his decision on Nuri. Even if this was pro-Nuri propaganda, it still reflected a much wider frustration and longing to return to the days of sidarat. The pamphlet thus made a veiled threat that unless the shah complied with what "the high and the low desire," he would be scandalized and put to shame.

> Shah! By God, the time for thy being a man is fast passing, and the misery of the people has already passed all bounds. Take heed of thy ways, relieve the affliction of thy people or hold thy subjects absolved, if they take measures to bring about what high and low desire. Put away thy intoxicating drinks, or we have that in hand which if made known will

make thee hide thy face for shame. Five hundred of these pamphlets
have been written and will be dispersed throughout every province.

No specific course was proposed, nor could it be said for certain what
sensitive secret could put the shah to shame save for distribution of pamphlets, but the threat of further action was bound to be interpreted as one
of subversion and popular unrest.

Though Ya'qub Khan denied that he was the author of the pamphlet,
he was nevertheless recognized as the ringleader. At the personal request
of the shah, the Russian embassy without resistance terminated his services. His property was auctioned, and he was forced into exile. The charges
of subversion may have been strengthened by the fact that Ya'qub maintained contacts with the British embassy in the hope of eventually facilitating Malkum's return. As much as can be understood from Alison's
muted report, it appears that he approached the envoy with the "avowed
object" of interesting the British mission in his son, who was then in exile
in Baghdad. For unspecified reasons, perhaps a basic distrust in Malkum and
his father, Alison refused to cooperate.[71]

Ya'qub was not remorseful about his and his son's involvement in the
Faramush-khana, nor did he absolve the shah and his ministers of the
accusations of misgovernment. In two letters written just before his expulsion, one to the shah and another to one of his senior ministers,
presumably Farrukh Khan Amin al-Dawla, Ya'qub came dangerously close
to making the criticism cited in the clandestine pamphlet. "Every hour that
loyal minister insists on my departure," he wrote sarcastically. "God
willing my departure will cure all ills of the government and the nation."

In his letter to the shah—which he self-mockingly called the "petition
of an old traitor"—Ya'qub even more poignantly put the blame on himself
and his son for trying to bring together in the Faramush-khana all the
"accomplished and insightful" men of Iran in order to garner support for
the shah's reform wishes. What greater betrayal could the members of the
Faramush-khana have committed to become the objects of His Majesty's
"inward and outward aversion"? Referring to the circumstances surrounding his son's exile, he insisted that although there had been an "opportunity
for disobedience" (*imkan-i tamarrud*), Malkum had complied with the
royal wishes and left the country. He must have "lost his wits," Ya'qub
agreed with the shah. But even the ban on the Faramush-khana, in Ya'qub's
view, was "too late." Like watches and fabrics imported from Europe, the
Faramush-khanah could no longer be thrown out and discredited. Moreover, he viewed the government's "violent" crackdown on the Faramush-
khana "prior to [any signs] of revolt" as completely out of place. "If His

Majesty would have become the supporter, the follower and the patron of this organization then he could have enjoyed his reign," he added with obvious regret. "In the entire land of Iran there is not a single person who would sincerely pledge an oath of loyalty to His Majesty. But if all the people of Iran vowed an oath of loyalty and sacrifice [in the Faramush-khana], his Majesty would have been released from the yoke of bondage."

Though put in slightly naive terms, Ya'qub's statement was clear about the Faramush-khana's effort to forge for the shah a new national constituency that would be reformist in outlook and responsive to the ever-growing demands for material development and social justice. Malkum's masonic secularism primarily aimed, one may presume, to outweigh the entrenched Qajar aristocracy and liberate the shah from subordination to the conservative elite. It was this elusive chance that Ya'qub believed the shah was about to miss. "His Majesty is rejecting his own good fortune and combating his own army. No doubt he will lose. Against this organization [literally, "setup" (basat), meaning Faramush-khana] he has no [alternative] organization, and instead of all these people whom he has now denounced, by God, he has not a single [true] servant."

Faramush-khana's shift toward radicalism, Ya'qub implied, was thus justifiable. Though he insisted that his secret society "ha[d] nothing to do with the Babis," he did not deny that "a thousand organizations such as the Babis' would be absorbed and transformed" by it. He denied the rumors that the Faramush-khana's objective was to assassinate the shah but added, alarmingly, that if this *were* the objective the members could easily have carried it out "a thousand times." Quoting a verse from Sa'di, the celebrated thirteenth-century Persian poet, he ended on an even gloomier note: "Let me present to you in all honesty. From now on I would not trust people's fear. 'Thou who art wise, fear him who fears you' [az an kaz tu tarsad bi-tars ay hakim]."[72]

It is a small wonder that with such an ominous warning the shah, suspicious of his own ministers' membership in the "Tehran lodge" and "apprehensive of incurring the hostility of his chief supporters," issued a double-edged public decree in the *Ruznama-yi Dawlat-i 'Alliya-yi Iran* of 29 May 1862 stressing his wishes that the "opinion of his subjects from high to low should harmonize, and every person as far as his nature permits [should] be free from all faults and errors." The subjects were called upon to "obey the faith," and be "submissive" not only to the royal commands but also in "observance of their duties" and in seeking their "daily subsistence." The emphasis on obedience and conformity in the shah's public declaration was followed by a warning against any "institution" whose members, in spite of earlier prohibitions, "persevered in maintaining it [i.e., the Faramush-khana]." Their conduct was "highly disapproved" of by the shah, who exiled the "chief promoter" but graciously allowed the innocent victims of this "exhibition of jugglery and charlatanry" to remain free because they were not aware of the extent of the royal displeasure. Only the few who persisted were "worthy of punishment," and they were therefore arrested and imprisoned "while others fled to foreign countries."[73]

For all intents and purposes, by mid-1862 the Faramush-khana episode had reached its end. It did not, as Ya'qub Khan had wished, endure like European watches and fabrics. The crackdown was successful to the extent that it ejected all organized elements of dissent beyond the Iranian frontiers. It took another three decades before any concrete movement of dissent could gather momentum, and then under different circumstances. Malkum returned to the Persian political scene less than a decade later, but with far less originality and flair. He conformed with the Qajar establishment but could never again earn the shah's full confidence. His later career was marred by subservience to often futile European concession-hunting enterprises cynically motivated by personal financial gain. Even the London publication, in the early 1890s, of the dissident paper *Qanun* did not fully restore his reputation as an advocate of restrained monarchy. All the same, his views, as apparent first through the propaganda of Faramush-khana and later articulated in the *Qanun*, came to capture the attention of the men of the constitutional period. Malkum himself, perhaps because of his Armenian background and certainly because of lack of family consequence, never managed to reach a high office matching his ambitions.

Breaking away from ideas of political modernization by the mid-1860s, the shah gave way to the conservative element so completely as to become almost their captive. Although he tried to balance off the power of individual ministers by constantly reshuffling the government officials, and although some pro-reform figures lingered in various government posts, by and large the shah's effort to overcome the monopoly of power enjoyed by the Qajar elite proved unsuccessful. Consequently, his approach to public affairs turned more personal and reverted to the most patrimonial mode of monarchy. In 1864, for example, in response to mounting public criticism of his ministers, the shah tried to break the bureaucratic barrier by introducing the "petition box" (literally, "the box of justice," *sanduq-i 'adalat*). The scheme, which owed its creation chiefly to the shah's "distrust toward his own ministers," was a reminder to all of the shah's most ancient function. Perhaps with some inspiration from the legend of the Sasanian ruler Khusraw I, Anushiravan, and his "chain of justice," the shah, as the supreme upholder of the social order, sought to create an "impartial administration of justice." The key to the sealed petition box, declared the public announcement of 27 July, would remain in the shah's hands. Even the archetype of the oppressed subject in Persian literature from the reign of Khusraw to the time of the Saljuq ruler, Sultan Sanjar—the old woman who was robbed of her property and had her most basic rights trampled— was promised perfect justice. "Not even a feeble old woman will be oppressed in the whole of Persia," declared the royal rescript, "and should she be subjected to ill-treatment, on the case being represented to His Majesty a full stop without delay will be put on that oppression and tyranny."[74] The "box of justice" was a vivid example of the shah's relapse into the world of traditional kingship once the domestic and foreign demands for reforms disappeared. Symbolic punishments, such as those that were administered during the Tehran riots, could only be complemented by symbolic justice. The few other institutional reforms still in infancy were abandoned in favor of informal and often haphazard methods of government.

Gobineau's assessment in July 1863 summed up the shah's predicament. He believed the shah was reproaching his ministers for deficiencies for which he himself was primarily responsible. Contrary to the royal hopes, Gobineau asserted, Iran did not prosper under direct rule, the army was in a miserable state, and the income stagnated.

> The shah is aware of the extent of the problem. Yet he has sufficient free spirit [l'esprit assez ouvert] to prevent him from renouncing certain habits of his. His primary education has made him consider these habits as his leisurely prerogative [d'heureuses prerogatives]. He has become too Europeanized to be able to rule like his father with a clear conscience, but not enough to allow him to adopt sincerely a new discipline of foreign ideas. As a result every now and then his hesitation makes him regret the dismissal of his ex-prime minister, and he constantly threatens his current advisers that he will call him back.[75]

As Gobineau correctly observed, the conflict between the old and the new in the shah's mind was rooted in his "leisurely prerogatives." This could best be associated, one may argue, with the "feast" aspect of his rule and the pleasures he increasingly felt he was entitled to enjoy while discharging his kingly duties. The "hesitations" and "regrets" were thus reflective of a state of mind, a struggle between loyalty to a fatherly figure that urged steadfastness, duty, and "fight," as opposed to his own "free spirit," which tended to opt for pleasure and "feast."

THE ROYAL PREROGATIVE

As late as October 1864, six years into the shah's direct rule, the British envoy could still find ample evidence to complain of the "want of an energetic man at the head of the affairs." The shah, he explained, was not "equal to the task of the holding the reins of government." His "constitutional excitability requires frequent change of scene, while application to business impairs his health as well as his temper." However, Alison believed, "suspicion and jealousy" prevented the shah from rendering to a sole minister the conduct of public affairs. As Farrukh Khan Amin al-Dawla, then the minister of interior, had confessed, neither he nor "any of the other ministers had any real power." Although his pro-reform counsels were always received by the shah with favor, "they were invariably buffeted not only by the intrigues of his own colleagues but also by those of the immediate attendants on the royal person who enjoyed the intimacy and confidence of the king and possess[ed] great influence."[76] The shah himself was not excluded from the prevailing stalemate, but at least he could rest assured that no minister would monopolize the power. No case could better demonstrate the never-ending contest between the king and his faction-ridden government than the episode that ended with the death of Nuri under suspicious circumstances.

In March 1865, when the shah revived his periodic threat of bringing Nuri back to power, there was a predictable "disquietude" among the ministers in office. This time the ex-premier was even permitted to reside in Qum, a place dangerously close to the capital and thus not easily accepted by the guardians of the status quo. The shah had declared that from the beginning of the new Persian year (21 March) he would relinquish direct rule and appoint a prime minister and that he had summoned Nuri with the view of having him "reinstated in his former office" seven years after his dismissal. Thus it was with "great satisfaction" that the news of Nuri's sudden death on 9 March 1865 was received by the Tehran political elite. This was as much as the British envoy knew, or was willing to reveal. Under the circumstances, however, it is hard not to read between the lines of his characteristically brief report and detect foul play.[77] One may speculate that Nuri was indeed murdered in secret by his political opponents who felt that their lives and positions would be jeopardized in the event of his return to power. Yet no one seemed particularly anxious to raise embarrassing questions about the untimely death. Even the shah seems to have treated the suspicious death of his ex-premier with gracious indifference. It is hard to believe that he himself perpetrated the crime (if indeed there was one), but there is a possibility that he contributed to Nuri's death by deliberately exposing him to his opponents. He must have been perfectly aware of the repercussions of Nuri's transfer to Qum when he declared his wishes to reinstate him in office. Whether foul play or not, one can hardly resist thinking that the shah could only have been gratified at the death of an ex-servant who had caused him much trouble in and out of office. Yet he must equally have feared the conspiratorial capacities of those who were the obvious beneficiaries of Nuri's demise. On a subliminal level, it may be suggested, Nuri's death may have freed the shah at least temporarily from the shadow of a dominant fatherly figure.

On 23 March, when he appointed Muhammad Khan Qajar to a post "equivalent to that of the grand vizier" with a new title, *sipahsalar a'zam* (grand commander of the army) and allowed him to wear the "tasseled robe ornamented with precious stones," the shah no doubt was sending a message to the conservatives headed by Mustawfi al-Mamalik that he intended to carry on with his original plan, albeit in a modified form. At one time an ally of Nuri, Muhammad Khan Qajar had turned down the shah's offer of premiership "with more prudence than ambition." The fate of the two last premiers, as Alison put it, "had no doubt its due weight in bringing him to this decision." Muhammad Khan's premiership, held in combination with the title of *sipahsalar*, seemed dangerously similar to Amir Kabir's or to Nuri's when the latter assumed full power toward the end of his term. It had become clear to him, as well as to the shah, that he would not be able to form a viable government by excluding other powerful ministers. The shah thus seems to have been persuaded to agree to a compromise. The triumvirate that was eventually formed was dominated by the old guard—the "old bones," as Malkum had put it. It was headed by Muhammad Khan, who also served as minister of war, and included Mustawfi al-Mamalik as finance minister and Sa'id Khan as minister for foreign affairs. Moreover, Amin al-Dawla, the last of the early reform-minded statesmen, was quietly left out of the government and sent back to the exile of his estate in Kashan. It was obvious that in his desire to strike a balance within the government the shah had surrendered to the wishes of his conservative ministers.

The new acting premier, though not on a par with Nuri or Amir Kabir, nevertheless was a military man with the potential to monopolize the bureaucracy and the army. Moreover, he was a Davalu, the "elder branch" of the Qajars, and the only one of that tribal division to rise to prominence since the brief premiership of Allah-yar Khan Asaf al-Dawla in 1826–1827. Not distinguished for high administrative talents or for bureaucratic skills, he was known for his somewhat rough and summary proceedings. Moreover, the Qajar khan had gratified His Majesty before his appointment with the presentation of a "large sum in money," a practice that became ominously synonymous with high-ranking (and later with middle- and low-ranking) appointments as the shah felt less troubled ethically by the flagrant habit of auctioning off government posts to their highest bidders. By appointing a Qajar khan as premier the shah no doubt wanted to avoid commissioning yet another member of the faction-ridden divan.[78] The shah's rescript, insisting on the tripartite nature of the new government—much similar to his intended division of labor at the outset of Nuri's premiership—pronounced the royal wishes to relinquish everyday affairs to his ministers. With typical self-righteousness, the rescript complained that having devoted time to affairs of the state, "we have not had leisure to devote our attention to many special matters, particularly to the administration of our royal prerogative. Many of our important plans thus has been postponed, and in truth we have thought it a pity that our valuable time should be spent any longer in the management of the affairs which by the help of God might be honorably and efficiently managed by our distinguished servants." Although the three ministers were expected to act "like a single person," Muhammad Khan, the acting premier, was to become "the object of hope and fear and obedience to the people."[79]

The most urgent prerogative, as it turned out, was an even greater craving for hunting, and the "important plans" whose postponement the shah lamented were nothing other than his incessant, almost insane, wanderings in the saddle along the picturesque slopes and gorges of the Alburz. The shah "has taken to himself to his favorite pastime of shooting," reported Alison, "and is not expected to return to his capital for some time."[80] No wonder that the tripartite arrangement could only last for little more than a year. In March 1866 a "commotion" in Tehran caused by men who publicly advocated that "all religions are absurd" was soon followed by several "tumults" in the capital in May, again caused by the scarcity of provisions. Though there were still enough Babis to be blamed for the trouble, there was no longer a Nuri to be accused of provoking them. The situation was so sensitive that Mahd 'Ulya, who was "greatly alarmed," telegraphed for the speedy return of the shah from the tour of the Caspian and herself ordered the royal granaries to be opened.[81] Unrest in the capital was enough to turn the shah's easily provoked suspicion against Muhammad Khan, who quickly came to replace his unfortunate predecessor in the shah's psyche. In June 1866 the shah dismissed the acting premier and suppressed the post of premiership for the second time. Moreover, the incident seems to have given the shah a chance to revive the earlier arrangement and try to strike a balance between the conservative and the moderately reform-minded elements. A few ministers were added to the cabinet, and Amin al-Dawla was restored to the post of "minister of the royal presence" (*vazir-i huzur-i khassa*), a demoted version of minister of the court. But the most striking of the shah's improvised schemes was his elimination of the office of interior minister altogether. To compensate, he divided the provincial and other responsibilities of the interior minister among all other ministers. Whereas Astarabad, Khurasan, and a host of smaller governments came under the supervision of the war minister, the finance minister, Mustawfi al-Mamalik, was given the supervision of Azarbaijan, Kurdistan, and few other minor governments, as well as the control of numerous departments in the royal palace. The ministers of the royal presence, foreign affairs, public works, justice, and commerce were also given provincial and miscellaneous functions entirely alien to their ministerial responsibilities.

The rescript of 2 Safar 1283/16 June 1866 announcing the new arrangement was indeed a testimony to the shah's reluctance to allow concentration of power and resources in the hand of any one minister, even at the expense of introducing greater confusion into the administration. The new arrangement also revealed the shah's resistance to the formation of a governmental framework that would require institutional limits on his own power. The bizarre improvisation was rooted as much in the shah's fears and insecurities as in his financial self-interest. Unwilling to restrict his "royal prerogatives," which in reality meant an even greater dose of the "feast," the shah thus opted for even greater factionalism among the bureaucratic barons of this newly emerging oligarchy.[82] The new, makeshift arrangement may have been conceived as a coup de grace against Mustawfi al-Mamalik, ending his monopoly over the finances by allowing every minister a degree of autonomy in raising income from the provinces assigned to him. In effect a fiefdom (*tuyul*) was created for every department of the government. The shah had adopted a curious combination of the old and the new that increasingly was becoming a hallmark of his desperate reign. The new arrangement would have seemed incomplete had the shah not introduced a princely component to the provincial administration. Adopting measures from the time of his great-grandfather, Fath 'Ali Shah, the shah in conjunction with devolving the central government began to assign substantial provincial governorships to his remaining sons. Along with his powerful uncles, who traditionally were the candidates for provincial posts, from the mid-1860s the shah's sons, Muzaffar al-Din Mirza and Mas'ud Mirza, were sent out to govern important provinces.

Whether because of Muhammad Khan's failure to comply with the new regulations, the opposition of fellow ministers to his promotion, or his enormous wealth accumulated as the war minister, he soon found himself in the post of trustee of the shrine of Imam Riza in Mashhad, a position synonymous with respectful but often interminable exile. In a royal tour to Khurasan a year later the shah treated him with great favor, giving rise to speculation that he would soon return to power. But the shah's favor proved fatal, a kiss of death strikingly similar to that bestowed upon Nuri a while ago. Only two days after the royal interview in Mashhad, the Qajar khan "died suddenly of a stroke of apoplexy." Even the usually secretive Alison was prepared to admit that Muhammad Khan's return to power "was very much dreaded by the party in office," no doubt a reference to Mustawfi al-Mamalik and Mirza Sa'id Khan, minister of foreign affairs. Muhammad Khan was "supposed by some people," reported Alison "to have come to his end by foul means. He had accumulated great wealth by his rapacity and parsimony but his death will, in other respects, be regretted by the shah as depriving him of an attached and useful minister."[83] Alison's veiled remark no doubt pointed at the shah's fulfilled wishes to appropriate Muhammad Khan's wealth, a powerful enough motive to condone the khan's secret murder.

In little more than two years, the two most powerful candidates for premiership disappeared from the political scene. Whether the deaths were the shah's own doing or the result of his minister's sinister maneuvers, he seems to have been firmly placed in a political trap from which he could not easily escape. The bureaucratic establishment killed off most reform initiatives, destroyed the old office of sidarat, and even drew the limits of the shah's "royal prerogative." The Qajar elite, an assortment of conservative statesmen, princes, and courtiers of a new generation, managed to cling to power in a complex game of favor and privilege in which one could hardly determine the winner or the loser. When in the late 1860s Mirza Husayn Khan Mushir al-Dawla, the Persian ambassador in Istanbul, began to emerge as a serious candidate for premiership, with grand reforming plans, he seemed the shah's best chance to free himself from the stagnant world of royal politics.

The expediency of maintaining royal sway over the provinces seemed an additional incentive for the shah to deal with the yet unresolved question of apparency. After the death of Amir Qasim in 1858 he had resisted both domestic and foreign pressures, mainly from the British side, to appoint an heir apparent, hoping that Jayran might bear him a new son. But his wishes proved illusive. In January 1860, shortly before Jayran's death, Rawlinson reported that "no single lady in the royal harem has proved pregnant for the last two years. It is generally believed that there is some constitutional derangement which will cause the direct descendants of Nasir al-Din Shah to be confined to the four sons now alone living, namely Muzaffar al-Din Mirza, Kamran Mirza, and two sons of *kaniz* [concubine]: Sultan Mas'ud Mirza and Sultan Husain Mirza."[84]

The cause and nature of the "constitutional derangement" remains unknown, but whatever it was it must have been connected to the shah's infertility, a condition that lasted at least for the next three decades of his life. Whether the shah's infertility was the outcome of a psychosomatic trauma or a hereditary infirmity that caused the death of so many of his offspring is impossible to say. What is certain is that he was greatly agonized by the fact that he could no longer procreate and have a large royal family on the scale of his progenitors. Although he must have preserved his sexual potency, since there is no evidence to the contrary, he nevertheless ought to have felt that he was no longer seen by his subjects as a perfect monarch. The dominant sexual culture of the time, especially within the super-productive Qajar house, no doubt contributed to such a self-image; hence, one may conclude, his restless desire to demonstrate his manliness on the hunting ground and on the throne by a display of vigor or violence.

By 1860 the shah knew he either had to postpone indefinitely the appointment of an heir apparent or to nominate a new one from among his surviving sons. Because of his maternal Qajar descent, Muzaffar al-Din Mirza was the most eligible, though by no means the shah's choice. Nasir al-Din disliked Muzaffar al-Din Mirza in part because of his son's maternal relatives. The shah responded to repeated British reminders with "his characteristic jealousy and suspicion," arguing that Muzaffar al-Din Mirza's nomination would inevitably give undue prominence to his son's maternal relatives. The prince's mother, Shukuh al-Saltana, whom the shah equally disliked, was the daughter of Fathullah Mirza, thirty-fifth son of Fath 'Ali Shah. There was some justification for the shah's concern, especially given the old tension that existed between the ruling house of 'Abbas Mirza and other sons of Fath 'Ali Shah. Moreover, the shah's concern for Muzaffar al-Din's apparency seems to have deepened because of Fath 'Ali Mirza's presumed Shaykhi leanings, more specifically his adherence to his relative Hajji Muhammad Karim Khan, the Shaykhi leader of Kirman and himself of Qajar ancestry. In the shah's mind such a connection was enough to bring about Muzaffar al-Din's eventual adherence to Shaykhism, a sectarian tendency that at the time had not yet distanced itself fully from its ideological sibling and rival, the Babi movement.[85]

The shah's contempt for Muzaffar al-Din had other personal roots. One can surmise that the sickly and unanimated prince reminded his royal father of his own unhappy childhood and "weak constitution." One can almost observe in his treatment of Muzaffar al-Din a pattern similar to Muhammad Shah's treatment of Nasir al-Din during the uncertain years of his apparency—the same coldness and rejection, dislike for the mother, and favor toward a rival brother of non-Qajar maternal descent. The subject of the shah's affection was his youngest son, Kamran Mirza, who was lately born to the daughter of the royal architect. For Nasir al-Din Shah, Kamran Mirza carried the same favor as 'Abbas Mirza (III) did for Muhammad Shah. It is not perhaps an accident that while discussing with Rawlinson the question of apparency and possible appointment of a regent—a circumstance very similar to Nasir al-Din's own position prior to 1848—the shah showed the British envoy documents that tended "to keep alive his suspicion" toward the exiled 'Abbas Mirza. Among them he presented a notebook by his father in which there were "various memoranda with royal handwriting expressive of affection to his younger son [i.e., 'Abbas Mirza] and indicating a desire to appoint him successor to the throne." Nasir al-Din even read one of the entries in Muhammad Shah's hand to the curious Rawlinson: "This day my Lord, the Hajee [Mirza Aqasi], assured me he had ascertained [i.e., by intuitive means] that my little pet, Abbas, would be one day the Shah of Persia, and my heart has been light ever since." Nasir al-Din confessed in a rare moment of truth that he "has ever before him the phantom of his crowned brother reigning in his place."[86] It was perhaps this "phantom" that was now casting its shadow over the miserable Muzaffar al-Din Mirza. He was not only a constant reminder of the shah's most unhappy days but also a shadow of the shah's hated brother.

Multifaceted as were the origins of shah's dislike for his eligible son, the circumstances were bound to modify them. In February 1860 Nasir al-Din had told Rawlinson that since he "was not destined to have anymore children" and that "he had been so unfortunate . . . in his previous nominations," he did not "wish to provoke fortune further by placing either of his remaining sons in the envied but fatal position."[87] Yet the royal expediency dictated otherwise. More than a year later, in May 1861, Muzaffar al-Din was named "de facto governor" of Azarbaijan, an appointment widely interpreted as a prelude to his nomination (see Pl. 23). Accompanied by 'Aziz Khan Sardar Kull as his chief steward, the prince thus began a tenure as governor of Azarbaijan that lasted exactly thirty-five years. A year later, on 21 May 1862, Muzaffar al-Din's nomination as heir to the throne was made official. Without even having bothered to summon him to the capital, the shah invested the nomination on the prince by proxy in a military camp in the plain of Ujan.[88] The royal favor looked more like a respected exile. It was as though the shah had overcome his inner resistance to the nomination by rewarding himself with the pleasure of not seeing his son for a long time. Seldom again was Muzaffar al-Din permitted to pay a visit to his father. When he did, it was not free from friction. For most of the time even his governorship in Azarbaijan was not real. Almost always "advised" by powerful stewards (pishkars) who were fully loyal to the shah and directly in contact with him, the crown prince seldom was given real responsibility during his long rehearsal for the throne. Each time he was given the privilege of governing the province on his own, he was pushed aside by his scolding father, who accused him of incompetence, corruption, and indulgence.

The decision to nominate Muzaffar al-Din Mirza nevertheless put an end to years of uncertainty and ambivalence. It also effectively ended speculation about the old claimants, Bahman Mirza and 'Abbas Mirza, whose claims were entertained by the Russian and British governments, respectively. The shah's decision to confirm the right of Qajar primogeniture to apparency must also have pleased Mahd 'Ulya and the Qajar aristocracy, even though the shah's harem may not have unanimously shared such sentiments. The shah's wives soon resigned themselves to the unwelcome reality that power and royal favor were no longer achievable by means of bearing new sons for the shah. The shah's infertility, combined with the nomination of Muzaffar al-Din, had the effect of terminating the traditional harem contest for promoting rival candidates for apparency. Instead the shah's wives, particularly of lower ranks, sought new channels by which to gain the shah's favor. Not surprisingly, the shah's curious infatuation with the page boys of his private court (khalwat) began shortly after the question of succession was settled. The first of the two Malijaks (malijak, literally, "little sparrow" in Kurdish, a term of endearment conferred by the shah on his favorite page boy) received royal attention as early as the mid-1860s. The son of a Kurdish shepherd from Garrus whose sister, Amina Aqdas, served first as the maid and then as the rival to the shah's favorite wife, Anis al-Dawla, later became the focus of royal affection. It was through Amina Aqdas that this Malijak was first introduced to the court. He came to substitute for the shah the place of a favorite son, one that after the death of Amir Qasim had remained vacant. Later, in the 1880s, the first Malijak was replaced by his son, Ghulam 'Ali 'Aziz al-Sultan, in the shah's heart, an operation designed and carried out by Amina Aqdas to insure her effective and enduring control over her royal master.[89]

The appointment of prince governors nevertheless was part of the shah's effort to reconstruct a new model of government. Not only was Muzaffar al-Din Mirza sent to Azarbaijan, but almost simultaneously in 1862 his brother Mas'ud Mirza (first with the title Yamin al-Dawla and, later, Zill al-Sultan [see Pl. 24]) was appointed to the government of Fars, the second most important provincial seat in the land. Being appointed to the government of Isfahan in 1865, Mas'ud Mirza became as enduring a figure in the center and south of Iran as was Muzaffar al-Din in Azarbaijan. Although the size of his government, at one time including sixteen large and small provinces throughout central, southern, and western Iran, altered dramatically according to the shah's favor or fear, Mas'ud Mirza maintained his hold over Isfahan all the way up to 1907, when he was eventually forced out of office by the coming of the Constitutional Revolution.

Mas'ud Mirza's tenure in the south meant to counterbalance his brother's government in Azarbaijan, a pattern almost identical with Fath 'Ali Shah's allocation of provincial posts among his powerful sons. A man of entirely different disposition to Muzaffar al-Din, Mas'ud Mirza proved to be a capable administrator, ruthless and cunning and with a passion for hunting no less out of control than his father's. It was no accident that in 1869 he was given the title of Zill al-Sultan, "the shadow of the king," for none of the shah's sons inherited the father's political resiliency or complexity of character as did Mas'ud Mirza. His daring conduct and his tyrannical methods of government were tolerated by the shah not only because the prince took advantage of his father's guilty conscience but because the shah found in him an assertiveness and candor missing in Muzaffar al-Din. As the shah's oldest son, Mas'ud Mirza could always remind the shah that even though his mother was a low-born *kaniz*, she was no less Qajar than Jayran, and thus the rule of primogeniture would apply to him even more than it did to Amir Qasim. Over the years the shah's rather subdued behavior toward his son's constant nagging could only be taken as a way of consoling Zill al-Sultan for the inevitable injustice that he sustained on the question of succession.

Yet the shah's Faridun-like assignment of large chunks of his kingdom to his sons could not, and did not, have the same disastrous outcome as in *Shahnama*'s epic-tragedy. With the same resiliency with which he resisted the emergence of another independent sidarat in the center, the shah also resisted the emergence of autonomous prince-governors in provinces, even if this meant sacking Zill al-Sultan in 1887 from all his posts save for governorship of Isfahan or angrily recalling Muzaffar al-Din Mirza to the capital on numerous occasions. He avoided princely insurrection and political turmoil by his sons and uncles (and later his half-brothers 'Abbas Mirza III, who after his rehabilitation in 1871 was given the title Mulk Ara; Muhammad Taqi Mirza Rukn al-Dawla; and 'Abd al-Samad Mirza 'Izz al-Dawla) by monitoring, erratic as they were, their political conduct, their personal lives, their sources of income, and their military capabilities.

Perhaps more effective than any single factor in the shah's exercising his hold over the princely rule in provinces of his Guarded Domains was the introduction of modern means of communication in Iran—namely, the telegraphic system. Becoming operational in 1865, the growing telegraph network revolutionized the method of command and surveillance, permitting him rapid and direct contact with the provinces. In 1861, when the first experimental telegraphic line between Tehran and Karaj, a distance of thirty miles, was established by Austrian engineers serving in Dar al-Funun, the British envoy considered it no more than a "toy" to please the shah. Even if this was the case at the outset, the shah soon realized the potential for this remarkable instrument of direct rule that could connect him not only to the provincial centers of his own land but also with the capitals of neighboring countries and beyond. No technological innovation in modern times left the same impact on the political life of Iran (and other countries of the Middle East). Of all the economic and political reform plans and modernization measures undertaken in the Nasiri period, the telegraph proved the most successful. The new era in the political career of Nasir al-Din Shah was thus inaugurated not by the growth of the shah's power, the decline of the sidarat, nor even the shift in British and Russian policies toward Iran in the 1860s and 1870s but rather by the establishment of the telegraphic lines. By September 1869, only eight years after Iran's first experimental telegraph, the British Indo-European line had been in full operation for four years, and the first line between Tehran and Julfa owned by the Persian government and constructed by the German engineer, Mr. Siemens, had become operational.[90]

The shah's efforts to maintain a delicate balance between the old and the new, between the conservatives and the modernizers, and between the center and the periphery, was thus consolidated with the new lines of communication. In the following decades the impact of the telegraph became more apparent, but even in the short term its effect on Iran's relation with her neighbors was immense. Swift contact with London, St. Petersburg, Bombay, and Istanbul to a large extent diminished the foreign envoys' role as the chief initiators of their countries' policies toward Iran. The telegraph allowed diplomacy to be conducted in the capitals and by foreign ministers. Thus, room for independent maneuvers by envoys such as Sheil, Murray, and Dolgorouki, whose self-initiated actions in the past generated much friction with the host government, was noticeably diminished. Perhaps more important for Iran's future, the new means of communication allowed the Persian government, and above all the shah himself, to open a dialogue with the higher authorities in foreign capitals not only via their representatives in Tehran but soon after through Persian envoys. In the following years such methods of communication proved to be a great asset to the shah in maintaining a balance, fragile though it was, between the two neighboring powers. Here, too, as in his domestic policy, he utilized selective means of modernity to preserve a delicate equilibrium. Through modern technology and selective reforms in his administration as well as by expediency and negotiation or, as a last resort, by coercion, he was still hoping to maintain the same "cycle of equity" whose upkeep he considered his chief kingly duty.

Epilogue: Remnants of a Reign

By 1871, when Nasir al-Din was forty years old, he had ruled over Iran for more than twenty-three years. During this time he consolidated his throne and achieved considerable political maturity. He remained on the throne for another quarter of a century before he was assassinated on 1 May 1896. The latter part of his reign deserves a separate study that would look, among other things, at aspects of the Qajar court and culture under his rule. The external and domestic forces of change in the succeeding decades were immense, yet it was the first phase of Nasir al-Din's rule that set the pace for the remainder of his years. In the crucial period between 1848 and 1871, the patterns of domestic and foreign policy were set, and the position of the monarchy vis-à-vis the state and society was determined. In some ways the model of autocracy that was set in the early Nasiri era was still visible even in the monarchy of the Pahlavi period.[1]

The shah's private life, too, continued to be dominated by the same routine that had marked his childhood and youth. Even though Nasir al-Din experienced spells of exhaustion and repeated emotional setbacks in his final years, he remained essentially the same man, with the same habits and temperament. The haphazard mix of the public and the private—the inevitable outcome of structural weaknesses in the first part of his rule—left its permanent mark on the shah's conduct and on his court. His personality, with all its fears and trepidation, bore the enduring signs of this ominous amalgamation.

PRECARIOUS ORDER WITHIN

The tenor of the shah's political behavior in the decades that followed was remarkably even. For the rest of his reign Nasir al-Din did not engage in any major diplomatic or military wrangles with the neighboring powers, nor did he wage wars for territorial gain. The period between the end of the Marv expedition in 1860–1861 and the Regie protest in 1891–1892 was uneventful on the domestic front. In spite of endemic corruption, the oppressive behavior of agents of the state, chronic famine, ravaging epidemics, and the stagnant, if not declining, economy, there were very few major urban riots, peasant revolts, religious insurrections, or massive political crises.[2] In 1873 a palace revolt staged by the conservative Qajar nobility and its bureaucratic and clerical allies in conjunction with the harem accelerated the repeal of the Reuter Concession and forced the shah, under pressure, to dismiss his reform-minded premier, Mirza Husayn Khan Mushir al-Dawla. Over the course of the following years, however, the shah gradually regained lost ground, dismantling the conservative alliance and reinstating Mushir al-Dawla at the ministerial level, though he never again served as prime minister.

It had taken some four decades since the Babi revolt of 1848–1852 before a serious crisis such as the Regie protest could successfully shake the pillars of Nasir al-Din's throne. Events such as the 1880 Kurdish revolt of the Naqshbandi leader Shaykh 'Ubaydullah and his allies, for instance, had only a minor impact on the stability of the Qajar government. Soundly defeated by the shah's army (in spite of initial Ottoman support for 'Ubaydullah), the revolt stands out in the chronicles of the late Qajar period not only because it was a rare victory against a frontier rebel but also because the Qajar court chroniclers had few other events by which they could glorify their patron.[3]

The paucity of major revolts, however, should not be taken as evidence of a lack of low-intensity conflicts in the cities and in the countryside. The official Persian records, the reports of foreign consuls and native "news writers," and the occasional testimonies of the populace indicate a considerable degree of violence and oppression by local authorities as well as by a variety of nomadic forces on the periphery. In spite of Russian annexation of the Central Asian khanates of Bukhara, Marv, and Khiva, bothersome Turkoman incursions continued to plague the northeastern provinces of Khurasan, Mazandaran, and Astarabad. The anxiety over Afghanistan and the Afghan incursions into central Khurasan dragged on for another decade after the 1856 war. They finally came to an end when the British sponsored a fragile unification of the previously nonintegrated Afghanistan. In the western and northwestern provinces of Iran, incursions and banditry on the frontier by local Arab and Kurdish tribes constantly clouded Perso-Ottoman relations and drained the limited resources of the Persian government.

In central and southern Iran—notably Isfahan, Fars, and Kirman provinces—it was primarily the Bakhtiyari, the Qashqa'i, and the confederacy of Khamsa that undermined the power of the central government and engendered instability outside and inside the cities. Shiraz, the provincial

capital of Fars, was frequently the scene of violent clashes, not only between the highly polarized city wards on the old Haydari-Ni'mati pattern of division but also among the local notables and powerful chiefs of
the surrounding tribes. In Isfahan, the seat of the provincial government
of Zill al-Sultan, the powerful Bakhtiyari confederacy was kept precariously under check through skillful, though ruthless, juxtapositions of
the tribal chiefs, as well as other incentives and punitive measures. Thanks
to Nasir al-Din's efforts, haphazard though they were, at no time during
the remaining years of his reign were any of the peripheral powers, nomadic or otherwise, potent enough to challenge the existence of the central government—a crowning achievement for the shah and the direct
result of the consolidation efforts implemented during the first phase of
his rule.[4]

The shah's success in achieving relative tranquility went only so far as
to guarantee his survival at the center of his own universe. The same
balance between chaos and order observable in domestic affairs was at work
in the shah's treatment of the central administration. In an endless game
of chess-like maneuvers and countermaneuvers, dismissals, reinstate-
ments, grants of royal favor (*iltifat*), infliction of royal wrath (*ghazab*),
exiles, secret murders (most notoriously by means of a poisonous brew
known as "Qajar coffee" [*qahva-yi Qajar*]), palace intrigue, bribery, annual auctioning of offices (provincial governorships as well as ministerial
appointments), extortion in the guise of gifts (*pishkish*) and estate taxes
imposed on deceased members of the government and court, and compromise and coercion, the shah was able to walk a tightrope. This precarious
arrangement survived in spite of its susceptibility to all manner of mischief
and abuse, the shah's personal greed, and the misdeeds of his ministers and
courtiers, his harem, his sons and uncles, and their relatives, dependents,
clients, and servants.

Yet for a long time the shah's Persian chessboard lacked a vizier.[5] His
efforts to eliminate the powerful office of the sidarat remained a distinctive
characteristic of his reign up to the late 1880s and the rise of 'Ali Asghar
Khan Amin al-Sultan. Earlier, Husayn Khan Mushir al-Dawla had tried to
revitalize the office within the framework of a Western-style administration. Appointed sadr a'zam in 1871, he had been reinstated, in the aftermath
of the 1873 revolt, as minister of war and, later, in other ministerial
capacities, only to see his reform initiatives nullified by the conservative
faction led by Mustawfi al-Mamalik. The shah nevertheless selectively
benefited from Mushir al-Dawla's reform measures to the same extent that
he had benefited earlier from Amir Kabir's reforms.

Nearly all the measures introduced by Mushir al-Dawla to rationalize the government apparatus, to restrict the abuses of the officeholders, to implement a code of administrative law, to regulate the judicial process and government courts, and to allow a limited degree of consultative representation on the model of the neighboring Ottoman Empire were ultimately compromised by the shah and modified to suit his own wishes. The shah took into account not only his "royal prerogative" but also his undiminished concern with appeasing the foreign interests and the conservative establishment, made up of the Qajar aristocracy, the bureaucratic class, and the 'ulama. The fate of the Consultative Council, the organ revitalized by Mushir al-Dawla to interact with his ministerial council, testifies to the way the shah purposefully modified the reform measures. The Consultative Council (*majlis-i dar al-shura*), which up to the end of the Nasiri period met irregularly and under different names (in the true spirit of Nasir al-Din's resistance to bureaucratic consistency), was deprived of an effective role in the affairs of the state beyond advising the shah on matters of domestic, and occasionally foreign, policy. Though the council did more than simply rubber-stamp the shah's often erratic decisions, and though it was more than a mere dumping ground for defunct notables and less desirable elements in the shah's government who entertained suspect reformist views, it was to a great extent deprived of its original functions as a legislative body charged with the task of codifying the secular practices (*'urf*) into an administrative body of law (*qanun*).[6]

Throughout all the years following the final dismissal of Mushir al-Dawla in 1881, the shah managed to resist all institutional measures that placed restrictions on his inconsistent and capricious conduct. This conscious desire to circumvent any long-term administrative procedure in effect placed a heavy burden on the shah's own shoulders, making him directly responsible for all decisions, great and small. All matters—financial, administrative, diplomatic, military, as well as private and personal—were to be brought to his attention, and his personal decisions were to be implemented at all levels. The ministers in charge were often no more than executive officers with ill-defined responsibilities and doubtful authority who were held accountable for failures essentially caused by royal intrusion into their ministerial spheres. To compensate for the inefficiency of the administrative apparatus, the shah's short-lived improvisations and his efforts to build alternative means of redressing popular grievances provided only superficial remedies. The various methods of receiving popular petitions (*'arayiz*) and responding to them, the symbolic punishment of corrupt low- and middle-ranking officials, the declarations guaranteeing individual rights to life and property, even the fostering of a limited degree of tolerance for recognized religious minorities could not substantially reverse the deep-rooted malaise of the system. Nor could these, or other, similar measures, build an enduring institutional framework free from the shah's constant adjustments and intrusions. They only helped to perpetuate a precarious balance built by the shah, dependent on the shah, and ultimately made for the shah. For all forty-eight years of his rule he barely managed to rise above the prosaic trees of autographs, directives, decrees, and budget lists to see the complexity of the governmental forest through which he maneuvered throughout his political career. He remained excruciatingly unimaginative, even when it came to envisioning bureaucratic practices that would have eased his own burden. Nasir al-Din's concept of kingship and society thus, remarkably, remained as static as it was unarticulated. He was discharging the same functions that the time-honored Persian theory of government required of the king. It was on the person of the shah, rather than any institutional device, that the prosperity or the ruin of the state and the country depended, and it was his personal conduct and judgment that maintained the delicate balance between the government and the people.

Yet Nasir al-Din Shah's task as a monarch on the threshold of a changing age was far more formidable than that of his predecessors, for he had to deal not only with the traditional components of power that helped preserve the balance of the state but also with the new forces represented by foreign powers, technological advances, and ideological dissent. This newly emerging interrelation between the domestic and foreign elements, between the old and the new, became even more volatile once the shah began to consolidate his power by dismantling the intermediary agents that had stood between him and his subjects.

The termination of the first phase of lukewarm reforms in the early 1860s effectively put an end to the growth of any political alternative to what Nasir al-Din acknowledged as being an "autocratic monarchy" (*saltanat-i mustaqilla*). The elements of political and religious dissent were either co-opted by the shah's expanding government, particularly by the diplomatic service, or relegated to the political wilderness of neighboring lands. After the exile of the Babi leadership to Baghdad in 1852 (later to the remoteness of Edirne in 1863 and then beyond, to Palestine and Cyprus, in 1868), the subsequent decades saw little organized resistance within Iran. Random Babi persecutions were often initiated by the 'ulama and received the shah's support. His deep fear of a recurring Babi revolt was not substantially obviated by Baha'ullah's statements that he and the moderate

Babis who adhered to him as Baha'is had abandoned (if they had ever entertained) any wish to overthrow the Qajars and assassinate the shah.

Baha'ullah's call for moderation in the nascent Baha'i doctrine, particularly after his 1869 exile to 'Akka, came to represent a moral ethos increasingly disengaged from political involvement as it fit his essentially mystical worldview. Nasir al-Din Shah never recognized the sincerity of Baha'ullah's disclaimers and his doctrinal dissociation from the still politically active Azali-Babi minority. Under the nominal leadership of his brother and contender for primacy, Mirza Yahya Subh Azal, the Azali Babis, at least in theory, remained committed to the prospect of a messianic revolt against the Qajars; yet, compared to the Baha'is, they were molested less by the 'ulama and the government, for they had no compunctions about practicing the time-honored Shi'ite tradition of dissimulation (ta-qiyya). In spite of the doctrinal and political reorientation of the Baha'i majority toward a tacit recognition of the Qajar monarchy, the Babi idea of dual opposition to the state and the 'ulama remained a major source of popular dissent in Persian society long before the arrival of Western-inspired ideologies.[7]

Alternative forces of dissent did not appear in earnest until the time of the Regie protest (1891–1892), when sectors of the mercantile community, having secured the support of high-ranking 'ulama and the backing of small but active dissident circles in large cities, successfully mobilized the urban population against the Qajar state, particularly its sale of concessions to foreign concerns. So far as Nasir al-Din Shah was concerned, the significance of the Regie protest lay primarily in the fact that, for the first time since the Babi insurrections of the late 1840s, not only were his arbitrary conduct and personal greed severely criticized, but his legitimacy as the ruler was questioned.[8]

The highly critical statements of Sayyid Jamal al-Din Asadabadi (better known as "Afghani") against the shah, though in part the outcome of a personal vendetta, exemplified a body of dissident literature that for the first time called openly for the downfall of Nasir al-Din Shah. This literature was not against the monarchy per se, nor even openly against the Qajar dynasty. Rather, it disqualified Nasir al-Din for his misgovernment, his personal profligacy and self-indulgence, the corruption of his ministers and officials, the decline of the country, the vulnerability of its citizens, and above all for the shah's giving in to the wishes of foreign powers. Though obviously inspired by the then-current Western themes of reform and accountability of the ruler, the spirit of the Regie protest was still profoundly influenced by the ancient notion of justice and the king's duty.

Nasir al-Din was blamed for disturbing the delicate balance between the efficiency and integrity of the state and the prosperity and welfare of the subjects. He was also held culpable for undermining the equally ancient, and equally Persian, tradition of harmony between the twin pillars of sociopolitical stability—the state and the good faith. The shah was blamed by the 'ulama primarily for allowing foreign intrusion into the Guarded Domains, an incidence of neglect that in their eyes, as in the eyes of their traditional or tactical allies, was tantamount to a serious breach of the most important royal duty—the defense of the kingdom and the faith.

Unlike the lay dissidents, however, the 'ulama seldom called for Nasir al-Din's downfall. They, as well as the shah, were well aware of the organic links that tied these two ancient institutions together. The advice of the Zoroastrian priest Tansar in the Sassanian book of council to the kings— that kingship and good religion were siblings that could not survive without each other's support—still echoed in the political milieu of late-nineteenth-century Iran. There was common ground between Nasir al-Din Shah, who granted the tobacco monopoly to the Regie company and then was obliged under the threat of a popular revolt to repeal it, and Mirza Hasan Shirazi, the celebrated mujtahid and "supreme exemplar" who was obliged to sanction the boycott on the use of tobacco as long as it remained the monopoly of the British-owned company. For both of them the need for state-religion interdependency were still very much alive. No doubt it was this awareness that brought the Regie protest to its end once the shah recognized, as he had done on other critical occasions throughout his reign, the importance of sustaining correct relations with the religious establishment. In spite of his earlier blunders, the shah's political astuteness saved him from certain revolution—and one with uncertain consequences.

A certain level of tension did exist between the state and some powerful mujtahids, and clashes between the 'ulama and agents of the Qajar state did occur. Yet it is wrong to believe that such conflicts were anything more than disputes over the boundaries of clerical influence. At no time during the Qajar period—not even during the reign of Fath 'Ali Shah, which is considered the golden age of Usuli mujtahids—did the 'ulama ever put forth a serious political claim, theoretically or practically, against the position and authority of the monarch; nor did they ever call, individually or collectively, for the downfall of the ruler, let alone for the destruction of the institution of monarchy. On the contrary, the 'ulama of the Qajar era were often explicit in their defense of the monarchy and its necessity to protect the "pale of Islam" (*biyza-yi Islam*) against all manner of dissenters, heretics, and foreign infidels. If the shah was ever cautioned by the 'ulama on issues beyond their personal or collective concern, it was to remind him of his duty to protect the faith, by which they primarily meant the *shari'a* and the institutions traditionally falling under their purview.

What did remain formidable for Nasir al-Din Shah in his dealings with the religious establishment was not a dispute over legitimacy (as misconstrued by some and misrepresented by others) but rather the need for a balance between clerical concerns and his own political and personal interests. Such territorial challenges by the 'ulama frequently weakened the shah's resolve to implement reforms and persuaded him to take sides with the conservatives in his own government who warned him against modernization in areas of social and economic life not mandated to the monarchy.

Perhaps the most prominent reason for the paucity of educational and judicial reforms in the Nasiri era and the resistance to new aspects of Europe's material culture was the shah's realistic apprehension of intruding into the 'ulama's sphere. Nasir al-Din was daring in introducing symbolic manifestations of modernity in areas independent of the clergy. The introduction of the telegraph; the adoption of Western-style military uniforms and, later, civilian dress; royal European tours; even the publication of his travel accounts, in which he often explicitly recorded his dealings with foreign heads of state, partaking at their tables and engaging in discussions with unveiled women of royalty, were steps in a secular direction. The clergy, for all their puritanical grumbling, were obliged to ignore the shah's measures and go along with his wishes as long as he avoided intruding into their jealously guarded domain. But if the above measures and other innovations of the Nasiri period or the scandals surrounding the shah's personal life and those of his courtiers and officials—from the royal favorite, Malijak, to the shah's premier, Amin al-Sultan—were tolerated, it was because the shah conspicuously avoided confrontation with the 'ulama on issues of great sensitivity.

The 'ulama's monopoly over religious courts, in their view, included jurisdiction over the law of "contracts," both civil and commercial, "unilateral obligations," and aspects of penal law that fell within the religious duty of "enjoining the good and prohibiting the evil." From Mushir al-Dawla's time or after, no judicial reform ever took firm hold, primarily because the shah was well aware of the possibility of clerical revolt. In a typically Qajar compromise, the boundaries between customary law (*'urf*) and religious law (*shar'*) thus remained deliberately unmarked so as to allow the government ample room in which to introduce minuscule legal reforms. Yet even by the end of the Nasiri era there was no legal codification of any significance, nor was the judicial machinery of the state capable of extending any meaningful jurisdiction over the mujtahids' courts. The idea of the dispensation of justice by the king in the Persian theory of government remained, as always, a quest for preserving social equilibrium, not a direct administration of justice, which was largely the domain of the 'ulama.[9]

Similarly, the growth of secular education was severely hampered by the 'ulama's claim over the very concept and availability of knowledge. With the exception of Dar al-Funun, the only secular institution of higher education for most of the Nasiri era, no modern elementary, intermediary, or advanced school was established in Iran before the last decade of the nineteenth century. In contrast to Ottoman and Egyptian reformers, Nasir al-Din remained ambivalent, if not unenthusiastic, about even a limited introduction of Western education. He took some pride in Dar al-Funun, the brainchild of his slain minister Amir Kabir, often visiting classrooms and monitoring students' progress (see Pl. 31). But he could never be persuaded to create, or support others in creating, similar institutions. Nor did he ever appreciate fully the potential of modern education as a vehicle for secularism. In this regard, his concern about the hazards of Western knowledge corresponded well with the 'ulama's conservative views. Public education in the European fashion, the shah believed, was an invitation to social innovation and, ultimately, political trouble. His ban on traveling abroad except for diplomatic or other government-sponsored missions, a policy he began to enforce somewhat haphazardly toward the end of his reign, kept to a bare minimum the number of graduates of Western institutions in the government. The graduates of Dar al-Funun, too, were hardly so numerous as to reverse the hegemony of the old-fashioned bureaucrats in the state administration. Up to the end of the Nasiri era the definition of education, as far as the majority of the population was concerned, barely transcended the traditional concept of the Qur'anic school (*maktab*) and the seminary (*madrasa*). Within the confines of the *madrasa*, too, the 'ulama were able to repel all elements of dissent that could potentially reform the old scholastic education. The students of philosophy (*hikmat*) and the followers of speculative Sufism and Shaykhism were isolated or relegated to the academic periphery, and the Usuli obsession with jurisprudence reigned supreme within the *madrasa* system.

Beyond the 'ulama's opposition, it is difficult to attribute the staggering absence of modern education to anything but the shah's personal convictions and limited perspective on the state's public responsibilities. No doubt the shrinking finances of the Qajar state contributed to the persistence of his attitude; yet this aspect should not be exaggerated beyond proportion. In spite of financial troubles endemic to the Qajar state, the shah was capable of financing preferred projects: communications, the army, urban development, and, of course, palace construction. Nor was he short of advisers urging him to modernize in the areas of education and the judiciary. He listened to them, but never attentively enough to act upon their advice. Instead, he encouraged those aspects of traditional education that, although not representative of mainstream Usuli scholasticism, were in no way detrimental to it. His patronage of philosophers (*hukama*), among them Mulla Hadi Sabzavari and Mirza Husyan Jilva, and occasional partiality toward Hajji Mirza Karim Khan Kirmani, the leader of Kirman's Shaykhis, were two examples. His desire to preserve the existing balance accounted for such equalizing patronage, yet he could hardly condone as drastic a change as the creation of a modern school or court system.[10]

FROM DEFIANCE TO DEFERENCE

Aside from his dealings with the bureaucrats, the 'ulama, and the tribal khans in the domestic arena, the shah's transactions with European powers continued to play a formidable part in his quest for security. Foreign relations, perhaps more than any other factor, affected not only the shah's political well-being but also Qajar political life and Iran's territorial integrity. The latter half of Nasir al-Din's reign proved to be every bit as daunting as the first half. The foreign presence was not limited to diplomatic and military matters but extended into economic penetration of the home markets and (from the shah's traditional viewpoint) the permeation of his subjects' minds with new ideas and institutions. With understandable dismay Nasir al-Din Shah began to realize that the power of the Western economies and political ideas could be as menacing to the stability of his throne as the brute power of Russian cannons and British gunboats and as inevitable as the presence of the diplomats who promoted the one and dissuaded him from pursuing the other. Despite the cumulative experience of his predecessors, it still took Nasir al-Din the first two decades of his rule to come to grips with this reality.

If Nasir al-Din scored high marks in any area beyond the preservation of domestic stability, it would have to be in his handling of foreign policy in the age of high imperialism, when he had the least room to maneuver. The futility of confronting the European powers on the battlefield or at the negotiating table convinced the shah, even more than it did his predecessors, that the foreign presence and its all-encompassing consequences were inescapable facts of life. But in the process he also learned that, if handled with skill, the imperial rivalry between the powers could be used to the benefit of his throne. By closely supervising the conduct of foreign policy for most of the period after Nuri, the shah managed to play off his two powerful neighbors against each other, often with considerable mastery, and, within his limited means, to capitalize on their imperial fears and strategic preoccupations.

The balance that was achieved almost up to the middle of the 1880s was precarious and swung wildly from one pole to the other. Nevertheless, the shah's was a remarkable achievement when compared to the ominous prospects of his Muslim neighbor, the Ottoman Sultan 'Abd al-Hamid II (1876–1909), or the risky modernization gambles of Khedive Isma'il (1863–79) of Egypt. The shah often successfully employed his bargaining power in the bipolar politics of the Anglo-Russian "cold war" to sustain his country's territorial integrity when all the rulers in comparable positions were fast losing territory and sovereignty to imperial Europe. The Ottoman loss of the Balkans and North Africa, the British occupation of Egypt, the French colonization of North Africa, the Russian annexation of the Central Asian khanates, and the virtual control of a united Afghanistan and the Persian Gulf by British India were foreboding messages that Nasir al-Din could digest only with a mixture of sober fatalism and sanguine indulgence.[11]

Yet the shah was not entirely oblivious of the need to upgrade his military capability in the land and in sea. Among many abortive attempts aimed at improving Iran's southern defense, in 1859, two years after Iran's defeat in the war with England, he was hoping to seek U.S. support in order to build up a naval presence in the Persian Gulf. In what appears to be Iran's first attempt to purchase arms from the United States, Nasir al-Din instructed his minister for foreign affairs, Mirza Sa'id Khan, to negotiate through the Persian envoy to Istanbul, Mirza Husayn Khan (later Mushir al-Dawla), the possibility of procuring from the United States a fleet of warships and merchant ships to be employed in the Persian Gulf. In his letter Sa'id Khan, acknowledging "the perfect skill of the government of the United States in this area," asked Husayn Khan to ascertain, preferably in secret, from his U.S. counterpart in Istanbul the cost of such a fleet, as well as the necessary manpower, training, and maintenance. On the margin of Sa'id Khan's letter the shah added in his own hand: "God willing, I wish to gradually purchase warships and launch them in the Persian Gulf. I regard purchase of ships from the United States a necessity." His wish list included "three warships, one with thirty guns and two others with twenty guns," a covetous reflection, perhaps, upon what the British fleet had done to the port of Muhammara in 1857. Four months later, in another dispatch, Sa'id Khan informed the Persian envoy to Istanbul that the shah had seen the report of his negotiation with the United States' envoy but that the royal mind was perturbed by the high prices, which were beyond Iran's capacity. Husayn Khan was told that for the time being he should not pursue the matter further. Yet in the same dispatch the envoy was informed that the Persian envoy to Paris, Hasan 'Ali Khan Garrusi, had been asked to send an emissary to the United States to follow up the negotiations. Perhaps, he speculated, "a better deal can be worked out."[12]

It was concern with British protest rather than the high prices that discouraged the shah to abandon the project temporarily, but he did not forget it altogether. In 1883 the shah finally did overcome the British "discountenance," as Curzon put it, and acquired a warship named Persepolis from Germany. The 600-ton ship armed with four Krupp guns was designed, in the view of Curzon—who did a careful inspection of the ship—for the double purpose of "bombarding refractory fishing villages, or intimidat[ing] local governors and sheiks, and of convoying cargoes of dates and pilgrims." The dual function, creating fear and carrying the faithful, bespoke a typical Qajar compromise. Yet in reality, by exercising its guns and spending its powder, the ship served only to convey to the shah's subjects along the Persian Gulf littoral "an idea of the overwhelming importance of their royal master." The guns of the Persepolis "have never yet fired in anger," observed Curzon in 1890, "but the general terror inspired by the four Krupps is so great, that immediately upon her appearance any disturbance as a rule ceases." To the acute but condescending English observer whose country ruled the waves, the naval strength of Persia was no more than a case of *ex nihilo nihil fit* ("from nothing, nothing is produced").[13] More appropriately, however, Persepolis seemed the *magni nominis umbra,* as the precarious Qajar reign resembled the shadow of once a great name.

A shadow or not, the concern with frontiers was real. In the decades following war with England over Herat, Nasir al-Din's concern for the Afghan threat to the security of Khurasan remained unchanged. In 1862, for instance, he was utterly distressed by the news of Dust Muhammad Khan's renewed effort to annex Herat to his territorial construct, which was then taking shape as a united Afghanistan under British auspices. The shah wished to keep Herat an independent principality off limits to the ambitious warlord. Stressing the need for Anglo-Persian cooperation to stabilize Herat's volatile politics, the shah insisted in a handwritten note to the

Persian envoy in London that Dust Muhammad Khan had to be stopped; "otherwise under no circumstances the Persian government could remain unalarmed and is entitled to be concerned." The tortured diplomatic language to which the shah had become accustomed nevertheless betrayed his youthful ambitions. Complaining in another note about London's slowness in responding to his previous inquires about Herat, he reminded the Foreign Office through his own envoy that if the British continued to ignore his concerns, "then the Persian government has no choice but to relinquish British cooperation and inevitably try to reassert its own rights." Then, he added, "the British could not claim again that Iran acted in breach of the treaty and is motivated by its own ambitions."[14]

To be sure, the shah did not wish to engage in another disastrous confrontation with Britain, but he was not entirely passive in response to their policies. Be that as it may, the shah realized that the loss of territory along the periphery was inevitable for the survival of the center. The 1860–1861 Marv campaign—in the course of which the indefensibility of the Central Asian vassal khanate by Iran's meager forces became ever more apparent—convinced the shah of the wisdom of accepting Russia's takeover of the troublesome Turkoman territory. By the 1880s the Russian annexation of the northeastern frontier relieved Iran considerably of the Uzbek-Turkoman menace that for close to four centuries had ravaged the provinces of Khurasan and Mazandaran. Likewise, the settling of Sistan's frontiers with British India (after prolonged and often acrimonious negotiations); the implicit abandonment of the Persian claim over the island of Bahrain; the successful reassertion of Persian sovereignty over Bandar 'Abbas, the northeastern shores of the Persian Gulf and the Gulf of Oman; and the demarcation of the western frontiers with the Ottoman Empire in the aftermath of the Erzerum treaty of 1847 gave the shah greater stature as the undisputed ruler of the Guarded Domains of Iran with recognized international boundaries.[15]

Enhanced stature and recognized boundaries, however, did not automatically guarantee the security of the land or of the throne. Nasir al-Din had to work hard to preserve both of them. During the 1870s and 1880s he fought every case related to Iran's territorial disputes with its neighbors with remarkable persistence and diplomatic skill. Territorial compromise, no matter how minor, was anathema to the ancient ethos of kingship and, in Nasir al-Din's eyes, constituted caving in to imperial powers and their predictable demands for further concessions. He was largely justified in his assessment, even though the fear of territorial losses became a formidable barrier to the shah's overall agenda to modernize. The construction of the

Indo-European telegraph line, which made the British presence more acute in the major cities and in remote places, and the subsequent disputes with the British envoys and subjects over jurisdiction, ownership, and confrontation with local authorities alerted Nasir al-Din to the hazards of an unrestrained Western presence. But even if he could temporarily persuade the European powers and their subjects to comply with his wishes and respect his reservations, he could not permanently bar their infiltration of his realms.

Soon after the repeal of the famous Reuter Concession, and with increasing consistency from 1879 onward, the British pressed for economic concessions aimed at making Iran's domestic markets further accessible to Britain. The idea of constructing a railway network was intermittently entertained by the British but then abandoned for fear that it would provide the Russians with access to the south. But the opening of the Karun River and access to the central province of Isfahan were the immediate objectives of the British and the subject of their exhaustive negotiations with the shah and his ministers. It is hard to believe that the British economic drive for new markets was entirely free from long-term strategic concerns in the southern part of Iran. Zill al-Sultan's welcoming gestures toward the British—in the course of which he mutely presented himself as an alternative to his uncooperative father and his feeble brother, Muzaffar al-Din Mirza, in the event of a future partitioning of Iran—only emboldened the British.

The shah thus had little choice but to cling to the telegraph lines. They connected him to London and St. Petersburg, often over the heads of the reluctant ministers plenipotentiary, who resented being bypassed by the shah but could not refuse to transmit his distress messages to their foreign ministers. On more than one occasion the British foreign minister was informed by the shah that if Britain pressed its demands for concessions, the Russians would retaliate by not only seeking similar concessions but also annexing Iran's northern provinces entirely. All the land beyond Mount Damavand, he repeatedly warned with dramatic effect, would belong to Russia.

Whether the royal fears were realistic or whether he was merely playing on British Russophobia, Nasir al-Din was able to procrastinate for no less than fourteen years before eventually giving in to the persuasive diplomacy of the energetic British envoy, Henry Drummond Wolff. In 1888 he finally put his seal of approval on a concession that for the first time allowed the British to navigate upstream along the Karun River and into the Iranian interior to Shushtar, from where goods could be shipped overland to

Isfahan. It was hoped that the easier access to the commercial markets of central Iran and the creation of a commercial shipping line operating along the coast of the Persian Gulf and the banks of the Karun River would boost the economy of southern Iran and counterbalance the thriving Russian trade in the north. The Karun concession was hailed by the British as a significant breakthrough, for it marked not only the arrival in earnest of European capital investment but also a notable shift in the shah's defiant position. The slow upward course of British steamers on the sleepy waters of the Karun, however, symbolized the obstacles to transforming Iran's southern markets.

Out of the relics of the fateful Reuter Concession, however, the shrewd British minister Wolff fashioned another major concession in 1890 for the creation of the Imperial Bank of Persia—the most influential and enduring enterprise granted to foreigners in the Nasiri period and, in the history of modern Iran, second in importance only to the oil concession of 1901. The Imperial Bank's operations, which included the issuance of bank notes, control of the money supply, and other standard functions of a central bank, left a profound impact on Iran's financial markets in long-distance trade and on the relations between the government and the economic community. The impressive portrait of the Persian sovereign on the bank notes, be-jeweled, smiling, and mustachioed, was intended to imprint upon the minds of his subjects the image of a confident king, mighty and majestic. Together with postage stamps, which also bore the shah's portrait, the bank notes familiarized the public with his face as had never before been done with coins, almanacs, or bas-reliefs.[16]

The realities of the financial market dictated against such a majestic image. The swift dislodging of indigenous moneylenders by the Imperial Bank, the introduction of new banking regulations, and the massive bor-rowing by the government and merchants—and later landlords and no-bility—resulted in greater financial dependency on foreign capital. The terms for borrowing from the Imperial Bank were easier than those of local bankers, but the penalties were stiffer. As a result, huge financial losses, bankruptcies, and the ruin of family fortunes became commonplace, even more so than in the traditional setting of the Persian bazaar. The man whose face was pictured on the bank notes could not escape blame for the part he played. Regardless of the bank's advantages in regulating the market, reducing the ruinous interest rates traditionally imposed on bor-rowers, and providing the conveniences and reliability of a modern banking system, association with foreign enterprises carried liabilities. It tarnished the sovereign's image of economic omnipotence, traditionally symbolized by coins struck in his name. The bank notes carrying the shah's portrait faced considerable resistance among the populace—even though they carried the lofty, but essentially puzzling, name "Imperial Bank of Persia" (*bank-i shahanshahi-yi Iran*)—before finally replacing coins as the chief means of monetary exchange.

The coins of the royal mint were no less helpful in boosting the shah's image even before the days of the Imperial Bank. In the 1880s, the chronic oversupply of copper coins in low denominations and silver coins in high denominations undermined confidence in metal currency entirely. Farmed out to an entrepreneur and leading merchant with a checkered record, Hajji Muhammad Hasan Amin al-Zarb, the royal mint had its income augmented by the seemingly ingenious device of lowering the copper and silver standards. The steady decline in the price of silver in the international market further lowered the value of the Persian silver-based currency. The shah could not avoid the cumulative resentment of merchants, who had suffered ruin in international trade from the collapsing exchange rate; the consumer public, now more dependent than ever on European goods (particularly cotton fabrics); and urban notables, whose distrust of the European bank caused them to hoard their cash savings. Amin al-Sultan's partnership in the income of the royal mint, as a proxy for the shah, had turned the operation into a shameless racket in the eyes of the public. The shah was reproached behind the bankers' benches and the retailers' counters in the bazaar and from the pulpits of the mosques for what he considered his royal prerogative. The public viewed the concessions—whether domestic or foreign, whether related to the royal mint or the Imperial Bank—as harmful royal infringements into the market, motivated by sheer greed, and contrary to the honest discharge of the monarch's duties.[17]

In spite of all the criticism leveled at the shah in his own time (and later in the history books), his record of resisting European economic penetration was not meager. British demands for greater economic concessions were replicated by the Russians with even greater vehemence, but the shah and the seemingly weak government of Iran often resisted persuasions and threats on both fronts. This resistance should not be explained purely in terms of the balance of power between the two imperial neighbors. Nor can it be said that it was the Anglo-Russian desire to maintain Iran as a buffer state that ensured the survival of the Persian throne and the territorial integrity of Iran. Indeed, it is possible to argue that the idea of a buffer state was advanced by European policy makers on both sides only when it became clear that they could neither advance their imperial ambitions in Iran beyond a certain point nor disengage from Iran's political arena altogether. But at no time in the Nasiri period (and afterward up to the rise of Riza Shah) was this admission equated with a sincere desire to hold back their economic and territorial objectives. For these policy makers, from Palmerston to Salisbury, from Gorchakov to Giers, and for the Qajar statesmen who cynically subscribed to the thesis of the buffer state and the modern historians who parroted it uncritically, the boundaries of the buffer state were respected only as long as it was impossible to cross them. Students of foreign policy often have been unwilling to acknowledge the domestic resistance that the Persian state, despite its inherent weaknesses, put up against imperial penetration, territorial and otherwise.

The role of Nasir al-Din in this respect can best be appreciated when it is taken into account that in 1907, only a decade after his death, Russia and Britain concluded their first secret accord for the partitioning of Iran. Referring euphemistically to "zones of influence," this accord was further cemented and enhanced in the treaty of 1915, at the outbreak of the First World War. Soon thereafter, the temporary Russian withdrawal from the Persian scene after the Bolshevik revolution of 1917 led to the infamous 1919 Anglo-Persian agreement. Only nominally different in its comprehensiveness from the 1914 Egyptian protectorate or from the mandates drawn by the powers for neighboring Iraq and other previously Arab provinces of the defunct Ottoman Empire, the 1919 agreement, which was not ratified even by the moribund Persian nationalist resistance, was a testimony to the British appetite for dominance in the very country it had earlier defined innocuously as a buffer state. Before 1917 the Russian tsarist empire was every bit as willing to occupy, and subsequently annex, Iran's northern provinces.

It is important not to fall into the trap of regal adulation nor to remain indifferent to the changing moods in the foreign policies of the neighboring powers at the turn of the twentieth century. Neither should one disregard the historical circumstances that brought about a new set of economic necessities in an already overstretched and outplayed Great Game. Nonetheless, one must take note of Nasir al-Din's contributions. Even when operating out of pure personal interests or merely a desire to buttress his derelict house, he was still capable of maintaining the balance between the imperial powers—a balance he had learned to appreciate and ultimately to master. He guarded his universe jealously, at times with narrow-mindedness, and preserved it almost intact, albeit at the cost of closing its doors often on the positive aspects of modernity.

A PERSONAL UNIVERSE

As far as expediency permitted him, Nasir al-Din resisted the pressures to become absorbed into the neighboring imperial systems of the late nineteenth century—but not without a price. What the shah learned about the West and from the West in the following decades he often tried to keep from his subjects. The fruits of Europe's forbidden tree could only be consumed by the shah and his retinue, the small circle of trusted courtiers and their children, who were permitted to learn the skills needed to deal with the West. Even prior to his first European tour in 1873, the shah had long been fascinated by Europe, particularly by the mystique of its pleasure, opulence, and good life—aspects of material culture most accessible and comprehensible to a monarch such as him.

In spite of his extensive reading about the geography and history of Europe, and in spite of three visits to that continent (in 1873, 1878, and 1889), the shah's view of the exotic lands he traversed barely transcended bewilderment at their great achievements. He looked at Europe through his own spectacles but was remarkably good at adjusting himself on the surface to what Europe wanted from him, an exotic king from an exotic land. He showed great interest in European royalty and whatever was of interest to them: palaces and royal gardens, military parades, lavish receptions, exhausting balls, and tedious toasts. Moreover, prosaic and impersonal though his travelogues were, he recorded with remarkable constancy his accounts of world exhibitions (two of which he visited, in Vienna and Paris), public parks, zoological gardens, aquariums, museums, theaters, music halls, the circus, armories, cannon foundries, hunting lodges, and the inevitable fire engine drills. Describing the countryside, plants, flowers, exotic animals, wild game, food, dress, and women, he presented to his Persian readers a mystery tour of ultimate good taste. He appreciated those things he believed were important and that his mental eye was trained to see. He admired the orderliness of everyday life, the cleanliness of the streets and public places, the endurance of European structures, the speed of the trains, and other achievements in technology and communication. Yet, in spite of his advisers' persuasion, he consistently refused to appreciate the intellectual and scientific complexity that was behind Western material culture, the secrets that made all those achievements possible.

An example of his naivete, his attempt to purchase wholesale the West's material progress, came through in his granting of the Reuter Concession, a bargain designed to bring material progress to Iran via a single European entrepreneur with dubious abilities. In exchange for a fixed sum paid to the

Persian government, the concessionaire, Baron Julius von Reuter, was authorized to develop and utilize all the natural and mineral resources of Iran, its agricultural potential, communications, banking, and modern industry. The concession was finalized during the shah's first European tour and no doubt was influenced by his early perception of Western technology as a purchasable commodity. It seemed as if the shah's typical caution and tact, which stubbornly resisted European capital and diplomacy at home, were lost in Europe to the lure of financial incentives offered to him and his ministers or overshadowed by the persuasive power of his hosts. Later, the hazards of European economic penetration turned his unripe enthusiasm to suspicious ambivalence. Here again a sense of destiny governed his attitude. Progress in science and technology, the shah seems to have been convinced toward the end of his reign, was destined for Europe but not essentially transferable or even suitable for his country. He did not like the smokestacks of the Victorian steel mills, the noise of the textile factories, nor the gloomy appearance of the shipyards. Nor did he care to see his subjects turning into laborers in depressing industrial cities such as those he visited in England and Germany, no doubt with some concern for the inevitable political consequences of industrialization.[18]

Nasir al-Din had no illusions about Europe's military might, however, nor did he harbor any about its economic power and diplomacy. The experience of his early years gave him an appreciation for the motives and the strategy of European powers, and he was avid in learning about their future ambitions. In spite of his condemnation of European powers early in his reign for their impudent encroachment into his kingdom, later in life he tended to look upon imperial domination in other places as an inevitable right of the powerful. Yet when it came to his own throne he expected deference and circumspection. Increasingly he viewed himself and his dynasty as occupying a position on a par with European royalty. In the age of empires he wanted to be considered as the ruler of one—a weaker one, no doubt, but an ancient monarchy with a distinct history and identity nevertheless.

The European states, and even more the European press and the public, enhanced such an image. They gave him all due attention to which an "Oriental monarch" from an ancient kingdom could possibly have aspired at the height of a European preoccupation with monarchies. Yet he was received by the royalty and by commoners with an air of amusement and condescension peculiar to the rapidly advancing Europe of the late nineteenth century. With thrilling fanfare Europe wanted to demonstrate to the bewildered shah of Persia all its charm and splendor in exchange for his awed praise. Nasir al-Din dutifully performed the part assigned to him. He was courteous and clever, deferential toward the ladies, correct at the table, and bold in the saddle. He appreciated with gratefulness what he was offered, even if it meant enduring long, stuffy royal balls, sitting through concerts, operas and performances, and listening to music alien to his ear. Even more torturous was sitting through incomprehensible sermons and speeches given in his honor, reviewing in full regalia endless military parades, and eating dishes that seemed suspiciously un-Islamic. In most instances he emerged with grace, somewhat in contrast to his uncouth entourage, as a true royal with all the splendor attached to the popular image of the Persian shah even in the last quarter of the nineteenth century.[19]

Respect and attention were what Nasir al-Din consciously sought in order to combat the battered image of his country as a land about to be devoured by its powerful neighbors. He rubbed shoulders with the tsar in St. Petersburg, dined with the emperor in Vienna, was received by the Prince of Wales in the Victoria train station. On each of his two visits to England, in 1873 and 1889, he was invited twice to Windsor to converse amicably with the reclusive Queen Victoria (see Pl. 29), who had been afraid her guest might not be able to master English table manners but was pleasantly surprised that the shah's only oddity during their interview was his consumption of a large amount of fruit in a typically Persian manner. The shah also held discussions with presidents of republics, prime ministers, and policy makers, negotiated with industrialists and concession hunters, conversed with celebrities, actresses, singers, and courtesans, and exchanged old memories with European friends. He even felt safe enough to mingle occasionally with the public, something he never found suitable or safe to do in his own country.

Beyond pure self-indulgence and gratification to the royal ego, Nasir al-Din Shah also earned a good deal of international prestige. To Western eyes he was still a king from a legendary land familiar mainly through travel accounts or works such as Montesquieu's Lettres persanes, Goethe's West-ostlicher Divan, and Morier's Hajji Baba. The classical Greek view of the Persians and Persian kingship also found a new resonance during the shah's visits, and so did the Persian legacy of kingship, as the British raj consciously presented itself in India as the heir to an Indo-Persian royal tradition. Set against this historical stage, Nasir al-Din Shah was received and recognized by European royalty and statesmen as a royal in his own right.

Seeking international recognition was a wise investment, for which the real credit goes to Mushir al-Dawla, who persuaded the shah to take the first journey in the face of a conservative resistance to see the "king of Islam" in the land of infidels. He fulfilled the shah's long-standing dream of visiting *farangistan*, not only to allow him to see Europe's advances but also to have Persian sovereignty and independence acknowledged. After the shah's first visit with the Russian tsar or the British sovereign, it was no longer easy for foreign power holders to write off Iran as yet another pawn in the imperial game. Nasir al-Din was aware of this "public relations" task and did not fail to perform it. The occasional moments of embarrassment and farcical disgrace caused by the unfamiliarity of his entourage with terse European court protocol, though disturbing to European sensibilities in the Kremlin, the Borg, and Buckingham Palace alike, were treated only as amusing nuisances associated with any Oriental monarch.

The shah's visits, particularly in 1873 (when they were treated as major events by the press and the public), gave some satisfaction to a confident Europe that, if it so wished, it could be gracious and benevolent to an ancient, decaying monarchy, honor its sovereignty, and celebrate its sorties into the world of modernity—a world Europe avidly celebrated as "civilization." The lavish welcoming ceremony in Paris in 1873 on the occasion of the shah's visit might also have hinted at an element of nostalgia for lost French royal panache after the demise of the Second Empire. A procession of elephants in front of the shah's cavalcade in the Champs Elysées was a spectacle that sought to present to a prosperous Europe the glamour of the shah of Persia and his extravagance, almost in the spirit of a circus.

The military music that was commissioned on the occasion of the shah's visit to Vienna in 1873—from no less distinguished a composer than Johann Strauss (II)—to be played as the Persian national anthem reflected an effort to tailor for the Persian monarchy a "civilized" musical outfit. The Austrians' utter surprise at Iran's lack of a national anthem was as great, one might imagine, as the British's utter bafflement as to how to standardize the Persian national and royal flags—itself the subject of a long correspondence between Lord Chamberlain and the British mission in Tehran. The prevailing sense of standard formalities and regimented ceremony in European courts could hardly digest the Qajar informality and seemingly playful decadence. But if the table manners of his entourage were not always up to the sterling standards of the English court, or if the shah's uncles fell asleep during the final act of Covent Garden's most recent production, or if the shah himself was at a loss for words in his French reply to the Lord Mayor of London during the City Hall banquet, the Persian guests were still dazzled by the magnificence of the Royal Albert Hall when, in 1873, Strauss's Persian national anthem was performed for the first time under the glare of electrical projectors. Europe was too intoxicated with dumbfounded praise of its Persian guests to remind them of their precarious condition back home. When he *was* reminded, the shah's reaction hardly went beyond the pristine notion of "progress" as a device to be purchased and brought to Iran the way he purchased and shipped home crystal wares, ornate furniture, run-of-the-mill paintings of the English countryside, binoculars, Verundel hunting rifles, Sheffield pen-knives, and women's petticoats and negligees.

Visits to Europe were part of a larger process of Nasir al-Din's intellectual reorientation. His early fascination with things Western—gadgets, dresses and outfits, paintings and architecture, firearms and horse carriages—gradually took a more serious turn, not only in his wish to create a telegraph service independent of the British Indo-European line but also in his desire to build a railway network. For decades the construction of a railroad was the subject of long and arduous negotiations with European governments and entrepreneurs, who ephemerally appeared on the Persian horizon with blueprints of ambitious and often self-serving projects. Reiterating the dream that long had occupied all Middle Eastern reformers, Nasir al-Din viewed the railroad as a gateway to progress and a powerful means of control over provincial governments and economies. Ever since the early 1860s, when the construction of a railroad in the Middle East had become a serious possibility, the shah's attraction to such projects complemented the enthusiasm of reformist statesmen in his court.[20]

An enduring obstacle toward realizing such projects, however, proved to be the resistance of Iran's two powerful neighbors. The British held the view that the construction of a railroad across Iran's north-south axis would result in an unwise exposure of their interests in the Persian Gulf to an inevitable Russian threat—a concern encouraged by the inherent Russophobia in British foreign policy. The Russians, by contrast, saw a railroad enterprise initiated by the British as one more factor in their rivals' ever-growing presence in Iran. Europeans from other countries, too, were viewed as potential allies of one or the other power and were treated as such. The endemic debate about Iran's railroad (which was concluded only in the 1930s, when the state-funded national network was constructed under Riza Shah Pahlavi) should be seen as a classic case of incapacitating power rivalry. As time passed, the shah's enthusiasm for the railroad was dampened by a peculiar sense of "technophobia" as he witnessed, with silent displeasure, the gradual disappearance of the old world around him. By the end of Nasir al-Din's reign the only railroad constructed in Iran was the Belgian-built, narrow-gauge, five-mile-long line that connected the capital to the pilgrimage town of Shah 'Abd al-'Azim.

It is true that modern communication—above all the telegraph network—dramatically increased the royal authority and presence throughout the kingdom, but it also increased the foreign presence and allowed the shah's subjects to contact each other swiftly, both at home and abroad. For a king deeply imbued with the duty of protecting his throne and his land from outside threats, it was only natural to view the physical presence of foreigners—some involved in investment and technology, others in the guise of merchants, soldiers, missionaries, technicians, engineers, physicians, and functionaries of foreign concerns—as an inevitable hazard to social stability and political endurance. Such attitudes were complemented, almost from the outset of the shah's reign, by a fatalistic disbelief in his subjects' ability to learn the secrets of modern technology. It was as though the traditional man within him, despite all his fascination with the West and despite all the self-education that had resulted from long hours of reading tedious geographical texts and travelogues, valued his subjects as mere artisans and merchants of the bazaar who could only engage in the professions of their forefathers and were governed by the equally ancient norms of their society. The shah's frame of reference in defining the society over which he ruled was strikingly static.

If the shah needed further arguments against industrialization, they were often provided by the grim view he held of Europe's industrial setup: the ugly smokestacks on the horizon, the suffocating air, the gloom and dampness, the regimented lifestyle, and the arduous working hours. Like many of his counterparts in the non-Western world, he saw some ultimate advantage in the prevailing international economic order, albeit with a sense of resignation. Supplying Europe's giant industrial machine with raw material gave a boost to the domestic economy of Iran and resulted in the selective prosperity of the merchant class. The export of cash crops—cotton, silk, opium, and tobacco, among others—benefited the shah, who learned to rely increasingly on the revenue from customs to compensate for the diminishing state income from other sources. The increasing volume of imports of European goods, whether fabrics, luxury goods, or weapons, did not seem particularly perturbing to the shah, who, in the true spirit of Victorian free trade and laissez-faire, preferred to remain the recipient of Western industrial products. The trouble that would ensue by manufacturing the same products at home seemed to him, and many of his statesmen, not worth the effort. Not surprisingly, up to the very end of Nasir al-Din's reign, none of the Western innovations so meticulously catalogued by the shah's minister of press and publication, Muhammad Hasan Khan I'timad al-Saltana, in his almanac, entitled *al-Ma'athir wa'l-Athar*, ever spilled over into the public domain. The gas lamp (followed by its electric counterpart), the horse carriage, and other such amenities remained expensive royal toys, whereas cotton mills, textile plants, glass factories, foundries, and armories, if they ever materialized into anything beyond rough blueprints, suffered a sorry fate emblematic of the shah's technophobia.

The shah's fascination with Europe thus remained decidedly nontechnical. His attraction to European history, world geography, and new discoveries, as well as current affairs, the various royal houses and their private scandals, and even the mundane curiosities covered in the European press, resulted in no distinct practical application. Nasir al-Din commissioned a substantial body of historical and geographical translations almost exclusively for his own personal use and out of the reach of the public. The biographies of Alexander of Macedonia, Peter I, Frederick the Great, Christopher Columbus, and Napoleon Bonaparte, together with numerous other volumes in history, travel, geography, and popular literature, were translated in the royal dragoman's bureau, read by the shah, and shelved in the royal library. The shah was well aware of the power of words and perhaps could have foreseen the outcome of the press revolution that started soon after his death.[21]

From his favorite pastime, reading historical and geographical works, he did not always learn the conventional "lessons of history" absorbed by any dilettante of his time. He embraced history at times and under circumstances reminiscent of his earlier fascination with Persian romance stories. On riding excursions, while the shah paused to partake of a huge lunch on a scenic hilltop in the vicinity of the capital, his exhausted and annoyed dragoman, I'timad al-Saltana, would typically read to his royal master a chapter from a multi-tome history of an empire as endangered as his own or a biography of a political leader who managed to conquer or reform on a scale never possible for the shah. Such readings were punctuated by the shah's occasional viewing of the panorama through his field glass, by the grumbling of his favorite page boy, Malijak, or by the cries of the master of the hunt when he sighted game. As abruptly as I'timad al-Saltana was interrupted in his scholarly endeavors, so could he be summoned to the private quarters with a remedy under his arms to ease the royal mind in the middle of a restless night. Disgusted with the rivalries among the women of the harem and their scolding tongues, the shah may have also taken refuge in the pages of history.[22]

Beyond their purely informative value for Nasir al-Din, the "lessons of history" provided above all an insight into the volatile nature of political power. Translated into the realities of his own surroundings, this boiled down to a lesson in political survival. The history of modern Europe demonstrated to him, above all, the hazards of military adventurism, popular revolution, and diplomacy. Contemporary accounts from the Ottoman Empire and Egypt confirmed for the shah the hazards of rapid modernization and overreliance on Europe.

Quite naturally, the shah viewed history from his own elevated position and associated with the ruler rather than the ruled. He was thus bound to admire Napoleon I, who came out of the anarchy of the French Revolution to create an expanding empire in deadly competition with the British and the Russians. But it was for Peter the Great of Russia that he reserved special praise. Like the shah, the Russian emperor started as a weak and vulnerable ruler; by his own initiative, he turned his backward country into a powerful empire. The shah's admiration for Frederick the Great of Prussia, whose biography he read in Persian, was even greater. Frederick's miserable childhood and youth, in which he was ill-treated and despised, as the shah had been by his own father, contrasted dramatically with his unexpected qualities of leadership he displayed once on the throne. Nasir al-Din must have found this comparable to his own story. No doubt he shrank from the example of these role models in the area of domestic reform, nor could he imitate them in military accomplishments. Yet Nasir al-Din Shah may have seen in his own rule a parallel with Frederick's "enlightened despotism." Finally, in the life of Louis XIV, with which he was familiar through I'timad al-Saltana's translations of Voltaire, the shah could admire the complementary qualities of royal grandeur, military might, and artistic patronage. Louis, too, had been a boy-king who liberated himself from the yoke of a powerful minister, Mazarin, and a manipulative mother to reduce the power of the French nobility and to become, in due course, an absolute ruler, *le Roi Soleil*, with self-assumed attributes not unlike those of the Persian Pivot of the Universe.

Other rulers and dynasties were not absent from Nasir al-Din's growing historical library: biographies of Catherine II (known in Persian accounts as *khurshid kulah* ["sun-crowned"]), Nicholas I, and Alexander II of Russia (both contemporaries of the shah), as well as a few works of classical history, including Herodotus. The shah's reading of European history, random though it was, reflected something of his self-image. Yet one can also trace a clever effort on the part of his enlightened confidant and cultural adviser, I'timad al-Saltana, to educate the shah and broaden his political horizons by exposing him to European history and literature. Himself a historian and a great advocate of French culture, I'timad al-Saltana over the years injected a fair dose of critical historiography into the shah's readings, including at least two of Voltaire's works and a Persian translation of Hammer-Purgstall's *Geschichte des Osmanischen Reiches*. Translations such as Voltaire's *La Princesse de Babylone* and Cervantes's *Don Quixote* (from a Russian translation), among the works commissioned by I'timad al-Saltana and patronized by the shah, may have served an entertaining purpose, but they were doubtless included by the royal dragoman for their critical content. Whether the shah appreciated the French philosopher's sarcastic critique of the cultural values of his time in *La Princesse*, or whether he could see in the anachronistic conduct of the fictional Spanish nobleman a farcical image of his own situation, is not known. The simple acknowledgment in the royal hand, "Read in its entirety" (*tamaman mulahiza shud*), at the end of a manuscript compiled for him by a royal translator of Voltaire's writings on Iran reveals nothing of the shah's deeper impressions.[23]

If I'timad al-Saltana's assertions in his memoirs regarding the shah's intellectual progress are to be relied upon, however, the impact of European cultural trends on him seems to have been limited at best. His readings of history, political essays, and modern literature did not radically transform his worldview or his approach to government and society. Nor did the analytical or allegorical contents of these works, as the case may have been, trouble him deeply. In a typically self-righteous way he sought in history books, royal biographies, newspaper articles, and European fiction confirmation of his own political deeds and justification for prolonging the status quo. He was too conscious of the hazards of liberalism to seek in the pages of history any message other than the legitimacy of prevailing power: "Might is right" seems to have been his perception.

The shah was very conscious of his own place and mindful of how he would be judged by comparison with his great predecessors in Persian history. His interest in men of destiny, the powerful rulers of modern Europe, was complemented by an enthusiasm for eminent figures in Iran's past. Isma'il I, 'Abbas I, Nadir Shah, and Aqa Muhammad Khan, among the more recent rulers, were admired by the shah, who viewed them as men of authority and vision. His self-image as a great ruler must no doubt have been modified through the decades, but Nasir al-Din did not cast off the presumption of strong rule even if he could no longer fulfill its essential precondition: military glory and conquest. He clearly viewed himself as being in the same league as his illustrious predecessors—a continuation of the same royal tradition. His patronage of historical writings, among them Muhammad Taqi Sipihr's *Nasikh al-Tawarikh* (which was started under Muhammad Shah), was further proof of his conscious effort to nurture a sense of national identity based on monarchical continuity. Sipihr traced this national identity in the story of Shi'ism, which constituted the greatest part of his account. "The King of the Shi'ites," as Nasir al-Din tended to view himself, was thus a corporate part of the Shi'ite story and represented its contemporary political dominance. If the 'ulama legitimized their authority as collective deputies of the Imam in the sphere of religion, it was only natural for Nasir al-Din, not unlike his grandfather, 'Abbas Mirza, to view himself as the political representative of the Imam and nurture a sense of national history accordingly.

Complementing the religious side, there was also a literary Persian historical consciousness favored by Nasir al-Din Shah. Jalal al-Din Mirza's *Nama-yi Khusravan* presented a history based on Persian monarchy, with its roots in mythological and pre-Islamic kingship, and was written in an effortless style of pure Persian. In both this work and in Sipihr's *Nasikh al-Tawarikh*, Nasir al-Din was presented as a benevolent patron, a natural link in the enduring chain of monarchy, both the defender of the faith and the heir to the glories of the past. One can see in the 1860s the earliest traces of a new official historical consciousness, to which Nasir al-Din contributed as patron and from which he benefited by consolidating his image and his authority. At a time when all the material manifestations of political power were visibly dwindling, the symbolic instruments of monarchy, among them historical legitimacy, seemed particularly crucial to Nasir al-Din and his dynasty.

The shah's political outlook was partially secularized by his study of modern history, though it was not entirely immune from his deep-seated fatalism. His belief in the forces of the zodiac and their impact on his throne was complemented by firm religious submission to the divine will. Though it is wrong to assume that he was entirely devoid of a causal view of the world in matters related to everyday life, on the broader historic plain he saw the rise and fall of the powers, the hegemony of some states over others, and material calamity and the decay of nations as outcomes of unavoidable acts of Providence, a tendency in harmony with the ancient view of temporal power in Persian literature. In this respect Nasir al-Din's view remained traditional even if he learned, or believed that he instinctively knew, the European art of diplomacy, the *pulitikat-i farang* in Qajar parlance.

This curious mix of political pragmatism and predestination went hand in hand with the shah's heartfelt religiosity. All his life he remained genuinely Shi'ite, with a lifelong dedication to 'Ali, the first Imam. He perpetuated the popular cult that surrounded 'Ali and other saints and martyrs of Shi'ism. The breed of popular religion that Nasir al-Din consciously embraced and successfully patronized was at variance with the legalistic religion of the Shi'ite 'ulama and often served as an effective weapon to beat them at their own game.

The shah's visit in 1871 to the Shi'ite shrines of Iraq, his first foreign tour (and his earliest exposure to the Ottoman modernizing efforts of the Tanzimat era), was a conscious display of his religiosity. It was also the fulfillment of his pious wish to pay homage to his patron saint. In the shrine of 'Ali in Najaf he truly behaved as if he were the king of the Shi'ites and was received as such by the dignitaries, the 'ulama, the public, and even the Ottoman officials. He ordered the private treasury of 'Ali's shrine, which had remained closed since Nadir Shah's capture of the city in 1733, to be opened and inspected in his presence. He also ordered extensive renovation and beautification of 'Ali's shrine, the shrine of Husayn in Karbala, and other Shi'ite sites, with all expenses to be paid from the royal purse. In formal audiences with the leading mujtahids of the 'Atabat in both holy cities and under the domes that held the caskets of the slain Imams, he appeared clearly at home. In the shrine of the "king of Najaf" (*shah-i Najaf*), as 'Ali is known in the popular Shi'ite literature, Nasir al-Din, the "king of the Shi'ites," offered his royal *jiqqa*, a massive diamond hat pin the Qajar shah wore as sign of his royal authority, to be hung above the Imam's tomb. The symbolism of such royal gestures could hardly escape those who witnessed or read about them in the shah's diary, which was published shortly after his return to Iran.[24]

The shah's expressions of religiosity beyond regular prayer and fasting, which he keenly recorded in all his travel diaries, also included an active patronage of the *ta'ziya*, the Shi'ite passion plays commemorating the martyrdom of Husayn and the sufferings of his house. A thriving aspect of popular religion in Qajar Iran, these plays were performed during the holy month of Muharram in a mixed spirit of mournfulness and fanfare. The shah's love for the *ta'ziya* cannot be attributed merely to a fondness for dramatic arts nor to a mundane desire to glance through binoculars at the nobility, particularly the women, sitting in private boxes reserved for "society." A deeper reason for the shah's consistent support for the *ta'ziya* was a conscious desire to preserve an alternative form of Shi'ism, even in the face of the 'ulama's vociferous disapproval. The legalistic Shi'ism championed by the jurists was a jealously guarded monopoly over which the government had little control. Their study of law was a dry, arcane, and highly specialized field that, even when popularized from mosque pulpits, seldom inspired lay audiences.

It is not accidental, therefore, that beginning in Safavid times and continuing throughout the Qajar period the state actively patronized the melodic recitation over the pulpit of the Shi'ite tragedies (*masa'ib* and *marathi*, popularly known as *rawza khawani*). The *ta'ziya* was a logical, and inevitable, extension of these dramatic recitations that offered the shah and the Qajar state, rather than the 'ulama, the chance to display their dedication to Shi'ism and its martyred saints in full view of the multitudes. The construction of "amphitheaters" (*takkiyas*) such as the magnificent Takkiya Dawlat (the state theater), built in 1868 for the purpose of staging these religious plays, was a crucial means of displaying royal dedication to religion (see Pl. 28). One of the greatest edifices built under Qajar rule, the Takkiya Dawlat (which was later razed under Riza Shah's modernization drive to make room, ironically, for his growing state bureaucracy) was the brainchild of Nasir al-Din himself. In the construction of the building itself, its circular stage, and its semipermanent dome, the shah may have been inspired by the structure of European concert halls, which he (or his French architectural adviser, Richard, and Dust 'Ali Khan Muayyir al-Mamalik) found suitable for the *ta'ziya* performance.

Nasir al-Din's patronage of art and literature and his own artistic creativity further glamorized and enhanced his image as the pivot of the Persian universe. The expansion and reconstruction of the capital on the model of all great rulers (from the Persian 'Abbas I to the French Napoleon III) started in earnest in 1867 with the removal of the old city walls and the construction of boulevards and royal buildings, whose tasteful Perso-European style reflected the spirit of the age. With the same eclectic taste Nasir al-Din built the Shams al-'Imarah (the Sun Palace), a curious palace gateway and royal veranda on the eastern side of the Gulistan complex that was reflective of Nasir al-Din's desire for structural grandiosity (see Pl. 26). The building's Perso-European style, though less evident than that of Takkiya Dawlat, was equally a monument to the shah's inauguration of the age of the feast (*bazm*).[25]

Nasir al-Din's religiosity never conflicted with his private life. Almost simultaneous with the building of Takkiya Dawlat he also built entirely new women's quarters in the Gulistan complex to house his growing harem. Later on he built other villas and residential complexes in royal gardens and in the capital. The size of the harem, however, did not always correspond directly to its influence. Under Nasir al-Din it was neither as glamorous nor as sensual as appeared in the Western imagination, nor was it as isolated as the Qajar court wished to keep it. To be sure, Nasir al-Din was not a creature of his harem, at least after the 1860s, nor was he a puritan unfamiliar with the pleasures of the flesh. But for him the harem remained primarily a refuge from the strains of the outside world and the closest he could come to enjoying a sense of family. Never again did he experience the amorous passion he had had for Jayran, but he did try to nurture, among his many wives and daughters in the harem, some elements of individuality. The design of the new andarun, which allocated to each woman a separate living unit (in contrast to the old arrangement), was one indication of this emerging individuality (see Pl. 25). So was the function of each woman in relation to the shah and others. Remarkably, the prevailing division of labor among women and their hierarchy (which was based on status and seniority) was seldom disturbed by the shah's whimsical swings of favoritism. By no means were all the shah's wives objects of his sensual attention, though a few of them certainly qualified as wives on those grounds. The shah's refined sense of aesthetics often stopped at the harem's doorsteps, judging by the taste and outfits of his wives in comparison to those of other women of the time.

In the latter years of his reign, the shah complained of the stress caused by the rivalry among his wives and their unending demands on him. There were a number of influential wives of peasant background to whom he felt particularly attached. Contrary to princesses and other members of the nobility, these women of low birth—a trait they shared with Jayran— better indulged the shah's undernourished emotional needs. Two of them in particular, Fatima Sultan Anis al-Dawla (d. 1897) and Zubayda Amina Aqdas (d. 1893), brought into the royal harem a certain plebeian mentality and lifestyle—and, in the case of the latter, a degree of vulgarity and homeliness—that appealed to the shah because of their simplicity.

Jealously guarded by the eunuchs, both black and white, the royal harem remained out of reach except to the closest of the shah's male relatives. The Qajar desire to exercise strict control over the women and their contacts with the outside world was not rooted merely in the wish to keep the royal honor (namus) intact. There were too many embarrassing secrets, personal and political, lurking in the serene surroundings of the royal harem that could damage any ruler beyond repair. But neither the conspicuous walls of the andarun nor the zeal of the eunuchs, who often developed close bonds with the women they served, could impose total seclusion upon the shah's wives. Through their family members, attendants, physicians, agents, and occasionally their lovers, the women wielded power, owned and controlled property, received petitions, and pleaded with the shah and his ministers.

With uneven success the shah tried to exert greater control over the harem's political interventions, and there were relatively fewer plots hatched after 1858 behind the thick walls of the royal andarun to hasten the downfall or death of high-ranking statesmen. The only figure comparable to Mahd 'Ulya in terms of political influence and ambition was Nasir al-Din's respected wife and head of the harem, Anis al-Dawla. Remarkably, she collaborated in the anti–Mushir al-Dawla palace coup together with the Qajar princes and some of the 'ulama immediately after Mahd 'Ulya's death in 1873. In her action she must have been motivated by a desire to demonstrate her supremacy over the harem as well as by a grudge against the premier over the shah's European trip, though the decision in Moscow to exclude her, together with other royal women, from the remainder of the royal tour was primarily the shah's. In spite of this early episode of intrigue, Anis al-Dawla has often been credited with championing ordinary people's causes and criticizing the shah for his personal excesses, such as his infatuation with Malijak. For instance, abiding by the ban on the use of tobacco declared in 1891 by the chief mujtahid, Mirza Hasan Shirazi, Anis al-Dawla prohibited the smoking of the water pipe in the harem in clear defiance of the shah. Her decision no doubt helped persuade the monarch to repeal the Regie Concession. Her position symbolized the harem's wish to be treated as an indispensable component of the Qajar body politic.

Anis al-Dawla's benign influence on the shah was often offset by Amina Aqdas, a capable woman with the nature of an intriguer. Like Anis al-Dawla, she too was elevated from the lowest social ranks to become the shah's private maid and later his treasurer and confidant. This division of responsibility may suggest a deliberate effort by the shah to forestall total supremacy by any one of his wives. Nevertheless, playing on the shah's many weaknesses and indulging his many emotional cravings, Amina Aqdas carved out her own niche and often achieved her petty ends. She took charge first of the shah's favorite cat, Babri Khan, which for a while remained the focus of acute royal affection. Soon after Babri's destruction by Amin Aqdas's rivals, she began promoting her infant nephew, Malijak II, who almost immediately became the object of the shah's intense infatuation. Amin Aqdas allied herself with the shah's influential chief butler and later court minister, Mirza Ibrahim Amin al-Sultan, and was influential in the elevation of his son, 'Ali Asghar Khan Amin al-Sultan, to the premiership. After the death of Amina Aqdas, the premier found a new ally in Khanum Bashi, a harem debutante in her teens who had learned to indulge the increasingly childish cravings of her sixty-three-year-old royal husband.[26]

The last decade of Nasir al-Din's reign was almost dominated by 'Ali Asghar Amin al-Sultan. A master of political maneuvering, he was the product of the inner court (khalwat). A son of the shah's trusted butler from a Georgian slave origin, he rose from the rank of a young page boy to minister of court at the age of twenty-five and soon after to the premiership. His rapid ascent was due not only to his own abilities and the support of the harem but also to the shah's wish to raise to high office an insider from his own household. Amin al-Sultan successfully capitalized on the shah's fear of independent-minded ministers from the divan background, whether reformist or conservative, and presented himself as a benign appendage to the throne. He monopolized numerous offices that were committed to his stewardship and used them to cultivate a lucrative racket with shares for the shah, himself, and other willing partners. His official appointment as sadr a'zam, however, came only after the death in 1886 of the powerful accountant general, Mirza Yusuf Mustawfi al-Mamalik. For more than four decades Mustawfi al-Mamalik had successfully preserved his administrative hegemony and opposed all premiers from Amir Kabir to Mushir al-Dawla. At the same time, he wisely and consistently shunned the title of sadr-i a'zam in favor of the modest but subtle title of aqa (master). For the last five years of his life Mustawfi al-Mamalik was practically the chief administrator of the Qajar state. In typically makeshift fashion, largely contrived by the shah, he shared the responsibilities of government with Amin al-Sultan and other minor scions of the Qajar bureaucracy.

An able negotiator and a shrewd politician, Amin al-Sultan moved quickly to consolidate his premiership after the demise of Mustawfi al-Mamalik by acting as a valuable agent of the shah in all domestic and foreign affairs. Their relationship turned into a complex game of power in which both parties, the shah and his premier, took advantage of each other. Amin al-Sultan's periodic vacillations between pro-British and pro-Russian positions may have been motivated by the dictates of a pragmatic and expedient foreign policy in accordance with the shah's wishes, but they were also fueled by concerns for his own political survival. In order to keep Amin al-Sultan in a chronic state of anxiety, the shah resorted to his customary habit of counterbalancing the premier's power. He promoted his own younger son, Kamran Mirza Na'ib al-Saltana, to the dual positions of war minister and governor of Tehran. The dreary domestic politics of the last years of Nasir al-Din Shah were confined to factional quarrels between the two men and their cronies, each party holding on to its bureaucratic and military fiefdoms.[27]

By the early 1890s the shah seemed more than ever cornered by the contingencies of the same precarious balance he had managed to maintain over the past three decades of his reign. Exhausted by all the years of attending to the affairs of the government and the court and dealing with the foreign powers and the wrangling of state bureaucrats, he grew conspicuously more indifferent to his duties. Narcissistic proclivities for kingly glory and an urge for opulence vied in the royal mind with an even greater sense of distrust toward the public and a desire for solitude. Haunted by the painful memories of his past and bored with the formalities of his royal facade, he sought emotional comfort in the puerile company of Ghulam 'Ali 'Aziz al-Sultan, the second Malijak (see Pl. 30). Indulging his page boy's juvenile mischiefs and banal pursuits, he seemingly reenacted his own troubled childhood, with Malijak playing the sickly and despised son and himself the affectionate father that he had never had. Malijak's rude and rowdy conduct, a source of serious embarrassment to the shah's etiquette-bound and seniority-conscious court, was condoned by the shah with a mixture of delicacy and delight. He seemed to be taunting the Qajar bureaucrats, the nobility, and the princely class for all the negligence they had displayed toward him before his accession, and all the manipulation and deceit afterward—a belated rebellion, perhaps, but one deeply motivated by his forlorn need for emotional care and normal human attachment. With all of Malijak's miserable maladjustments, his infamously unhygienic look, and his utterly outrageous whims, he was the one person with whom the shah did not need to present a kingly appearance. He was a wild offshoot of the royal persona, grafted and nurtured to bear all the maladies of his master's tortured psyche.[28]

CHAOS REVISITED

The shah's self-engrossing world, composed of Malijak and Khanum Bashi, fostered further alienation and delinquency. A political system so heavily built on the personality of the monarch and his ability to preserve the balance at all levels, foreign and domestic, could not withstand the assaults of a changing and hostile era. No matter how anxiously the shah and his decaying establishment tried to detain the forces of foreign intervention and popular discontent, they could not withhold them forever. The shah's diplomatic acrobatics, likewise, could not save him from pressure from his mighty neighbors. In the absence of any institutional setup answerable to public criticism, the shah, even when Amin al-Sultan was officially in charge of the government, could not escape the blame for all the problems that engulfed Iran in the closing decade of the nineteenth century. It was natural for his subjects, especially the western-educated few, to see him as the man whose rule, now aided by better communication, an improved police apparatus, and growing control over the elite and the commoners, was the cause of their destitution and their country's stagnation. Nasir al-Din's monarchy was built on the symbolism of might and sovereignty and on the images of the shah's religiosity and rectitude. Once these powerful symbols were compromised by forces within and beyond the ruler's control, it was only to be expected that his legitimacy would erode and that he would have to face the consequences. The kingly glory (farr-i shahi) upheld by the old Persian idea of kingship as the source of royal legitimacy could no longer be sustained once the sense of order had been lost to the perception of corruption and disarray. In his final years, signs of fatigue and frustration in the shah's conduct contributed to the general sense of despair.

The shah was assassinated on 18 Dhu al-Qa'da 1313 Q./1 May 1896 in the shrine of Shah 'Abd al-'Azim, on the eve of the fiftieth anniversary of his accession to the Qajar throne (according to the lunar Islamic calendar). The event could not have been more symbolic of the forces that culminated in the Constitutional Revolution (1906–1911). The assassin, Mirza Riza Kirmani (see Pl. 32), was an impoverished petty merchant turned agitator enraged by the wrongs he suffered at the hands of Kamran Mirza's henchmen and animated by the acid criticism of the dissident clique in exile.

The shah was shot inside the shrine, where he had come to pay homage to the popular Shi'ite saint in thanksgiving for a half-century of rule. For the first time, it is reported, he allowed ordinary folk to stay inside the shrine during the royal visit rather than having it declared off limits. In a manner typical of all petitioners, Mirza Riza approached the shah's retinue when the monarch had completed his prayer in front of the saint's tomb and was about to exit the shrine. Reaching toward the shah to hand him his petition scroll, the assassin then drew a small revolver and fired several shots point blank, hitting his victim in the heart. Within minutes the shah was dead, but legend has it that he lasted long enough to ask to be carried next to Jayran's tomb a few steps away. The scene was not far from the spot where, in 1890, Sayyid Jamal al-Din Afghani (Asadabadi) had been arrested and dragged out of the sanctuary by royal decree and subsequently expelled from Iran on charges of sedition and conspiracy. Mirza Riza's choice of location, as he later confessed, was symbolic, as he sought to avenge the dishonor brought upon his master.

Faced with the prospect of instant panic and anarchy—familiar consequences of any royal death—Amin al-Sultan arranged for the shah's body to be spirited away secretly to the royal carriage. Sitting beside the shah's seated corpse all the way to Gulistan Palace, he manipulated his master's lifeless limbs, his hands and his drooping head, as though he were waving and nodding to the anxious crowd that gathered along the road to the capital. He must have found this feat of puppetry with the dead Nasir al-Din far less arduous than with the living one. As the chief officer of the state, Amin al-Sultan was quick to utilize the necessary means for a smooth transition of the crown. He consulted with the Russian and British envoys, who reaffirmed their countries' commitment to Muzaffar al-Din's accession, demanded that the princes of the royal family, most notably Zill al-Sultan, declare their loyalty to the new shah, and assigned the Persian Cossack brigade, headed by a Russian officer, to maintain security in the capital. The provinces remained calm. Shortly thereafter, Muzaffar al-Din arrived from Tabriz and ascended the throne on 8 June 1896, and Nasir al-Din's assassination soon became an ominous incident best relegated to the repository of popular memory.

The shrewd Amin al-Sultan even instructed the royal *ta'ziya* performers to include an opening act in their repertoire portraying the good deeds of the "martyr king" (*shah-i shahid*), as Nasir al-Din soon came to be remembered by the public. The exercise was apparently aimed at calming the public anxiety heightened by the act of regicide. Cynical as it may sound, the assassination was a convenient incident nevertheless, most of all for an heir apparent who had grown old and ill in the isolation of his provincial capital. To the credit of Amin al-Sultan (and that of his slain master), never before in Qajar history was a succession carried through so uneventfully. The premier, however, could not entirely escape the customary Qajar treatment of kingmakers. In November 1896 he was dismissed from office and sent into exile at his private estate in Qum. In keeping with the same civility that made an uneventful accession possible, the new shah spared Amin al-Sultan from the dreadful end that had befallen his predecessors.

Nasir al-Din's assassination was the first instance of regicide in Iran since Aqa Muhammad Khan's murder in 1798, almost a century earlier.

Unlike most would-be and actual royal assassins in Iran's dynastic past (but like Nasir al-Din's unsuccessful Babi assailants more than four decades earlier), Mirza Riza was a lay subject, a *ra'iyat*. He was neither a vengeful khan of a rival tribe nor a pretender to the throne or servant of the court. Nasir al-Din Shah did not lose his crown on the run from a foreign or domestic enemy, as had so many shahs before and after him. He was murdered for his deeds, for being seen as the cause of all the country's ills. To be sure, Sayyid Jamal al-Din Afghani's personal animosity toward Nasir al-Din—owing to the former's maltreatment and expulsion from Iran in 1890—was the primary cause. But there was enough resentment within Iran and abroad to make the regicide possible. Afghani's pronouncements calling for the downfall of Nasir al-Din Shah during the Regie protest aimed at the shah's personal misconduct, avarice, debauchery, and intemperance and still more at his dereliction of duty in guarding his subjects against injustice and protecting his land against the ravages of infidels. Iran's material and moral decay and the impoverishment and ignorance of its people, as maintained frequently in the clandestine pamphlets of the late nineteenth century, were perceived as the outcome of the shah's tyranny and neglect and of his self-serving desire to retain crafty and corrupt statesmen such as Amin al-Sultan in power.

Given the rising tide of criticism, the shah's celebration of his jubilee may be seen as his symbolic attempt to glorify the monarchy and renew the covenant of kingship with his subjects at a time when the pillars of traditional rule were shaky. Nasir al-Din may have intended to announce on the occasion one of his periodic, often ephemeral, administrative reform measures in response to growing criticism at home. He may also have been contemplating Amin al-Sultan's dismissal at the end of a seven-year cycle that had started in 1889 with his official nomination as the *sadr a'zam*. Rumors of such royal designs abounded in the court circles and coincided with the curious circumstances of the shah's assassination, making it inevitable that the incident would capture the public imagination. Speculation about the causes behind the shah's murder went so far as to identify the premier as an accomplice in the crime.[29]

The account of Mirza Riza's interrogation, a rare testimony to the assassin's state of mind (as well as the spite his master, Sayyid Jamal al-Din Afghani, reserved for the shah), rules out the plausibility of such a conspiracy. There is no reason to doubt that it was the "stocks and chains" by which Mirza Riza previously had been bound in the Qajar jail, and the "agonies" that he had endured at the hands of government agents, that incited him to "cut down the tree" of Nasir al-Din's reign. Quoting a proverbial verse from Rumi's *Masnavi,* he replied to his interrogator, "The fish begins to stink at the head, not at the tail." With a tortured, almost melancholic, spirit such as Mirza Riza's, an inducement by Afghani and his associates went a long way. They had apparently managed to convince Mirza Riza that the shah posed a major obstacle to the long-cherished dream of pan-Islamism, which Afghani wished to see fulfilled under the auspices of the Ottoman Sultan 'Abd al-Hamid. "By reason of the long duration of his reign and his venerable age," the sultan reportedly had said to Afghani, "Nasir al-Din Shah has acquired a power and prestige such that, if he is firm, the Shi'ite divines and the people of Persia will not move to support our ideas or accomplish our aims. We must therefore think of some plan for dealing with him personally."[30] Even if Afghani, or Mirza Riza, exaggerated the extent of the sultan's insinuation, this statement was symptomatic of the anti-Nasir al-Din feelings within the circle of Afghani's adherents in Istanbul.

Beyond Afghani, two dissident intellectuals in particular stood out as promoters of anti-Qajar sentiment: Mirza Aqa Khan Kirmani, the celebrated writer and radical activist, and his erudite cohort, Shaykh Ahmad Ruhi Kirmani. They were both of Babi background, but by the 1890s they had probably abandoned their earlier beliefs in favor of a mélange of Persian nationalism, liberal constitutionalism and, in the case of the former, agnostic socialism. Though there is no direct evidence to implicate the two Kirmani dissidents in the shah's assassination, it is hard to believe they were not a source of intellectual encouragement to Mirza Riza, their co-citizen and comrade. In his interrogation Mirza Riza hinted at such inspiration. Mirza Aqa Khan may not have shared all of Afghani's pan-Islamic ideals, but he did harbor a similar hatred for Nasir al-Din and his house. From his writings one can sense an element of desperate opportunism peculiar to Afghani's politics, blended with the romantic idealism typical of the revolutionaries of his time. By eliminating Nasir al-Din, he probably believed, he would deliver Iran from the yoke of a willful tyrant who, as he saw it, obstructed the way to "progress" and "civilization." For sure, the assassination cleared the path for the coming of a revolution.

The Persian activists were arrested in Istanbul even before the assassination on charges of conspiracy and extradited to Iran afterwards, together with a third presumed accomplice, Mirza Hasan Khabir al-Mulk. Afghani was detained briefly but escaped arrest and punishment presumably because of his contacts in the Porte and his friendship with the sultan. 'Abd al-Hamid must have been horrified by the prospects of a reprisal by Afghani's adherents similar to what had befallen Nasir al-Din. Afghani remained under virtual house arrest in his "golden cage" in the months prior to his death in March 1897. In July 1896 the newly nominated Qajar heir apparent and viceroy of Azarbaijan, Muhammad 'Ali Mirza, secretly executed Mirza Aqa Khan and his associates in Tabriz and despatched their stuffed heads to Tehran to his newly crowned father, Muzaffar al-Din Shah. Whether motivated by a drive for hasty vengeance for the blood of his grandfather, a desire to secure the honor of his house, or perhaps a deep intolerance for political dissent, Muhammad 'Ali Mirza's act incurred the enmity of many future Constitutionalists. The butchery of the Bagh-i Shah royal garden some twelve years later on the occasion of the royalist coup and the bombardment of the Majlis and the arrest of Constitutionalist leaders in July 1908 was a fitting complement to Muhammad 'Ali Mirza's record.

Mirza Riza's inevitable execution came shortly after the death of his associates. He was publicly hanged in Tehran in August 1896. Some three months earlier Nasir al-Din's funeral had taken place with all the pomp and circumstance of a European burial ceremony. His casket, embellished with ostrich feathers and wrapped in black satin, was carried through Tehran streets in a royal procession and placed in the Takkiya Dawlat for public tribute. He was buried in the shrine of Shah 'Abd al-'Azim, a short distance from the scene of his assassination (see Pl. 33).[31]

LEGACY OF A LONG REIGN

The fantasy of the shah's jubilee was shattered by the grim reality of his assassination. This symbolic finale to Nasir al-Din's long reign could not help but have a sobering effect on the minds of his subjects, a poignant reminder of monarchy's vulnerability in the face of discontent and despair. His assassin proudly declared, "I have rendered a service to all creatures, and to the nation and the state alike. I have watered this seed, and it is beginning to sprout. All men were asleep, and they are now awakening."[32] It was another decade before the storm of the Constitutional Revolution could water the seed of dissent. The desperate attempt by Muhammad 'Ali Shah (1907–1909) to suppress the revolutionary process and restore old-fashioned absolutism on the model of his grandfather was a mistake that cost him his crown. For the first time in modern Persian history a monarch was dethroned by means of a popular revolution, this despite the fact that throughout the civil war with the Constitutionalist forces (1908–1909) he had the backing of the conservative Shi'ite clergy and the military and moral support of tsarist Russia. His minor son and successor, Sultan Ahmad

Shah (1909–1925), was little more than a nominal ruler—a "constitutional monarch," as he preferred to call himself—who clung precariously to the diminishing residue of Qajar legitimacy before being driven into voluntary exile. Iran's new strongman and popular hero, Riza Khan, an officer in the Persian Cossack brigade who rose meteorically to become the Sardar Sipah, the commander of the armed forces, and later an all-powerful prime minister, proved an even more potent threat to the moribund Qajar monarchy. By 1925 he had mustered enough power and credibility to coerce the Majlis to sanction the demise of the Qajar dynasty and, soon thereafter, his investiture as the founder of the Pahlavi monarchy.

Yet the memories of the Qajar past lingered. In particular the age of Nasir al-Din Shah, the "martyr king," was remembered with nostalgia. Ironically, during the Constitutional period Nasir al-Din's assassin was hailed as an emancipator, and the two slain Kirmani dissidents, Mirza Aqa Khan and Shaykh Ahmad Ruhi, were exalted as precursors of the revolution. Such ambivalence, crediting both the assassin and his victim, was symbolic of a dilemma in the collective psyche of the era. The Constitutional Revolution shattered the sense of universal order that was traditionally symbolized by the monarchy. Even though the ten-year reign of Muzaffar al-Din Shah was marked by greater cultural receptivity, social mobility, and openness toward the West than Nasir al-Din's reign, it was also viewed as an era of monarchical decline. Under Muzaffar al-Din the weaknesses of the monarchy were more manifest in the face of growing foreign domination and domestic discontent. The revolutionary momentum further heightened these pressures and transformed the familiar patterns of material life and social interaction. The Constitutional Revolution in effect dislodged the two pillars of sociopolitical stability in Persian society, the Qajar monarchy and the Shi'ite clerical establishment, without being able to replace them effectively with modern democratic institutions. The traditional Persian model of state-religion symbiosis that had prevailed under the Qajars for more than a century disappeared. The Nasiri period thus loomed large as an age of stability and security that reflected the conservative values and expectations of a vast majority of the population. At the same time it was criticized by advocates of modernity as an age of decadence and corruption, a time when the chance for reform and equality with the West was missed. This dual image is well represented in Pahlavi portrayals of Nasir al-Din and his era. The state-sponsored historical literature consistently scorned and ridiculed him as an ignoble tyrant (if not a traitor) who neither resisted infiltration by foreign powers nor sought to modernize the country. But there remained among the elite of the early

Pahlavi era many, some of them products of the Nasiri period, who regarded with fascination the personality and traditional power of the Qajar shah, which stood in stark contrast to the image of a blunt and uncompromising Riza Shah and his drive for modernization.

Yet in spite of the apparent reproach reserved for the Qajar shah and his entire dynasty, the themes of Nasir al-Din's reign persisted in some respects throughout the Pahlavi period and had lasting consequences. The most obvious was the enduring desire of the Pahlavi monarchy to prevail over the premiership. The tension to which this old struggle gave rise, most notably in the Musaddiq era, remained a major obstacle to the growth of democratic institutions in Iran. Nasir al-Din Shah had reduced the office of premiership merely to that of an executive agent and a domesticated component of his court. A century after the fall of Amir Kabir, Musaddiq's premiership was still up against the same royal challenges that had brought down his predecessors, from Hajji Ibrahim I'timad al-Dawla at the outset of the nineteenth century to Mirza 'Ali Khan Amin al-Dawla at the beginning of the twentieth. Even during the Constitutional Revolution, the Majlis remained distrustful of an effective government and consistently tried to subordinate it to excessive legislative interventions. In effect the Majlis assumed the shah's, and particularly Nasir al-Din's, role, hence contributing to the weakness of the executive branch in the post-Constitutional period. In the Pahlavi era reliance on royal power continued to pose an impediment to the growth of the government as an independent institution. In essence this was a return to the Nasiri model, which ultimately exposed the Pahlavi shahs, Riza Shah and then Muhammad Riza Shah, to predicaments similar to those that had baffled their Qajar predecessor decades earlier. Ironically, the very statesmen of the Pahlavi era who resisted the royal monopoly, most notably Muhammad Musaddiq and Ahmad Qawam, initially had been trained in the Nasiri administration and still relied on the discretion and resourcefulness of their Qajar bureaucratic background to master a Pahlavi shah. Other statesmen of the period who were of a similar background, Mahdi Quli Hidayat and even Muhammad 'Ali Furughi, both premiers under Riza Shah, entertained no such ambitions, though they, too, looked at the Nasiri era with nostalgic ambivalence.

There were other enduring themes reminiscent of the Nasiri period. With little change, Iran's strategic position down to the time of the Islamic Revolution (and even thereafter to the collapse of the Soviet Union and the end of the Cold War) remained as it had been in the Qajar era. During Nasir al-Din's reign, Iran's diplomacy of appeasement was ever more refined once the shah became aware of the fragility of his country's existence amid a bipolar power rivalry. The Pahlavi state, having much greater resources with which to conduct an independent diplomacy, did not, and perhaps could not, deliver Iran from these strategic entanglements, first between Britain and the Soviet Union and later, from the 1950s onward, between the United States and the Soviet Union. Pahlavi Iran was influenced more powerfully during the Cold War by the concerns and interests of super-powers than Qajar Iran had been during the Great Game. The Qajars were viewed by the British—and the Pahlavis by the Americans—as necessary means for the preservation of strategic and economic Western interests against the advances of Iran's northern neighbor. Oil as a new source of income added to the power of the Pahlavi state in a way inconceivable in Qajar times, when income from the land and trade had been the two traditional sources of government revenue.

Even Iran of the post-revolutionary era holds its affinity with the Qajar period. Although in the 1990s it has been relieved of the Russian presence on its northern borders (thanks to the disintegration of the Soviet Union some 270 years after Peter the Great's occupation of Gilan in 1721), and although British India has long been relegated to the history books (and nostalgic television series), the legacy of the imperial past still haunts the Islamic Republic and its neighbors. Supremacy over the Persian Gulf is still the bone of contention between Iran and the only remaining superpower, the United States, and a source of dispute with Iran's southern neighbors. Long after the days of the Qajars, revolutionary Iran was still forced to fight an atrocious war with Iraq for eight years (1980–1988) over a strategic waterway and a persecuted Shi'ite population that have remained at the heart of Perso-Ottoman strife. And the Iraqi regime tried to take advantage of Iran's revolutionary chaos the same way its Ottoman predecessor had done as early as the sixteenth century. Not unlike Britain's strategic con-cerns that required it to unite Afghanistan and the sheikhdoms of the Persian Gulf, economic contingencies in the late twentieth century still require the presence of Western powers in the Persian Gulf to insure an uninterrupted flow of cheap oil and, if need be, build regional alliances and issue Desert Storms upon transgressors.

No less than the Persian Gulf region, Iran's eastern neighbor has been hit by the superpowers' security pursuits. The latest and most disastrous episode of Russian expansionism in Afghanistan was a belated fulfillment of the prophecies of the Victorian strategists. Yet more than 120 years after the Qajars were forced to relinquish their claims, the destructive occupation of Afghanistan by one superpower, the Soviet Union, and the covert intervention of another, the United States, only helped unravel the self-serving designs of an ex-superpower, Great Britain. Afghanistan is no more united in the 1990s than it was in the 1850s. Nasir al-Din Shah's wish for a divided Afghanistan seems to have come true after all as the only gloomy alternative to the devastating factional feuds now being waged among Afghanistan's postmodern warlords.

Placed in the center of this quandary, Iran still tries to take advantage of its strategic position, its natural resources, and its revolutionary drive. It tries to utilize the residue of the old power rivalries between Russia and the West, between the United States and Europe, between the West and the Far East, and between the West and the Islamic world. Haphazard and desperate though its efforts may seem, Iran still aspires to remain a regional power, and the forces of Islamic religious resurgence surely blow enough wind into its sails to keep it afloat.

Yet beyond its regional objectives, and more importantly for Iran's socio-political stability, the future of the Islamic Republic still hangs in the balance. The revolution no doubt succeeded in destroying, at least for now, the exceedingly overblown and untenable royal pivot of Iran's ancient universe, which had been resented and resisted since Nasir al-Din Shah's time but never before so forcefully rejected. But that in the annals of Iran's long history one of the ancient twins, the "good religion," finally devoured its sibling, the kingship, there lies a discomforting irony. The irony is not that revolution removed an archaic institution from Iran's political arena, but that it substituted an even more oppressive and arbitrary institution: the "guardianship of the jurist," the premise by which Ayatullah Khomeini consecrated his hegemony and that of his successors. In view of its dwindling economic resources, exploding demographics, international isolation, political, religious, and gender repression, and the closing of Iran's social and cultural horizons under the weight of a monolithic and paranoiac ideology, it is not difficult to foresee a fierce disruption of Iran's "cycle of equity." Without a strong state at its core—almost always a mark of its identity and stability—the un-Guarded Domains of future Iran may experience ethnic and political convulsions more severe and destructive than it ever witnessed in its Qajar or Pahlavi past. Or, as it has done many times in its turbulent history, Iran may weather the current menace and regenerate itself with a new national ethos and a new pivot to its political universe, one that will be less arbitrary and self-indulgent than its past monarchy and more tolerant, accountable, and relevant than its present guardian jurist.

Abbreviations

AFAD   Isfahaniyan, K., and Q. Rushani (Za'faranlu), eds. *Majmu'a-yi As-nad va Madarik-i Farrukh Khan Amin al-Dawla.* 5 vols. Tehran, 1346–1357/1967–1978.

CNBL   Correspondence of the Imperial Majesty Nasir al-Din Shah of Persia from 1848 to 1896 (original and translation), British Library, BL Or 11665 and Or 11665*.

DDG   Gobineau, Comte Joseph A. de. *Les Depeches Diplomatiques du Comte de Gobineau en Perse.* Ed. A. D. Hytier. Geneve and Paris, 1959.

EI²   *The Encyclopedia of Islam.* 2d ed., Leiden, 1960– .

EIr   *Encylopaedia Iranica.* Ed. E. Yarshater. London and Costa Mesa, Calif., 1982– .

FO   Great Britain, The Public Record Office, Foreign Office, General Correspondence.

FOCP   *British Documents on Foreign Affairs: Reports and Papers from Foreign Office Confidential Prints.* Series B: The Near East and Middle East, 1856–1914. Vol. X (Persia: 1856–1885). New York, 1984.

NTQ   Sipihr, Mirza Muhammad Taqi [Lisan al-Mulk]. *Nasikh al-Tawarikh: Qajariya.* Ed. M. B. Bihbudi. 4 vols. Tehran, 1344/1965.

RSN   Hidayat, Riza Quli Khan [Lala-bashi]. *Rawdat al-Safa-yi Nasiri.* 3d ed., Vols. IX–X. Tehran, 1338–1339/1959–1960.

SHA   'Abbas Mirza Mulk Ara. *Sharh-i Hal-i 'Abbas Mirza Mulkara.* Ed. 'A. Nava'i and 'A. Iqbal. 2d ed. Tehran, 1355/1976.

SML   Qasim Ghani, Collection of Qajar Documents, Manuscripts and Archives, Sterling Memorial Library, Yale University. Series 1–9.

ST   I'timad al-Saltana, Muhammad Hasan Khan, *Sadr al-Tawarikh.* Ed. M. Mushiri. Tehran, 1349/1970.

VI   *Ruznama-yi Vaqayi'-i Ittifaqiya* (Tehran Weekly Gazette). nos. 1–473 (1267–1277/1851–1860). Later published as *Ruznama-yi Dawlat-i 'Alliya-yi Iran.*

Notes

1. For a general history of the early Qajar period see P. Averey, G. Hambly, and C. Melville eds., *The Cambridge History of Iran*, vol. 7 (Cambridge, 1991), 3–174; E. Bosworth and C. Hillenbrand, eds., *Qajar Iran: Political, Social and Cultural Changes, 1800–1925* (Edinburgh, 1983); *The Encyclopedia of Islam*, 2d ed. (Leiden, 1960– ; hereinafter *EI2*), "Kadjar" (A.K.S. Lambton), later published in idem., *Qajar Persia* (Austin, 1987). See also 'Abd al-Razzaq Dunbuli, *Ma'thir-i Sultaniya* (Tabriz, 1241/1825), 2d ed. (Tehran, 1351 Sh./1972), English trans. H. Jones Brydges, *The Dynasty of the Kajars* (London, 1833); H. Fasa'i, *Farsnama-yi Nasiri*, 2 vols. in one (Tehran, 1312–1313/1894–1895), English trans. H. Busse, *History of Persia Under Qajar Rule* (New York, 1972), 1–281; R. G. Watson, *A History of Persia* (London, 1866).

2. See for example Hidayat, Riza Quli Khan Lalabashi, *Rawdat al-Safa-yi Nasiri*, 3d ed. (Tehran, 1338–1339/1959–1960; hereinafter *RSN*), IX, 7–127, and Muhammad Hasan Khan I'timad al-Saltana, *al-Ma'athir wa'l-Athar* (Tehran, 1306/1888), 295. Nadir Shah Afshar (1736–1747) was responsible for the destruction of the Qajar chief, Fath 'Ali Khan, the commander-in-chief of the last effective Safavid ruler, Tahmasp II (1722–1732). Fath 'Ali Khan's son, Muhammad Hasan, lost his life in war with Karim Khan Zand (1750–1779). Muhammad Hasan's son, a brother of Aqa Muhammad Khan, died during successive conflicts with the Zands while taking refuge with the Turkoman Yamut tribes of northwestern Iran. On the Qajar struggle for supremacy and the internal feud between its rival houses in the eighteenth century, see L. Lockhart, *The Fall of the Safavi Dynasty and the Afghan Occupation of Persia* (Cambridge, 1958), 122–23, 280; Lockhart, *Nadir Shah*, (London, 1938), 14–15, 24–27,243–44; and J. R. Perry, *Karim Khan Zand, A History of Iran, 1747–1779*, (Chicago, 1979), 62–78, 137–149.

3. See G.R.G. Hambly, "Agha Mohammad Khan and the Establishment of the Qajar Dynasty," *Journal of the Royal Asian Society* 50 (1963), 161–174; *Cambridge History of Iran* VII, 104–43 (R. G. Hambly); and E. Yarshater, ed., *Encyclopaedia Iranica* (London and Costa Mesa, Calif., 1982– ; hereinafter *EIr*), "Aga Mohammad Khan Qajar" (J. R. Perry).

4. In spite of a wealth of Persian and European primary sources on Fath 'Ali Shah and his reign, the subject still awaits a full-length treatment. *Cambridge History of Iran* (VII, 144–169 [R. G. Hambly]) is the most thorough so far. Among many European contemporary accounts, J. Malcolm, *The History of Persia*, 2 vols. (London, 1815) and Jones Brydges, *Dynasty of the Kajars*, are more systematic. Among Persian studies S. Nafisi, *Tarikh-i Ijtima'i va Siyasi-yi Iran dar dawra-yi*

Ma'asir, 2 vols., 2nd ed. (Tehran, 1344/1965), covers most important Persian accounts. See also *Tahqiq dar Bara-yi Zindigi, Ahval, Amal, Afkar va Divan-i Kamil-i Ash'ar-i Fath 'Ali Shah Qajar (Khaqan)*, ed. H. Gul Muhammadi (Tehran, 1370/1992).

5. Within the Qajar administration the Mazandaran faction was dominated by Nuri and 'Aliabadi families, the Iraq 'Ajam faction by Farahani and Ashtiyani families and their clients, the Azarbaijan faction at times by Caucasian officials of Iravani and Georgian backgrounds and at other times by Kurdish and Azarbaijani chiefs in the Qajar service, and the Fars-Isfahan faction by Ibrahim Khan I'timad al-Dawla and his family of Fars and later by the Sadr Isfahani family of Isfahan. For some description of these factions see K. Sasani, *Siyasatgaran-i Dawra-yi Qajar*, 2 vols. (Tehran, 1346/1967), and Muhammad Hasan Khan I'timad al-Saltana, *Sadr al-Tawarikh*, ed. M. Mushiri (Tehran, 1349/1970; hereinafter *ST*). See also *EIr:* "Ebrahim Khan Kalantar, E'temad-al-dawla" (A. Amanat); "Amin-al-dawla, 'Abdullah Khan" (A. Amanat); and "Aqasi, Hajji Mirza 'Abbas Iravani" (A. Amanat). On the Qajar administeration see C. Meredith, "Early Qajar Administration: An Analysis of Its Development and functions," *Iranian Studies* 4 (1971), 59–84; also S. Bakhash, "Evolution of Qajar Bureaucracy: 1779–1879," *Middle East Studies* 7 (1971), 139–168.

6. On religious developments in the early Qajar period see H. Algar, *Religion and State in Iran, 1785–1906: The Role of the Ulama in the Qajar Period* (Berkeley and Los Angeles, 1969); Algar, "Shi'ism and Iran in the Eighteenth Century," *Studies in Eighteenth Century Islamic History*, ed. Neff and R. Owen (Carbondale, Ill., 1977), 288–302; A. Amanat, *Resurrection and Renewal: Making of the Babi Movement in Iran, 1844–1850* (Ithaca, 1989); Amanat, "In Between *Madrasa* and the Marketplace: The Designation of Clerical Leadership in Modern Shi'ism," *Authority and Political Culture in Shi'ism*, ed. S. Arjomand (Albany, 1988), 98–132; S. Arjomand, "The Shi'ite Heirocracy and the State in Pre-modern Iran: 1785–1890," *European Journal of Sociology* 22 (1981), 40–78; A.K.S. Lambton, "A Nineteenth Century Interpretation of *Jihad*," *Studia Islamica* 22 (1970), 181–192.

7. Royal favors (*iltifat*) to the members of the elite and privileged classes ranged from appointing them to a position (*mansab*) with salary (*mawajib*), provisions (*suyursat*), and pension (*mustamarri*), to granting a land tenure (*tuyul*) with exemption from taxation, to an array of symbolic gestures such as granting a ceremonial robe (*khil'at*), a title (*laqab*), a decoration (*nishan*), or a cash bonus (*sala*). Royal approbations expressed in private audience and ranking in the public levees (*salam*) were also highly valued in the etiquette-conscious Qajar court, as was a person's access to the shah and the degree to which he was in the confidence of the monarch.

8. On the Persian theory of government see A.K.S. Lambton, "Justice in the Medieval Persian Theory of Kingship," *Studia Islamica* 17 (1962), 91–119; Lambton, *State and Government in Medieval Islam* (Oxford, 1981); Lambton, "The Dilemma of Government in Islamic Persia: The *Siyast-nama* of Nizam al-Mulk," *Iran* 22 (1984), 55–66; E.I.J. Rosenthal, *Political Thought in Medieval Islam* (Cambrige, 1985). For aspects of monarchy in Iran see E. Abrahamian, "Oriental Despotism: The case of Qajar Iran," *International Journal of Middle East Studies* V (1974), 3–31, and S. A. Arjomand, *The Shadow of God and the Hidden Imam:*

Religion, Political Order and Societal Change in Shi'ite Iran from the Beginning to 1890 (Chicago, 1984).

9. Following the Safavid tradition, some basic categories of titles in the early Qajar period represented the functions and duties of their holders. The servants of the state often held titles ending with *dawla;* thus *i'timad al-dawla,* "trust of the state," was the title of the chief minister, or "grand vizier" (*sadr-i a'zam*), and *mu'tamad al-dawla* ("trustee of state") came to be that of the chief state registrar; later, *mushir al-dawla* ("state counsel") became the title of the minister in charge of foreign affairs. Titles ending with *saltana* denoted courtly position, whereas those ending with *sultan* often denoted attachment to the shah's personal retinue. Yet even in Fath 'Ali Shah's time, titles were vastly usurped by the emerging Qajar nobility and princes of the royal family. For a general discussion of titles see *EIr:* "Alqab" (A. Ashraf) and the cited sources; S. Sultan al-Qura'i, *Ism-i Ashhar, Kitabshinakht-i Alqab-i Dawra-yi Nasir al-Din Shah* (Tehran, 1355/1976).

10. On the economy, demography, and trade of early Qajar Iran, see A. Amanat, ed., *Cities and Trade: Consul Abbott on the Economy and Society of Iran, 1847–1866* (London, 1983) and cited sources; A. Ashraf, "Historical Obstacles to the Development of a Bourgeoisie in Iran," *Iranian Studies* II (1969), 54–79; A. Ashraf and H. Hekmat, "Merchants and Artisans and the Developmental Processes of Nineteenth-Century Iran," *The Islamic Middle East, 700–1900,* ed. A. L. Udovitch (Princeton, 1981); *EIr:* "Commerce, Qajar period" (W. Floor); W. M. Floor, "The Merchants (*tujjar*) in Qajar Iran," *Zeitsschrift der Deutschen morgenlandischen Gesellschaft* 129 (1976), 101–135; G. Gilbar, "The Persian Economy in the mid-19th Century," *Die Welt des Islams* 19 (1979), no. 1–4, 196–211; G. Hambly, "An Introduction to the Economic Organization of Early Qajar Iran," *Iran* 2 (1964), 69–81; C. Issawi, ed., *The Economic History of Iran, 1800–1914,* (Chicago, 1971); A.K.S. Lambton, "Persian Trade under the Early Qajars," ed. D. S. Richards, *Islam and the Trade of Asia* (Oxford, 1970), 215–244, reprinted in Lambton, *Qajar Persia,* 108–139.

11. For the Tehran citadel and the palaces, see Y. Zuka', *Tarikhcha-yi Sakhtimanha-yi Arg-i Saltanati va Rahnama-yi Kakh-i Gulistan* (Tehran, 1349/1970).

12. For cities in the early Qajar period see, in addition to the sources cited above, *Cambridge History of Iran,* VII, 542–589; M. Ettehadieh, "Patterns in Urban Development: The Growth of Tehran (1852–1903)," *Qajar Iran,* 199–212.

13. See M. Minovi, ed., *Nama-yi Tansar bi Gushnasp,* 2d ed. (Tehran, 1354/1975) 89, 204–205; Hamdullah Mustawfi, *Nazhat al-Qulub,* ed. M. Dabir-Siyaqi (Tehran, 1336/1957), 19–28.

14. On Perso-Ottoman relations in the early Qajar period see B. Masters, "The Treaties of Erzurum (1823 and 1848) and the Changing Status of Iranians in the Ottoman Empire," *Iranian Studies* 22 (1989), 51–62. See also *Ansnad va Mukatibat-i Tarikhi-yi Iran (Qajariya),* ed. M. R. Nasiri, vols. 1–2 (Tehran, 1366–1368/1987–1989); Vizarat-i Umur-i Kharija, Daftar-i Mutala'at-i Siyasi va Bayn al-Milali, *Guzida-yi Asnad-i Siyasi-i Iran va 'Usmani: Dawra-yi Qajariya* (Tehran, 1369/1990), I (1211–1270 Q./1796–1853). See also *EIr:* "Dawlatshah, Muhammad 'Ali Mirza" (A. Amanat).

15. On the Russo-Persian relations in the early Qajar period see M. Atkin, *Russia and Iran, 1780–1828* (Minneapolis, 1980); *Cambridge History of Iran,* VII,

326–41 (F. Kazemzadeh); A. Tajbakhsh, *Tarikh-i Ravabit-i Iran va Rusiyya dar Nima-yi Avval-i Qarn-i Nuzdahum* (Tabriz, 1337/1958). For the Russo-Persian wars, see also A. Amanat, "'Russian Intrusion into the Guarded Domain': Reflections of a Qajar Statesman on European Expansion," *Journal of the American Oriental Society* 113.1 (1993), 35–56, and the cited sources; Muhammad Sadiq Vaqayi'nigar, *Ahang-i Surush: Tarikh-i Jangha-yi Iran va Rus: Yaddashtha-yi Mirza Muhammad Sadiq Vaqayi'nigar (Huma) Marvazi*, ed. A. H. Azar (Tehran, 1369/1990).

16. On Anglo-Persian relations in the early Qajar period see *Cambridge History of Iran*, VII, 374–394 (R. Greaves); E. Ingram, *The Beginning of the Great Game in Asia, 1828–1834* (Oxford, 1979); J. B. Kelly, *Britian and the Persian Gulf, 1795–1880* (Oxford, 1968); D. Wright, *The English Amongst the Persians* (London, 1977); and M. E. Yapp, *Strategies of British India: Britain, Iran and Afghanistan, 1798–1850* (Oxford, 1980). See also M. Mahmud, *Tarikh-i Ravabit-i Siyasi-yi Iran va Ingilis dar Qarn-i Nuzdahum-i Miladi*, 8 vols., (Tehran, 1328/1949), I–III; and A. Tahiri, *Tarikh-i Ravabit-i Bazargani va Siyasi Ingilis va Iran*, 2 vols., (Tehran, 1354/1975).

17. The totemistic appellation may have originated in the flock-keeping and camelbreeding occupations of the respective clans in the pastures of the northeastern province of Astarabad, the original homeland of the eastern Qajars. It may also have been reminiscent of the insignia of the fifteenth-century Aq-Quyunlu, to whom the Quvanlu looked as their historical ancestors. On the origins and early history of the Qajar tribe see Dunbuli, *Ma'athir*, 4–16, and English trans. Jones Brydge, *Dynasty of the Qajars*, 1–15; *RSN*, IX, 4–13; Mirza Muhammad Taqi Sipihr (Lisan al-Mulk), *Nasikh al-Tawarikh: Qajariya*, ed. M. B. Bihbudi (Tehran, 1344/1965; hereinafter *NTQ*), I, 7–29. In their attempt to trace the origins of the ruling tribe, these accounts often do not hesitate to cross the frontiers of history into legend. Muhammad Hasan I'timad al-Saltana, in *Durrar al-Tijan fi Tarikh Bani Ashkan*, (Tehran, 1308–1311/1890–1893), makes every effort to link Qajars to the Parthian dynasty of the pre-Islamic era. Mas'ud Mirza, Zill al-Sultan, who gives a lengthy account of the early Qajars (*Tarikh-i Sarguzasht-i Mas'udi* [Tehran, 1325/1907], 4–17), admits that his historical research only proved to him this verse of Hafiz: "With no one I saw a trace of that untraceable, either I lack insight or he has no trace." See also Malcolm (*The History of Persia*, 2 vols., [London, 1815], II, 116, 125, 262), who erroneously traces the origins of Qajar tribal divisions in the villages of Armenia. For a modern assessments see *EI2*: "Kadjar (Turcoman tribe)" by F. Sumer, and "Kadjar (dynasty)" by A.K.S. Lambton, especially 389–390.

18. See Hambly, "Agha Mohammad Khan," 139–161. Also *RSN*, IX, 129–156, 215–217.

19. Sultan Ahmad Mirza 'Azud al-Dawla, *Tarikh-i 'Azudi*, ed. 'A. Nava'i (Tehran, 1355/1976), 94–95.

20. *NTQ*, II, 140–146. Cf. 'Azud al-Dawla, *Tarikh-i 'Azudi*, 321. Not surprisingly, there is some confusion concerning the exact number of Fath 'Ali's sons and daughters and their order of seniority. *NTQ*, (II, 140) gives the total of 260 children, 103 of whom (57 sons and 46 daughters) survived their father.

21. 'Azud al-Dawla, *Tarikh-i 'Azudi*, appendix. I, 175–298. *NTQ* (III, 140) gives the total of 685 surviving grandchildren in 1834.

22. *NTQ,* II, 140. Cf. *RSN,* X, 99, and 'Azud al-Dawla, *Tarikh-i 'Azudi,* 167. Fazlullah Khavari's unpublished work *Tarikh Dhul-Qarnayn* and its supplement, *Takmala-yi Tarikh Dhul-Qarnayan,* represent the most complete account devoted to the history of Fath 'Ali Shah's house.

23. See 'Azud al-Dawla, *Tarikh-i 'Azudi* (12–16) for the shah's disgust with the his senior wives' quarrels over their ranking in the private levee (*salam*) held in the *andarun,* which eventually led to the abolishment of this custom.

24. Ibid., 16.

25. See for instance John McNeill's assertion in 1842 that "the late Shah [Fath 'Ali], and even his predecessor, Aqa Muhammad Khan, had laid it down as a principle in the selection of the Heir to the Throne , that he should be descended from Kajars by his mother as well as by his father" (FO 60/86, no. 8, McNeill to Earl of Aberdeen, Tehran, 14 February 1842).

26. See P. W. Avery, "An Enquiry into the Outbreak of the Second Russo-Persian War, 1826–28," *Iran and Islam,* ed. C. E. Bosworth, (Edinburgh, 1971), 17–45. For opposite views, see N. Najmi, *Iran dar Miyan-i Tufan ya Sharh Zindigani-yi 'Abbas Mirza Na'ib al-Saltana* (Tehran, 1336/1957).

27. For the English text see J. C. Hurewitz, *The Middle East and North Africa in World Politics,* 2 vols. (New Haven, 1975–79), 197–199.

28. Hurewitz, *Middle East,* I, 233.

29. Jahangir Mirza, *Tarikh-i Naw,* ed. 'A. Iqbal (Tehran, 1327/1948), 208.

30. The joint agreement of the powers concerning the new nomination is evident in Palmerston's message to the Russian tsar on the question of secession (Palmerston to Bligh, 5 September 1834, cited in V. Chirol, *The Middle Eastern Question or Some Political Problems of Indian Defence,* [London, 1903], 437). See also Ingram (*Great Game,* 300–327) for an account of the British involvement during the crisis of succession.

CHAPTER 1: THE CHILD OF TURKMANCHAY

1. 'Azud al-Dawla, *Tarikh-i 'Azudi,* 94–95; cf. *RSN,* X, 172–173, 577–579 and *NTQ,* I, 312. *Tarikh 'Azudi* (43) also recounts Fath 'Ali Shah's curious dream, on the night of Muhammad Mirza's wedding with Malik Jahan, in which the shah saw his grandson castrated. This, too, may be interpreted as a sign of the ruler's concern with the success of his genealogical scheme.

2. I'timad al-Saltana, *Ma'athir,* 9.

3. *RSN,* X, 14.

4. Ibid., X, 742.

5. *ST,* 178, n. 1 (by M. Mushiri).

6. Several specimens of Muhammad Shah's calligraphy have survived. One good example is in British Library collection (BL, MS 4936. no. 3). See also C. Rieu, *Catalogue of the Persian Manuscripts in the British Museum (Supplement)* (London, 1895), 257, no. 403). On the margin of a piece executed in *nasti'aliq* style, Farhad Mirza Mu'tamad al-Dawla testifies that the piece was written by his brother Muhammad Shah in 1261 Q./1845 as a calligraphic lesson for him.

7. J. B. Fraser, *A Winter Journey (Tatar) from Constantinople to Tehran,* 2 vols., (London, 1838), 179–181.

8. A descendent of an old family of bureaucrats from Farahan with a record of service going back to Safavid times, Mirza Buzurg was trained in Shiraz under his uncle, who was minister to the ill-fated Lutf 'Ali Khan, the last of the Zand rulers. Ever since the appointment of Mirza Buzurg as the tutor and minister to the young 'Abbas Mirza, the tutor's interest in poetry and mysticism (a legacy of the eighteenth-century literary revival) made the provincial capital Tabriz a haven for a few literati and Sufis, particularly of the persecuted Ni'matullahi order. A critical study of the Qa'im Maqams remains to be done. *ST* (115–151) is the most extensive. Among recent accounts, Khan Malik Sasani (*Siyasatgaran-i Dawra-yi Qajar,* [Tehran, 1346/1967], II, 2–60) and F. Adamiyat ("Sarnivisht-i Qa'im Maqam," *Maqalat-i Tarikhi,* 2d ed. [Tehran, 1362/1983], 9–36) contain new material but suffer from the authors' biases and misjudgments. See also Ma'sum 'Ali Shah Shirazi [Na'ib al-Sadr], *Tara'iq al-Haqa'iq,* 2d ed., ed. M. J. Mahjub, 3 vols (Tehran, 1345/1966), III, 276–279. Of European accounts, Fraser (*A Winter Journey,* 181–188) and Algar (*Religion,* 73–81) provide some interesting details.

9. Jahangir Mirza, the author of *Tarikh-i Naw,* Mahmud Mirza, the author of a comprehensive biographical dictionary, and Farhad Mirza, author of several literary works, are better known. But other sons of 'Abbas Mirza, in the tradition of their father, were patrons of literature and scholarship.

10. 'Azud al-Dawla, *Tarikh-i 'Azudi,* 28. Devotion to Sufi adepts, especially Ni'matullahis, was not rare among the Qajar ruling elite of the early nineteenth century. Contrary to official state support for the 'ulama, and in spite of recurring Sufi persecutions, dervishes were occasionally admitted to service in provincial courts. Sufi scholars such as Mulla Riza Hamadani, Kawthar 'Ali Shah, were prominent in Tabriz. Both Qa'im Maqams held special admiration for Kawthar 'Ali, among whose devotees in the Qajar *andarun* was the mother of Malik Jahan, though there is no evidence that Malik Jahan herself entertained such Sufi inclinations. For Kawthar 'Ali see Ma'sum 'Ali Shah, *Tara'iq al-Haqa'iq,* III, 264–266, and R. Gramlich, *Die Schiitischen Derwischorden Persiens,* 2 vols (Wiesbaden, 1975–1976), I, 41–43.

11. Jahangir Mirza, *Tarikh-i Naw,* 13.

12. See *EIr:* "Aqasi, Hajji Mirza 'Abbas Iravani" (A. Amanat) and cited sources.

13. 'Azud al-Dawla, *Tarikh-i 'Azudi,* 61–62.

14. Ibid., 64.

15. Ibid., 64–65.

16. For his account see M. Bamdad, *Sharh-i Hal-i Rijal-i Iran dar Qarn-i 12, 13, 14 Hijri,* 6 vols. (Tehran, 1347–1355/1968–1974), II, 118–120.

17. For Malik Jahan's lineage and family see, among other accounts, 'Azud al-Dawla, *Tarikh-i 'Azudi,* 72, 94 and appendix, 244–245; and *RSN,* X, 172.

18. Perhaps the first since the ill-fated Khayr al-Nisa Khanum Mahd 'Ulya, wife of Muhammad Khudabanda and mother of 'Abbas I, who was murdered by the Qizilbash in 1579. P. Jackson and L. Lockhart, *The Cambridge History of Iran,* VI, (Cambridge, 1986), [H. Rumer], 255, 344.

19. Jahangir Mirza, *Tarikh-i Naw,* 201–240.

20. *NTQ,* III, 146.

21. Ibid.

22. See Adamiyat, "Sarnivesht-i Qa'im Maqam," *Maqalat-i Tarikhi*, 9–36, which is based on intentional readings of John Campbell's correspondence (F.O. 60/37–39 [1835]). See also Jahangir Mirza, *Tarikh-i Naw*, 236–240; I. Safa'i ed., *Yaksad Sanad-i Tarikhi*, (Tehran, 1352/1973), letters no. 3–9, (13–29); and *ST*, 135–151.

23. *ST*, 137.

24. *NTQ*, III, 147.

25. Jahangir Mirza, *Tarikh-i Naw*, 248–249 cf. *RSN*, X, 173.

26. Ibid., 249; cf. FO 60/36, Ellis to Palmerston, no. 8, Tehran, 6 October 1835, enclosure: Memorandum from Captain Campbell.

27. *RSN*, X, 174.

28. W. Stuart, *Journal of a Residence in Northern Persia and in the Adjacent Provinces of Turkey* (London, 1835), 136.

29. W. Stuart, *Journal of Two Years Travel in Persia*, 2 vols. (London, 1854), II, 236.

30. J. E. Polak, *Persien, das Land und Seine Bewohner, Ethnographische Scilderungen*, 2 vols. (Leipzig, 1865), II, 3; Persian trans., *Safarnama-yi Pulak: Iran va Iranian*, trans. K. Jahandari (Tehran, 1361/1982), 270.

31. *RSN*, X, 199, and *NTQ*, II, 262.

32. *NTQ*, II, 262 and *RSN* X, 199. For the causes, development, and consequences of the first Herat expedition, see M. Ittihadiya, *Gushihha-i az Ravabit-i Kharaji-yi Iran, 1200–1280 Hijri-yi Qamari* (Tehran, 1355/1976), 53–116. See also H. Rawlinson, *England and Russia in the East* (London, 1875).

33. *NTQ*, II, 262 and *RSN*, X, 199.

34. *RSN*, X, 199 cf. H. C. Brugsch, *Reise der Kgl. Preussischen Gesandschaft nach Persien 1860 und 1861*, 2 vols. (Leipzig, 1862–1863), I; Persian trans. *Safari bi Darbar-i Sultan-i Sahibqaran*, trans. M. Kurdbachih (Tehran, 1367/1988) I, 89–90. Brugsch quotes the tsar as saying to young Nasir al-Din Mirza that the diamond ring is a token of the tsar's support for the crown prince whenever in the future he finds himself in trouble. This counsel Nasir al-Din found useful when he reached the throne in 1848.

35. F.O. 60/56, McNeill to Backhouse, Private, Tehran, 31 January 1838, enclosure: Bonham to McNeill, Tabriz, 2 January 1838. Mirza Taqi Khan's point concerning change in the Russian treatment is evident in the elaborate protocol observed in the first embassy. See Mirza Mustafa Afshar Baha' al-Mulk, "Ahvalat-i Safar-i Mirza Mas'ud," *Nashriya-i Vizarat-i Umur-i Kharija*, III, no. 3, (Shahrivar 1345/1966), 180–322. Later published as *Safarnamih-yi Khusraw Mirza bi Pitirzburg*, M. Gulbun ed., (Tehran, 1349/1970), 208–243.

36. *RSN*, 200–201.

37. Polak, *Persein*, I, 258–259; Persian trans., 179.

38. Ibid. Persian trans., 179–180. Cf. 'Abdullah Mustawfi, *Sharh-i Zindigani-yi Man ya Tarikh-i Ijtima'i va Idari-yi Dawra-yi Qajariya*, 2d ed., 3 vols. (Tehran, 1343/1964), I, 387–389.

39. Polak, *Persien*, I, 230; Persian trans. 161. In spite of a close attachment to his mother and an extensive account of his paternal linage, Zill al-Sultan does not

elaborate on his maternal side. He no doubt regarded his mother's humble origins as an obvious weakness in the way of his ambitions for the throne (*Tarikh-i Sarguzasht-i Mas'udi*, 1–17).

40. Muhammad Hasan Khan I'timad al-Saltana, *Ruznama-yi Khatirat-i I'timad al-Saltana*, ed. I. Afshar (Tehran, 1345/1976), 141. She was Ghulam Husayn Sadiq al-Saltana's mother.

41. Carla Serena, *Hommes et Choses en Perse*, (Paris, 1883). Persian trans. *Adamha va A'inha*, trans. 'A. Sa'idi, (Tehran, 1362/1983), 77.

42. See *EIr*: "Amin al-Soltan, Ebrahim" (A. Amanat).

43. *NTQ*, III, 147.

44. Ibid., II, 333.

45. Ibid., III, 333. See also Ittihadiya, *Ravabit*, 99–114.

46. F.O. 60/56, McNeill to Backhouse, Private, Tehran, 31 January 1838, enclosure: Bonham to McNeill, Tabriz, 2 January 1838.

47. Ibid. Mirza Taqi Khan further confided to Bonham the intentions of the Persian peace mission to Europe headed by Husayn Khan Ajudanbashi and the complaints it would lodge in London concerning the conduct of the British diplomats in Iran, a piece of intelligence that he must have disclosed, one may assume, out of desperation rather than sympathy for the British. Similar observations by Mirza Taqi Khan appear in Bonham's dispatches during this period. See, for instance, F.O. 60/66 and 69, Bonham to Sheil, May to July 1839.

48. *RSN*, X, 172 and *NTQ*, III, 135–141.

49. This was after the premature death, at the age of six, of another son from the same mother and by the same name (i.e., 'Abbas Mirza II), who had been named after the shah's father, 'Abbas Mirza I. (*NTQ*, III, 141 and *ST*, 189–190 [quoting Allah Quli Khan Ilkhani]).

50. Polak, *Persien*, II, 1–2; Persian trans., 270.

51. 'Abbas Mirza Mulk Ara, *Sharh-i Hal-i 'Abbas Mirza Mulkara*. Ed. 'A. Nava'i and 'A. Iqbal, 2d ed. (Tehran, 1355/1976), 43, 124 (hereinafter *SHA*).

52. Ibid., 124.

53. Joseph A. Comte de Gobineau, *Correspondance entre le Comte de Gobineau et le Comte de Prokesch-Osten (1854–1876)* (Paris, 1933), 70.

54. *ST*, 179.

55. Polak, *Persien*, II, 1–2; Persian trans., 270.

56. Ibid.

57. For his account, see below. Also Ittihadiya, *Ravabit*, 134–158.

58. For his account, see Bamdad, *Rijal-i Iran*, VI, 93 and Dust-'Ali Khan Mu'ayyir al-Mamalik, *Rijal-i 'Asr-i Nasiri* (Tehran, 1361/1982), 33–42.

59. Mu'ayyir al-Mamalik, *Rijal*, 36 (account related by 'Ismat al-Dawla, Nasir al-Din's daughter, to his own son, Dust 'Ali Khan Mu'ayyir al-Mamalik). Cf. G. N. Curzon, *Persia and the Persian Question* (2 vols. [London, 1892], I, 394) which implies the same hardship.

60. Polak, *Persien*, II, 2–3; Persian trans., 271.

61. A. D. Soltykov, *Voyage en Perse*, (Paris, 1851); Persian trans. 86.

62. Ibid., plate 15; Persian trans. 85.

63. Ibid., plate 16; Persian trans., 85.

64. F.O. 60/86, McNeill to Aberdeen, no. 8, Tehran, 14 February 1842 and Aberdeen to Sheil, no. 2, London, 4 July 1842, enclosure: Bligh to Nesselrode.

65. F.O. 60/90, Sheil to Aberdeen, no. 5, near Tehran, 6 September 1842.

66. Safa'i, *Yaksad Sanad*, no. 17, p. 40.

67. Ibid.

68. Aqa Mahdi Navvab Tihrani, *Risala-yi Dustur al-A'qab*, in Sasani, *Siyasatgaran*, II, 95.

69. See *EIr:* "Aqasi."

70. Navvab Tihrani, *Dustur al-A'qab*, in Sasani, *Siyasatgaran* II, 77.

71. 'Azud al-Dawla, *Tarikh-i 'Azudi*, 52.

72. 'A. Nava'i, "Vali'ahdha-yi Nasir al-Din Shah," *Yadgar*, 55–56. For Madam Gulsaz, see below.

73. *RSN*, X, 287.

74. FO 60/114, Sheil to Aberdeen, no. 74, Camp near Tehran, 30 June 1845.

75. Dust 'Ali Khan Mu'ayyir al-Mamalik, *Yaddashtha-i az Zindigani-yi Khususi-yi Nasir al-Din Shah*, 2d ed. (Tehran, 1362/1983), 22. Recollections of Nasir al-Din Shah in the gathering of his wives.

76. *RSN*, X, 288–289.

77. *NTQ*, II, 61.

78. FO 60/114, no. 74.

79. FO 60/114, Sheil to Aberdeen, no. 77, Camp near Tehran, 12 July 1845.

80. FO 60/115, Sheil to Aberdeen, no. 98, Camp near Tehran, 10 August 1845.

81. FO 60/115, same to same, no. 112, Tehran, 30 September 1845.

82. FO 60/115, same to same, no. 115, Tehran, 15 October 1845.

83. See *EIr:* "Allah-qoli Khan Ilkhani" (A. Amanat) and cited sources. Also FO 60/115, no. 115.

84. FO 60/115, Sheil to Aberdeen, no. 122, Tehran, 30 October 1845.

85. FO 60/115, same to same, no. 124, Tehran, 31 October 1845.

86. Ibid.

87. Ibid.

88. FO 60/116, same to same, no. 129, Tehran, 20 November 1845.

89. Ibid.

90. FO 60/116, same to same, no. 130, Tehran, 20 November 1845.

91. Ibid. enclosure no. 1: Aqasi to Muhammad Shah.

92. Ibid. enclosure no. 2: Muhammad Shah to Aqasi.

93. FO 60/116, no. 130.

94. Ibid., enclosure no. 4: Sheil to Heir Apparent.

95. Ibid., enclosure no. 3: Muhammad Shah to Heir Apparent.

96. FO 60/116, Sheil to Aberdeen, no. 139, Tehran, 29 November 1845.

97. Nuri's wife was a maternal cousin of Malik Jahan ('Azud al-Dawla, *Tarikh-i 'Azudi*, 72, 92, 243, 302).

98. *NTQ*, III, 70 cf. *ST*, 236.

99. Reference to amicable relations with the British appears in FO 60/138. Farrant to Palmerston, no. 80, Tehran, 19 September 1848.

100. *NTQ*, III, 71.

101. Ibid. III, 86–87.

102. FO 60/132. Farrant to Palmerston, no. 6, Tehran, 20 October 1847.

103. Ibid.

104. Ibid.

105. FO 60/136, same to same, no. 10, Tehran, 26 January 1848.

106. Ibid.

107. Ibid.

CHAPTER 2: A MIRROR FOR THE PRINCE

1. 'Abbas Mirza to Muhammad Mirza, letter no. 5, Mashhad, n.d. (1249 Q./1833), "Wasaya-yi Na'ib al-Saltana, 'Abbas Mirza," Naw-Bahar 13 (1301/1922), 5, in Najmi, Iran dar Miyan-i Tufan, 334.

2. 'Abbas Mirza to Malik Jahan [Malika Jahan], Mashhad, 1249 Q./1833 in Najmi, Iran dar Miyan-i Tufan, 335–336.

3. For her account see C. Serena, Souvenirs Personnels. Mon voyage. Une Européenne en Perse, (Paris, 1881); 'A. Iqbal, "Madam Hajji 'Abbas Gulsaz," Yadgar, III, no. 6–7 (February–March 1947), 106–109. After his accession Nasir al-Din appointed Madam Gulsaz to the position of interpreter to the royal harem. She died in 1878 in Tehran.

4. The decline of this office, a telling symptom of the state's loosening grip over the religious establishment, is studied in S. A. Arjomand, "The Mujtahid of the Age and the Mulla-bashi: An Intermediate Stage in the Institutionalization of Religious Authority in Shi'ite Iran," Authority and Political Culture in Shi'ism, S. A. Arjomand ed., (Albany, 1988), 80–97. The office of mulla-bashi, originally being the chief of the religious corps, was once occupied by the celebrated scholar of the late seventeenth century, Mulla Muhammad Baqir Majlisi, but by Qajar times it had been diminished to a court function of overseeing the education of the crown prince.

5. Aqa Buzurg [Muhammad Muhsin] Tihrani, Al-Dhari'a ila Tasanif al-Shi'a, 25 vols., (Najaf and Tehran, 1968–1978), I, 381.

6. Mulla Mahmud Nizam al-'Ulama Mulla-bashi Tabrizi, Al-Shihab al-Thaqib fi Radd al-Nawasib (Tabriz, 1270 Q./1853). See Tihrani, Dhari'a, XIV, 253; cf. K. Mushar, Fihrist-i Kitabha-yi Chappi-yi Farsi, 3 vols. (Tehran, 1352/1973), II, 2180.

7. Mirza Asadullah Mazandarani (Fazil), Zuhur al-Haqq, vol. III (Tehran, n.d. [1944 ?]), 10.

8. Farhad Mirza Mu'tamad al-Dawla, Munsha'at, ed. and comp. Fursat al-Dawla Shirazi, (Bombay, 1318 Q./1900), 65.

9. I'timad al-Saltana, Ma'athir, 161.

10. Farhad Mirza, Munsha'at, 66.

11. FO 60/116, Sheil to Aberdeen, no. 129, Tehran, 20 November 1845.

12. Mirza Ibrahim was the uncle of the renowned statesman and reformer of the late nineteenth-century Mirza Malkam Khan. For his account see F. Naura'i, Tahqiq dar Afkar-i Mirza Malkam Khan Nazim al-Dawla, (Tehran, 1352/1973), 2–5, and F. Adamiyat, Amir Kabir va Iran, 3d ed., (Tehran, 1348/1969), 373, 542–543.

13. FO 60/121, Sheil to Aberdeen, no. 29, Tehran, 17 March 1846.

14. Mirza 'Ali Khan Amin al-Dawla, *Khatirat-i Siyasi-yi Mirza 'Ali Khan Amin al-Dawla*, ed. H. Farmanfarma'yan [Farmayan], (Tehran, 1341/1962), 3.

15. Curzon, *Persia and the Persian Question*, I, 397.

16. Amin al-Dawla, *Khatirat-i Siyasi*, 13.

17. FO 60/138, Farrant to Palmerston, no. 97, Tehran, 28 October 1848.

18. For his account and a list of his works see his autobiography in Riza Quli Khan Hidayat [Lala–bashi], *Majma' al-Fusaha*, ed. M. Musaffa, 6 vols. (Tehran, 1336–1340/1957–1961), VI, 1209–1211; E. G. Browne, *Literary History of Persia*, 4 vols., (Cambridge, 1928); E. Edwards, *Catalogue of the Persian Printed Books in the British Museum*, (London, 1922), 631–632; and Bamdad, *Rijal-i Iran*, II, 39–42.

19. Note particularly in 'Abbas Mirza's *Sarh-i Hall* his obvious ease with the use of language and frequent citations of appropriate classical verses.

20. For further discussion see Y. Aryanpur, *Az Saba ta Nima*, 2 vols. (Tehran, 1354/1975). See also Amanat, "Russian Intrusion," 36–55.

21. Nadir Mirza, *Tarikh va Jughrafi-yi Dar al-Saltana-yi Tabriz*, 2d ed., ed M. Mushiri, (Tehran, 1351/1972), 176.

22. The title of 'Abd al-Latif Tasuji's translation, *Hazar u Yak Shab* (Tabriz, 1261 Q./1845) is a rendering of *One Thousand and One Nights*, the original name of this ancient Perso-Indian collection of tales otherwise known as *Arabian Nights* (J. Rypka, *History of Iranian Literature* [Dordrecht, 1968] 663–669). The impact of this edition on the Persian public can be gauged by the numerous editions produced in the nineteenth century. See K. Mushar, *Mu'allifin-i Kutub-i Chappi (Farsi va 'Arabi)*, 6 vols. (Tehran, 1340–1344/1961–1965) III, 933.

23. Y. Zuka' ("Mirza Abul-Hasan Khan Sani' al-Mulk Ghaffari," *Hunar va Mardum*, I, no. 10 [Murdad 1342/August 1963], 14–27 and no. 11 [Shahrivar 1342/September 1963], 16–33 [25–26]), citing Ahmad Munshi Razi Badayi' Nigar [II], *Badayi' al-Tawarikh* (MS 122/1 and 122/2, Library of the Faculty of Law and Political Sciences [Danishkadih-yi Huquq va 'Ulum-i Siyasi], Tehran University).

24. For Tasuji's biography see M. Qazvini, "Wafiyat-i Ma'asirin," *Yadgar*, V, no. 8–9 (March–April 1949), 68–71, partially citing an important letter by Yahya Dawlatabadi; M. T. Malik al-Shu'ara Bahar, *Sabk-shinasi*, 3 vols., (Tehran, 1337/1958), III, 369–370; M. J. Mahjub, "Tarjama-yi Farsi *Alf Laylat wa'l Layla*," *Sukhan*, 11 (1339/1960), no. 1, 34–53; and Aryanpur, *Az Saba ta Nima*, II, 182–185. Dawlatabadi's reference to Tasuji's tutorship of the crown prince is too equivocal to be taken beyond what is implied in the text. After Nasir al-Din's accession, for reasons unknown, he immigrated to the 'Atabat, were he died in the 1880s. Circumstantial evidence may suggest that Tasuji's unorthodox beliefs led to his removal by Mirza Taqi Khan Amir Kabir.

25. He was introduced to Nasir al-Din by one of his aides du comp (Hidayat, *Majma' al-Fusaha*, IV, 406).

26. For Surush's biography see two introductions by Jalal al-Din Huma'i and Muhammad Ja'far Mahjub to Surush Isfahani, *Divan-i Surush, Shams al-Shu'ara*, ed. M. J. Mahjub, 2 vols. (Tehran, 1339/1960), 1–90, 91–208.

27. Of major religious works cited in *Divan-i Surush*, the long but incomplete poem "Urdibihishtnama," composed in 1854 in five parts, is fully devoted to 'Ali's battles and is not free from exaggerations associated with the Ahl-i Haqq, a

semi-independent rustic religion of western Iran. For other panegyrics in honor of 'Ali see Hidayat, *Majma' al-Fusaha*, IV, 407–429. For Surush's expulsion from Isfahan see *Divan-i Surush* (Introduction), I, 7–8, 101–102.

28. Hidayat, *Majma' al-Fusaha*, IV, 415.

29. Ibid., IV, 409.

30. Ibid., IV, 409. Surush's poetical corpus included two other interesting items commissioned by Nasir al-Din. Even before his appointment as poet laureate, he attempted to compose in the style of *Shahnama* (and perhaps in competition with Saba) an epic history of the Qajar tribe. Reference to these untraceable works of Surush appears in Sayyid Ahmad Divan-Bagi Shriazi, *Hadiqat al-Shu'ara*, 'A. Nava'i ed., 3 vols. (Tehran, 1364–1366/1985–1987), I, 767–773, which includes the editor's citations from Mirza Tahir Shi'ri, *Ganj-i Shaygan*, in the notes. See also Jalal al-Din Huma'i's introduction to *Divan-i Surush*, 19.

31. Hidayat, *Majma' al-Fusaha*, V, 855–856. Other panegyrics in honor of Nasir al-Din appear in Qa'ani Shirazi, *Divan-i Qa'ani Shirazi* (Tehran, 1270 Q./1853), 2d ed., ed. M. J. Mahjub (Tehran, 1336/1957). See also D. C. Phillott, trans., *Selection from Qa'ani* (ed. Muhammad Kazim Shirazi [Calcutta, 1907], 3) for circumstances of his acquaintance with the crown prince.

32. Hidayat, *Majma' al-Fusaha*, IV, 189.

33. Aryanpur, *Az Saba ta Nima*, I, 133; cf. Hidayat, *Majma' al-Fusaha*, V, 515.

34. For the tradition of fight and feast, see O. M. Davidson, *Poet and Hero in the Persian Book of Kings* (Ithaca, 1994), 156–167; Rypka, *History*, 142, 148.

35. *NTQ*, III, 148. Jamshid is the Pishdadid king of the *Shahnama*, and Rustam is the renowned king maker and symbol of physical strength. Qa'an is the Persianized version of the title of the Chinese Mongol emperors, and Hatam is the legendary Arab chief of the Tayy, known for his generosity.

36. Serena, *Hommes*; Persian trans., 81.

37. Mirza Nasrullah Damavandi, *Al-Tuhfat al-Nasiriya fi Ma'rafat al-Ilahiya*, Tehran University Central Library, MS no. 2653, 37 folio, 1264 Q./1848. The author refers to two other works of his. See also A. Munzavi, *Fihrist-i Nuskhaha-yi Khatti-yi Farsi*, 6 vols. (Tehran, 1348–1353/1969–1974), II/2, 1566 and Tihrani, *Dhari'a*, XXIV, 101.

38. Sayyid Ja'far Kashfi Darabi, *Tuhfat al-Muluk fi'l-Sayr wa'l Suluk* (Tehran, 1273 Q./1856). For a discussion on the content, see Arjomand, "The Shi'ite Heirocracy," 40–78. For Kashfi see also Amanat, *Resurrection and Renewal*, 46–47, 247–248, and cited sources.

39. Mirza Asadullah Shahkhasti Mazandarani [Nadir], *Khasa'il al-Muluk*, Tehran University Central Library, MS no. 4972, (1256 Q./1840). See M. T. Danishpazhuh, *Fihrist-i Kitabkhanih-yi Danishgah-i Tihran*, (Tihran, 1345/1966), XV, 4071.

40. Muhammad Ja'far Marvazi, *Tuhfa-yi Nasiri*, Milli Library (Kitabkhana-yi Milli), MS no. 913F, 1254 Q./1838. This copy probably belonged to the royal library. See also Munzavi, *Fihrist*, II/2, 1566, and Tihrani, *Dhari'a*, IX, 1297. For a thorough bibliographical survey of the reform literature and the genre of mirrors in the nineteenth century, see I. Afshar's introduction to M. Shafi' Qazvini, *Qanun-i Qazvini*, ed. I. Afshar (Tehran, 1370/1991), vii–xii.

41. Muhammad Sadiq Marvazi, *'Ahdnama-yi Malik-i Ashtar*, Milli Library, MS no. 151F. This copy belonged to the royal library and bears Nasir al-Din's seal. See Munzavi, *Fihrist*, II/2, 1573. Muhammad Sadiq is also the author of a general history and two works of mirrors dedicated to 'Abbas Mirza. See Munzavi, *Fihrist*, II/ 2, 1561, 1641, and B. Atabay, ed., *Fihrist-i Tarikh, Safarnama, Siyahatnama, Ruznama va Jughrafiya-yi Khatti-yi Kitabkhana-yi Saltanati* (Tehran, 1356/ 1977), 317. For the list of Persian translations of *'Ahdnama*, see Munzavi, *Fihrist*, II/2, 1572–1574. The most well known in the Qajar period is by Muhammad Ibrahim Navvab Tihrani, Badayi' Nigar, published in his *Makhzan al-Insha'* (Tehran 1273 Q./1856). For the Arabic text and a more recent translation see 'Ali Naqi Fayz al-Islam, *Nahj al-Balagha*, A. M. Razi, ed. (Tehran, 1326/1947), no. 53, 979–1026. For the English translation see *Nahjul Balagha, Book of Eloquence*, Sayed Ali Reza trans., 3d ed. (Elmhurst, 1984), 534–549.

42. Fayz al-Islam, *Nahj al-Balagha*, 1004–1005; cf. Ali Reza, *Nahjul Balagha*, 540–541.

43. Fayz al-Islam, *Nahj al-Balagha*, 990–991; cf. Ali Reza, *Nahjul Balagha*, 536.

44. Fayz al-Islam, *Nahj al-Balagha*, 1018–1019; cf. Ali Reza, *Nahjul Balagha*, 545.

45. *Jahan Nama*, trans. Mirza Muhammad Husayn Farahani Dabir al-Mulk (from Turkish translation by Musa Jan Davud Khan of the original French), Majlis Library, MS 287, 1272 Q./1860. The copier of this manuscript noted that he had earlier produced three copies of the same work for Nasir al-Din Shah. See Munzavi, *Fihrist*, VI, 3961–3962 for various copies.

46. Rafa'il Flughun, *Jahan Nama*, Milli Library, MS 336 F, 1266 Q./1849–1850. The author's name may be a Persian rendering of Raphael Flannighan. He was an early student of Persian in Tabriz. The copy in the Milli Library probably belonged to Nasir al-Din. Another copy of the same work is entitled *Jahan Ara'* (see Munzavi, *Fihrist*, VI, 3961). This work was published as Rafa'il Flughun, *Jughrafiya-yi Jahan Nama* (Tabriz, 1267 Q./1850).

47. Idvard Burjis [Edward Burgess], *Jughrafiya-yi 'Alam*, Milli Library, MS no. 540, 1267 Q./1851 (probably belonged to Nasir al-Din Shah). See 'A. Anvari, comp., *Fihrist-i Nusakh-i Khatti-yi Kitabkhanih-yi Milli* (Tehran, 1347/1968), II, 32. See also C. Burgess and E. Burgess, *Letters From Persia Written by Charles and Edward Burgess, 1828–1855*, ed. B. Schwartz (New York, 1942), 95–96, Edward Burgess to George Burgess (of New York), Tabriz, 2 February 1847. Edward Burgess also prepared for Bahman Mirza a collection of travelogues on China entitled *Ahval-i Chin* (Milli Library, MS 895/1F, 1263 Q./1845). See Burgess, *Letters*, 85, Edward Burgess to George Burgess, Tabriz, 5 January 1847.

48. Burgess, *Letters*, 93, Edward Burgess to George Burgess, Tabriz, 5 January 1847.

49. Ibid., 93, same to same, Tabriz, 5 January 1847.

50. Ibid., 62, same to same, Tabriz, 30 June 1844.

51. Ibid., 103, same to same, Tabriz, 6 May 1848.

52. Ibid., 102, same to same, Tabriz, 4 April 1848.

53. Ibid., 103, same to same, Tabriz, 6 May 1848.

54. Ibid., 103–104, same to same, Tabriz, 17 September 1848. The royal

autograph granting him the post was not even sealed, since the royal seal had not yet been engraved.

55. Mirza Muhammad Lavasani, *Mir'at al-Ard*, Majlis Library (Kitabkhana-yi Majlis-i Shawra-yi Milli), MS 702. See Munzavi, *Fihrist*, VI, 4050.

56. See Mustafa Afshar, "Ahvalat-i Safar-i Mirza Mas'ud," 179–323 and his *Safarnamih*.

57. Riza Quli Mirza and Najaf Quli Mirza, *Rumuz al-Siyaha* (The Mysteries of Traveling), Milli Library, MS no. 96f, 1840. This copy probably belonged to the royal library. See Munzavi, *Fihrist*, VI, 4001–4002. The published edition appears as Riza Quli Mirza, *Safarnama Riza Quli Mirza Na'ib al-Iyala*, ed. A. Farman-farma'i Qajar (Tehran, 1346/1967). The English translation as A. Kayat, trans., *Journal of a Residence in England*, 2 vols. (London, 1839 [private circulation]). See also J. B. Fraser, *Narrative of the Residence of the Persian Princes in London, in 1835 and 1836*, 2 vols. (London, 1838). One should also not rule out the possibility of Nasir al-Din's access to Mir 'Abd al-Latif Shushtari's geographical account, *Tuhfat al-'alam* (Tehran, 1263 Q./1847). There is no trace of manuscripts in Iranian libraries of other early Persian travel accounts such as by Mirza Abul-Hasan Shirazi's *Hayrat Nama*, covering his 1809 European visit, and Mirza Abu Talib Isfahani's account of his 1801 European tour entitled *Masir-i Talibi*.

58. Mahmud Mirza Qajar, *Akhbar-i Muhammadi* (Muhammadan accounts), Milli Library, MS no. 578F. This was an abridged version of another work by the same author. Muhammad Sadiq Marvazi, Vaqayi' Nigar, *Tarikh-i Jahan Ara*, Gulistan Library (Kitabkhana-yi Saltanati), MS no. 140, 1233 Q./1817. See Atabay, *Fihrist-i Tarikh*, 317 and Munzavi, *Fihrist*, VI, 4305–4346. Fazullah Khavari, *Tarikh-i Dhul-Qarnayan*, Milli Libary, MS. 1771f., 1262 Q./1846. See Munzavi, *Fihrist*, VI, 4242–4243.

59. *Tarikh-i Napilun*, Gulistan Library, MS no. 187/1976, 90 illutrations, 1260 Q./1844. See *Fihrist-i Tarikh*, 425.

60. Burgess, *Letters*, 93. Edward Burgess to George Burgess, Tabriz, 5 January 1847.

61. J. Richard, "Journal," 29 March 1844 and 10 October 1844, in Khalil Saqafi [A'lam al-Dawla], *Maqalat-i Gunagun* (Tehran, 1322/1943), 44 and 113–114. Richard's memoirs are only partially available in Persian translation in the above work. The French original remains unpublished and unaccessible.

62. Richard, letter to anon., 29 October 1849 cf. "Journal," 10 June 1845 in Saqafi, *Maqalat*, 88–90 and 45–46.

63. *RSN*, X, 346; cf. FO 60/138, Farrant to Palmerston, no. 16, Tehran, 18 January 1847.

64. *RSN*, IX, 678.

65. Amin al-Dawla, *Khatirat-i Siyasi*, 13. On Hajji Bizhan see *RSN*, X, 360, 465, 505. As a reward for his services, he was later given the post of head servant in the Shah's inner court.

66. FO 60/140, Robert Stevens to Palmerston, no. 3, Tabriz, 16 February 1848.

67. FO 60/140, same to same, no. 6, Tabriz, 10 March 1848.

68. FO 60/140, no. 3; cf. same to same, no. 11, Tabriz, March 16 1848.

69. FO 60/140, same to same, no. 14, Tabriz, 3 May 1848.

70. FO 60/140, same to same, no. 15, Tabriz, 5 May 1848.

71. Burgess, *Letters*, 102, Edward Burgess to George Burgess, Tabriz, 4 April 1848.

72. FO 60/140, Robert Stevens to Palmerston, no. 17, Tabriz, 4 June 1848.

73. FO 60/140, same to same, no. 20, Tabriz, 20 June 1848, enclosure no.1: George A. Stevens to Consul Stevens, 16 June 1848.

74. FO 60/140, no. 20.

75. Nadir Mirza, *Tabriz*, 176.

76. FO 60/140, no. 20.

77. Nadir Mirza, *Tabriz*, 176.

78. FO 60/140, no. 20, enclosure no. 1.

79. FO 60/140, no. 20.

80. Ibid.

81. FO 60/140, same to same, no. 21, Tabriz, 21 June 1848.

82. Mulla Muhammad Taqi Mamaqani, *risala* (treatise), cited in part in M. Mudarrisi Chahardihi, *Shaykhigari va Babigarai*, 2d ed. (Tehran, 1351/1972), 311. Muhammad Taqi was the son of the prominent Shaykhi *mujtahid* of Tabriz Mulla Muhammad Mamaqani, himself an inquisitor in the trial of Tabriz and later the co-author of the *fatwa* of the execution of the Bab in 1850. Muhammad Taqi compiled the *risala* at Nasir al-Din Shah's request, presumably in 1873. For further detail see Amanat, *Resurrection and Renewal*, 386–387, 399–400.

83. Mudarrisi, *Shaykhigari*, 315; cf. E. G. Browne, *Materials for the Study of the Babi Religion* (Cambridge, 1918), 249 (English trans. 252), and Amanat, *Resurrection and Renewal*, 385–34.

84. Official government report cited in Browne, *Materials*, 249 (English trans., 252).

85. *RSN*, X, 423. The Babi-Baha'-i accounts are varied on this point. They assign the initiative of sitting at the head or top of the room to the Bab himself. See E. G. Browne, ed., *Nuqtatu'l-Kaf [Nuqtat al-Kaf] Compiled by Hajji Mirza Jani of Kashah* (London and Leiden, 1910), 134, and Shaykh Muhammad Nabil Zarandi, *The Dawn-Breakers, Nabil's Narrative of the Early Days of the Baha'i Revelation*, ed. and trans. Shoghi Effendi (Wilmette, Ill., 1932), 315.

86. *RSN*, X, 424.

87. Ibid., 425.

88. Ibid., 427. *Kitab al-Hidaya*, a popular elementary text in Arabic syntax, is part of a compilation of fifteen rudimentary works in Arabic gammer known as *Jama' al-Muqaddimat*. This book, in use in the nineteenth century, may have been studied by Nasir al-Din under Mulla-bashi.

89. Browne, *Nuqtatu'l-Kaf*, 135–137.

90. Ibid., 135; cf. *RSN*, X, 427.

91. Mamaqani, *risala* in Mudarrisi, *Shaykhigari va Babigari*, 312; cf. Browne, *Nuqtatu'l-Kaf*, 135.

92. For William Cormick's account see Browne, *Material*, 260–262, and Amanat, *Resurrection anad Renewal*, 109, 391–392.

93. *RSN*, X, 428.

94. Ibid. Cf. Browne, *Nuqtatu'l-Kaf*, 138.

CHAPTER 3: ASCENDING THE HHRONE

1. Brugsch, *Reise;* Persian trans., 90.

2. F.O. 60/138, Farrant to Palmerston, no. 86, 29 September 1848, enclosure: Abbott, to Farrant, Tabriz, 10 September 1848. See also *NTQ*, III, 180–181 and *RSN*, X, 352.

3. F.O. 60/138, Farrant to Palmerston, no.78, camp near Tehran, 5 September 1848. See also Mahdi Quli Hidayat, Mukhbir al-Saltana, *Guzarish-i Iran*, III (Tehran, 1333 Q./1914), 44; *RSN*, X, 354 and *NTQ*, III, 133, 137.

4. I'timad al-Saltana, *Ruznama*, 249; 16 Jumada al-Ula 1300 Q./April 1883.

5. F.O. 60/138, Farrant to Palmerston, no.77, camp near Tehran, 4 September 1848.

6. F.O. 60/138, same to same, no. 78, camp near Tehran, 5 September 1848.

7. F.O. 60/138, no. 77.

8. F.O. 60/138, no. 86, enclosure no. 1.

9. Ibid., enclosure no.2: Abbott to Farrant, Tabriz, 14 September 1848.

10. *RSN*, X, 358 and *NTQ*, III, 182.

11. The rate of exchange in 1848 was slightly less than two tumans for one pound sterling (Issawi, *Economic History*, 343).

12. F.O. 60/140, Stevens to Palmerston, no. 40, Tabriz, 26 September 1848.

13. *NTQ*, III, 183.

14. As an incentive, it was agreed that the equivalent of the interest be paid annually as pension to the financiers ('A. Iqbal, *Mirza Taqi Khan Amir Kabir*, ed. I. Afshar [Tehran, 1340/1961], 90–91 citing Shaykh al-Mashayikh Mu'izzi's *Navadir al-Amir*). On the margin (91), Qasim Ghani notes that one of the merchants was probably a certain Hajji Shaykh Qasim, father of Shaykh Muhsin Khan Mu'taman al-Mulk, later Mushir al-Dawla (IV). A. Gilanshah (*Yaksad va Panjah Sal Saltanat dar Iran* [Tehran, 1340/1961] (23) identifies another merchant, Hajji 'Ali-Baba Anarchi. See also *Namaha-yi Amir Kabir bi Inzimam-i Risala-yi Navadir al-Amir*, ed. 'Ali Al Davud (Tehran, 1371/1993).

15. F.O. 60/138, Farrant to Palmerston, no. 90, Tehran, 3 October 1848, containing excerpts of Abbott's report to Farrant, Tabriz, 26 September 1848. *RSN* (X, 358) gives the detailed list of the assembled troops and their commanders and puts the total number as high as 30,000.

16. *RSN*, X, 359 and *NTQ*, III, 183–184; cf. F.O. 60/140, Stevens to Palmerston, no. 45, Tabriz, 9 October 1848. Soon after Aqasi's downfall, 'Ali-Khan was dismissed and sent into exile, and two of his brothers, governors of Kirmanshah and Zanjan, later met the same fate. Perhaps concerned with repercussions for the Azarbaijan army, Nasir al-Din refrained from confiscating their possessions.

17. For the evolution of the office see *EIr:* "Amir-i Nizam" (A.Amanat).

18. For Amir Kabir's early career see three biographies: Iqbal, *Amir Kabir;* Adamiyat, *Amir Kabir;* and H. Makki, *Zindagani-yi Mirza Taqi Khan Amir Kabir*, 5th ed. (Tehran, 1360/1981). See also Watson, *History*, and *EIr:* "Amir(-i) Kabir" (H. Algar). An admixture of fact and fiction surrounds his early life, stressing his humble origins and his striving for excellence. See for example Mu'izzi, *Navadir*

al-Amir, in Al Davud, *Namaha;* and A. Hashimi Rafsanjani, *Amir Kabir ya Qahraman-i Mubariza ba Isti'mar*, 2d ed. (Tehran, 1362/1983).

19. Aqasi to Mirza Taqi Khan Vazir Nizam, cited in Makki, *Amir Kabir*, 72 originally belonging to Raf'at al-Mulk, *Darya-yi Ma'rifat*, MS. 138.

20. F.O. 60/140, no. 40.

21. Ibid.

22. Adamiyat, *Amir Kabir*, 193.

23. Iqbal, *Amir Kabir*, 97.

24. Ibid. 99.

25. *NTQ*, IV, 185–186.

26. F.O. 60/137, Farrant to Palmerston, no. 79, Camp near Tehran, 6 September 1848 cf. *RSN*, X, 352–353.

27. *NTQ*, III, 152–154.

28. F.O. 60/138, Farrant to Palmerston, no. 81, Tehran, 19 September 1848.

29. *RSN*, X, 353.

30. *NTQ*, III, 159. Aside from Farrant's references, most of the information about the council is recorded by Sipihr, himself an eyewitness and possibly a participant. Writing for Nasir al-Din Shah during the premiership of Mirza Aqa Khan Nuri, an opponent of the council, he is careful not to credit the chiefs of the republic for any achievements.

31. F.O. 60/138, no. 81, enclosure: Farrant to Queen Mother, n.d..

32. F.O. 60/138, no. 81, enclosure: Queen Mother to Farrant, 18 September 1848.

33. FO 60/138, no. 81; cf. *NTQ*, III, 161.

34. *NTQ*, III, 161.

35. F.O. 60/138, no. 81. The two priests could very well have been Mirza Abul-Qasim, the Imam Jum'a of Tehran, and Mirza Mahmud Mujtahid, another influential cleric in Tehran.

36. *NTQ*, III, 186.

37. Muhammad Ja'far Khurmuji, *Haqayiq al-Akhbair-i Nasiri*, ed. H. Khadiv Jam (Tehran, 1344/1965), 44.

38. Mirza Fazlullah Nuri, *Tazkara-yi Ahval*, MS cited in Iqbal, *Amir Kabir*, 101.

39. F.O. 60/138, Farrant to Palmerston, no. 91, Tehran, 3 October 1848. Besides the above-mentioned passage in the Persian sources, there is no reference in the contemporary Foreign Office files that confirms Nuri's request for protection. As in other cases, the British and the Russian representatives preferred to keep protégé status for their collaborators as vague as possible lest they deprive themselves of this effective weapon of diplomatic pressure. Whenever circumstances required they could add to or delete from their list of protégés at will, a practice that was a constant source of animosity with the Persian state.

40. F.O. 60/138, Farrant to Palmerston, no. 92, Tehran, 23 October 1848.

41. *NTQ*, III, 189.

42. F.O. 60/138, no. 92.

43. *RSN*, X, 361.

44. *NTQ*, III, 190 and *RSN*, X, 362.

45. F.O. 60/138, Farrant to Palmerston, no. 96, Tehran, 27 October 1848, enclosure no. 2.

46. The suggestion that the *atabak-i a'zam* presumably was Amir Kabir's honorary tutorship of Nasir al-Din's infant son and heir apparent, Mahmud Mirza, son of Galin, is too far-fetched. See Qasim Ghani's note on Iqbal, *Amir Kabir*, 108n.

47. 'Azud al-Dawla, *Tarikh-i 'Azudi*, 163.

48. *RSN*, IX, 356–357; cf. Dunbuli, *Ma'athir*, 49.

49. Remarkably, the first verifiable usage of the title *atabak* back in Saljuq times is in reference to the celebrated Persian minister Nizam al-Mulk, who at the outset of the minor Malik Shah's accession in 1072 was bestowed with the additional office of *atabak-i a'zam*. See *EI2*: "Atabak" (C. Cohen) and A.K.S. Lambton, *Continuity and Change in Medieval Persia* (Albany, 1988), 229–233. Contrary to Cohen's assumption, the office of *atabak* continued under the Ilkhanids and beyond. A member of the Juvayni family, Baha' al-Din Juvayni, son of Shams al-Din Sahib Divan, held the title of *atabak*. In Safavid times, the *ataliq*, and the more common *lala*, often chosen from the Qizilbash chiefs, served the same functions of tutorship and guardianship to the minor Safavid princes. See Iskandar Bayg Turkaman Munshi, *'Alam Ara-yi 'Abbasi*, I. Afshar ed., 2nd ed. (Tehran, 1350/1971), I, 134, 290; II, 1213, and *Cambridge History of Iran*, VI, 366 (R. M. Savory).

50. After the collapse of the Safavids in 1722, Fath 'Ali Khan Qajar, the patriarch of the Quvanlu, served as the *na'ib al-saltana* (viceroy) and *vakil al-dawla* (the representative of the state) for the young and inexperienced Tahmasp II before being slain by Nadir, who replaced him in the office. See Lockhart, *The Fall of the Safavi Dynasty*, and R. Sha'bani, *Tarikh-i Ijtima'i-yi Iran dar 'Asr-i Afshariya* (Tehran, 1365/1986), 40–43, 78–79. Vakil al-Dawla, the proclaimed position of Karim Khan Zand (later *vakil al-ra'aya:* the representative of the subjects), also rooted in the same notion of *atabak*. See Perry, *Karim Khan Zand*, 214–220.

51. Of all the contemporary or near-contemporary sources, Persian and European, only Hidayat on one occasion acknowledges that Mirza Taqi Khan Amir Nizam was granted the title of *amir-(i) kabir*. In most other existing correspondence, official records and historical accounts, Mirza Taqi Khan is often addressed as prime minister (*sadr-i a'zam*) and more often as *amir nizam*. One exception is the correspondence of the French minister in Tehran, Comte de Sartige. On two occasions in 1848–1849 he addressed Amir Nizam as Amir Kabir (see Makki, *Amir Kabir*, 90–94). It is only from the late nineteenth century and increasingly after the 1920s that Amir Nizam came to be known as Amir Kabir, particularly in the literature critical of Nasir al-Din Shah and laudatory of his slain minister. The early occurrences in the late Nasiri period must have been in subtle defiance of the then holder of the title of *amir kabir*, Kamran Mirza, Nasir al-Din's son and dreaded war minister. For reasons of historical currency, throughout the rest of this work the title *amir kabir* is preferred over *amir nizam*.

52. See *EI2*: "al-Amir al-Kabir" (D. Ayalon) for Turco-Mamluk usage.

53. *RSN*, IX, 357, 443, 462.

54. Ibid., 565.

55. F.O. 60/138, Farrant to Palmerston, no. 75, camp near Tehran, 31 August 1848.

56. F.O. 60/138, Farrant to Palmerston, no. 97, 28 October 1848, Tehran.

57. Ibid.

58. *NTQ*, III, 188–189, 233. Many of Ardabili's allies in the Iraq 'Ajam party, the original province of Amir Nizam, were co-opted, at least temporarily. Among them, Mirza Yusuf Mustawfi al-Mamalik and Hasan 'Ali Khan Garrusi are known to us.

59. Persian correspondence on this affair appears in Makki, *Amir Kabir*, 90–99. For background and further discussion see Adamiyat, *Amir Kabir*, 547–567.

60. Although Comte de Sartige was an appointee of Goiso (of Louis Philippe's time), he was confirmed in office after the proclamation of the Republic and remained in his post until the break in relations less than two years later.

61. F.O. 60/138, Farrant to Palmerston, no. 95, Tehran 27 October 1848. The reply of President Cavaignac of France acknowledging Nasir al-Din Shah's accession (enclosed in Sartige to Amir Kabir, Makki, *Amir Kabir*, 98–99) was written two weeks prior to Louis Napoleon's takeover in December 1848.

62. For a typical justification of Amir Kabir's political behavior, see Adamiyat's well-documented but partisan treatment of the Franco-Persian affairs that led to the break in relations (*Amir Kabir*, 556–567).

63. F.O. 60/138, Farrant to Palmerston, no. 97, 25 October 1848.

64. F.O. 60/144, Farrant to Palmerston, no. 4, Tehran, 26 January 1849.

65. SML, fold. 12, no. 110, n.d. [apparently written in February 1849]. See also Muhammad Hasan Jabiri Ansari (*Agahi-yi Shahan az Kar-i Jahan*, 4 vols. [Isfahan, 1314/ 1935] III, 88–89 for Malikzada's recollection of Amir Kabir's unwillingness to consummate the marriage in the days immediately following their wedding.

66. SML, fold. 12, no. 101, n.d..

67. F.O. 60/144, Farrant to Palmerston, no. 12, Tehran, 12 February 1849.

68. *EI2*: "al-Atabak al-Kabir."

69. F.O. 60/144, no. 4.

70. Ibid.

71. F.O. 60/144, Farrant to Palmerston, no. 14, Tehran, 26 February 1849. Based on information given to Farrant by Dolgorouki.

72. F.O. 60/144, Farrant to Palmerston, no. 15, confidential, Tehran, 26 February 1849. Amir Kabir's reply to Bahman Mirza (20 February 1849) is enclosed.

73. Ibid. Sheil at a later date attributed this threat to a later incident involving the army mutiny in Tehran. See below.

74. *NTQ*, III, 229.

75. Watson, *History*, 376.

76. F.O. 60/144, Farrant to Palmerston, no. 18, Tehran, 17 March 1849. *NTQ* (III, 231) gives the figure of 5,000, which probably is an exaggeration.

77. F.O. 60/144, no. 18.

78. *NTQ*, III, 230.

79. F.O. 60/144, no. 18.

80. Amir Kabir to Nasir al-Din Shah, Makki, *Amir Kabir*, 126.

81. Ibid.

82. SML, III A, no. 90.

83. Watson, *History*, 377; *NTQ*, III, 231–232. Sipihr's figure of 50,000 seems to be an exaggeration.

84. F.O. 60/144, no. 18; cf. *NTQ*, III, 231–232.

85. Watson, *History*, 377.

86. F.O. 60/144, no. 18.

87. F.O. 60/144, Farrant to Palmerston, no. 19, Tehran, 18 March 1849.

88. Isma'il Khan Farrash-bashi (chief of the *farrash*s: functionaries of the outer court), who probably had earlier advocated Amir Kabir's dismissal, was fined heavily and sent into exile. Ironically, Isma'il Khan, the executioner of Amir Kabir's mentor, Qa'im Maqam, in 1835, was succeeded in office by Hajji 'Ali Khan Maragha'i (later Hajib al-Dawla and I'timad al-Saltana I), the future executioner of Amir Kabir himself. Agha Bahram, the chief magistrate [*amir-i divan*], a high-ranking Qarabaghi eunuch, was exiled to Kirmanshah on charges of secret collaboration with Sadr al-Mamalik Ardabili. The latter himself was implicated in the mutiny and was sent to the same city. Muhammad 'Ali Bayg, son of Nasir al-Din's old Georgian tutor, Bizhan Khan, was also dismissed. *NTQ*, III, 233; *RSN*, X, 402; and Jahangir Mirza, *Tarikh-i Naw*, 334.

89. See *VI*, 24 (17 Ramadan 1267/1851) for an account of the disciplinary action against 150 members of the Qahramaniya regiment, including an unspecified number of executions (also cited in Iqbal, *Amir Kabir*, 11–13). For a revealing account of Vazir Nizam's character and conduct, see J. P. Ferrier, "Situation de la Perse en 1851," *Revue Orientale et Algerienne*, 1 (Paris, 1852), 141–159, partially cited in M. Momen, *The Babi and Baha'i Religions, 1844–1944, Some Contemporary Western Accounts* (Oxford, 1981), 504–505. Other regiments were pardoned in 1851 on account of their bravery in wars in Khurasan and Zanjan.

90. *ST*, 236.

91. F.O. 60/144, no. 18.

92. SML, III A, no. 165, also cited in Iqbal, *Amir Kabir*, 132–133.

93. *RSN*, X, 388–389.

94. Watson, *History*, 378.

95. Ibid. 383; cf. F.O. 60/146, Sheil to Palmerston, no. 14, Tehran, 15 December 1849.

96. Russian Ministry of Foreign Affairs, file no. 178 (Tehran, 1849) 435–438. Dolgorouki to Nesselrode, no. 80, 10 October 1849, cited in M. S. Ivanov, *Babidskie vosstaniya v Irane (1848–1852)* (Moscow, 1939), 149–151, document no. 10. For the Egyptian crisis of 1839–1841, see M. S. Anderson, *The Eastern Question, 1774–1923* (London, 1966).

97. SML, III A, no. 170.

98. F.O. 60/146, no. 14.

99. Ibid.

100. F.O. 60/144, Farrant to Palmerston, no. 29, Tehran, 25 April 1849.

101. F.O. 60/146, no. 14.

CHAPTER 4: THE SHAH AND HIS ATABAK

1. Mirza Ahmad Sharif Shirazi Divanbaygi, *Tarikh-i Qajariya*, in Muhammad Khan-Bahadur, "Yak Shakhs-i Muhimm ya Mirza Taqi Khan Atabak," *Armaghan* XV (1313/1934), no. 4, 296.

2. For further discussion see A. Amanat, "The Downfall of Mirza Taqi Khan Amir Kabir and the Problem of Ministerial Authority in Qajar Iran," *International Journal of Middle East Studies* 23 (1991), 577–599.

3. Of the great variety of issues raised in more than 500 surviving private notes addressed by Amir Kabir to Nasir al-Din, a large number deal with official matters, domestic and foreign policies, army, finance, and appointments in court and government. An equally large number, however, are devoted to personal matters related to the shah, Amir Kabir himself, and the royal family. Treating them as mere private notes exchanged to maintain a constant line of communication, Amir Kabir shows little hesitation in blending the official with the personal and even less in expressing his momentary reactions. Except for SML (Ghani Collection), selections of other collections in Majlis Library, Gulistan Library, and private collections are published in Iqbal, *Amir Kabir*, Makki, *Amir Kabir*, Adamiyat, *Amir Kabir* and Al Davud, *Namaha*. Our view of the relationship between the shah and his minister remains inevitably lopsided because Nasir al-Din's private notes to Amir Kabir did not survive except on few occasions. Their summary, often cryptic references to current events and issues and hurried, often ungrammatical style, makes their full use formidable. They are always undated and written in a difficult *shikasta*, usually by Amir Kabir himself.

4. Makki, *Amir Kabir*, 231.

5. Ibid., 229. Makki somewhat inappropriately interprets the allusion to a reference to Isma'il I.

6. Ibid., 235.

7. SML, III A, nos. 13, 14, 40, 49, 101, and 178.

8. Ibid., no. 51; cf. nos. 80, 112, 138, and 156.

9. Makki, *Amir Kabir*, 266.

10. Ibid.

11. Ibid., 267–268.

12. Ibid., 268.

13. SML. III A, no. 201.

14. Ibid., no. 175.

15. Ibid., no. 183.

16. Ibid., no. 85.

17. Ibid., no. 140.

18. Ibid., no.180.

19. Ibid., no. 182.

20. Ibid., no. 73.

21. Ibid., no. 86.

22. Ibid., no. 109.

23. Ibid., no. 209.

24. Makki, *Amir Kabir*, 339. For Sulayman Khan see Bamdad, *Rijal*, II, 115.

25. SML, III A, no. 12.

26. Ibid., no. 27.

27. Ibid., no. 65.

28. Ibid., no. 75.

29. Makki, *Amir Kabir*, 336.

30. Ibid., 108.

31. Ibid., 109.

32. Ibid., 338.

33. SML, III A, no. 8.

34. Makki, *Amir Kabir*, 107–108.

35. SML, III A, no. 21.

36. Ibid., no. 114.

37. Ibid., no. 204.

38. Ibid., no. 1.

39. Ibid., no. 4.

40. Ibid., no. 72.

41. Makki, *Amir Kabir*, 270.

42. SML, III A, no. 6.

43. SML, III A, no. 136. *Kurur* is 500,000. Amir Kabir places Iran's population at 9 million, which is perhaps exaggerated compared to other estimates of 6 to 7 million.

44. Makki, *Amir Kabir*, 116.

45. SML, III A, no. 101.

46. Ibid., no. 206. He was presumably writing from halfway to Shamiran, in the northern outskirts of the capital.

47. Makki, *Amir Kabir*, 335.

48. SML, III A, no. 123.

49. Ibid., no. 194. Even consulting the Qur'an (*istikhara*) may not produce the auspicious result for the prime minister in seeking the right time to reply to foreign envoys' correspondence (ibid., no. 31).

50. Ibid., no. 86.

51. Makki, *Amir Kabir*, 230.

52. Khan Malik Sasani, *Dast-i Pinhan-i Siyasat-i Ingilis dar Iran* (The Invisible Hand of the British Policy in Iran) (Tehran [?], n.d.), 26. Like many other anecdotes related in this book, the rhetorical trappings are often the figments of the author's mind. He makes his Amir Kabir say to Nasir al-Din: "This fellow [i.e., Malcolm] has thought that by [producing] such nonsensical stuff he can meddle with a nation's sanctities and rob them of their honor and [national] pride and encroach upon their country." The real Amir Kabir could hardly have known the contents of Malcolm's *History*, nor would his pro-British proclivities have made him think in these anachronistic terms more suitable to 1950s sentiments. The gradual development of Amir Kabir's legend deserves a separate study.

53. Makki, *Amir Kabir*, 212. For Muhammad Shah's earlier *farman* and excerpts of further correspondence see 205–213. Translations appear in F.O. 84/774. Farrant to Palmerston, 2 February 1849 in Kelly, *Persian Gulf*, 604.

54. Makki, *Amir Kabir*, 213. As in many other diplomatic instances of the period, the British used the implementation of the ban on the slave trade as a leverage to exert pressure over the Tehran government. See Kelly, *Persian Gulf*, 593–613 and Adamiyat, *Amir Kabir*, 510–528.

55. Makki, *Amir Kabir*, 337–338.

56. For Mustawfi al-Mamalik's possible involvement in the downfall of Amir Nizam see *ST*, 295–296.

57. SML, III A, no. 16.

58. Ibid., no. 59.

59. Gulistan Library, album 108/161, Jahan Khanum Mahd 'Ulya to Nasir al-Din Shah, n.d. in Sasani, Siyasatgaran, II, 47.

60. Mahd 'Ulya to 'Ayn al-Mulk, in Adamiyat, Amir Kabir, 661–662.

61. Ibid.

62. Ibid.

63. Later reports ascribed Mahd 'Ulya's cool relations with the shah and the premier to her "lustfulness" and even some unrequited sexual passes at Amir Kabir. The veracity of these reports can be seriously questioned, but it is hard not to believe that even milder versions of such rumors would have a serious effect on Nasir al-Din's sentiments. See, for instance, Bamdad (Rijal, IV, 326–327), which is typical of the sex biases of the secondary sources. Other allegations of "women's deceit and craftiness" in reference to Mahd 'Ulya are detectable in Adamiyat (e.g., Amir Kabir, 658, 702).

64. Mahd 'Ulya to 'Ayn al-Mulk, Adamiyat, Amir Kabir, 662–663.

65. Nasir al-Din's alleged attempt to slay his mother, and Amir Kabir's involvement, has been reported by more than one source. Mu'ayyir al-Mamalik (Yaddashtha, 175–176) even quotes Nasir al-Din Shah on this point (the second edition of this work [Tehran, 1362/1983] omitted this confession altogether). See also ST, 216, and Gilanshah, Yaksad va Panjah Sal, 45–46.

66. Mahd 'Ulya to Nasir al-Din Shah, Gulistan Library, album no. 161/108, in Sasani, Siyasatgaran I, 47–48.

67. See SHA, 43–47, and 'A. Iqbal's introduction 17–24. See also F.O. 60/163, Sheil to Palmerston, no. 182, Tehran, 30 October 1851. Earlier cases of British support for the disfavored members of the royal family include the three sons of Husayn 'Ali Mirza, who took refuge in England and later were on British pension in Iraq; 'Alishah Zill al-Sultan and other princes of Fath 'Ali Shah house; and, later, Farhad Mirza and Hajji Sayf al-Dawla. Before his departure from Iran in 1852, foreign support for 'Abbas Mirza was never extended beyond letters of caution to the Persian government.

68. SML, Series IIIA, no. 191.

69. NTQ, III, 381.

70. Majlis Library, SHA, 21–22 (introduction by Iqbal).

71. Muhammad Hasan Khan I'timad al-Saltana, Khalsa Mashhur bi Khwab-nama, ed. M. Katira'i (Tehran, 1348/1969) 35–36.

72. Ibid., 36. This work of semifictional "confessions" of the premiers of the Qajar dynasty who are put on trial by the past rulers of Iran, the product of the author's fantastic "dream," was written anonymously to compensate for what I'timad al-Saltana could not disclose in official histories produced under his auspices. The reliability of many reports in this work is debateable. The above passage, presumably related by his father, however, is too specific to be a fabrication or even hearsay.

73. Ahmad Shirazi, Tarikh-i Qajariya, in Khan Bahadur, "Yak Shakhs," Armaghan, 295.

74. Ibid.

75. Gulistan Library, Adamiyat, Amir Kabir, 675.

76. F.O. 60/169, Sheil to Palmerston, no. 9, Tehran, 16 January 1852, enclosure no. 2, Nasir al-Din Shah to Amir Nizam (translated by Ronald Thomson). Sheil enclosed this and another autograph (see below) with his report in which he conveyed the news of Amir Kabir's murder so that Palmerston could "form an estimate of the monarch's character." Originals of these letters were confided to him by Amir Kabir himself and were returned to him "at his request on his departure from Tehran." The fallen premier must have taken them into exile, one may surmise, as tokens of his master's one-time gratitude.

77. Gulistan Library, collection no. 249, in Iqbal, *Amir Kabir*, 312–313.

78. Ibid. 313–314.

79. F.O. 60/169, Sheil to Palmerston, Tehran, 16 January 1852, enclosure no 3: autograph note from the Shah to the Ameer-i Nezam (written the 15th or 16th November 1852). Attached to this enclosure is a list of the regular and irregular infantry presumably sent by the shah to Amir Kabir in conjunction with instructions in the above note. The recapitulated version of this autograph appears in *NTQ*, III, 384.

80. *NTQ*, III, 384–385.

81. Gulistan Library, collection no. 249, 22 Muharram 1268 Q./15 January 1852, in Iqbal, *Amir Kabir*, 319–320.

82. For the Foreign Office's conditional consent to the lifting of Nuri's British protection, see Chapter 8.

83. Gulistan Library, Muharram 1268 Q./January 1852, in Sasani, *Siyasatgaran*, 2–3, and Iqbal, *Amir Kabir*, 315–317; cf. *NTQ*, III, 385. Date in the original mistakenly entered 1267/1851—presumably, as Iqbal asserts, as a result of Amir Kabir's emotional stress. Only Amir Kabir's responses to the twelve conditions set forward have survived.

84. Mirza Muhammad 'Ali Shirazi to foreign envoys in Tehran, 24 Muharram 1268/19 November 1851, Iran Ministry of Foreign Affairs (Vizarat Umur Kharija Iran), copies of foreign correspondence (*savad-i mukatibat*), vol. 19, in Adamiyat, *Amir Kabir*, 690.

85. F.O. 60/64, Sheil to Palmerston, no. 203, Tehran, 18 November 1851.

86. Gulistan Library, album no. 161, document 108 in Sasani, *Siyasatgaran*, I, 3–4.

87. *NTQ*, III, 385–387.

88. Ibid.

89. F.O. 60/169, Sheil to Palmerston, no. 9, Tehran, 16 January 1852, enclosure: Statement showing Iran's troop strength (attached to the letter of Nasir al-Din Shah to Amir Kabir, 15 or 16 November 1851).

90. F.O. 60/164, Sheil to Palmerston, no. 203, Tehran, 18 November 1851.

91. F.O. 60/164, Sheil to Palmerston no. 209, Tehran, 21 November 1851.

92. Gulistan Library, Album 249, in Iqbal, *Amir Kabir*, 322–323. The verse is from a *qasida* in praise of 'Ali, the First Imam, by the sixteenth-century Indo-Persian poet 'Urfi Shirazi (*Qasa'id-i 'Urfi* [Lucknow, 1966], 15).

93. See *EIr*: "Amin-al-Dawla, 'Abdullah Khan" (A. Amanat) and "Aqasi."

94. *NTQ*, III, 387–388.

95. F.O. 60/164, no. 209.

96. Ibid.

97. Ibid.

98. F.O. 60/164, Sheil to Palmerston, no. 214, Tehran, 26 November 1851, enclosure: Sheil to Dolgorouki, Tehran, 21 November 1851.

99. Ibid.

100. F.O. 60/164, no. 209.

101. Mirza Aqa Khan Nuri to Persian minister plenipotentiary in St. Petersburg, Ministry of Foreign Affairs, copies of correspondence, in Iqbal, *Amir Kabir*, 336–337.

102. F.O. 60/164, no. 209.

103. Ibid.

104. Sheil, *Glimpses*, 250.

105. *Vaqayi'-i Ittifaqiya (VI)*, no. 42, Thursday 26 Muharram 1268 Q./21 November 1851.

106. Persian Minister of Foreign Affairs to Foreign Envoys, Iran Ministry of Foreign Affairs, copy of correspondence, 26 Muharram 1268 Q./21 November 1851, Adamiyat, *Amir Kabir*, 704–705.

107. *VI*, no. 44, 10 Safar 1268 Q./7 December 1852.

108. F.O. 60/164, Sheil to Palmerston, no. 212, Tehran, 22 November 1851.

109. F.O. 60/164, no. 212.

110. F.O. 60/164, no. 214.

111. F.O. 60/164, Sheil to Palmerston, no. 214, enclosure no. 5: Meerza Tekkee Khan (Ameer Nizam) to Lt. Colonel Sheil, 22 November 1851. Another translation of the same letter, with minor variations, is enclosed in F.O. 60/209, Murray to Clarendon, no. 63, Baghdad, 14 July 1856. It bears the date Thursday 28 Muharram 1268 Q./22 November 1851. The Christian date corresponds to the Thursday, but 28 Muharram falls on Friday. This, however, could be an error in reading the date in Persian, which ought to be 27 Muharram. Ironically, at the height of the Anglo-Persian dispute over granting diplomatic asylum to the celebrated Hashim Khan Nuri and his wife Parvin Khanum, which led to the break in relations between the two countries and contributed to the war of 1857 (see Chapter 7), Murray, the British minister in Tehran (after the break residing in Baghdad), produced this letter to prove to London the advisability of maintaining the practice of giving protection to Persian subjects.

112. This phrase, appearing in the Murray's translation (see above), seems to be a more accurate translation than "I have not power to write more" in the above translation.

113. No reference could be found in any Foreign Office files that indicates an acknowledgment of Sheil's error. Yet a postmortem examination of Sheil's dispatches after Amir Kabir's execution would have revealed to London some inconsistencies in the envoy's reporting. Watson (*History*, 401–402), who as secretary of the mission had access to all correspondence, preferred not to make reference to Amir Kabir's written petition, though an undertone of remorse is discernible in his pages. Remarkably, there is no mention in Adamiyat's *Amir Kabir* (pp. 702–711) either, though perhaps for different reasons. Although he made ample use of Sheil's dispatch (F.O. 60/164, no. 214) and its enclosures (e.g., p. 723), there is no reference to enclosure 5, which contains the text of Amir Kabir's petition. Such selective treatment is not uncharacteristic of Adamiyat's overall idolization of Amir Kabir.

No matter how desperate and demoralized his heroic but ahistorical Amir Kabir was, he could not have been allowed by his biographer to seek refuge in a foreign mission, least of all a British one.

114. Sheil, *Glimpses*, 251. The use of the present tense in the last sentence is problematic, since it *could* confirm the author's prior knowledge of what might befall Amir Kabir, a confirmation that would contradict Justin Sheil's later claim that he was totally uninformed.

115. Ibid.

116. Gulistan Library, Album 249, in Iqbal, *Amir Kabir*, 327–329.

117. Iqbal, *Amir Kabir*, 331.

118. Sheil, *Glimpses*, 251.

119. F.O. 60/164, Sheil to Palmerston, no. 249, Tehran, 22 December 1851.

120. Ibid.

121. Nuri to Persian minister in Petersburg, in Iqbal, *Amir Kabir*, 338–339.

122. Ibid.; cf. Watson, *History*, 402.

123. Richard, "Journal," 18 January 1852, in Saqafi, *Yaddashtha*, 84–85.

124. Munshi, *'Alam Ara-yi 'Abbasi*, I, 400–405. Cahen (*EI2*: "Atabak") alludes to the frequency with which *atabaks* were later destroyed by their masters.

125. See Chapter 3 for Amir Kabir's reference to 'Abbas I. Three manuscript copies of Munshi, *'Alam Ara-yi 'Abbasi* existed in the Gulistan Library (Munzavi, *Fihrist*, VI, nos. 45162, 45213, 45233).

126. For the circumstances that led to I'timad al-Dawla's downfall and execution see among other sources Fasa'i, *Farsnama*, I, 249–250 citing Fazlullah Khavari, *Tarikh-i Dhul-Qarnayn*, and *EIr*, "Ebrahim Khan Kalantar Širazi" (A. Amanat).

127. Adamiyat, *Amir Kabir*, 713.

128. For conflicting accounts of Amir Nizam's last hours, see Iqbal, *Amir Kabir*, 341–360 and Adamiyat, *Amir Kabir*, 713–720. See also Amanat, "Downfall," 592–596.

129. F.O. 60/169, Sheil to Palmerston, no. 9, Tehran, 16 January 1852.

130. F.O. 248/147, Malmesbury to Sheil, no. 9, confidential, Foreign Office, 23 March 1852, enclosure no. 5. (The English transcription of the Persian translation of the same letter appears as enclosure no. 6.) The Persian text and facsimile of Malmesbury's protest, apparently taken from the Gulistan Library collection, appear in Sasani, *Siyasatgaran*, I, 5–7. The correspondence concerning Amir Kabir's murder received special attention in London. In May Malmesbury even laid before Queen Victoria Sheil's dispatch of 22 March 1852, in which the Persian government's justifications were explained (Malmesbury to Sheil, no. 11, Foreign Office, 7 May 1852).

131. FO 248/147. Malmesbury to Sheil, no. 9, Foreign Office, 23 March 1852, enclosure: Seymour to Granville, no. 78, confidential, St. Petersburg, 28 February 1852. Passages of Nuri's response through the Persian envoy to St. Petersburg are quoted above in this chapter. See also Iqbal, *Amir Kabir*, 335–340 for the full text of Nuri's response.

132. Adamiyat, *Amir Kabir*, 726.

133. Watson, *History*, 405.

134. Persian minister of foreign affairs to Mirza Shafi' Khan, in Sasani, *Siyasatgaran*, I, 7–11. This source also produces the facsimile of Nasir al-Din's draft of the note to Mirza Shafi' Khan in his own hand (pp. 8–9).

135. *VI*, no. 50, 23 Rabi' al-Awwal 1268 Q./16 January 1852.

136. *VI*, no. 52, 7 Rabi' al-Thani 1268 Q./30 January 1852.

137. Three exceptions are worth mentioning. The account by Mirza Ahmad Sharif Shirazi Divan-Baygi never saw the light of day (Khan Bahadur "Yak Shakhs," *Armaghan*, XV, no. 5, 356). Khurmuji's account (*Haqayiq*, 103–106) apparently disenchanted its royal patron for the mention of the execution. The passage in *ST* by Mirza Ghulam-Husayn Adib al-Saltana, 'Ali Khan Farrash-bashi's son, giving a revealing account of his father's involvement, was censored in the final version by his brother Muhammad Hasan Khan I'timad al-Saltana (see Iqbal, *Amir Kabir*, 343–347, and Adamiyat, *Amir Kabir*, 714–717; cf. *ST*, 218).

138. Watson, *History*, 405–406.

139. Nasir al-Din Shah, *Safarnama-yi 'Iraq-i 'Ajam* (Tehran, 1311 Q./1894, reprint, Tehran, 1362/1983), 61–62.

140. Adamiyat, *Amir Kabir*, 26, n. 1.

141. Gobineau cited in Iqbal, *Amir Kabir*, 369–370.

142. Farhad Mirza Mu'tamad al-Dawla, *Zanbil* (Tehran, 1318/1901), 154, 356. All three epigrams equal 1268 according to *abjad* numerological computation.

CHAPTER 5: A NARROW ESCAPE

1. Richard to anonymous friend in Rhodes, 18 January 1852, in Saqafi, *Maqalat*, 86.

2. F.O. 60/169, Sheil to Earl of Granville, no. 20, Tehran, 22 February 1852.

3. Born to an old family from the Nur region in Mazandaran, Nuri's father joined the army of Aqa Muhammad Khan Qajar at the outset of his struggle for the throne in the 1780s. His service to the Qajars was acknowledged by Fath 'Ali Shah, who once remarked that the Nuri family was as close to him as the robe he wore ('Azud al-Dawla, *Tarikh-i 'Azudi*, 72).

4. Joseph A. Comte de Gobineau, *Trois ans en Asie (de 1855 a 1858)*, 2 vols. (Paris, 1859) II, 303–304. For Nuri's biography and relevant sources, see EIr: "E'temad al-Dawla, Aqa Khan Nuri" (A. Amanat). Nuri's life and personality have been the subject of much distortion and hostile treatment, primarily because of his involvement in the fall of Amir Kabir. Sasani, *Siyasatgaran*, I, 1–58 (in spite of some valuable documentation) and Adamiyat, *Amir Kabir*, (especially 647–746) are two examples. A more balanced treatment appears in J. Qa'im Maqami, "Payan-i kar-i Mirza Aqa Khan I'timad al-Dawla Nuri," *Barrasiha-yi Tarikhi* III (1347/1968), no. 3, 96–114 and no. 5, 119–144.

5. Gulistan Library, file 108/162, in Sasani, *Siyasatgaran*, I, 17.

6. FO 60/169. Sheil to Granville, no. 15, Tehran, 18 February 1852; cf. Gobineau, *Trois ans en Asie*, I, 305. Though of little consequence during Nuri's years, Sa'id Khan clung to the job for years to come and performed to Nasir al-Din's satisfaction. His pronounced proclivities toward Russia in later years were condoned after 1858 and compensated by the shah's own proximity to the British.

7. F.O. 60/170, Sheil to Granville. no. 58, Tehran, 11 May 1852. The prince in question was probably Farhad Mirza. For him and other protégés of the British mission who occasioned Sheil's observation, see below.

8. Gulistan Library, file 108/162 in Sasani, *Siyasatgaran*, I, 17 and 20. Sasani speaks of an unspecified diary by Nasir al-Din that recorded the names of the women in the company of the shah. Arghuniya, previously the property of one of Fath 'Ali Shah's grandsons, was renamed Davudiya after Nuri's son. Mount Qaf, the mythological mountain at the end of inhabited land, is a metaphor for a remote and inaccessible place.

9. Correspondence of the Imperial Majesty Nasir al-Din Shah of Persia from 1848 to 1896 (original and translation), British Library, BL Or 11665 and Or 11665 (hereinafter CNBL). Nasir al-Din Shah to Nuri, n.d. [circa 1854]. A *tar* is a six-string long-handled Persian lute played with a plectrum.

10. Gulistan Library, file 108/162 and 163, Nuri to Nasir al-Din Shah, Sasani, *Siyasatgaran*, 18–20.

11. CNBL. no. 7, Nasir al-Din Shah to Nuri, n.d. [circa 1856]; cf. ibid. no. 15, wherein Nasir al-Din inquires about Nuri's health: "Write two words about your health to assure me."

12. *VI*, no. 80, 25 Shawwal 1268 Q./12 August 1852.

13. The *Standard* (of London), 7 October 1852, citing the report of the paper's Istanbul correspondent of 23 September 1852, Momen, *Babi and Baha'i Religions*, 129.

14. F.O. 60/171, Sheil to Malmesbury, no. 99, Camp near Tehran, 16 August 1852.

15. Ibid; cf. the *Standard*, 7 October 1852, in Momen, *Babi and Baha'i Religions*, 129.

16. F.O. 60/171, no. 99.

17. Besides the account in the special issue (supplement to no. 80, n.d.), other issues of *VI* (no. 81, 3 Dhulqa'da 1268 Q./26 August 1852 and no. 82, 10 Dhulqa'da 1268 Q./3 September 1852) covered the incident in full but with omissions and biases. These reports are the basis for *RSN* (especially X, 544–550) and most other Persian accounts.

18. Sheil, *Glimpses*, 275.

19. F.O. 60/171, no. 99 and Sheil, *Glimpses*, 274.

20. The death of Isma'il II (1577) was a result of palace intrigue. The assassinations of Nadir (1747) and Aqa Muhammad Khan Qajar (1797), by contrast, were works of army chiefs and domestic servants. Likewise, the Afshar and Zand pretenders to the throne were often slain by rival contestants and their supporters.

21. Sheil, *Glimpses*, 274–275.

22. F.O. 60/171, no. 99.

23. *NTQ*, IV, 37.

24. F.O. 60/171, no. 99.

25. For his account see Amanat, *Resurrection and Renewal*, 280–281, 383–386 and cited sources.

26. Zarandi, *Dawn-Breakers*, 599, and *VI* (no. 82), which identifies Muhammad Sadiq as a Zanjani.

27. Zarandi, *Dawn-Breakers*, 599–601. The incompetent planning and ineffective execution of the attempt has often been upheld by the later Baha'i sources to prove its spontaneity, its "folly," and the assassins' "frenzy of despair;" an assertion necessary in later decades to deny a preconceived conspiracy and essentially to demonstrate Baha'ullah's innocence. (See also E. G. Browne, ed. and trans., *The Tarikh-i Jadid or New History of Mirza 'Ali Muhammad the Bab* (Cambridge, 1893) 315–317.

28. Mazandarani, *Zuhur al-Haqq*, III, 298–300.

29. 'Ali Quli Mirza I'tizad al-Saltana, *al-Mutanabbi'in*, partially published and edited by 'A. Nava'i as *Fitna-yi Bab* (Tehran, 1351/1972). Note no. 97 (p. 275), inserted on the margin of the original manuscript by an informed and sympathetic reader, provides details on Qumi.

30. Zarandi, *Dawn-Breakers*, 599.

31. Ibid., 602–603; cf. *VI*, no. 81. See also Dossier no. 1582, Dolgorouki to Seniavin, no. 56, 12 August 1852 (Russian calendar)/24 August 1852, Tehran, in Ivanov, *Babidskie*, appendix. English trans. F. Kazemzadeh, "Excerpts from Dispatches Written during 1848–1852 by Prince Dolgoroukov, Russian Minister to Persia," *World Order* (Fall 1966), 17–24.

32. According to one report, the mutilated body of Sadiq Tabrizi, split and hung from a pillar outside the city gate, was recognized by a young boy, who led the warden of the neighborhood to Sulayman's house. Another account holds the servant of a Babi household responsible. More likely, however, it was Sulayman's Babi reputation, well known in court circles, that caused his arrest.

33. *VI*, no. 82; cf. *NTQ*, IV 38–39 and F.O. 60/171. Sheil to Malmesbury, no. 110, Tehran, 22 August 1852.

34. F.O. 60/171, no. 110 and *VI*, no. 82.

35. Dossier no. 1582, Dolgorouki to Seniavin, 11 August 1852 in Ivanov, *Babidskie*, no. 24; English trans. Kazemzadeh, "Excerpts," 23–24.

36. CNBL, Nasir al-Din Shah to Nuri, no. 11, n.d. [c. August 1852], n.p. [Niyavaran].

37. The village of Zarkanda was assigned as *tuyul* (fiefdom) to the Russian mission (as Qulhak was to the British), administered by the Russian envoy, and was considered part of the summer compound of the mission and therefore protected by diplomatic immunity.

38. Dolgorouki no. 23.

39. F.O. 60/171, no. 110; cf. I'tizad al-Saltana, *Fitna-yi Bab*, 103 and *NTQ*, IV, 39. Momen (*Babi and Baha'i Religions*, 135) treats the above account as "rather fanciful" in an apparent effort to deny the Babis' militancy and their "unorthodox" beliefs, which ran contrary to the passive picture of the Babi movement he presented in his book. 'Azim was open and unapologetic in admitting his beliefs and actions. In an interview with I'tizad al-Saltana (*Fitna-yi Bab*, 103–105), shortly after his interrogation, in "direct language and with eloquent speech" he gave the prince a full account of the way he fled certain arrest during the persecution of the 1850s. There is no reason he should not have adopted the same standard of frankness during the interrogation by Nuri. However, it is possible that Nuri's claim to 'Azim's acceptance of sole responsibility for the plot was an exaggeration obviously beneficial to him.

40. *Oesterreichischer Soldatenfreund,* no. 291, 12 October 1852 cited in E. G. Browne, *Materials,* 268.

41. *VI,* no. 82 and *NTQ,* IV, 40.

42. F.O. 60/171, Sheil to Malmesbury, no. 111, Tehran, 27 August 1852.

43. Ibid.

44. *VI,* no. 82 and *NTQ,* IV, 41–42. For Hajji Mirza Jani see Amanat, *Resurrection and Renewal,* 344–348.

45. Two of the Bab's secretaries, Sayyid Husayn Yazdi and Mulla 'Abd al-Karim Qazvini (the former executed at the hands of 'Aziz Khan and his officers), and several veterans of the Babi wars, the so-called "remnants of the sword" (including Lutf 'Ali Shirazi, an ex-government official who served as the chronicler of the Tabarsi episode), were among the victims. Three Nuris were also executed, including Mirza Sulayman-Quli, brother of the chief of the royal "runners" (*shatir-bashi*), who was close to Baha'ullah, and a cousin of the latter.

46. Dossier no. 158, Dolgorouki to Seniavin, 11 August 1852 OS (23 August) cited in Ivanov, *Babidskie,* no. 55. English trans. Kazemzadeh, "Excerpts," 17–24.

47. For her biography and the circumstances of her death see Amanat, *Resurrection and Renewal* (295–331), and the cited sources. The mujtahids' hesitation may have been more out of fear of endorsing the execution of a formidable Babi, herself from an important mujtahid family, whose uncle, Mulla Muhammad Taqi Baraghani, earlier was the victim of Babi outrage.

48. *VI,* no. 85, 1 Dhul-Hijja 1268 Q./27 October 1852.

49. Dolgorouki, Dossier no. 1582, no. 55.

50. *VI,* no. 83, 17 Dhul-Qa'da 1268/September 1852; cf. ibid., no. 82.

51. Zarandi, *Dawn-Breakers,* 635–637 and 646–650.

52. Ibid., 598.

53. Ibid., 636.

54. Nasir al-Din Shah to Zill al-Sultan on the margin of an official report by Zill al-Sultan, n.d., Khurumi Collection, Tehran. "Burning someone's father" is a common term of abuse in this context, alluding to the application of harsh measures and dissemination.

55. F.O. 60/171, Sheil to Malmesbury, no. 100, camp near Tehran, 16 August 1852.

56. F.O. 60/171, same to same, no. 108, camp near Tehran, 22 August 1852. Sheil attributes Dolgorouki's reluctance to defend Khadija not only to her pro-British sentiments but also to motives he could not "expose in a despatch."

57. *SHA,* 24–25 (introduction by Iqbal). English translation (with some modifications) in F.O. 60/172, Sheil to Malmesbury, no. 115, camp near Tehran, 3 September 1852, enclosure no. 2: Translation of Autograph from the Shah to Sadr Azim.

58. F.O. 60/172, no. 115, enclosure no. 2: translation, forty eight of the chief notables of the court to Colonel Sheil and Prince Dolgorouki, 26 August 1852.

59. Ibid., enclosure no. 3.

60. *SHA,* 49–50.

61. F.O. 60/172, no. 115.

62. Sheil and Dolgorouki to Persian Minister of Foreign Affairs, 12 Dhul-Qa'da

1268/28 August 1852, in *SHA*, 25–26 (Introduction by Iqbal). The English text was not included in Sheil's enclosures to Foreign Office.

63. Nuri to Sheil and Dolgorouki (Marginal note by Nasir al-Din Shah), Iran Ministry of Foreign Affairs, *SHA*, 27–28 (Introduction by Iqbal). English trans. F.O. 60/172, no. 115, enclosure no. 5: Sadr A'zam to Colonel Sheil, Tehran, 29 August 1852. Nizam al-Mulk, was regarded as the model of ministerial wisdom.

64. *SHA*, 50–51.

65. Ibid. 51–53. See also ibid. 32–39 (Introduction by Iqbal) and F.O. 60/172, Sheil to Malmesbury, no. 116, camp near Tehran, 5 September 1852 and no. 127, same to same, camp near Tehran, 13 September 1852.

66. F.O. 173, Sheil to Malmesbury, no. 156, Tehran, 13 October 1852. Henry Rawlinson, then the British consul-general in Baghdad, was instrumental in arriving at an understanding with the Ottoman *vali*. See ibid., enclosure no. 1: Rawlinson to Pasha of Baghdad.

67. Zarandi, *Dawn-Breakers*, 638–642 and F.O. 60/173, Sheil to Malmesbury, no. 143, Tehran, 2 October 1852.

68. F.O. 60/173, Sheil to Malmesbury, no. 158, Tehran, 20 October 1852.

69. Ibid.

CHAPTER 6: PLAYING THE POWER GAME

1. FO 60/169, Sheil to Palmerston, no. 2, Tehran, 1 January 1852.

2. FO 60/169, same to same, no. 12, Tehran, 20 January 1852, enclosure: Sheil to Sadr A'zam, 11 January 1852.

3. Ibid., enclosure no. 1: Sadr A'zam to Sheil, 14 January 1852.

4. *NTQ*, IV, 43–48.

5. FO 60/169, no. 12, enclosure no. 2: Sheil to Sadr A'zam, 16 January 1852.

6. FO 60/169, Sheil to Earl of Granville, no. 14, Tehran, 14 February 1852, enclosure no. 5: Sheil to Sadr A'zam.

7. Ibid., enclosure no. 7: Translation of an autograph letter from the Shah of Persia to the Sadr A'zim, 1852.

8. Ibid., enclosure no. 8: Sheil to Sadr A'zam.

9. FO 60/169, same to same, no. 16, Tehran, 20 February 1852. The last comment must have been said, no doubt, with Nuri's failure to keep his promises concerning Amir Kabir's safety in mind.

10. FO 60/169, same to same, no. 29, Tehran, 5 March 1852. See also *NTQ*, IV, 48.

11. FO 60/169, same to same, no. 35, Tehran, 22 March 1852, enclosure no. 1: Autograph note of the Shah to Sadr A'zem. For reasons unexplained in Sheil's dispatch, this royal autograph, like many others addressed to the premier in this period, ended up in the hands of the British minister. One may assume the shah deliberately used the Nuri channel in order to communicate his wishes to the British envoy without being obliged to work within the framework of official correspondence. Yet the contents of some of the notes were so sensitive that their having been divulged to the British minister could only be attributed to Nuri's sheer betrayal of the shah with the aim of securing his own shaky position.

12. FO 60/170, same to same, no. 43, Tehran, 10 April 1852.

13. Ibid.

14. FO 60/170, same to same, no. 44, Tehran, 10 April 1852.

15. FO 60/170, same to same, no. 67, camp near Tehran, 7 June 1852.

16. FO 60/171, same to same, no. 104, camp near Tehran, 19 August 1852.

17. FO 60/178, same to same, no. 23, Tehran, 30 January 1853, enclosure no. 4: Engagement contracted by the Persian government relative to Herat. Also Hurewitz, *Middle East* I, 305–306.

18. FO 60/178, same to same, no. 2, Tehran, 5 January 1853, enclosure no. 4: The Shah to Sayd Muhammad Khan.

19. FO 60/178, no. 23.

20. FO 60/178, same to same, no. 4, Tehran, 6 January 1853.

21. FO 60/173, Sheil to Malmesbury, no. 180, Tehran, 10 December 1852.

22. FO 60/178, Sheil to Malmesbury, no. 12, Tehran, 13 January 1853.

23. Ibid., enclosure: Sadr Azam to Sheil and Dolgorouki, 12 January 1852.

24. CNBL, Nasir al-Din to Nuri, no. 40, n.d.. The event alluded to is the massacre of Karbala in 1843 by Najib Pasha, the Ottoman governor of Iraq. The date of the note is thus 1853 which corresponds to the Sultaniya gathering.

25. FO 60/179, Thomson to Lord Russell, no. 16, Tehran, 7 April 1853.

26. FO 60/181, Thomson to Clarendon, camp near Tehran, 8 August 1853, enclosure: Copy of Thomson to Stratford de Radcliffe.

27. FO 60/181, same to same, no. 78, camp near Tehran, 9 August 1853.

28. FO 60/181, same to same, no. 82, camp near Tehran, 14 August 1853.

29. FO 60/181, Thomson to Clarendon, no. 102, camp Arjeen (near Sultaniya), 21 September 1853.

30. FO 60/181, same to same, no. 105, camp near Tehran, 5 October 1853.

31. FO 60/181, same to same, no. 107, camp near Tehran, 3 October 1853.

32. FO 60/169, Sheil to Granville, no. 26, 3 March 1852.

33. FO 60/169, same to same, no. 28, Tehran, 3 March 1852.

34. Not to be mistaken with Muhammad Hasan Khan Sardar Iravani, Sar-i Aslan.

35. FO 60/170, Sheil to Malmesbury, no. 68, camp near Tehran, 7 June 1852.

36. Ibid.

37. FO 60/170, same to same, no. 73, camp near Tehran, 22 June 1852.

38. FO 60/170, same to same, no. 93, camp near Tehran, 10 August 1852.

39. FO 60/170, Sheil to Malmesbury, no. 58, Tehran, 11 May 1852, enclosure no. 1: Autograph note from the Shah to the Sadr A'zim written on 10 May 1852.

40. Muhammad Hasan Khan I'timad al-Saltana (*Tarikh-i Muntazam-i Nasiri*, 2d ed., ed. M. I. Rizvani, 3 vols. [Tehran, 1363–1367/1984–1988], III, 1644) identifies him as Mirza 'Ali Naqi Farahani, but Mirza Shafi', the Persian representative in London, gives Azarbaijan as his origin (FO 60/172, Sheil to Malmesbury, no. 128, camp near Tehran, 15 September 1852, enclosure: Shafi' Khan to Malmesbury, 15 July 1852).

41. FO 60/170, Sheil to Malmesbury, no. 65, Tehran, 18 May 1852.

42. FO 60/172, no. 128.

43. FO 60/172, Sheil to Malmesbury, no. 136, 28 September 1852, enclosure no. 4: Autograph note from the Shah to Sadr A'zam. On the margin it is inserted that the autograph note is evidently not the shah's own composition.

44. Ibid., enclosure no. 8: Autograph of the shah to the Sadr A'zam.

45. Ibid.

46. FO 60/178, Sheil to Malmesbury, no. 10, confidential, Tehran, 10 January 1853, enclosure no. 1: Autograph letter from the shah to the Sadr A'zam.

47. FO 60/181, Thomson to Clarendon, no. 94, camp near Tehran, 4 September 1853.

48. FO 60/182, Thomson to Clarendon, no. 129, camp near Tehran, 5 November 1853. See also A.K.S. Lambton, "The Study of the Role of the Merchant in Mid-Nineteenth Century Persia: The Case of Hajji 'Abd al-Karim," in *Qajar Persia*, 164–193 (177–178). In her study the author, in spite of looking at all other aspects of the case, did not discuss the British political motives for pursuing 'Abd al-Karim's claims even after he renounced his essentially false claim to British citizenship. Lambton seems to agree with Thomson's grounds for suspending relations: that he "had exhausted every argument and been constantly met with evasive replies" in presenting 'Abd al-Karim's case and demanding satisfaction for the ensuing incident from the Persian government. Thomson's claims of 'Abd al-Karim's entitlement to British protection, considering the evidence Lambton herself presented in the article, were entirely unjustified. Such an obvious lapse of judgment on Lambton's part could only be attributed to her conscious desire to minimize, if not altogether ignore, the effects of British diplomatic harassment in Iran and instead present the case of Hajji 'Abd al-Karim as a purely commercial dispute.

49. CNBL, Nasir al-Din Shah to Nuri, no. 39. n.d. [15 November 1853].

50. CNBL, Nasir al-Din Shah to Nuri, no. 38, 1270 Q./15 October 1853.

51. For Tehran's influential mayor, Mahmud Khan Kalantar, and his connections with the *lutis*, see H. G. Migeod, "Die Lutis, Ein Ferment des stadtischen Lebens in Persien," *Journal of Economic and Social History of the Orient*, II (1959) 82–91. See also below Chapter 9.

52. CNBL, Nasir al-Din Shah to Nuri, no. 36, n.d..

53. CNBL, Nasir al-Din Shah to Nuri, no. 18., 1270 Q./1853.

54. CNBL, Nasir al-Din Shah to Nuri, no. 33, 1270 Q./late October–early November 1853.

55. CNBL, Nasir al-Din Shah to Nuri, no.31. n.d. [late October 1853].

56. CNBL, Nasir al-Din Shah to Nuri, no. 27, 1270 Q./late October 1853.

57. CNBL, Nasir al-Din Shah to Nuri, no. 28, n.d. [1853]. This note is a response to FO 60/182, no. 129, enclosure no. 16: Thomson to Nuri, 27 October 1853, or enclosure no. 17: same to same, 31 October 1853. Both letters are devoid of diplomatic amenities and contain threats of a break in relations.

58. CNBL, Nasir al-Din Shah to Nuri, no. 24, n.d. [early November 1853].

59. FO 60/182, same to same, no. 130, camp near Tehran, 8 November 1853, enclosure no. 2: An autograph note from the Shah to the Sadr A'zam, 7 November 1853. By the shah's instruction a copy of this note was to be sent to Thomson.

60. FO 60/182, Thomson to Clarendon, Tehran, 13 November 1853.

61. FO 60/178, Sheil to Malmesbury, no. 15, 14 January 1853.

62. FO 60/179, Thomson to Clarendon, no. 31, camp near Tehran, 11 May 1853.

63. FO 60/182, same to same, no. 132, camp near Tehran, 11 November 1853 cf. Arkhiv vneshnei politiki Rossi (hereafter AVPR), fond (f.) Kantseliaria MID, Perpiska s Tegeranom, 1853. d. 75, 1, 238, in M. Volodarsky, "Persia's Foreign Policy Between the Two Herat Crises, 1831–1856," *Middle East Studies* 21 (1985), 111–151 (137).

64. FO 60/182, Thomson to Clarendon, no. 149, Tehran, 24 November 1853.

65. FO 60/182, same to same, no. 150, Tehran, 26 November 1853.

66. Watson, *History*, 416.

67. CNBL, Nasir al-Din Shah to Nuri, no. 41. In response to a weekly report (*ruznamcha*) dated Jumada al-Awwal 1271 Q./February 1854.

68. Watson, *History*, 417.

69. CNBL, Nasir al-Din Shah to Nuri, nos. 19–20, Sha'ban 1270 Q./June 1854.

70. SML, Nuri to Sadiq Nuri, I, nos. 145–146, n.d. [1854].

71. CNBL, Nasir al-Din Shah to Nuri, no. 44, n.d. [late August–early September 1853]. Cf. F.O. 60/181, Thomson to Clarendon, no. 84, camp near Tehran, 15 August 1853 and no. 95, camp near Tehran, 8 September 1853.

72. Farhad Mirza to Faridun Mirza, Rabi' al-Awwal 1270 Q./December 1853 in Farhad Mirza, *Munsha'at*, 31–40 (38).

73. Thomson to Nuri, 3 Rabi' al-Thani 1271 Q./23 December 1854, in M. H. Muhaddis, ed., *Mukatibat-i Iran va Ingilis dar Bara-yi Panahandigi-yi Farhad Mirza* (Tehran, 1360/1982), 13.

74. Nuri to Thomson, 29 Rabi' al-Awwal 1271 Q./20 December 1854, and same to same, 10 Rabi' al-Thani 1271 Q./1 January 1855 in Muhaddis, *Mukatibat*, 5–11, 40–42.

75. Nasir al-Din Shah to Nuri, Rabi' al-Thani 1271 Q./January 1855, in Muhaddis, *Mukatibat*, 36–38.

76. The third-century *Letter of Tansar* recommended outright favor for the virtuous few, absolute intimidation for evildoers and seditious ones, and "a combination of benevolence and coercion" for the majority of the subjects (Minuvi. *Nama-yi Tansar*, 63). The thirteenth-century Nasir al-Din Tusi advised rulers to supplement kindness with awe (*haybat*) in order to secure "the aura and splendor of kingship" (Nasir al-Din Tusi, *Akhlaq-i Nasiri* [Laknaw, 1883], 445). English, trans., *The Nasirean Ethics*, trans. G. M. Wickens (London, 1964), 233.

77. Muhaddis, *Mukatibat*, 37–38.

78. Nasir al-Din Shah quoted in Nuri to Thomson, 18 Rabi' al-Thani 1271 Q./7 January 1855 in Muhaddis, *Mukatibat*, 71–72.

CHAPTER 7: YOUTHFUL AMBITIONS

1. Watson, *History*, 118.

2. Murray to Dalhousie, 5 May 1855, Dalhousie Papers: 6/168/2664 in B. English, *John Company's Last War* (London, 1971), 42.

3. Watson, *History*, 118.

4. H. Maxwell, *The Honorable Sir Charles Murray, K.C.B., a Memoir* (Edinburgh and London, 1898), 52–70, 148–165.

5. C. Murray, *Bird of the Prairie* (London, 1844).

6. F.O. 60/202, Murray to Clarendon, no. 7, Tehran, 20 April 1855.

7. *British Documents on Foreign Affairs: Reports and Papers from Foreign Office Confidential Print*, Series B: The Near East and Middle East, 1856–1914 (Persia: 1856–1885) (New York, 1984), X, doc. 27., Murray to Clarendon, no. 37, Oroomiah, 22 March 1856. (Hereinafter *FOCP*.)

8. F.O. 60/202, Murray to Clarendon, no. 22, camp near Tehran, 18 June 1855.

9. F.O. 60/203, same to same, no.28, camp near Tehran, 9 July 1855. To "eat dirt" (*guh khurdan*) is a literal translation of a vulgar Persian expression of insult meaning humiliating retraction of an action or a claim.

10. F.O. 60/203, same to same, no. 35, camp near Tehran, 24 July 1855.

11. F.O. 60/203, same to same, no. 52, camp near Tehran, 17 September 1855.

12. F.O. 60/204, same to same, no. 77, secret and confidential, camp near Tehran, 29 October 1855; cf. no. 72, camp near Tehran, 19 October 1855.

13. F.O. 60/204, no. 77, enclosure: Translation of a Memorandum given by the Persian Government. Murray specified that the shah himself dictated the memorandum.

14. F.O. 60/204, no. 77.

15. Murray to Dalhousie, 5 May 1855, Dalhousie Papers in English, *John Company's Last War*, 43.

16. CNBL, Nasir al-Din Shah to Nuri, no. 14. 18 Rabi'al-Awwal 1272 Q./28 November 1855.

17. F.O. 60/204, Murray to Clarendon, no. 84, Tehran, 17 November 1855, enclosure no. 2: Nuri to Murray (containing the shah's autograph note), 4 November 1855. Persian text, Nuri to Murray, no. 2, 24 Safar 1272 Q., in M. Gharavi ed., *Majara-yi Dawlat-i Inglis va Mirza Hashim Khan* (Tehran, 1363/1984) 24. The source of the correspondence on the Hashim Khan affair is not mentioned by the editor. It may be that this collection was one of several copies of the correspondence provided by royal order for distribution among foreign legations in Tehran.

18. F.O. 60/198, Thomson to Clarendon, camp near Tehran, 15 July 1854. For Hashim Khan see also Bamdad, *Rijal*, IV, 417–421.

19. F.O. 60/204, Murray to Clarendon, no. 80, Tehran, 9 November 1855.

20. F.O. 60/204, same to same, no. 84.

21. Ibid., enclosure no. 3, 6 November 1855; cf. Persian text, no. 2, 24 Safar 1272 Q. in Gharavi, *Hashim Khan*, 20.

22. F.O. 60/204, no. 84, enclosure no. 4: 6 November 1855 cf. Persian text, no. 4, 25 Safar 1272 Q. in Gharavi, *Hashim Khan*, 24.

23. F.O. 60/204, no. 84, enclosure no. 5, 8 November 1855 cf. Persian text, no. 5, 27 Safar 1272 Q., in Gharavi, *Hashim Khan*, 26–27.

24. F.O. 60/204, no. 84, enclosure no. 6, 11 November 1855; cf. Persian text, no. 6, in Gharavi, *Hashim Khan*, 30–34.

25. Murray to Dalhousie, 1 December 1855, Dalhousie's papers: 6/179/3, English, *John Company's Last War*, 48; Maxwell, *Murray*, 256 n. Maxwell's remark is in response to current suspicions in England: "Murray got mixed up with

some woman there, didn't he?" said one of his acquaintances, "I don't remember much about it, but I am pretty sure there was a woman at the bottom of the trouble."

26. F.O. 60/204, no. 84. enclosure no. 9, 17 December 1855; cf. Persian text, no. 9, 5 Rabi' al-Awwal 1272 Q., in Gharavi, *Hashim Khan*, 42–23.

27. F.O. 60/204, no. 84, enclosure no. 10, 17 December 1855; cf. Persian text, no. 11, in Gharavi, *Hashim Khan*, 48–49.

28. F.O. 60/204, no. 84, enclosure no. 11, 17 November 1855.

29. F.O. 60/204, same to same, no. 86, Tehran, 20 November 1855.

30. F.O. 60/204, same to same, no. 88, Tehran, 28 November 1855, enclosure no. 2, 22 November 1855; cf. Persian text, no. 29, in Gharavi, *Hashim Khan*, 101–102.

31. F.O. 60/204, no. 88, enclosure no. 4, Murray to Sa'id Khan containing memorandum in response to the shah's autograph, 23 November 1855; cf. Persian text, no. 16, 13 Rabi' al-Awwal 1272 Q., in Gharavi, *Hashim Khan*, 62–64.

32. F.O. 60/204, no. 88, enclosure no. 7: Nasir al-Din Shah to Sa'id Khan (to be sent to Murray), 26 November 1855; cf. Persian text, no. 15, 25 (?) Rabi' al-Awwal 1272 Q., in Gharavi, *Hashim Khan*, 58–59. The Foreign Office's translation has been slightly modified. This autograph note corresponds to the dream quoted above.

33. F.O. 60/204, no. 88, enclosure no. 8: Murray to Sa'id Khan, 27 November 1855; cf. no. 21, 16 Rabi' al-Awwal 1272 Q. in Gharavi, *Hashim Khan*, 78–79.

34. F.O. 60/204, same to same, no. 91, Tehran, 1 December 1855.

35. It is probably this transfer of the documents from Tehran to Tabriz and then to Baghdad that created the most enduring damage resulting from the break in relations. The archive of the British embassy in Tehran, now in PRO, contains not a single file of the original Persian correspondence and other Persian documents exchanged between the Persian government and the British embassy. One may assume that after they had been transferred to Baghdad they were eventually lost or destroyed, but there is some evidence that Murray in Baghdad had access to the original documents and possibly was himself responsible for their loss. The fate of the Persian files of the British embassy in Tehran remains a mystery, and their loss a great handicap for the history of the period.

36. F.O. 60/204, same to same, no. 95, Kan, 6 December 1855.

37. F.O. 60/208, same to same, Tabriz, no. 26, 22 February 1856, enclosure: Translation of the Shah's autograph to the Sadr A'zam, December 1855. See also Maxwell, *Murray*, 249–250. This autograph must have been written concomitant with the shah's dream, hence the reference to "vexation" during the night. The date given must be an approximate one. The brackets in reference to Sultan Husayn are original in the English translation.

38. F.O. 60/204, same to same, no. 79, Secret and Confidential, camp near Tehran, 2 November 1855; cf. Mirza Malkum Khan, *Majmu'a-yi Asar-i Mirza Malkum Khan*, ed. M. Muhit Tabataba'i (Tehran, 1327/1948), *jim*.

39. W. S. Blunt, *Secret History of the English Occupation of Egypt* (London, 1903), 83. For a biography of Malkum Khan, see H. Algar, *Mirza Malkum Khan, a Study in the History of Iranian Modernism* (Berkeley and Los Angeles, 1973).

40. Malkum, *Majmu'a*, pp. *lam-ha*.

41. Louis Antoine de Bourrienne's *Memoires* (Paris, 1829) was a popular biography of Napoleon written by his private secretary. It was translated into Persian in 1252/1836 from the English edition (*Memoirs of Napoleon Bonaparte*, [London, 1836]) by Muhammad Riza Muhandis[-bashi] Tabrizi as *Tarikh-i Napil'un* (Gulistan Library, MS no. 185/732 [Atabay, *Fihrist-i Tarikh*, 418]). The translator was among early Persian graduates of engineering from England who translated a number of French works into Persian, including Voltaire's. On the inside cover Nasir al-Din made some sketches of Napoleon mounted and on foot and entered comments on the margins of the manuscript. The above note appears on the margin of p. 12. There are two other biographies of Napoleon in the Gulistan Library. *Luy 'Il* (the year of crocodile) is the fifth year in the Turco-Mongolian cyclical calendar, which rotates every twelve years. This calendar was observed along with the lunar Islamic calendar by the Qajar court up to the end of the Nasiri period. The Mirror Hall is the main hall of audience in the Gulistan Palace. Ghulam-Husayn Yuz-bashi, the bearer of the good news, was also promoted to the rank of *sartip* (I'timad al-Saltana, *Muntazam-i Nasiri*, III, 1793–1794). Wishing the blindness of the enemy is an abusive proverb in Persian. One hundred and ten cannon shots were fired because the *abjad* numerical value of '*Ali*, the name of the Third Shi'ite Imam, is 110. An emblem of royal power, the Naqara-khana (the house of the kettledrum) performed traditional Persian military music on drums and trumpets at five regular intervals daily and on special occasions. The cause of the crown prince's immature death probably was cholera. The quoted verse is a common supplication (part of Qur'an, 2:153) often recited for the dead. For Nuri's account of the arrival of the Herat news, see K. Isfahaniyan and Q. Rushani (Za'faranlu), eds., *Majm'a-yi Asnad va Madarik-i Farrukh Khan Amin al-Dawla* (Tehran, 1346–1357/1967–1978), I, 153–154 (hereinafter *AFAD*). Nuri to Farrukh Khan, 4 Rabi' al-Awwal 1273/2 November 1856. The shah presented the events as though they happened on 2 November, but it is certain that he was informed of the victory earlier.

42. "Sharh-i Hal-i Kamal al-Mulk az Zaban-i Khudash," in Q. Ghani, *Yad-dashtha-yi Duktur Qasim Ghani*, 12 vols. (London, 1980–1984) V, 26–37. For the painting see Zuka', *Tarikhcha*, 217.

43. Rawlinson, *England and Russia*, 84–86.

44. Hurewitz, *Middle East*, I, 310. For diplomatic aspects of the Herat crisis see Kelly, *Persian Gulf*, 452–466, and Ittihadiya, *Ravabit*, 117–197.

45. F.O. 60/210, Murray to Clarendon, no. 108, Confidential, Baghdad, 20 November 1856.

46. *VI*, no. 304, 28 Rabi' al-Awwal 1273 Q./December 1856. Murray believes the Belgian weekly in question may very well be the *Independence Belge* or, alternatively, the *Nord* (FO 60/210, Murray to Clarendon, no. 126, Baghdad, 22 December 1856). The candid tone of the article presumably was not regarded by the shah and Nuri as damaging to Nasir al-Din's public image.

47. *VI*, no. 304.

48. Comte Joseph A. de Gobineau, *Les Depeches Diplomatiques du Comte de Gobineau en Perse*, ed. A. D. Hytier (Geneve and Paris, 1959), 79 (hereinafter *DDG*), Gobineau to Walewski, no. 23, Tehran, 7 April 1857. For the first Herat crisis

see Kelly, *Persian Gulf*, 290–353; A. Amanat, "'Pishva-yi Ummat' va Vazir-i Mukhtar-i 'Bi-Tadlis-i' Ingilis: Murasala-yi Hajj Sayyid Muhammad Baqir Shafti, Hujjat al-Islam, va Sir Jan Maknil [Sir John McNeill] dar Qaziya-yi Lashkarkashi-i Muhammad Shah bi Harat," *Iranshinasi* II, 1 (1369/1991), 11–41; and M. Itti-hadiya, *Ravabit*, 53–116.

49. *VI*, no. 304.

50. F.O. 60/209, Murray to Clarendon, no. 57, Baghdad, 21 June 1856.

51. F.O. 60/208, Murray to Clarendon, no. 5, Tabriz, 8 January 1856.

52. F.O. 60/208, same to same, no. 5, Tabriz, 8 January 1856.

53. Thomson to Sadr A'zam, no. 15, 15 Rabi' al-Awwal I 1271 Q./5 January 1855, in Muhaddis, *Mukatibat*, 56–57. Also nos. 16, 17, and 31.

54. F.O. 60/204, Murray to Clarendon, no. 97, Kend (Kan) near Tehran, 6 December 1855.

55. *FOPC*, X, doc. 39, Stevens to Clarendon, no. 14, Tehran, 31 March 1856. Consul Stevens learned of this communication through his agents around Nuri.

56. *AFAD*, I, 64, Nuri to Amin al-Mulk, 4 Dhul-Hijja 1272/5 August 1856.

57. British Library, Manuscript Copies of Sixty Treaties and Other Persian Documents, MS Or. 4679, no. 58: "Surat-i Taqrirat-i . . . Sadr 'Azam Huzur-i Sarkar-i A'lahazrat etc." (Minutes of prime minister's presentations to His Majesty [Nasir al-Din Shah]). Also published as *Qararha va Qarardadha*, S. Vahidniya ed., (Tehran, 1362/1983), 268.

58. *FOCP*, X, doc. 38, Stevens to Redcliffe, Tehran, 31 March 1856.

59. Ibid., doc. 37, Murray to Clarendon, Oroomiah, 22 March 1856.

60. Ibid., doc. 35, Clarendon to Murray, Foreign Office, 15 May 1856.

61. Ibid., doc. 46, Clarendon to Redcliffe, Telegraphic, Foreign Office, 24 May 1856.

62. Ibid., doc. 24, Murray to Clarendon, no. 34, Tabriz, 7 March, 1856, in-cluding no. 1, Stevens to Murray, Tehran, 28 February 1856.

63. Ibid., doc. 51, Stevens to Clarendon, no. 29, camp near Tehran, 19 May 1856.

64. Ibid., doc. 52, Stevens to Clarendon, no. 26, Tehran, 11 May 1856.

65. *AFAD*, I, 48–49, Nasir al-Din Shah to Emperor of France, n.d.

66. Gobineau, *Prokesch*, 43, Tehran, 19 September 1855.

67. *AFAD*, I, 25–26, "Kitabcha-yi Dastur al-'Amal." At the end of the doc-ument, Nuri added: "Seen word by word and approved by this servant of the throne in Shawwal 1272 Q. (June–July 1856). Let it be admissible to the royal sight. May God ease off our burden." The shah inserted his usual approval. On the Persian view of the Indian revolt, see below.

68. *FOCP*, X, doc. 82, Stevens to Clarendon, no. 43, camp near Tehran, 10 July 1856; *AFAD*, I, no. 14, "List of the horses presented," Dhul-Qa'da 1272 Q./July 1856.

69. *AFAD*, I, 38–39, "Separate instruction about concluding treaties with [other] states."

70. FO 60/208, no. 26.

71. *AFAD* I, 114–115, 171, 193, 211, 220–221, 247, 422; II, 118, 233, 301. For the establishment of relations with the United States, see "Report no. 1648, [to

accompany bill H.R. 6743], Commercial Relations with Persia," House of Representatives, 47th Congress, 1st session, 1–4.

72. The shah may have also noted the Ostend Manifesto, issued in the same year by the U.S. envoys to Europe. The threat that the United States would take Cuba by military force if Spain refused to sell it had caused great excitement in the European press.

73. *AFAD*, I, 66–71, Nuri to Amin al-Mulk, 12 Dhul-Hijja 1272 Q./August 1856. On the margin the shah's instruction.

74. Ibid., I, 70.

75. Ibid., I, 136. Nuri to Amin al-Mulk, Tehran, 16 Safar 1273 Q./16 October 1856.

76. Ibid. I, 138. The shah's autograph dated 16 Safar 1273 Q./16 October 1856.

77. Ibid. I, 153–154. Nuri to Amin al-Mulk, 4 Rabi' al-Awwal 1273 Q./2 October 1856.

78. Ibid. I, 157. Nuri to Amin al-Mulk, 7 Rabi' al-Awwal 1273 Q./5 November 1856.

79. Ibid. I, 155. Nuri to Amin al-Mulk, 5 Rabi' al-Awwal 1273 Q./3 November 1856. Nasir al-Din's first crown prince, Sultan Mahmud Mirza, had died in 1266 Q./1851.

80. Ghani, *Yaddashtha*, IX, 366–367. The text of the epinicium is quoted in full in Husam al-Saltana's letter to his brother Ardishir Mirza Rukn al-Dawla, Herat, November 1856. For the *salam* held on that occasion, see *NTQ*, IV, 205–208. Salm and Tur were sons of Faridun, the legendary King of the Kayanid dynasty in the *Shahnama*, who jointly murdured their younger brother Iraj.

81. *AFAD*, I, 163–165. Nuri to Amin al-Mulk, 20 Rabi' al-Awwal 1273 Q./18 November 1856. This was perhaps one of the earliest instances of the use of the term *millat* in its modern sense to denote the nation.

82. *AFAD*, I, 175–178, Nuri to Amin al-Mulk, 3 Rabi' al-Thani 1273 Q./1 December 1856, II, no. 19, 29–32; Mirza Najaf Bahadur Khan Hindi to Nasir al-Din Shah, Mashhad, circa Dhul-Qa'da 1272 Q./August 1856, no. 20, 32–34; same to same, Tehran (?), November 1856 (?). For petitions by Afghan chiefs see nos. 16–18, 25–29. Girishg is on the bank of the Hilmand River some 100 miles south of Herat on the road to Kandahar.

83. *NTQ*, IV, 208–211 and *RSN*, X, 702–704. *Ghaza* is the localized offensive waged against infidels on the frontiers of the Abode of Islam (*Dar al-Islam*). *Jihad* is the holy war, often defensive, to be fought by all eligible Muslims. Sani' al-Mulk's portrait of 'Ali with a radiant halo around his face and dressed in Arab attire, green turban and shawl, holding his double-edged saber on his lap, became the most popular icon of Shi'ite Iran ever since its creation. It was first described in *VI*, 14 Rabi' al-Thani 1273 Q./1 December 1856.

84. *FOCP*, X, doc. 129, Clarendon to Persian Minister of Foreign Affairs, Foreign Office, 10 October 1856.

85. *FOCP*, X, doc. 135, Clarendon to Redcliffe, Foreign Office, 28 October 1856. Murray's list of demands appears in doc. 105, Murray to Clarendon, Baghdad, 18 August 1856. The demand for Bandar 'Abbas is more clearly spelled out in doc. 130, same to same, no. 46, Foreign Office, 14 October 1856.

86. Ibid., doc. 126, Clarendon to Murray, no. 44, Secret and Confidential, Foreign Office, 10 October 1856; doc. 160, same to Smith, Foreign Office, 19 November 1856; doc. 231, same to Wodehouse, no. 1, Foreign Office, 3 January 1857.

87. *FOCP*, X, doc. 162, Stevens to Clarendon, no. 71, camp near Tehran, 13 October 1856.

88. Ibid., doc. 167, same to same, no. 75, camp near Tehran, 18 October 1856.

89. CNBL, Nasir al-Din Shah to Nuri, no. 9, n.d. [1856].

90. CNBL, Nasir al-Din Shah to Nuri, no. 1, n.d. [November 1856].

91. *AFAD*, I, 192, Shah to Amin al-Mulk, 20 Rabi' al-Awwal 1273/18 November 1856. On the margin is the shah's note and the autograph.

92. *VI*, no. 311, 18 Jumada al-Ula 1273 Q./January 1857.

93. *RSN*, X, 731–733 and *NTQ*, IV, 276–279, 283–284. Kirmani's *Nasiriya* is dated 18 Rajab 1273 Q./March 1857. It appears in Hajji Muhammad Karim Khan Kirmani, *Majma' al-Rasa'il* (Kirman, 1386/1966).

94. For the Anglo-Persian war see A. Ballard, "The Persian War of 1856–57," *Blackwood Magazine* (Edinburgh, September 1861); English, *John Company's Last War*, 60–120; G. H. Hunt, *Outram and Havelock's Campaign (1857)*, (London, 1857); Kelly, *Persian Gulf*, 452–499; J. F. Standish, "The Persian War of 1856–1857," *Middle East Studies*, vol. 3 (1966), no. 1, 18–45; M. Volodarsky, "Russian Diplomacy During the Anglo-Persian Conflict of 1855–1857," *Central Asian Survey*, vol. 6 (1987), no. 2; 43–54. See Also *RSN*, X, 719–763; Kurmuji, *Haqayiq*, 197–212.

95. CNBL, no. 36, Nasir al-Din Shah to Nuri, n.d. [early 1857]. On the margin Nuri states that the shah's note had arrived a day after Stevens' departure from Tehran in disguise. The verse quoted, the last hemistich from a quatrain by Shah Nazar, an Isma'ili poet, portrayed the shah's desperate mood:

> Either we will pound at the enemy's head with stone,
> Or he will hang us from the gallows.
> In short, in this house [i.e., the world] of many tricks,
> Dying in honor is better than two hundred lives in disgrace.

96. *DDG*, 67, Gobineau to Walewski, no. 15, Tehran, 20 February 1858.

97. Ironically, Darya-yi Nur's companion piece, Kuh-i Nur (mountain of light)—both snatched away by Nadir in 1739 from the Mughal ruler of India as war booty—had, in a symbolic turn of fortune, become the centerpiece of the British crown.

98. CNBL, Nasir al-Din Shah to Nuri, nos. 5–6, n.d. [late 1856].

99. Ibid., nos. 5–6. For the cost of the Herat campaigns see *AFAD*, I, 175, Nuri to Amin al-Mulk, 1 December. 1856 (with Shah's autograph on the margin).

100. *AFAD*, I, 211–212. Shah to Amin al-Mulk, 24 Rabi' al-Thani 1273 Q./ December 1857. Photograph of the rescript in Husayn b. 'Abdullah Sarabi, *Makhzan al-Waqayi', Safarnamih-yi Farrukh Khan Amin al-Dawla*, eds. K. Isfahaniyan and Q. Rushani, 2nd ed. (Tehran, 1361/1982), ill. no. 2.

101. *AFAD*, I, 212–213, same to same, 24 Rabi' al-Thani 1273 Q./December 1856. Photograph in Sarabi, *Makhzan*, ill. no. 1.

102. *VI*, no. 312, 25 Jumada al-'Ula 1273 Q./21 January 1857.

103. *AFAD*, I, 236, same to same, 9 Jumada al-Ula 1273 Q./4 January 1857. Shah's autograph in the margin appears with a note promising great rewards in exchange for sincere service.

104. Ibid., 216, Nuri to Amin al-Mulk, 25 Rabi' al-Thani 1273 Q./22 December 1856; ibid., 243–244, Nuri to Malkum, 19 Jumada al-Ula 1273 Q./14 January 1857; ibid., 272–273, Nuri to Amin al-Mulk, 15 Rajab 1273 Q./12 March 1857.

105. *DDG*, 80, Gobineau to Walewski, no. 23, Tehran, 7 April 1857.

106. *AFAD*, I, 338, Nuri to Amin al-Mulk, Tehran, 7 Ramadan 1273 Q./June 1857, and ibid. 350, Nuri to Amin al-Mulk, Tehran, 8 Ramadan 1273 Q./June 1857.

107. Ibid, 291, Nuri to Amin al-Mulk, 24 Rajab 1273 Q./21 March 1857.

108. Ibid., 316, same to same, 29 Sa'ban 1273 Q./25 April 1857.

109. Watson, *History*, 447.

110. For the treaty's English text see Hurewitz, *Middle East*, I, 341–343. For the Persian, see Sarabi, *Makhzan*, 219–225.

111. Later accusations of haste in the conclusion of the treaty and the advantages that supposedly could have been earned from delaying it were often based on an erroneous assumption about the time and circumstances of the Indian Mutiny. The loss of Herat, which never was under direct Persian control (at least after Nadir's downfall), is lamented by some modern Persian histories as a great tragedy, often with blissful disregard for the fact that the general attitude in Herat was deeply divided on the question of Persian domination. In contrast, Murad Mirza Husam al-Saltana was often portrayed as the hero of Herat and the true bearer of the militarism of 'Abbas Mirza and Nadir, though often Aqa Muhammad Khan is omitted from the list of great warlords in Iran's modern history. For a specimen, see N. Najmi, *Fatih-i Harat, Murad Mirza Husam al-Saltana* (Tehran, 1367/1988), and the inevitable K. Sasani, *Siyasatgaran*, I, 28–32. In the absence of nonpartisan and documented histories, these "patriotic" accounts hold sway over Persian minds up to the present.

112. *AFAD*, I, 415–417, Amin al-Mulk to Nasir al-Din Shah, n.d. [c. April 1857]. Some months later, when Murray got hold of a copy of the report through his spies, he had little difficulty in guessing in what direction Napoleon III aimed.

113. Ibid., 343, Nasir al-Din Shah to Napoleon III, 7 Ramadan 1273 Q./3 May 1857. For Napoleon's further correspondence, see below.

114. Ibid., 414–415, Amin al-Mulk's report to the shah. For Amin al-Mulk's account of his visit to England, see Sarabi, *Makhzan*.

115. Ibid., 384, Nasir al-Din Shah to Nuri, 3 Shawwal 1273 Q./30 May 1857; ibid., 385, Nasir al-Din Shah to Amin al-Mulk, Shawwal 1273 Q./May–June 1857.

116. Ibid., 420, Amin al-Mulk's report to the shah.

117. F.O. 60/218, Murray to Clarendon, no. 36, Baghdad, 7 May 1857; cf. *NTQ*, IV, 350. The report of the Russian charge d'affaires cited in the report of the Persian minister in St. Petersburg (*AFAD*, II, no. 52, Qasim Khan Vali to Mirza Sa'id Khan, 28 Ramadan 1273 Q./May 1857) makes it clear that the shah was present.

118. F.O. 60/212, Stevens to Murray, no. 6, Tehran, 18 January 1856, and Stevens to Clarendon, no. 58, Tehran, 2 October 1856.

119. F.O. 60/217, Murray to Clarendon, no. 22, Baghdad, 10 April 1857, and *AFAD*, I, 270–271, Nuri to Amin al-Mulk, 24 Jumada al-Thani 1857 Q./20 April 1857.

120. *DDG*, 95–96, Gobineau to Walewski, no. 29, Tehran, 20 May 1857, and 98–99; ibid., same to same, Tehran, 20 May 1857, and F.O. 60/217, no. 22.

121. *AFAD*, I, 355. Nuri to Amin al-Mulk, 25 Ramadan 1273 Q./21 May 1857.

122. *AFAD*, III, 197–199, "Draft of the account to be published in the paper."

123. *DDG*, 125, Gobineau to Walewski, no. 40, Chizar, 22 July 1857.

124. *DDG*, 126, no. 40; *AFAD*, II, 161, Nuri to Amin al-Mulk, 6 Dhul-Hijja 1273 Q./28 August 1857.

125. *AFAD*, II, 154, no. 85, Murray to Nuri, n.d. [19 July 1857]; ibid., 154–155, no. 86, Nuri to Murray, n.d. [18 July 1857]; ibid. III, 199–202, "Draft of the account to be published in the paper." *DDG*, 119–125, Gobineau to Walewski, no. 38, Chizar, 16 July 1857; F.O. 60/218, Murray to Clarendon, no. 58, camp near Tehran, 20 July 1857.

126. *AFAD*, II, no. 68, Nuri to Murray, 5 Dhul-Qa'da 1273 Q./27 July 1857.

127. Ibid., II, 103–104, no. 53; 125–126; ibid., no. 66, 3 Dhul-Qa'da 1273 Q. /1 July 1857.

128. *DDG*, 124, Gobineau to Walewski, no. 39, Chizar, 18 July 1857; ibid. 137–139, same to same, no. 46, Chizar, 5 October 1857; ibid., 140–142, same to same, no. 47, Tehran, 20 October 1857.

129. F.O. 60/230, Murray to Clarendon, no. 8, Secret and Confidential, Tehran, 16 March 1858, enclosure: Translation of Sadr A'zam's letter to Mirza Sadiq Khan.

130. F.O. 60/220, Murray to Clarendon, no. 148, Tehran, 20 December 1857; cf. *DDG*, 154, Gobineau to Walewski, 24 December 1857. Translation in F.O. 60/229, same to same, no. 7, 27 January 1858.

CHAPTER 8: ABOLISHING THE SIDARAT

1. Mu'ayyir al-Mamalik, *Yaddashtha*, 38–39.

2. Polak, *Persien*, II, 34–35; Persian trans., 290.

3. F.O. 60/210, Murray to Clarendon, Baghdad, 3 November 1856.

4. *DDG*, 100–101. Gobineau to Walewski, no. 32, Tehran, 7 June 1857; Qa'im Maqami, "Payan-i Kar," I, 135.

5. Amin al-Dawla, *Khatirat-i Siyasi*, 15.

6. Ibid.

7. *FOCP*, 181–182. Wodehouse to Clarendon, no. 27, St. Petersburg, 10 January 1857. Oddly enough, no mention of Muzaffar al-Din is made, as though the British ambassador or Russian Foreign minister were not aware of his existence.

8. *DDG*, 106–107. Gobineau to Walewski, no. 34, Tehran, 15 June 1857.

9. *DDG*, 107–112. Gobineau to Walewski, no. 35, Tehran, 15 June 1857 cf. F.O. 60/218, Murray to Clarendon, no. 79, camp near Tehran, 19 August 1857. Nizamiya survived well into the present century, having been turned in the 1920s into a fashionable restaurant, Luqantih (Turkish *lukanta* meaning restaurant). It was demolished in the mid-1970s. Earlier many of the wall paintings were auctioned or destroyed, but one was preserved in the Iran Bastan Museum.

10. F.O. 60/218, Murray to Clarendon, no. 54, Hamadan, 4 July 1857, enclosure: The Shah's autograph.

11. *AFAD*, II, 174–75, no. 103, Nuri to Amin al-Mulk, 24 Dhul-Hijja 1273

Q./20 August 1857; *DDG*, no. 35; F.O. 60/219, Murray to Clarendon, no. 114, Secret and Confidential, camp near Tehran, 5 October 1857.

12. *AFAD*, II, 149, no. 79, Nuri to Amin al-Mulk, 1 Dhul-Qa'da 1273 Q./23 June 1857.

13. F.O. 60/218, Murray to Clarendon, no. 55, Hamadan, 4 July 1857. Later, Sitara married twice, the second time with a middle-rank court functionary with a dubious reputation (I'timad al-Saltana, *Ruznama*, 601).

14. F.O. 60/218, no. 55 cf. *DDG*, 117–18, Gobineau to Walewski, no. 37, Chizar, 5 July 1857.

15. *AFAD*, 131–34, no. 69, Nuri to Amin al-Mulk, 5 Dhul-Qa'da 1273 Q./27 June 1857; ibid., no. 103.

16. Ibid., no. 69.

17. For Nasir al-Din's offspring, see I'timad al-Saltana, *Ma'athir*, 11–15.

18. See above, Chapter Seven.

19. *VI*, no. 341.

20. *AFAD*, 236–237, no. 153, Nuri to Amin al-Mulk, 19 Muharram 1274 Q./10 September 1857.

21. F.O. 60/218, no. 79; ibid., no. 99, same to same, camp near Tehran, 25 September 1857.

22. F.O. 60/214, same to same, camp near Tehran, 5 October 1857.

23. F.O. 60/229, Murray to Clarendon, no. 5, Secret Intelligence Series, 15 February 1858.

24. F.O. 60/230, same to same, no. 45, Tehran, 20 March 1858. Reference to Austrian physician is no doubt to Joseph Polak, who then was appointed as the royal physician.

25. F.O. 60/231, Murray to Malmesbury, no. 12, Secret and Confidential, Tehran, 14 April 1858.

26. F.O. 60/232, same to same, no. 99, camp near Tehran, 1 July 1858.

27. Aqa Buzurg [Muhammad Muhsin] Tihrani, *Tabaqat A'lam al-Shi'a*, I: *Nuqaba al-Bashar fi al-Qarn al-Rabi' al-'Ashar* (Najaf, 1373 Q./1954), 881–883.

28. F.O. 60/232, same to same, no. 15, Secret Intelligence Series, camp near Tehran, 2 June 1858.

29. F.O. 60/232, same to same, no. 16, Secret Intelligence Series, camp near Tehran, 15 June 1858.

30. *AFAD*, III, no. 22, 39–43, Nuri to Amin al-Mulk, 10 Dhul-Qa'da 1274 Q./23 June 1858.

31. F.O. 60/232, no. 16.

32. *AFAD*, III, no. 22.

33. In a note to the prince, Mahd 'Ulya complained of I'tizad al-Saltana's neglect, which she attributed to the bad influence of one of the shah's powerful granduncles, an ally of Nuri. Mahd 'Ulya's note called for the prince's help in throwing a party for the shah in her garden in Shah 'Abd al-'Azim, but it is obvious that she had no direct access to the shah. "Profoundly anxious" about his son's health, she urged I'tizad al-Saltana for help, as she was certain her chief eunuch would be denied any accurate information on the matter. Mahd 'Ulya to I'tizad al-Saltana, Shah 'Abd al-'Azim, n.d. (circa 1858), album of Qajar women's

correspondence, Khurumi Collection of Qajar correspondence and documents, Tehran.

34. CNBL, Nasir al-Din Shah to Nuri, no. 45, n.d. (circa June 1858).

35. Polak, *Persien*, II, 34–35; Persian trans., 290.

36. CNBL, Nasir al-Din Shah to Nuri, no. 25, n.d. (circa late July 1858).

37. F.O. 60/232, no. 97.

38. Polak, *Persien*, II, 194–195; Persian trans., 398; H. Lavi, *Tarikh-i Yahud-i Iran*, 3 vols. (Tehran, 1339/1960), III, 743–751, based on Kuhan Sidq's notes and other unspecified sources. Lavi's rendering is not reliable. Not unlike a few Jewish dignitaries of the time, the Jewish medical brothers maintained a dual religious identity, Islam for the public and Judaism in private.

39. Polak had spotted some curable cases of brain inflammation among children. Moreover, incurability of the disease was no protection against charges of intentional maltreatment. Inevitably, treatment of the heir apparent was a highly sensitive issue, not only because of the punishment physicians might receive upon the death of their distinguished patients but also because of the tense political climate surrounding the heir apparent's illness. The shah could express hollow optimism in his reply to Nuri because no physician, including Polak, dared either to openly communicate to him the bad news nor to point out the futility of any treatment.

40. Lavi, *Yahud*, 748–750, and Polak, *Persien*, II; Persian trans., 412.

41. *AFAD*, III, 370–375, Nuri to Amin al-Mulk, no. 188, 22 Dhul-Qa'da 1274 Q./May 1858.

42. Pichon to Walewski, file 19, no. 189, Tehran, 1 September 1858, in Qa'im Maqami, "Payan-i Kar," 131–132. For kings' encounters with reality on the hunting ground, see A. Amanat, "'Bar Taq-i Ivan-i Faridun': Dawlat va Ra'iyat dar Dida-yi Sa'di," *Iranshinasi*, III (1370/ 1991), no. 1, 170–172.

43. F.O. 60/232, Murray to Malmesbury, no. 116, camp near Tehran, 31 August 1858.

44. CNBL, Nasir al-Din Shah to Nuri, no. 50 (written in the shah's own hand and dated 1275 Q./1858, bearing the royal seal at the top). Also in Muhammad Hasan Khan I'timad al-Saltana, *Mir'at al-Buldan-i Nasiri*, 4 vols. (Tehran, 1294–1297 Q./1877–1880), II, 226. A translation appears in F.O. 60/232, Murray to Malmesbury, no. 116, camp near Tehran, 31 August 1858, enclosure no. 2: Translation of His Majesty's Autograph to Sadr A'zam.

45. CNBL, Nuri to Nasir al-Din Shah, no. 42, n.d. (31 June 1858) in Nuri's own hand.

46. Ibid., Nasir al-Din Shah to Nuri, no. 43, n.d. (31 August 1858) written in the shah's own hand.

47. Polak, *Persien*, II, 34–35; Persian trans., 290.

48. CNBL, Nasir al-Din Shah to Nuri, no. 37, n.d. (19 Muharram 1275 Q./10 September 1858).

49. Qa'im Maqami, "Payan-i Kar," 38.

50. F.O. 60/169, Sheil to Palmerston, no. 9, Tehran, 16 January 1852, enclosure no. 2: Nasir al-Din Shah to Amir Nizam (trans. Ronald Thamson).

51. See "Naqqashiha-yi Nasir al-Din Shah," *Nashriya-yi Vizarat-i Umur-i Kharija*, III, no. 3 (Shahrivar 1345/1966), 49–64, figures 3 and 4. See also I. Afshar,

"Naqashiha-yi Nasir al-Din Shah," *Chihil Sal Tarikh-i Iran dar Dawra-yi Pad-ishahi-yi Nasir al-Din Shah* (critical edition of I'timad al-Saltana, *Ma'athir*), 2d. ed., 3 vols. (Tehran, 1363–1368/1984–1989), III, 831–886 (839–841). These sketches belong to the Nasiri albums preserved in Iran Ministry of Foreign Affairs. Oddly enough, the shah seems to have reversed the sequence of the sketches. He first captioned the second sketch the mournful Nuris, as though it preceded the first sketch, the joyful Nuris. This no doubt was an oversight, for at no time after Nuri's downfall was there a moment of joy.

52. F.O. 248/147, Granville to Sheil, no. 7, Foreign Office, 8 January 1852.

53. F.O. 60/232, no. 116. For Murray's proposals see below.

54. F.O. 60/232, no. 116, enclosure no. 1: Murray to Minister for Foreign Affairs, 1 September 1858, and M. Anitchkov to Minister of Foreign Affairs, Iran Ministry of Foreign Affairs, file 6059, in Qa'im Maqami, "Payan-i Kar," 138–139.

55. F.O. 60/233, Doria to Malmesbury, no. 9, Tehran, 30 October 1858. See also Pichon to Walewski, file 29, no. 220 in Qa'im Maqami, "Payan-i Kar," 143–144, and Mirza Fazlullah Nuri, *Tazkara-yi Tarikhi*, in ibid., 73.

56. Nuri to Mirza Muhammad Mahdi Nuri, n.p. (Yazd), n.d. (1862) in Qa'im Maqami, "Payan-i Kar," II, 131.

57. Ibid.

CHAPTER 9: BALANCING THE OLD AND THE NEW

1. *AFAD*, I, 409–411, "Draft of interview with Napoleon III the French emperor," n.d. [April 1857].

2. *AFAD*, I, 434–437, "Letter de Napoleon III au Shah de Perse," Palais des Tuileries, 12 Avril 1858.

3. Ibid. III, 278–279, Shah to Napoleon, n.d. [c. June 1857].

4. FO 60/232. Murray to Malmesbury, no. 116, camp near Tehran, 31 August 1858.

5. *VI*, no. 397, 23 Muharram 1275 Q./3 September 1858 and no. 398, 7 Safar 1275 Q./September 1858.

6. For early administrative reforms see F. Adamiyat, *Andishah-yi Taraqqi va Hukumat-i Qanun, 'Asr-i Sipahsalar* (Tehran, 1351/1972), 53–57 and S. Bakhash, *Iran: Monarchy, Bureaucracy and Reform under the Qajars*, (London, 1978), 76–83.

7. *Kitabcha-yi Majlis-i Maslahat-khana* (Handbook of the Consultative Council) together with Nasir al-Din Shah's rescript, Tehran, 1276 Q./1859 in Adamiyat, *Taraqqi*, 57–60.

8. The presence of 'Abd al-Latif Tasuji, the translator of *One Thousand and One Nights* from Arabic to Persian and a companion of the young Nasir al-Din in Tabriz; Riza Quli Khan Hidayat, now the principle of Dar al-Funun; Muhammad Taqi Sipihr, the court historian; Muhammad Ibrahim Badayi'-nigar, an enlightened literate; Mirza Riza Muhandis-bashi, a translator of many European works into Persian commissioned by the shah; Husayn Khan Nizam al-Dawla, one-time ambassador extraordinaire to European courts in the late 1830s; and possibly Malkum Khan reflected a mix of conservative and pro-reform elements in the Council. See also Adamiyat, *Tarraqi*, 60–62.

9. FO 60/247, Rawlinson to Wood, no. 5, Tehran, 5 January 1860; cf. Doria to Stanly, no. 50, Tehran, 25 April 1859.

10. The text of the *Kitabcha-yi Ghaybi* and its three supplementary treatises: *Rafiq va Vazir* ("The Friend and the Minister"), a fictional dialogue between a reformist and a conservative minister; *Tanzim-i Lashkar va Majlis-i Idara* ("Army Reform and the Administrative Council"); and *Daftar-i Qanun* ("A Manual of Law") appear in Malkum Khan, *Majmu'a-yi Athar*, 1–52, 53–71, 98–117, 118–166, respectively. They all were produced between 1858 and 1861 and unless proven otherwise their authorship by Malkum should not be doubted, except perhaps for *Tanzim-i Lashkar* (see below). For a discussion of these works see Adamiyat, *Tarraqi*, 29–33; Algar, *Malkum*, 25–36; Bakhash, *Monarchy*, 4–12; *Majmu'a* (introduction by Muhit Tabataba'i); and F. Naura'i, *Tahqiq*, 58–71. Algar's *Malkum* does little justice to Malkum's influence on the Qajar polity and its critical assessment of the realities of his time.

11. Malkum, *Majmu'a*, 4–7, 14–18, 24, 26.

12. Blonnet to Walewski, Tehran, September 1861, cited in J. Qa'im Maqami, "Chand Sanad Marbut bi Tarikh-i Faramush-khana dar Iran," *Yaghma* 16, no. 9 (1342/1963): 404–405. For a discussion of Faramush-khana and its membership, see also Adamiyat, *Taraqqi*, 63–75; Algar, *Malkum*, 34–55; and M. Katira'i's partisan but still useful *Framasunari dar Iran* (Tehran, 1347/1968), 60–82, 159–193.

13. FO 60/258, Alison to Russell, no. 120, Tehran, 1 November 1861; Husayn Khan Mushir al-Dawla to Mirza Sa'id Khan Mu'taman al-Mulk, Istanbul, 1279 Q./1862, in F. Adamiyat, *Fikr-i Azadi va Muqaddima-yi Nahzat-i Mashrutiyat* (Tehran, 1340/1961), 96; SML. IV, folder 17, no. 25. Mirza Sa'id Khan to Husayn Khan Mushir al-Dawla, Tehran, 1 Jumada al-Thani 1279 Q./December 1862.

14. Ibrahim Badayi'-nigar, *'Ibrat al-Nazirin wa 'Ibrat al-Hadirin*, in Sasani, *Siyasatgaran*, I, 146–147.

15. Joseph A. Comte de Gobineau, *Religions et philosophies dans l'Asie Centrale*, 2d ed. (Paris, 1957), 273.

16. Malkum, *Majmu'a*, 115; cf. Adamiyat, *Tarraqi*, 60n. See also *AFAD* (III, 330–350), which identifies Malkum's *Tanzim-i Lashkar* as that of Farrukh Khan Amin al-Dawla: "This booklet was written by His Excellency Farrukh Khan Amin al-Dawla at the behest of His Majesty, who requested information about the restructuring of the army and the council of reforms."

17. FO 60/239, Alison to Russell, no. 107, camp near Tehran, 17 September 1859. Though the accused Babi was not identified, the reference to Nuri's "relatives" in Baghdad raises an intriguing question. The two Babi brothers Mirza Husayn 'Ali Nuri, with the title Baha' [later Baha'ullah], and Mirza Musa [later entitled Kalim], were distant relatives of Nuri through marriage. They may have received, like many other Persian exiles in Iraq, a pension from the Persian government, in their case as compensation for confiscation of their properties. Yet it is difficult to believe they were behind the alleged plot. In Baghdad, Baha'ullah had become a voice of moderation and an advocate of peaceful reconstruction of the Babi network. Even the more radical tendency within the Babi movement, which later was identified with Mirza Yahya Nuri, entitled Subh Azal (Baha'ullah's younger brother), although committed to the movement's revolutionary objectives, found

it difficult to actualize an assassination attempt. The memories of the ghastly horrors that had followed their earlier attempt in 1852 were still alive. Yet the forces of dissent survived. No doubt there were many Babi radicals in Iran, and in the Babi nucleus in Baghdad, who still anticipated the occurrence of the "insurrection" (*khuruj*) to vanquish the Qajar throne and replace it with the "kingdom of the Imam of the Age," or, rather, that of the Babi messiah, "He whom God shall manifest." But whatever the origin of these rumors, the conspirators were obviously capitalizing on a vast reservoir of public discontent.

18. FO 60/238. Alison to Russell, no. 21, 1 March 1859; ibid., same to same, no. 39, Tehran, 31 March 1859; ibid., same to same, no. 49, Tehran, 25 April 1859, and ibid., same to same, no. 65, Tehran, 26 May 1859.

19. FO 60//238, Doria to Stanly, no. 51, Tehran, 27 April 1859.

20. FO 60/240, Same to same, no. 128, Tehran, 1 November 1859.

21. For Rawlinson biography see George Rawlinson, *A Memoir of Major-General Sir Henry Creswicke Rawlinson* (London, 1898) and Wright, *English,* 22–23, 56–57, 155–157. For his critique of the British policy in Iran and Afghanistan, see Rawlinson, *England and Russia.* For his deciphering of the Bisutun rock inscription and other scholarly contributions, see E. A. Wallias Budge, *The Rise and Progress of Assyriology* (London, 1925) and Seton Lloyd, *Foundations in the Dust* (London, 1947), 143–167.

22. Rawlinson, *England and Russia,* 97.

23. FO 60/247, Rawlinson to Wood, no. 2, Secret and Confidential, Tehran, 5 January 1860.

24. FO 60/247, same to same, no. 9, Secret and Confidential, Tehran, 29 February 1860; cf. "Report of the Consultative Council" (*ruznama-yi maslahat-khanih*), Iran National Archives, cited in F. Adamiyat and H. Natiq, *Afkar-i Ijtima'i va Siyasi va Iqtisadi dar Asari-i Muntashir Nashuda-yi Dawran-i Qajar* (Tehran, 1356/1977), 204–207.

25. FO 60/247. no. 9.

26. Ibid.

27. Ibid.

28. Ibid.

29. Ibid. Enclosure: "curious document," n.d., n.p..

30. FO 60/248, same to same, no. 11, Secret and Confidential, Tehran, 30 March 1860.

31. FO 60/248, same to same, no. 60, Tehran, 23 April 1860.

32. Rawlinson, *England and Russia,* 99–100.

33. FO 60/249, Pelly to Russell, no. 99, camp near Tehran, 12 June 1860.

34. FO 60/249, Pelly to Russell, Tehran, 25 May 1860. The prince in question was probably Firuz Mirza, an uncle of the shah.

35. FO 60/249, Rawlinson to Russell, no. 81, Tehran, 14 May 1860; FO 60/270. Eastwick to Russell, no. 3, Tehran, 16 December 1862. Though Ja'far Khan may have died of old age, at least two of his prominent successors, Muhammad Khan Sipahsalar and, later, Husayn Khan Mushir al-Dawla, died in the same post from suspected foul play.

36. FO 60/249, Pelly to Russell, no. 92, Tehran, 25 May 1860. The earlier

forecast appears in FO 60/247, Rawlinson to Wood, no. 4, Secret and Confidential, Tehran, 30 January 1860. Rawlinson acknowledges a similar prediction during Nuri's downfall.

37. In the ancient rite of "New Year king" (*mir-i nawruzi*) on the first day of Nawruz, the solar Persian new year festival at the occurrence of the spring equinox, a commoner was put on the throne for the duration of the day in order to avoid the evil of the cosmic chaos preceding the establishment of the new order. On 7 Dhul-Qa'da 1001 Q. (August 1592), upon the appearance of a comet, the royal astrologer advised 'Abbas I to abdicate temporarily. The shah was replaced on the throne for three days by a Nuqtavi "heretic" who immediately upon the conclusion of the conjunction was put to death. See *Tarikh-i Jalal-i Munajjim Yazdi*, cited in S. Kiya, *Nuqtaviyan ya Pisikhaniyan, Iran Kawdih*, no. 13, 1320 Yazgirdi/1951, 42–43. This account, as given in Iskandar Bayg Munshi, '*Alam Ara* (I, 473–477), must have been known to Nasir al-Din Shah. See also A. Amanat, "The Nuqtawi Movement of Mahmud Pisikhani and His Persian Cycle of Mystical-Materialism," *Essays in Mediaeval Isma'ili History and Thought*, ed. F. Daftary (Cambridge, 1996), 281–298.

38. FO 60/249, Pelly to Russell, no. 15, Secret and Confidential, camp near Goolhak, 15 June 1860.

39. FO 60/249, same to same, no. 15, Secret and Confidential, camp near Tehran, 15 June 1860.

40. Though a common title for all rulers, *sahib-qaran* was often emphasized in reference to Nasir al-Din in the literature of the period, probably with an eye toward beating numerous odds.

41. FO 60/250, Pelly to Russell, no. 19, Secret and Confidential, camp near Tehran, 16 July 1860. The impact of the 1852 assassination attempt was permanent. On later occasions the shah's lifelong fears caused the death of other innocent victims. In 1871 the young Babi emissary Mirza Buzurg Nishaburi (with the epithet Badi') was also put to death after being spotted by the shah on a hilltop in the vicinity of the Niyavaran palace waving a scroll containing Baha'ullah's letter to the shah (known as the Tablet of the Sultan of Iran). In 1896, when he was assured of the fortuitous conjunction for the celebration of his jubilee, the shah had a fatal encounter with an assassin hiding a revolver underneath a petition scroll.

42. For Alison's biography see Wright, *English*, 23–28, and cited sources.

43. FO 60/249, Rawlinson to Wood, Separate, Qazvin, 23 May 1860, enclosure: Translation of a Memorandum drawn up by HM the Shah of Persia with Remarks by Sir Henry Rawlinson.

44. FO 60/238, same to same, no. 59, 30 April 1859.

45. Brugsch, *Reise*; Persian trans., II, 601–602.

46. E. B. Eastwick, *Journal of a Diplomat's Three Years' Residence in Persia*, 2 vols. (London, 1864), I, 288–20. Alison (FO 60/256, Alison to Russell, no. 27, Tehran, 3 March 1861) gives a summary version playing down the severity of the riots. See also Brugsch, *Reise*; Persian trans., II, 602–605.

47. Brugsch, *Reise*; Persian trans. II, 605.

48. Brugsch, *Reise*; Persian trans. II, 605–69. See also Farhad Mirza's unpublished notes cited in Adamiyat, *Tarraqi*, 79.

49. FO 60/256, Alison to Russell, no. 27, Tehran, 3 March 1861. For the events leading to the Tehran riot see Migeod, "Die Luti" 82–91.

50. FO 60/256, same to same, no. 37, 3 April 1861. Alison "merely informed" Amin al-Dawla of what had occurred.

51. Brugsch, *Reise;* Persian trans., I, 184 and II, 605; cf. FO 60/258, same to same, Separate, Tehran, 11 November 1861 (list of 32 items prepared by Edward Eastwick).

52. FO 60/251, same to same, no. 66, Tehran, 4 December 1860; FO 60/283, same to same, no. 62, camp near Tehran, 26 July 1864; FO 60/290, same to same, no. 78, Ghulhak, 24 July 1865.

53. Brugsch, *Reise;* Persian trans., I, 183–184.

54. FO 60/257, Alison to Russell, no. 81, Camp near Baladeh, 3 August 1861.

55. Blonnet to Walewski, October 1861, cited in J. Qa'im-maqami, "Chand Sanad," 404–405.

56. Gobineau, *Religions,* 274.

57. FO 60/258, Alison to Russell, no. 120, Tehran, 1 November 1861. Though it is unlikely that the house in question was that of Sulayman Khan Tabrizi in Sarchishma quarter, which served as the Babi headquarters in 1852, it is possible that some Babis had entered the Faramush-khanih.

58. *Ruznama-yi Dawlat-i 'Alliya-yi Iran* no. 501, 12 Rabi' al-Thani 1278 Q./18 October 1861. FO 60/258 (no. 120) translates it as, "If any person should so much as mention the word 'freemason,' he will be punished."

59. Malkum, *Majmu'a* (suppl. to page *lam ji,m*) quoting a treatise entitled *Madaniyat* by Mirza Muhammad Khan Nazim Daftar, one of Malkum's followers.

60. I. Ra'in, *Faramushkhana va Farmasunari dar Iran,* 3 vols., (Tehran, 1357/1978), I, 508 and Algar, *Malkum,* 53.

61. Blunt, *Secret History,* 84.

62. For the constitutions and proceedings of the Consultative Council see Adamiyat and Natiq, *Afkar,* 190–215.

63. Malkum, "Daftar-i Qanun," *Majmu'a,* 149–150, and Adamiyat and Natiq, *Afkar,* 215–220.

64. Malkum, "Daftar-i Qanun," *Majmu'a,* 123.

65. FO 60/267, same to same, no. 68, Secret, Tehran, 28 May 1862.

66. Ibid. Enclosure: "Anonymous Letter delivered to the Shah on the 18th of May 1862," translated by E. Eastwick. No trace of the original Persian has yet been found. Correspondence of the Iranian Archive (*Asnad-i Iran*) cited in Adamiyat and Natiq, *Afkar* (171–180), only makes it clear that pamphlets were distributed.

67. A master builder of some taste, Dust 'Ali later built Bagh Firdaws in the vicinity of Tajrish for himself and Shams al-'Imara in the Gulistan complex for Nasir al-Din. He was also the builder of the famous Takiyya Dawlat, the enormous amphitheater adjacent to the Arg in an innovative style to house the passion plays of the Muharram. For Dust 'Ali Khan see Mu'ayyir al-Mamalik, *Rijal,* 33–48, 143–150; I'timad al-Saltana, *Ma'athir,* 17; Afshar, *Chihil Sal,* I, 96–97 and II, 477.

68. For his account see I'timad al-Saltana, *Ma'athir,* 38.

69. Eastwick must have rendered "Prophet," somewhat inaccurately, in place

of the [Hidden] Imam, the most plausible figure the writer could have mentioned. For the 'ulama's dealings with foreign envoys see, for example, Amanat, "Pishvay-i Ummat" 11–41.

70. Failing to appreciate the subtlety of the address to the shah, Eastwick translated what probably in original Persian was *"ay shah-i kamran"* as "Kamran Shah." The rest of the passage is rendered in archaic English, which may indicate the admonishing tone of the original.

71. FO 60/266, same to same, no. 61, Tehran, 9 May 1962. To prove his sincerity and worth, Ya'qub had already provided Alison with sensitive documents, including a copy of the 1855 Perso-Russian secret treaty. He seems to have remained in the Russian service, however. Soon afterward he was in the Central Asian khanates on a mission reporting on the political situation to St. Petersburg.

72. Ya'qub Khan to Nasir al-Din Shah, Iran National Archive, cited in Adamiyat and Natiq, *Afkar*, 172–178. Ya'qub quoted the first hemistich of a verse passage by Sa'di's *Bustan* with a haunting moral: "Thou who art wise, fear him who fears you/Even if you can conquer hundreds like him. See when the cat is desperate/It claws at a tiger's eye. The snake will bite the shepherd/For it fears its brain to be blown apart by his stone."

73. FO 60/267. Same to same, no. 89, camp near Tehran, 24 June 1862 and enclosure: "Translation of an article in the Tehran Gazette of the 29th May 1862."

74. FO 60/283, Alison to Russell, no. 55, Tehran, 16 July 1864 and enclosure: "Translation of an official proclamation to all classes in Persia, 9 July 1864." For the Petition box, see M. Ettehadieh Nezam-Mafi, "The Council for Investigation of Grievamas: A Case Study of Nineteenth Century Iranian Social History," *Iranian Studies* 22 (1989), 51–62.

75. *DDG*, 254, Gobineau to Thouvenel, no. 64, Tehran, 5 July 1863.

76. FO 60/258, Alison to Russell, no. 95, Secret, Gulhak, 13 October 1864.

77. FO 60/289, same to same, no. 29, Tehran, 14 March 1865; ibid., no. 28, same to same, no. 39, Tehran, 28 March 1865. The suspicious circumstances of Nuri's death remained unnoticed by later historians, among others by Qa'im Maqami ("Payan-i Kar"). As on similar occasions, Persian contemporary sources are completely silent on the ex-premier's fate.

78. FO 60/289, no. 29.

79. FO 60/289, same to same, no. 38, Tehran, 25 March 1865, enclosure no. 2.

80. FO 60/289, no. 39.

81. FO 60/296, Alison to the Earl of Clarendon, no. 35, Tehran 13 March 1866 and ibid., same to same, no. 49, Tehran, 5 May 1866.

82. FO 60/297, same to same, no. 82, Gulhak, 28 June 1866, and enclosure no. 2: "Regulations laid down by the Shah for the guidance of His Ministers on the 2nd Safar 1283 [Q.], 16 June 1866."

83. FO 60/305, Alison to Stanly, no. 57, Gulhak, 1 July 1867. Alison's report was based on the report of Thomson, who accompanied the shah on the Khurasan tour.

84. FO 60/247, no. 4.

85. FO 60/247, Rawlinson to Russell, no. 30, Tehran, 20 February 1860.

86. Ibid.

87. FO 60/247, no. 30.

88. FO 60/256, Alison to Russell, no. 47, Tehran, 3 May 1861; FO 60/267, same to same, Tehran, 23 May 1862, and enclosure: "Translation of Mirza Sa'id Khan to Mr Alison, 21 May 1862 Announcing Nomination." Appointment to the governorship was apparently made on 1 May 1861. Thirty-five years later, on 1 May 1896, Nasir al-Din was assassinated.

89. For the Malijaks see, among other accounts, *EIr:* "'Aziz al-Soltan" (A. Amanat).

90. FO 60/320. Thomson to Clarendon, no. 58, 22 September 1869.

EPILOGUE

1. Aspects of the political history of the late Nasir al-Din Shah period have been studied in P. Avery, *Modern Iran* (London, 1965); S. Bakhash, *Bureaucracy and Reform; Cambridge History of Iran*, VII, 174–198 (N. R. Keddie and M. Amanat); A. R. Sheikholeslami, "The Central Structure of Authority in Iran, 1871–1896," Ph.D. Dissertation, University of California, Los Angeles, 1975; H. G. Migeod, *Die persische Gesellschaft unter Nasiru'd-Din Sah (1848–1896)* (Berlin, 1990); and G. Nashat, *The Origins of Modern Reform in Iran, 1870–1880* (Urbana, 1982). For personal perspectives of the history of the period see, among others, M. Q. Hidayat, *Khatirat va Khatarat* (Tehran, 1344/1965); Mustawfi, *Sharh-i Zindagani*, I. See also *EI2:* "Nasir al-Din Shah" (A. Amanat) and cited sources.

2. For epidemics and famine see H. Natiq, "Ta'thir-i Ijtima'i va Iqtisadi-yi Bimari-yi Vaba dar Dawra-yi Qajar," *Musibat-i Vaba va Bala-yi Hukumat* (Tehran, 1358/1979), 9–46; S. Okazaki, "The Great Famine of 1870–1871," *Bulletin of the School of Oriental and African Studies* 49 (1986), 183–192.

3. For Shaykh 'Ubaydullah's revolt in the Persian chronicles, see I'timad al-Saltana, *Muntazam*, I, 476–478; and *M'athir*, I, 79–80. For studies of Shaykh 'Ubaydullah's movement, see R. Olson, *The Emergence of Kurdish Nationalism, 1880–1925*, Austin, 1989, 1–25. See also *EIr:* "Amir Nizam Garrusi" (A. Amanat).

4. On the treatment of tribes in the late Nasiri period see *Cambridge History of Iran*, VII, 506–541 (R. Tapper); G. R. Garthwaite, *Khans and Shahs: A Documentary Analysis of Bakhtiyari in Iran* (Cambridge, 1983); B. Spooner, "Who Are the Baluch?" *Qajar Iran*, 93–110. See also L. Beck, *The Qashqa'is of Iran* (New Haven, 1986); *EI2:* "Ilat" (A.K.S. Lambton); and P. Oberling, *The Qashqa'i Nomads of Fars* (Paris/The Hague, 1974).

5. *Farzin* is the original Persian term for the chess piece that came to be known in the West as the queen.

6. For the Mushir al-Dawla period, see F. Adamiyat, *Taraqqi*; idem., *Fikr-i Azadi*; Bakhash, *Monarchy, Bureaucracy*; 77–304; M. Farhad-Mu'tamad, *Tarikh-i Ravabit-i Iran va 'Usmani* (Tehran, n.d.); A. Karny, "The Premiership of Mirza Hosein Khan and His Reforms in Iran, 1872–1873," *Asian and African Studies* 10 (1974–1975), 127–156; Nashat, *Origins of Modern Reform*. See also *Hukumat-i Sayaha: Asnad-i Mahramana va Siyasi-yi Mirza Husayn Khan Sipahsalar*, ed. M. R. 'Abbasi (Tehran, 1372/1993).

7. On later Babi-Baha'i developments, see H. Balyuzi, *Baha'u'llah, the King of Glory* (Oxford, 1980); A. Bausani, *Persia Religiosa* (Milan, 1959); M. Bayat, *Iran's First Revolution: Shi'ism and the Constitutional Revolution* (New York,

1991); idem, *Mysticism and Dissent: Socioreligious Thought in Qajar Iran* (Syracuse, 1982); *EIr:* "Baha'-Allah" (J. Cole), " 'Abd-al-Baha" (D. MacEoin) and cited sources; Momen, *Babi and Baha'i Religions.* See also Amanat, *Resurrection and Renewal,* 405–416; J. Cole, "Iranian Millenarianism and Democratic Thought in the 19th Century," *International Journal of Middle East Studies,* 24 (1992), 1–26; P. Smith, *The Babi and Baha'i Religions: From Messianism to a World Religion* (Cambridge and New York, 1987).

8. Studies on the Regie concession and its repeal include F. Adamiyat, *Shurish bar Imtiyaznama-yi Rizhi* (Tehran, 1360/1981); F. Kazemzadeh, *Russia and Britain in Persia, 1864–1914: A Study in Imperialism* (New Haven, 1968), 241–301; N. R. Keddie, *Religion and Rebellion in Iran: The Tobacco Protest of 1891–92* (London, 1966); Lambton, "The Tobacco Regie: A Prelude to Revolution," in *Qajar Persia,* 223–276.

9. On the 'ulama in the late Qajar period, see Algar, *Religion and State,* 169–239; J. Cole, "Imami Jurisprudence and the Role of the Ulama: Mortaza Ansari on Emulating the Supreme Exemplar," *Religion and Politics in Iran,* ed. N. R. Keddie (New Haven, 1983), 33–46; and D. MacEoin, "Changes in Charismatic Authority in Qajar Shi'ism," *Qajar Iran,* 148–176. See also Amanat, "In between the *Madrasa* and the Marketplace," 98–132. On Afghani see E. G. Browne, *The Persian Revolution of 1905–1909* (Cambridge, 1910), 1–58; and N. R. Keddie, *Sayyid Jamal ad-Din "al-Afghani": A Political Biography* (Berkeley and Los Angeles, 1972).

10. On modern education in the late Nasiri period, see *EIr:* "Dar al-fonun" (J. Gurney and N. Nabavi); M. Mahbubi Ardakani, *Tarikh-i Mu'assasat-i Tamadduni-yi Jadid dar Iran,* 2 vols. (Tehran, 1357/1978). On the judiciary, in addition to the works cited on Mushir al-Dawla, see W. Floor, "Change and Development in the Judicial System of Qajar Iran (1800–1925)," *Qajar Iran,* 113–147.

11. For overviews of late-nineteenth-century relations between Iran and the European powers, see *Cambridge History of Iran,* VII, 374–425 (R. L. Greaves); Curzon, *Persia and the Persian Question,* I, 1–25, II, 585–634; R. L. Greaves, *Persia and the Defence of India, 1884–1892* (London, 1959); Kazemzadeh, *Russia and Britain.* See also 'A. Hushang-Mahdavi, *Tarikh-i Ravabit-i Khariji-yi Iran* (Tehran, 1349/1970); B. Martin, *German-Persian Diplomatic Relations, 1873–1912* ('s-Gravenhage, 1959); R. K. Ramazani, *Foreign Policy of Iran, 1500–1941* (Charlottesville, 1966).

12. SML, IV, no. 38, Mirza Sa'id Khan to Mirza Husayn Khan (shah's note on the margin), Tehran, Safar 1276 Q./September 1859; ibid., IV, no. 37, same to same, Tehran, 12 Rajab 1276 Q./25 January 1860.

13. Curzon, *Persia,* II, 394–396.

14. SML, VI, no. 38, Nasir al-Din Shah to Iran Minister for Foreign Affairs, 1279 Q./1862; ibid., VI, no. 44, same to same [to be conveyed to Mirza Husayn Khan, then residing in London], 1279 Q./1862.

15. On the demarcation of the eastern boundaries of Iran in the late nineteenth century, see *Eastern Persia, An Account of the Journeys of the Persian Boundary Commission, 1870–1–2,* ed. F. J. Goldsmid, 2 vols. (London, 1876); Kazemzadeh, *Russia and Britain,* 386–447.

16. On the Imperial Bank see Issawi, *Economic History*, 346–355; G. Jones, *Banking and Empire in Iran: The History of the British Bank of the Middle East,* vol. I (Cambridge, 1986); Kazemzadeh, *Russia and Britain,* 268–276; I. Taymuri, *'Asr-i Bikhabari ya Tarikh-i Imtiyazat dar Iran* (Tehran, 1332/1953), 178–212.

17. On coin depreciation see Amin al-Dawla, *Khatirat-i Siyasi,* 58–59, 69–71, 135–139, 182–184, 195–201; Mustawfi, *Zindagani-yi Man,* 395–402; EIr: "Amin al-Zarb" (A. Enayat); J. Rabino, "Banking in Persia," in Issawi, *Economic History,* 348–356.

18. On Reuter and other concessions see L. E. Frechtling, "The Reuter Concession in Persia," in Issawi, *Economic History,* 177–184; Kazemzadeh, *Russia and Britain,* 100–147; Taymuri, *'Asr-i Bikhabari,* esp. 97–150.

19. For Nasir al-Din's first European tour see his *Ruznama-yi Safar-i Farangistan* (Tehran, 1291 Q./1874); J. W. Redhouse, trans., *The Diary of H.M. the Shah of Persia* (London, 1874). For the second tour see idem, *Ruznama-yi Safar-i Duvvum-i Farangistan* (Bombay, 1295 Q./1878), 2d ed. (Tehran, 1296 Q./1879), reprint ed. I. Afshar (Tehran 1363/ 1984); A. Houtum-Schindler and L. de Norman, trans., *A Diary Kept by His Majesty the Shah of Persia, during His Journey to Europe in 1878* (London, 1879). For the third tour see idem, *Ruznama-yi Safar-i Sivvum-i Farangistan (The Third Tour of the Shah of Persia in Europe)* (Bombay, n.d. [1891]). For a private version of the journals he kept during the third tour, see idem. *Khatirat-i Nasir al-Din Shah dar Safar-i Sivvum-i Farangistan,* ed. I Rizvani, 3 vols. (Tehran 1369–1371/1990–1993). For a summary of the European reception of Nasir al-Din see D. Wright, *The Persians Amongst the English* (London, 1985), 121–140.

20. On aborted railway projects see Issawi, *Economic History,* 184–194; Kazemzadeh, *Russia and Britain,* 100–240.

21. The shah's interest in geography and topography is well evident in his own travel accounts. For an account of his domestic travels see Nasir al-Din Shah, *Ruznama-yi Safar-i Gilan,* ed. M. Sutudah, Tehran 1367/1988; idem, *Ruznama-yi Safar-i Mazandaran,* Tehran 1294 Q./1877, reprint, Tehran, 1356/1977; *Safarnama-yi 'Iraq-i 'Ajam;* idem, *Safarnama-yi Khurasan* (second visit), Tehran 1303 Q./1885, reprint 1354/ 1975.

22. The secret journal of I'timad al-Saltana (*Ruznama-yi Khatirat*), covering the inner workings of the Persian court and government and the personality of Nasir al-Din and his courtiers and officials between 1881 and 1896, remains a valuable source for the study of late-Nasiri court and culture, the theme of a companion volume to the present one. For a discussion of I'timad al-Saltana and his journal, see I. Afshar, introduction to *Ruznama,* 2–22; Sasani, *Siyasatgaran,* I, 169–184. See also EIr: "E'temad-al-Saltana" (A. Amanat).

23. *'Aqida-yi Vultir darbara-yi Iran va Hind,* trans. Avanis Zargarbashi Masihi, Milli Library, Tehran, no. 378 f, 24 folios, dated 1301 Q./1883–1884. The shah read this compilation on the first day of his trip to Jajrud in 1302 Q./1884. He was inspired to sketch on the manuscript a black-and-white bust of Voltaire.

24. For Nasir al-Din's visit to Ottoman Iraq see his *Safarnama-yi Karbala va Najaf* (n.p. [Tehran], 1287 Q./1870), 2d ed. as *Safarnama-yi 'Atabat,* ed. I. Afshar (Tehran, 1363/1984). For a comparable Persian view of pilgrimage to foreign lands

in this period see F. Farmayan and R. A. McDaniel's excellent translation and edition of Muhammad Husayn Husayni Farahani, *A Shi'ite Pilgrimage to Mecca, (1885–1886)* (Austin, 1990) and the cited sources.

25. On *ta'ziya* and Takkiya Dawlat see J. Calmard, "Le Mecenat des Representations de Ta'ziye," *Le Monde iranien et l'Islam* 2 (1974), 73–126 and 4 (1976), 133–162; P. Chelkowski, *Ta'ziyeh: Ritual and Drama in Iran* (New York, 1979); idem, "Majlis-i Shahinshah-i Iran Nasir al-Din Shah," in Bosworth and Hillenbrand, *Qajar Iran*, 229–242.

26. For the shah's harem and private life in later years see Mu'ayyir al-Mamlik, *Yaddashtha*, and his other works; Taj al-Saltana, *Khatirat-i Taj al-Saltana*, ed. M. Ittihadiya (Nizam-Mafi) and S. Sa'dvandiyan (Tehran, 1361/1982), English translation as *Crowning Anguish: The Memoirs of a Persian Princess from the Harem to Modernity, 1884–1914*, ed. A. Amanat, trans. A. Vanzan and A. Neshati (Washington, D.C., 1993). See also *EIr:* "Anis al-Dawla" and "Amin Aqdas" (G. Nashat). For the Nasiri court see *EIr:* "Court, iv. Qajar Period" (A. Amanat).

27. On Amin al-Sultan see *EIr,* "Amin-al-Soltan, Mirza 'Ali Asgar" (J. Calmard) and cited sources; see also Amin al-Dawla, *Khatirat*, 119–219.

28. On Malijak see I'timad al-Saltana, *Ruznama* (index); *EIr:* "'Aziz-al-Soltan" and cited sources; Amin al-Dawla, *Khatirat*, 86–88, 111–112, 123–125; B. Afrasiyabi, ed. *Shah-i Dhul-Qarnayn va Khatirat-i Malijak*, (Tehran, 1368/1987); Taj al-Saltana, *Crowning Anguish* (index).

29. There is an extensive literature on the assassination of Nasir al-Din. In addition to general sources for the period see 'Ali Khan Zahir al-Dawla, *Tarikh-i Bi Durugh* (Tehran, 1362/1983); Browne, *Persian Revolution*, 59–98; Taj al-Saltana, *Crowning Anguish*, 214–220.

30. Browne, *Persian Revolution*, 65, 83.

31. For the social and intellectual development in the post–Nasir al-Din Shah period and the prelude to the Constitutional Revolution see among others E. Abrahamian, *Iran Between Two Revolutions* (Princeton, 1982); and *EIr:* "Constitutional Revolution, i. Intellectual Background" (A. Amanat) and cited sources.

32. Browne, *Persian Revolution*, 91.

Bibliography

UNPUBLISHED PERSIAN SOURCES

Anonymous. *Tarikh-i Napil'un.* Gulistan Library, MS no. 187/1976, 90 illus., 1260 Q./1844.

Burin [Bourrienne, Louis A. F. de,]. *Tarikh-i Napilun.* Trans. Muhammad Riza Muhandis[-bashi] Tabrizi. Gulistan Library, MS no. 185/732, 1252 Q./1836.

Burjis, Idvard. [Burgess, Edward]. *Jughrafiya-yi 'Alam.* Milli Library, MS no. 540, 1267 Q./1851.

Dabir al-Mulk, Mirza Muhammad Husayn Farahani, trans. [from Turkish trans. by Musa Jan Davud Khan of French original]. *Jahan Nama.* Majlis Library, MS no. 287, 1272 Q./1860.

Damavandi, Mirza Nasrullah. *Al-Tuhfat al-Nasiriya fi Ma'rafat al-Ilahiya.* Tehran University Central Library, MS no. 2653, 37 folio, 1264 Q./ 1848.

Flughun, Rafa'il. *Jahan Nama.* Milli Library, MS no. 336F, 1266 Q./1849–1850.

Ghani, Qasim. Collection of Qajar Documents. Manuscripts and Archives, Sterling Memorial Library [Abbreviated as SML], Yale University. Series 1–9.

Hizar u Yak Shab (Persian trans. of *The One Thousand and One Nights*). Trans. 'Abd al-Latif Tasuji and Shams al-Shu'ar Surush Isfahani, illustr. Abul-Hasan Ghaffari Kashani, Sani' al-Mulk. 6 vols., completed 1276 Q./ 1859. Gulistan Library, MSS nos. 2240–2244 and 679.

Khavari, Fazullah. *Tarikh-i Dhul-Qarnayan.* Milli Libary, MS no. 1771F, 1262Q./ 1846.

Khurumi, Hisam al-Din. Collection of Qajar Correspondence and Documents. Tehran.

Lavasani, Mirza Muhammad. *Mir'at al-Ard.* Majlis Library, MS no. 702.

Mahmud Mirza Qajar. *Akhbar-i Muhammadi.* Milli Library, MS no. 578F.

Manuscript Collection of Persian Autographs and Other Documents. British Library, Or. 4936.

Manuscript Copies of Sixty Treaties and Other Persian Documents. British Library, Or. 4679.

Marvazi, Muhammad Ja'far. *Tuhfa-yi Nasiri.* Milli Library, MS no. 913F, 1254 Q./ 1838.

Marvazi, Muhammad Sadiq [Vaqayi' Nigar]. *'Ahdnama-yi Malik-i Ashtar.* Milli Library, MS no. 151F.

———. *Tarikh-i Jahan Ara.* Gulistan Library, MS no. 140, dated 1233 Q./ 1817.

Nasir al-Din Shah Qajar. Correspondence of the Imperial Majesty Nasir al-Din Shah of Persia from 1848 to 1896 (original and translation). British Library, BL Or. 11665 and Or. 11665*.

Qajar Portraits and Drawings. British Library, Or. 4938.
Riza Quli Mirza [and Najaf Quli Mirza]. *Rumuz al-Siyaha*. Milli Library, MS no. 96f, 1256 Q./1840.
Shahkhasti Mazandarani [Nadir], Mirza Asadullah. *Khasa'il al-Muluk*. Tehran University Central Library, MS no. 4972, 1256 Q./1840.

UNPUBLISHED EUROPEAN SOURCES

Great Britain, The Public Record Office, Foreign Office, General Correspondence: FO 60 Series, vols. 36, 37, 38, 39 (1835); 56 (1838); 66, 69 (1839); 86, 90 (1842); 114, 115, 116 (1845); 121 (1846); 132 (1847); 136, 138, 140 (1848); 144, 146 (1849); 163, 164 (1851); 169, 170, 171, 172, 173 (1852); 178, 179, 181, 182 (1853); 198 (1854); 202, 203, 204 (1855); 208, 209, 210, 212 (1856); 214, 217, 218, 219, 220 (1857); 229, 230, 231, 232, 233 (1858); 238, 239, 240, (1859); 247, 248, 249, 250, 251 (1860); 256, 257, 258 (1861); 266, 267, 270 (1862); 283 (1864); 289, 290 (1865); 296, 297 (1866); 305 (1867); 320 (1869).
FO 248 Series, vol. 147 (1852).
United States, House of Representatives, 47th Congress, 1st session. Report no. 1648, [to accompany bill H.R. 6743], Commercial Relations with Persia.

PUBLISHED WORKS IN PERSIAN AND ARABIC

'Abbas Mirza Mulk Ara. *Sharh-i Hal-i 'Abbas Mirza Mulkara*. Ed. 'A. Nava'i and 'A. Iqbal. 2d ed. Tehran, 1355/1976.
'Abbasi, M. R., ed. *Hukumat-i Sayaha: Asnad-i Mahramana va Siyasi-yi Mirza Husayn Khan Sipahsalar*. Tehran, 1372/1993.
Adamiyat, F. *Amir Kabir va Iran*. 3d ed. Tehran, 1348/1969.
———. *Andishah-yi Taraqqi va Hukumat-i Qanun, 'Asr-i Sipahsalar*. Tehran, 1351/1972.
———. *Fikr-i Azadi va Muqaddima-yi Nahzat-i Mashrutiyat-i Iran*. Tehran, 1340/1961.
———. *Maqalat-i Tarikhi*. 2d ed. Tehran, 1362/1983.
———. *Shurish bar Imtiyaznama-yi Rizhi*. Tehran, 1360/1981.
Adamiyat, F., and H. Natiq. *Afkar-i Ijtima'i va Siyasi va Iqtisadi dar Asari-i Muntashir Nashuda-yi Dawran-i Qajar*. Tehran, 1356/1977.
Afrasiyabi, B., ed. *Shah-i Dhul-Qarnayn va Khatirat-i Malijak*. Tehran, 1368/1987.
Afshar, I. *Ganjina-yi 'Aksha-yi Iran*. Tehran, 1992.
Afshar, I. [and H. Mahbubi Ardakani], ed. *Chihil Sal Tarikh-i Iran dar Dawra-yi Padishahi-yi Nasir al-Din Shah* (critical edition of Muhammad Hasan Khan I'timad al-Saltana, *Al-Ma'athir wa'l-Athar*). 2d. ed., 3 vols. Tehran, 1363–1368/1984–1989.
Afshar, Mirza Mustafa [Baha' al-Mulk]. "Ahvalat-i Safar-i Mirza Mas'ud," *Nashriya-i Vizarat-i Umur-i Kharija* III, no. 3, (Shahrivar 1345/1966), 180–322.
———. *Safarnama-yi Khusraw Mirza bi Pitirzburgh*. Ed. M. Gulbun. Tehran, 1349/1970.

Al Davud, 'Ali, ed. *Namaha-yi Amir Kabir bi Inzimam-i Risala-yi Navadir al-Amir.* Tehran, 1371/1993.

Amanat, A. "'Bar Taq-i Ivan-i Faridun': Dawlat va Ra'iyat dar Dida-yi Sa'di." *Iranshinasi* III (1370/1991), no. 1, 170–172.

———. "'Pishva-yi Ummat' va Vazir-i Mukhtar-i 'Bi-Tadlis-i' Ingilis: Murasala-yi Hajj Sayyid Muhammad Baqir Shafti, Hujjat al-Islam, va Sir Jan Maknil [Sir John McNeill] dar Qaziya-yi Lashkarkashi-i Muhammad Shah bi Harat." *Iranshinasi* II (1369/1991), no. 1, 11–41.

Amin al-Dawla, Farrukh Khan. See Isfahaniyan, K.

Amin al-Dawla, Mirza 'Ali Khan. *Khatirat-i Siyasi-yi Mirza 'Ali Khan Amin al-Dawla.* Ed. H. Farmanfarma'yan [Farmayan]. Tehran, 1341/1962.

Anonymous. "Naqqashiha-yi Nasir al-Din Shah." *Nashriya-yi Vizarat-i Umur-i Kharija* 3 (1345/ 1966), 49–64.

———. *Tehran-i Qadim.* Tehran, 1372/ 1993.

Anvari, 'A. *Fihrist-i Nusakh-i Khatti-yi Kitabkhana-yi Milli.* II, Tehran, 1347/ 1968.

Aryanpur, Y. *Az Saba ta Nima.* 2 vols. Tehran, 1354/1975.

Atabay, B. *Fihrist-i Albumha-yi Kitabkhana-yi Saltanati.* Tehran, 1357/1978.

———. *Fihrist-i Divanha-yi Khatti va Kitab-i Hizar u Yak Shab-i Kitabkhana-yi Saltanati.* 2 vols. Tehran, 1355/ 1976.

———. *Fihrist-i Tarikh, Safarnama, Siyahatnama, Ruznama va Jughrafiya-yi Khatti-yi Kitabkhana-yi Saltanati.* Tehran, 1356/1977.

'Azud al-Dawla, Sultan Ahmad Mirza. *Tarikh-i 'Azudi.* Ed. 'A. Nava'i. Tehran, 1355/1976.

Bahar, M. T. [Malik al-Shu'ara]. *Sabk-Shinasi.* 3 vols. Tehran, 1337/1958.

Bamdad, M. *Sharh-i Hal-i Rijal-i Iran dar Qarn-i 12, 13, 14 Hijri.* 6 vols. Tehran, 1347–1355/1968–1974.

Browne, E. G., ed. *Nuqtatu'l-Kaf [Nuqtat al-Kaf] Compiled by Hajji Mirza Jani of Kashah.* London and Leiden, 1910.

Burugsh, H. [H. C. Brugsch]. *Safari bi Darbar-i Sultan-i Sahibqaran.* Trans. M. Kurdbachih. 2 vols. Tehran, 1367/1988.

Danishpazuh, M. T. *Fihrist-i Kitabkhana-yi Danishgah-i Tehran.* Tehran, 1345/ 1966.

Divan-Bagi Shriazi, Sayyid Ahmad. *Hadiqat al-Shu'ara.* 'A. Nava'i ed. 3 vols. Tehran, 1364–66/1985–87.

Dunbuli, 'Abd al-Razzaq [Maftun]. *Ma'thir-i Sultaniya.* Tabriz, 1241 Q./1825. 2d ed. Tehran, 1351/1972. (For English trans., see H. Jones Brydges).

Farhad Mirza Qajar [Mu'tamad al-Dawla]. *Munsha'at.* Ed. Fursat al-Dawla Shirazi. Bombay, 1318/1900.

———. *Zanbil.* Tehran, 1318/1901.

Farhad-Mu'tamad, M. *Tarikh-i Ravabit-i Iran va 'Usmani.* Tehran, n.d..

Fasa'i, H. *Farsnama-yi Nasiri.* 2 vols. in one. Tehran, 1312–1313 Q./1894–1895. (For English trans., see H. Busse).

Fath 'Ali Shah Qajar. *Tahqiq dar Bara-yi Zindigi, Ahval, Amal, Afkar va Divan-i Kamil-i Ash'ar-i Fath 'Ali Shah Qajar (Khaqan).* Ed. H. Gul Muhammadi. Tehran, 1370/1992.

Fayz al-Islam, 'Ali Naqi., trans. *Nahj al-Balagha.* Ed. A. M. Razi. Tehran, 1326/1947.

Flughun, Rafa'il. *Jughrafiya-yi Jahan Nama.* Tabriz, 1267 Q./1850.

Ghani, Q. *Yaddashtha-yi Duktur Qasim Ghani.* 12 vols., London, 1980–1984.

Gharavi, M., ed. *Majara-yi Dawlat-i Inglis va Mirza Hashim Khan.* Tehran, 1363/1984.

Gilanshah, G. *Yaksad va Panjah Sal Saltanat dar Iran.* Tehran, 1340/1961.

Hashimi Rafsanjani, A. *Amir Kabir ya Qahraman-i Mubariza ba Isti'mar.* 2d ed. Tehran, 1362/1983.

Hidayat, Mahdi Quli [Mukhbir al-Saltana]. *Guzarish-i Iran.* Vol. III. Tehran, 1333/1914.

———. *Khatirat va Khatarat.* Tehran, 1344/1965.

Hidayat, Riza Quli Khan [Lala-bashi]. *Majma' al-Fusaha.* Ed. M. Musaffa. 6 vols. Tehran, 1336–1340/1957–1961.

———. *Rawdat al-Safa-yi Nasiri.* 3d ed. Vols. IX–X. Tehran, 1338–1339/1959–1960.

Hushang-Mahdavi, 'A. *Tarikh-i Ravabit-i Khariji-yi Iran.* Tehran, 1349/1970.

Iqbal, 'A. "Madam Hajji 'Abbas Gulsaz." *Yadgar* III, no. 6–7 (February–March 1947), 106–109.

———. *Mirza Taqi Khan Amir Kabir.* Ed. I. Afshar. Tehran, 1340/1961.

Iran, Government of. *Ruznama-yi Dawlat-i 'Alliya-yi Iran.* Nos. 472–650, repr. J. Kiyanfar, 2 vols. Tehran, 1370–1372/1991–1993.

———. *Ruznama-yi Vaqayi'-i Ittifaqiya.* Nos. 1– 473. 1267–1277 Q./1851–1860.

———. *Sharaf va Sharafat, Dawra-yi Ruznamaha-yi.* 2d ed. Tehran, 1363/1984.

Isfahaniyan, K., and Q. Rushani (Za'faranlu), eds. *Majmu'a-yi Asnad va Madarik-i Farrukh Khan Amin al-Dawla.* 5 vols. Tehran, 1346–1357/1967–1978.

I'timad al-Saltana, Muhammad Hasan Khan [Sani' al-Dawla]. *Al-Ma'athir wa'l-Athar.* Tehran, 1306 Q./1888.

———. *Durrar al-Tijan fi Tarikh Bani Ashkan.* Tehran, 1308–1311 Q./1890–93.

———. *Khalsa Mashhur bi Khwabnama.* Ed. M. Katira'i. Tehran, 1348/1969.

———. *Mir'at al-Buldan-i Nasiri.* 4 vols. Tehran, 1294–1297 Q./1877–1880.

———. *Ruznama-yi Khatirat-i I'timad al-Saltana.* Ed. I. Afshar. Tehran, 1345/1976.

———. *Ruznama-yi Mir'at al-Safar va Mishkwat al-Hazar.* Repr. I. Afshar and 'A. Faradi. Tehran, 1363/1984.

———. *Sadr al-Tawarikh.* Ed. M. Mushiri. Tehran, 1349/1970.

———. *Tarikh-i Muntazam-i Nasiri.* 2d ed. Ed. M. I. Rizvani. 3 vols. Tehran, 1363–1367/1984–1988.

I'tizad al-Saltana, 'Ali Quli Mirza. *Al-Mutanabbi'in* (partially published and edited by 'A. Nava'i as *Fitna-yi Bab*). Tehran, 1351/1972.

Ittihadiya, M. *Gushihha-i az Ravabit-i Khariji-yi Iran, 1200–1280 Hijri-yi Qamari.* Tehran, 1355/1976.

Jabiri Ansari, Muhammad Hasan. *Agahi-yi Shahan az Kar-i Jahan.* 4 vols. Isfahan, 1314/1935.

Jahangir Mirza Qajar. *Tarikh-i Naw.* Ed. 'A. Iqbal. Tehran, 1327/1948.

Karimzada Tabrizi, M. 'A. *Ahval va Athar-i Naqqashan-i Qadim-i Iran va Barkhi az Mashahir-i Nigargar-i Hind va 'Usmani.* 3 vols. London, 1985–1991.

Kashfi Darabi, Sayyid Ja'far. *Tuhfat al-Muluk fi'l-Sayr wa'l Suluk.* Tehran, 1273 Q./1856.

Katira'i, M. *Framasunari dar Iran.* Tehran, 1347/1968.

Khan-Bahadur, Muhammad. "Yak Shakhs-i Muhimm ya Mirza Taqi Khan Atabak." *Armaghan* XV (1313/1934), 208–217, 286–296, 355–360.

Khurmuji, Muhammad Ja'far. *Haqayiq al-Akhbai-i Nasiri.* Ed. H. Khadiv Jam. Tehran, 1344/1965.

Kirmani, Hajji Muhammad Karim Khan. *Majma' al-Rasa'il.* Kirman, 1386/1966.

Kiya, S. *Nuqtaviyan ya Pisikhaniyan. Iran Kawdih,* 13, 1320 Yazdgirdi/1951.

Lavi, H. *Tarikh-i Yahud-i Iran.* 3 vols. Tehran, 1339/1960.

Mahbubi Ardakani, M. *Tarikh-i Mu'assasat-i Tamadduni-yi Jadid dar Iran.* 2 vols. Tehran, 1357/1978.

Mahjub, M. J. "Tarjama-yi Farsi *Alf Laylat wa'l Layla.*" *Sukhan* 11 (1339/1960), no. 1, 34–53.

Mahmud, M. *Tarikh-i Ravabit-i Siyasi-yi Iran va Ingilis dar Qarn-i Nuzdahum-i Miladi.* 8 vols. Tehran, 1328/1949.

Makki, H. *Zindagani-yi Mirza Taqi Khan Amir Kabir.* 5th ed. Tehran, 1360/1981.

Malkum Khan, Mirza. *Majmu'a-yi Asar-i Mirza Malkum Khan.* Ed. M. Muhit Tabataba'i. Tehran, 1327/1948.

Marvazi, Muhammad Sadiq [Vaqayi'-Nigar]. *Ahang-i Surush: Tarikh-i Jangha-yi Iran va Rus: Yaddashtha-yi Mirza Muhammad Sadiq Vaqayi'-Nigar (Huma) Marvazi.* Ed. A. H. Azar. Tehran, 1369/1990.

Ma'sum 'Ali Shah Shirazi [Na'ib al-Sadr]. *Tara'iq al-Haqa'iq.* 2d ed. Ed. M. J. Mahjub. 3 vols. Tehran, 1345/1966.

Mazandarani, Mirza Asadullah [Fazil]. *Zuhur al-Haqq.* Vol. III. Tehran, n.d. [1944?].

Minovi, M., ed. *Nama-yi Tansar bi Gushnasp.* 2d ed. Tehran, 1354/1975.

Mu'ayyir al-Mamalik, Dust-'Ali Khan. *Rijal-i 'Asr-i Nasiri.* Tehran, 1361/1982.

———. *Yaddashtha-i az Zindigani-yi Khususi-yi Nasir al-Din Shah.* 2d ed. Tehran, 1362/1983.

Mudarrisi Chahardihi, M. *Shaykhigari va Babigari.* 2d ed. Tehran, 1351/1972.

Muhaddis, M. H., ed. *Mukatibat-i Iran va Ingilis dar bara-yi Panahandigi-yi Farhad Mirza.* Tehran, 1360/1982.

Mulla-bashi Tabrizi, Mulla Mahmud Nizam al-'Ulama. *Al-Shihab al-Thaqib fi Radd al-Nawasib.* Tabriz, 1270 Q./1853.

Munshi, Iskandar Bayg Turkaman. *'Alam Ara-yi 'Abbasi.* 2nd ed. Ed. I. Afshar. Tehran, 1350/ 1971.

Munzavi, A. *Fihrist-i Nuskhaha-yi Khatti-yi Farsi.* 6 vols. Tehran, 1348–1353/ 1969–1974.

Mushar, K. *Fihrist-i Kitabha-yi Chappi-yi Farsi.* 2d ed. 3 vols. Tehran, 1352/1973.

———. *Mu'allifin-i Kutub-i Chappi (Farsi va 'Arabi).* 6 vols. Tehran, 1340–44/ 1961–1965.

Mustawfi, 'Abdullah. *Sharh-i Zindigani-yi Man ya Tarikh-i Ijtima'i va Idari-yi Dawra-yi Qajariya.* 2d ed. 3 vols. Tehran, 1343/1964.

Mustawfi, Hamdullah. *Nazhat al-Qulub*. Ed. M. Dabirsiyaqi. Tehran, 1336/1957.

Nadir Mirza. *Tarikh va Jughrafi-yi Dar al-Saltana-yi Tabriz*. 2d ed. Ed. M. Mushiri. Tehran, 1351/1972.

Nafisi, S. *Tarikh-i Ijtima'i va Siayasi-yi Iran dar dawra-yi Ma'asir*. 2 vols. 2d ed. Tehran, 1344/1965.

Najmi, N. *Fatih-i Harat, Murad Mirza Husam al-Saltana*. Tehran, 1367/1988.

———. *Iran dar Miyan-i Tufan ya Sharh-i Zindigani-yi 'Abbas Mirza Na'ib al-Saltana*. Tehran, 1336/1957.

Nasir al-Din Shah Qajar. *Khatirat-i Nasir al-Din Shah dar Safar-i Sivvum-i Farangistan*. Ed. I. Rizvani. 3 vols. Tehran, 1369–1373/1990–1994.

———. "Naqqashiha-yi Nasir al-Din Shah." *Nashriya-yi Vizarat-i Umur-i Kharija* III, no. 3, (Shahrivar 1345/1966), 49–64.

———. *Ruznama-yi Safar-i Duvvum-i Farangistan*. Bombay, 1295 Q./1878. 2d ed. Tehran, 1296 Q./1879. 3d ed. Ed. I. Afshar. Tehran 1363/1984. (See also Nasir ud-Din Shah for English translation.)

———. *Ruznama-yi Safar-i Farangistan*. Tehran, 1291 Q./1874 (Also see Nasir ud-Din Shah for English translation.)

———. *Ruznama-yi Safar-i Gilan*. Ed. M. Sutudah. Tehran, 1367/1988.

———. *Ruznama-yi Safar-i Mazandaran*. Tehran, 1294 Q./1877 (reprint, Tehran, 1356/1977).

———. *Ruznama-yi Safar-i Sivvum-i Farangistan (The Third Tour of the Shah of Persia in Europe)*. Bombay, n.d. [1891].

———. *Safarnama-yi 'Iraq-i 'Ajam*. Tehran, 1311 Q./1894 (reprint, Tehran, 1362/1983).

———. *Safarnama-yi Karbala va Najaf*. n.p. [Tehran], 1287 Q./1870. 2d ed. as *Safarnama-yi 'Atabat*. Ed. I. Afshar. Tehran, 1363/1984.

———. *Safarnama-yi Khurasan* (second visit). Tehran, 1303 Q./1885 (reprint, 1354/1975).

Nasiri, M. R., ed. *Ansnad va Mukatibat-i Tarikhi-yi Iran (Qajariya)*. 2 vols., Tehran, 1366–1368/1987–1989.

Natiq, H. *Musibat-i Vaba va Bala-yi Hukumat*. Tehran, 1358/1979.

Naura'i, F. *Tahqiq dar Afkar-i Mirza Malkam Khan Nazim al-Dawla*. Tehran, 1352/1973.

Nava'i, 'A., ed. *Fitna-yi Bab*. 1351/1972. (See also I'tizad al-Saltana.)

———. "Vali'ahdha-yi Nasir al-Din Shah." *Yadgar* III, no. 10, 55–67.

Navvab Tihrani, Muhammad Ibrahim [Baday'i-Nigar]. *Makhzan al-Insha'*. Tehran 1273 Q./1856.

Pulak, J. [Polak, J.] *Safarnama-yi Pulak; Iran va Iranian*. Trans. K. Jahandari. Tehran, 1361/1982.

Qa'ani Shirazi. *Divan-i Qa'ani Shirazi*. Tehran, 1270 Q./1853. 2d ed. Ed. M. J. Mahjub. Tehran, 1336/1957.

Qa'im Maqami, J. "Chand Sanad Marbut bi Tarikh-i Faramushkhana dar Iran." *Yaghma* 16 (1342/1963), no. 9, 404–405.

———. "Payan-i Kar-i Mirza Aqa Khan I'timad al-Dawla Nuri." *Barrasiha-yi Tarikhi*, III (1347/1968), no. 3, 96–114, and no. 5, 119–144.

Qazvini, M. "Wafiyat-i Ma'asirin." *Yadgar* V no. 8–9 (1328/1949), 68–71.

Qazvini, Muhammad Shafi'. *Qanun-i Qazvini*. Ed. I. Afshar. Tehran, 1370/1991.

Ra'in, I. *Faramushkhana va Farmasunari dar Iran*. 3 vols., Tehran, 1357/1978.

Riza Quli Mirza Qajar. *Safarnama-yi Riza Quli Mirza Na'ib al-Iyala*. Ed. A. Farmanfarma'i Qajar. Tehran, 1346/1967.

Ruznama. See Iran, Government of.

Safa'i, I. *Yaksad Sanad-i Tarikhi*. Tehran, 1352/1973.

Saqafi, Khalil [A'lam al-Dawla]. *Maqalat-i Gunagun*. Tehran, 1322/1943.

Sarabi, Husayn b. 'Abdullah. *Makhzan al-Vaqayi', Safarnama-yi Farrukh Khan Amin al-Dawla*. Ed. K. Isfahaniyan and Q. Rushani. 2d ed. Tehran, 1361/1982.

Sasani. Khan Malik. *Dast-i Pinhan-i Siyasat-i Ingilis dar Iran*. Tehran (?), n.d..

——. *Siyasatgaran-i Dawra-yi Qajar*. 2 vols. Tehran, 1346/1967.

Sha'bani, R. *Tarikh-i Ijtima'i-yi Iran dar 'Asr-i Afshariya*. Tehran, 1365/1986.

Sharaf. See Iran, Government.

Shushtari, Mir 'Abd al-Latif. *Tuhfat al-'Alam*. Tehran, 1263 Q./1847.

Sipihr, Mirza Muhammad Taqi [Lisan al-Mulk]. *Nasikh al-Tawarikh: Qajariya*. Ed. M. B. Bihbudi. 4 vols. Tehran, 1344/1965.

Sirina, K. [Serena, C.]. *Adamha va A'inha*. Trans. A. Sa'idi. Tehran, 1362/1983.

Surush Isfahani. *Divan-i Surush, Shams al-Shu'ara*. Ed. M. J. Mahjub. 2 vols. Tehran, 1339/1960.

Sultan al-Qura'i, S. *Ism-i Ashhar, Kitabshinakht-i Alqab-i Dawra-yi Nasir al-Din Shah*. Tehran, 1355/1976.

Tahiri, A. *Tarikh-i Ravabit-i Bazargani va Siyasi Ingilis va Iran*. 2 vols. Tehran, 1354/1975.

Taj al-Saltana. *Khatirat-i Taj al-Saltana*. Ed. M. Ittihadiya (Nizam-Mafi) and S. Sa'dvandiyan. Tehran, 1361/1982. (For English translation, see Taj al-Saltana.)

Tajbakhsh, A. *Tarikh-i Ravabit-i Iran va Rusiyya dar Nima-yi Avval-i Qarn-i Nuzdahum*. Tabriz, 1337/1958.

Tasuji, 'Abd al-Latif., trans. *Hazar u Yak Shab*. Tabriz, 1261 Q./1845.

Taymuri, I. *'Asr-i Bikhabari ya Tarikh-i Imtiyazat dar Iran*. Tehran, 1332/1953.

Tihrani, Aqa Buzurg [Muhammad Muhsin]. *Al-Dhari'a ila Tasanif al-Shi'a*. 25 vols. Najaf and Tehran, 1968–1978.

——. *Tabaqat A'lam al-Shi'a*. I: *Nuqaba al-Bashar fi al-Qarn al-Rabi' al-'Ashar*. Najaf, 1373 Q./1954.

Tusi, Nasir al-Din. *Akhlaq-i Nasiri*. Laknaw, 1883.

'Urfi Shirazi. *Qasa'id-i 'Urfi*. Lucknow, 1966.

Vahidniya, S., ed. *Qararha va Qarardadha*. Tehran, 1362/1983.

Vizarat-i Umur-i Kharija, Darfat-i Mutala'at-i Siyasi va Bayn al-Milali. *Guzida-yi Asnad-i Siyasi-i Iran va 'Usmani: Dawra-yi Qajariya*. I: 1211–1270 Q./1796–1853. Tehran, 1369/1990.

Zahir al-Dawla, 'Ali Khan. *Tarikh-i Bi Durugh*. Tehran, 1362/1983.

Zill al-Sultan, Mas'ud Mirza. *Tarikh-i Sarguzasht-i Mas'udi*. Tehran, 1325 Q./1907.

Zuka', Y. "Mirza Abul-Hasan Khan Sani' al-Mulk Ghaffari." *Hunar va Mardum*, I, no. 10 [Murdad 1342/August 1963], 14–27, and no. 11 [Shahrivar 1342/September 1963], 16–33.

————. *Tarikhcha-yi Sakhtimanha-yi Arg-i Saltanati va Rahnama-yi Kakh-i Gulistan.* Tehran, 1349/1970.

PUBLISHED WORKS IN EUROPEAN LANGUAGES

Abrahamian, E. *Iran Between Two Revolutions.* Princeton, 1982.
————. "Oriental Despotism: The Case of Qajar Iran." *International Journal of Middle East Studies* V (1974), 3–31.
Algar, H. "Amir(-i) Kabir." *Encyclopaedia Iranica.*
————. "Dar al-fonun." *Encyclopaedia Iranica.*
————. *Mirza Malkum Khan: A Study in the History of Iranian Modernism.* Berkeley and Los Angeles, 1973.
————. *Religion and State in Iran, 1785–1906: The Role of the Ulama in the Qajar Period.* Berkeley and Los Angeles, 1969.
————. "Shi'ism and Iran in the Eighteenth Century." *Studies in Eighteenth Century Islamic History.* Ed. Neff and R. Owen. Carbondale, Ill., 1977, 288–302.
Ali Reza, Sayed, trans. *Nahjul Balagha, Book of Eloquence.* 3d ed. Elmhurst, 1984.
Amanat. A. "Allah-qoli Khan Ilkhani." *Encyclopaedia Iranica.*
————. "Amin-al-dawla, 'Abdollah Khan." *Encyclopaedia Iranica.*
————. "Amin-al-soltan, Ebrahim Khan." *Encyclopaedia Iranica.*
————. "Amir(-i) Nezam [office]." *Encyclopaedia Iranica.*
————. "Amir Nezam Garrusi." *Encyclopaedia Iranica.*
————. "Aqasi, Hajji Mirza 'Abbas Iravani." *Encyclopaedia Iranica.*
————. " 'Aziz-al-soltan." *Encyclopaedia Iranica.*
————, ed. *Cities and Trade: Consul Abbott on the Economy and Society of Iran, 1847–1866.* London, 1983.
————. "Constitutional Revolution, i. Intellectual Background." *Encyclopaedia Iranica.*
————. "Court, iv. Qajar Period." *Encyclopaedia Iranica.*
————, ed. *Crowning Anguish: The Memoirs of a Persian Princess from the Harem to Modernity, 1884–1914.* Trans. A. Vanzan and A. Neshati. Washington, D.C., 1993. (See also Taj al-Saltana.)
————. "Dawlatshah, Mohammad 'Ali Mirza." *Encyclopaedia Iranica.*
————. "The Downfall of Mirza Taqi Khan Amir Kabir and the Problem of Ministerial Authority in Qajar Iran." *International Journal of Middle East Studies* 23 (1991), 577–599.
————. "Ebrahim Khan Kalantar, E'-temad-al-dawla." *Encyclopaedia Iranica.*
————. "E'temad-al-dawla, Aqa Khan Nuri." *Encyclopaedia Iranica.*
————. "E'temad-al-saltana, Mohammad Hasan Khan." *Encyclopaedia Iranica.*
————. "In Between *Madrasa* and the Marketplace: The Designation of Clerical Leadership in Modern Shi'ism." *Authority and Political Culture in Shi'ism.* Ed. S. A. Arjomand. Albany, 1988. 98–132.
————. "Nasir al-Din Shah." *Encyclopedia of Islam,* 2d. ed.
————. "The Nuqtawi Movement of Mahmud Pisikhani and his Persian Cycle of Mystical-Materialism." *Essays in Mediaeval Isma'ili History and Thought.* Ed. F. Daftary. Cambridge, 1995, 281–297.

————. *Resurrection and Renewal: The Making of the Babi Movement in Iran, 1844–1850*. Ithaca, 1989.

————. "'Russian Intrusion into the Guarded Domain': Reflections of a Qajar Statesman on European Expansion." *Journal of the American Oriental Society* 113.1 (1993), 35–56.

Anderson, M. S. *The Eastern Question, 1774–1923*. London, 1966.

Arjomand, S. A. "The Mujtahid of the Age and the Mulla-bashi: An Intermediate Stage in the Institutionalization of Religious Authority in Shi'ite Iran." *Authority and Political Culture in Shi'ism*. Ed. S. A. Arjomand. Albany, 1988. 80–97.

————. *The Shadow of God and the Hidden Imam: Religion, Political Order and Societal Change in Shicite Iran from the Beginning to 1890*. Chicago, 1984.

————. "The Shi'ite Heirocracy and the State in Pre-modern Iran: 1785–1890." *European Journal of Sociology* 22 (1981), 40–78.

Ashraf, A. "Alqab." *Encyclopaedia Iranica*.

————. "Historical Obstacles to the Development of a Bourgeoisie in Iran." *Iranian Studies* II (1969), 54–79.

Ashraf, A., and H. Hekmat. "Merchants and Artisans and the Developmental Precesses of Nineteenth Century Iran." *The Islamic Middle East, 700–1900*. Ed. A. L. Udovitch. Princeton, 1981.

Atkin, M. *Russia and Iran, 1780–1828*. Minneapolis, 1980.

Averey, P., G. Hambly, and C. Melville, eds. *The Cambridge History of Iran*. 7 vols. VII. Cambridge, 1991.

Avery, P. W. "An Enquiry into the Outbreak of the Second Russo-Persian War, 1826–28." *Iran and Islam*. Ed. C. E. Bosworth. Edinburgh, 1971. 17–45.

————. *Modern Iran*. London, 1965.

Ayalon, D. "al-Amir al-Kabir." *Encyclopadia of Islam*. 2d ed.

Bakhash, S. "Evolution of Qajar Bureaucracy: 1779–1879." *Middle East Studies* 7 (1971), 139–168.

————. *Iran: Monarchy, Bureaucracy and Reform under the Qajars*. London, 1978.

Ballard, A. "The Persian War of 1856–1857." *Blackwood Magazine* (September 1861).

Balyuzi, H. *Baha'u'llah the King of Glory*. Oxford, 1980.

Bausani, A. *Persia Religiosa*. Milan, 1959.

Bayat, M. *Iran's First Revolution: Shi'ism and the Cosntitutional Revolution*. New York, 1991.

————. *Mysticism and Dissent: Socioreligious Thought in Qajar Iran*. Syracuse, 1982.

Beck, L. *The Qashqa'is of Iran*. New Haven, 1986.

Benjamin, S.G.W. *Persia and the Persians*. London, 1887.

Blunt, W. S. *Secret History of the English Occupation of Egypt*. London, 1903.

Bosworth, E. and C. Hillenbrand, eds. *Qajar Iran: Political, Social and Cultural Changes, 1800–1925*. Edinburgh, 1983.

Bourrienne, Louis Antoine de. *Memoires*. Paris, 1829.

————. *Memoirs of Napoleon Bonaparte*, London, 1836.

Browne, Edward G. *Literary History of Persia*. 4 vols. Cambridge, 1928.

———. *Materials for the Study of the Babi Religion.* Cambridge, 1918.

———. *The Persian Revolution of 1905–1909.* Cambridge, 1910. New edition ed. A. Amanat. Washington D.C., 1995.

———, ed. and trans. *The Tarikh-i Jadid or New History of Mirza 'Ali Muhammad the Bab.* Cambridge, 1893.

Brugsch, H. C. *Reise der Kgl. Preussischen Gesandschaft nach Persien 1860 und 1861.* 2 vols. Leipzig, 1862–1863. (For Persian trans. see Brugush.)

Burgess, Charles, and Edward Burgess. *Letters From Persia Written by Charles and Edward Burgess, 1828–1855.* Ed. B. Schwartz. New York, 1942.

Busse, H., trans. *History of Persia Under Qajar Rule.* New York, 1972.

Calmard, J. "Amin-al-soltan, Mirza 'Ali Asgar Khan." *Encyclopaedia Iranica.*

———. "Le Mecenat des Representations de Ta'ziye." *Le Monde iranien et l'Islam,* 2 (1974), 73–126, and 4 (1976), 133–162.

Chelkowski, P. "Majlis-i Shahinshah-i Iran Nasir al-Din Shah." *Qajar Iran: Political, Social and Cultural Changes, 1800–1925.* Eds. E. Bosworth, and C. Hillenbrand. Edinburgh, 1983, 229–242.

———. *Ta'ziyeh: Ritual and Drama in Iran.* New York, 1979.

Chirol, V. *The Middle Eastern Question or Some Political Problems of Indian Defence.* London, 1903.

Cohen, C. "Atabak." *Encyclopedia of Islam.* 2d ed.

Cole, J. "Baha' Allah." *Encyclopaedia Iranica.*

———. "Imami Jurisprudence and the Role of the Ulama: Mortaza Ansari on Emulating the Supreme Exemplar." *Religion and Politics in Iran.* Ed. N. R. Keddie. New Haven, 1983. 33–46.

———. "Iranian Millenarianism and Democratic Thought in the 19th Century." *International Journal of Middle East Studies,* 24 (1992), 1–26.

Coste, P., and E. Flandin. *Voyage en Perse.* 8 vols., Paris, 1843–1854.

Curzon, G. N. *Persia and the Persian Question.* 2 vols. London, 1892.

Davison, O. M. *Poet and Hero in the Persian Book of Kings.* Ithaca, 1994.

Dubeux, L. *La Perse.* Paris, 1841.

Eastwick, B. E. *Journal of a Diplomat's Three Years' Residence in Persia.* 2 vols. London, 1864.

Edwards, E. *Catalogue of the Persian Printed Books in the British Museum.* London, 1922.

Enayat, A. "Amin al-Zarb." *Encyclopaedia Iranica.*

Encyclopaedia Iranica. Ed. E. Yarshater. London and Costa Mesa, Calif., 1982– .

The Encyclopedia of Islam. 2d ed., Leiden, 1960– .

English, B. *John Company's Last War.* London, 1971.

Ettehadieh, M. "Patterns in Urban Development; the Growth of Tehran (1852–1903)." *Qajar Iran: Political, Social and Cultural Changes, 1800–1925.* Eds. E. Bosworth and C. Hillenbrand. Edinburgh, 1983, 199–212.

Farahani, Muhammad Husayn Husayni. *A Shi'ite Pilgrimage to Mecca, (1885–1886).* Eds. F. Farmayan and R. A. McDaniel. Austin, 1990.

Ferrier, J. P. "Situation de la Perse en 1851." *Revue Orientale et Algerienne,* 1 (Paris, 1852), 141–159.

Floor, W. "Change and Development in the Judicial System of Qajar Iran (1800–1925)," *Qajar Iran: Political, Social and Cultural Changes, 1800–1925.* Eds. E. Bosworth and C. Hillenbrand. Edinburgh, 1983, 113–147.

———. "Commerce, Qajar period." *Encyclopaedia Iranica*.

———. "The Merchants (*tujjar*) in Qajar Iran." *Zeitsschrift der Deutschen morgenlandischen Gesellschaft* 129 (1976), 101–135.

Fraser, J. B. *Narrative of the Residence of the Persian Princes in London, in 1835 and 1836.* 2 vols., London, 1838.

———. *A Winter Journey (Tatar) from Constantinople to Tehran.* 2 vols. London, 1838.

Garthwaite, G. R. *Khans and Shahs: A Documentary Analysis of Bakhtiyari in Iran.* Cambridge, 1983.

Gilbar, G. "The Persian Economy in the mid-19th Century." *Die Welt des Islams* 19 (1979), no. 1–4, 196–211.

Gobineau, Comte Joseph A. de. *Correspondance entre le Comte de Gobineau et le Comte de Prokesch-Osten (1854–1876).* Paris, 1933.

———. *Les Depeches Diplomatiques du Comte de Gobineau en Perse.* Ed. A. D. Hytier. Geneve and Paris, 1959.

———. *Religions et philosophies dans l'Asie Centrale.* 2d ed. Paris, 1957.

———. *Trois ans en Asie (de 1855 à 1858).* 2 vols. Paris, 1856.

Goldsmid, F. J. *Eastern Persia, An Account of the Journeys of the Persian Boundary Commission, 1870–1–2.* 2 vols. London, 1876.

Gramlich, R. *Die Schiitischen Derwischorden Persiens.* 2 vols. Wiesbaden, 1975–1976.

The Graphic, an Illustrated Weekly Newspaper. Vol. VIII. London, 1873.

Great Britain, Foreign Office. *British Documents on Foreign Affairs: Reports and Papers from Foreign Office Confidential Prints.* Series B: The Near East and Middle East, 1856–1914. X (Persia: 1856–1885). New York, 1984.

Greaves, R. L. *Persia and the Defence of India, 1884–1892.* London, 1959.

Habsburg and Feldman. *Islamic Works of Art.* New York, 1990.

Hambly, G.R.G. "Agha Mohammad Khan and the Establishment of the Qajar Dynasty." *Journal of the Royal Asian Society* 50 (1963), 161–174.

———. "An Introduction to the Economic Organization of Early Qajar Iran." *Iran* 2 (1964), 69–81.

Hunt, G. H. *Outram and Havelock's Campaign (1857).* London, 1857.

Hurewitz, J. C. *The Middle East and North Africa in World Politics.* 2 vols. New Haven, 1975–1979.

Ingram, E. *The Beginning of Great Game in Asia, 1828–1834.* Oxford, 1979.

Issawi, C. *The Economic History of Iran, 1800–1914.* Chicago, 1971.

Ivanov, M. S. *Babidskie vosstaniya v Irane (1848–1852).* Moscow, 1939.

Jackson, P., and L. Lockhart. *The Cambridge History of Iran.* Vol. VI. Cambridge, 1986.

Jones, G. *Banking and Empire in Iran: The History of the British Bank of the Middle East.* 2 vols. Cambridge, 1986–1987.

Jones Brydges, Harford. *The Dynasty of the Kajars.* London, 1833.

Karny, A. "The Premiership of Mirza Hosein Khan and His Reforms in Iran, 1872–1873." *Asian and African Studies* 10 (1974–75), 127–156.

Kayat, A., trans. *Journal of a Residence in England.* 2 vols. London, 1839 [private circulation].

Kazemzadeh, F. "Excerpts from Dispatches Written During 1848–52 by Prince Dolgoroukov, Russian Minister to Persia." *World Order* (Fall 1966), 17–24.

————. *Russia and Britain in Persia, 1864–1914: A Study in Imperialism.* New Haven, 1968.

Keddie, N. R. *Religion and Rebellion in Iran: The Tobacco Protest of 1891–92.* London, 1966.

————. *Sayyid Jamal ad-Din "al-Afghani": A Political Biography.* Berkeley and Los Angeles, 1972.

Kelly, J. B. *Britian and the Persian Gulf, 1795–1880.* Oxford, 1968.

Lambton, A.K.S. *Continuity and Change in Medieval Persia.* Albany, 1988.

————. "The Dilemma of Government in Islamic Persia: The *Siyast-nama* of Nizam al- Mulk." *Iran* 22 (1984), 55–66.

————. "Ilat." *Encyclopedia of Islam.*

————. "Justice in the Medieval Persian Theory of Kingship." *Studia Islamica* 17 (1962), 91–119.

————. "A Nineteenth Century Interpretation of *Jihad.*" *Studia Islamica* 22 (1970), 181–192.

————. "Persian Trade under the Early Qajars." *Islam and the Trade of Asia.* Ed. D. S. Richards. Oxford, 1970, 215–244.

————. *Qajar Persia.* London and Austin, 1987.

————. *State and Government in Medieval Islam.* Oxford, 1981.

Lloyd, Seton. *Foundation in the Dust.* London, 1947.

Lockhart, L. *The Fall of the Safavi Dynasty and the Afghan Occupation of Persia.* Cambridge, 1958.

————. *Nadir Shah.* London, 1938.

MacEoin, D. "'Abd al-Baha." *Encyclopaedia Iranica.*

————. "Changes in Charismatic Authority in Qajar Shi'ism." *Qajar Iran: Political, Social and Cultural Changes, 1800–1925.* Eds. E. Bosworth and C. Hillenbrand. Edinburgh, 1983, 148–176.

Malcolm, J. *The History of Persia.* 2 vols. London, 1815.

Martin, B. *German-Persian Diplomatic Relations, 1873–1912.* 's-Gravenhage, 1959.

Masters, B. "The Treaties of Enzurum (1823 and 1848) and the Changing Status of Iranians in the Ottoman Empire." *Iranian Studies* 24 (1991), 3–17.

Maxwell, H. *The Honorable Sir Charles Murray, K.C.B., A Memoir.* Edinburgh and London, 1898.

Meredith, C. "Early Qajar Administration: An Analysis of its Development and Functions." *Iranian Studies* 4 (1971), 59–84.

Migeod, H. G. "Die Lutis, Ein Ferment des stadtischen Lebens in Persien." *Journal of Economic and Social History of the Orient,* II (1959), 82–91.

————. *Die persische Gesellschaft unter Nasiru'd-Din Sah (1848–1896).* Berlin, 1990.

Momen, M. *The Babi and Baha'i Religions, 1844–1944, Some Contemporary Western Accounts.* Oxford, 1981.

Murray, C. *Bird of the Prairie.* London, 1844.

Nashat, G. "Anis al-Dawla." *Encyclopaedia Iranica.*

————. *The Origins of Modern Reform in Iran, 1870–1880.* Urbana, 1982.

Nasir ud-Din Shah [Nasir al-Din Shah]. *A Diary Kept by His Majesty the Shah of Persia, during His Journey to Europe in 1878.* Trans. A. Houtum-Schindler and L. de Norman. London, 1879.

————. *The Diary of H.M. the Shah of Persia.* Trans. J. W. Redhouse. London, 1874.

Oberling, P. *The Qashqa'i Nomads of Fars.* Paris/The Hague, 1974.

Okazaki, S. "The Great Persian Famine of 1870–1871." *Bulletin of the School of Oriental and African Studies* 49 (1986), 183–192.

Olson, R. *The Emergence of Kurdish Nationalism, 1880–1925.* Austin, 1989.

Pakravan, A. *Tehran de Jadis.* Geneve, 1971.

Perry, J. R. "Aga Mohammad Khan Qajar." *Encyclopaedia Iranica.*

————. *Karim Khan Zand, A History of Iran, 1747–1779.* Chicago, 1979.

Phillott, D. C., trans. *Selection from Qa'ani.* Ed. Muhammad Kazim Shirazi. Calcutta, 1907.

Polak, J. E. *Persien, das Land und Seine Bewohner, Ethnographische Scilderungen.* 2 vols. Leipzig, 1865. (For Persian trans. see Pulak.)

Ramazani, R. K. *Foreign Policy of Iran, 1500–1941.* Charlottesville, 1966.

Rawlinson, G. *A Memoir of Major-General Sir Henry Creswicke Rawlinson.* London, 1898.

Rawlinson, H. *England and Russia in the East.* London, 1875.

Rieu, C. *Catalogue of the Persian Manuscripts in the British Museum (Supplement).* London, 1895.

Rosenthal, E.I.J. *Political Thought in Medieval Islam.* Cambridge, 1985.

Rypka, J. *History of Iranian Literature.* Dordrecht, 1968.

Serena, Carla. *Hommes et Choses en Perse.* Paris, 1883. (For Persian translation, see Sirina.)

————. *Souvenirs Personnels. Mon voyage. Une Européenne en Perse.* Paris, 1881.

Sheikholeslami, A. R. "The Central Structure of Authority in Iran, 1871–1896." Ph.D. Dissertation, University of California, Los Angeles, 1975.

Slaby, H. *Bindenschild und Sonnenlowe: Die Geschichte der osterreilchisch-iranischen Beziehungen bis zur Gegenwart.* Graz, 1982.

Smith, Peter. *The Babi and Baha'i Religions: From Messianism to a World Religion.* Cambridge and New York, 1987.

Soltykov, A. D. *Voyage en Perse.* Paris, 1851.

Standish, J. F. "The Persian War of 1856–1857." *Middle East Studies* 3 (1966), no. 1, 18–45.

Stuart, W. *Journal of a Residence in Northern Persia and in the Adjacent Provinces of Turkey.* London, 1835.

————. *Journal of Two Years Travel in Persia.* 2 vols. London, 1854.

Sumer, F. "Kadjar [Turcoman tribe]." *Encyclopedia of Islam.* 2d ed.

Taj al-Saltana. *Crowning Anguish: The Memoirs of a Persian Princess from the Harem to Modernity, 1884–1914.* Ed. A. Amanat, trans. A. Vanzan and A. Neshati. Washington, D.C., 1993.

Thornton, L. *Images de Perse: Le Voyage du Colonel F. Colombari a la cour du Chah de Perse de 1833 a 1848.* Paris, 1981.

Volodarsky, M. "Persia's Foreign Policy Between the two Herat Crises, 1831–1856." *Middle East Studies* 21 (1985), 111–151.

————. "Russian Diplomacy During the Anglo-Persian Conflict of 1855–1857." *Central Asian* Survey 6 (1987), no. 2, 43–54.

Wallias Budge, E. A. *The Rise and Progress of Assyriology.* London, 1925.

Watson, R. G. *A History of Persia*. London, 1966.

Wickens, G. M., trans. *The Nasirean Ethics*. London, 1964.

Wright, D. *The English Amongst the Persians*. London, 1977.

———. *The Persians Amongst the English*. London, 1985.

Yapp, M. E. *Strategies of British India: Britain, Iran and Afghanistan, 1798–1850*. Oxford, 1980.

Zarandi, Shaykh Muhammad Nabil. *The Dawn-Breakers, Nabil's Narrative of the Early Days of the Baha'i Revelation*. Ed. and trans. Shoghi Effendi. Wilmette, Ill., 1932.

Index

Text: 10/13 Aldus
Display: Aldus
Index: Patricia Deminna
Map: Bill Nelson
Composition: Braun-Brumfield